CompTIA.

Network+

Certification Study Guide, Sixth Edition
(Exam N10-006)

Glen E. Clarke

Mc
Graw
Hill
Education

New York   Chicago   San Francisco   Athens
London   Madrid   Mexico City   Milan
New Delhi   Singapore   Sydney   Toronto

Cataloging-in-Publication Data is on file with the Library of Congress

McGraw-Hill Education books are available at special quantity discounts to use as premiums and sales promotions, or for use in corporate training programs. To contact a representative, please visit the Contact Us pages at www.mhprofessional.com.

CompTIA Network+® Certification Study Guide, Sixth Edition (Exam N10-006)

1234567890 DOC/DOC 1098765

ISBN: Book p/n 978-0-07-184756-8 and DVD p/n 978-0-07-184755-1
of set 978-0-07-184888-6

MHID: Book p/n 0-07-184756-1 and DVD p/n 0-07-184755-3
of set 0-07-184888-6

Sponsoring Editor *Timothy Green*	**Copy Editor** *Lisa McCoy*	**Illustration** *Cenveo Publisher Services*
Editorial Supervisor *Jody McKenzie*	**Proofreader** *Paul Tyler*	**Art Director, Cover** *Jeff Weeks*
Project Editor *LeeAnn Pickrell*	**Indexer** *Karin Arrigoni*	**Cover Designer** *Jeff Weeks*
Acquisitions Coordinator *Amy Stonebraker*	**Production Supervisor** *James Kussow*	
Technical Editor *Edward Tetz*	**Composition** *Cenveo® Publisher Services*	

To my beautiful wife, Tanya,
for all her love and support.

Glen E. Clarke, MCSE, MCSD, MCITP, MCT, CCNA, CEH, CHFI, SCNP, CISSO, Security+, Network+, A+ is an independent trainer and consultant, focusing on network security and security auditing services. Glen spends most of his time delivering certified courses on CCNA, Windows Server, SQL Server, Exchange Server, Visual Basic .NET, and ASP.NET. Glen also teaches a number of security-related courses covering topics such as ethical hacking and countermeasure, computer forensics and investigation, information system security officer, vulnerability testing, firewall design, and packet analysis topics.

Glen is an experienced author and technical editor whose published work has been nominated for referenceware excellence awards in 2003 and 2004. Glen has worked on a number of certification titles, including topics on A+ certification, Cisco's CCENT and CCNA certification, and Network+ and Security+ certification. Glen is author of the *CompTIA Security+ Certification Study Guide, Second Edition* (McGraw-Hill Education, 2014).

When he's not working, Glen loves to spend quality time with his wife, Tanya, and their four children, Sara, Brendon, Ashlyn, and Rebecca. He is an active member of the High Technology Crime Investigation Association (HTCIA). You can visit Glen online at www .gleneclarke.com, or contact him at glenclarke@accesswave.ca.

About the Contributor

Robb H. Tracy (CNA, CNE, CNI, CompTIA A+, CompTIA Network+, CompTIA Security+, CompTIA Linux+) has been a professional technology instructor and courseware developer since 1996. He has designed and implemented technical training products and curricula for major hardware and software vendors, including Novell, Micron Technology, TestOut, Messaging Architects, and Motorola. Robb previously served on CompTIA's Network+ Advisory Committee, where he helped define the objectives that make up the CompTIA Network+ certification. He is a cofounder of Nebo Technical Institute, Inc., a leading provider of information technology training and consulting. Robb is the author of *Novell Certified Linux Engineer (Novell CLE) Study Guide* (Novell Press, 2005), *Novell Certified Linux Engineer 9 (CLE 9) Study Guide* (Novell Press, 2006), *Linux+ Certification Study Guide* (McGraw-Hill Education, 2008), *LPIC-1/CompTIA Linux+ Certification Exam Guide* (McGraw-Hill Education, 2011), *CompTIA Network+ Certification Practice Exams* (McGraw-Hill Education, 2012), and *LPI Linux Essentials Certification All-in-One Exam Guide* (McGraw-Hill Education, 2013).

About the Technical Editor

Edward Tetz graduated in 1990 from Saint Lawrence College in Cornwall, Ontario, with a degree in business administration. He spent a short time in computer sales and support. In 1994 he added training to his repertoire. Since 2002, Edward has been a computer consultant specializing in enterprise infrastructure in Halifax, Nova Scotia, and Ottawa, Ontario. Edward has continued to increase and improve his knowledge and skills through industry-recognized certifications.

Some of the certifications Edward holds include Cisco Certified Network Associate (CCNA), VMware Certified Professional (VCP), A+, ITIL Foundations Certificate in IT Service Management (IT Infrastructure Library), Microsoft Certified Trainer (MCT), Microsoft Certified Systems Engineer (MCSE), Microsoft Certified Database Administrator (MCDBA), and Chauncey Group's Certified Technical Trainer (CTT). During his work experience, he has supported Apple Macintosh, IBM OS/2, Linux, Novell NetWare, and all Microsoft operating systems from MS-DOS to Windows 2012, as well as hardware from most of the major vendors.

Becoming a CompTIA Certified IT Professional Is Easy

It's also the best way to reach greater professional opportunities and rewards.

Why Get CompTIA Certified?

Growing Demand

Labor estimates predict some technology fields will experience growth of more than 20% by the year 2020. (Source: CompTIA's *Ninth Annual Information Security Trends Study,* 2012: online survey of 500 U.S. IT and business executives responsible for information security policies and procedures.) CompTIA certification qualifies the skills required to join this workforce.

Higher Salaries

IT professionals with certifications on their resume command better jobs, earn higher salaries, and have more doors open to new multi-industry opportunities.

Verified Strengths

91% of hiring managers indicate CompTIA certifications are valuable in validating IT expertise, making certification the best way to demonstrate your competency and knowledge to employers. (Source: CompTIA's *Employer Perceptions of IT Training and Certification* study, 2011.)

Universal Skills

CompTIA certifications are vendor neutral—which means that certified professionals can proficiently work with an extensive variety of hardware and software found in most organizations.

Learn	Certify	Work
Learn more about what the exam covers by reviewing the following:	Purchase a voucher at a Pearson VUE testing center or at CompTIAstore.com.	Congratulations on your CompTIA certification!
• Exam objectives for key study points.	• Register for your exam at a Pearson VUE testing center.	• Make sure to add your certification to your resume.
• Sample questions for a general overview of what to expect on the exam and examples of question format.	• Visit pearsonvue.com/CompTIA to find the closest testing center to you.	• Check out the CompTIA Certification Roadmap to plan your next career move.
• Visit online forums, like LinkedIn, to see what other IT professionals say about CompTIA exams.	• Schedule the exam online. You will be required to enter your voucher number or provide payment information at registration.	
	• Take your certification exam.	

Learn More: Certification.CompTIA.org/networkplus

CompTIA Disclaimer

CONTENTS AT A GLANCE

CONTENTS

The objective of this study guide is to prepare you for the Network+ certification exam by familiarizing you with the technology or body of knowledge tested on the exam. Because the primary focus of the book is to help you pass the certification exam, we don't always cover every aspect of the related technology. Some aspects of the technology are only covered to the extent necessary to help you understand what you need to know to pass the exam, but we hope this book will serve you as a valuable professional resource after your exam.

In This Book

This book is organized in such a way as to serve as an in-depth review for the CompTIA Network+ certification exam for both experienced network professionals and newcomers to the world of network technologies. Each chapter covers a major aspect of the certification exam, with an emphasis on the "why" as well as the "how to" of working with and supporting networking environments.

On the DVD

For more information on the DVD, please see the appendix "About the DVD" at the back of the book.

Exam Readiness Checklist

At the end of the introduction you will find an Exam Readiness Checklist. This table has been constructed to allow you to cross-reference the official exam objectives with the objectives as they are presented and covered in this book. The checklist also allows you to gauge your level of expertise on each objective at the outset of your studies. This should allow you to check your progress and make sure you spend the time you need on more difficult or unfamiliar sections. References have been provided for the objective exactly as the vendor presents it, along with the relevant chapter number.

In Every Chapter

We've created a set of chapter components that call your attention to important items, reinforce important points, and provide helpful exam-taking hints. Take a look at what you'll find in every chapter:

- Every chapter begins with **Certification Objectives**—what you need to know in order to pass the section on the exam dealing with the chapter topic. The Objective headings identify the objectives within the chapter, so you'll always know an objective when you see it!

- **Exam Watch** notes call attention to information about, and potential pitfalls in, the exam. These helpful hints are written by authors who have taken the exams and received their certification—who better to tell you what to worry about? They know what you're about to go through!

| The operative phrase to watch for on the exam is "exclusive use." | Questions using this phrase are most likely referring to a private cloud solution. |

- **Step-by-Step Exercises** are interspersed throughout the chapters. These are typically designed as hands-on exercises that allow you to get a feel for the real-world experience you need in order to pass the exams. They help you master skills that are likely to be an area of focus on the exam. Don't just read through the exercises; they are hands-on practice that you should be comfortable completing. Learning by doing is an effective way to increase your competency with a product.

- **On the Job** notes describe the issues that come up most often in real-world settings. They provide a valuable perspective on certification- and product-related topics. They point out common mistakes and address questions that have arisen from on-the-job discussions and experience.

- **Inside the Exam** sidebars highlight some of the most common and confusing problems that students encounter when taking a live exam. Designed to anticipate what the exam will emphasize, getting inside the exam will help ensure you know what you need to know to pass the exam. You can get a leg up on how to respond to those difficult-to-understand questions by focusing extra attention on these sidebars.

- ■ The **Certification Summary** is a succinct review of the chapter and a restatement of salient points regarding the exam.

 ■ The **Two-Minute Drill** at the end of every chapter is a checklist of the main points of the chapter. It can be used for last-minute review.

 ■ The **Self Test** offers questions similar to those found on the certification exams. The answers to these questions, as well as explanations of the answers, can be found at the end of each chapter. By taking the Self Test after completing each chapter, you'll reinforce what you've learned from that chapter while becoming familiar with the structure of the exam questions.

Some Pointers

Once you've finished reading this book, set aside some time to do a thorough review. You might want to return to the book several times and make use of all the methods it offers for reviewing the material:

1. *Re-read all the Two-Minute Drills, or have someone quiz you.* You also can use the drills as a way to do a quick cram before the exam. You might want to make some flash cards out of 3 × 5 index cards that have the Two-Minute Drill material on them.

2. *Re-read all the Exam Watch notes and Inside the Exam elements.* Remember that these notes are written by authors who have taken the exam and passed. They know what you should expect—and what you should be on the lookout for.

3. *Re-take the Self Tests.* Taking the tests right after you've read the chapter is a good idea, because the questions help reinforce what you've just learned. However, it's an even better idea to go back later and do all the questions in the book in one sitting. Pretend that you're taking the live exam. When you go through the questions the first time, you should mark your answers on a separate piece of paper. That way, you can run through the questions as many times as you need to until you feel comfortable with the material.

4. *Complete the Exercises.* Did you do the exercises when you read through each chapter? If not, do them! These exercises are designed to cover exam topics, and there's no better way to get to know this material than by practicing. Be sure you understand why you are performing each step in each exercise. If there is something you are not clear on, re-read that section in the chapter.

ACKNOWLEDGMENTS

I would like to thank the wonderful people at McGraw-Hill Education, especially Timothy Green and Stephanie Evans, for their extreme patience and support—you guys are a great team to work with! I thank Timothy Green for giving me the opportunity to work with him once again and for this project—it has been a phenomenal experience! Thank you to a close friend and former coworker, Ed Tetz, for great feedback and encouraging ideas as the technical editor.

A special thank you to my wife, Tanya, who has been extremely supportive and loving through the many hours of writing this book. I would also like to thank my four children, Sara, Brendon, Ashlyn, and Rebecca, for helping Daddy enjoy the simple things—playing hockey, skating on the rink, going for walks in the mall, and, Sara, I cannot forget movie night! I love the time I spend with all four of you!

If you are new to certifications, we have some good news and some bad news. The good news is that a computer industry certification is one of the most valuable credentials you can earn. It sets you apart from the crowd and marks you as a valuable asset to your employer. You will gain the respect of your peers, and certification can have a wonderful effect on your income.

The bad news is that certification exams are not easy. You may think you will read through some study material, memorize a few facts, and pass the examinations. After all, these certification exams are just computer-based, multiple-choice tests, so they must be easy. If you believe this, you are wrong. Unlike many "multiple-guess" tests you have been exposed to in school, the questions on certification examinations go beyond simple factual knowledge.

The purpose of this introduction is to teach you how to take a computer certification examination. To be successful, you need to know something about the purpose and structure of these tests. We will also look at the latest innovations in computerized testing. Using *simulations* and *adaptive testing,* the computer industry is enhancing both the validity and security of the certification process. These factors have some important effects on how you should prepare for an exam, as well as your approach to each question during the test.

We will begin by looking at the purpose, focus, and structure of certification tests, and we will examine the effect these factors have on the kinds of questions you will face on your certification exams. We will define the structure of examination questions and investigate some common formats. Next, we will present a strategy for answering these questions. Finally, we will give some specific guidelines on what you should do on the day of your test.

The Value of Certification

The CompTIA Network+ certification program, like the certification programs from Microsoft, Cisco, Oracle, and other software vendors, is maintained for the ultimate purpose of increasing the corporation's profits through the creation of skilled workers. A successful certification program accomplishes this goal by helping to create a pool of certification questions that not only test the knowledge of the candidate, but also test their skills.

Vendor certification has become increasingly popular over the years because it helps employers find qualified workers, and it helps software vendors, such as Microsoft, sell their products. A number of employers are looking for IT professionals who hold IT certifications, and a number of individuals are overlooked because they don't hold the required certification.

A marked characteristic of the computer certification program is an emphasis on performing specific job tasks rather than merely gathering knowledge. It may come as a shock, but most potential employers do not care how much you know about the theory of operating systems, networking, or database design. As one IT manager put it, "I don't really care what my employees know about the theory of our network. We don't need someone to sit at a desk and think about it. We need people who can actually do something to make it work better."

CompTIA's Network+ certification program will be testing you on current network implementations in wide use today, including network-related hardware and software. The job task orientation of certification is almost as obvious, but testing real-world job skills using a computer-based test is not an easy test. In Network+, CompTIA have created a great certification exam that ensures a candidate knows the basics of networking.

Test Structure and Specifications

The 2015 version of the CompTIA Network+ Certification exam is exam number N10-006. You can book your exam online at www.pearsonvue.com. The Network+ exam cost is approximately US$277, but the price may be different in your country. The exam is approximately 90 questions, and you have 90 minutes to complete the exam. The passing score is 720 on a scale of 100 to 900. It is recommended, not required, that you have your A+ certification and 9 months' networking experience before taking the exam.

The topics that you are tested on are divided into domains. The following table shows the different domains and the corresponding percentage of exam questions based on that domain.

Domain	% of Examination
1.0 Network architecture	22%
2.0 Network operations	20%
3.0 Network security	18%
4.0 Troubleshooting	24%
5.0 Industry standards, practices, and network theory	16%
Total	**100%**

The Network+ exam is known as a form test; this is the type of test that we are most familiar with. A form test is made up of a number of multiple-choice questions, and you can go to previous questions at any point. For the CompTIA certification, a form consists of 90 questions and allows for 90 minutes to complete it.

The CompTIA Network+ exam is a form-based test where each correct answer gives you the same amount of points. The score is on a scale from 100 to 900, and a score of 720 must be obtained in order to pass. An interesting and useful characteristic of a form test is that you can mark a question you have doubts about as you take the test. Assuming you have time left when you finish all the questions, you can return and spend more time on the questions you have marked as doubtful.

Question Types

Computerized test questions can be presented in a number of ways. Some of the possible formats for questions are listed next, and you may find any of the following types of questions on your Network+ certification exam.

True/False

We are all familiar with true/false questions, but because of the inherent 50 percent chance of choosing the correct answer, you will most likely not see true/false questions on your Network+ certification exam.

Multiple Choice

The majority of Network+ certification questions are in the multiple-choice format, with either a single correct answer or multiple correct answers that need to be selected. One interesting variation on multiple-choice questions with multiple correct answers is whether or not the candidate is told how many answers are correct—you might be told to select all that apply.

Graphical Questions

One or more graphical elements are sometimes used as exhibits to help present or clarify an exam question. These elements may take the form of a network diagram or pictures of networking components on which you are being tested. It is often easier to present the concepts required for a complex performance-based scenario with a graphic than it is with words. Expect to see some graphical questions on your Network+ exam.

Test questions known as *hotspots* actually incorporate graphics as part of the answer. These questions ask the certification candidate to click a location or graphical element to answer the question. As an example, you might be shown the diagram of a network and asked to click on an appropriate location for a router. The answer is correct if the candidate clicks within the hotspot that defines the correct location. The Network+ exam has a few of these graphical hotspot questions, and most are asking you to identify network types, such as a bus or star network. As with the graphical questions, expect only a couple of hotspot questions during your exam.

Free Response Questions

Another kind of question you sometimes see on certification examinations requires a *free response* or type-in answer. This type of question might present a TCP/IP network scenario and ask the candidate to calculate and enter the correct subnet mask in dotted decimal notation. However, the CompTIA Network+ exam most likely will not contain any free response questions.

Scenario-Based Questions

CompTIA certification exams have gotten more difficult in recent years. The exams not only test you on your technical knowledge through knowledge-based questions, but they now have scenario-based questions that present you with a situation and you need to give the best answer based on that situation.

Knowledge-based questions are fairly straightforward and simply expect you to understand or know a particular concept. Knowledge-based objectives typically use verbs such as *list* and *identify* and tend to test only what you know, not what you can do. For example:

Objective:
5.9 Compare and contrast the following ports and protocols
Which of the following ports is used by POP3 to read e-mail?

    A. 80

    B. 443

    C. 143

    D. 110

Correct answer: D.

The Network+ exam consists of a mix of knowledge-based and scenario-based multiple-choice questions that can be answered fairly quickly if you know your stuff. These questions can be tricky at times, but always narrow it down by eliminating the choices you know are not correct first.

Other objectives use action verbs such as *install, configure,* and *troubleshoot* to define job tasks. These objectives can often be tested with either a knowledge-based question or a scenario-based question. CompTIA are focused on presenting more scenario-based questions where you will need to read about a situation and make an informed decision. For example:

You want to ensure you have a reliable tape backup scheme that is not susceptible to fire and water hazards. You are backing up three Windows servers and would like to completely back up the entire system. Which of the following is the most reliable backup method?

    A. Configure the backup program to back up the user files and operating system files; complete a test restore of the backup; and store the backup tapes offsite in a fireproof vault.

    B. Configure the backup program to back up the entire hard drive of each server, and store the backup tapes offsite in a fireproof vault.

    C. Copy the user files to another server; configure the backup program to back up the operating system files; and store the backup tapes offsite in a fireproof vault.

    D. Configure the backup program to back up the user files and operating system files, and store the backup tapes offsite in a fireproof vault.

Correct answer: A.

Even in this simple example, the superiority of the scenario-based question is obvious. Whereas the knowledge-based question asks for a single fact, the scenario-based question presents a real-life situation and requires that you make a decision based on this scenario. Thus, scenario-based questions give more bang (validity) for the test author's buck (individual question).

Performance-Based Questions

The new CompTIA certification exams now include what is known as performance-based questions. These questions typically involve a graphical element to the question that you need to interact with. For example, you may be presented with a network diagram and need to drag the correct IP addresses to different devices in the diagram. Or you may need to place the network device, such as a router or switch, in the correct location.

Another example of a performance-based question you may receive may list different network services on one side of the screen, and you need to drag the appropriate port number to the appropriate network service. In order to help you prepare for these style questions, we have placed samples on the accompanying material for this book and are including videos of yours truly demonstrating how to answer these style questions on the real exam!

Study Strategies

There are a number of different ways to study for the different types of questions you will see on a CompTIA Network+ certification examination. The following section outlines some of the methods you can use to prepare for the different types of questions.

Knowledge-Based Questions

Knowledge-based questions require that you memorize facts. There are hundreds of facts inherent in every content area of every Network+ certification examination. There are several tricks to memorizing facts:

- **Repetition** The more times your brain is exposed to a fact, the more likely you are to remember it. Flash cards are a wonderful tool for repetition. Either make your own flash cards on paper or download a flash card program and develop your own questions.

- **Association** Connecting facts within a logical framework makes them easier to remember. Try using mnemonics, such as "All People Seem To Need Data Processing" to remember the seven layers of the OSI model in order.

- **Motor association** It is often easier to remember something if you write it down or perform some other physical act, such as clicking on a practice test answer. You will find that hands-on experience with the product or concept being tested is a great way to develop motor association.

We have said that the emphasis of CompTIA certification is job performance, and that there are very few knowledge-based questions on CompTIA certification exams. Why should you waste a lot of time learning filenames, IP address formulas, and other minutiae? Read on.

Scenario-Based Questions

Most of the questions you will face on a CompTIA certification exam are scenario-based questions. We have discussed the superiority of these questions over simple knowledge-based questions, but you should remember that the job task orientation of CompTIA certification extends the knowledge you need to pass the exams; it does not replace this knowledge. Therefore, the first step in preparing for scenario questions is to absorb as many facts relating to the exam content areas as you can. In other words, go back to the previous section and follow the steps to prepare for an exam composed of knowledge-based questions.

The second step is to familiarize yourself with the format of the questions you are likely to see on the exam. You can do this by answering the questions in this study guide and by doing the practice tests that accompany this study guide. The day of your test is not the time to be surprised by the complicated construction of some exam questions.

At best, these scenario-based questions really do test certification candidates at a higher cognitive level than knowledge-based questions do. At worst, these questions can test your reading comprehension and test-taking ability rather than your ability to administer networks. Be sure to get in the habit of reading the question carefully to determine what is being asked.

The third step in preparing for CompTIA scenario questions is to adopt the following attitude: scenario-based questions are just knowledge-based questions with a little story wrapped around them.

To answer a scenario-based question, you have to sift through the story to the underlying facts of the situation and apply your knowledge to determine the correct answer. This may sound silly at first, but the process we go through in solving real-life problems is quite similar. The key concept is that every scenario-based question (and every real-life problem) has a fact at its center, and if we can identify that fact, we can answer the question.

Exam Readiness Checklist

Exam Objective	Ch #	Beginner	Intermediate	Advanced
1.0 Network architecture				
1.1 Explain the functions and applications of various network devices	*3*			
Router	3			
Switch	3			
Multilayer switch	3			
Firewall	3			
HIDS	3			
IDS/IPS	3			
Access point (wireless/wired)	3			
Content filter	3			
Load balancer	3			
Hub	3			
Analog modem	3			
Packet shaper	3			
VPN concentrator	3			
1.2 Compare and contrast the use of networking services and applications	*11*			
VPN	11			
Site to site/host to site/host to host	11			
Protocols	11			
TACACS/RADIUS	11			
RAS	11			
Web services	5			
Unified voice services	5			
Network controllers	5			
1.3 Install and configure the following networking services/applications	*9*			
DHCP	9			
Static vs. dynamic IP addressing	9			
Reservations	9			
Scopes	9			

Exam Readiness Checklist

Exam Objective	Ch #	Beginner	Intermediate	Advanced
Leases	9			
Options (DNS servers, suffixes)	9			
IP helper/DHCP relay	9			
DNS	9			
DNS servers	9			
DNS records (A, MX, AAAA, CNAME, PTR)	9			
Dynamic DNS	9			
Proxy/reverse proxy	9			
NAT	9			
PAT	9			
SNAT	9			
DNAT	9			
Port forwarding	9			
1.4 Explain the characteristics and benefits of various WAN technologies	12			
Fiber	12			
SONET	12			
DWDM	12			
CWDM	12			
Frame relay	12			
Satellite	12			
Broadband cable	12			
DSL/ADSL	12			
ISDN	12			
ATM	12			
PPP/Multilink PPP	12			
MPLS	12			
GSM/CDMA	12			
LTE/4G	12			
HSPA+	12			

Exam Readiness Checklist

Exam Objective	Ch #	Beginner	Intermediate	Advanced
3G	12			
Edge	12			
Dial-up	12			
WiMAX	12			
Metro-Ethernet	12			
Leased lines	12			
T-1	12			
T-3	12			
E-1	12			
E-3	12			
OC3	12			
OC12	12			
Circuit switch vs. packet switch	12			
1.5 Install and properly terminate various cable types and connectors using appropriate tools	1			
Copper connectors	1			
RJ-11	1			
RJ-45	1			
RJ-48C	1			
DB-9/RS-232	1			
DB-25	1			
UTP coupler	1			
BNC coupler	1			
BNC	1			
F-connector	1			
110 block	3			
66 block	3			
Copper cables	1			
Shielded vs. unshielded	1			

Exam Readiness Checklist

Exam Objective	Ch #	Beginner	Intermediate	Advanced
CAT 3, CAT 5, CAT 5e, CAT 6, CAT 6a	1			
PVC vs. plenum	3			
RG-59	1			
RG-6	1			
Straight-through vs. crossover vs. rollover	1			
Fiber connectors	1			
ST	1			
SC	1			
LC	1			
MTRJ	1			
FC	1			
Fiber coupler	1			
Fiber cables	1			
Single mode	1			
Multimode	1			
APC vs. UPC	1			
Media converters	1			
Single-mode fiber to Ethernet	1			
Multimode fiber to Ethernet	1			
Fiber to coaxial	1			
Single-mode to multimode fiber	1			
Tools	18			
Cable crimpers	18			
Punch-down tool	18			
Wire strippers	18			
Snips	18			
OTDR	18			
Cable certifier	18			

Exam Readiness Checklist

Exam Objective	Ch #	Beginner	Intermediate	Advanced
1.6 Differentiate between common network topologies	1			
Mesh	1			
Partial	1			
Full	1			
Bus	1			
Ring	1			
Star	1			
Hybrid	1			
Point-to-point	1			
Point-to-multipoint	1			
Client-server	1			
Peer-to-peer	1			
1.7 Differentiate between network infrastructure implementations	1			
WAN	1			
MAN	1			
LAN	1			
WLAN	1			
Hotspot	1			
PAN	10			
Bluetooth	10			
IR	10			
NFC	10			
SCADA/ICS	3			
ICS server	3			
DCS/closed network	3			
Remote terminal unit	3			
Programmable logic controller	3			

Exam Readiness Checklist

Exam Objective	Ch #	Beginner	Intermediate	Advanced
Medianets	3			
VTC	3			
ISDN	11			
IP/SIP	5			
1.8 Given a scenario, implement and configure the appropriate addressing schema	5			
IPv6	5			
Auto-configuration	5			
DHCP6	5			
Link local	5			
Address structure	5			
Address compression	5			
Tunneling 6to4, 4to6	5			
IPv4	4			
Address structure	4			
Subnetting	8			
APIPA	4			
Classful A, B, C, D	4			
Classless	8			
Private vs. public	4			
NAT/PAT	5			
MAC addressing	4			
Multicast	4			
Unicast	4			
Broadcast	4			
Broadcast domains vs. collision domains	3			
1.9 Explain the basics of routing concepts and protocols	8			
Loopback interface	8			
Routing loops	8			

Exam Readiness Checklist

Exam Objective	Ch #	Beginner	Intermediate	Advanced
Routing tables	8			
Static vs. dynamic routes	8			
Default route	8			
Distance vector routing protocols	8			
RIP v2	8			
Hybrid routing protocols	8			
BGP	8			
Link state routing protocols	8			
OSPF	8			
IS-IS	8			
Interior vs. exterior gateway routing protocols	8			
Autonomous system numbers	8			
Route redistribution	8			
High availability	8			
VRRP	8			
Virtual IP	8			
HSRP	8			
Route aggregation	8			
Routing metrics	8			
Hop counts	8			
MTU, bandwidth	8			
Costs	8			
Latency	8			
Administrative distance	8			
SPB	8			
1.10 Identify the basics elements of unified communication technologies	9			
VoIP	9			
Video	9			

Exam Readiness Checklist

Exam Objective	Ch #	Beginner	Intermediate	Advanced
Real-time services	9			
Presence	9			
Multicast vs. unicast	9			
QoS	9			
DSCP	9			
COS	9			
Devices	9			
UC servers	9			
UC devices	9			
UC gateways	9			
1.11 Compare and contrast technologies that support cloud and virtualization	3			
Virtualization	3			
Virtual switches	3			
Virtual routers	3			
Virtual firewall	3			
Virtual vs. physical NICs	3			
Software-defined networking	3			
Storage area network	3			
iSCSI	3			
Jumbo frame	3			
Fibre Channel	3			
Network attached storage	3			
Cloud concepts	3			
Public IaaS, SaaS, PaaS	3			
Private IaaS, SaaS, PaaS	3			
Hybrid IaaS, SaaS, PaaS	3			
Community IaaS, SaaS, PaaS	3			

Exam Readiness Checklist

Exam Objective	Ch #	Beginner	Intermediate	Advanced
1.12 Given a set of requirements, implement a basic network	*13*			
List of requirements	13			
Device types/requirements	13			
Environment limitations	13			
Equipment limitations	13			
Compatibility requirements	13			
Wired/wireless considerations	13			
Security considerations	13			
2.0 Network operations				
2.1 Given a scenario, use appropriate monitoring tools	*17*			
Packet/network analyzer	17			
Interface monitoring tools	17			
Port scanner	17			
Top talkers/listeners	17			
SNMP management software	17			
Trap	17			
Get	17			
Walk	17			
MIBS	17			
Alerts	17			
E-mail	17			
SMS	17			
Packet flow monitoring	17			
SYSLOG	17			
SIEM	17			
Environmental monitoring tools	17			
Temperature	17			
Humidity	17			

Exam Readiness Checklist

Exam Objective	Ch #	Beginner	Intermediate	Advanced
Power monitoring tools	17			
Wireless survey tools	10			
Wireless analyzers	10			
2.2 Given a scenario, analyze metrics and reports from monitoring and tracking performance tools	*17*			
Baseline	17			
Bottleneck	17			
Log management	17			
Graphing	17			
Utilization	17			
Bandwidth	17			
Storage	17			
Network device CPU	17			
Network device memory	17			
Wireless channel utilization	10			
Link status	17			
Interface monitoring	17			
Errors	17			
Utilization	17			
Discards	17			
Packet drops	17			
Interface resets	17			
Speed and duplex	17			
2.3 Given a scenario, use appropriate resources to support configuration management	*14*			
Archives/backups	14			
Baselines	14			
On-boarding and off-boarding of mobile devices	14			
NAC	14			

Exam Readiness Checklist

Exam Objective	Ch #	Beginner	Intermediate	Advanced
Documentation	14			
Network diagrams (logical/physical)	14			
Asset management	14			
IP address utilization	14			
Vendor documentation	14			
Internal operating procedures/policies/standards	14			
2.4 Explain the importance of implementing network segmentation	*15*			
SCADA systems/industrial control systems	15			
Legacy systems	15			
Separate private/public networks	15			
Honeypot/honeynet	15			
Testing lab	15			
Load balancing	15			
Performance optimization	15			
Security	15			
Compliance	15			
2.5 Given a scenario, install and apply patches and updates	*14*			
OS updates	14			
Firmware updates	14			
Driver updates	14			
Feature changes/updates	14			
Major vs. minor updates	14			
Vulnerability patches	14			
Upgrading vs. downgrading	14			
Configuration backup	14			
2.6 Given a scenario, configure a switch using proper features	*7*			
VLAN	7			
Native VLAN/default VLAN	7			
VTP	7			

Exam Readiness Checklist

Exam Objective	Ch #	Beginner	Intermediate	Advanced
Spanning Tree (802.1d)/Rapid Spanning Tree (802.1w)	7			
Flooding	7			
Forwarding/blocking	7			
Filtering	7			
Interface configuration	7			
Trunking/802.1q	7			
Tag vs. untag VLANs	7			
Port bonding (LACP)	7			
Port mirroring (local vs. remote)	7			
Speed and duplexing	7			
IP address assignment	7			
VLAN assignment	7			
Default gateway	7			
PoE and PoE+ (802.3af, 802.3at)	7			
Switch management	7			
User/passwords	7			
AAA configuration	7			
Console	7			
Virtual terminals	7			
In-band/out-of-band management	7			
Managed vs. unmanaged	7			
2.7 Install and configure wireless LAN infrastructure and implement the appropriate technologies in support of wireless capable devices	*10*			
Small office/home office wireless router	10			
Wireless access points	10			
Device density	10			
Roaming	10			
Wireless controllers	10			
Wireless bridge	10			

Exam Readiness Checklist

Exam Objective	Ch #	Beginner	Intermediate	Advanced
Site surveys	10			
Heat maps	10			
Frequencies	10			
2.4 GHz	10			
5.0 GHz	10			
Channels	10			
Goodput	10			
Connection types	10			
802.11a-ht	10			
802.11g-ht	10			
Antenna placement	10			
Antenna types	10			
Omnidirectional	10			
Unidirectional	10			
MIMO/MUMIMO	10			
Signal strength	10			
Coverage	10			
Differences between device antennas	10			
SSID broadcast	10			
Topologies	10			
Ad hoc	10			
Mesh	10			
Infrastructure	10			
Mobile devices	10			
Cell phones	10			
Laptops	10			
Tablets	10			
Gaming devices	10			
Media devices	10			

Exam Readiness Checklist

Exam Objective	Ch #	Beginner	Intermediate	Advanced
3.0 Network security				
3.1 Compare and contrast risk-related concepts	*15*			
Disaster recovery	15			
Business continuity	15			
Battery backups/UPS	15			
First responders	15			
Data breach	15			
End-user awareness and training	15			
Single point of failure	15			
Critical nodes	15			
Critical assets	15			
Redundancy	15			
Adherence to standards and policies	15			
Vulnerability scanning	15			
Penetration testing	15			
3.2 Compare and contrast common network vulnerabilities and threats	*15*			
Attacks/threats	15			
Denial of service	15			
Distributed DoS	15			
Reflective/amplified	15			
Friendly/unintentional DoS	15			
Physical attack	15			
ARP cache poisoning	15			
Packet/protocol abuse	15			
Spoofing	15			
Wireless	15			
Evil twin	10			
Rogue AP	10			

Exam Readiness Checklist

Exam Objective	Ch #	Beginner	Intermediate	Advanced
War driving	10			
War chalking	10			
Bluejacking	10			
Bluesnarfing	10			
WPA/WEP/WPS attacks	10			
Brute force	10			
Session hijacking	10			
Social engineering	15			
Man-in-the-middle	15			
VLAN hopping	15			
Compromised system	15			
Effect of malware on the network	15			
Insider threat/malicious employee	15			
Zero-day attacks	15			
Vulnerabilities	15			
Unnecessary running services	15			
Open ports	15			
Unpatched/legacy systems	15			
Unencrypted channels	15			
Clear-text credentials	15			
Unsecure protocols	15			
TEMPEST/RF emanation	15			
3.3 Given a scenario, implement network hardening techniques	*16*			
Antimalware software	16			
Host-based	16			
Cloud-/server-based	16			
Network-based	16			
Switch port security	16			
DHCP snooping	16			

Exam Readiness Checklist

Exam Objective	Ch #	Beginner	Intermediate	Advanced
ARP inspection	16			
MAC address filtering	16			
VLAN assignments	16			
Security policies	16			
Disable unneeded network services	16			
Use secure protocols	16			
SSH	16			
SNMPv3	16			
TLS/SSL	16			
SFTP	16			
HTTPS	16			
IPSec	16			
Access lists	16			
Web/content filtering	16			
Port filtering	16			
IP filtering	16			
Implicit deny	16			
Wireless security	10			
WEP	10			
WPA/WPA2	10			
TKIP/AES	10			
802.1x	10			
TLS/TTLS	10			
MAC filtering	10			
User authentication	11			
CHAP/MSCHAP	11			
PAP	11			
EAP	11			
Kerberos	11			

Exam Readiness Checklist

Exam Objective	Ch #	Beginner	Intermediate	Advanced
Multifactor authentication	11			
Two-factor authentication	11			
Single sign-on	11			
Hashes	15			
MD5	15			
SHA	15			
3.4 Compare and contrast physical security controls	*16*			
Mantraps	16			
Network closets	16			
Video monitoring	16			
IP cameras/CCTVs	16			
Door access controls	16			
Proximity readers/key fob	16			
Biometrics	16			
Keypad/cipher locks	16			
Security guard	16			
3.5 Given a scenario, install and configure a basic firewall	*16*			
Types of firewalls	16			
Host-based	16			
Network-based	16			
Software vs. hardware	16			
Application aware/context aware	16			
Small office/home office firewall	16			
Stateful vs. stateless inspection	16			
UTM	16			
Settings/techniques	16			
ACL	16			
Virtual wire vs. routed	16			

Exam Readiness Checklist

Exam Objective	Ch #	Beginner	Intermediate	Advanced
DMZ	16			
Implicit deny	16			
Block/allow	16			
Firewall placement	16			
3.6 Explain the purpose of various network access control models	*16*			
802.1x	16			
Posture assessment	16			
Guest network	16			
Persistent vs. non-persistent agents	16			
Quarantine network	16			
Edge vs. access control	16			
3.7 Summarize basic forensic concepts	*16*			
First responder	16			
Secure the area	16			
Escalate when necessary	16			
Document the scene	16			
e-discovery	16			
Evidence/data collection	16			
Chain of custody	16			
Data transport	16			
Forensics report	16			
Legal hold	16			
4.0 Troubleshooting				
4.1 Given a scenario, implement the following network troubleshooting methodology	*18*			
Identify the problem	18			
Gather information	18			
Duplicate the problem, if possible	18			
Question users	18			

Exam Readiness Checklist

Exam Objective	Ch #	Beginner	Intermediate	Advanced
Identify symptoms	18			
Determine if anything has changed	18			
Approach multiple problems individually	18			
Establish a theory of probable cause	18			
Question the obvious	18			
Consider multiple approaches	18			
Test the theory to determine cause	18			
Once theory is confirmed, determine next steps to resolve problem	18			
If theory is not confirmed, re-establish new theory or escalate	18			
Establish a plan of action to resolve the problem and identify potential effects	18			
Implement the solution or escalate as necessary	18			
Verify full system functionality and, if applicable, implement preventative measures	18			
Document findings, actions, and outcomes	18			
4.2 Given a scenario, analyze and interpret the output of troubleshooting tools	*18*			
Command-line tools	6			
ipconfig	6			
netstat	6			
ifconfig	6			
ping/ping6/ping -6	6			
tracert/tracert -6/traceroute6/traceroute -6	6			
nbtstat	6			
nslookup	6			
arp	6			
mac address lookup table	6			
pathping	6			
Line testers	18			
Certifiers	18			
Multimeter	18			
Cable tester	18			

Exam Readiness Checklist

Exam Objective	Ch #	Beginner	Intermediate	Advanced
Light meter	18			
Toner probe	18			
Speed test sites	18			
Looking glass sites	18			
Wi-Fi analyzer	18			
Protocol analyzer	18			
4.3 Given a scenario, troubleshoot and resolve common wireless issues	*10*			
Signal loss	10			
Interference	10			
Overlapping channels	10			
Mismatched channels	10			
Signal-to-noise ratio	10			
Device saturation	10			
Bandwidth saturation	10			
Untested updates	10			
Wrong SSID	10			
Power levels	10			
Open networks	10			
Rogue access point	10			
Wrong antenna type	10			
Incompatibilities	10			
Wrong encryption	10			
Bounce	10			
MIMO	10			
AP placement	10			
AP configurations	10			
LWAPP	10			
Thin vs. thick	10			

Exam Readiness Checklist

Exam Objective	Ch #	Beginner	Intermediate	Advanced
Environmental factors	10			
Concrete walls	10			
Window film	10			
Metal studs	10			
Wireless standard–related issues	10			
Throughput	10			
Frequency	10			
Distance	10			
Channels	10			
4.4 Given a scenario, troubleshoot and resolve common copper cable issues	*18*			
Shorts	18			
Opens	18			
Incorrect termination (mismatched standards)	18			
Straight-through	18			
Crossover	18			
Crosstalk	18			
Near end	18			
Far end	18			
EMI/RFI	18			
Distance limitations	18			
Attenuation/Db loss	18			
Bad connector	18			
Bad wiring	18			
Split pairs	18			
Tx/Rx reverse	18			
Cable placement	18			
Bad SFP/GBIC – cable or transceiver	18			

Exam Readiness Checklist

Exam Objective	Ch #	Beginner	Intermediate	Advanced
4.5 Given a scenario, troubleshoot and resolve common fiber cable issues	*18*			
Attenuation/Db loss	18			
SFP/GBIC – cable mismatch	18			
Bad SFP/GBIC – cable or transceiver	18			
Wavelength mismatch	18			
Fiber type mismatch	18			
Dirty connectors	18			
Connector mismatch	18			
Bend radius limitations	18			
Distance limitations	18			
4.6 Given a scenario, troubleshoot and resolve common network issues	*18*			
Incorrect IP configuration/default gateway	18			
Broadcast storms/switching loop	18			
Duplicate IP	18			
Speed and duplex mismatch	18			
End-to-end connectivity	18			
Incorrect VLAN assignment	18			
Hardware failure	18			
Misconfigured DHCP	18			
Misconfigured DNS	18			
Incorrect interface/interface misconfiguration	18			
Cable placement	18			
Interface errors	18			
Simultaneous wired/wireless connections	18			
Discovering neighboring devices/nodes	18			
Power failure/power anomalies	18			
MTU/MTU black hole	18			
Missing IP routes	18			

Exam Readiness Checklist

Exam Objective	Ch #	Beginner	Intermediate	Advanced
NIC teaming misconfiguration	18			
Active-active vs. active-passive	18			
Multicast vs. broadcast	18			
4.7 Given a scenario, troubleshoot and resolve common security issues	*18*			
Misconfigured firewall	18			
Misconfigured ACLs/applications	18			
Malware	18			
Denial of service	18			
Open/closed ports	18			
ICMP-related issues	18			
Ping of death	18			
Unreachable default gateway	18			
Unpatched firmware/OSs	18			
Malicious users	18			
Trusted	18			
Untrusted users	18			
Packet sniffing	18			
Authentication issues	18			
TACACS/RADIUS misconfigurations	18			
Default passwords/settings	18			
Improper access/backdoor access	18			
ARP issues	18			
Banner grabbing/OUI	18			
Domain/local group configurations	18			
Jamming	18			
4.8 Given a scenario, troubleshoot and resolve common WAN issues	*18*			
Loss of Internet connectivity	18			
Interface errors	18			
Split horizon	18			

Exam Readiness Checklist

Exam Objective	Ch #	Beginner	Intermediate	Advanced
DNS issues	18			
Interference	18			
Router configurations	18			
Customer premise equipment	18			
Smart jack/NIU	18			
Demarc	18			
Loopback	18			
CSU/DSU	18			
Copper line drivers/repeaters	18			
Company security policy	18			
Throttling	18			
Blocking	18			
Fair access policy/utilization limits	18			
Satellite issues	18			
Latency	18			
5.0 Industry standards, practices, and network theory				
5.1 Analyze a scenario and determine the corresponding OSI layer	2			
Layer 1 – Physical	2			
Layer 2 – Data link	2			
Layer 3 – Network	2			
Layer 4 – Transport	2			
Layer 5 – Session	2			
Layer 6 – Presentation	2			
Layer 7 – Application	2			
5.2 Explain the basics of network theory and concepts	1			
Encapsulation/de-encapsulation	2			
Modulation techniques	1			
Multiplexing	1			
De-multiplexing	1			

Exam Readiness Checklist

Exam Objective	Ch #	Beginner	Intermediate	Advanced
Analog and digital techniques	1			
TDM	1			
Numbering systems	4			
Binary	4			
Hexadecimal	5			
Octal	4			
Broadband/base band	1			
Bit rates vs. baud rate	1			
Sampling size	1			
CDMA/CD and CSMA/CA	1			
Carrier detect/sense	1			
Wavelength	1			
TCP/IP suite	5			
ICMP	5			
UDP	5			
TCP	5			
Collision	1			
5.3 Given a scenario, deploy the appropriate wireless standard	*10*			
802.11a	10			
802.11b	10			
802.11g	10			
802.11n	10			
802.11ac	10			
5.4 Given a scenario, deploy the appropriate wired connectivity standard	*1*			
Ethernet standards	1			
10BaseT	1			
100BaseT	1			
1000BaseT	1			

Exam Readiness Checklist

Exam Objective	Ch #	Beginner	Intermediate	Advanced
1000BaseTX	1			
10GBaseT	1			
100BaseFX	1			
10Base2	1			
10GBaseSR	1			
10GBaseER	1			
10GBaseSW	1			
IEEE 1901-2013	1			
Wiring standards	1			
EIA/TIA 568A/568B	1			
Broadband standards	1			
DOCSIS	1			
5.5 Given a scenario, implement the appropriate policies or procedures	*15*			
Security policies	15			
Consent to monitoring	15			
Network policies	15			
Acceptable use policy	15			
Standard business documents	15			
SLA	15			
MOU	15			
MSA (was MLA, but changed to MSA as per v5 of objectives)	15			
SOW	15			
5.6 Summarize safety practices	*14*			
Electrical safety	14			
Grounding	14			
ESD	14			
Static	14			

Exam Readiness Checklist

Exam Objective	Ch #	Beginner	Intermediate	Advanced
Installation safety	14			
Lifting equipment	14			
Rack installation	14			
Placement	14			
Tool safety	14			
MSDS	14			
Emergency procedures	14			
Building layout	14			
Fire escape plan	14			
Safety/emergency exits	14			
Fail open/fail close	14			
Emergency alert system	14			
Fire suppression systems	14			
HVAC	14			
5.7 Given a scenario, install and configure equipment in the appropriate location using best practices	3			
Intermediate distribution frame	3			
Main distribution frame	3			
Cable management	3			
Patch panels	3			
Power management	3			
Power converters	3			
Circuits	3			
UPS	3			
Inverters	3			
Power redundancy	3			
Device placement	3			
Air flow	3			
Cable trays	3			

Exam Readiness Checklist

Exam Objective	Ch #	Beginner	Intermediate	Advanced
Rack systems	3			
Server rail racks	3			
Two-post racks	3			
Four-post racks	3			
Free-standing racks	3			
Labeling	3			
Port labeling	3			
System labeling	3			
Circuit labeling	3			
Naming conventions	3			
Patch panel labeling	3			
Rack monitoring	3			
Rack security	3			
5.8 Explain the basics of change management procedures	*14*			
Document reason for a change	14			
Change request	14			
Configuration procedures	14			
Rollback process	14			
Potential impact	14			
Notification	14			
Approval process	14			
Maintenance window	14			
Authorized downtime	14			
Notification of change	14			
Documentation	14			
Network configurations	14			
Additions to network	14			
Physical location changes	14			

Exam Readiness Checklist

Exam Objective	Ch #	Beginner	Intermediate	Advanced
5.9 Compare and contrast the following ports and protocols	4			
80 HTTP	4			
443 HTTPS	4			
137-139 NetBIOS	4			
110 POP	4			
143 IMAP	4			
25 SMTP	4			
5060/5061 SIP	4			
2427/2727 MGCP	4			
5004/5005 RTP	4			
1720 H.323	4			
TCP	5			
Connection-oriented	5			
UDP	5			
Connectionless	5			
5.10 Given a scenario, configure and apply the appropriate ports and protocols	4			
20, 21 FTP	4			
161 SNMP	4			
22 SSH	4			
23 Telnet	4			
53 DNS	4			
67, 68 DHCP	4			
69 TFTP	4			
445 SMB	4			
3389 RDP	4			

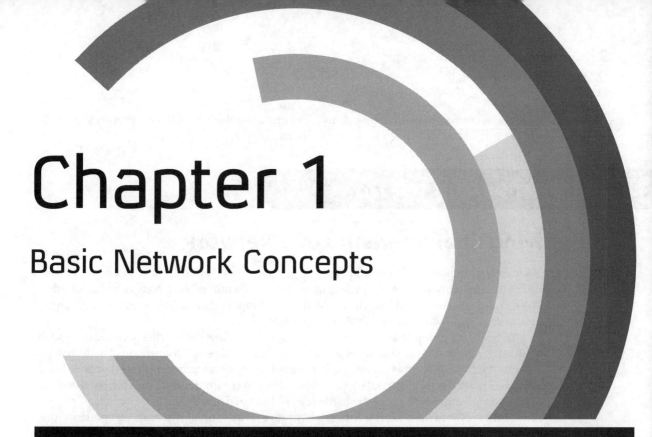

Chapter 1

Basic Network Concepts

Knowing how computers communicate in a network environment is essential to passing the Network+ certification exam and successfully troubleshooting networking issues. This chapter introduces you to the basics of what makes a network tick, and covers topics and terminology that will set the foundation for the rest of your studies.

We will look at the various topologies, network operating systems, and common terminology used in day-to-day discussions between IT professionals. In this chapter, you will learn the purpose of a network; the different types of networks; network topologies, cables, and connectors; and network architectures. You will finish the chapter by learning about some of the most popular network operating systems.

Identifying Characteristics of a Network

More and more people are building home and small office networks now as a result of the low cost of networking devices such as hubs and home routers. As a Network+ Certified Professional, you will need to ensure that you can support these small, medium, and large networks, so you will start by learning some basic terms.

A network is a group of systems that are connected to allow the sharing of resources—such as files or printers—or the sharing of services—such as an Internet connection. There are two aspects of setting up a network: the hardware used to connect the systems together and the software installed on the computers that allows them to communicate. This chapter is designed to give you an understanding of the hardware used to build a network, and later chapters discuss the software needed. The network hardware is made up of two basic components: the entities that want to share the information or resources, such as servers and workstations, and the medium that enables the entities to communicate, which is a cable or a wireless device.

Servers, Workstations, and Hosts

A typical network involves having users sit at workstations, running such applications as word processors or spreadsheet programs. The workstation also is known as a client, which is just a basic computer running a client operating system, such as Windows 7 or Linux. These users typically store their files on a central server so that they can share the files with other users on the network. The server is a special computer that contains more disk space and memory than is found on client workstations and has special software installed that allows it to function as a server. This special software can provide file and print services, webpages to clients, or e-mail functionality to the company.

The term *host* refers to any computer or device that is connected to a network and sends or receives information on that network. A host can be a server, a workstation, a printer with its own network card, or a device such as a router. We can summarize by saying that any system or device that is connected to the network is known as a host.

WANs, LANs, and MANs

Some other terms that you will hear often are LAN, WAN, and MAN. A *local area network (LAN)* typically is confined to a single building, such as an office building, your home network, or a college campus. A *wide area network (WAN)* spans multiple geographic locations and is typically made up of multiple LANs. For example, I have a company with an office in Halifax, Nova Scotia, that has 100 computers all connected together. This would be considered a LAN. Now if we expand the company and create an office in Toronto, the network in Toronto also would be considered a LAN. If we want to allow the two offices to share information with one another, we would connect the two LANs together, creating a WAN.

The term *metropolitan area network (MAN)* is not used often anymore; it refers to a network that exists within a single city or metropolitan area. If we had two different buildings within a city that were connected together, it would be considered a MAN.

Another common network acronym we see is WLAN, which stands for *wireless LAN.* A wireless LAN is a wireless network that is made up of a hotspot created by a wireless access point. You can connect wireless devices such as laptops, tablets, and mobile phones to the wireless network by connecting them to the wireless access point so that they can access resources such as the Internet. You will learn more about wireless networks in Chapter 10.

Types of Networks

Organizations of different sizes, structures, and budgets need different types of networks. The network needs for a local newspaper company would be different from the needs of a multinational company. Networks can be divided into one of two categories: peer-to-peer or server-based.

Peer-to-Peer

A *peer-to-peer* network has no dedicated servers; instead, a number of workstations are connected together for the purpose of sharing information or devices. When there is no dedicated server, all workstations are considered equal; any one of them can participate as the client or the server. Peer-to-peer networks are designed to satisfy the networking needs of home networks or of small companies that do not want to spend a lot of money on a dedicated server but still want to have the capability to share information or devices. For example, a small accounting firm with three employees that needs to access customer data from any of the three systems or print to one printer from any of the three systems may not want to spend a lot of money on a dedicated server. A small peer-to-peer network will allow these three computers to share the printer and the customer information with one another (see Figure 1-1). The extra cost of a server was not incurred because the existing client systems were networked together to create the peer-to-peer network.

Most of the modern operating systems, such as Windows 7 and Windows 8, already have built-in peer-to-peer networking capabilities, which is why building a peer-to-peer network would be a "cheap" network solution. The disadvantage of a peer-to-peer network is the lack of centralized administration—with peer-to-peer networks, you need to build user accounts and configure security on each system.

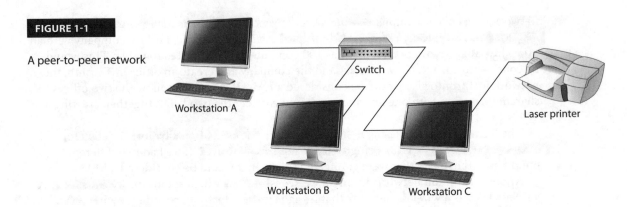

FIGURE 1-1

A peer-to-peer network

It is important to note that peer-to-peer networks are designed for fewer than ten systems, and with Microsoft client operating systems such as Windows 8, only ten concurrent network connections to those clients are allowed. This means that if you have 15 or 20 employees, for example, you eventually will need to implement a server-based network.

The Microsoft term for a peer-to-peer network is a *workgroup*. Be aware that peer-to-peer networks typically consist of fewer than ten systems.

Client-Server Networks

A big disadvantage of peer-to-peer networking is that you can't do your day-to-day administration in a single place. With peer-to-peer networking, user accounts typically are created on all the systems, and data files are stored throughout all the systems. This leads to a more complicated environment and makes your job harder as a network administrator. Usually, after four or five systems have been networked, the need for a dedicated server to store all of the user accounts and data files becomes apparent—this is known as a *client-server* network (see Figure 1-2).

The advantage of a client-server network is that the data files that will be used by all of the users are stored on the one server. This will give you a central point to set up permissions on the data files, and it will give you a central point from which to back up all of the data in case data loss should occur. With a client-server network, the network server stores a list of users who may use network resources, and usually holds the resources as well.

The server in a client-server network may provide a number of different services. The services it will offer to the network usually are decided by the server's role. There are a number of different roles that a server could play on a network:

- File and print servers
- Application servers

FIGURE 1-2

A client-server network

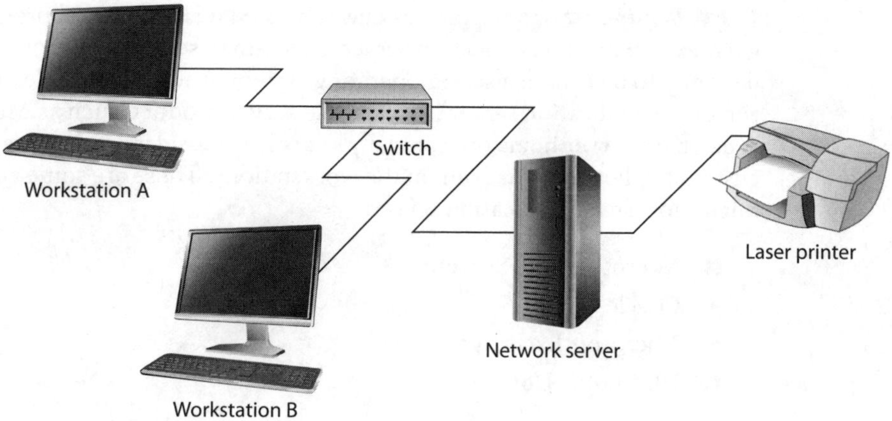

Workstation A

Switch

Workstation B

Network server

Laser printer

- Web servers
- Directory servers

File and print servers control and share printers and files among clients on the network. File and print servers were the original reason to have a network; a large number of users needed access to the same files, so the files were placed on a server, and all clients were connected to the server when they needed to work with the files. File servers often have the following characteristics:

- Large amounts of memory
- Fast hard disks
- Multiple central processing units (CPUs)
- Fast input/output (I/O) buses
- High-capacity tape drives
- Fast network adapters
- Redundant power supplies
- Hot-swappable hard disks and power supplies

File and print servers also check the access control list (ACL) of each resource before allowing a user to access a file or use a printer. If the user or a group to which the user belongs is not listed in the ACL, the user is not allowed to use the resource, and an "access denied" message appears on the user's screen.

Application servers are servers that run some form of special program on the server. A good example of an application server is an e-mail server. The e-mail server software is designed to be run on a server operating system. Another example of software that would run on an application server is a database server product, such as Microsoft SQL Server. A database server holds the company's core business data and typically gives this data to custom applications that run on the workstations. These are some applications that you might find on an application server:

■ Microsoft SQL Server
■ Oracle
■ Microsoft Exchange Server
■ IBM Lotus Domino

Web servers run the Hypertext Transfer Protocol (HTTP) and are designed to publish information on the Internet or the corporate intranet. Web servers are popular in today's businesses because they host web applications (websites) for the organization. These web applications could be designed for internal use, or they could be used to publish information to the rest of the world on the Internet. Examples of web server software are Microsoft's Internet Information Services (IIS) that runs on Windows, or Apache web server software that runs on UNIX/Linux and Windows.

Directory servers hold a list of the user accounts that are allowed to log on to the network. This list of user accounts is stored in a database known as the directory database and can store information about these user accounts, such as address, city, phone number, and fax number. A directory service is designed to be a central database that can be used to store everything about such objects as users and printers.

In a server-based network environment, the centralized administration comes from the fact that the directory server stores all user accounts in its directory database. When a user sits at a client machine to log on to the network, the logon request is sent to this directory server. If the user name and password exist in the directory database, the client is allowed to access network resources.

It is important to note that a server can have numerous roles at the same time. A server can be a file and print server, as well as an application server, or it can be a file, print, and directory server all at the same time. Because a single server can perform multiple roles, a company will not need to purchase an additional server every time a new product or feature is implemented on the network, and this fact reduces the cost of a server-based network.

Internet, Intranet, and Extranet

Internet, intranet, and extranet are three terms that describe "Internet-type" applications that are used by an organization, but how do you know if a web application is part of your intranet or part of the Internet?

Internet

If you wish to expose information to everyone in the world, then you would build an Internet-type application. An Internet-type application uses Internet protocols such as HTTP, File Transfer Protocol (FTP), or Simple Mail Transfer Protocol (SMTP) and is available to persons anywhere on the Internet. We use the Internet and web applications as ways to extend who the application can reach. For example, I no longer need to go to the bank to transfer funds. Because the bank has built a website on the Internet, I can do that from the comfort of my own home.

Intranet

An application is considered to be on the company's intranet if it is using Internet-type protocols such as HTTP or FTP but the application is available only within the company. The information on a company's intranet would not be accessible to persons on the Internet because it is not for public use. For example, a few years ago I was sitting with my banking officer going over my account and noticed that the bank had moved all of its customer account information to a website and that the banking officer was using a web browser to retrieve my account details. Although the application was being used by a web browser, it was still an "internal" application meant only for banking officers.

Extranet

From time to time, an application that has been built for the company's intranet and used by internal employees will need to be extended to select business partners or customers. If you extend your intranet out to select business partners or customers, you have created an extranet. An extranet cannot be used by anyone external to the company except for those selected individuals.

This section has introduced you to some terms such as peer-to-peer versus server-based networking, Internet, intranet, and extranet; now let's look at how the network is laid out with the different network topologies.

CERTIFICATION OBJECTIVE 1.02

Identifying Network Topologies

This section will introduce you to a number of different network topologies, but this topic is a lead-in to a bigger topic introduced later in the chapter: network architecture. A network architecture is made up of a topology, a cable type, and an access method. Before we can discuss network architectures, we need to specify what the different types of topologies, cables, and access methods are.

A network topology is the physical layout of computers, cables, and other components on a network. There are a number of different network topologies, and a network may be built using multiple topologies. The different types of network layouts are

- Bus topology
- Star topology
- Mesh topology
- Ring topology
- Hybrid topology
- Wireless topology

Bus Topologies

A bus topology uses one cable as a main trunk to connect all of the systems together (shown in Figure 1-3). A bus topology is easy to set up and requires no additional hardware, such as a hub. The cable is also called a trunk, a backbone, or a segment.

With a bus topology, when a computer sends out a signal, the signal travels the cable length in both directions. When the signal reaches the end of the cable length, it bounces back and returns in the direction it came from. This is known as signal bounce. Signal bounce is a problem, because if another signal is sent on the cable length at the same time, the two signals will collide and be destroyed and then must be retransmitted. For this reason, at each end of the cable there is a terminator. The terminator is designed to absorb the signal when the signal reaches the end, preventing signal bounce. If there is no termination, the entire network fails because of signal bounce, which also means that if there is ever a break in the cable, you will have unterminated ends and the entire network will go down.

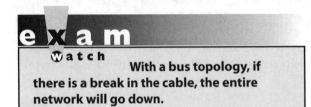

e x a m
ⓦatⓒh   **With a bus topology, if there is a break in the cable, the entire network will go down.**

A bus is a passive topology, which means that the workstations on the bus are not responsible for regenerating the signal as it passes by them. Since the workstations do not

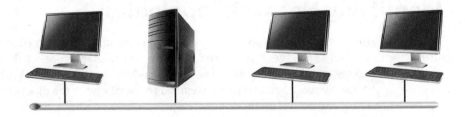

FIGURE 1-3

With a bus topology, all systems are connected to one linear cable.

play an active role, the workstations are not a requirement of a functioning bus, which means that if a workstation fails, the bus does not fail.

Advantages of a Bus Topology

One advantage of a bus topology is cost. A bus topology uses less cable than a star topology or a mesh topology, and you do not need to purchase any additional devices such as hubs. Another advantage of a bus topology is the ease of installation. With a bus topology, you simply connect the workstation to the cable segment or backbone. You only need the amount of cable necessary to connect the workstation to the backbone. The most economical choice for a network topology is a bus topology, because it is easy to work with and few additional devices are required. Most importantly, if a computer fails, the network stays functional.

Disadvantages of a Bus Topology

The main disadvantage of a bus topology is the difficulty in troubleshooting it. When the network goes down, it is usually due to a break in the cable segment. With a large network, this problem can be tough to isolate.

Scalability is an important consideration in the dynamic world of networking. Being able to make changes easily within the size and layout of your network can be important in future productivity or downtime. The bus topology is not very scalable.

Star Topologies

In a star topology, all computers are connected through one central device known as a hub or a switch, as illustrated in Figure 1-4. Each workstation has a cable that goes from the network card to the hub device. One of the major benefits of a star topology is that a break in the cable causes only the workstation that is connected to the cable to go down, not the entire network, as with a bus topology. Star topologies are popular in today's networking environments.

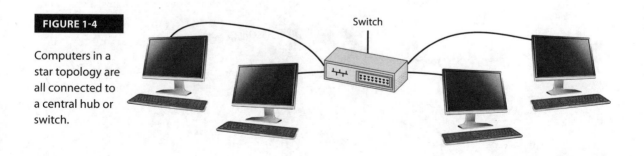

FIGURE 1-4

Computers in a star topology are all connected to a central hub or switch.

Switch

Advantages of a Star Topology

One advantage of a star topology is scalability and ease of adding another system to the network. If you need to add another workstation to the network with a star topology, you simply connect that system to an unused port on the hub. As mentioned, another benefit is the fact that if there is a break in the cable, it affects only the system that is connected to that cable. Figure 1-5 shows a hub with a few ports available.

Centralizing network components can make an administrator's life much easier in the long run. Centralized management and monitoring of network traffic can be vital to network success.

ⓦatch With a star topology, if there is a break in the cable, only the system connected to that cable is affected. Today's networks use switches instead of hubs.

With a star configuration, it is also easy to add or change configurations because all of the connections come to a central point.

Disadvantages of a Star Topology

On the flip side, if the hub fails in a star topology, the entire network comes down, so we still have a central point of failure. But this is a much easier problem to troubleshoot than trying to find a cable break with a bus topology.

Another disadvantage of a star topology is cost. To connect each workstation to the network, you will need to ensure that there is a hub with an available port, and you will need to ensure that you have enough cable to go from the workstation to the hub. Today, cost is increasingly less of a disadvantage because of the low prices of devices such as hubs and switches.

FIGURE 1-5

A five-port hub with four available ports

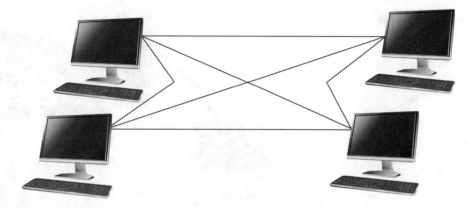

FIGURE 1-6

Computers in a mesh topology are connected to every other computer on the network.

Mesh Topologies How does it differ from P2P?

A mesh topology is not very common in computer networking today, but you must understand the concept for the exam. In a mesh topology, every workstation is connected to every other component of the network, as illustrated in Figure 1-6.

Advantages of a Mesh Topology

The biggest advantage of a mesh topology is fault tolerance, meaning that if there is a break in a cable segment, traffic can be rerouted through a different pathway because there are multiple pathways to send data from one system to another. This fault tolerance means that it is almost impossible for the network to go down due to a cable fault.

Disadvantages of a Mesh Topology

A disadvantage of a mesh topology is the cost of the additional cabling and network interfaces to create the multiple pathways between each system. A mesh topology is hard to administer and manage because of the numerous connections.

It is important to note that there are two major types of mesh topologies—a *full mesh* topology, which involves each system connecting to every other system to create the redundant pathways, or a *partial mesh* topology, where the system is connected to multiple systems, but not to all other systems.

Ring Topologies

In a ring topology, all computers are connected via a cable that loops in a ring or circle. As shown in Figure 1-7, a ring topology is a circle that has no start and no end. Because there are no ends, terminators are not necessary in a ring topology. Signals travel in one direction on a ring while they are passed from one computer to the next, with each computer regenerating the signal so that it may travel the distance required.

A ring topology

Advantages of a Ring Topology

A major advantage of a ring topology is that signal degeneration is low because each workstation is responsible for regenerating the signal. With the other topologies, as the signal travels the wire, it gets weaker and weaker as a result of outside interference; eventually, it becomes unreadable if the destination system is too far away. Because each workstation in a ring topology regenerates the signal, the signal is stronger when it reaches its destination and seldom needs to be retransmitted.

Disadvantages of a Ring Topology

The biggest problem with ring topologies of the past was that if one computer failed or the cable link was broken, the entire network could go down. With newer technology, however, this isn't always the case. The concept of a ring topology today is that the ring will not be broken when a system is disconnected; only that system is dropped from the ring because the ring is more of a logical ring than a physical ring nowadays.

Hybrid Topologies

It is important to note that it is typical for networks to implement a mixture of topologies to form a hybrid topology. For example, a popular hybrid topology is a star-bus topology, in

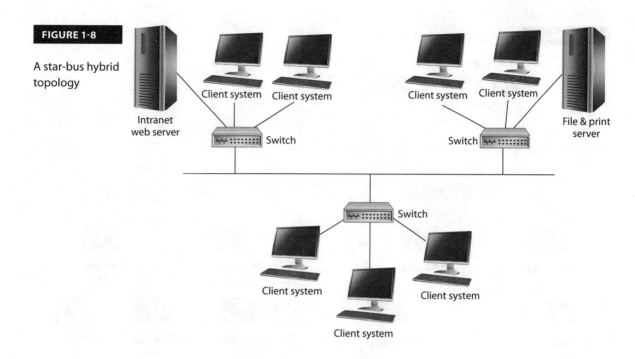

FIGURE 1-8

A star-bus hybrid topology

which a number of star topologies are connected by a central bus, as shown in Figure 1-8. This is a popular topology because the bus will connect hubs that are spread out over distances.

Another popular hybrid topology is the star-ring topology. The star-ring topology is popular because it looks like a star but acts as a ring. For example, there is a network architecture known as Token Ring (more on this later, in the section "Network Architectures") that uses a central "hub" type device, but the internal wiring makes a ring. Physically, it looks like a star, but logically, it acts like a ring topology.

Wireless Topologies

A wireless topology is one in which only a few cables are used to connect systems. The network is made up of transmitters that broadcast the packets using radio frequencies. The network contains special transmitters called *cells,* or *wireless access points,* which extend a radio sphere in the shape of a bubble around the transmitter. This bubble can extend to multiple rooms, and possibly even floors, in a building. The PCs and network devices have a special transmitter-receiver, which allows them to receive broadcasts and transmit requested data back to the access point. The access point is connected to the physical

FIGURE 1-9   A wireless network topology

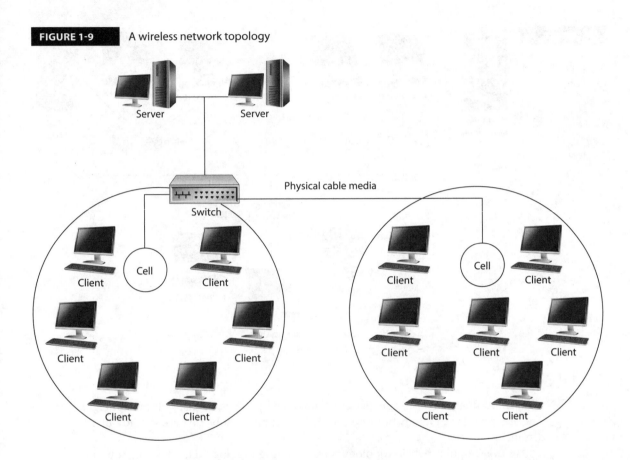

network by a cable, which allows it, and any wireless clients, to communicate with systems on the wired network. A wireless network topology is shown in Figure 1-9.

Notice in Figure 1-9 that the wireless cells, or access points, are connected to the network through the hub or switch, which is connected to the rest of the wired network. Also notice that the clients do not have cables connecting them to the network. These are wireless clients, and they will get access to the network through the wireless cell (or access point).

Another option for wireless networks is the use of a radio antenna on or near the building, which allows one cell to cover the building and the surrounding area. This approach is best in a campus-type arrangement, where many buildings that need to be included in the cell are in a close geographical area.

Wireless networks also can consist of infrared communications, similar to a remote-control TV, but this type of communication is slow and requires a direct line of sight—as well as close proximity—for the communication to work. Infrared mainly is used only between two systems. Infrared is not used often as a complete networking solution and should not be considered as an option for an entire network; it is useful only between laptops or a laptop and a printer.

Advantages of a Wireless Topology

The nice thing about wireless networks is the lack of cabling. The wireless network requires only base backbone segments to connect the wireless cells to the wired network, if there is one. Once these are set up, the PC and network devices also need special transmitter-receiver network interface cards, which allow the PCs and devices to communicate with the cell and then through the cell to the servers.

Troubleshooting failed devices and cells is easy and makes failed components easy to find and replace.

Disadvantages of a Wireless Topology

Disadvantages of wireless networks include a greater chance of signal interference, blockage, and interception. Other devices and machinery that emit radio frequencies, or "noise," can cause interference and static, which can disrupt the bubble of communication around the cell. Another source of noise is lightning during storms. This is the same static you hear when lightning strikes while you are speaking on a phone.

Blockage can occur in structures that are made of thick stone or metal, which do not allow radio frequencies to pass through easily. This drawback usually can be overcome somewhat by changing the frequency the devices use to a higher frequency. You can determine early if this is going to be a problem in your building by trying to use a radio inside the building to pick up some radio stations. If the radio will not pick them up, the building material is too thick to allow radio frequencies to pass through the walls. This problem can be overcome by installing a cell in each room where a PC or network device will be placed.

exam ⓦatch

For the Network+ exam you need to be able to visually recognize the different network topologies from a network diagram.

Another major disadvantage with wireless networks is signal interception. Signal interception means unwanted third parties could intercept wireless communications without physically being on the premises; they would simply have to be within the signal range. One of the key steps to securing wireless communication is to limit who can connect to the network and to encrypt the traffic in transit. You will learn about wireless security in Chapter 10.

Point-to-Point and Point-to-Multipoint

There are two popular layouts for topologies: they are point-to-point or point-to-multipoint. A *point-to-point* topology—also known as host to host—is one system connected directly to another system. In the past, these systems would connect directly through the serial ports with a null modem cable, but these days, you could connect them using a crossover cable or a wireless connection.

A *point-to-multipoint* topology uses a central device that connects all the devices together. This topology is popular with wireless networks. With point-to-multipoint, when the central device sends data, it is received by all devices connected to it. But if one of the devices that is connected sends data, then it is received by only the destination system.

Segments and Backbones

With the various topologies you've looked at, you have seen the words "segment" and "backbone" mentioned a couple of times. A network segment is a cable length (or multiple cable lengths) that is uninterrupted by network connectivity devices, such as bridges and routers. A single network is often broken into multiple network segments through the use of a bridge or router to cut down on network traffic, as shown in Figure 1-10.

In Figure 1-10, notice that there are three network segments, named Segment A, Segment B, and Segment C. Also notice that each network segment could have a number

FIGURE 1-10 A single network broken into multiple network segments

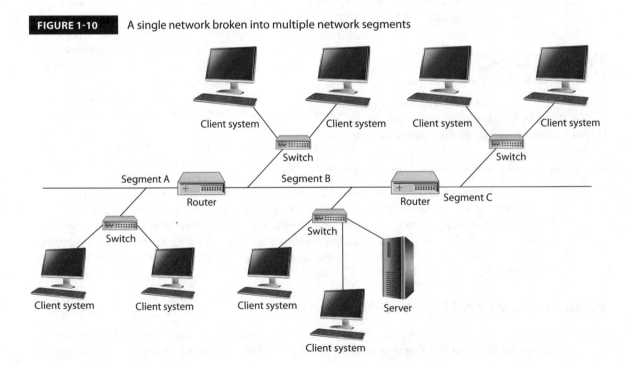

FIGURE 1-11

A network backbone with drop cables connecting the computers

Drop cable

Backbone

of clients and servers, all connected through a number of hubs that are then connected to a backbone. This is just one possible solution involving network segments.

A backbone is the main cable segment or trunk in the network. In a bus network, you might see a main cable trunk that has smaller cables connecting the workstations. These smaller cables, known as *drop cables*, connect the workstations to the backbone. Figure 1-11 shows a backbone with drop cables.

Another example of a backbone is a satellite linking geographically dispersed LANs, making a WAN. Such a backbone is an example of a wireless communications network, whereas the previous examples all used cable as the medium.

CERTIFICATION OBJECTIVE 1.03

Network Media and Connectors

Now that you have learned that networks are built using a bus, star, or ring topology, let's take a look at how the systems will be connected in the topology that you choose. Cabling is the medium for the transmission of data between hosts on the LANs. LANs can be connected together using a variety of cable types, such as unshielded twisted-pair, coax, or fiber. Each cable type has its own advantages and disadvantages, which you will examine in this section.

Three primary types of cable media can be used to connect systems to a network—coaxial cable, twisted-pair cable, and fiber-optic cable. Transmission rates that can be supported on each of these physical media are measured in millions of bits per second, or megabits per second (Mbps).

FIGURE 1-12

A coaxial cable

Coaxial Cable

Coaxial, or coax, cable looks like the cable used to bring the cable TV signal to your television. One strand (a solid-core copper wire) runs down the middle of the cable. Around that strand is a layer of insulation, and covering that insulation is braided wire and metal foil, which shields against electromagnetic interference. A final layer of insulation covers the braided wire. Because of the layers of insulation, coaxial cable is more resistant to outside interference than other cabling, such as unshielded twisted-pair (UTP) cable. Figure 1-12 shows a coaxial cable with the copper core and the layers of insulation.

e x a m

ⓦatch   **Both thinnet and thicknet have a transfer rate of 10 Mbps.**

There are two types of coax cabling: thinnet and thicknet. The two differ in thickness and maximum cable distance that the signal can travel. Let's take a look at thinnet and thicknet.

Thinnet

This refers to RG-58 cabling, which is a flexible coaxial cable about a quarter-inch thick. Thinnet is used for short-distance communication and is flexible enough to facilitate routing between workstations. Thinnet connects directly to a workstation's network adapter card using a Bayonet Neill–Concelman (BNC) connector and uses the network adapter card's internal transceiver. The maximum length of thinnet is 185 meters. Figure 1-13 displays thinnet coaxial cabling and the BNC connector on the end.

Thicknet

This coaxial cable, also known as RG-8, gets its name by being a thicker cable than thinnet. Thicknet cable is about a half-inch thick and can support data transfer over longer distances than thinnet. Thicknet has a maximum cable length of 500 meters and usually is used as a backbone to connect several smaller thinnet-based networks. Due to its thickness, this cable is

FIGURE 1-13

Thinnet coaxial cable with a BNC connector

	Coax Type	Cable Grade	Thickness	Maximum Distance	Transfer Rate	Connector Used to Connect NIC to Cable Type
TABLE 1-1 Thinnet Versus Thicknet	Thinnet	RG-58	0.25 in	185 m	10 Mbps	BNC
	Thicknet	RG-8	0.5 in	500 m	10 Mbps	AUI

harder to work with than thinnet cable. A transceiver often is connected directly to the thicknet cable using a connector known as a vampire tap. Connection from the transceiver to the network adapter card is made using a drop cable to connect to the attachment unit interface (AUI) port connector. Table 1-1 summarizes the characteristics of thicknet and thinnet.

Twisted-Pair Cable

Coaxial cable is not as popular today as it was a few years ago; today, the popularity contest is dominated by twisted-pair cabling. Twisted-pair cabling gets its name from the four pairs of wires that are twisted to help reduce crosstalk or interference from outside electrical devices. (Crosstalk is interference from adjacent wires.) Figure 1-14 shows a twisted-pair cable. Just as there are two forms of coaxial cable, there are two forms of twisted-pair cabling—unshielded twisted-pair (UTP) and shielded twisted-pair (STP).

FIGURE 1-14

Unshielded twisted-pair cable

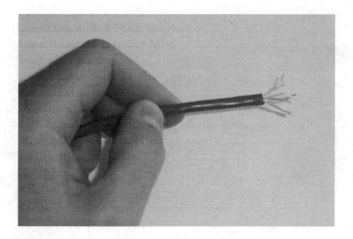

Unshielded Twisted-Pair Cable Unshielded twisted-pair (UTP) cables are familiar to you if you have worked with telephone cable. The typical twisted-pair cable for network use contains four pairs of wires. Each member of the pair of wires contained in the cable is twisted around the other. The twists in the wires help shield against electromagnetic interference. The maximum distance of UTP is 100 meters, with the exception of CAT 6, which has a maximum distance of 100 meters when used in 10/100/1000BaseT environments, but has a maximum distance of 55 meters when used with 10GBaseT networks.

UTP cable uses small plastic connectors designated as registered jack 45, or most often referred to as RJ-45. RJ-45 is similar to the phone connectors, except that instead of four wires, as found in the home system, the network RJ-45 connector contains eight contacts, one for each wire in a UTP cable. The bottom cable in Figure 1-15 is an RJ-45 connector.

It can be easy to confuse the RJ-45 connector with the RJ-11 connector. The RJ-11 connector is a telephone connector, and is shown in the top of Figure 1-15. In an RJ-11 connector, there are four contacts; hence, there are four wires found in the telephone cable. With RJ-45 and RJ-11, you will need a special crimping tool when creating the cables to make contact between the pins in the connector and the wires inside the cable.

UTP cable is easier to install than coaxial because you can pull it around corners more easily due to its flexibility and small size. Twisted-pair cable is more susceptible to interference than coaxial is, however, and should not be used in environments containing large electrical or electronic devices.

UTP cabling has different flavors, known as grades or categories. Each category of UTP cabling was designed for a specific type of communication or transfer rate. Table 1-2 summarizes the different UTP categories—the most popular today being CAT 5e, which can reach transfer rates of over 1000 Mbps or 1 gigabit per second (Gbps).

FIGURE 1-15

An RJ-11 connector and an RJ-45 connector

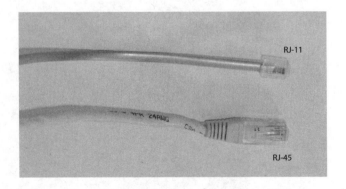

RJ-11

24AWG

RJ-45

TABLE 1-2

Different UTP
Category Cabling

UTP Category	Purpose	Transfer Rate
Category 1	Voice only	
Category 2	Data	4 Mbps
Category 3	Data	10 Mbps
Category 4	Data	16 Mbps
Category 5	Data	100 Mbps
Category 5e	Data	1 Gbps (1000 Mbps)
Category 6	Data	10 Gbps
Category 6a	Data	10 Gbps

The difference between CAT 6 and CAT 6a is that with CAT 6 cabling, the maximum distance allowed for the cable length is reduced to 55 meters when connected to 10 Gbps networks, while CAT 6a can run at a maximum distance of 100 meters with 10 Gbps networks due to reduced crosstalk measures built into the cabling.

Wiring Standards

It is important to understand the order of the wires within the RJ-45 connector for both the Network+ exam and in the real world if you intend on creating (also known as crimping) your own cables. Let's start with some basics comparing a straight-through cable with a crossover cable.

Straight-Through Cables   CAT 5 UTP cabling usually uses only four wires when sending and receiving information on the network. The four wires of the eight that are used are wires 1, 2, 3, and 6. Figure 1-16 shows the meaning of the pins on a computer and the pins on a hub (or switch), which is what you typically will be connecting the computers to. When you configure the wire for the same pin at either end of the cable, this is known as a straight-through cable.

FIGURE 1-16

Pinout diagram for a
straight-through cable

Computer   Hub/Switch

Wire   Wire

TX+ ① ———————— ① RX+
TX− ② ———————— ② RX−
RX+ ③ ———————— ③ TX+
RX− ⑥ ———————— ⑥ TX−

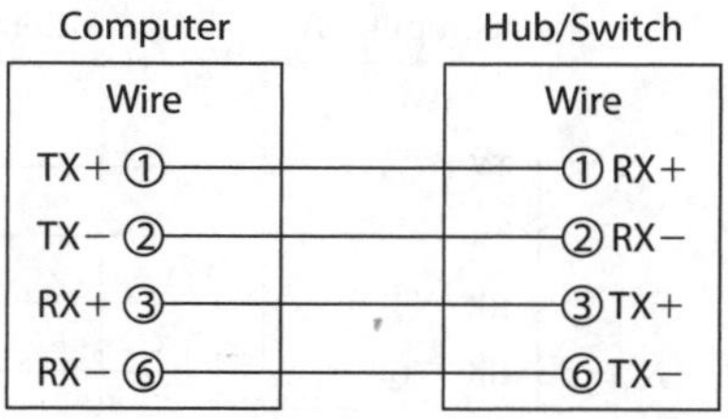

You will notice in the figure that wires 1 and 2 are used to transmit data (TX) from the computer, while wires 3 and 6 are used to receive information (RX) on the computer. You will also notice that the transmit pin on the computer is connected to the receive pin (RX) on the hub via wires 1 and 2. This is important because we want to make sure that data sent from the computer is received at the network hub. We also want to make sure that data sent from the hub is received at the computer, so you will notice that the TX pins on the hub are connected to the RX pins on the computer through wires 3 and 6. This will allow the computer to receive information from the hub.

The last thing to note about Figure 1-16 is that pin 1 on the computer is connected to pin 1 on the hub by the same wire, thus the term *straight-through.* You will notice that all pins are matched straight through to the other side in Figure 1-16.

Crossover Cables   At some point, you may need to connect two computer systems directly together without the use of a hub, from network card to network card. You would not be able to use a straight-through cable for this because the transmit pin on one computer would be connected to the transmit pin on another computer, as shown in Figure 1-17. How could a computer pick up the data if it was not sent to the receive pins? This will not work, so we need to change the wiring of the cable to what is known as a crossover cable.

In order to connect two systems directly together without the use of a hub, you will need to create a crossover cable by switching wires 1 and 2 with wires 3 and 6 at one end of the cable, as shown in Figure 1-18. You will notice that the transmit pins on Computer A are connected to the receive pins on Computer B, thus allowing Computer A to send data to Computer B. The same applies for Computer B to send data to Computer A—pins A and B on Computer B are wired to pins 3 and 6 on Computer A so that Computer A can receive data from Computer B.

For the Network+ exam, you should be familiar with the scenarios that require a

e x a m

ⓦ a t c h   **For the Network+ exam, remember that to create a crossover cable, wires 1 and 2 are switched with wires 3 and 6 on one end of the cable. Also know that a crossover cable is used to connect similar devices together, such as two switches.**

FIGURE 1-17

Using a straight-through cable to connect two computers will not work.

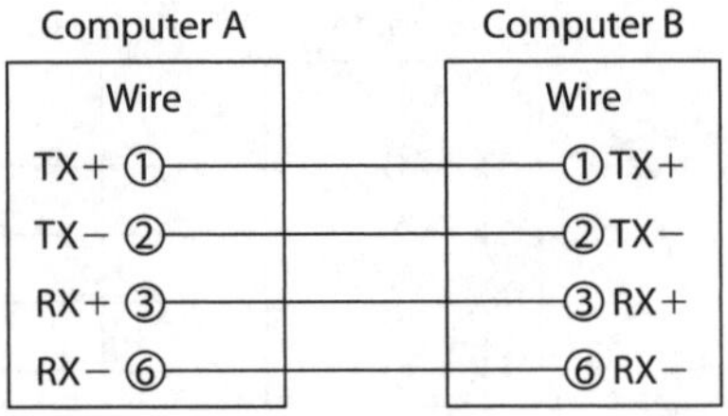

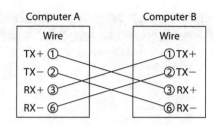

FIGURE 1-18

Pinout diagram of a crossover cable

crossover cable. You will need to use a crossover cable when connecting similar devices together, such as

- Connecting a computer to a computer
- Connecting a switch to another switch
- Connecting a switch to a hub
- Connecting a router to a router
- Connecting a router to a computer

T1 Crossover   A T1/E1 crossover is created for the same reasons you use other crossover type cables, but is used to connect to T1 interfaces. With a T1 crossover cable, the wires that are crossed are different from those of a normal network cable—wires 1 and 2, which are connected to the receive pins, are switched with wires 4 and 5 (transmit pins) at the opposite end of the cable.

568A and 568B Standards   Although only four of the wires are used to send and receive data in most environments today, some of the newer standards use all eight wires. Therefore, it is important to know the order of all eight wires in a UTP cable. There are two popular wiring standards today: 568A and 568B. If the goal is to create a straight-through cable, you would use the same wiring standard on each end (for example, 568B), but if you wanted to create a crossover cable, you would configure one end of the cable using the 568A wiring scheme, while the other end is set up using the 568B wiring scheme. Table 1-3 shows the wire order for the 568B standard of a straight-through cable at both ends.

Following this standard and what you have learned of crossover cables, you would switch wires 1 and 2 with wires 3 and 6 at one end to create a crossover cable. After switching the wires on one end, you would have a cable that has the order of wires shown in Table 1-4.

watch   The Network+ exam is sure to test you on the order of wires in 568B and 568A standards. Be sure to know the order and know that to create a crossover cable, you would wire one end as 568B and the other as 568A.

TABLE 1-3		
The 568B Wiring Standard for a Straight-through Cable		

Wire	Connector #1 (568B)	Connector #2 (568B)
1	White wire/orange stripe (white-orange)	White wire/orange stripe (white-orange)
2	Orange wire	Orange wire
3	White wire/green stripe (white-green)	White wire/green stripe (white-green)
4	Blue wire	Blue wire
5	White wire/blue stripe (white-blue)	White wire/blue stripe (white-blue)
6	Green wire	Green wire
7	White wire/brown stripe (white-brown)	White wire/brown stripe (white-brown)
8	Brown wire	Brown wire

Before moving on to other cable types, apply what you have learned by crimping (creating) your own CAT 5 cable. To create your own network cable, you will need to have a crimper like the one shown in Figure 1-19.

When you select a crimping tool, you want to make sure that you have one that has a built-in crimper as well as a wire stripper and a wire cutter. Exercise 1-1 demonstrates the steps needed to crimp your own CAT 5 cable.

TABLE 1-4		
Using 568A and 568B at Either End to Create a Crossover Cable		

Wire	Connector #1 (568B)	Connector #2 (568A)
1	White wire/orange stripe (white-orange)	White wire/green stripe (white-green)
2	Orange wire	Green wire
3	White wire/green stripe (white-green)	White wire/orange stripe (white-orange)
4	Blue wire	Blue wire
5	White wire/blue stripe (white-blue)	White wire/blue stripe (white-blue)
6	Green wire	Orange wire
7	White wire/brown stripe (white-brown)	White wire/brown stripe (white-brown)
8	Brown wire	Brown wire

FIGURE 1-19

A crimping tool

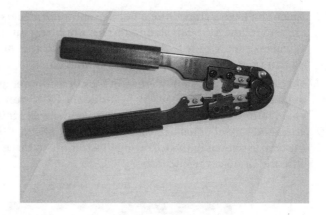

EXERCISE 1-1

Crimping a Category 5 Cable

In this exercise, you will learn how to crimp your own CAT 5 cable. To complete this exercise, you will need to have a crimping tool, a piece of CAT 5 cabling, some RJ-45 connectors, and a little bit of patience! To create a CAT 5 cable, do the following:

1. Ensure that you have a clean-cut end on the cable by using your wire cutters to cut a little off the end of the CAT 5 cable.

2. Once you have cut a clean end on the cable, strip about an inch off the outer jacket from the cable using the wire-stripper portion of your crimping tool, as shown in the next illustration. After stripping the outer jacket off, make sure that you have not cut into any of the individual wires. If you have, cut a clean end off the cable again and start from the beginning.

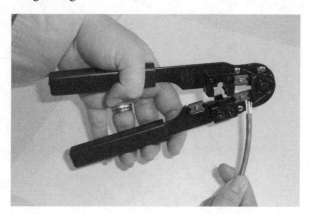

3. Once you have stripped the outer jacket off the cable, order the wires from left to right to follow the 568B standard. This is where your patience will come in, because it will take some time to get the wires in the correct order and placed tightly together so that they will go inside the RJ-45 connector.

4. Once you have the wires aligned in the correct order and you have them all nice and snug together so that they will fit inside the RJ-45 connector, you are ready to insert them into the connector. Before inserting the wires into the connector, make sure their ends are of equal length; if they are not, just cut the tips a bit with your wire cutters, as shown in the following illustration, to be certain that they will fit nicely into the RJ-45 connector.

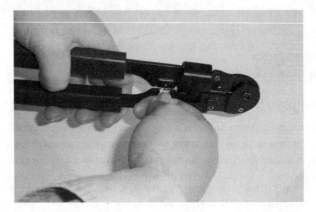

5. Slide the wires into the RJ-45 connector, as shown in the next illustration, and make sure that all wires are touching the metal contacts inside the RJ-45 connector by looking at the end of the connector. This is where mistakes happen frequently; there is usually one wire in the middle that is not pushed up to the end of the connector.

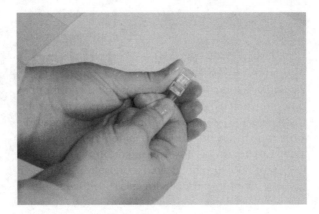

6. Once you are certain that all wires have made contact, you can "crimp" the wire, which will enclose the RJ-45 connector on the wires, creating a permanent fit. Insert the connector into the crimping tool and squeeze the handle tight, as seen in the following illustration.

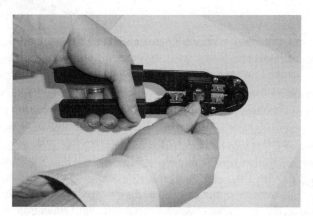

Rollover   A rollover cable is a popular cable type in the networking world and is used to connect to a Cisco device such as a router or a switch. Also known as a console cable, this cable connects the computer's serial port to the console port of the router or switch. Once the network administrator connects to the console port, he or she is then able to configure the router or switch.

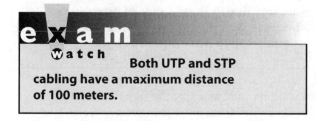

Both UTP and STP cabling have a maximum distance of 100 meters.

Shielded Twisted-Pair Cable

Shielded twisted-pair (STP) cable is similar to UTP cabling, but it differs from UTP in that it uses a layer of insulation within the protective jacket, which helps maintain the quality of the signal.

Fiber-Optic Cable

The third type of cabling that we want to discuss is fiber-optic cabling. Fiber-optic cabling is unlike coax and twisted-pair, because both of those types have a copper wire that carries the electrical signal. Fiber-optic cables use optical fibers that carry digital data signals in the form of modulated pulses of light. An optical fiber consists of an extremely thin cylinder of glass, called the core, surrounded by a concentric layer of glass, known as the cladding.

There are two fibers per cable—one to transmit and one to receive. The core also can be an optical-quality clear plastic, and the cladding can be made up of gel that reflects signals back into the fiber to reduce signal loss.

There are two types of fiber-optic cables: single-mode fiber (SMF) and multimode fiber (MMF).

Single-mode Fiber   Uses a single ray of light, known as a mode, to carry the transmission over long distances.

Multimode Fiber   Uses multiple rays of light (modes) simultaneously, with each ray of light running at a different reflection angle to carry the transmission over short distances.

APC vs. UPC   *Angle-polished connectors (APC)* and *ultra-polished connectors (UPC)* are not necessarily fiber-optic cable types, but describe how the ends of the fiber-optic cables are configured. With UPC, polished ends reflect the light back down the core toward the source, where it hits the connector, causing a slight degradation in performance. APC has a polished end with an 8-degree angle, which changes the light reflection when it hits the connector so that it goes toward the cladding instead of back to the source of the light.

e x a m

ⓦ a t c h   **You have learned of two electrical phenomena that can disrupt a signal traveling along your network: crosstalk and outside electrical noise. Crosstalk is caused by electrical fields in adjacent wires, which induce false signals in a wire. Outside electrical noise comes from lights, motors, radio systems, and many other sources. Fiber-optic cables are immune to these types of interference because they do not carry electrical signals—they carry pulses of light.**

Fiber-optic cable supports up to 1000 stations and can carry the signal for many kilometers. Fiber-optic cables are also highly secure from outside interference, such as radio transmitters, arc welders, fluorescent lights, and other sources of electrical noise. On the other hand, fiber-optic cable is by far the most expensive of these cabling methods, and a small network is unlikely to need these features. Depending on local labor rates and building codes, installing fiber-optic cable can cost as much as $500 per network node.

Fiber-optic cables can use many types of connectors, but the Network+ exam is concerned only with the two major connector types: the straight-tip (ST) connector and the subscriber (SC) connector. The ST connector is based on the BNC-style connector, but has a fiber-optic cable instead of a copper cable. The SC connector is square and somewhat

FIGURE 1-20

Fiber-optic ST and
SC connector types

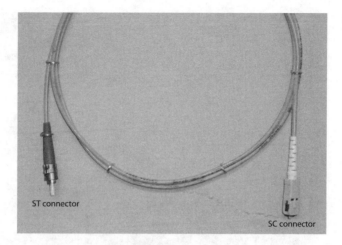

similar to an RJ-45 connector. Figure 1-20 shows the ST (the connector on the left side) and the SC (the connector on the right side) types.

Regardless of the connector type, the fiber-optic cable still functions at the same speed, which is typically 1000 Mbps and faster. The only thing that you need to worry about for the exam is that the connector matches the device to which it is being connected, since the two connector types are not interchangeable.

When preparing for the Network+ exam, it is sometimes helpful to have a table listing the differences between the different cable types. Table 1-5 summarizes the different cable types—be sure to review it for the Network+ exam.

Connector Types

Now that you have an understanding of the different cable types, I want to discuss the connectors that are used on the ends of the cables to connect the cable to a network device.

TABLE 1-5

Summary of
Cable Types

Cable	Max Distance	Transfer Rate	Connector Used
Thinnet	185 m	10 Mbps	BNC
Thicknet	500 m	10 Mbps	AUI
CAT 3 (UTP)	100 m	10 Mbps	RJ-45
CAT 5 (UTP)	100 m	100 Mbps	RJ-45
CAT 5e	100 m	1 Gbps	RJ-45
CAT 6	100 m	10 Gbps	RJ-45
Fiber	2 km	1+ Gbps	SC, ST

A 50-ohm BNC
terminator and T
connector

Terminator

T-connector

In this section, you will learn about the different connectors for coaxial, twisted-pair, and
fiber-optic cabling.

Coaxial Connectors

We have discussed coaxial cabling, and you saw the BNC connector that goes on the end of
the cable and connects to the network card, but there are a few other BNC connector types
you should be familiar with. The BNC-T connector is used to connect to coax cable from
either side so that the cable length can continue on, while a third end of the connector tees
out to have a cable length connect to the network card on the client machine. Figure 1-21
displays the BNC-T connector being placed on a network card.

We also discussed the terminator that needs to go at both ends of the coax cable. For
example, if we use the BNC-T connector to connect our last system to the network, we would
need to terminate one of the ends on the T-connector, also shown in Figure 1-21. Notice that the
terminator goes on one end of the T-connector and the coax cable connects into the other end.

Twisted-Pair Connectors

We have discussed two major twisted-pair connectors: the RJ-11 for four-wire telephone
cable and the RJ-45 for eight-wire network cables. There are also UTP couplers, which
are female connectors on both ends that allow you to join two cable lengths together and
reach greater distances, although not exceeding 100 meters. Figure 1-22 shows an RJ-45
UTP coupler connecting two cable lengths together. There are also BNC couplers that are
designed to connect two coaxial cable lengths together, and a fiber-optic coupler that is
designed to connect two lengths of fiber-optic cabling together.

A UTP coupler

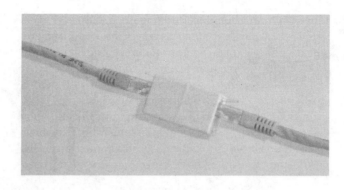

Other Connectors

There are a number of additional connector types that you will come across in networking environments, some of which are listed here.

F-type connector   Also known as an F-connector, this is used by coax cabling and is the connector style that connects to your TV.

Fiber Local Connector (LC) and Mechanical-Transfer Registered Jack
(MT-RJ)   These are additional fiber-optic connector types that are similar to the registered jack and fiber SC shape. The fiber LC is preferred for communications exceeding 1 Gbps due to its small form factor.

FC and RJ-48C   The FC connector is a special fiber-optic connector that is designed to be used in environments that have a high level of vibrations and are not as common as SC and LC connectors.

The RJ-48C connector is a registered jack connector (like RJ-45) used by T1 devices. You will learn more about T1 connections in Chapter 12.

Universal Serial Bus (USB)   This is a high-speed serial bus that supports 127 devices in the chain. USB uses a standard connector type that is used by most devices, including mice, printers, network cards, digital cameras, and flash drives. There are three USB standards: USB 1.1, which has a transfer rate of 12 Mbps; USB 2.0, which has a transfer rate of 480 Mbps; and USB 3.0, which has a transfer rate of approximately 5 Gbps. There are a number of different USB connectors, including Type A and Type B. Type A connectors connect to the computer, whereas Type B connectors connect to the device. Figure 1-23 displays these two connector styles. There are also Mini USB and Micro USB connectors, each with an A and B version.

IEEE 1394 (FireWire)   This is an ultra-high-speed bus that supports 63 devices in the chain and is ideal for real-time applications and devices, such as for video. FireWire has two

USB Type A and Type B
connectors

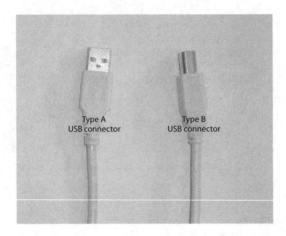

standards: 1394a, which has a transfer rate of 400 Mbps, and 1394b, which has a transfer rate of 800 Mbps.

DB-9 (RS-232) and DB-25   This is the standard for connections using the serial port on a computer. The serial port was a popular way to achieve a point-to-point connection between two hosts, or was used for modems. The RS-232 standard defines a transfer rate of 20,000 bits per second, but serial devices support higher transfer rates.

DB-25 is a port type used by different types of devices. There is a male DB-25 port that is a serial port like the DB-9, but larger. There is also a DB-25 female parallel port that is used by older printers.

Networking over Power Lines

In recent years, a new type of network media has appeared in which the power lines running to your house and through your home are used to carry network data. The following technologies are used to carry data over the power lines.

Broadband over Powerline   Broadband over powerline (BPL), also known as IEEE 1901-2013, is a fairly new technology that allows Internet service providers to supply high-speed Internet to your home using the power lines connected to your house. This has become common in areas where the cable company or phone company is not able to deliver high-speed Internet to customers due to limitations on the existing network infrastructure.

With BPL, you are given a special modem from the service provider that connects to a power outlet in the home, and then a cable connects to your computer or home router.

Ethernet over Powerline   A similar technology that home users are starting to adopt is the concept of connecting a computer to your network by connecting it to a network adapter that

FIGURE 1-24

An Ethernet over
Powerline adapter

is plugged into a power outlet (see Figure 1-24). This allows you to network with other systems through the existing power lines in the home. This is a great solution if you have systems that are too far to run a network cable and you do not want to use wireless networking. As long as there is a power outlet close to the PC, you can connect the PC to a power network adapter and then plug it into the power outlet. You would also connect your network switch to a power network adapter at the other end of the building.

Ethernet over HDMI　You can also use the High-Definition Multimedia Interface (HDMI) cable as an Ethernet network cable to deliver networking data to a device. This is similar to how the cable company uses the coax cable to deliver TV channels and Internet data to your house.

DOCSIS　Data Over Cable Service Interface Specification (DOCSIS) is a broadband standard that cable companies use to offer high-speed Internet over their existing cable system using hybrid fiber-coaxial (HFC) infrastructure.

Media Converters

When you have the wrong type of cabling to connect to a device, you can use a media converter (see Figure 1-25) to change the connector. Different types of media converters are available. The following are some common examples of media converters.

Single-mode Fiber to Ethernet　A single-mode fiber to Ethernet converter allows you to connect single-mode fiber-optic cable to the UTP cabling used by Ethernet networks.

FIGURE 1-25

A media converter

Multimode Fiber to Ethernet   A multimode fiber to Ethernet converter allows you to connect multimode fiber-optic cable to the UTP cabling used by Ethernet networks.

Fiber Optic to Coaxial   If you need to connect fiber-optic cabling to a device that has a coax connector on it, you can use a fiber optic to coaxial media converter.

Single-mode to Multimode Fiber Optic   If you need to switch single-mode fiber-optic cabling to multimode fiber-optic cabling, you can use the single-mode to multimode fiber-optic media converter.

INSIDE THE EXAM

Bonding and MPLS

The Network+ exam expects you to be familiar with the following network technologies as they relate to network media and increasing network performance.

Bonding   Also known as channel bonding, bonding is a technology that allows you to join the bandwidth of multiple network cards installed in a single system or device to get better network performance, or throughput.

MPLS   Multiprotocol Label Switching (MPLS) is a technology that allows you to assign a label to data, and the network device makes routing decisions based on the label and not by examining the header of the packet. This allows for better throughput, as you have taken away the work of analyzing the header of a packet.

CERTIFICATION OBJECTIVE 1.04

Access Methods

You now know that a network uses a topology—which is the layout of the network—and you know that some form of media such as cabling connects all hosts on the network. We have discussed the three major types of cabling: coax, twisted-pair, and fiber-optic cabling.

This section will identify various access methods. An access method determines how a host will place data on the wire—does the host have to wait its turn or can it just place the data on the wire whenever it wants? The answer is determined by three major access methods: CSMA/CD, CSMA/CA, and token passing. Let's look at each of these access methods.

CSMA/CD

Carrier sense multiple access with collision detection (CSMA/CD) is one of the most popular access methods in use today. With CSMA/CD, every host has equal access to the wire and can place data on the wire when the wire is free from traffic. If a host wishes to place data on the wire, it will "sense" the wire and determine whether a signal is already present. If there is, the host will wait to transmit the data; if the wire is free, the host will send the data, as shown in Figure 1-26.

| FIGURE 1-26 | A host "sensing" the wire to see if it is free of traffic |

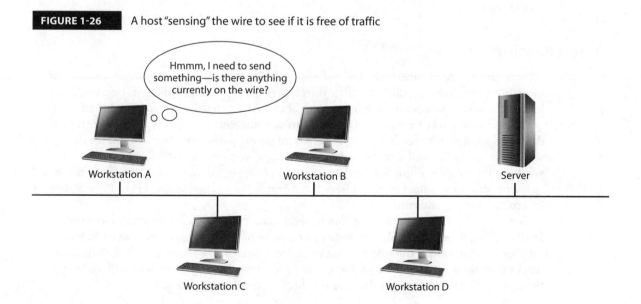

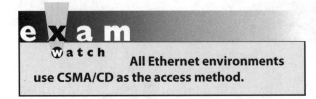

The problem with the process just described is that if two systems "sense" the wire at the same time, they will both send data at the same time if the wire is free. When the two pieces of data are sent on the wire at the same time, they will collide with one another and the data will be destroyed. If the data is destroyed in transit, the data will need to be retransmitted. Consequently, after a collision, each host will wait a variable length of time before retransmitting the data (they don't want the data to collide again), thereby preventing a collision the second time. When a system determines that the data has collided and then retransmits the data, that is known as collision detection.

To summarize, with CSMA/CD, before a host sends data on the network, it will "sense" (CS) the wire to ensure that it is free of traffic. Multiple systems have equal access to the wire (MA), and if there is a collision, a host will detect that collision (CD) and retransmit the data.

CSMA/CA

Carrier sense multiple access with collision avoidance (CSMA/CA) is not as popular as CSMA/CD, and for good reason. With CSMA/CA, before a host sends data on the wire, it will "sense" the wire to see if it is free of signals. If the wire is free, the host will try to "avoid" a collision by sending a signal out, letting all others know they should wait before sending data. This helps prevent collisions from occurring, but is sending more data out on the wire.

Token Passing

With both CSMA/CD and CSMA/CA, the possibility of collisions is always there, and the more hosts that are placed on the wire, the greater the chances of collisions because you have more systems "waiting'" for the wire to become free so that they can send their data.

Token passing takes a totally different approach in determining how a system can place data on the wire. With token passing, there is an empty packet running around on the wire—the "token." In order to place data on the wire, you need to wait for the token; once you have the token and it is free of data, you can place your data on the wire. Since there is only one token and a host needs to have the token to "talk," it is impossible to have collisions in a token-passing environment.

For example, if Workstation 1 wants to send data on the wire, the workstation would wait for the token, which is circling the network millions of times per second. Once the token reaches Workstation 1, the workstation takes the token off the network, fills it with data, marks the token as being used so that no other systems try to fill the token with data, and then places the token back on the wire heading for the destination host.

All systems will look at the data, but they will not process it, since it is not destined for them. However, the system that is the intended destination will read the data and send the token back to the sender as a confirmation. Once the token has reached the original sender, the token is unflagged as being used and released as an empty token onto the network.

Modulation Techniques

Modulation is the term used to alter a property or characteristic of a communication signal. There are two types of modulation:

- **Digital modulation** Digital modulation involves converting a digital signal to an analog signal so that the data can travel over an analog line. At the end of the line the signal is converted back to a digital signal.
- **Analog modulation** Analog modulation involves transferring an analog signal over an analog line using different frequencies.

Multiplexing and De-multiplexing

Multiplexing is a communication technique used to allow multiple signals, or streams of data, to use a shared medium such as a network cable or telephone line. Multiplexing allows multiple data sources to place the signal on the medium and share the medium, while de-multiplexing removes the signal from the shared line. One of the benefits is to have the cost of the network medium shared by the sources of the data streams. There are two ways that multiplexing occurs:

- **Time Division Multiplexing (TDM)** With TDM, each of the data sources is given equal time slots on the medium to transfer data during non-overlapping times.
- **Frequency Division Multiplexing (FDM)** With FDM, each source is assigned a different frequency within the medium so that each can deliver their data at the same time in separated discrete frequencies.

Bit Rates vs. Baud Rate

The serial port can be used for communication, and most serial devices are measured with either a bit rate or a baud rate. It is important to note that the two are different ratings and not the same thing.

The bit rate identifies how many bits can be transferred across the line and is measured in bits per second (bps). Many network technologies measure their transfer rate like this, for example, 100 Megabits per second (100 Mbps). The bits are created in the signal by changing the voltage of the signal—for example, a +3 voltage would be a 1 bit, while a lower voltage of +0.2 would take the binary value of 0.

The baud rate is the number of changes in voltage within the signal per second. The baud rate can sometimes be the same as the bit rate, but if a technology has more changes to the signal per second than the actual bits represented, then the baud rate will differ from the bit rate.

Sampling Size and Wavelength   Two networking terms you should know for the Network+ certification exam are sampling size and wavelength. Sampling size is the amount of data that is being analyzed to determine speed, bandwidth, or wavelength. Wavelength is the distance between two adjacent waves in a signal.

CERTIFICATION OBJECTIVE 1.05

Network Architectures

This section will discuss the different network architectures that are popular in today's networking environments. This section is very important from an exam point of view as well, so be sure to understand how the different architectures are pieced together.

Before we can discuss the different network architectures, we need to define two terms: broadband and baseband transmissions.

Baseband and Broadband

Two different techniques may be used to transmit the signal along the network wire— baseband communication and broadband communication. Let's take a look at each of these techniques.

Baseband

Baseband sends digital signals through the media as a single channel that uses the entire bandwidth of the media. The signal is delivered as a pulse of electricity or light, depending on the type of cabling being used. Baseband communication is also bidirectional, which means that the same channel can be used to send and receive signals.

Broadband

Broadband sends information in the form of an analog signal, which flows as electromagnetic waves or optical waves. Each transmission is assigned to a portion of the bandwidth, known as a frequency, so unlike baseband communication, it is possible to have multiple transmissions at the same time, with each transmission assigned its own channel or frequency. Broadband communication is unidirectional, so in order to send and receive, two pathways need to be used. This can be accomplished either by assigning a frequency for sending and a frequency for receiving along the same cable or by using two cables: one for sending and one for receiving.

Ethernet

I first want to point out that network architecture is something that came about one day when someone sat down and said, "We are going to design a network architecture; let's use CAT 3 cabling, a star topology, and CSMA/CD as an access method. Oh, and let's call this architecture 10BaseT!"

10BaseT was the name assigned to the architecture because 10 Mbps is the transfer rate of the network, baseband communication is the technique used to transmit the signal, and the T means our cable type—in this case, twisted-pair. Now, we have discussed different types of twisted-pair cabling, but CAT 3 is the one that runs at 10 Mbps, so it is the cable used in 10BaseT.

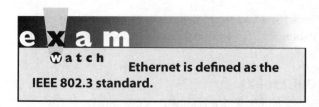

Ethernet is defined as the IEEE 802.3 standard.

The first types of network architecture we will look at are the different Ethernet architectures. When designing networks, one of the first decisions we usually make is: "Do we want to use Ethernet or the competing network architecture, Token Ring?" If we decide to use Ethernet, the next question is: "What flavor of Ethernet?" This section will help you understand the different flavors of Ethernet.

10Base2

The 10Base2 Ethernet architecture is a network that runs at 10 Mbps and uses baseband transmissions. 10Base2 typically is implemented as a bus topology, but it could be a mix of a bus and a star topology. The cable type that we use is determined by the character at the end of the name of the architecture—in this case, a 2. The 2 implies 200 meters. Now, what type of cable is limited to approximately 200 m? You got it; thinnet is limited to approximately 200 m (185 m, to be exact). The only characteristic we have not mentioned is the access method that is used. All Ethernet environments use CSMA/CD to put data on the wire.

10Base5

The 10Base5 Ethernet architecture runs at 10 Mbps and uses baseband transmission as well. It was also implemented as a bus topology. The cable it uses is limited to approximately 500 meters, which is thicknet, and it uses CSMA/CD as the access method. The thicker copper core in the wire allows the signal to travel farther than is possible with thinnet.

10Base2 and 10Base5 follow what is known as the 5-4-3 rule, which means that there can be only five network segments in total, joined by four repeaters (more on repeaters in Chapter 3), but only three of those network segments can be populated with nodes.

10BaseT

The 10BaseT Ethernet architecture runs at 10 Mbps and uses baseband transmission. It uses a star topology with a hub or switch at the center, allowing all systems to connect to one another. The cable it uses is CAT 3 UTP, which is the UTP cable type that runs at 10 Mbps. Keep in mind that most cable types are backward compatible, so you could have CAT 5 UTP cabling in a 10BaseT environment. But because the network cards and hubs are running at 10 Mbps, that is the maximum transfer speed you will get, even though the cable supports more. Like all Ethernet environments, 10BaseT uses CSMA/CD as the access method.

10BaseFL

The 10BaseFL Ethernet architecture allows for a 10 Mbps Ethernet environment that runs on fiber-optic cabling. The fiber-optic cabling is used as a backbone to allow the network to reach greater distances.

Fast Ethernet (100BaseT and 100BaseFX)

These two standards are part of the 100BaseX family, which is known as fast Ethernet. The different fast Ethernet flavors run at 100 Mbps, use a star topology, and use CSMA/CD as an access method, but differ in the type of cabling used. 100BaseTX (also known as 100BaseT) uses two pairs (four wires) in the CAT 5 cabling, while 100BaseT4 uses UTP cabling using all four pairs (eight wires). 100BaseFX uses two strands of fiber-optic instead of twisted-pair cabling.

Gigabit Ethernet

Gigabit Ethernet is becoming the de facto standard for network architectures today. With Gigabit Ethernet, we can reach transfer rates of 1000 Mbps (1 Gbps), using traditional media such as coaxial, twisted-pair, and fiber-optic cabling. Gigabit Ethernet has two standards known as IEEE 802.3z and IEEE 802.3ab (more on the IEEE standards in Chapter 2) defining the technologies.

IEEE 802.3z The IEEE 802.3z standard, known as 1000BaseX, defines Gigabit Ethernet that runs over fiber-optic cabling or coaxial cabling. Three types of Gigabit Ethernet fall under this standard:

■ **1000BaseSX** The Gigabit Ethernet architecture that runs at 1000 Mbps over multimode fiber-optic cabling. This architecture is designed for short distances of up to 550 meters.

- **1000BaseLX**   The Gigabit Ethernet architecture that runs at 1000 Mbps over single-mode fiber-optic cabling. This architecture supports distances up to 3 kilometers.
- **1000BaseCX**   The Gigabit Ethernet architecture that runs at 1000 Mbps over coaxial cable and supports distances of up to 25 meters.

IEEE 802.3ab   The IEEE 802.3ab standard, known as 1000BaseT or 1000BaseTX, defines Gigabit Ethernet that runs over twisted-pair cabling and uses characteristics of 100BaseTX networking, including the use of RJ-45 connectors and the CSMA/CD access method. Like 100BaseTX, 1000BaseTX uses CAT 5e or CAT 6 unshielded twisted-pair; the difference is that 100BaseTX runs over two pairs (four wires) while 1000BaseTX runs over four pairs (all eight wires).

10-Gigabit Ethernet

Standards for 10-Gigabit Ethernet (10,000 Mbps) have been developed that use fiber-optic cabling or UTP:

- **10GBaseSR**   Runs at 10 Gbps and uses "short-range" multimode fiber-optic cable, which has a maximum distance of 400 meters (depending on fiber type used).
- **10GBaseLR**   Runs at 10 Gbps and uses "long-range" single-mode fiber-optic cable, which has a maximum distance of 10 kilometers.
- **10GBaseER**   Runs at 10 Gbps and uses "extra-long-range" single-mode fiber-optic cable, which has a maximum distance of 40 kilometers.
- **10GBaseT**   Runs at 10 Gbps using CAT 6a UTP cabling, which has a maximum distance of 100 meters.

There are special WAN versions of 10-Gigabit Ethernet that use fiber-optic cabling to connect to a Synchronous Optical Network (SONET) network (more on SONET in Chapter 12).

Be sure to focus on the 100 Mbps, 1000 Mbps (1 Gbps), and 10 Gbps architectures for the Network+ exam. Ensure you are familiar with the speeds, cable types, connectors, and maximum distance of each architecture.

- **10GBaseSW**   The 10-Gigabit Ethernet standard for short-range, multimode fiber-optic cable, which has a maximum distance of 100 meters.
- **10GBaseLW**   The 10-Gigabit Ethernet standard for long-range, single-mode fiber-optic cable, which has a maximum distance of 10 kilometers.

- **10GBaseEW**   The 10-Gigabit Ethernet standard for extended-range, single-mode fiber-optic cable, which has a distance of up to 40 kilometers.

Token Ring

A big competitor to Ethernet in the past was Token Ring, which runs at 4, 16, and 100 Mbps. Token Ring is a network architecture that uses a ring topology (physically, it looks like a star but is wired logically as a ring) and can use many forms of cables. IBM Token Ring has its own proprietary cable types, while more modern implementations of Token Ring can use CAT 3 or CAT 5 UTP cabling. Token Ring uses the token-passing access method.

Looking at Token Ring networks today, you may wonder where the "ring" topology is because the network appears to have a star topology. The reason this network architecture appears to use a star topology is that all hosts are connected to a central device that looks similar to a hub, but with Token Ring, this device is called a multistation access unit (MAU or MSAU). The ring is the internal communication path within the wiring.

e x a m
ⓦ a t c h   **Token Ring is defined as the IEEE 802.5 standard.**

Token Ring uses token passing; thus, it is impossible to have collisions in a token-passing environment, because the MAUs do not have collision lights like an Ethernet hub does (remember that Ethernet uses CSMA/CD and there is potential for collisions).

FDDI

Fiber distributed data interface (FDDI) is a network architecture that uses fiber-optic cabling, token passing, and a ring topology, but FDDI also uses two counter-rotating rings for fault tolerance on the network. For more information on FDDI, please refer to Chapter 12.

Once again, a table summarizing the core facts is always useful when preparing for an exam. Table 1-6 summarizes the popular network architectures. Be sure to review these before taking the Network+ exam.

TABLE 1-6

Network
Architecture
Summary

Network Architecture	Topology	Cable	Transfer Rate	Access Method
10Base2	Bus	Thinnet	10 Mbps	CSMA/CD
10Base5	Bus	Thicknet	10 Mbps	CSMA/CD
10BaseT	Star	CAT 3	10 Mbps	CSMA/CD
100BaseT	Star	CAT 5	100 Mbps	CSMA/CD
1000BaseTX	Star	CAT 5, 5e, 6	1 Gbps	CSMA/CD
10GBaseLR	Star	Fiber optic (single mode)	10 Gbps	CSMA/CD
Token Ring	Star ring	UTP	4 /16/100 Mbps	Token passing

INSIDE THE EXAM

Unraveling the Ethernet Jargon

Most people get confused by the jargon used to describe the various Ethernet types, but Ethernet is explained easily by breaking down the name of the architecture. Ethernet types follow a ##BaseXX naming convention and are designated as follows:

- ## stands for the speed of the network; examples are 10 (for 10 Mbps), 100 (for 100 Mbps), 1000 (for 1000 Mbps or 1 Gbps), and 10G (for 10 Gbps).

- Base stands for baseband transmission.

- XX stands for the cable type or medium:

    - For example, if there is a 5 at the end of the architecture name, 5 represents the cable medium thicknet. The 5 in the name indicates the maximum length of thicknet, which is 500 meters. A 2 at the end of the name would mean that the medium is thinnet, which

gets its name from the fact that thinnet has a maximum length of 200 meters (actually, 185 meters).

- T stands for twisted-pair cabling and can be further categorized to show the number of pairs; for example, 10BaseT4 requires four pairs of wires from a twisted-pair cable.

- F is for fiber-optic cable.

- X represents a higher grade of connection, and 100BaseTX is twisted-pair cabling that can use either UTP or STP at 100 Mbps. With fiber-optic cable such as 100Base-FX, the speed is quicker than with standard 10BaseF.

If we look at 100BaseTX, for example, the 100 means 100 Mbps using baseband transmission and twisted-pair cable. Since we know that the speed is 100 Mbps, we also can assume that the type of twisted-pair cable will be at least CAT 5.

EXERCISE 1-2

Identifying the Different Network Architectures

In this exercise, you will review the different network architectures by filling in the table. After reading the description, specify which network architecture should be used.

Description	Network Technology to Use
I want to have a network that runs at 10 Mbps, using a star topology and UTP cabling. What architecture should I use?	
I want to have a 1000 Mbps network that uses my existing CAT 5 cabling. What type of network architecture should I use?	
As a network technician, I want to build a network that uses an architecture that runs at 1000 Mbps and can handle a distance of about 1 kilometer. What network architecture should I use?	
I want to have a network that runs at 100 Mbps, using a star topology and UTP cabling. What architecture should I use?	
I want to build a network that runs at 10 Gbps and can span about 100 meters. What network architecture should I use?	

INSIDE THE EXAM

The Role of Network Topology, Cabling, and Connectors

A thorough understanding of how network topology, cabling, and connectors coexist is a valuable skill set to possess for the Network+ exam. This is especially the case if you are a network engineer who must design and implement a network from the ground up. You must know the characteristics of each network topology and be able to apply them in each unique situation you encounter.

For example, let's say you are designing a network for a small investment firm with ten users and a minimal budget. Instantly, you may be thinking "star topology," which is relatively inexpensive and easy to implement for smaller networks such as this one.

Your choice of network topology also dictates other characteristics of the network, such as what your choice of cabling will be and whether additional hardware is required.

In our example, we have implemented a star topology, which is conducive to twisted-pair cabling—more importantly, of at least CAT 5 UTP. The UTP cables will be connected to a network hub or switch using an RJ-45 connector, which leads us to our final specification: the network connector. Just as the network topology dictates the choice of cabling, it also dictates our choice of connector. The RJ-45 connector is the cornerstone of twisted-pair cabling.

Although this example seems fairly straightforward, the secret lies in understanding the characteristics of each type of network, such as cable types, connectors, and supporting devices. This will come in handy during your Network+ exam, which will definitely test your knowledge of these concepts.

CERTIFICATION OBJECTIVE 1.06

Network Operating Systems

Now that you have a general idea of the network topologies, cable types, and network architectures, let's look at the network operating system (NOS). We focus on the two most widely used network operating systems available today:

- Windows Server 2012
- UNIX

Once you have connected the cables to the hubs and the clients to the cables, it is time to install a network operating system. The network operating system is responsible for providing services to clients on the network. These services could be the sharing of files or printers; the server could be providing name resolution through DNS services or logon services by acting as a directory server.

Let's take a look at some of the popular network operating systems that provide network services to their clients. For this discussion, we will use the term Windows Server 2012 to describe our Windows Server, but the concepts apply to any Windows Server version, including Windows Server 2008 R2.

Windows Servers

Developed from the Virtual Memory System (VMS) platform many years ago, Microsoft created a Windows Server OS named Windows NT that has progressed to Windows Server 2012. Windows Server operating systems have grown into popular network operating systems that provide a number of built-in network services, including

- **File and print services** These allow the administrator to share files and printers among Windows clients.
- **DNS and WINS services** These allow the administrator to configure DNS and NetBIOS name resolution.
- **DHCP services** These allow the administrator to configure the server to assign IP addresses to clients on the network.
- **Directory services** These allow the administrator to build a central list of objects, such as user accounts that may be used by clients to log on to the network. Microsoft's directory service is known as Active Directory.
- **Web services** These allow the administrator to build Internet or corporate intranet sites that are hosted on the server.

- **E-mail services**   These allow the administrator to configure the server to send e-mail using SMTP. This feature was designed to allow application developers to build e-mail functionality into their applications.
- **Group policies**   These allow an administrator to deploy settings down to the client operating systems from a central point. Some of the types of settings that can be applied to clients through group policies are folder redirection, file permissions, user rights, and installation of software.

We will look at those network services in a later chapter; the point now is that the network operating systems usually come with these features and all you need to do is install and configure them on the server.

One of the major factors that led to the popularity of the Windows-based server operating systems is that Microsoft developed a user interface on the server that was similar to the Windows client operating systems. With Windows Server 2008 and 2012, Microsoft also provides a "Server Core" installation option that does not include a graphical user interface. Figure 1-27 displays the user interface of a Windows server.

The fact that the user interface on the server operating system is the same as that on the client operating system means that the learning curve for the server operating system is dramatically reduced. The other thing that led to the rapid growth of the installed base

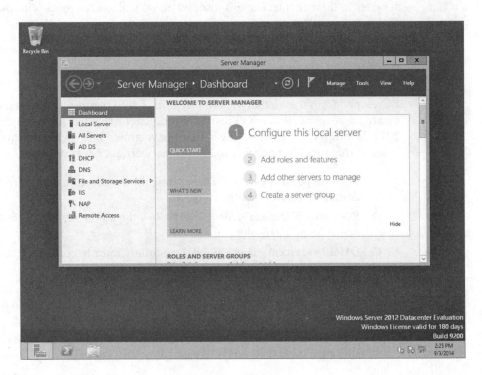

FIGURE 1-27

The Windows server user interface

for Windows-based servers is the fact that Windows servers made it easy to configure the services that were mentioned previously. For example, to install a Domain Name System (DNS) or Dynamic Host Configuration Protocol (DHCP) server, you simply go to Server Manager in Windows Server 2008 or Windows Server 2012.

EXERCISE 1-3

Video

Installing DNS on a Windows Server

This exercise shows you how to install the DNS service on Windows Server 2012. The exercise is designed to demonstrate the ease of use of the operating system, rather than to demonstrate how to configure DNS. To install DNS, do the following:

1. Start the 2012ServerA VM and log on as Administrator.
2. Launch Server Manager by choosing the Server Manager icon in the task bar.
3. Once Server Manager is loaded, choose Manage | Add Roles And Features.
4. On the Before You Begin screen, choose Next.
5. Ensure role-based or feature-based installation is selected and choose Next.
6. Ensure that your server is selected on the Select Destination Server page and choose Next.
7. On the Select Server Roles page, select DNS Server and choose Next.
8. Choose Next on the Select Feature page.
9. Choose Finish to complete the installation of the DNS server.

Clients and Resources

A major component of successful networking with NOS is the client operating system. The client operating system needs to have client software installed known as the redirector. The term *redirector* comes from the fact that when the client makes the request for a network resource, the redirector redirects the request from the local system to the network server. Whether the workstations are in a workgroup environment (peer-to-peer) or a client-server environment, you need to have client software installed on the client operating systems to connect to the servers. Some examples of client operating systems that can connect to a Windows server are Windows 7, Windows 8, Mac OS X, and UNIX and Linux.

Directory Services

With Windows servers, the server that holds the central list of user accounts that may log on to the network is called a domain controller. Microsoft calls the database of user accounts that resides on domain controllers the Active Directory Database. Active Directory is Microsoft's implementation of a directory service. Typically, when users log on to the network, they will sit at a client machine and type in a user name and password. In the Microsoft world, this user name and password combination is sent to the domain controller so that the domain controller can verify that the logon information is correct. If the logon information is correct, the user is allowed to use network resources to which they have been given access. A directory service also enables users to locate objects on the network such as printers because the directory stores more than user accounts—it stores additional network objects such as printers and folders so that users can search the directory for these objects.

UNIX/Linux

Originally developed by Bell Labs, UNIX is a popular operating system that provides powerful networking and database management. UNIX boasts three key features that make it powerful: multitasking, multiusers, and networking capabilities.

UNIX is a powerful multitasking operating system that can run many processes in the background while enabling users to work in the foreground on an application. The last feature, networking capability, has been standard for some time. UNIX has been the leader in creating many successful applications that have made their way to other platforms such as Windows. UNIX has a popular cousin, known as Linux, which has picked up some market share as both a server and a client. Figure 1-28 displays the Linux operating system.

FIGURE 1-28

The Linux user interface

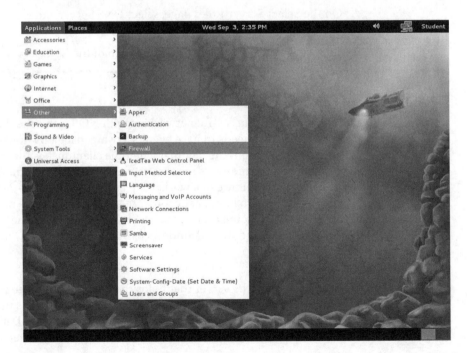

Clients and Resources

Today's versions of UNIX, and especially Linux, are different from the older versions. Today, like Windows, most Linux versions have a graphical shell loaded automatically that allows a user to use the operating system with a mouse. Most versions also have programs automatically installed that allow you to configure the operating system and change its settings. In addition, popular programs are installed, such as a word processor and a spreadsheet. Although most people have traditionally associated Linux and UNIX with the command line only, you can do a lot from the graphical shell as well.

Directory Services

The UNIX and Linux standard directory service is Network Information Service (NIS), which has been superseded by NIS+ and Lightweight Directory Access Protocol (LDAP). As a matter of fact, Microsoft Services for UNIX includes an NIS service that allows UNIX and Linux clients to authenticate to Active Directory. These services also allow the objects from Active Directory to be copied or synchronized with the NIS directory, allowing UNIX clients to authenticate with NIS if the account was built originally in the other directory. Similar to Active Directory, NIS is a central repository of network resources (for example, users, groups, and printers) that is synchronized to other UNIX and Linux servers on the network.

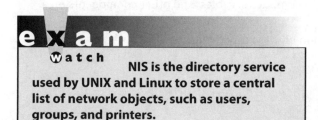

NIS is the directory service used by UNIX and Linux to store a central list of network objects, such as users, groups, and printers.

CERTIFICATION SUMMARY

This chapter plays a significant role in this book. It serves as an introduction to some key elements of networking, such as network topologies, cabling, and network architectures. Understanding the basic network structure requires a little knowledge of computing and information sharing. First, remember that for a network to exist, we need to have two things: the entities that want to share information or resources and the medium that enables the entities to communicate (a cable, such as coaxial or unshielded twisted-pair, or a wireless network). In this chapter, you looked at the various topologies that exist in networks: bus, star, ring, mesh, and wireless. You also looked at network terms, such as segments and backbones.

In addition, you looked at the various networking media and connectors. Knowing the different grades of cable can be important for the exam, as well as knowing what connectors go with what type of cabling. Make sure to review this before taking your exam.

You also learned about some of the network operating systems for client-server networks: Windows Server and UNIX.

TWO-MINUTE DRILL

Identifying Characteristics of a Network

❑ A network is made up of two basic components: the entities that need to share information or resources and the medium that enables the entities to communicate.

❑ A peer-to-peer network has a number of workstations that connect to one another for the purpose of sharing resources. There is no dedicated server on a peer-to-peer network.

❑ A server-based network has a central server installed, with each client requesting resources from the server.

Identifying Network Topologies

❑ Topology is the physical layout of computers, cables, and other components on a network.

❑ Many networks are a combination of these topologies:

1. Bus
2. Star
3. Mesh
4. Ring
5. Wireless

❑ A bus topology uses a main trunk to connect multiple computers. If there is a break in a cable, it will bring the entire network down.

❑ In a star topology, all computers are connected through one central hub or switch. If there is a break in a cable, only the host that is connected to that cable is affected.

❑ With a mesh topology, every workstation has a connection to every other component of the network. This type of topology is seen more commonly in something like the nationwide telephone networks.

❑ In a ring topology, all computers are connected in a ring with no beginning or end. Each system in the ring regenerates the signal.

❑ In a wireless topology, radio frequencies are used instead of physical cables. Wireless clients connect to cells, or access points, through the use of a wireless network card.

❑ A backbone is the main cable segment in the network.

Network Media and Connectors

❑ Cabling is the LAN's transmission medium.

❑ Three primary types of physical media can be used: coaxial cable, twisted-pair cable, and fiber-optic cable.

❑ Coax uses a copper core that carries an electrical signal. There are two types of coax: thinnet and thicknet. Hosts connect to thinnet through BNC connectors, whereas vampire taps and drop cables are used to connect to thicknet.

❑ Twisted-pair cabling is similar to telephone cable, but there are eight wires instead of four. Telephone cables use an RJ-11 connector, whereas network cabling uses an RJ-45 connector.

❑ Fiber-optic cabling has a glass or clear-plastic core that carries pulses of light. The straight tip (ST) and subscriber connector (SC) are used with fiber-optic cabling.

Access Methods

❑ An access method determines how systems access the network or place data on the wire.

❑ CSMA/CD is the access method used by Ethernet networks and involves a host sensing traffic on the wire. When the wire is free of traffic, the host can send its data.

❑ Token passing is the access method used by Token Ring. When a system on a Token Ring network wants to send data, it must wait to receive the token.

Network Architectures

❑ A network architecture is made up of a certain cable type, access method, and topology.

❑ Two popular Ethernet architectures are 1000BaseT and 100BaseT. 1000BaseT uses twisted-pair cabling at 1000 Mbps (CAT 6) and uses CSMA/CD as the access method. 100BaseT runs at 100 Mbps using CAT 5 UTP cabling. Both architectures use a star topology.

❑ Token Ring is a network architecture that uses token passing as the access method and is configured in a star topology.

Network Operating Systems

❑ The two most widely used network operating systems available are Microsoft Windows Server 2008 R2 and Windows Server 2012 and UNIX/Linux.

SELF TEST

The following questions will help you measure your understanding of the material presented in this chapter. Read all the choices carefully, because there may be more than one correct answer, but you will need to select the most correct answer.

Identifying Characteristics of a Network

1. In which type of network is there no dedicated server, with each node on the network being an equal resource for sharing and receiving information?
   A. Client-server
   B. Peer-to-peer
   C. Windows Server 2012
   D. Novell NetWare 6.*x*

2. What is the Microsoft term for a peer-to-peer network?
   A. Client-server
   B. Domain
   C. Workgroup
   D. Active Directory

3. A company has offices in Halifax and Toronto. Both networks are connected to allow the two locations to communicate. This is considered what type of network?
   A. LAN
   B. JAN
   C. MAN
   D. WAN

4. Which type of server is responsible for storing files for users on the network?
   A. File and print server
   B. Web server
   C. Directory server
   D. Application server

Identifying Network Topologies

5. The physical layout of computers, cables, and other components on a network is known as what?
   A. Segment
   B. Backbone
   C. Topology
   D. Protocol

6. Which topology has a centralized location in which all of the cables come together to a central point such that a failure at this point brings down the entire network?
   A. Bus
   B. Star
   C. Mesh
   D. Ring
   E. Wireless

7. Which topology has a layout in which every workstation or peripheral has a direct connection to every other workstation or peripheral on the network?
   A. Bus
   B. Star
   C. Mesh
   D. Ring
   E. Wireless

Network Media and Connectors

8. You have four switches connected together with twisted-pair cabling. Systems connected to switch two cannot seem to communicate with the rest of the network. What could be the problem?
   A. It is not using a straight-through cable to connect to the other switches.
   B. It is using an LC connector to connect to the other switches.
   C. It is using an ST connector to connect to the other switches.
   D. It is not using a crossover to connect to the other switches.

9. Which cable type sends the signal as pulses of light through a glass core?
   A. Thinnet
   B. Thicknet
   C. Fiber-optic
   D. CAT 5e

10. What is the maximum distance of CAT 3 UTP cabling?

   A. 100 meters

   B. 185 meters

   C. 250 meters

   D. 500 meters

11. You wish to install a 100BaseT network. What type of cabling will you use?

   A. CAT 3 UTP

   B. CAT 5 UTP

   C. Thinnet

   D. Fiber-optic

12. Fiber-optic cabling uses which types of connectors? (Select two.)

   A. SC

   B. RJ-45

   C. BNC

   D. ST

13. What is the maximum distance of single-mode fiber (SMF)?

   A. 300 meters

   B. 500 meters

   C. 2 kilometers

   D. 850 meters

14. Which cable type is immune to outside interference and crosstalk?

   A. Thinnet

   B. Thicknet

   C. Twisted-pair

   D. Fiber-optic

15. You want to create a crossover cable to connect two systems directly together. Which wires would you have to switch at one end of the cable?

   A. Wires 1 and 2 with wires 3 and 6

   B. Wires 2 and 3 with wires 6 and 8

   C. Wires 1 and 2 with wires 3 and 4

   D. Wires 2 and 3 with wires 3 and 6

Access Methods

16. Which access method does 100BaseT use?

   A. Baseband

   B. CSMA/CD

   C. CSMA/CA

   D. Token passing

17. Which access method does Token Ring use?

    A. Baseband

    B. CSMA/CD

    C. CSMA/CA

    D. Token passing

Network Architectures

18. Which network architecture is defined as the IEEE 802.3 standard?

    A. Token Ring

    B. FDDI

    C. Fiber

    D. Ethernet

19. Which network architecture uses single-mode fiber-optic cabling?

    A. 1000BaseLX

    B. 1000BaseSX

    C. 1000BaseCX

    D. 1000BaseTX

20. Which type of cabling is used in a 10BaseFL network?

    A. STP

    B. CAT 3 UTP

    C. Thinnet

    D. Thicknet

    E. Fiber-optic

21. Which Gigabit architecture uses multimode fiber cabling?

    A. 1000BaseLX

    B. 1000BaseSX

    C. 1000BaseCX

    D. 1000BaseTX

Network Operating Systems

22. Which network operating system was developed from the VMS platform?

    A. NetWare

    B. UNIX

    C. Windows 95

    D. Windows NT

23. Which operating system was originally developed by Bell Labs and has multitasking, multiuser, and built-in networking capabilities?

A. UNIX

B. Windows NT

C. Windows 95

D. NetWare

24. Microsoft's directory service is called _____?

A. Active Directory

B. NDS

C. DNS

D. StreetTalk

Performance-Based Question Review: See the performance-based question sample from the author included with the accompanying media.

SELF TEST ANSWERS

Identifying Characteristics of a Network

1. ☑ **B.** A peer-to-peer network has no dedicated servers. There are no hierarchical differences between the workstations in the network; each workstation can decide which resources are shared on the network. In a peer-to-peer network, all workstations are clients and servers at the same time.

   ☒ **A** is incorrect because this network type has a dedicated server. **C** and **D** are incorrect because Windows Server 2012 and Novell NetWare 6.*x* constitute the server portion of the client-server network.

2. ☑   **C.** The Microsoft term for a peer-to-peer network is a workgroup environment. If you have not installed your Windows clients in a domain (client-server), then they are in a workgroup environment.

☒   **A** is incorrect because a client-server network is the opposite of a peer-to-peer network; a client-server network uses a central server. **B** is incorrect because domain is the term for a Microsoft server–based environment. **D** is incorrect because Active Directory is the term for Microsoft's implementation of a directory server.

3. ☑   **D.** Two remote offices that are spread over geographic distances constitute a wide area network (WAN).

☒   **A** is incorrect because it is the opposite of a WAN; a LAN is a network in a single geographic location. **B** is incorrect because there is no such thing in networking as a JAN. **C** is incorrect because this is a metropolitan area network.

4. ☑   **A.** A file and print server is responsible for providing files and printers to users on the network.

☒   **B, C,** and **D** are incorrect because they are each their own type of server. A web server will host websites; a directory server contains a central list of objects, such as user accounts on the network; and an application server runs a form of networking application, such as an e-mail or a database server program.

Identifying Network Topologies

5. ☑   **C.** The topology is the physical layout of computers, cables, and other components on a network. Many networks are a combination of the various topologies.

☒   **A** is incorrect because a segment is a part of a LAN that is separated by routers or bridges from the rest of the LAN. **B** is incorrect because a backbone is the main part of cabling that joins all of the segments together and handles the bulk of the network traffic. **D** is incorrect because a protocol is a set of rules governing the communication between PCs; a protocol can be thought of as similar to a language.

6. ☑   **B.** In a star topology, all computers are connected through one central hub or switch. A star topology actually comes from the days of the mainframe system. The mainframe system had a centralized point at which the terminals connected.

☒   **A** is incorrect because a bus topology uses one cable to connect multiple computers. **C** is incorrect because the mesh network has every PC connected to every other PC and can resemble a spider's web. **D** is incorrect because a ring topology resembles a circle or ring. **E** is incorrect because there is no physical cabling to represent the topology; it is represented by a bubble or cell.

7. ☑   **C.** A mesh topology is not very common in computer networking, but you have to know it for the exam. The mesh topology is seen more often with something like the nationwide telephone network. With a mesh topology, every workstation has a connection to every other component of the network.

☒ **A** is incorrect because a bus topology uses one cable to connect multiple computers. **B** is incorrect because a star topology is made up of a central point or hub, with cables coming from the hub and extending to the PCs. **D** is incorrect because this topology resembles a circle or ring. **E** is incorrect because there is no physical cabling to represent the topology; it is represented by a bubble or cell.

Network Media and Connectors

8. ☑ **D.** When connecting similar devices, you should use a crossover cable, which switches the placement of the transmit and receive wires on one end of the cable to allow similar devices such as two switches to communicate.
☒ **A, B,** and **C** are incorrect. LC and ST connectors are used with fiber-optic cabling; a straight-through cable would not be used to connect two switches together.

9. ☑ **C.** Fiber-optic cabling sends pulses of light through a glass core.
☒ **A, B,** and **D** are incorrect because each carries an electrical signal.

10. ☑ **A.** All twisted-pair cabling is limited to 100 meters.
☒ **B** is incorrect because 185 meters is the maximum distance of thinnet cabling; **D** is incorrect because 500 meters is the maximum distance of thicknet cabling. **C** is incorrect; there is no cable type that has a 250-meter maximum distance.

11. ☑ **B.** 100BaseT uses twisted-pair that runs at 100 Mbps. CAT 5 is the twisted-pair cabling type that runs at 100 Mbps.
☒ **A** is incorrect because CAT 3 runs at 10 Mbps. **C** is incorrect because thinnet runs at 10 Mbps and is known as 10Base2. **D** is incorrect. Although fiber optic can run at 100 Mbps, it is not used in 100BaseT.

12. ☑ **A** and **D.** Fiber-optic cabling uses a number of connector styles, two of which are the SC and ST connectors.
☒ **B** and **C** are incorrect. RJ-45 is used by twisted-pair cabling, and BNC is used by thinnet.

13. ☑ **C.** Single-mode fiber-optic cabling has a maximum distance of approximately 2 km.
☒ **A, B,** and **D** are incorrect distances for single-mode fiber, although 300 meters is the maximum distance of multimode fiber.

14. ☑ **D.** Fiber-optic cabling is immune to outside interference and crosstalk.
☒ **A, B,** and **C** are incorrect. Thinnet, thicknet, and twisted-pair cabling are susceptible to outside interference.

15. ☑ **A.** To create a crossover cable, you would switch wires 1 and 2 with wires 3 and 6 on one end of the cable.
☒ **B, C,** and **D** are incorrect. These combinations are not used to create crossover cables.

Access Methods

16. ☑ **B.** Carrier sense multiple access with collision detection (CSMA/CD) is the access method that 100BaseT uses. With CSMA/CD, a host will sense the wire to see if it is free; only if the wire is free of data will the host send data.

    ☒ **A, C,** and **D** are incorrect. Baseband is not an access method. CSMA/CA and token passing are access methods, but are not used by 100BaseT.

17. ☑ **D.** Token Ring uses the token-passing access method. With token passing, a host must have the token before submitting data on the wire.

    ☒ **A, B,** and **C** are incorrect. Baseband is not an access method, CSMA/CA is used in AppleTalk networks, and CSMA/CD is used in Ethernet environments.

Network Architectures

18. ☑ **D.** Ethernet (CSMA/CD) is defined by IEEE 802.3.

    ☒ **A, B,** and **C** are incorrect. These architectures are not defined by 802.3, but be aware that Token Ring is defined by IEEE 802.5.

19. ☑ **A.** 1000BaseLX uses single-mode fiber-optic cabling.

    ☒ **B, C,** and **D** are incorrect. 1000BaseSX uses multimode fiber-optic cabling, 1000BaseCX uses coaxial cabling, and 1000BaseTX uses CAT 5e or higher.

20. ☑ **E.** 10BaseFL uses fiber-optic cabling. Remember to watch the characters at the end of the architecture name to determine what the cable type is—"FL" is for fiber link.

    ☒ **A, B, C,** and **D** are incorrect. STP, thinnet, thicknet, and CAT 3 UTP are all cable types, but are not used in 10BaseFL.

21. ☑ **B.** 1000BaseSX uses multimode fiber cabling. Remember that multimode cannot go as far as single mode, and also the "SX" in the architecture is for "short range"—multimode for short range; single mode for long range.

    ☒ **A, C,** and **D** are incorrect. 1000BaseLX uses single-mode fiber, 1000BaseCX uses coaxial cable, and 1000BaseTX uses twisted-pair.

Network Operating Systems

22. ☑ **D.** Developed from the VMS platform many years ago, Microsoft Windows Server operating systems are based on Windows NT technology, which is based on the VMS platform.

    ☒ **A, B,** and **C** are incorrect. The graphical interface and look and feel of the other operating systems in the Windows family made Windows NT popular among users and network administrators. Windows 95 was simply a great enhancement of Windows for Workgroups. NetWare and UNIX were not based on VMS.

23. ☑ **A.** Originally developed at Bell Labs, UNIX is a popular, powerful operating system for networking and database management. UNIX boasts three key features that make it powerful: multitasking, multiuser, and networking capabilities.
☒ **B, C,** and **D** are incorrect. Windows 95 and NT were developed by Microsoft; NetWare was developed by Novell.

24. ☑ **A.** Active Directory is the name of Microsoft's directory service.
☒ **B, C,** and **D** are incorrect. Novell's directory service is known as NDS, DNS is the name of a service that performs FQDN-to-IP address name resolution, and StreetTalk is Banyan's directory service.

Chapter 2

Network Protocols and Standards

CERTIFICATION OBJECTIVE 2.01

Network Protocols

Understanding the concepts of networking protocols is critical to being able to troubleshoot communication problems in networking environments. This section will introduce you to four common network protocols found in networking environments and the difference between routable and nonroutable protocols.

A network protocol is a language that is used by systems that wish to communicate with one another. Let's look at an example of a communication problem that could occur when two persons who want to talk are not speaking the same language. Let's say you are traveling the country on your summer vacation and stop in a fast food restaurant. When ordering your favorite meal, you would need to ensure that you speak the same language as the person taking the order. If you speak English and the waiter speaks French, you would be giving your order, but the waiter would not be able to understand you. The same thing will happen on the network when two systems use two totally different protocols—everyone is talking, but no one is communicating. The first step to networking is making sure that the two systems that are trying to talk have the same protocol installed.

Four of the major protocols found in networking environments today are

- NetBEUI
- IPX/SPX
- AppleTalk
- TCP/IP

NetBEUI

NetBIOS Extended User Interface (NetBEUI) is a transport protocol developed by IBM but adopted by Microsoft for use in earlier versions of Windows and DOS. NetBEUI commonly was found in smaller networks due to the fact that it is a nonroutable protocol. A *nonroutable protocol* is a protocol that sends data, but the data is unable to cross a router to reach other networks; communication is limited to the local area network (LAN) only. The fact that NetBEUI is a nonroutable protocol has limited its use on networks dramatically.

NetBEUI was first implemented with LAN Manager networks and became popular in smaller Microsoft networks back with Windows 3.11, Windows 95, and Windows 98. It is no longer supported in Windows 7. NetBEUI is an extremely efficient and simple protocol with little overhead because of its inability to route packets. One of the major advantages of NetBEUI is that it is extremely simple to install and configure. Minimal configuration is required to allow the protocol to work—you install it, specify a unique computer name, and it works!

 The Network+ exam does not expect you to know the details of NetBEUI, but know that NetBEUI is a nonroutable protocol.

What Is NetBIOS?

NetBEUI has a close friend, *NetBIOS* (short for *Network Basic Input/Output System*), with which it works closely when communicating with systems on the network. NetBIOS is an application programming interface (API) that is used to make network calls to remote systems. When you install NetBEUI, it includes the NetBIOS protocol, and NetBEUI relies on NetBIOS for session management functionality. Also, NetBIOS is nonroutable, but may be installed with other routable protocols, such as IPX/SPX or TCP/IP, to allow NetBIOS traffic to travel across networks. NetBIOS has two communication modes:

- **Session mode** This is used for connection-oriented communication in which NetBIOS is responsible for establishing a session with the target system, monitoring the session to detect any errors in transmission, and then recovering from those errors by retransmitting any data that went missing or was corrupt.
- **Datagram mode** This is used for connectionless communication in which a session is not needed. Datagram mode also is used by NetBIOS broadcasts. Datagram mode does not support error detection and correction services, which are the responsibility of the application using NetBIOS.

Now that you understand a little bit about NetBIOS, here are some important things to keep in mind regarding NetBIOS and NetBEUI:

- NetBIOS is a session protocol, whereas NetBEUI is a transport protocol (more on session and transport later in this chapter, when you learn about the OSI model).
- NetBIOS is used by other protocols as well, such as TCP/IP.
- Since NetBIOS is not a transport protocol, it does not directly support routing, but depends on one of two transport protocols—TCP/IP or IPX/SPX—to do this.
- NetBIOS uses NetBIOS names as a method of identifying systems on the network. A NetBIOS name, also known as a computer name, can be a maximum of 16 bytes long— 15 bytes for the name and 1 byte for the NetBIOS name suffix (a code at the end of the name representing the running service). The NetBIOS computer name must be unique on the LAN.

IPX/SPX

Internetwork Packet Exchange/Sequenced Packet Exchange (IPX/SPX) is a protocol suite (which means there are many protocols in one) that was developed by Novell and was popular on older NetWare networks. However, newer versions of NetWare (NetWare 5.*x* and later) have moved away from it and are using TCP/IP as the preferred protocol. Microsoft refers to IPX/SPX as NWLink (NetWare Link).

The IPX protocol of the IPX/SPX protocol suite is responsible for the routing of information across the network. IPX/SPX is a routable protocol, so its addressing scheme must be able to identify each system on the network and the network itself using a network ID. The network administrator assigns each network a network ID. An IPX network ID is an eight-character hexadecimal value—for example, 0BADBEEF. A complete IPX address is made up of the network ID, a period (.), and then the six-byte Media Access Control (MAC) address of the network card (a unique address burned into the network card) in the system. For example, the computer I am sitting at right now has a MAC address of 00-90-4B-4C-C1-59. If my system were connected to network ID 0BADBEEF, then my IPX network address would be 0BADBEEF.00904B4CC159. The fact that the MAC address is used means that there is no need to have it resolved when communication occurs—which will make the protocol more efficient than other protocols such as TCP/IP, which does require the IP address to be resolved to a MAC address.

IPX/SPX is not as easy to configure as NetBEUI. When doing an IPX installation, you will need to be familiar with configuration issues such as the network number and frame type:

■ **Network number**   This is the number assigned to the Novell network segment. It is a hexadecimal value, with a maximum of eight digits.

■ **Frame type**   This is the format of the packet that is used by the network. It is important to make sure that all systems on the network are configured for the same frame type. For example, if I want to connect to SERVER1, which uses the frame type 802.2, then I would need to ensure that my frame type was set to 802.2—otherwise, I would not be able to communicate with SERVER1. The four major frame types are 802.2, 802.3, ETHERNET_SNAP, and ETHERNET_II.

While IPX is responsible for the routing of packets, it is also a connectionless, unreliable transport. Unreliable means IPX packets are sent to a destination without requiring the destination to acknowledge receiving those packets. Connectionless means that no session is established between sender and receiver before transmitting data.

SPX is the protocol in the IPX/SPX protocol suite that is responsible for reliable delivery. SPX is a connection-oriented protocol that will ensure packets that are not received at the destination are retransmitted on the wire.

AppleTalk

AppleTalk is a routable protocol that is used primarily in Macintosh environments to connect multiple systems together in a network environment. AppleTalk was implemented in two phases, known as phase 1 and phase 2:

■ **Phase 1**   This was designed for small workgroup environments and, therefore, supports a much smaller number of nodes on the network. Phase 1 supports nonextended networks; each network segment can be assigned only a single network number, and only one zone is allowed in a nonextended network. A zone is a logical grouping of nodes—the network administrator will assign nodes to a particular zone.

- **Phase 2** This was designed for larger networks and supports more than 200 hosts on the network. Phase 2 supports extended networks, thereby allowing one network segment to be assigned multiple network numbers and allowing for multiple zones on that network segment. Each node is part of a single zone on an extended network.

TCP/IP

Transmission Control Protocol/Internet Protocol (TCP/IP) is the most common network protocol suite used today. A routable protocol, TCP/IP is the protocol on which the Internet is built. TCP/IP is robust and commonly is associated with UNIX, Linux, Windows, and Mac OS systems.

TCP/IP originally was designed in the 1970s to be used by the Defense Advanced Research Projects Agency (DARPA) and the U.S. Department of Defense (DOD) to connect dissimilar systems across the country. This design required the capability to cope with unstable network conditions. Therefore, the design of TCP/IP included the capability to reroute packets.

One of the major advantages of TCP/IP was the fact that it could be used to connect heterogeneous (dissimilar) environments together, which is why it has become the protocol of the Internet—but what are its drawbacks? TCP/IP has two major drawbacks:

- **Configuration** TCP/IP requires configuration, and to administer it, you need to be familiar with IP addresses, subnet masks, and default gateways—not complicated topics once you are familiar with them, but there is a bit of a learning curve compared to installing NetBEUI.

- **Security** Because communication was a design goal of TCP/IP, it is an unsecure protocol. If security is a concern, you need to make certain that you implement additional technologies to secure the network traffic or systems running TCP/IP. For example, if you want to ensure that other individuals cannot read the data sent to your web server, you would use Secure Sockets Layer (SSL) with the website—which would encrypt traffic between a client and your web server. You will be introduced to network security in more detail in Chapter 15, but be aware that security could be an issue for TCP/IP if not handled appropriately.

exam

watch The Network+ exam focuses on TCP/IP as the core protocol suite. Note that Chapters 4, 5, 6, and 8 go into more detail on TCP/IP—please be sure to spend a lot of time with those chapters to prepare for the exam.

Routable vs. Nonroutable Protocols

We have discussed each of the four major protocols, and you have learned that NetBEUI is a nonroutable protocol, whereas IPX/SPX, AppleTalk, and TCP/IP are routable protocols. What exactly is a routable protocol? A routable protocol is a protocol whose packets may leave your network, pass through your router, and be delivered to a remote network, as shown in Figure 2-1.

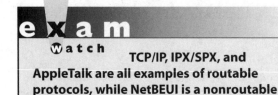

TCP/IP, IPX/SPX, and AppleTalk are all examples of routable protocols, while NetBEUI is a nonroutable protocol.

A nonroutable protocol does not have the capability to send packets across a router from one network to another network. This is due to the fact that this is a simple protocol and does not accommodate addressing patterns in the packets that give knowledge of multiple networks. For example, NetBEUI uses NetBIOS names to send data back and forth, but a NETBIOS name does not identify "what network" the destination system exists on, whereas TCP/IP and IPX/SPX both have a network ID portion to their addressing schemes that identifies "what network" the destination system exists on.

When a nonroutable packet reaches the router, the router discards it, as shown in Figure 2-2, because there is no routing information in the packet, such as a layer-3 destination address.

FIGURE 2-1   A routable protocol sending data through a router

Workstation A
Switch
Router
Internet
Router
Switch
Workstation A

Workstation B
Network server
Network server
Workstation B

Company XYZ
Company ABC

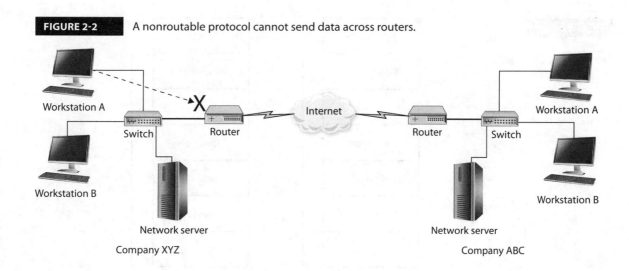

FIGURE 2-2   A nonroutable protocol cannot send data across routers.

The OSI Model

In the early 1980s, the International Organization for Standardization (ISO) defined a standard, or set of rules, for manufacturers of networking components that would allow these networking components to communicate in dissimilar environments. This standard is known as the Open Systems Interconnect (OSI) model and is made up of seven layers. Each layer of the OSI model is responsible for a specific function or task within the stages of network communication. The seven layers, from highest to lowest, are application, presentation, session, transport, network, data link, and physical. Network communication starts at the application layer of the OSI model (on the sending system) and works its way down through the layers to the physical layer. The information then passes along the communication medium to the receiving computer, which works its way back up the layers starting at the physical layer. Figure 2-3 shows an example of packets being transmitted down through the OSI layers of the sending computer, across the medium, and back up the OSI layers on the receiving computer. Be sure to refer to this figure frequently when going through this section.

Each layer of the OSI model is responsible for certain functions within the process of sending data from one system to another. Each layer is responsible for communicating with

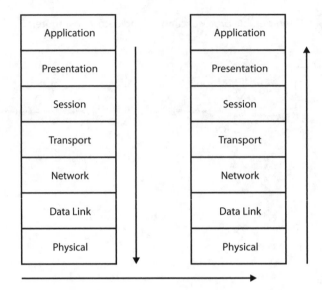

FIGURE 2-3

Layers of the OSI model

the layers immediately above it and below it. For example, the presentation layer will receive information from the application layer, format it appropriately, and then pass it to the session layer. The presentation layer will never deal directly with the network or data link layers.

Let's look at the layers from the point of view of two computers that will send data between each other: COMPUTER1 and SERVER1 are going to exchange data on the network. COMPUTER1 is the sending computer, and SERVER1 is the receiving computer, as shown in Figure 2-4. The data exchange starts with COMPUTER1 sending a request to SERVER1. It is important to notice as you progress through the layers that whatever function is performed at a layer on the sending system must be undone at the same layer on the receiving system. For example, if the presentation layer compresses the data on the sending system, the presentation layer will decompress the data on the receiving system before passing it up to the application layer.

e x a m

ⓦ a t c h   The Network+ exam is sure to test your knowledge of the OSI model and each of its layers, so be familiar with this for the exam! You should also note that the data has special terms assigned to it once it reaches different layers—at layer 4, the data is called a *segment;* at layer 3, the data is called a *packet;* and at layer 2, the data is called a *frame.*

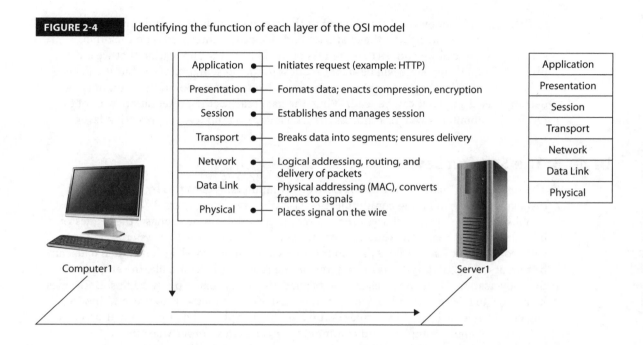

FIGURE 2-4 Identifying the function of each layer of the OSI model

Layer 7: The Application Layer

The application layer running on the sending system (COMPUTER1) is responsible for the actual request being made. This could be any type of networking request—a web request using a web browser (HTTP), an e-mail delivery request using Simple Mail Transport Protocol (SMTP), or a file system request using the network client redirector software. On the receiving system, the application layer would be responsible for passing the request to the appropriate application or service on that system. In our example, we will assume that you are sitting at COMPUTER1 and you have typed the address of SERVER1 into your web browser to create an HTTP request.

Layer 6: The Presentation Layer

After the request is made, the application layer passes the data down to the presentation layer, where it is formatted so that the data (or request) can be interpreted by the receiving system. When the presentation layer receives data from the application layer, it makes sure the data is in the proper format—if it is not, the presentation layer converts the data accordingly. On the receiving system, when the presentation layer receives network data from the session layer, it makes sure the data is in the proper format and once again converts it if it is not.

Formatting functions that could occur at the presentation layer include compression, encryption, and ensuring that the character code set can be interpreted on the other side. For example, if we choose to compress our data from the application that we are using, the application layer will pass that request to the presentation layer, but it will be the presentation layer that does the compression. Now, at some point, this data must be decompressed so that it can be read. When the data reaches the presentation layer of the receiving computer, it will decompress the data and pass it up to the application layer.

Layer 5: The Session Layer

The session layer manages the dialog between computers. It does this by establishing, managing, and terminating communications between two computers. When a session is established, three distinct phases are involved. In the establishment phase, the requestor initiates the service and the rules for communication between the two systems. These rules could include such things as who transmits and when, as well as how much data can be sent at a time. Both systems must agree on the rules; the rules are like the etiquette of the conversation. Once the rules are established, the data transfer phase begins. Both sides know how to talk to each other, what are the most efficient methods to use, and how to detect errors, all because of the rules defined in the first phase. Finally, termination occurs when the session is complete, and communication ends in an orderly fashion.

In our example, COMPUTER1 creates a session with SERVER1 at this point, and they agree on the rules of the conversation.

Layer 4: The Transport Layer

The transport layer handles functions such as reliable and unreliable delivery of the data. For reliable transport protocols, the transport layer works hard to ensure reliable delivery of data to its destinations. On the sending system, the transport layer is responsible for breaking the data into smaller parts, known as segments, so that if retransmission is required, only the missing segments will be sent. Missing segments are detected when the transport layer receives acknowledgments (ACKs) from the remote system upon receiving the packets. At the receiving system, the transport layer is responsible for opening all of the packets and reconstructing the original message.

Another function of the transport layer is segment sequencing. Sequencing is a connection-oriented service that takes segments that are received out of order and resequences them in the right order. For example, if I send you five packets and you receive the packets in this order (by their sequence number): 3, 1, 4, 2, 5, the transport layer will read the sequence numbers and assemble them in the correct order.

The transport layer also enables the option of specifying a "service address," known as a *port address.* The port address allows the services or applications that are running on the systems to specify what application the request came from and what application the request

TCP is an example of a transport layer protocol responsible for reliable delivery, whereas User Datagram Protocol (UDP) is an example of a transport layer protocol responsible for unreliable delivery.

is headed for by having each application use a unique port address on the system. All modern operating systems run many programs at once, and each network program has a unique service address. Service addresses that are well defined (by networking standards, for example) are called well-known addresses. Service addresses also are called sockets or ports by protocols such as TCP/IP.

At this point in our example, the request is broken into segments in preparation for being delivered across the network, and transport-layer information (such as the transport protocol being used and any additional transport information) is appended to the request. In this example, because we are dealing with a TCP/IP application, the source port and destination port are added.

INSIDE THE EXAM

Connection-Oriented Communication

Connection-oriented communication ensures reliable delivery of data from the sender to the receiver. When establishing these services, the protocol must perform some sort of handshaking function. Handshaking takes place at the beginning of a communication session. During this process, the two computers determine the rules for communication, such as transmission speed and which ports to use. Handshaking also determines the proper way to terminate the session when finished. This ensures that communication ends in an orderly manner.

A session is a reliable dialog between two computers. Because connection-oriented services can provide reliable communication, they are used when two computers need to communicate in a session. Sessions are maintained until the two computers decide

that they are finished communicating. A session is just like a telephone call. You set up a telephone call by dialing (handshaking), speak to the other person (exchange data), say "Goodbye," and hang up when finished.

Connectionless Communication

Connectionless communication is a form of communication in which the sending system does not "introduce" itself—it just fires the data off. Also, the destination computer does not notify the source when the information is received. This type of communication can be unreliable because there is no notification to guarantee delivery. Connectionless communication can be faster than connection-oriented communication because the overhead of managing the session is not there, and after the information is sent, there is no second step to ensure it was received properly.

Layer 3: The Network Layer

The network layer is responsible for managing logical addressing information in the packets and the delivery, or routing, of those packets by using information stored in a routing table. The routing table is a list of available destinations that are stored in memory on the routers (more on routing in Chapter 8).

The network layer is responsible for working with logical addresses. Logical addresses uniquely identify a system on the network, and at the same time identify the network that the system resides on. This is unlike a MAC address (the physical address burned into the network card), because a MAC address just gives the system a unique address and does not specify or imply what network the system lives on. The logical address is used by network-layer protocols to deliver the packets to the correct network.

In our example, the request is coming from a web browser and is destined for a web server, both of which are applications that run on TCP/IP. At this point, the network layer will add the source address (the IP address of the sending system) and the destination address (the IP address of the destination system) to the packet so that the receiving system will know where the packet came from.

w a t c h   **Remember that layer 3 of the OSI model handles logical addressing and routing. An example of a logical address is an IP address, which takes the form of 192.168.3.24. An IP address is also known as a layer-3 address.**

Layer 2: The Data Link Layer

The data link layer is responsible for converting the data from a packet to a pattern of electrical bit signals that will be used to send the data across the communication medium. On the receiving system, the electrical signals will be converted to packets by the data link layer and then passed up to the network layer for further processing. The data link layer is divided into two sublayers:

- **Logical link control (LLC)** This is responsible for error correction and control functions.
- **Media Access Control (MAC)** This determines the physical addressing of the hosts. It also determines how the host places traffic on the medium—for example, CSMA/CD versus token passing.

The MAC sublayer maintains physical device addresses (commonly referred to as MAC addresses) for communicating with other devices on the network. These physical addresses are burned into the network cards and constitute the low-level address used to determine the source and destination of network traffic.

exam

watch   For the Network+ exam, remember that a MAC address is the physical address assigned to the network card and is known as a layer-2 address. An example of a MAC address is 00-02-3F-6B-25-13.

In our example, once the sending system's network layer appends the IP address information, the data link layer will append the MAC address information for the sending and receiving systems. This layer will also prepare the data for the wire by converting the packets to binary signals. On the receiving system, the data link layer will convert the signals passed to it by the physical layer to data and then pass the packets to the network layer for further processing.

Note for the exam that the network access methods and architectures you learned about in the last chapter run at layer 2 of the OSI model. For example, Ethernet and Token Ring network architectures are defined at layer 2 of the OSI model.

Layer 1: The Physical Layer

The bottom layer of the OSI hierarchy is concerned only with moving bits of data on and off the network medium. This includes the physical topology (or structure) of the network, the electrical and physical aspects of the medium used, and encoding and timing of bit transmission and reception.

In our example, once the network layer has appended the logical addresses and passed the data to the data link layer, where the MAC addresses have been appended and the data was converted to electrical signals, the data is then passed to the physical layer so that it can be released on the communication medium. On the receiving system, the physical layer will pick the data up off the wire and pass it to the data link layer, where it will ensure that the signal is destined for that system by reading the destination MAC address.

exam

watch   Remember for the Network+ exam that anything that works with the electrical signal runs at layer 1 of the OSI model. This includes the network cables and connectors you learned about in the last chapter.

Data Encapsulation

The term *data encapsulation* refers to the fact that as data is passed down the seven layers of the OSI model, header information is added to the message. For example, when the information reaches layer 4 of the OSI model, a layer-4 header is added, which contains protocol information for that layer, such as the port number. On the sending system, the layer-4 header is added and then the data is passed down to layer 3, where the layer-3 header is added to the left side of the data and layer-4 header. The layer-3 header contains

FIGURE 2-5

Each layer of the OSI
model adds a header.

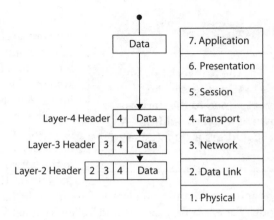

the layer-3 protocol information, such as the layer-3 source and destination address. Once the layer-3 header is applied, the message is then passed down to layer 2, where the layer-2 header is assigned, and contains the source and destination MAC addresses (layer-2 addresses).

On the receiving system, the message is passed up the OSI model. The receiving system strips the layer-2 header off and reads the destination MAC address to ensure this system is the destination of the message. Once the layer-2 header is read, the message is then passed up to the layer-3 protocol, which reads the layer-3 header (as shown in Figure 2-5). This process continues up the seven layers of the OSI model and is known as *de-encapsulation*.

Now that you have been introduced to the seven-layer OSI model, let's try an exercise to put your newfound knowledge to the test.

EXERCISE 2-1

Mixing and Matching OSI Model Definitions

In this exercise, you will take a look at some terms and match them with their appropriate definitions. This exercise is designed to give you the opportunity to identify the purpose of each layer of the OSI model.

Definition	Layer
_____ Responsible for the logical addressing and delivery of the packets.	A. Session
_____ Responsible for formatting the message.	B. Physical

Definition	Layer
_____ Responsible for physical addressing and converting the data packets to electrical signals.	C. Application
_____ Responsible for creating, managing, and ending a dialog.	D. Network
_____ Responsible for reliable delivery, sequencing, and breaking the message into packets.	E. Data link
_____ Responsible for placing or removing the signal on and off the wire.	F. Presentation
_____ Responsible for initiating or receiving the network request.	G. Transport

Protocols and the OSI Layers

Different protocols work at different levels of the OSI model. Here, we look at a few of the main protocols for this exam, apply them to the OSI model, and see how they fit in the OSI model's seven layers. For more information on protocols and services, check out Chapter 5.

IPX

IPX is an extremely fast, streamlined protocol that is not connection oriented. IPX was once fairly common because of its widespread use on Novell NetWare. This is a routable protocol that is located at the network layer of the OSI model. Because it is also an unreliable connectionless transport, IPX also applies to layer 4—the transport layer. Remember, unreliable means data is sent without acknowledgment of receipt, and connectionless means that a session is not established before transmitting. IPX is capable of being run over both Ethernet and Token Ring networks using the appropriate network interface card (NIC). For a number of years, IPX over Ethernet was the default use of NICs.

watch Although IPX runs at layer 3 (network layer) and layer 4 (transport layer), the Network+ exam places it at layer 3.

SPX

Sequenced Packet Exchange (SPX) is a transport protocol used by IPX for connection-oriented communication. It is responsible for breaking the message into manageable packets and ensuring the data reaches the destination. SPX is equivalent to TCP in the TCP/IP protocol suite. Because SPX runs at the transport layer, it is considered a layer-4 protocol.

IP

The *Internet Protocol (IP)* in the TCP/IP protocol suite performs the same routing functions that IPX does for the IPX/SPX protocol suite. IP is responsible for the logical addressing and routing of messages across the network. It does not ensure the delivery of the packets; that is the responsibility of higher-layer protocols, such as TCP.

IP is a network-layer protocol and is responsible for logical addressing—as a result, an IP address is referred to as a layer-3 address.

The logical address that IP uses is known as an IP address and it looks similar to 192.168.3.200—which is different from the physical address (MAC address), which looks like 00-02-3F-6B-25-13. The logical address is responsible for identifying the network the system resides on, along with an address for the system, whereas a MAC address is flat and identifies only the physical system on the LAN—not "where" the system resides.

IP is fully capable of running over either Token Ring or Ethernet networks, as long as an appropriate NIC is used. IP over Ethernet is the most common implementation in networking today because Ethernet is much less expensive than Token Ring and because TCP/IP is used widely on the Internet.

TCP

The *Transmission Control Protocol (TCP)* is a transport-layer protocol that is responsible for breaking the data into manageable packets and ensuring that the packets reach their destination. TCP is considered a connection-oriented protocol, which means that it relies on a session being established first. This is different from a connectionless communication, which just sends the data out and if it reaches the destination, great; if not, no big deal. With connection-oriented protocols, a session is established through introductions. ("Hi, I'm Glen Clarke. Nice to meet you, I am going to send you some data.") Connection-oriented protocols will monitor that session to ensure that the packets have reached their destination.

UDP

The *User Datagram Protocol (UDP)* is part of the TCP/IP protocol suite and is similar to TCP. When you send data on a TCP/IP network and you need a connection-oriented conversation, the TCP protocol is used. But what protocol do we use if we want to have a connectionless, unacknowledged conversation? UDP. Both TCP and UDP are layer-4 protocols. IP is used to deliver both types of data, but TCP and UDP determine whether the delivery is connection oriented or not.

TCP and UDP run at the transport layer of the OSI model and are therefore considered layer-4 protocols.

NFS

The *Network File System (NFS)* is a protocol for file sharing that enables a user to use network disks as though they were connected to the local machine. NFS was created by Sun Microsystems for use on Solaris, Sun's version of UNIX. NFS is still used frequently in the UNIX and Linux worlds (it is used universally by the UNIX community), and is available for use with nearly all operating systems. Vendor and third-party software products enable other operating systems to use NFS. It has gained acceptance with many companies and can be added to nearly any operating system. In addition to file sharing, NFS enables you to share printers. It is located in the application layer of the OSI model and is considered a member of the TCP/IP protocol suite. The primary reason to use the NFS protocol is to access resources located on a UNIX server or to share resources with someone working on a UNIX workstation.

SMB/CIFS

Microsoft's Server Message Block (SMB) is the file-sharing protocol found on Windows systems. It is used to provide shared files, printers, and serial ports on the network.

SMB is used primarily for file and printer sharing in Microsoft and is considered an application-layer protocol. It is important to note the SMB has been replaced by *Common Internet File System (CIFS)*, which has been the file-sharing protocol since Windows 2000.

NCP

The *Network Control Protocol (NCP)* is a negotiation protocol that is responsible for negotiating options over the Point-to-Point (PPP) protocol for different network-layer protocols.

SMTP

The *Simple Mail Transport Protocol (SMTP)* is the protocol for sending Internet e-mail messages. SMTP uses a well-defined syntax for transferring messages. An SMTP session includes initializing the connection, sending the destination e-mail address, sending the source e-mail address, sending the subject, and sending the body of the e-mail message.

e x a m

ⓦ a t c h   **SMTP is an application-layer protocol for sending e-mail on the Internet.**

FTP and TFTP

The *File Transfer Protocol (FTP)* is a standardized method of transferring files between two machines. FTP is a connection-oriented protocol, which means that the protocol verifies that packets successfully reach their destinations.

The *Trivial File Transfer Protocol (TFTP)* has the same purpose and function as FTP, except that it is not a connection-oriented protocol and does not verify that packets reached their destinations. By not verifying that data has been successfully transferred to its destination and therefore requiring less overhead to send data, TFTP is able to operate faster than FTP. TFTP has no authentication mechanism, whereas FTP can require a user name and password.

TCP/IP, IPX/SPX, and AppleTalk are routable protocols; NetBEUI is nonroutable.

DLC and HDLC

Data Link Control (DLC) is part of the data link layer (layer 2) of the OSI model and is responsible for identifying a system with a unique 48-bit MAC address.

The *High-level Data Link Control (HDLC)* protocol is a common serial-link protocol used on the serial ports of routers to allow the router to communicate over a point-to-point serial link. HDLC is responsible for encapsulating the packet and sending the data to the other end of the serial link (typically another router).

Video

EXERCISE 2-2

Viewing Protocol Information with Network Monitor

In this exercise, you will install a network-monitoring tool known as Network Monitor, which you can download from Microsoft's website. You will look at network traffic that was captured previously in a file. The example is that a user has entered a credit card number into a website and you have captured the traffic. Your goal is to find the credit card number in the packet.

Let's start the exercise by installing the Network Monitor software on your system. These steps were written for Network Monitor, but you could perform similar steps using monitoring software such as Wireshark. Be sure to check out the video of this exercise found in the accompanying material for this book!

Installing Network Monitor

1. Download and install the latest version of Microsoft Network Monitor from Microsoft's website.

Viewing Packet Data with Network Monitor

2. Start Network Monitor by launching the program with the shortcut found on the desktop.

3. Once Network Monitor is started, open a capture file by choosing File | Open | Capture.

4. In the Open dialog box, open the HTTPTraffic.cap file located in the LabFiles\PacketCaptures folder.

5. The contents of the packet capture are displayed. Notice that there are 24 frames (numbers listed down the left) captured and that frame 16 is the actual HTTP Post Request, which is the form's information posted to the server. This is the phase where the credit card number was submitted. We will use frame 16 as our learning tool to view network traffic.

6. Select frame 16 to view the details of the traffic at the bottom of the screen.

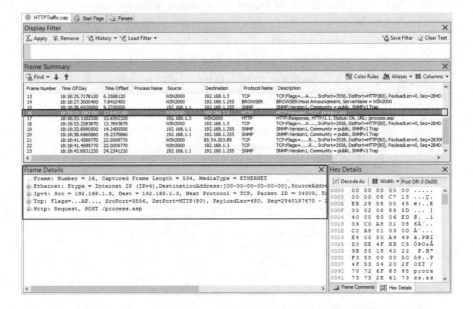

7. The window is divided into a number of panes; the middle pane is the Frame Summary pane listing all the frames (or packets) that have been captured. Below the Frame Summary is the Frame Details pane, which is used to display the details of the selected frame. Beside the Frame Details pane is the hex data for that frame. Ensure that frame 16 is still selected in the Frame Summary pane so that you can investigate your packet.

8. In the Frame Details pane, double-click Ethernet, which will expand the Ethernet section showing you the source and destination Ethernet addresses or MAC addresses (shown in the accompanying illustration).

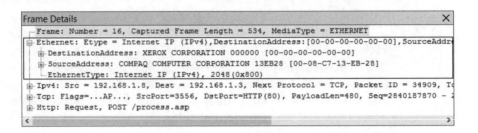

```
Frame Details                                                        ×
   Frame: Number = 16, Captured Frame Length = 534, MediaType = ETHERNET
  Ethernet: Etype = Internet IP (IPv4),DestinationAddress:[00-00-00-00-00-00],SourceAddr
    DestinationAddress: XEROX CORPORATION 000000 [00-00-00-00-00-00]
    SourceAddress: COMPAQ COMPUTER CORPORATION 13EB28 [00-08-C7-13-EB-28]
    EthernetType: Internet IP (IPv4), 2048(0x800)
  Ipv4: Src = 192.168.1.8, Dest = 192.168.1.3, Next Protocol = TCP, Packet ID = 34909, T
  Tcp: Flags=...AP..., SrcPort=3556, DstPort=HTTP(80), PayloadLen=480, Seq=2840187870 - 2
  Http: Request, POST /process.asp
```

9. Record the source MAC address, which is the system that sent the packet, in the blanks.

Source MAC address: _____

What layer of the OSI model does this information pertain to? _____

10. Below the Ethernet section is the protocol information. What layer-3 protocol is this network traffic using? _____

11. If you answered IPv4 in the preceding question, you are correct! If you double-click the IPv4 section, you will see what layer-3 addresses (IP addresses) are the source of the packet and the destination of the packet.

```
Frame Details                                                        ×
   Frame: Number = 16, Captured Frame Length = 534, MediaType = ETHERNET
  Ethernet: Etype = Internet IP (IPv4),DestinationAddress:[00-00-00-00-00-00],SourceAddre
  Ipv4: Src = 192.168.1.8, Dest = 192.168.1.3, Next Protocol = TCP, Packet ID = 34909, T
    Versions: IPv4, Internet Protocol; Header Length = 20
    DifferentiatedServicesField: DSCP: 0, ECN: 0
    TotalLength: 520 (0x208)
    Identification: 34909 (0x885D)
    FragmentFlags: 16384 (0x4000)
    TimeToLive: 128 (0x80)
    NextProtocol: TCP, 6(0x6)
    Checksum: 60726 (0xED36)
    SourceAddress: 192.168.1.8
    DestinationAddress: 192.168.1.3
  Tcp: Flags=...AP..., SrcPort=3556, DstPort=HTTP(80), PayloadLen=480, Seq=2840187870 - 2
  Http: Request, POST /process.asp
```

12. Fill in the following information:

Where is the packet headed? _____

Where did the packet come from? _____

Hint: View the source and destination addresses.

13. You also can see what transport protocol was used by IP. Two lines above the source IP address, you can see that IP is using TCP, a connection-oriented, layer-4 protocol, to ensure that the packet reaches the destination.

14. If you double-click the IP heading, you will collapse the IP details. Let's look at the application protocol information for this packet. You want to see the credit card number that was typed into the webpage. In the Frame Details pane, double-click HTTP to expand the detailed application information.

15. Select the last piece of information for HTTP, which is the HTTP Payload data (packet data). When you expand out the payload data, you can see that there is a field called CCNumber; this is the credit card number contained in the packet. Select it and it will also highlight the CCNumber in the hex pane.

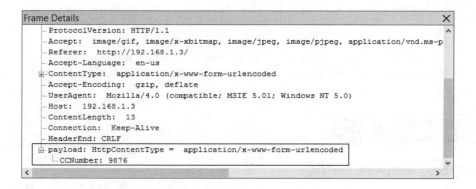

16. What is the credit card number? _____
17. Close Network Monitor.

This exercise has shown you how to view layer-2 information in a packet, such as the source and destination MAC addresses. It has also shown you how to view logical address information, such as the source and destination IP addresses, which were found with layer-3 information. You also saw how the layer-3 protocol (IP) relies on TCP to ensure delivery of the information. Finally, you viewed the application information that was submitted with the request. This will hopefully show you why it is important to ensure that you are using an encryption protocol to encrypt the data typed into an application.

It is important to understand the protocols, services, and applications that we deal with every day and what layer of the OSI model those products may be working with. Table 2-1

| TABLE 2-1 | OSI Layers for Popular Protocols and Services |

OSI Layer	Protocols, Services, Methods, and Layers
Application	FTP, SMTP, Telnet
Presentation	JPEG, GIF, MPEG
Session	NFS, RPC
Transport	TCP, UDP, SPX, IPX
Network	IPX, IP
Data Link	Ethernet, Token Ring
Physical	Twisted-pair, thinnet coax, adapter unit interface (AUI), network interface card

summarizes some of the popular protocols, services, and applications that are found in networking environments and specifies what layer of the OSI model they run at.

Video

EXERCISE 2-3

Analyzing Network Traffic

Your manager has been recording network traffic to your web server and has noticed that someone has been submitting fake data into the online store. She wants you to open one of the packet captures stored in Lab2.cap (located in your LabFiles\PacketCaptures folder) and analyze one of the packets. She would like you to report back to her the following information:

Source MAC Address: _____

Source IP Address: _____

Destination IP Address: _____

Fake Credit Card Number Used: _____

If you have trouble with this lab, look back to the exercise walk-through you did to learn where to find information about layer-2 and layer-3 addresses and where to find the specific application data.

CERTIFICATION OBJECTIVE 2.03

802 Project Standards

The Institute of Electrical and Electronics Engineers (IEEE) is a large and respected professional organization that is also active in defining standards. The 802 committee of the IEEE defines one set of standards dear to the hearts of most network professionals. Twelve subcommittees of the 802 committee define low-level LAN and wide area network (WAN) access protocols. Most of the protocols defined by the 802 committee reside in the physical and data link layers of the OSI model.

IEEE 802 Categories

As the use of LANs increased, standards were needed to define consistency and compatibility among vendors. The IEEE began a project in February 1980, known as Project 802 for the year and month it began. IEEE 802 is a set of standards given to the various LAN architectures, such as Ethernet, Token Ring, and ArcNet, by the LAN standards committee. The goal of the committee was to define more of the OSI's data link layer, which already contained the LLC and MAC sublayers. Several 802 subcommittee protocols are at the heart of PC networking. Although there are a number of 802 project categories, the exam focuses on only a few of them, which are discussed in this section.

802.3 Based on the original Ethernet network from DIX (Digital-Intel-Xerox), 802.3 is the standard for Ethernet networks today. The only difference between 802.3 Ethernet and DIX Ethernet V.2 is the frame type. The two Ethernet networks can use the same physical network, but devices on one standard cannot communicate with devices on the other standard.

The MAC sublayer uses carrier sense multiple access with collision detection (CSMA/CD) for access to the physical medium. CSMA/CD keeps devices on the network from interfering with one another when trying to transmit. To reduce collisions, CSMA/CD devices listen to the network before transmitting. If the network is "quiet" (no other devices are transmitting), the device can send its data. Because two devices can think the network is clear and start transmitting at the same time (which would result in a collision), all devices listen as they transmit. If a device detects another device transmitting at the same time, a collision occurs. The device stops transmitting and sends a signal to alert other nodes about the collision. Then, all the nodes stop transmitting and wait a random amount of time before they begin the process again.

Remember that Ethernet is defined by the IEEE 802.3 standard.

CSMA/CD doesn't stop collisions from happening, but it helps manage the situations when they do occur. In fact, collisions are a normal part of Ethernet operation. You need to become concerned only when collisions begin to occur frequently.

Ethernet has evolved over the years to include a number of popular specifications. These specifications are based, in part, on the media variety they employ, such as coaxial, twisted-pair, and fiber-optic cabling:

- The 10Base5 specification, commonly referred to as thicknet, was the original Ethernet specification. It has a maximum distance of 500 meters (approximately 1640 feet) with a maximum speed of 10 Mbps.

- The 10Base2 specification, commonly referred to as thinnet, uses a thinner coaxial cable than 10Base5. It has a maximum distance of 185 meters (approximately 607 feet) with a maximum speed of 10 Mbps.

- The 10BaseT specification uses twisted-pair cabling with a maximum distance of 100 meters (approximately 328 feet) with a speed of 10 to 100 Mbps.

A number of Ethernet standards have been developed in the 802.3 category, as shown in Table 2-2.

802.5 Although Token Ring was first designed in the late 1960s, IBM's token-passing implementation did not become IEEE standard 802.5 until 1985.

The Token Ring IEEE 802.5 standard passes a special frame known as a token around the network. This token is generated by the first computer that comes online on the Token Ring network. When another workstation wants to transmit data, it grabs the token and then begins transmitting. This computer will send a data frame on the network with the address of the destination computer. The destination computer receives the data frame, modifies it, and

TABLE 2-2   Popular Ethernet IEEE 802.3 Project Standards

IEEE Project Standard	Description
802.3	Ethernet (CSMA/CD)
802.3u	Fast Ethernet (100 Mbps)
802.3z	Gigabit Ethernet over fiber-optic cabling or coaxial cabling
802.3ab	Gigabit Ethernet over twisted-pair cabling
802.3ae	10-Gigabit Ethernet

sends it on the network back to the destination computer, indicating successful transmission of data. When the workstation has finished transmitting, the token is released back to the network. This ensures that workstations will not communicate on the network simultaneously, as in the CSMA/CD access method.

802.11   The IEEE 802.11 standard addresses wireless networking (discussed in Chapter 10). This includes the wireless access point (WAP) devices and the wireless NICs that are used to send and receive broadcasts from the cell or WAP device.

The WAPs and wireless NICs can be set to use different frequencies to allow for cell overlap. This is not the same technology used by cell phones to manage movement of PCs or mobile devices. The wireless NIC is set to a specific frequency and must be changed manually in order to communicate with another cell. This means that a PC cannot be moved from one cell area to another without changing the frequency, unless, for some reason, the cells operate on the same frequency and have no overlap of coverage area.

Important wireless standards in the IEEE 802.11 category include the following:

■ **802.11a**   Supports speeds of 54 Mbps at frequencies ranging from 5.725 GHz to 5.850 GHz. 802.11a wireless components are not compatible with 802.11b devices.

■ **802.11b**   Supports speeds of 11 Mbps at frequency ranges of 2.400 GHz to 2.4835 GHz. 802.11b wireless components are compatible with 802.11g devices, which use an enhancement of the 802.11b standard.

■ **802.11g**   Supports speeds of 54 Mbps at the same frequency range as 802.11b, which allows devices from the two standards to coexist. For example, I have an 802.11b wireless access point, but I am connected to it with my 802.11g wireless network card. I am getting only the 11 Mbps transfer rate because it is the lowest common denominator between the two standards.

■ **802.11n**   A wireless project that runs at 5 GHz or 2.4 GHz and is backward compatible with 802.11a/b/g standards. The goal of 802.11n is to increase the

Project	Description
802.1	Internetworking
802.2	Logical link control
802.3	Ethernet
802.4	Token bus
802.5	Token Ring
802.6	Metropolitan area network (MAN)
802.7	Broadband technology
802.8	Fiber-optic technology
802.9	Voice and data integration
802.10	Network security
802.11	Wireless networking
802.12	Demand priority networking

ⓌⒶⓉⒸⒽ **Expect to be asked about the IEEE standards on the exam, especially the ones that pertain to Ethernet, Token Ring, and wireless.**

bandwidth and the range. 802.11n has data transfer rates of over 150 Mbps with one antenna and up to 600 Mbps with four antennas!

You will need to be familiar with the IEEE 802 projects that have been mentioned, as the exam will focus on those, but you should be familiar with the other 802 standards as well. Table 2-3 lists most of the 802 project standards.

CERTIFICATION SUMMARY

In this chapter, you have learned about network protocols, such as NetBEUI, IPX/SPX, and TCP/IP. You have learned about the advantages and disadvantages of these protocols, which ones are routable, and which ones are nonroutable. You also learned that TCP/IP is the protocol being used today and the one you need to know for the Network+ certification exam!

You have also learned that in order for all of the different manufacturers of networking components to build technologies that will work together, some standards had to be defined. There are two major standards that manufacturers follow: the 802 project models and the OSI model. In this chapter, you looked at each layer of the OSI model and what functions they perform. An easy way to remember the layers (application, presentation, session, transport, network, data link, and physical) is with the sentence, "All People Seem To Need Data Processing."

TWO-MINUTE DRILL

Network Protocols

❑ Packets and protocols are the fundamental building blocks of data transmission over the network.

❑ Internetwork Packet Exchange/Sequenced Packet Exchange (IPX/SPX) is the protocol most commonly used with older versions of Novell NetWare.

❑ The Transmission Control Protocol/Internet Protocol (TCP/IP) is the most common protocol used today. TCP/IP, a routable protocol, is the protocol on which the Internet is built.

❑ The NetBIOS Extended User Interface (NetBEUI) is a transport protocol commonly found in smaller peer-to-peer networks.

❑ NetBEUI is a nonroutable protocol.

❑ AppleTalk is a routable protocol used in Macintosh environments.

The OSI Model

❑ The Open Systems Interconnect (OSI) model is a seven-layer model that defines the function of network protocols and devices.

❑ The seven layers of the OSI model, from highest to lowest, are application, presentation, session, transport, network, data link, and physical.

❑ SMTP, HTTP, Telnet, and FTP are all examples of application-layer (layer-7) protocols.

❑ Compression and encryption are examples of functions that can be performed at the presentation layer (layer 6).

❑ The session layer (layer 5) is responsible for the creation of sessions and the management of those sessions.

❑ The transport layer (layer 4) is responsible for the reliability of the transmission, including breaking the data down into manageable sizes using acknowledgments and packet sequence numbers to ensure that data arrives at the destination and is pieced together in the correct order. Examples of layer-4 protocols are TCP, UDP, and SPX.

❑ Layer 3, known as the network layer, performs logical addressing and delivery functions. Examples of layer-3 protocols are IP and IPX.

❑ The data link layer, layer 2, is responsible for physical addressing and converting the packets to electrical signals. Any device that works with MAC addresses runs at this layer.

❑ The first layer of the OSI model, located at the bottom, is known as the physical layer and is responsible for carrying the signal. Your network media and architectures are defined at this level.

❑ An IP address is known as a layer-3 address and looks similar to 192.168.45.6.

❑ A MAC address is known as a layer-2 address and looks similar to 00-02-3F-6B-25-13.

❑ A port address is known as a layer-4 address and looks similar to 80 (web server port).

802 Project Standards

❑ The Institute of Electrical and Electronics Engineers (IEEE) has created project groups that define networking standards.

❑ 802.3 is the Ethernet (CSMA/CD) standard.

❑ 802.5 defines the Token Ring standard.

❑ 802.11 defines the wireless standard.

SELF TEST

The following questions will help you measure your understanding of the material presented in this chapter. Read all the choices carefully because there may appear to be more than one correct answer and you need to choose the best answer.

Network Protocols

1. What is the name given to languages that are used for network communication?
   A. NIC
   B. Segment
   C. Protocol
   D. Cable

2. Which protocol used on the Internet gives each computer a unique address?
   A. IPX/SPX
   B. TCP/IP

    C. NetBEUI

    D. DLC

3. Which of the following protocols is a nonroutable protocol?

    A. IPX/SPX

    B. TCP/IP

    C. NetBEUI

    D. AppleTalk

4. Which protocol was developed by IBM and used primarily in Microsoft workgroup environments?

    A. NetBEUI

    B. TCP/IP

    C. IPX/SPX

    D. AppleTalk

5. Which protocol configures hosts in zones on the network?

    A. IPX/SPX

    B. TCP/IP

    C. NetBEUI

    D. AppleTalk

The OSI Model

6. Which of the following is not a layer in the OSI model?

    A. Physical

    B. Transport

    C. Network

    D. Data transmission

7. Which of the following protocols are layer-3 protocols? (Choose two.)

    A. IPX

    B. TCP

    C. IP

    D. SPX

8. Which of the following represents a layer-2 address?

    A. COMPUTER1

    B. 00-02-3F-6B-25-13

    C. 192.168.3.200

    D. www.gleneclarke.com

9. Which of the following functions can be performed at layer 6 of the OSI model? (Select all that apply.)
   A. Routing of the message
   B. Compression
   C. Encryption
   D. Converting the message to a format that is understood by the destination

10. Which of the following protocols are transport-layer protocols? (Choose two.)
   A. IPX
   B. TCP
   C. IP
   D. SPX

11. Which of the following represents a layer-3 address?
   A. COMPUTER1
   B. 00-02-3F-6B-25-13
   C. 192.168.3.200
   D. www.gleneclarke.com

12. Which of the following represents an application-layer protocol?
   A. SMTP
   B. IP
   C. SPX
   D. TCP

13. Which layer of the OSI model is responsible for converting the packet to an electrical signal that will be placed on the wire?
   A. Layer 1
   B. Layer 4
   C. Layer 3
   D. Layer 2

802 Project Standards

14. Which 802 project standard defines Gigabit Ethernet using fiber-optic cabling?
   A. 802.5
   B. 802.3z
   C. 802.3ab
   D. 802.11g

15. Which 802 project standard defines Token Ring?
   A. 802.5
   B. 802.3z

    C. 802.3ab

    D. 802.11g

16. Which 802 project standard defines 10-Gigabit Ethernet?

    A. 802.3z

    B. 802.3ae

    C. 802.3ab

    D. 802.11g

17. Which 802 project standard defines wireless at speeds of 54 Mbps and a frequency range of 2.4 GHz?

    A. 802.11a

    B. 802.11b

    C. 802.11c

    D. 802.11g

Performance-Based Question Review: See the performance-based question sample from the author included with the accompanying media.

SELF TEST ANSWERS

Network Protocols

1. ☑   **C.** A protocol is the network language used by two systems to communicate across the network.
  ☒   **A, B,** and **D** are incorrect because a NIC is a network card, which is not a language—it is a network device. The segment is the term for a part of network cabling on one side of a router or bridge. The cable is not a language; it is the network medium used to carry the signals.

2.   ☑   **B.** TCP/IP is the protocol of the Internet, and each system is assigned a unique IP address.
  ☒   **A, C,** and **D** are incorrect. IPX/SPX is the protocol developed by Novell for use in NetWare environments, NetBEUI was developed by IBM and used in Microsoft workgroup environments, and DLC is a protocol used to connect to printers.

3. ☑ **C.** NetBEUI is a nonroutable protocol.

   ☒ **A, B,** and **D** are incorrect because IPX/SPX, TCP/IP, and AppleTalk are all routable protocols.

4. ☑ **A.** NetBEUI was developed by IBM and used primarily in Microsoft workgroup environments.

   ☒ **B, C,** and **D** are incorrect. TCP/IP is the protocol of the Internet, IPX/SPX was developed by Novell, and AppleTalk was developed by Apple.

5. ☑ **D.** The AppleTalk protocol configures hosts into zones.

   ☒ **A, B,** and **C** are incorrect. IPX/SPX, TCP/IP, and NetBEUI do not use zones to organize nodes on the network.

The OSI Model

6. ☑ **D.** Data transmission is not a layer of the OSI model.

   ☒ **A, B,** and **C** are incorrect because physical, transport, and network are all layers of the OSI model.

7. ☑ **A and C.** IP is the network-layer protocol in the TCP/IP protocol suite, and IPX is the network-layer protocol in the IPX/SPX protocol suite.

   ☒ **B and D** are incorrect because TCP and SPX are transport-layer protocols.

8. ☑ **B.** 00-02-3F-6B-25-13 is an example of a MAC address, which is a layer-2 address.

   ☒ **A, C,** and **D** are incorrect. COMPUTER1 is an example of a NetBIOS name (computer name); 192.168.3.200 is an example of an IP address, which is a layer-3 address; and www.gleneclarke. com is an example of a DNS name.

9. ☑ **B, C,** and **D.** They are all examples of data formatting that is performed at the presentation layer.

   ☒ **A** is incorrect because the routing of the message is handled by the network layer, which is layer 3.

10. ☑ **B and D.** TCP is the transport protocol responsible for reliable delivery in the TCP/IP protocol suite, whereas SPX performs the same function in the IPX/SPX protocol suite.

    ☒ **A and C** are incorrect. IPX and IP are network-layer protocols responsible for the addressing and delivery of data.

11. ☑ **C.** 192.168.3.200 is an example of an IP address that is a layer-3 protocol; thus, this is a layer-3 address.

    ☒ **A, B,** and **D** are incorrect. COMPUTER1 is a computer name, 00-02-3F-6B-25-13 is an example of a MAC address (layer-2 address), and www.gleneclarke.com is an example of a DNS-style name.

12. ☑ **A.** An application-layer protocol is responsible for initiating some form of request. SMTP is used to send e-mail from server to server.

    ☒ **B, C,** and **D** are incorrect. IP is a layer-3 address (network layer); SPX and TCP are transport-layer protocols.

13. ☑ **D.** Layer 2 (the data link layer) is responsible for converting the packet to an electrical signal.
   ☒ **A, B,** and **C** are incorrect. Layer 1 (physical layer) is responsible for placing the signal on the wire, layer 4 (transport layer) is responsible for reliable delivery, and layer 3 (network layer) is responsible for logical addressing, routing, and delivery.

802 Project Standards

14. ☑ **B.** Gigabit Ethernet over fiber is defined in the IEEE 802.3z project standard.
   ☒ **A, C,** and **D** are incorrect. The 802.5 standard defines Token Ring, 802.3ab defines Gigabit Ethernet over twisted-pair, and 802.11g defines wireless at 54 Mbps.

15. ☑ **A.** The IEEE 802.5 project standard defines Token Ring.
   ☒ **B, C,** and **D** are incorrect. 802.3z defines Gigabit Ethernet over fiber, 802.3ab defines Gigabit Ethernet over twisted-pair, and 802.11g defines wireless at 54 Mbps.

16. ☑ **B.** The IEEE 802.3ae standard defines 10-Gigabit Ethernet.
   ☒ **A, C,** and **D** are incorrect. 802.3z defines Gigabit Ethernet over fiber, 802.3ab defines Gigabit Ethernet over twisted-pair, and 802.11g defines wireless at 54 Mbps.

17. ☑ **D.** 802.11g defines a wireless standard at 54 Mbps while maintaining compatibility with 802.11b by being on the same frequency.
   ☒ **A, B,** and **C** are incorrect. 802.11a is at 54 Mbps, but is not at a frequency of 2.4 GHz; 802.11b is at 11 Mbps and is compatible with 802.11g, because it runs at the same frequency; and both are Wi-Fi compatible. 802.11c is not a wireless standard.

Chapter 3

Networking Components

I n this chapter, you will learn about popular networking components found in a local area network (LAN) environment, such as network cards, hubs, switches, routers, and other network devices. This chapter is a critical chapter, not only for the Network+ exam, but also for the real world. Be sure to take your time and understand all the concepts presented in this chapter.

CERTIFICATION OBJECTIVE 3.01

Network Interface Cards

The *network interface card (NIC),* or network card, is a device installed on the system that is responsible for sending and receiving data on the network. It is responsible for preparing data from the system to be transported on the wire by converting the outbound data from a parallel format (due to the width of the bus architecture that the card is sitting in) to electrical signals that will travel along the network media. On the receiving end, the network card is responsible for receiving the electrical signal and converting it to data that the system understands.

The network card also is known as a network adapter; it can be installed in the system after the system has been purchased, or the system can come with a network card built in. A system that comes with a network card built in is said to have an integrated network card. Figure 3-1 shows an integrated network card port on the side of a laptop; desktop computers typically have the port on the back of the computer.

Transceivers

A *transceiver* is that portion of the network interface that actually transmits and receives electrical signals across the transmission media. When the signal is traveling along the length of the wire, the transceiver picks the signal up and verifies that the data is destined

FIGURE 3-1

An integrated
network card on
a system

FIGURE 3-2

RJ-45 and BNC onboard transceivers on a network card

for the local system. If the data is destined for the local system, the data is passed up to the system for processing; if it is not, it is discarded. There are two types of transceivers: onboard and external.

Onboard Transceivers

Onboard transceivers are built onto the network interface card. With these transceivers, the media connector is built right on the back of the NIC. Common examples of this type include RJ-45 receptacles for twisted-pair cable. Figure 3-2 shows an RJ-45 transceiver and Bayonet Neill–Concelman (BNC) connectors for thinnet coaxial cable.

External Transceivers

With an *external* transceiver, the actual media connection is made external to the network card using a small device that attaches to the NIC via an extension cable. These connections use an attachment unit interface (AUI) connector, also called a Digital-Intel-Xerox (DIX) connector, on the back of the network card. The AUI connector is a female 15-pin D-connector that looks very much like a joystick port and typically is used to connect a workstation to thicknet cabling. Figure 3-3 shows a transceiver connected to the AUI port on a Cisco device that has an RJ-45 port on it.

Transceiver Configuration

A number of network cards have multiple types of connectors on the back of the card (called combo cards in this case) to allow you to use different types of cabling to connect the system

A transceiver
connected to an
AUI port

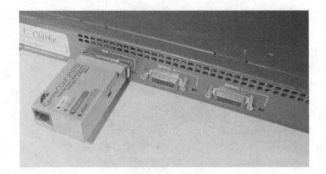

to the network. The transceiver type that is being used by the network card is typically set to the "auto" setting, which means that the card can sense which transceiver you are using and will configure itself to use that transceiver. When troubleshooting to find out why the card is not working, the "auto" setting is the first thing you should change. When I have problems connecting to a network, I usually change the transceiver setting to the actual one I am using. For example, if you are using the RJ-45 connector, you will want to change the setting to something like TP (for twisted-pair) or TX, as shown in Figure 3-4. During configuration, the different transceivers can be referred to in the following ways:

■ **DIX or AUI**   The card uses an external thicknet transceiver.

Changing the
transceiver type
through the network
card properties

■ **Coax, 10Base2, or BNC**   The card has an onboard thinnet Ethernet connector known as a BNC connector.

■ **TP, TX, UTP, 10BaseT, or 100BaseT**   The card has an onboard RJ-45 connector.

Another setting that I normally have no problem with but have had trouble with recently is the transfer rate of the network card. A number of today's network cards support 10 Mbps, 100 Mbps, and even 1000 Mbps. Most of the time, these network cards are set to "auto" in order to detect the speed at which the card will run—the card derives its speed from the device it is connected to. For example, if you have a 10/100 Mbps network card but plug it into a 10 Mbps hub, it will run at 10 Mbps—not the full 100 Mbps—because the card detects the speed of the device it is connected to.

A few years back, I had a problem when the network card was not able to auto-configure itself. After troubleshooting for a little bit, I went to the network card properties and forced the speed of the network card to 100 Mbps (shown in Figure 3-5)—and voilà! It worked beautifully.

Another setting you may want to configure on your network card is the transmission method. The three transmission methods are as follows:

■ **Simplex**   Allows communication in one direction only. You can only send or receive with a simplex device—not both.

FIGURE 3-5

Changing the network card rate from auto to 100 Mbps

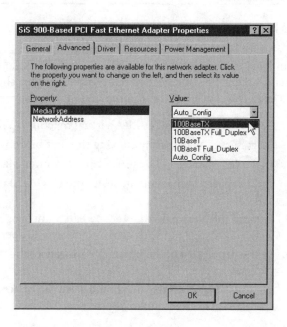

- **Half duplex**   Allows communication in both directions (send and receive), but not at the same time. A network card set to half duplex will not be able to receive data while sending data. Using the half-duplex setting can slow down communication if your device supports full duplex.

- **Full duplex**   Allows communication in both directions at the same time. If a network card supports full duplex, it will be able to receive data when data is being sent because all four pairs of wires are used. If a network card that supports full duplex is set to full duplex, you will notice a big difference in throughput if the device is set to half duplex instead.

Make sure you are familiar with the differences between simplex, half duplex, and full duplex.

Most network cards are set to auto. You may want to force the setting to the full-duplex mode to be sure that you are getting full-duplex communication. You can change the communication method through the network card properties in Device Manager. Looking back at Figure 3-5, notice that there is a Full_Duplex setting that could be used.

EXERCISE 3-1

Configuring a Network Card

In this exercise, you will learn how to configure a number of different settings on a network card in Device Manager. The dialog boxes are particular to the device driver; you may have different screens on your system, but the general idea should be the same. To see a video of this exercise, check out the accompanying material for this book.

1. Switch to the 2012SERVERA virtual machine (VM).
2. Start Server Manager by clicking the first button on the task bar.
3. In Server Manager, choose Tools | Computer Management.
4. In Computer Management, select the Device Manager node on the left side of the screen.
5. Expand the Network Adapters category and select your network card in the list. Right-click your network card and choose Properties.
6. In the properties of the network card, select the Advanced tab to set your network card settings.
7. On the Advanced tab, you should see a list of properties that may include transceiver, transfer speed, and duplex properties. You may also see settings such as Wake On

LAN and Jumbo Frame. The settings that appear on the Advanced tab will depend on your driver.

8. Click OK.
9. Close Device Manager.

MAC Address

Each network card has a unique address that is burned into the card by its manufacturer. This unique address, known as a Media Access Control (MAC) address, is used in the header of the packet for the source and destination addresses of the packet. The MAC address is a 48-bit address displayed in a hexadecimal format that looks similar to 00-90-4B-4C-C1-59 or sometimes 00:90:4B:4C:C1:59.

The MAC address is made up of 12 characters and is in hexadecimal format. The first half of the MAC address is the manufacturer's address, while the last half of the address is the unique address assigned to that network card by the manufacturer (shown in Figure 3-6). The combination of the manufacturer ID and the unique address ensures that the MAC address is unique.

To view your MAC address on your Windows system, you can go to a command prompt and type **ipconfig /all**. You will notice the MAC address of the network card listed within the output as the physical address. To view your MAC address in Linux, go to a terminal prompt and type **ifconfig**. Exercise 3-2 demonstrates how to view your MAC address and then how to use the Internet to determine the manufacturer of the network card by using the first six characters of the MAC address.

A MAC address is a 48-bit address burned into the network card and is used to send data from one network card to another. A MAC address looks similar to 00-90-4B-4C-C1-59.

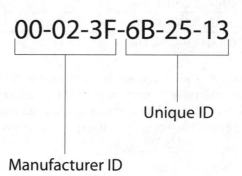

FIGURE 3-6

Identifying the manufacturer ID of the MAC address

00-02-3F-6B-25-13

Unique ID

Manufacturer ID

EXERCISE 3-2

Determining Your Local Machine's MAC Address

In this exercise, you will learn how to determine the MAC address of your computer using Windows 8. You will then go to www.coffer.com/mac_find/ to determine the manufacturer of your network card.

1. To open a command-prompt window, go to the Start screen, type **cmd**, and then press ENTER.

2. When the command prompt appears, type **ipconfig /all** to view your TCP/IP settings and MAC address.

3. Record your MAC address here:

   Physical Address: _____

4. Once you have recorded the MAC address, start Internet Explorer and navigate to www.coffer.com/mac_find/. This site is used to input the first six characters of the MAC address, which represents the address of the manufacturer of the card, and the site will tell you who manufactured it.

5. Once you access this site, fill in the "MAC Address or Vendor to look for" text box with the first six characters of your MAC address, and click the String button. For example, the first six characters of my MAC address are 00-90-4B, so I would type **00-90-4B**.

6. In the middle of the page, your network card manufacturer will be displayed. In my example, the manufacturer of all cards starting with 00-90-4B appears to be Gemtek Technology Co.

7. Take a few minutes and search for manufacturers of the following MAC addresses. Once you find the manufacturer, fill in the table.

MAC Address	Manufacturer
00-B0-D0-B1-ED-51	
00-0D-60-48-53-9E	
00-A0-C9-C3-D2-E2	

8. Now that you have searched for the vendor of a MAC address by using the manufacturer ID portion of the MAC address, let's search by manufacturer! In the String To Search For text box, type **Intel** and click the String button. Record the first five manufacturer IDs in the spaces provided.

   i. _____

   ii. _____

iii. _____

iv. _____

v. _____

9. Close the browser when you have finished.

The MAC address is also known as the MAC-48 address or the EUI-48 address, and is used with most networking technologies such as Ethernet, Token Ring, fiber distributed data interface (FDDI), and wireless. The IEEE has trademarked the names MAC-48 and EUI-48 and another address format known as EUI-64. EUI stands for *Extended Unique Identifier.* The EUI-64 address is an address scheme used by technologies such as FireWire and IPv6. To learn more about IPv6 address formats, check out Chapter 5.

e x a m

ⓌatcH   **The MAC address is also known as the hardware address or physical address of the network card. Be sure to remember for the exam that the MAC address is known as a layer-2 address.**

Troubleshooting Network Cards

Along with installing and configuring the network card, you should be familiar with some common steps involved in troubleshooting connectivity issues. When problems arise in connecting to the network, one of the first things you want to do is check to see that the "link" light is on at the back of the network card. If the link light is on, you may want to make sure that there is activity by looking at the activity light. The activity light should be blinking when there is network activity. If these lights are not on, you will need to reconfigure the cards or replace them if reconfiguration doesn't work. You also may want to try updating the driver for the network card if you are having problems with the device.

Testing

If there is one thing you will do often, it is testing to be sure any updates or changes you made are working properly. Once your network card has been installed, you have to connect the cable to it. Some network cards have multiple transceivers on them. You must connect the appropriate cable for the network into the correct transceiver type.

Once the cable has been connected, you can check a couple of things to see whether the card is operating properly. The first of these is the link light on the back of the card. Some older network cards do not have this feature, but newer ones do. You should see a light next to the transceiver. Some 10 Mbps cards have an activity light and a connection light. Some

10/100 Mbps cards have both a 10 Mbps light and a 100 Mbps light, along with the activity light, which tells you the speed at which you are connected.

Once you have verified that the link light is on, which proves to you that there is a physical connection, the next thing you need to do is troubleshoot connectivity issues. Most networks run TCP/IP, so you will likely start pinging addresses on the network. For more troubleshooting tips on TCP/IP, refer to Chapter 6.

Network Card Diagnostics

Another direction to take when troubleshooting the network card is to use a diagnostic program to run a series of tests on the network adapter. You can use generic diagnostic programs or vendor-supplied diagnostics. Diagnostic programs run a variety of tests on the hardware of the card, including the transceiver, and perform a communication test (such as a loopback test).

Loopback Test

The loopback test tests communication in and out of the card. A stream of data is sent out and loops back around into the card. The input is then compared to see whether the data received is the same as that sent.

Some cards can run an internal loopback test as a method of troubleshooting communication problems. Others must have a loopback adapter that plugs into the card. This way, the data actually is sent out of the card and loops around and comes back into the card as though it were received from another device. Sometimes this is a more accurate and realistic test of the card.

Drivers

When you install a network card on a Windows system, Plug and Play recognizes and configures the hardware by loading the appropriate driver. A driver is a piece of software that enables the operating system to communicate with the device. There are different types of drivers for modems, sound cards, and just about any other component in a computer. If a driver needs updating in Device Manager, it will show with an Unknown Device icon (yellow question mark).

From time to time, you might want to update the drivers for your various devices. Manufacturers update their drivers if problems are found in current versions. You can update the driver for your network card through Device Manager with Windows operating systems. Once in Device Manager, you will need to locate the device and then right-click and choose Update Driver, as shown in Figure 3-7. Once you choose the Update Driver command, you will need to browse to the location of the driver file.

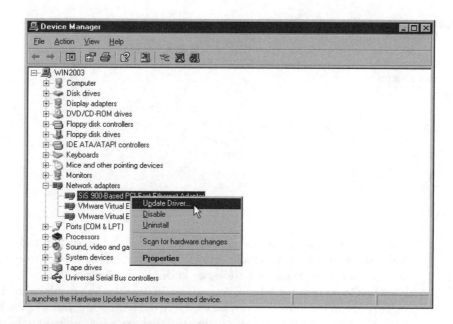

FIGURE 3-7

Updating a network card driver in Windows

CERTIFICATION OBJECTIVE 3.02

Hubs, MAUs, and Repeaters

Once you have the network card inserted into the computer system or network device, you will need to connect each of the systems together using devices such as hubs, repeaters, or MAUs. You will need to be familiar with each of these networking devices for the Network+ exam, as well as being familiar with the layers of the OSI model that these devices run at.

Hubs

Hubs are one of the most important components of a network because they act as a central point for all network devices to connect to. You can easily remember the layout of a hub if you think of a wheel and picture how the spokes radiate out from the hub of the wheel. In a network, each spoke is a connection, and the hub of the wheel is the hub of the network where all of the cables come together.

The Role of Hubs in Networking

The hub, also known as a concentrator, is responsible for providing all systems with a central point of connection. When a computer sends a piece of data to another computer,

FIGURE 3-8

A five-port hub used
to connect systems
together

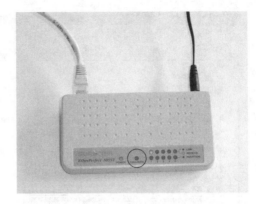

the electrical signal leaves the network card of the sending system and reaches the hub. The hub then sends the signal to all ports so that all systems can check to see whether the data is destined for them. Figure 3-8 shows an example of a five-port hub.

When looking at Figure 3-8, you will notice that the hub displays link lights for each active port on the hub. This can be used in troubleshooting, just like the link light on the back of a network card. You also will notice that there is a collision indicator on the hub, which indicates whether or not your network currently is having a lot of collisions. Once again, this could be useful when troubleshooting network problems—excessive collisions could lead to systems dropping off the network.

Cascading Hubs

Looking at Figure 3-9, you will notice that there is a switch on the hub to indicate that you wish to use the fifth port to cascade, or connect, to another hub. If you were to try to chain two hubs together with the switch set to normal, it would be similar to trying to connect

FIGURE 3-9

The uplink switch
on a hub

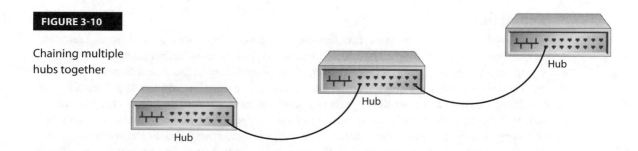

FIGURE 3-10

Chaining multiple hubs together

two computers together with a straight-through cable; it can't be done because you need to switch the send and receive wires on one end of the cable. We have discussed using a crossover cable, but manufacturers of hubs have given us a solution that eliminates the need for crossover cables by creating a port on the hub that is already crossed over; you simply need to switch the setting to use the fifth port as the cascade port. Also known as the uplink port, the cascade port connects to a normal port on the next hub.

If you wanted to connect three 24-port hubs together, you would need to uplink port 24 on the first hub to any port on the second hub (I usually uplink to the first port on the second hub), then use port 24 on the second hub to uplink to the first port on the third hub, as shown in Figure 3-10.

Before we get into the different types of hubs, a point that I want to stress (one that was mentioned earlier) is that a hub sends the signal to all ports on the hub. This means that if you have a 24-port hub linked to another 24-port hub and a workstation sends data to another workstation, the data will be sent to all 48 ports on the network. This leads to a lot of unneeded traffic and contention across the entire network that will slow down network performance. A solution would be to use a switch, which is the subject of an upcoming discussion.

Passive Hubs

The function of a *passive* hub is simply to receive data from one port and send it out to the other ports. For example, an eight-port hub receives data from port 3 and then resends that data to ports 1, 2, 4, 5, 6, 7, and 8.

A passive hub contains no power source or electrical components, there is no signal processing (such as when the hub receives the electrical signal), and there is no regenerating of the signal to ensure that it is readable at the destination. A passive hub simply attaches the ports internally and enables communication to flow through the network. Regeneration of the signal is a function of an active hub.

Active Hubs

An *active* hub provides the same functionality as a passive hub, with an additional feature. Active hubs amplify the signal before sending it to all of the destination ports on the hub. Using active hubs, you can increase the length of your network, because although the signal weakens with distance, when the active hub receives the signal, it rebuilds the data, allowing it once more to go a greater distance. It is important to remember that unshielded twisted-pair (UTP) cabling can be run a maximum of 100 meters. With an active hub, you can run this type of cable 100 meters on each side of the hub. An active hub has a power source and built-in repeaters to boost, or amplify, the signal. An active hub is also known as a *multiport repeater.*

Hybrid Hubs

A *hybrid* hub can use many different types of cables in addition to UTP cabling. A hybrid hub usually is cabled using thinnet or thicknet Ethernet along with popular cable types such as twisted-pair cabling. A few years ago, hybrid hubs were fairly popular. UTP seems to be the most popular type today, so you may not see the thinnet or thicknet connector on the hub. Figure 3-11 displays a hybrid hub.

w a t c h   **Hubs have been used in Ethernet environments, whereas Token Ring environments use MAUs. Also know that hubs run at layer 1 of the OSI model because they work with the electrical signal.**

FIGURE 3-11

A hybrid hub using UTP and thinnet cabling

Multistation Access Units

A *multistation access unit (MAU)* is a device to which multiple workstations are connected in order to communicate on a Token Ring network. This hub-type device has some features that make it a little bit different from a hub—for example, when the signal passes through the MAU, the MAU regenerates the signal so that it can travel a longer distance.

Because Token Ring networks use token passing instead of carrier sense multiple access with collision detection (CSMA/CD), there is no chance for collisions. Therefore, the first difference you will notice with MAUs over hubs is that a MAU does not have collision indicators on it because you can't have collisions on a Token Ring network.

Another major difference with a MAU is that MAUs don't actually use an uplink port. With Token Ring, there is a logical ring within the MAU, and when you connect to another MAU, you must complete a full ring structure again. Therefore, the Token Ring MAU has a ring-in port and a ring-out port. When you wish to connect two MAUs together, you must ring out of the first MAU and, with that cable, ring in to the second MAU. Then you must ring out of the second MAU and ring in to the first MAU, as shown in Figure 3-12.

FIGURE 3-12

Connecting two MAUs using ring-in and ring-out ports

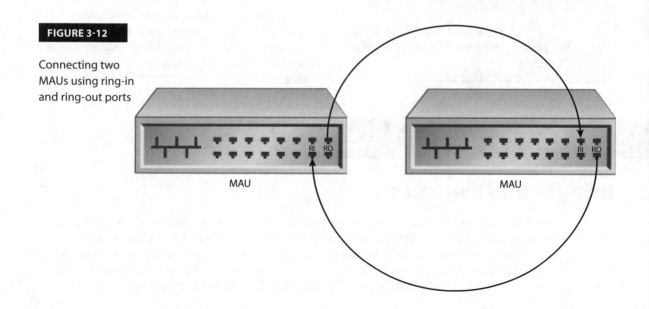

FIGURE 3-13 Using a repeater to regenerate the signal

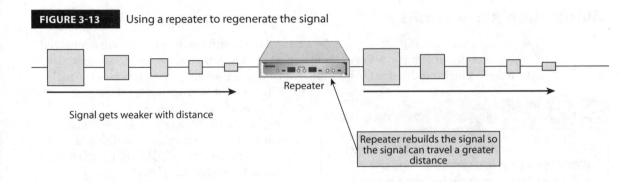

Repeater

Signal gets weaker with distance

Repeater rebuilds the signal so the signal can travel a greater distance

Repeaters

One of the pitfalls of networking environments is that the electrical signal becomes weaker as it travels as a result of outside interference. Eventually, if two systems are too far from one another, the signal is so weak that by the time it reaches the other side, it is unreadable. This is where repeaters come in.

If your network layout exceeds the normal specifications of the cable, you can use repeaters at different points and enable the signal to travel the distance. For example, if you are using thinnet cabling, you know that thinnet is limited to 185 meters. But what if you want to connect two systems together that are 235 meters apart? You would place a repeater somewhere before the 185-meter mark so that the repeater will regenerate, or rebuild, the signal, allowing it to travel the extra difference. Figure 3-13 shows a signal that is weakened over distance but is regenerated through the use of a repeater.

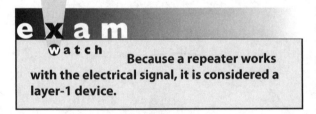

e x a m

ⓦatch **Because a repeater works with the electrical signal, it is considered a layer-1 device.**

CERTIFICATION OBJECTIVE 3.03

Bridges and Switches

Now that we have discussed some of the popular layer-1 devices, let's take a look at some popular layer-2 devices. Layer-2 devices are a little smarter than layer-1 devices in the sense that they actually can make decisions about where the electrical signal needs to go. Remember that a hub, which is a layer-1 device, forwards the signal to all ports on the hub, which will lead to traffic problems as you start adding hubs to the topology.

This section will introduce you to two layer-2 devices that often are used to filter network traffic. By filtering network traffic, we are conserving precious bandwidth on the network, which will have a huge impact on the overall performance of the network.

Bridges

A bridge is a network connectivity device that is used to break the network down into multiple network segments. A bridge runs at layer 2, the data link layer, and is used to filter traffic by only forwarding traffic to the destination network segment. Figure 3-14 shows an example of a bridged network.

Let's look at an example of how a bridge filters network traffic. Assume that you have just completed connecting the bridge to the network segments shown in Figure 3-14. When Workstation A sends data to Workstation F, the data will go out the network card of Workstation A and will travel the full length of segment 3 in both directions. The signal will reach the bridge, and the bridge will look at the destination MAC address of the packet. Once the bridge looks at the destination MAC address, it will compare that to the MAC addresses in its bridging table. The bridging table is a table in memory that lists all known MAC addresses and which network segment they live on. This table is critical to the bridge's filtering features. Since this is the first piece of data sent on the network, the MAC address for Workstation F is not in the bridging table, so the bridge will need to forward the data to both segment 1 and segment 2. It will not forward the information to network segment 3 because that is where the data came from, and if Workstation F existed on that network, it would already have the data.

When the bridge received the initial data from Workstation A, it recorded the MAC address of Workstation A and the network segment that Workstation A resides on in the

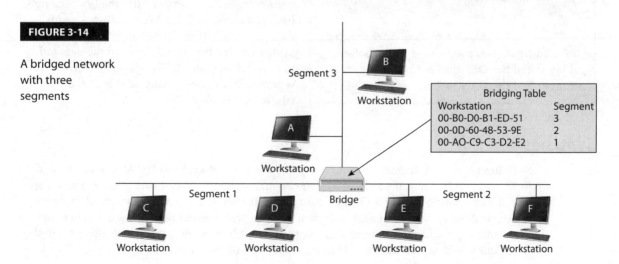

FIGURE 3-14

A bridged network with three segments

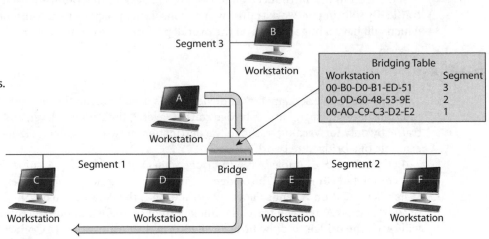

FIGURE 3-15

A bridge forwards the traffic only to the needed network segments.

bridging table. This way, if anyone sends data to Workstation A, the bridge will have an entry for Workstation A in the bridging table, and the bridge will forward the data only to network segment 3 and not to the other segments. Also note that when Workstation F replies to Workstation A, the data will need to pass through the bridge so the bridge will know what network segment Workstation F resides on and will record that MAC address in the bridging table.

e x a m

watch   Since a bridge works with a MAC address, and the MAC is a component of layer 2 of the OSI model, the bridge runs at layer 2 of the OSI model.

Over time, the bridging table will be filled with MAC addresses and their associated network segments. In our example, after the bridging table has been constructed, if Workstation A sends data to Workstation C, the data will reach the bridge and the bridge will forward the data only to network segment 1. This prevents network segment 2 from being congested with the traffic (shown in Figure 3-15).

Switches

Switches are one of the most common devices used on networks today. A hub sends the data to all ports on it. Thus, if you have a large network structure, this means you have probably linked a few hubs together, and when data is sent from one system to another, all computers see the traffic. This leads to a lot of network traffic, which eventually slows down network performance, not to mention the security concern of having the data sent to all ports on the hub! Figure 3-16 shows an example of a 24-port 10/100 Mbps switch.

FIGURE 3-16

A 24-port 10/100
Mbps switch

When you use a switch instead of a hub, the switch acts as a filtering device by
associating the MAC address of the system connected to the switch with the port on the
switch that the system is connected to. For example, in Figure 3-17, Computer A transmits
a frame to Computer C. The frame enters the switch from port 1 and then travels a direct
route to port 3, because the switch uses the destination MAC address of the frame and
knows that the MAC address is for the device connected to port 3. From port 3, the frame
is transmitted to Computer C. During this process, Computer B is unaware of the traffic

FIGURE 3-17

An example of a switch in
action

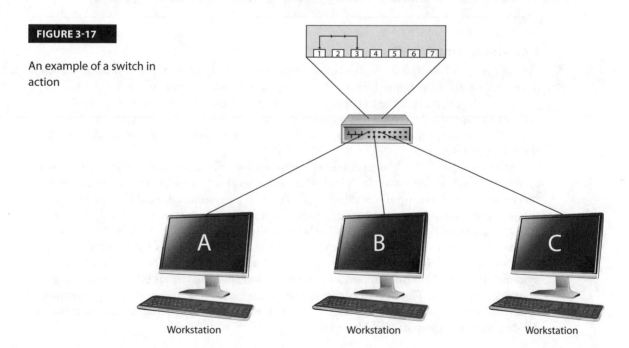

between Computers A and C because there is a direct path within the switch and no shared bandwidth.

It is a best practice to use switches whenever possible because of the increase in performance over a standard hub. Switches also offer more security since transmissions are not sent to every port on the switch, and because the administrator can control which stations can connect to each switch port via the port security feature on a switch. The bandwidth with a standard hub is shared by all users connected to the hub; however, with a switch, all users get the full network bandwidth. For example, a 100 Mbps network with a 24-port hub and 24 PCs allows each user to have 100/24 Mbps bandwidth; with a switch, however, each user would have a full 100 Mbps bandwidth.

exam
w a t c h   For the exam, know that bridges and switches are considered layer-2 devices. You can remember this easily because they both work with MAC addresses (layer-2 addresses). Also note that when data has a layer-2 header applied and is being processed by a layer-2 device, the data is called a "frame" instead of a "packet."

Understanding VLANs

Virtual LANs (VLANs) are a feature of most switches today, where the administrator groups ports on a switch by placing the ports in a *virtual LAN*. When a port is configured for a particular VLAN, it is unable to communicate with systems that are not on that VLAN without the use of a device such as a router. This is similar to the fact that if we had two physical networks, a machine could not send data from one network to the other without the use of a router.

The purpose of a VLAN is to cut down on broadcast traffic through the use of what are known as broadcast domains. Let's look at how this works. Normally, if we had a 24-port hub or switch and a computer wanted to send data to all systems, it would "broadcast" the data out onto the network. A broadcast will hit every port on that switch or hub. With a VLAN-supported switch, you can create VLANs that act as "broadcast" domains. This means that if Workstation A is on VLAN1, which is made up of ports 1 through 12 on the 24-port switch, when Workstation A sends broadcast traffic (traffic intended for all systems), it will be sent only to ports 1 through 12 because the virtual LAN is acting as a boundary for traffic. The benefit of this is that you are now able to minimize traffic within or across switches, which increases network throughput. Figure 3-18 shows a switch that is divided into two different VLANs.

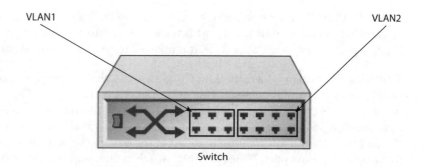

FIGURE 3-18

Ports on a switch associated with VLANs

VLAN1

VLAN2

Switch

To create the VLANs, the network administrator will need to run the configuration utility on the VLAN-supported switch. Also note that with a layer-1 switch, if a system needs to be moved from VLAN1 to VLAN2, there is no need to move systems around; you simply need to configure the port that the system is connected to from one VLAN to the other on the switch.

exam
ⓦatch

Know that a *multilayer* switch, such as a switch that runs at layer 2 and layer 3, provides the functionality of both a switch (layer 2) and a router (layer 3).

These are popular devices today, replacing the need to buy both a switch and a router, and are typically advertised as a "layer-3 switch."

Switch Features

Most enterprise-capable switches have a number of features that make the switch attractive to large organizations. The following is a listing of popular features incorporated into big-name switches, such as those from Cisco and Juniper Networks.

Spanning Tree Protocol The Spanning Tree Protocol (STP) runs at layer 2 and is designed to prevent loops on a network that could occur if you connect a number of switches together. For example, a loop is created if you connect Switch 1 to Switch 2 and then turn around and connect Switch 2 back to Switch 1 using a different cable and ports on the switches.

Having a loop on the network could cause the network to go down and creates instability in the switches. To prevent this, STP was designed. STP is a protocol that looks at all of the ports used to create a loop and then places one of those ports in a blocking state so that no data traffic can pass through the port. Once the port is in a blocking state, the loop is broken and the network becomes more stable.

The fact that the port is in a blocking state instead of being disabled means that if one of the other links goes down, the port is transitioned into a forwarding state automatically. When a port is in a forwarding state, it is allowed to send and receive data on the port.

Trunking   Trunking is a feature on Cisco switches that allows you to connect the switches together and then assign one of the ports as a trunk port. The trunk port is used to carry VLAN traffic to the other switch. VLANs are allowed to contain ports that are from multiple switches as members. If data is destined for all systems in the VLAN, the VLAN identification information is added to the data packet and then the switch sends the packet out the trunk port. When another switch receives the packet, it checks the VLAN identification information and then sends the data to all of its ports that are a member of that particular VLAN.

ISL and 802.1Q   When a switch assigns the VLAN identification information to a packet, this is known as tagging. Two popular protocols for tagging are the InterSwitch Link (ISL) and the IEEE 802.1Q protocol.

ISL is the Cisco-proprietary protocol for tagging packets and associating them with a particular VLAN on older switches, while 802.1Q is the IEEE standard for VLAN trunking. Newer Cisco and Juniper Networks switches use 802.1Q as the tagging method.

Port Mirroring   Port mirroring, also known as port monitoring, is a feature that allows the switch to send a copy of data that reaches certain ports to the mirrored, or monitored, port. Port monitoring allows an administrator to plug a workstation into the port that the copy of the data is being sent to and monitor the network traffic.

Port mirroring is an important feature of a switch because, by default, the switch filters traffic by only sending the data to the port that the destination system resides on. The switch's filtering feature will prevent the monitoring of traffic, so as a result, if the administrator wishes to monitor network traffic, he or she will need to enable port mirroring and then connect their workstation to the monitored port.

Port Security/Authentication   Port security is another important feature of the switch that allows the administrator to associate the MAC address of the system with the port to which it will connect. The administrator can also specify that if a system with a different MAC address connects to the port, the port is to be automatically disabled.

Port authentication will help increase the security of the network by allowing only authorized systems to connect to it—a critical feature of any switch!

Content Switch   A content switch is a special switch designed for optimizing data delivery to clients by incorporating features that improve performance, such as data-caching or load-balancing features on the switch. Here is an example of how the switch can load-balance traffic: If you connect two servers into the switch, the switch creates a virtual server using a virtual IP. When a request comes in to the virtual IP, the switch then forwards the request to one of the servers connected to the switch. The result is that the load is balanced across both servers and performance is increased.

CERTIFICATION OBJECTIVE 3.04

Routers and Brouters

Another popular network device is a network router. A *router* is responsible for sending data from one network to another, and is a layer-3 device. This section will introduce you to routers and brouters, which combine a bridge and a router.

Routers

Routers are layer-3 devices responsible for routing, or sending, data from one network to another. A router can have multiple network interfaces, as shown in Figure 3-19, with each network connecting either to a network or a wide area network (WAN) environment.

| FIGURE 3-19 | A Cisco 1604 router with LAN and WAN interfaces |

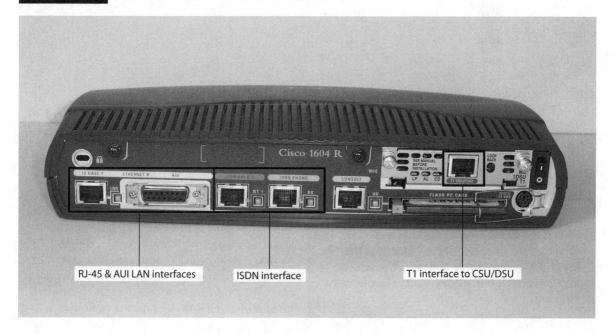

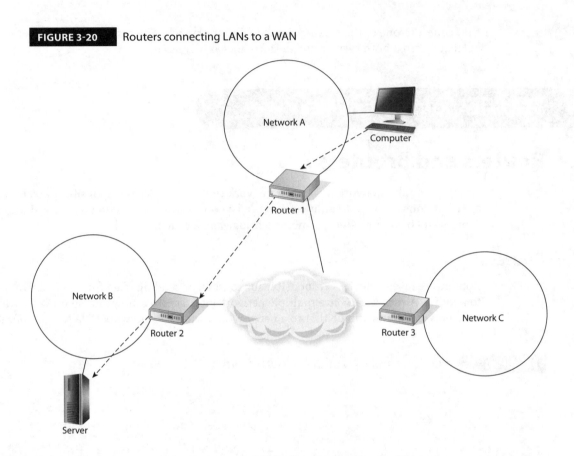

FIGURE 3-20 Routers connecting LANs to a WAN

Routers are typically used to connect the LAN to a WAN environment by having a network interface and a WAN interface connecting to each type of network. The router then passes data from one interface to the other.

Routers work with layer-3 addresses, which are logical addresses assigned to the systems that are used to determine how to reach the destination network. Routers use a routing table stored in memory to determine how to reach a system on a destination network. Figure 3-20 shows three networks connected by routers. In the figure, notice that if a system on Network A wants to send data to a system on Network B, it must leave Network A by means of Router 1, and

exam

watch

Remember for the Network+ exam that a router is a layer-3 device. Also note that when data has the layer-3 header (which contains the source and destination IP address), it is known as a "packet."

then Router 1 will send the data to Router 2. It is the responsibility of Router 2 to send the data to the destination computer.

Routers are a great way to filter network traffic as well, because they act as a broadcast domain. Traffic will not cross the router unless it is actually destined for a system on the remote network. Most router administrators do not allow broadcasts to pass through.

For more information on how routers work and how to manage them, be sure to check out Chapters 7 and 8.

Brouters

A number of network environments use multiple network protocols to support different network applications or services. If you need to route data for one protocol but need the bridging functionality for another protocol, instead of buying both a bridge and a router, you can purchase a brouter. A *brouter* is the combination of a bridge and a router, and it decides whether it needs to bridge the data or route the data according to the protocol being used. If the protocol is a nonroutable protocol, such as NetBEUI, the data will be bridged. If the protocol is TCP/IP or IPX/SPX, the data will be routed.

Collision Domains and Broadcast Domains

The Network+ certification exam now expects you to be familiar with the terms *collision domain* and *broadcast domain.* Let's start with a quick definition of each and then I will expand on the two terms a bit.

- **Collision domain**   A group of systems that could potentially have their data collide with one another.
- **Broadcast domain**   A group of systems that can receive one another's broadcast messages.

Collision Domain

A collision domain is a group of systems that could potentially have their data collide with one another. For example, if you are using a hub to connect five systems together on a network, because traffic is sent to all ports on the hub, it is possible that if another system sends data at the same time, the data could collide with what is already being transmitted on the network. For this reason, we consider all network ports on a hub (and any devices connected to those ports) as part of a single collision domain. Note that this also means when you cascade a hub off another hub, then all hubs are part of the same collision domain.

If you were using a switch to connect the five systems together, each port on the switch would create its own network segment (like a bridge breaks the network down into different network segments). When data is sent by a system connected to the switch, the switch only sends the data to the port that the destination system resides on. For this reason, if another system were to send data at the same time, the data would not collide. As a result, each port on the switch creates a separate collision domain.

Broadcast Domain

A broadcast domain is a group of systems that can receive one another's broadcast messages. When using a hub to connect five systems in a network environment, if one system sends a broadcast message, the message is received by all other systems connected to the hub. For this reason, all ports on the hub create a single broadcast domain.

Likewise, if all five systems were connected to a switch and one of the systems sent a broadcast message, the broadcast message would be received by all other systems on the network. Therefore, when using a switch, all ports are part of the same broadcast domain as well.

Be sure to know the difference between a broadcast domain and collision domain for the Network+ certification exam!

If you wanted to control which systems received one another's broadcast messages, you would have to use a router that does not forward broadcast messages on to other networks. For the Network+ exam, remember that a router is the device you use to create multiple broadcast domains. You could also use VLANs on a switch, with each VLAN being a different broadcast domain.

CERTIFICATION OBJECTIVE 3.05

Gateways and Security Devices

Two other types of devices that are found in networking environments are gateways and firewalls. This section discusses gateways and acts as an introduction to security devices such as firewalls and intrusion detection systems. For a more detailed discussion on security, see Chapters 15 and 16.

Gateways

A gateway is responsible for translating information from one format to another and can run at any layer of the OSI model, depending on what information the gateway translates. A typical use of a gateway is to ensure that systems in one environment can access information

FIGURE 3-21   A gateway translates data from one format to another.

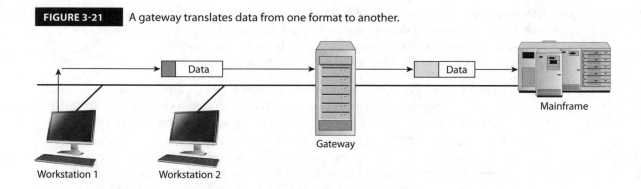

Workstation 1   Workstation 2   Gateway   Mainframe

in another environment. For example, you want to make sure that your PC environment can access information on the company's mainframe.

In Figure 3-21, notice that the information sent by Workstation 1 has been reformatted after reaching the gateway. Gateways do this by stripping the packet down to just the data and then rebuilding the packet so that it is understood at the destination.

It is also important to note that when you configure TCP/IP and you configure the "default gateway" setting, you are pointing to the address of the router on the network. It really has nothing to do with an actual "gateway" device.

Firewalls

Firewalls are a networking component responsible for protecting the network from outside intruders. The firewall is designed to block specific types of traffic while allowing certain information to pass through. For example, I have a firewall that blocks any data that tries to reach my network from the Internet unless it is HTTP traffic. The reason I have allowed HTTP traffic through the firewall is that I would like my customers to be able to view my website. The firewall administrator selectively chooses which traffic can and cannot pass through the firewall.

For more information on firewalls, refer to Chapter 16.

on the
Ọob

The home router you purchase for a home or small office has firewall features built in. I would highly recommend one to protect your systems from the Internet. To make sure that your computer is not connected directly into the Internet, put one of these devices between you and the outside world!

Intrusion Detection Systems

An *intrusion detection system (IDS)* is a security device that monitors system or network activity and then notifies the administrator of any suspicious activity. Intrusion detection systems are important devices that will complement other security devices such as firewalls. The IDS is an important device because it will notify you not only of suspicious activity against the firewall, but also of suspicious activity inside the network.

There are two types of intrusion detection systems:

■ **Host-based IDS (HIDS)**   Host-based intrusion detection systems monitor the local system for suspicious activity. A host-based IDS is typically a piece of software installed on the system and can only monitor activity on the system it was installed on.

■ **Network-based IDS (NIDS)**   A network-based IDS monitors network traffic for suspicious behavior. A network-based IDS is able to monitor the entire network and compare that traffic to known malicious traffic patterns. When a match is found, an alert can be triggered. Network-based IDSs can be software loaded on a system that monitors network traffic, or it can be a hardware device.

Intrusion detection systems can be either active or passive. An *active* IDS will monitor activity, log any suspicious activity, and then take some form of corrective action. For example, if a system is doing a port scan on the network, the IDS may log the activity but also disconnect the system creating the suspicious action from the network. Note that an active IDS is now known as an *intrusion prevention system (IPS)*.

A *passive* intrusion detection system does not take any corrective action when suspicious activity has been identified. The passive IDS will simply identify the activity and then log to a file any information needed during an investigation. The passive IDS does not take any corrective action.

EXERCISE 3-3

Identifying Network Components

In this exercise, you review the different network components by matching the term with the definition.

Definition	Component
_____ A layer-3 device responsible for sending data from one network to another.	A. Switch
_____ A layer-1 device that regenerates the signal.	B. Collision domain
_____ A layer-2 device used to connect all systems to the network.	C. VLAN
_____ A group of systems that can receive one another's broadcast messages.	D. Firewall

Definition	Component
_____ Responsible for translating information from one format to another.	E. Router
_____ Used to create communication boundaries on a switch.	F. Hub
_____ A group of systems that could potentially have their data collide with one another.	G. Repeater
_____ Used to protect a system or device from unwanted traffic.	H. Gateway
_____ A layer-1 device used to connect all systems to the network.	I. Broadcast domain

CERTIFICATION OBJECTIVE 3.06

Other Networking Devices

There are a few additional devices that you should be familiar with for the Network+ exam. These are devices that will connect you to a wireless network or a WAN environment. These devices are only quickly mentioned here because they appear again in the chapters on WAN and remote connectivity.

Wireless Access Points

Wireless access points (WAPs) are network devices that can be connected to the wired network to allow a wireless client to pass through and access the wired network and its resources. A wireless access point also is known as a cell, which is a device that transmits and receives radio frequencies between the PCs and network devices with wireless transmitters connected to them. The wireless access point is connected to a physical cable, which connects the WAP device to the rest of the network. Figure 3-22 shows an example of a Linksys home router that is a wireless access point as well. Notice the wireless antennas attached to the access point.

The typical home router is a multifunctional device; it acts as a wireless access point, firewall, switch, and router, all wrapped up in one device.

Analog Modems

There are other forms of networking devices beyond the typical network card; for instance, analog modems can be used to communicate with other systems across the public switched

A home router being used as a wireless access point

telephone network (PSTN). They are used to convert digital data from the PC to analog transmission so that the information can be transmitted over the analog phone lines. The modem on the receiving end is designed to convert the analog signal to a digital format readable by the system. For more information on modems, see Chapter 11.

CSU/DSU

A *channel service unit/data service unit* (CSU/DSU) is either one device or a pair of devices that allows an organization to get a very high-speed WAN connection from the telephone company, such as a T1 or T3 link. The CSU is used at the business end to get the connection to the WAN, and the DSU may be used at the provider's end to allow the CSU to connect. For more information on WAN technologies and CSU/DSUs, see Chapter 12.

ISDN

The Integrated Services Digital Network (ISDN) is a communication standard for sending voice and data over normal telephone lines or digital telephone lines. In order to connect to the ISDN lines, a system will need an ISDN modem, which doesn't really act like a modem because whereas a modem converts digital data to analog, the ISDN modem carries digital data from one digital system to another, and so it really is acting as a terminal adapter connecting you to the ISDN lines.

There are two popular types of ISDN connections:

■ **Basic rate interface (BRI)**   This is a 128 Kbps connection that is made up of two 64 Kbps channels (known as B-channels) and one 16 Kbps control channel (known as a D-channel).

■ **Primary rate interface (PRI)**   This is a 1.55 Mbps connection that is made up of twenty-three 64 Kbps channels (B-channels) and one 64 Kbps D-channel for signaling and control information.

Network Appliances

The Network+ exam expects you to be familiar with devices such as routers and switches, but also expects you to understand other types of network appliances. The following is a listing of common network appliances and their purpose:

■ **Encryption devices**   A common network device today is an encryption device. You can have encryption devices that just encrypt specific types of traffic or all network traffic.

■ **Load balancer**   A load balancer is a network appliance that allows you to split the workload (the request) for an application across many servers. This helps improve performance, as no single system is handling all the requests. This is a common appliance with websites.

■ **Proxy server**   A proxy server is a network device that is used to request Internet resources (such as webpages) on behalf of the internal users. The benefit of having all users send requests through the proxy server is that the proxy server can filter what websites the user can visit, cache the sites for quicker access in the future, log Internet activity, and control what protocols can be used to access Internet resources.

■ **Content filter**   A content filter appliance is responsible for filtering what type of content the user is allowed to access on the Internet. For example, you may wish to filter which URLs the users can visit.

■ **VPN concentrator**   A virtual private network (VPN) concentrator is a network appliance that allows multiple clients to establish a secure, encrypted VPN connection to the office network. The VPN concentrator is used to establish the encrypted tunnel, but also enforces policies such as requirements to connect to the VPN.

■ **Packet shaper**   A packet shaper, also known as a *traffic shaping* device, is responsible for delaying certain types of packets in order to make bandwidth available for other types of packets. For example, you may shape the network so that all packets but voice packets are delayed in order to give priority to voice traffic.

Virtualization

Virtualization technology has taken off over the last few years, with companies consolidating many existing servers down to one physical server and running each server in a virtual machine. The virtual machine uses resources such as random access memory (RAM) and hard disk space from the actual physical server.

The benefit of virtualization technology is that overall, companies use minimal resources such as memory, processor, and disk space on the actual physical server. For example, your company wants to have an e-mail server, so you spend thousands of dollars on this server, but once the e-mail server is installed and running, you are only using 30 percent of the RAM you purchased and 20 percent of the processing power. Then the company wants a database server and they go out and purchase a new physical server for you to install the database server software on. This doesn't make sense, as the original system you purchased is underutilized.

In today's day and age, you can use virtualization software that allows you to run both the e-mail server and database server on the same physical server. Products such as VMWare and Microsoft's Hyper-V allow you to run machines in a virtual environment. Figure 3-23 displays two systems running in a virtual environment.

FIGURE 3-23

A Windows 7 and Windows Server 2008 VM

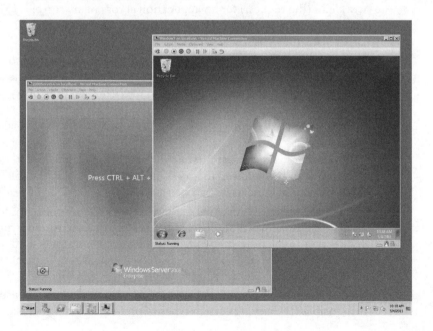

With virtualization software, you can virtualize a number of different types of network components. The following is a list of virtual network components:

- **Virtual switches**   Being able to create virtual switches allows you to place different virtual machines on different virtual networks.
- **Virtual routers**   You can connect different virtual switches together by virtual routers in order to route traffic between the different virtual switches (networks).
- **Virtual firewall**   You can also create virtual firewalls to control what traffic can enter or leave the different virtual networks.
- **Virtual vs. physical NICs**   Virtualization software typically allows you to create virtual network cards in each VM and then connect those virtual network cards to a virtual switch, or map it to a physical network card so that the VM can participate on the real network.
- **Software-defined networking**   Software-defined networking (SDN) is a networking strategy that separates networking functionality into either a control plane (a routing mechanism) or data plane (the different destinations).
- **Virtual desktops**   Companies can have users running virtual desktop systems, which are virtual machines stored on a central server and already configured for a group of applications the user would use.
- **Virtual servers**   One of the most common virtualization technologies is to run multiple servers on one physical server, saving on hardware cost and offering environmental benefits such as less power consumption due to the lower number of physical machines.
- **Virtual PBX**   Private branch exchange (PBX) systems are used by companies needing phone services for a number of employees within the business at one time. The PBX system is responsible for routing calls to the appropriate employee and offering mailbox features such as voice mail. A virtual PBX is offered by a service provider so that the company does not need to invest in PBX hardware.

Cloud Computing

Cloud computing is a huge trend today and is one of the new concepts you can expect to see a bit more of on the Network+ certification. The purpose of cloud computing is that instead of you purchasing all the server hardware and software you need to build a server or network (which costs thousands of dollars and is very time consuming to plan), you simply pay a cloud provider for hosting the services while you are responsible for the administration of those servers (typically through a web browser). There are huge benefits to cloud computing:

- **No hardware costs**   The huge benefit to cloud services is that you do not have to spend months planning for hardware and then purchasing the server hardware, knowing that the server is hosted somewhere across the Internet.

- **Scalability and high availability**   Most providers offer the option to add new servers at any time as your needs grow (scalability). They also provide high availability so that there is no single point of failure should a piece of hardware fail.

- **Focus on software configuration**   Within minutes of signing up for the service, you can have your server up and running. I had signed up for Office 365 (Office, Exchange, SharePoint, and Lync in the cloud) and had an e-mail server up in seconds and was sending e-mail in minutes (had to build the mailboxes and configure my domain name). The installation and configuration of an e-mail server is typically weeks of work!

Cloud Models

There are different types of cloud topologies that can be implemented, with each cloud implementation offering a solution to fit any company's needs. The following outlines the different types of cloud solutions:

- **Public**   A public cloud means that you will subscribe to a cloud service where hosting of the solution will occur across the Internet by a cloud provider. You will pay a monthly subscription fee to access cloud services. Types of cloud services could be paying for storage, or hosting of servers, or even hosting of applications that you connect to from across the Internet.

- **Private**   A private cloud is when you decide to host the cloud services within your own data center and inside your own firewalls. A reason to do this is for compliance or security reasons if your company cannot have the services hosted by a public provider. For example, your company may need to ensure that data is kept private (as in the health industry) so the organization decides to host those services in their own data center.

- **Hybrid**   A hybrid cloud solution involves having some of the services in a public cloud while other services are in a private cloud.

- **Community**   A community cloud is when multiple companies share the cost on a cloud service (whether hosted private or public) and share the same goals for the service. This may be a typical solution when collaborating with another company on a project.

Cloud Service Models

There are a number of different types of cloud service models that offer different solutions to clients. The cloud service model you choose will depend on the type of functionality you would like from the cloud:

- **Infrastructure as a Service (IaaS)**   Infrastructure as a Service is a cloud service model that allows cloud providers to provide infrastructure services, such as CPU processing power and storage, and services to customers, such as backups.

- **Software as a Service (SaaS)**   Software as a Service is a service model that involves providing software to end users through a web browser. For example, an employee can use Microsoft Word via the Office 365 software provided by the cloud.
- **Platform as a Service (PaaS)**   Platform as a Service is a cloud offering that is targeted toward developers and IT administrators who are responsible for developing solutions that are to reside in the cloud. Examples of PaaS are Cloud9, which provides an integrated development environment (IDE) to develop apps with Cloud9 tools. Microsoft Azure is another example of PaaS that allows the creation of websites, web services, and virtual machines.
- **Database as a Service (DBaaS)**   Database as a Service is a cloud service model that provides database services to customers. DBaaS allows cloud providers to provide database server instances to clients in order to allow the client to host and manage databases across the Internet.

It is important to note that the Network+ exam calls out models such as Private Software as a Service or Public Software as a Service. Understand that service models such as IaaS, SaaS, and PaaS can be a private cloud service, a public cloud service, or even a community-based service.

Storage Area Networks

A *storage area network (SAN)* is a dedicated network that allows you to centralize and access all data resources for your systems. The SAN allows you to group storage devices together and have them appear as if they are locally connected devices to the servers while the servers use that storage space for storing data.

Different technologies can be used to create storage area networks, and you need to be familiar with these for the Network+ exam:

- **iSCSI**   iSCSI is a protocol that is used to encapsulate *Small Computer System Interface (SCSI)* commands in an IP packet so that the command can be sent across an Ethernet network from the server to the storage device. iSCSI allows you to use remote storage without having to invest in specialized hardware because you are able to use the existing Ethernet network. The storage space will run on an *iSCSI target* while the servers that wish to access this space will need to have the *iSCSI initiator* software to connect to the target.
- **Jumbo frame**   Jumbo frames are any frame that has more than 1500 bytes of data in the frame (the default maximum size for Ethernet frames). Jumbo frames can have a maximum of 9000 bytes of data contained in the frame with the benefit being that using a jumbo frame can reduce overhead when sending large amounts of data.

■ **Fiber channel** A typical SAN will involve purchasing specialized equipment such as fiber channel switches (high-speed switches that carry storage communication), as well as special fiber channel interfaces and cables to connect to the fiber channel switch, which makes the creation of a SAN a costly adventure (unless using iSCSI). Fiber channel networks use the *Fiber Channel Protocol (FCP)* to transport the SCSI commands over the fiber channel network.

■ **Network-attached storage (NAS)** A network-attached storage device is a special device that is used to provide file storage to systems on the network. The NAS is normally its own computing device that has multiple hard drive bays and allows you to put multiple hard drives in the system and configure a redundant array of independent disks (RAID) with the drives. This NAS device is then used as the file server for the network—a central place for everyone to store and access documents.

SCADA/ICS and Medianets

In this section you will be introduced to SCADA and medianets—two new topics introduced to the Network+ certification objectives.

SCADA/ICS

Supervisory Control And Data Acquisition (SCADA) is a special system used in industrial environments to monitor and control remote industrial equipment. SCADA is a form of industrial control system (ICS) that can monitor and manage equipment such as that at a production plant. The following are terms related to SCADA and industrial control systems you should be familiar with:

■ **ICS server** An *industrial control system (ICS)* server is a system that receives information from the devices and then sends out supervisory commands to those devices on how they should function.

■ **DCS/closed network** A *distributed control system (DCS)*, also known as a closed network, is a type of control system used in plants that involves parts of the control system distributed to a number of systems on the network. The components are connected by a network to allow them to communicate.

■ **Remote terminal unit** The *remote terminal unit (RTU)* is an electronic device that allows equipment to connect to the DCS.

■ **Programmable logic controller** The *programmable logic controller (PLC)* is a device that is used to monitor and control machinery, typically machinery in an assembly line of a manufacturing plant. These PLC devices are rugged devices designed to handle ranges in temperature, are resistant to vibration, and are immune to electrical noise.

Medianets

A medianet is the term for a network that has been optimized for voice, video, webpages, and other forms of media in order to deliver a better "rich media" experience to users. Recent advances in network technologies, such as faster switches and better quality video streaming equipment, have made it more feasible for companies to incorporate voice and video in everyday business activity. The medianet is the network designed to handle those business goals.

A great example of a type of media that is common today is *video teleconferencing (VTC)*, which involves the use of voice, video, and other types of content in a conference call, such as screen sharing and PowerPoints being presented—all across the network. Having a network that has been tweaked for such content and offers quality of service has never been more desirable and more achievable.

Power Management

The network has grown to contain a wealth of different types of devices, including different types of power management devices that you need to be familiar with. The following are some key power management components:

- **Power converters**   A power converter is a device that converts power from one format to another—for example, the device may convert AC power to DC power, such as a power supply in a computer.
- **Inverters**   An inverter is the opposite of a converter and is responsible for converting DC power to AC power.
- **Circuits**   An electrical circuit is the pathway that an electrical current takes. When we want to stop that current, we typically go to the electrical box and switch the circuit breaker on (usually as a precaution when doing some electrical work).
- **UPS**   An *uninterruptible power supply (UPS)* is a device that provides emergency power to network equipment and servers when the power is lost. This UPS has limited charge, so it can only provide backup power for a short time, but enough time to gracefully shut down network devices to prevent data corruption.
- **Power redundancy**   One final consideration that should be made with power is to ensure that you have power redundancy. This is making sure that you have multiple power sources to your network equipment such as routers, switches, and servers. You can accomplish this by ensuring the equipment has *redundant power supplies (RPSs)*.

Wiring Distribution and Rack Systems

This chapter wouldn't be complete without a discussion of how the cabling for the network is configured. In Chapter 1 you learned about the different types of cables; this section will identify related terms you need to know for the exam.

Plenum vs. PVC

For the Network+ exam, you need to be familiar with the term plenum. *Plenum* refers to the space between the ceiling tiles and the floor located above them. This space is typically used to route power and network cables. It is important to use plenum-grade cables in this space because if there is a fire and you are not using plenum-grade cables, known as polyvinyl chloride (PVC) cabling, a toxin is released when it is burned that could be carried throughout the building, causing harm to individuals. Plenum-grade cabling uses a low-toxicity material for the jacket of the cable in case of fire.

Patch Panel

Most companies have network jacks located in the walls that allow systems to connect to the network. These jacks have cables connected to them that are then routed a long distance to a patch panel in a server room.

The patch panel then has a *patch cable* that connects the front of the patch panel to a port on a switch. Using a patch panel aids with cable management, as you can easily change which wall jack is connected to which switch. When a computer connects to the network jack in the wall, the patch cable is used to map that system to the port on the switch. The concept of the patch panel allows ease of administration and flexibility in moving systems from one switch to another without visiting the workstation. Figure 3-24 displays a patch panel. Another aspect of cable management is the fact that the racks that hold the servers have cable tracks that allow you to cleanly run cables through the rack. You will learn more about rack systems in the next section.

FIGURE 3-24

A typical patch panel

Cross-connects, MDF, and IDF

The Network+ exam expects you to know terms such as cross-connects, MDF, and IDF. When wiring the network, you will typically have the outside line coming into the building connect to a panel known as the *main distribution frame (MDF).* The MDF typically connects to other panels, known as *intermediate distribution frames (IDFs),* which are used to connect workstations to the network. The purpose of using MDF and IDF panels is to give the company flexibility when reorganizing the network in the future.

In a typical example, the MDF would connect to the cable coming from outside the building. Then there may be a separate IDF panel representing each floor in the building, with the workstations on a particular floor connecting to the panel associated with that floor.

@atch **For the Network+ exam, know that the patch cable that connects to the patch panel is called a horizontal cross-connect (HCC) cable. The cable that connects the MDF to the IDFs is called the vertical cross-connect (VCC) cable.**

Demarc, Demarc Extension, and Smartjack

The *demarc,* also known as the *demarc point,* is the point where the service provider equipment connects to your building. The term is used to identify who is responsible for a particular problem. For example, if the equipment that is faulty is on your company's side of the demarc point, then it is your company's problem to fix, while if the problem is on the service provider's side of the demarc point, then the responsibility to solve the problem falls into the service provider's hands.

The term *demarc extension* (Figure 3-25) refers to the area between the connection into your building (from the service provider) and your company's communication equipment. The demarc extension is typically a patch cable that connects the service provider's line to your company's network equipment.

FIGURE 3-25

Demarc point and demarc extension

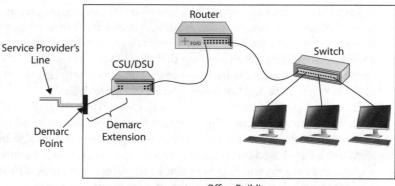

A *smartjack* is the term for a demarc point that serves as more than just a connection point, but also has the intelligence to perform diagnostics that help in troubleshooting situations.

Rack Systems

When designing your network environment, you will most likely design a rack system. The rack system is a special component that can host servers, routers, and switches in the rack-mountable system. This is a clean way to organize your network equipment.

The rack system is a metal system that has empty compartments for you to slide in a rack-mountable server, switch, or router on server rails (known as server rail racks) and then secure it in place. This allows you to easily add and remove the server as you wish. The compartments are typically 19 inches in width, making the servers much smaller devices than a typical tower-based server. The rack system is typically secured to the floor and the wall of the building.

The compartments are 1.75 inches in height and are known as a unit, or "U." A single rack system can have many units and is typically labeled as such. A typical rack system is 45U with a single blade server requiring approximately 10U. You would carefully plan the number of devices you could host in the rack system by the number of "U"s each device is and how many "U"s the rack itself is.

The rack system is usually either a two-post rack or a four-post rack. The name comes from the number of vertical posts that are used to support the rack system. A two-post rack was typically used for communication equipment, such as routers, while a four-post rack is used for server racks. The benefit of a four-post rack is that the mounting rails can be secured at the front and then at the back, while a two-post rack can only be mounted by the front panel holes. Many two-post racks come as free-standing racks, which means they usually have a deep base, giving stability so that the rack system does not need to be bolted to the floor.

You want to make sure that you space the servers in a rack so that you can get proper airflow and ensure that there is a panel on the side to run cables (known as a cable tray) to keep things clean and accessible. You also want to ensure that in a large data center you create hot and cold aisles, which is when creating rows of servers, the front of the servers take in cool air and the back of the servers have vents sending out hot air as part of their cooling system. You want to ensure that when creating the rows of servers, the fronts of two rows are facing cold air aisles (an aisle that does not have hot air pushed to it) and the backs of the servers are facing hot aisles (shown in Figure 3-26).

The last topic to discuss with regard to rack systems is rack monitoring and security. Rack monitoring involves using a system that allows you to monitor temperature, humidity, and power status in real time. The monitoring system should also be able to send alerts and have a web-based interface that allows you to configure the monitoring system. Some monitoring systems will also have smoke detectors, vibration sensors, and door-open sensors to help detect fire, vibrations, and intrusion incidents.

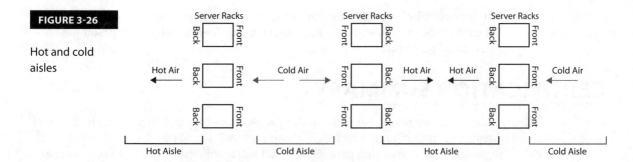

FIGURE 3-26

Hot and cold aisles

From a security point of view, you can install video surveillance equipment in the data center for monitoring who has access to the servers. You can also ensure that limited access to the servers is granted by locking down the server room and using proximity cards or biometrics for high-security needs. If you are hosting your servers in a shared data center, ensure that each individual rack is individually locked so that if someone does have access to the server room, they do not necessarily get access to the servers.

Device Placement and Labeling

The final topic for this chapter is a great day-to-day practice that should be followed—place the equipment in the appropriate location and label your network equipment to ensure that everything is well documented.

Ensure that you have all servers, routers, switches, and other network infrastructure equipment locked in the server room. Once the equipment has been secured, you should label all the equipment, ports, and connections so that you will understand the purpose of the equipment later on down the road.

The following outlines some items that should be labeled:

- **Port labeling**   Be sure to label ports, switches, and routers so that the purpose of each port is well documented. You can also label the network jacks in the wall and assign the same label to the corresponding port on the patch panel.

- **System labeling**   Ensure that you label each system and device. For example, put a small label on each server so that you know which server does what when looking at the server rack.

- **Circuit labeling**   The leased line coming into your office from your service provider is known as a communication circuit. That line will connect to the WAN port on the router (the CSU/DSU) and should be labeled with the Internet service provider (ISP) information.

- **Naming conventions**   Be sure to come up with a naming convention for your server names. For example, I may use the name TORFSACCT as the name for the Toronto file server for the accounting department.

■ **Patch panel labeling** As I mentioned earlier, it is a good idea to label the ports in the patch panel, which will help you know which network jack in the building each patch panel port corresponds to.

CERTIFICATION SUMMARY

In this chapter, you learned about some of the popular networking devices that are used to allow systems to communicate. The first of those devices is the network card. The network card is responsible for converting parallel data that is transmitted through the computer's bus to a serial bit stream to be sent on the wire. The network card uses a transceiver. Transceivers constitute that portion of the network interface that actually transmits and receives electrical signals across the transmission media and connects to the media. There are two types of transceivers: built in and external. The NIC usually has a built-in transceiver for twisted-pair and thinnet, but thicknet typically uses an external transceiver.

The network card uses the MAC address burned into the card by the manufacturer as an identifier to determine where the packet is destined for and where it came from. The system does this by adding the source MAC address and destination MAC address to the packet, which is read by networking devices to determine where the packet needs to go.

There are a few popular layer-1 devices, such as hubs, repeaters, and MAUs. Remember that these devices are considered layer 1 because they work with the electrical signals. Any data that reaches a layer-1 device will be sent to all ports on the device. A repeater is responsible for regenerating the electrical signal so that the signal may travel a greater distance. A MAU is used in a Token Ring environment and regenerates the signal with each system connected to the MAU. When connecting MAUs, you will need to ring out of one MAU and ring in to the second MAU; you will then ring out of the second MAU and ring in to the third MAU. Remember to ring out of the last one and ring in to the first MAU.

Bridges and switches are examples of layer-2 devices. A bridge is responsible for filtering network traffic by sending the data only to the network segment where the destination system resides. The bridge builds a bridging table, which has a list of destinations. A switch has replaced the network hub nowadays, and it filters traffic by sending data only to the port on the switch where the destination system is connected. You can increase network performance dramatically by changing your network hubs to switches. A number of switches support VLAN capabilities. A VLAN is used to create virtual networks out of ports on one or more switches. When data is broadcast on the VLAN, it is sent only to members of the VLAN, not the entire switch. Systems can communicate only with other systems on their VLAN and cannot communicate with systems on other VLANs without the use of a router.

Some other popular networking components are routers, gateways, and firewalls. Routers are layer-3 devices that are responsible for sending data from one network to another. A gateway is responsible for converting data from one format to another so that the data can be understood on both sides of the gateway. A firewall is a device that stops traffic from passing through it, protecting private network resources.

TWO-MINUTE DRILL

Network Interface Cards

❑ Network interface cards (NICs) function by converting parallel data from the computer to a serial bit stream sent on the network.

❑ The computer must have a software driver installed to enable it to interact with the NIC, just as it must for any other peripheral device.

❑ The Media Access Control (MAC) address, or hardware address, is a 12-digit number that is used to determine where the data is being sent and where it is coming from. The MAC address also is known as a layer-2 address and looks like 00-0D-60-48-53-9E.

❑ A computer bus is the term used for the speed and type of interface the computer uses with various types of interface cards and equipment. Popular bus architectures are ISA, PCI, and PCMCIA for laptops. When you install a network card, you will need to be familiar with what bus slot you will place the card into.

❑ The network card uses a transceiver to pick up the electrical signals and send electrical signals on the wire. There are two types of transceivers: built in and external. The transceivers for twisted-pair and thinnet usually are built into the network card, whereas the transceiver for thicknet is usually an external one.

❑ When you are configuring the network card, you may need to specify the transfer rate so that it supports the device you are connecting to. You also may need to specify the transceiver you intend to use, the transmission type, and whether to use half duplex or full duplex.

❑ Simplex transmissions allow data to be sent in only one direction. Half duplex allows data to be sent and received, but not at the same time. Full duplex allows data to be sent and received at the same time.

Hubs, MAUs, and Repeaters

❑ Hubs are the central location to which all cabling must connect in most topologies.

❑ When exam time comes, remember the difference between an active hub and a passive hub. An active hub contains electronic components to boost the signal. A passive hub does not.

❑ A multistation access unit (MAU) is a device to which multiple workstations are connected in order to communicate on a Token Ring network.

❑ Because the signal gets weaker over distance, repeaters are used to regenerate the signal so that it can continue in its travels.

❑ Hubs, MAUs, and repeaters are layer-1 devices.

Bridges and Switches

❑ A bridge is used to create multiple segments on the network. The bridge will forward network traffic only to the destination segment and not to all segments, thus acting as a filtering device to improve network performance.

❑ A switch filters network traffic by sending data only to the port on the switch where the destination system resides.

❑ Switches are replacing hubs, and network administrators who wish to improve network performance should replace their hubs with switches.

❑ Some switches support virtual LANs (VLANs). A VLAN is a group of ports on the switch that make up their own logical network. Systems on a particular VLAN can communicate only with other systems on the same VLAN unless a router is used. The VLAN also acts as a broadcast domain because broadcast traffic is sent only to ports in the VLAN where the sender of the broadcast traffic exists.

❑ Bridges and switches are layer-2 devices.

❑ Each port on a switch or bridge creates a separate collision domain.

Routers and Brouters

❑ A router is a layer-3 device that sends data from one network to another using a layer-3 address such as an IP address.

❑ Routers are used by routable protocols such as IPX/SPX, TCP/IP, and AppleTalk.

❑ Routers and VLANs are used to create separate broadcast domains.

❑ A brouter is a device that combines a bridge and a router. The brouter will act as a router for routable protocols, but will act as a bridge for nonroutable protocols such as NetBEUI.

Gateways and Security Devices

❑ A gateway is a device that is used to join dissimilar environments together.

❑ The gateway converts data from one side of the gateway to a format that the other side of the gateway will understand.

❑ A firewall is a device that blocks all network traffic from passing through in order to protect private network resources, although it may be configured to allow selected traffic to pass through. For example, most companies have a web server that publishes their website, so they will need to allow HTTP traffic to pass through the firewall.

Other Networking Devices

❑ Modems are used as remote connectivity devices to connect systems across telephone wires. The modem converts digital signals to analog on the sending computer and converts analog signals to digital on the receiving computer.

❑ CSU/DSU is a network device that allows an organization to connect to a high-speed link such as a T1 or T3.

❑ ISDN is a digital service that is used to connect systems over a digital phone line and to receive transmission rates faster than conventional modems.

SELF TEST

The following questions will help you measure your understanding of the material presented in this chapter. Read all of the choices carefully, because there might be more than one correct answer. Choose all correct answers for each question.

Network Interface Cards

1. What does a network interface card add to a computer's functionality?
   A. It provides faster communication between the CPU and the hard disk.
   B. It provides the capability to communicate across a phone line to another computer.
   C. It provides the capability to communicate with other computers across a network medium.
   D. It provides the capability to save more information on a diskette than normal.

2. If a card has the capability to connect to more than one kind of medium, you might have to set which of the following in order to ensure connectivity?
   A. IRQ setting
   B. Link light on/off setting
   C. Transceiver-type setting
   D. PCI setting

3. When troubleshooting to find out why a network card will not connect to the network, which of the following would you check first?
   A. Driver
   B. Link light
   C. Transceiver-type setting
   D. Switch

4. Which of the following is an example of a layer-2 address?
   A. 192.168.2.5
   B. COMPUTER100
   C. Computer100.glensworld.loc
   D. 00-0D-60-48-53-9E

5. What is an AUI connector?
   A. A 9-pin DB male connector
   B. A 15-pin D female connector
   C. A 25-pin D female connector
   D. Same as an RJ-45 connector

Hubs, MAUs, and Repeaters

6. Which of the following types of hubs does not regenerate the signal and therefore is not a repeater?
   A. Active hub
   B. Hybrid hub
   C. Passive hub
   D. Switching hub

7. Which network component is used to extend the distance the signal can travel by regenerating the signal?
   A. Passive hub
   B. NIC
   C. IRQ
   D. Repeater

8. Which type of hub enables more than one type of cable or medium to connect to it?
   A. Passive
   B. Active
   C. Hybrid
   D. Multistation access unit

9. Which network device is used to connect systems together in a Token Ring environment?
   A. Multisensing action unit
   B. Multistation access unit
   C. Multisplit add transmission unit
   D. Multistation action unit

10. When data is sent to a system on a hub, the data is sent to which port(s) on the hub?
    A. The port of the destination system
    B. All ports on the immediate hub, but not any linked hubs
    C. All ports on the immediate hub and any linked hubs
    D. All ports on only the linked hub

Bridges and Switches

11. Which type of network component enables each device to have the full bandwidth of the medium when transmitting?
  A. Hub
  B. Repeater
  C. Switch
  D. Transceiver

12. When data is sent to a known system on a switch, the data is sent to what port(s)?
  A. The port of the destination system
  B. All ports on the immediate switch, but not any uplinked switches
  C. All ports on the immediate switch and any uplinked switches
  D. All ports on the uplinked switch

13. Which layer of the OSI model does a bridge run at?
  A. Layer 4
  B. Layer 1
  C. Layer 3
  D. Layer 2

14. Which networking feature allows you to group ports on a switch to create a broadcast domain?
  A. WANs
  B. VLANs
  C. MANs
  D. CANs

Routers and Brouters

15. Which layer of the OSI model does a router run at?
  A. Layer 4
  B. Layer 1
  C. Layer 3
  D. Layer 2

16. Which networking device routes data used by a routable protocol but bridges data for nonroutable protocols?
  A. Router
  B. Bridge
  C. Gateway
  D. Brouter

17. Which of the following are nonroutable protocols?

A. NetBEUI

B. IPX

C. TCP/IP

D. AppleTalk

Gateways and Security Devices

18. Which of the following layers does a gateway run at? (Select the best answer.)

A. Layer 4

B. Layer 1

C. Layer 5

D. All layers

19. Which type of device is responsible for connecting dissimilar networking environments together?

A. Router

B. Bridge

C. Gateway

D. Switch

20. Which networking device is used to block unauthorized traffic from entering the network?

A. Bridge

B. Gateway

C. Switch

D. Firewall

Other Networking Devices

21. Which of the following devices is used to connect to digital phone lines?

A. ISDN modem

B. CSU/DSU

C. Modem

D. NIC

22. Which of the following devices is used to prepare the digital data for transmission over the PSTN?

A. ISDN modem

B. CSU/DSU

C. Modem

D. NIC

23. How many B-channels are in a BRI ISDN connection?
 A. 1
 B. 2
 C. 3
 D. 4

Performance-Based Question Review: See the performance-based question sample from the author included with the accompanying media.

SELF TEST ANSWERS

Network Interface Cards

1. ☑ **C.** A network card provides the capability to communicate with other computers across a network medium such as a CAT 5 cable. The network card connects to the cable using a transceiver, which is responsible for sending and receiving the electrical signals on the wire. Network interface cards (NICs) are known by a variety of names, including network adapters, network cards, network adapter boards, and media access cards. Regardless of the name, they function by enabling computers to communicate across a network. NICs are often defined by the following criteria: 1) the type of data link protocol they support, such as an Ethernet adapter or a Token Ring adapter; 2) the type of medium to which they connect, such as TP or thinnet; and 3) the data bus for which they were designed, such as ISA, PCI, or USB.

☒ **A, B,** and **D** are incorrect. **A** is incorrect because a NIC does not help increase the bus speed between the CPU and the hard drive; that would require a different, faster system bus that is based on the system clock, which controls the bus speed. **B** is incorrect because a NIC does not provide communications on a phone line—a modem does. **D** is incorrect since the NIC has no bearing or connection to the diskette drive.

2. ☑ **C.** The transceiver-type setting is required for network adapters that are capable of attaching to more than one media type. Typical cards of this nature include Ethernet cards that have both twisted-pair and coaxial connectors. This is one of the more common oversights in configuring a NIC and renders the card nonfunctional if configured for the wrong media connection. To alleviate this problem, some cards of this type have an auto setting that causes the card to search for the transceiver that has media connected to it. From a troubleshooting point of view, you should be prepared for the auto setting not to be working, and you may need to manually specify the transceiver type.

   ☒ **A** is incorrect because the IRQ setting allows you to specify that the IRQ should get the processor's attention, allowing the device to get some processing time. **B** and **D** are incorrect because the link light on/off setting and the PCI setting do not exist.

3. ☑ **B.** When troubleshooting any kind of problem, you want to check the easy stuff first. When it comes to network cards, the first thing you want to check is the link light on the back of the computer to verify that there is an actual connection to the network.

   ☒ **A, C,** and **D** are incorrect. Although the driver and switch are definitely things you should verify, they would not be at the top of my list. After verifying that there is a link, I would check the settings on the network card, such as the transceiver type; if that did not work, I would try replacing the driver with a newer version.

4. ☑ **D.** A layer-2 address is a MAC address and looks like 00-0D-60-48-53-9E.

   ☒ **A, B,** and **C** are incorrect. 192.168.2.5 is an example of an IP address, which is a layer-3 address. COMPUTER100 is an example of a NetBIOS name, and computer100.glensworld.loc is an example of a fully qualified domain name.

5. ☑ **B.** An AUI connector is a 15-pin D female connector that looks very much like a joystick port. With an external transceiver, the actual media connection is made external to the NIC using a small device that attaches via an extension cable. These types of connections use an attachment unit interface (AUI) connector, also called a Digital-Intel-Xerox (DIX) connector, on the back of the NIC.

   ☒ **A, C,** and **D** are incorrect. **A** is incorrect because a 9-pin male connector is found on the back of PCs and is the serial port. **C** is incorrect because a 25-pin connector is found on the back of a PC as the printer connection. **D** is incorrect because the RJ-45 is used with twisted-pair cable networks.

Hubs, MAUs, and Repeaters

6. ☑ **C.** The function of a passive hub is simply to receive data from one port of the hub and send it out to the other ports. For example, an eight-port hub receives data from port 3 and then resends that data to ports 1, 2, 4, 5, 6, 7, and 8. It is as simple as that. A passive hub contains no power source or electrical components. There is no signal processing. It simply attaches the ports internally and enables communication to flow through the network.

☒ **A, B,** and **D** are incorrect. **A** is incorrect because the active hub does regenerate the signal, since it is powered. **B** is incorrect because, even though the hybrid hub is powered, the only difference between it and a regular hub is that the hybrid hub has connectors for different media types. **D** is incorrect because a switch is always powered and, therefore, will regenerate the data signals.

7. ☑ **D.** Repeaters can be used to extend the length of the maximum distance of the different types of cables because when a signal reaches a repeater, the repeater regenerates the signal.
☒ **A, B,** and **C** are incorrect. **A** is incorrect because a passive hub does not regenerate signals, given that it is not powered. **B** is incorrect because a NIC generates a signal but does not regenerate a signal. **C** is incorrect because the IRQ is used to get the CPU's attention by interrupting it to perform processing.

8. ☑ **C.** A hybrid hub is one that can use many types of cables. A popular example of a hybrid hub is a hub that has connectors for thinnet and twisted-pair cabling.
☒ **A** and **B** are incorrect because active and passive hubs deal with the question of whether they will regenerate the signal or not; this has nothing to do with the connector types on the hub. **D** is incorrect because a MAU is for Token Ring networks and does not support multiple connector types.

9. ☑ **B.** A multistation access unit (MAU) is a hub-type device in Token Ring environments. Remember that the MAUs are connected together by a ring-in/ring-out feature.
☒ **A, C,** and **D** are incorrect because they are terms that were made up to trick you!

10. ☑ **C.** Remember that with hubs, when a data signal reaches the hub, the hub sends the signal throughout the entire network bus, which includes ports on that hub and any linked hubs. Hubs perform no filtering of traffic, which is what a switch offers!
☒ **A, B,** and **D** are incorrect because the signal will be sent to all ports on all linked hubs.

Bridges and Switches

11. ☑ **C.** Switching is a fairly involved process that allows the device to have the full bandwidth when transmitting.
☒ **A, B,** and **D** are incorrect. **A** is incorrect because the bandwidth is divided among all used ports on a hub. **B** is incorrect because a repeater does not split bandwidth, inasmuch as it is used only to receive signals on one cable and regenerate the signal on another cable. **D** is incorrect because a transceiver is the connection point on a NIC and does not allow for multiple users to send data through the transceiver. The bandwidth on the transceiver is dedicated to the PC in which the NIC is installed.

12. ☑ **A.** A switch is different from a hub in the sense that with a switch, the data is sent only to the port that hosts the destination system. This minimizes network traffic and increases throughput on the network.
☒ **B, C,** and **D** are incorrect because a switch will forward the signal only to the port on which the destination system resides.

13. ☑ **D.** Because a bridge works with MAC addresses, it is considered a layer-2 device.

    ☒ **A, B,** and **C** are incorrect. A hub and a repeater are examples of layer-1 devices; a router is an example of a layer-3 device.

14. ☑ **B.** A VLAN is a way to group ports on a switch so that each grouping is its own virtual network. Systems can communicate only with other systems on their own VLAN, which includes broadcast traffic. If a system sends broadcast traffic on the wire, it will be sent only to other ports on the same VLAN.

    ☒ **A, C,** and **D** are incorrect. WANs, MANs, and CANs are terms used for types of networks; they have nothing to do with features of a switch.

Routers and Brouters

15. ☑ **C.** A router runs at layer 3 of the OSI model.

    ☒ **A, B,** and **D** are incorrect. An example of a layer-1 device would be a hub or repeater, and an example of a layer-2 device would be a bridge or a switch. A gateway could run at any layer of the OSI model.

16. ☑ **D.** A brouter will route information using a routable protocol and will bridge information being sent using a nonroutable protocol.

    ☒ **A, B,** and **C** are incorrect. A router simply routes or sends data from one network to another, whereas a bridge filters data within the network by sending data to the appropriate segment within a network. A gateway is a device used to translate data from one format to another.

17. ☑ **A.** NetBEUI is an example of a nonroutable protocol.

    ☒ **B, C,** and **D** are incorrect because they are routable protocols.

Gateways and Security Devices

18. ☑ **D.** A gateway can run at any layer of the OSI model, such as layer 4, 5, 6, or 7, depending on what it is translating. It is very popular in the networking world for layers 4, 5, 6, and 7 to be used, but be aware that the gateway could run at any layer.

    ☒ **A, B,** and **C** are incorrect because a gateway can run at any layer.

19. ☑ **C.** A gateway is responsible for converting data from one format to another to allow dissimilar networking environments to communicate.

    ☒ **A, B,** and **D** are incorrect. A router sends, or routes, information from one network to another without reformatting. A bridge and a switch are filtering devices that run at layer 2.

20. ☑ **D.** A firewall is used to block unauthorized traffic from entering the network.

    ☒ **A, B,** and **C** are incorrect because these devices do not block traffic. A bridge and a switch are filtering devices that run at layer 2, whereas a gateway translates data.

Other Networking Devices

21. ☑ **A.** An ISDN modem is used for digital communication over digital or conventional phone lines.

☒ **B, C,** and **D** are incorrect. A CSU/DSU is used to connect to a high-speed WAN link, such as a T1 or T3 link. A modem is used to connect systems over an analog link, and a network card is used to connect a system to the network over network media.

22. ☑ **C.** A modem is responsible for converting digital data to analog and analog data to digital so that digital data can travel over analog lines.

☒ **A, B,** and **D** are incorrect. An ISDN modem is used for digital communication over digital or conventional phone lines. A CSU/DSU is used to connect to a high-speed WAN link, such as a T1 or T3 link. A network card is used to connect to another system over network media.

23. ☑ **B.** There are two B-channels in a BRI connection. Each channel is 64 Kbps, so a BRI connection is 128 Kbps.

☒ **A, C,** and **D** are incorrect because a BRI connection does not use one, three, or four B-channels.

Chapter 4

TCP/IP Addressing

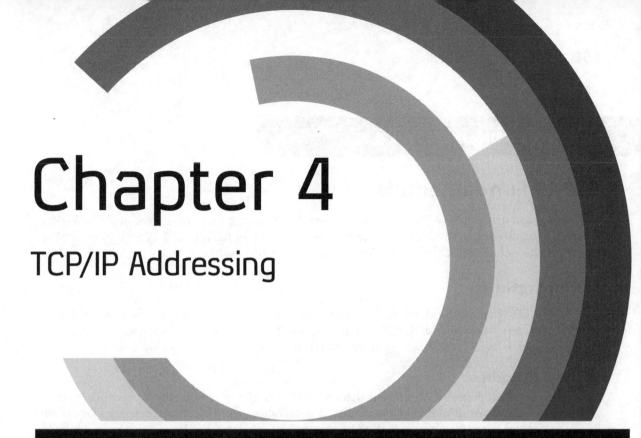

The most popular protocol suite in use today is Transmission Control Protocol/Internet Protocol (TCP/IP). The Internet and most company intranets currently use TCP/IP because of its popularity, flexibility, compatibility, and capability to perform in both small and large network implementations. TCP/IP can connect a diverse range of hosts, from mainframes, network servers, desktop computers, to handheld devices. The popularity of this protocol suite ensures you will encounter many TCP/IP-related questions throughout the Network+ exam. Although TCP/IP is the most commonly used protocol, it is not the easiest to configure, or even to understand. This chapter gives you an in-depth understanding of TCP/IP addressing and demonstrates how to configure TCP/IP on a system.

TCP/IP Fundamentals

Now that you have learned about some of the popular protocols that exist in the TCP/IP protocol suite, this section will introduce you to the configuration of TCP/IP by discussing the addressing scheme and rules for assigning an address to a system.

TCP/IP Settings

TCP/IP is a protocol that requires a little bit of knowledge to configure the systems properly. When you configure TCP/IP, you must know the settings for the IP address, subnet mask, and default gateway. Let's start with the IP address!

IP Address

The IP address is a 32-bit value that uniquely identifies the system on the network (or the Internet). An IP address looks similar in appearance to 192.168.1.15. There are four decimal values in an IP address separated by periods (.). Each decimal value is made up of 8 bits (1s and 0s), and there are four decimal values, so 8 bits times 4 equals the 32-bit address.

Since each of the decimal values is made up of 8 bits (for example, the 192), we refer to each of the decimal values as an octet. There are four octets in an IP address. It is very important to understand that the four octets in an IP address are divided into two parts—a network ID and a host ID. The subnet mask determines the number of bits that make up the network ID and the number of bits that make up the host ID. Let's see how this works.

Subnet Mask

When looking at a subnet mask, if there is a 255 in an octet, then the corresponding octet in the IP address is part of the network ID. For example, if I had an IP address of 192.168.1.15 and a subnet mask of 255.255.255.0, the first three octets would make up the network ID and the last octet would be the host ID. The network ID assigns a unique address to the network itself, while the host ID uniquely identifies the system on the network. Table 4-1 summarizes this example.

TABLE 4-1		Octet 1	Octet 2	Octet 3	Octet 4
Identifying the Network ID and Host ID Portions of an IP Address	IP address	192	168	1	15
	Subnet mask	255	255	255	0
	Address portion	N	N	N	H

TABLE 4-2		Octet 1	Octet 2	Octet 3	Octet 4
Identifying Two Systems on Different Networks Using the Subnet Masks	IP address 1	192	168	1	15
	Subnet mask	255	255	255	0
	IP address 2	192	198	45	10

You can see in Table 4-1 that the network ID (shown with an "N") is 192.168.1, and the host ID is the last octet with a value of 15. This means that this system is on the 192.168.1 network and any other system on the same network will have the same network ID.

To use a different example, if I had a subnet mask of 255.0.0.0, it would mean that the first octet of the IP address is used as the network ID portion, while the last three octets are the host ID portion of the IP address.

So what is the purpose of the subnet masks? Or better yet, why do we have a subnet mask that breaks the IP address into a network ID part and a host ID? The reason is so that when a system such as 192.168.1.15 with a subnet mask of 255.255.255.0 sends a piece of data to 192.198.45.10, the sending system first needs to determine whether the target computer exists on the same network or not. It does this by comparing the network IDs (Table 4-2); if the network IDs are the same, then both systems exist on the same network and one system can send to the other without the use of a router. If the systems exist on different networks, the data will need to be passed to the router so that the router can send the data to the other network.

Let's take a look at an exercise in which you will need to determine whether two systems are on the same network or not.

EXERCISE 4-1

Identifying Remote Systems

In this exercise, you will determine whether two systems exist on the same network or not by filling in the following table.

ComputerA (IP address)	ComputerA (Subnet mask)	ComputerB (IP address)	Same Network?
12.45.8.34	255.0.0.0	14.34.212.5	
131.107.4.78	255.255.0.0	131.108.45.112	
198.45.23.2	255.255.255.0	198.45.23.14	
26.45.78.5	255.0.0.0	28.45.78.15	
176.34.56.12	255.255.0.0	176.34.12.10	

FIGURE 4-1

Viewing your
TCP/IP settings

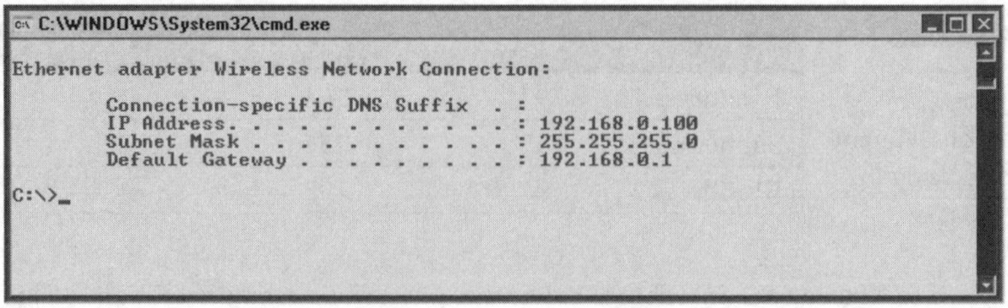

```
C:\WINDOWS\System32\cmd.exe                                       _ □ X

Ethernet adapter Wireless Network Connection:

        Connection-specific DNS Suffix  . :
        IP Address. . . . . . . . . . . : 192.168.0.100
        Subnet Mask . . . . . . . . . . : 255.255.255.0
        Default Gateway . . . . . . . . : 192.168.0.1

C:\>_
```

Default Gateway

When your system wants to send data to another system on the network, it looks at its own network ID and compares that to the destination system's IP address. If it appears that they both have the same network ID, the data is sent directly from your system to the destination system. If the two systems are on different networks, your system must pass the data to the router so that the router can send the data to the destination system's router.

The question now is how does your system know who the router is? The answer is "that is what the default gateway is." The default gateway is the IP address of the router that can send data from your network.

In order to communicate on the Internet, your system will need to be configured with an IP address, a subnet mask, and a default gateway. If you need to communicate only with other systems on your network, you will need only an IP address and a subnet mask.

To view your TCP/IP settings, you can go to a command prompt and type **ipconfig**—you should see output similar to that shown in Figure 4-1. You will learn more about TCP/IP-related commands later in this chapter and in Chapter 6.

CERTIFICATION OBJECTIVE 4.02

TCP/IP Addressing

This section will introduce you to the binary representation of an IP address and ensure that before you move on to the subnetting chapter (Chapter 8), you feel comfortable with converting binary values to decimal and address classes. The new Network+ exam expects you to be familiar with different numbering systems such as the binary system (0 or 1), decimal system (0 to 9), octal system (0 to 7), and hexadecimal system (0 to F). This chapter will focus on understanding the binary system and converting to decimal, while Chapter 5 will discuss the hexadecimal system and the octal system.

Understanding Binary

You know from the previous discussion that the IP address is a 32-bit address divided into four 8-bit blocks (called octets). The four octets are normally displayed as decimal values, but also have a binary representation that looks like

11000000 10101000 00000001 00001111

Notice that there are four sets of 8 bits (1 or 0), which make up the 32 bits (8×4 sets) of an IP address. Let's take a look at how you can determine the binary representation of an octet. The values of the 8 bits within the octet are shown in Table 4-3.

Looking at Table 4-3, you can see that the first bit in an octet (far right) has a decimal value of 1, the second bit has a decimal value of 2, the third bit has a decimal value of 4, and the values keep doubling with each additional bit. You can also see that the eighth bit has a decimal value of 128. The first bit is known as the least significant bit or low-order bit, while the eighth bit is known as the most significant bit or high-order bit.

Bit	8	7	6	5	4	3	2	1
Value	128	64	32	16	8	4	2	1

TABLE 4-3

Values Associated with Each Bit in an Octet

To calculate the binary value of an octet with a decimal number such as 192, you need to enable, or turn on, the bits that will add up to the number 192, as shown in Table 4-4.

Notice that the previous table has bit 8 and bit 7 turned on to give you a value of 128 + 64, which equals 192. The remaining bits will take an "off" state, which means they are not included in the calculation. A bit that has an on state takes a "1," and an off state takes a "0." So the combination of 8 bits to make the number 192 would be 11000000. Now that you know how to convert a decimal value to binary and a binary value to decimal, try out Exercise 4-2 and Exercise 4-3 before moving on to the section on address classes.

Bit	8	7	6	5	4	3	2	1
Value	128	64	32	16	8	4	2	1
State	On	On						

TABLE 4-4

Calculating the Decimal Value of 192 in Binary

EXERCISE 4-2

Converting Decimal to Binary

In this exercise, you will practice converting decimal values to binary values by filling out the following table.

Decimal	Binary
127	
131	
198	
224	
96	
192.168.1.100	
216.83.11.78	
202.14.45.0	

EXERCISE 4-3

Converting Binary to Decimal

In this exercise, you will practice converting binary values to decimal values by filling out the following table.

Binary	Decimal
10110101	
11000011	
10000111	
11111111	
10101011	
11000001.10000001.00001011.10100001	
00000111.10101001.00110101.10110101	
11000000.10100001.00000111.11111111	

Address Classes

Every IP address belongs to a distinct address class. The Internet community defined these classes to accommodate networks of various sizes. The class to which the IP address belongs initially determines the network ID and host ID portions of the address, along with the number of hosts that are supported on that network. The different class addresses are named class A, class B, class C, class D, and class E. This section details each class of addresses.

Class A Addresses

A class A address has a default subnet mask of 255.0.0.0, which means that the first octet is the network ID and the last three octets belong to the host ID portion of the address. Each octet can contain 256 possible values (0–255), so a class A address supports 16,777,216 hosts on the network (256 × 256 × 256). Actually, there are only 16,777,214 valid addresses to use on systems, because there are two addresses on each IP network you are not allowed to assign to systems because they are reserved. These are the addresses with all host bits set to 0s (the network ID) and all host bits set to 1s (the broadcast address). So with a class A address, you will not be able to assign n.0.0.0 or n.255.255.255 (where n is your network ID) to any hosts on the network.

You can always identify a class A address because the value of the first octet falls between the numbers 1 and 127. Although an address that starts with 127 is technically a class A address, you are not allowed to use any address that starts with 127 because it is reserved for the loopback address (more on the loopback address later). An example of a class A address is the IP address 12.56.87.34 because the first octet is 12, which falls in the range of 1–127.

Class B Addresses

Class B addresses have a default subnet mask of 255.255.0.0, which means that the first two octets are the network ID and the last two octets are the host ID portion of the address. This means that we can have 65,536 hosts (256 × 256) on the network. Oh, but wait! Don't forget to take off the two illegal addresses, so that gives us 65,534 addresses that can be assigned to hosts on the network.

Due to the number of hosts that are supported on a class B address, you usually find that a medium-sized company has a class B address. You can identify a class B address because the first octet starts with a number that falls between 128 and 191.

Class C Addresses

Class C addresses have a subnet mask of 255.255.255.0, which means that the first three octets are the network ID and the last octet is the host ID. Having only one octet as the host ID means that a class C address can support only 254 hosts (256 − 2) on the network.

You can identify a class C address because it has a value for the first octet that ranges between 192 and 223. For example, an IP address of 202.45.8.6 is a class C address because 202 falls between 192 and 223. You also know that this system has a subnet mask of 255.255.255.0 because it is a class C address.

exam

watch
Class C addresses have an IP address in which the value of the first octet is between 192 and 223. In addition, class C addresses have a default subnet mask of 255.255.255.0.

Class D Addresses

Class D addresses are used for special types of applications on the network known as multicasting applications. Multicasting applications send data to a number of systems at the same time by sending data to the multicast address, and anyone who has registered with that address will receive the data. A multicast address is what class D addresses are used for, so you will not be assigning them specifically to hosts on the network for normal network communication. Class D addresses have a value on the first octet that ranges from 224 to 239.

Class E Addresses

The funny thing about class E addresses is that they were designed for experimental purposes only, so you will never see a class E address on a network. Class E addresses have a first octet with a value that falls in the range of 240 to 247.

Now that you are familiar with the different address classes, take a look at Table 4-5, which summarizes them. Be sure to know them for the exam.

TABLE 4-5		First Octet Value	Subnet Mask	# of Hosts per Network
Reviewing Address Classes	Class A	1–127	255.0.0.0	16,777,214
	Class B	128–191	255.255.0.0	65,534
	Class C	192–223	255.255.255.0	254

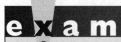

ⓦⓐⓣⓒⓗ **It's guaranteed that you will see questions on identifying class A, B, and C addresses on the exam. Be sure to know their default subnet masks as well.**

EXERCISE 4-4

Identifying Address Classes

In this exercise, you will practice identifying address classes for different IP addresses and their associated subnet masks. Fill in the following table.

IP Address	Subnet Mask	Address Class
27.56.89.234		
196.79.123.56		
130.49.34.23		
109.189.109.200		
189.90.23.100		
126.34.100.12		
14.198.120.100		

Loopback Address

You have learned that you are not allowed to have a host assigned an IP address that has a value of 127 in the first octet. This is because the class A address range of 127 has been reserved for the loopback address.

The loopback address is used to refer to the local system, also known as the localhost. If you want to verify that the TCP/IP software has initialized on the local system even though you may not have an IP address, you may ping the loopback address, which is typically referred to as 127.0.0.1.

o n t h e
ⓘ o b **You can test your own local system by typing** ping 127.0.0.1, ping localhost, **or** ping loopback **to verify that the TCP/IP protocol stack is functioning on your system.**

Private Addresses

Another type of address you need to be aware of is what is known as a private address. A *private* address is an address that can be assigned to a system but cannot be used for any kind of Internet connectivity. The private addresses are nonroutable addresses, so any system using them will not be able to route data across the Internet. The following three address ranges are private:

- 10.0.0.0–10.255.255.255
- 172.16.0.0–172.31.255.255
- 192.168.0.0–192.168.255.255

INSIDE THE EXAM

Illegal Addresses

A few IP addresses are illegal and cannot be assigned to hosts on the network. You might wonder why a class C address can have only 254 hosts and not 256, as would seem more likely, since an 8-bit number can have 256 possible values. The reason for this seeming discrepancy is that two of the addresses are lost from the available host pool. The first is an address that has all bits set to 0s in the host ID, which signifies the network ID of the network. The second is an address that has all bits set to 1s in the host ID, which signifies the broadcast address for the network. So, for example, in the class C network 200.158.157.*x*, the addresses 200.158.157.0 (the network ID) and 200.158.157.255 (the broadcast address) are not available to hosts, reducing the available number of hosts from 256 to 254.

Another illegal address is any system that has the first octet of 127; remember that this is reserved as the loopback address and you will

not be able to assign the address to any host. The following summarizes illegal addresses:

- **Any address starting with 127**   An IP address that starts with 127 is reserved for the loopback address and cannot be assigned to a system. An example of this illegal address is 127.50.10.23.

- **All host bits set to 0**   You are not allowed to assign a system an IP address that has all of the bits in the host ID portion set to 0 because this is the network ID. An example of this illegal address is 131.107.0.0.

- **All host bits set to 1**   You are not allowed to assign a system an IP address that has all the host bits set to 1 because this corresponds to the broadcast address of the network. An example of this type of illegal address is 131.107.255.255.

- **A duplicate address**   You are not allowed to assign a system an address that another system is using because this results in a duplicate IP address error.

Not being able to route data across the Internet when using these addresses will not pose a problem, because realistically, you will have these private addresses sitting behind a Network Address Translation (NAT) server that will translate the private address to a public address that can be routed on the Internet. For more information on NAT, refer to Chapter 5.

EXERCISE 4-5

Understanding Valid Addresses

In this exercise, you will practice identifying valid addresses by recording whether each of the following addresses is valid. A valid address is an address that can be assigned to a system on the network. If an address is invalid, you must specify why.

Address	Valid?
10.0.40.10	
127.54.67.89	
131.107.34.0	
45.12.0.0	
216.83.11.255	
63.256.4.78	
200.67.34.0	
131.107.23.255	

Addressing Schemes

When sending data on the network, there are different ways that the data can be sent to the destination. The data can be sent to a unicast address, a broadcast address, or a multicast address. The following outlines the difference between unicast, broadcast, and multicast:

- **Unicast** Sends information to one system. With the IP protocol, this is accomplished by sending data to the IP address of the intended destination system.
- **Broadcast** Sends information to all systems on the network. Data that is destined for all systems is sent by using the broadcast address for the network. An example of a broadcast address for a network is 192.168.2.255. The broadcast address is determined by setting all host bits to 1 and then converting the octet to a decimal number.

■ **Multicast** Sends information to a selected group of systems. Typically, this is accomplished by having the systems subscribe to a multicast address. Any data that is sent to the multicast address is then received by all systems subscribed to the address. Most multicast addresses start with 224.*x.y.z* and are considered class D addresses.

TCP/IP Ports

An application or process uses a TCP/IP port as an identifier for that application running on a system. When you send data from one computer to another, you send data to the port used by that application. For example, when you type the IP address of a website in your web browser, the web browser connects to the web server (or web application) running at that system by sending data to port 80 (shown in Figure 4-2). Port 80 is the default port of a web server. When the web server answers your request by sending the webpage to your browser, the browser is running on a particular port as well and the web server sends the page to the port of the web browser.

Server applications typically use low port numbers that fall under 1024, whereas client applications usually run on ports over 1024. There are three types of ports:

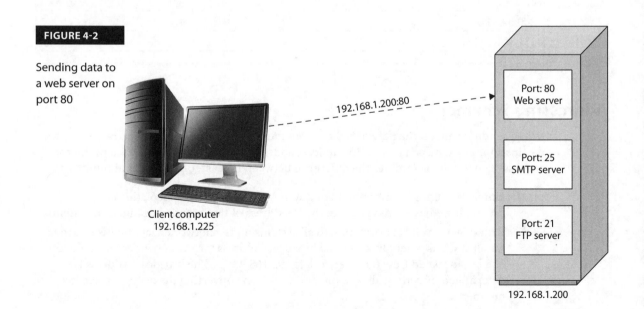

FIGURE 4-2

Sending data to a web server on port 80

192.168.1.200:80

Client computer
192.168.1.225

Port: 80
Web server

Port: 25
SMTP server

Port: 21
FTP server

192.168.1.200

■ **Well-known ports** Port numbers that are used by servers are known as *well-known* ports. Well-known port numbers range from 0 to 1023.

■ **Registered ports** These are ports assigned to certain applications or protocols. Registered ports range from 1024 to 49151.

■ **Dynamic ports** Dynamic ports are used by applications temporarily and range from 49152 to 65535. They are called dynamic ports because many times, the port is selected at runtime by the application and is different each time the program runs. For example, when you start Internet Explorer, it may use a different port number each time the program is started, but a web server uses the same port each time (port 80).

Table 4-6 is a list of well-known port numbers that are used by different types of applications or protocols. Be sure to know these for the Network+ exam.

TABLE 4-6 Ports Used by Popular Internet Applications

Port Number	Process	Description
20	FTP-DATA	File Transfer Protocol—used to transfer data from one machine to another
21	FTP	File Transfer Protocol—used for control messages of the FTP session
22	SSH	Secure Shell
23	TELNET	Telnet—used to create a terminal session
25	SMTP	Simple Mail Transfer Protocol—used to send e-mail across the Internet
53	DNS	Domain Name System—used to query DNS servers for the IP address of a remote system
67,68	DHCP	Used by Domain Host Configuration Protocol (DHCP) clients and servers to automatically configure clients
69	TFTP	Trivial File Transfer Protocol
80	HTTP	Hypertext Transfer Protocol—used to deliver webpages from a web server to the web client
110	POP3	Post Office Protocol, version 3—a protocol for reading e-mail over the Internet
119	NNTP	Network News Transfer Protocol—used to read news articles from a news server
123	NTP	Network Time Protocol—used to synchronize the time on systems

(Continued)

TABLE 4-6   Ports Used by Popular Internet Applications (*continued*)

Port Number	Process	Description
137–139	NetBIOS	Used by Windows systems for NetBIOS sessions
143	IMAP4	Internet Message Application Protocol, version 4—another Internet protocol for reading e-mail
443	HTTPS	Secure Hypertext Transfer Protocol—used to encrypt web traffic between a client and a server
5060/5061	SIP	Session Initiation Protocol—used to set up a Voice over IP (VoIP) call
2427/2727	MGCP	Media Gateway Control Protocol—a VoIP protocol used for controlling media gateways
5004/5005	RTP	Real-time Transport Protocol—used to send voice data between phones with VoIP communication
1720	H.323	An older protocol used to deliver audio and video data over a computer network
3389	RDP	Remote Desktop Protocol—used to remotely connect to and administer a system
445	SMB	Server Message Blocks—the Microsoft file-sharing protocol

EXERCISE 4-6

Viewing TCP/IP Port Values

In this exercise, you will look back to the packet capture that you viewed in Chapter 2 for the analysis of web traffic and identify the ports that were used by both the web browser (sending system) and the web server (the receiving system).

1. Start Network Monitor.
2. Once Network Monitor has started, open the HTTPTraffic.cap capture file from the LabFiles\PacketCaptures folder.
3. Double-click the frame in the packet capture that is posting form data to a web server (frame 16) to show the details of that packet.

4. In the Frame Details panel (bottom of screen), expand the TCP section by clicking the + sign beside it (as shown in the accompanying illustration).

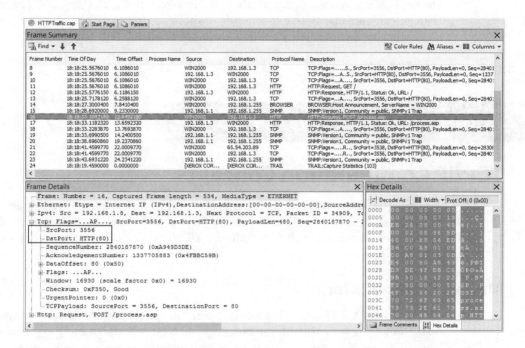

5. Notice that the source port and the destination port are shown. Record the following information in the spaces provided:

Source Port: _____

Destination Port: _____

6. You should have the following answers recorded in the preceding spaces:

Source Port: **3556**

Destination Port: **80**

7. Keep in mind that the destination port is port 80, which is the default port of a web server. You have found that the source port is 3556, which is a value above 1024. You have learned that a client application usually uses a value above 1024, so this is traffic of a web browser sending data to a web server.

8. Close Network Monitor and don't save any information if asked.

Another term that you will hear a lot is socket. A *socket* is the end point of communication and is made up of three components: the IP address of the system, the port number of the application, and the protocol that is being used—either TCP or UDP. The socket is how data is sent from one system to another, or more accurately, from one application to another. The following formula defines what a socket is:

```
Socket = IP address + Port number + Protocol (TCP or UDP)
```

CERTIFICATION OBJECTIVE 4.03

TCP/IP Configuration Concepts

You have learned what an IP address, a subnet mask, and a default gateway are used for, and you have learned all about the binary form of addressing, including class addresses. In this section, you will learn to configure TCP/IP on a client system both manually and as a DHCP client.

Manual Configuration

To configure TCP/IP on a Windows 8 client, you will go to the charm list (move the mouse to the bottom-right corner of the task bar) and choose Settings and then choose Control Panel. Choose Network And Internet as a category and then Network And Sharing Center.

Choose the Change Adapter Settings option on the left and then right-click your Ethernet connection and choose Properties. Select the Internet Protocol Version 4 (TCP/IPv4) and then choose Properties (shown in Figure 4-3).

To configure your system with a specific address, select Use The Following IP Address and then type the IP address, the subnet mask, and the default gateway; then choose OK. Once you have finished configuring TCP/IP, you will be able to communicate with network resources using the newly configured system.

Configuring a system manually is not the best approach to take on a network for a number of reasons:

- **Workload** The amount of work involved in manually configuring each system on the network is too much for any network administrator.
- **Typos** The potential for human error is great when inputting the parameters on multiple systems simply due to the fact that it is such a laborious task. It is also very easy to assign a duplicate address on the network, which would result in an error.

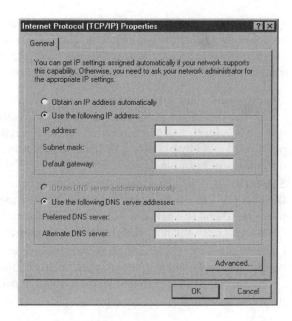

FIGURE 4-3

Changing TCP/IP
settings

- **Change management**   It is very hard to implement major changes to your IP
  infrastructure when you are manually configuring systems. For example, a change to
  a router address would require a lot of time to update the default gateway entry on
  the clients.

Dynamic Host Configuration Protocol (DHCP)

Configuring IP addressing on a large TCP/IP-based network can be a nightmare, especially
if machines are moved from one network to another frequently. DHCP can help with the
workload of configuring systems on a network by assigning addresses to systems on boot-up
automatically.

The process of dynamically assigning IP addresses is managed via a DHCP server. The
DHCP server is configured with a set of usable IP addresses, called a *scope*. The scope can
also include the subnet mask, IP addresses of the default gateway, DNS servers, Windows
Internet Naming Service (WINS) servers, and other necessary addresses. When a PC
comes online and is set up to use a DHCP server, it requests an IP address by transmitting a
broadcast request packet, looking for any DHCP servers on the network (known as DHCP
Discovery). The DHCP server responds with an offer containing an IP address that the
client can lease (known as the DHCP Offer). The client then accepts the offer by sending
a request message for that address from the DHCP server (known as the DHCP Request),

and then the server responds with an acknowledgment to the client that it has that address and additional settings for the lease time (known as the DHCP ACK). The DHCP server marks the IP address in its database as being in use so that it is not assigned again. When configuring the DHCP server, you will need to configure a scope with the following settings:

- ■ **IP addresses**   The DHCP server issues an IP address to each DHCP client system on the network. Each system connected to a TCP/IP-based network is identified by a unique IP address. As you learned in this chapter, the IP address consists of four 8-bit octets separated by periods. The IP address is normally shown in dotted-decimal notation—for example, 192.10.24.62.

- ■ **Subnet mask**   The IP address actually consists of two parts: the network ID and the host ID. The subnet mask is used to identify the part of the IP address that is the network ID and the part that is the host ID. Subnet masks assign 1s to the network ID bits and 0s to the host ID bits of the IP address.

- ■ **Default gateway**   A default gateway is required when the client system needs to communicate outside its own subnet. Normally, the default gateway is a router connected to the local subnet, which enables IP packets to be passed to other network segments.

Video

EXERCISE 4-7

Configuring TCP/IP to Use DHCP

In this exercise, you will learn how to configure TCP/IP on your Windows client to use DHCP.

1. Go to your Windows 8 system.
2. Go to the charm list (move the mouse to the bottom-right corner of task bar) and choose Settings.
3. Choose Control Panel.
4. Choose Network And Internet as a category.
5. Choose Network And Sharing Center.
6. Choose the Change Adapter Settings option on the left.
7. Right-click your Ethernet connection and choose Properties.
8. Select the Internet Protocol Version 4 (TCP/IPv4) and then choose Properties.
9. The TCP/IP Properties dialog box appears. To configure your system as a DHCP client, choose the Obtain An IP Address Automatically setting.
10. Click OK and close all windows.

Scope Options

A DHCP scope is the range of IP addresses and additional options that the DHCP server will hand out to the DHCP clients on the network. As previously mentioned, the IP address and subnet mask are required items that the DHCP scope must include. Another requirement in the scope is the lease duration. It specifies how long a DHCP client can use an IP address before it must renew it with the DHCP server. This duration can be set for an unlimited time period or for a predetermined time period. You have the option of configuring a scope to reserve a specific IP address for a DHCP client or even for a system on the network that is not DHCP enabled.

on the Job

Options within the DHCP scope can be configured for settings such as the DNS server, WINS server, router address, and domain name.

Servers

Several versions of Windows server products support DHCP server capabilities, including Windows Server 2008 and Windows Server 2012. The main factor to consider if you have multiple subnets is that your routers must comply with RFC 1542 so that a DHCP server can receive the broadcast message from a client. It is wise to keep in mind that if your DHCP server goes down and your DHCP clients cannot renew their lease, the clients will most likely not be able to access network resources.

One of the benefits of using multiple DHCP servers is redundancy. Redundancy can prevent your network from going down. If you decide to use multiple DHCP servers, you should place them on different subnets to achieve a higher degree of fault tolerance in case one of the subnets becomes unavailable. You can manage multiple servers on different subnets with the DHCP Console, the graphical utility used to maintain and configure DHCP servers in Windows.

on the Job

In most companies, two DHCP servers provide fault tolerance for IP addressing if one server fails or must be taken offline for maintenance. Each DHCP server has at least half of the available addresses in an active scope. The number of addresses on each DHCP server should be more than enough to provide addresses for all clients.

Supported Clients

The following operating systems can perform as DHCP clients on your network:

- Windows clients, such as Windows 7 and Windows 8
- Windows servers, such as Windows Server 2008 R2 or Windows Server 2012 (servers are typically assigned a static address though)

- Older Microsoft clients, such as Windows XP
- Non-Microsoft operating systems such as Linux

Of course, DHCP clients are not limited to Microsoft operating systems. Any system that conforms to RFC 1541 can be a DHCP client. For example, you can have a UNIX, Linux, or Mac OS client on the network that obtains an address from your DHCP server as well.

APIPA

Windows clients support a feature known as Automatic Private IP Addressing (APIPA), which, when a Windows client boots up and cannot contact a DHCP server, will configure itself automatically with a 169.254.*x*.*y* address. If there is something wrong with the DHCP server and none of the systems on the network can obtain an address, the clients will all assign themselves an address within the 169.254 address range and then be able to communicate with one another.

APIPA does not assign a default gateway, so you will be unable to access resources on a remote network and the Internet—but you can still communicate with systems on your network. When troubleshooting to find out why a machine cannot communicate on the network, watch for systems that have the 169.254.*x*.*y* address range because it means they could not find a DHCP server.

Boot Protocol

The Boot Protocol, known as BOOTP, is used by diskless workstations. When a diskless workstation boots, it does so using an Electrically Erasable Programmable Read-Only Memory (EEPROM) on the network card, which allows it to load basic drivers and connect to the network by obtaining an IP address automatically.

A BOOTP server, similar to a DHCP server, assigns the diskless workstation an address to allow it to participate on the network. You will see the term BOOTP a lot when it comes to DHCP and routers; a BOOTP-enabled router will allow the DHCP broadcast to cross the router so that a DHCP server can be found on the other side of the network.

The BOOTP server is usually the same as the DHCP server; the two are considered one and the same. Routers need to be BOOTP compatible to allow the DHCP requests to pass through the router to another segment; otherwise, you will require a DHCP server per network segment.

Domain Name System

One service that is used throughout networks and the Internet is the Domain Name System (DNS). Most users on the network connect to resources by using a friendly name, such as

FIGURE 4-4

Finding an IP
address using DNS

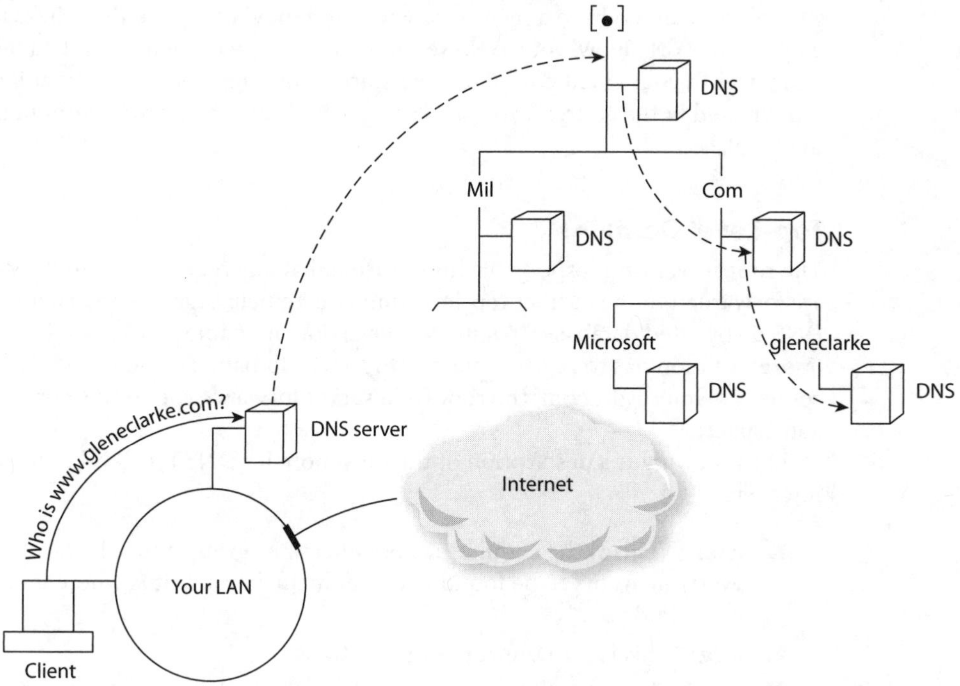

www.gleneclarke.com—this style of name, known as a fully qualified domain name (FQDN),
must be converted to an IP address before communication can occur. DNS is our solution to
converting FQDNs to IP addresses.

Let's walk through an example of a name being resolved. You are sitting in your office
on your network, and you try to connect to www.gleneclarke.com, which means that your
client computer will send a query to the DNS server (shown in Figure 4-4) in your office
asking, "Do you have an IP address for www.gleneclarke.com?" Your DNS server does not
know who www.gleneclarke.com is, so it will then go out and query the DNS root servers
and ask them if they have an IP address for www.gleneclarke.com. There are only about
13 DNS root servers on the Internet; they don't actually hold records for individual hosts,
but they do forward the request to the name servers at the next level down, which are the
.com name servers. DNS will find the IP address of the name requested by reading it from
right to left—in this case, .com is the far-right name part, so the request is forwarded to the
.com name servers. The .com name servers look at the request and say, "No, we don't have
a clue who www.gleneclarke.com is, but why don't you check out the gleneclarke.com name
servers—they might know."

Your DNS server then queries the name servers for gleneclarke.com and asks them,
"Do you have an IP address for www.gleneclarke.com?" In this case, the DNS servers for

gleneclarke.com do have a record for www, and they return the IP address to the DNS on your network. Now, your DNS server is smart—it will cache that data before sending an answer to your client computer that started the whole process so that if anyone else is interested in the address, your DNS server will have the answer without going out on the Web!

Top-Level Domains

The root servers are responsible for ensuring that any requests for an Internet resource are forwarded to the correct top-level domain. To help organize Internet resources in the DNS distributed database, specific top-level domain names are created, and a company or organization has to register under a top-level domain. For example, if you are trying to connect to microsoft.com, the root DNS server forwards you to the .com top-level domain namespace.

The following is a description of the most popular DNS top-level domains found on the Internet:

- **.com** This is the commercial organizations group and is by far the largest. Almost everyone wants to be found in this domain, because it is where most customers will try to find you.
- **.org** This is for nonprofit organizations.
- **.net** This is for networking organizations, such as island.net and nfs.net, as well as for Internet service providers, such as netzero.net.
- **.mil** This is for military organizations, such as army.mil and navy.mil.
- **.gov** This is for U.S. government offices only.
- **.edu** This is for educational organizations.

Country Domain Names

With only six top-level domain names and the requirement that all organizations register under one of those top levels if they want an Internet name, this soon became a problem because there were so many names to be registered and so few choices on the top levels. Eventually, top-level names were created for country domains; therefore, if you resided in a certain country, you could register under that country domain so that your customers could find you easily. Here are a few of the most common country domain names:

- **.ca** Canada
- **.ie** Ireland
- **.uk** United Kingdom
- **.us** United States

FIGURE 4-5

Managing a DNS server in Windows

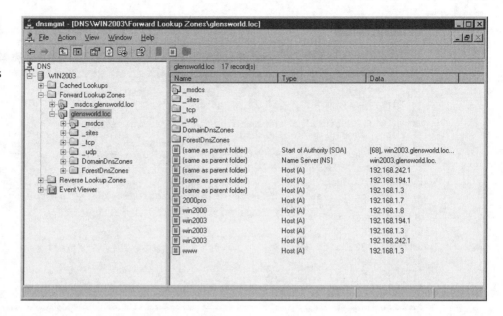

DNS Files

Most DNS servers maintain their DNS data in a number of files that exist on the hard disk of the server. In the old days, you managed the records by updating these text files, but today, most DNS server environments support a graphic tool like the one shown in Figure 4-5 to create the records for your DNS server. When you create the records graphically, the DNS files are updated. Windows servers store their DNS files in %systemroot%\system32\DNS.

For Windows servers running Active Directory, the DNS database can be integrated with Active Directory, which allows you to have the DNS data replicated with Active Directory and also allows the zone data to be modified in multiple locations, given that Active Directory is a multimaster environment. If the DNS database is integrated with Active Directory, it will not be located in the %systemroot%\system32\DNS directory, but will be stored within the Active Directory database.

Hosts File

Before DNS became a popular solution to hostname resolution, there was a more manual method of creating and modifying a file on the local hard disk of every system. This file would need to be updated on every system if a change was made to a server's IP address and you wanted the client applications to be aware of the change. This file, known as the hosts file, was located on each client system.

FIGURE 4-6   Looking at the hosts file on a Windows system

FIGURE 4-6   Looking at the hosts file on a Windows system

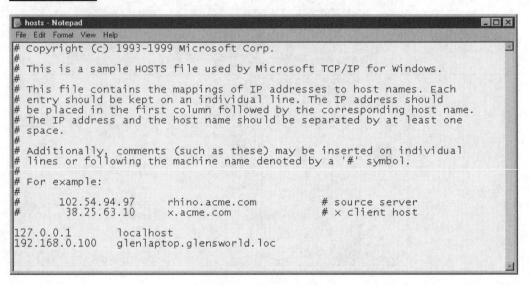

```
# Copyright (c) 1993-1999 Microsoft Corp.
#
# This is a sample HOSTS file used by Microsoft TCP/IP for Windows.
#
# This file contains the mappings of IP addresses to host names. Each
# entry should be kept on an individual line. The IP address should
# be placed in the first column followed by the corresponding host name.
# The IP address and the host name should be separated by at least one
# space.
#
# Additionally, comments (such as these) may be inserted on individual
# lines or following the machine name denoted by a '#' symbol.
#
# For example:
#
#      102.54.94.97     rhino.acme.com          # source server
#       38.25.63.10     x.acme.com              # x client host

127.0.0.1        localhost
192.168.0.100    glenlaptop.glensworld.loc
```

Before DNS servers became a standard, network administrators used to create a text file known as the hosts file, which was used to resolve the FQDN to matching IP addresses. This text file was stored locally on each system; in the Windows world, it is stored in the %systemroot%\system32\drivers\etc folder and contains two columns—one for the IP address and the other for the FQDN. Figure 4-6 displays the contents of a hosts file.

Windows Internet Naming Service

The Windows Internet Naming Service (WINS) provides name resolution for NetBIOS names to matching IP addresses and is popular on large Microsoft networks. WINS is similar to DNS, but contains a database of different-style names—NetBIOS names instead of fully qualified domain names.

When a WINS client boots up, it registers its names within the WINS database and then queries that server any time it needs to have a computer name resolved to a matching IP address. When the WINS client shuts down, it also deregisters its names from the WINS database so that another system can register the names while it is offline.

Before WINS, the LMHOSTS file was used to assist with remote NetBIOS name resolution. The LMHOSTS file is a static file that maps NetBIOS names to IP addresses. This is similar to the hosts file in functionality; the only difference is that the hosts file is used for mapping hostnames to IP addresses. To configure a client for DNS, follow the steps in Exercise 4-8.

EXERCISE 4-8

Configuring a Client for DNS

In this exercise, you will learn how to configure TCP/IP on your Windows client to use a DNS server for name resolution.

1. Go to your Windows 8 system.
2. Go to the charm list (move the mouse to the bottom-right corner of the task bar) and choose Settings.
3. Choose Control Panel.
4. Choose Network And Internet as a category.
5. Choose Network And Sharing Center.
6. Choose the Change Adapter Settings option on the left.
7. Right-click your Ethernet connection and choose Properties.
8. Select the Internet Protocol Version 4 (TCP/IPv4) and then choose Properties.
9. The TCP/IP Properties dialog box appears. To configure your system to use a specific DNS server, choose the Use The Following DNS Server Addresses setting.
10. In the Preferred DNS Server setting, type the IP address of the DNS server, for example, 10.0.0.1.
11. Click OK and close all windows.

Table 4-7 outlines the differences between WINS and DNS.

Name resolution is a very important part of troubleshooting networking problems—chances are a large percentage of communication problems come from name resolution. To help people troubleshoot name resolution in real life and on the Network+ exam, I usually draw for them Figure 4-8, which is a flow chart of the types of names and the technologies used

TABLE 4-7   Identifying Differences Between DNS and WINS

Feature	DNS	WINS
Purpose	Converts FQDNs to IP addresses	Converts NetBIOS names to IP addresses
Names	Hierarchical 255-character names	Flat 15-character names
Dynamic Registration	Yes, with dynamic DNS supported	Yes
Name Types	FQDN (ex: www.gleneclarke.com)	NetBIOS name (ex: COMPUTERA)

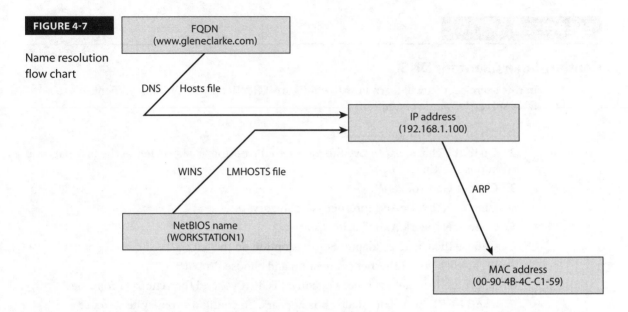

FIGURE 4-7

Name resolution
flow chart

to resolve them. For example, looking at Figure 4-7, you can see that Address Resolution Protocol (ARP) is used to convert IP addresses to Media Access Control (MAC) addresses, whereas DNS is used to convert the FQDN to the IP address—which is then converted to the MAC address by ARP.

Configuring a Linux Machine for TCP/IP

We have spent most of the examples talking about Windows operating systems and how to configure TCP/IP on Windows. Let's take some time now and focus on Linux, one of the biggest competitors of Microsoft Windows. The version of Linux that I have installed for this book is Red Hat Linux 8. If you have Red Hat Linux 9, you should be able to follow the same steps because there are not a lot of changes in this area between the two versions.

To download a free version of the most current version of Linux, visit www.linux.org.

To change your TCP/IP settings in Linux, you will need to log on to the computer with root-level access and then click the Red Hat button in the bottom-left corner of the screen. When the menu appears, select System Settings | Network, as shown in Figure 4-8.

Once the Network Configuration dialog box appears, click the Edit button to change the IP address that is assigned to the Ethernet device in the Linux machine. To statically assign an IP address, select the Statically Set IP Addresses option, as shown in Figure 4-9.

FIGURE 4-8

Selecting the network settings from the Red Hat menu

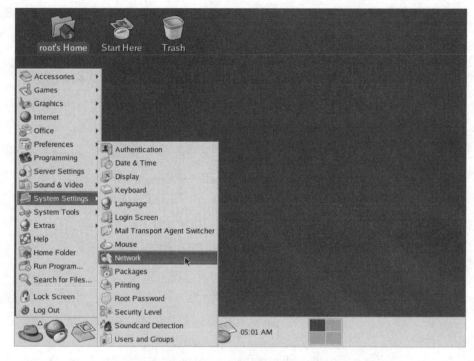

FIGURE 4-9

Configuring a Linux machine with a static IP address

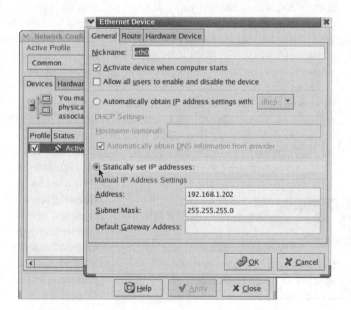

FIGURE 4-10

Configuring a Linux
machine as a DHCP client

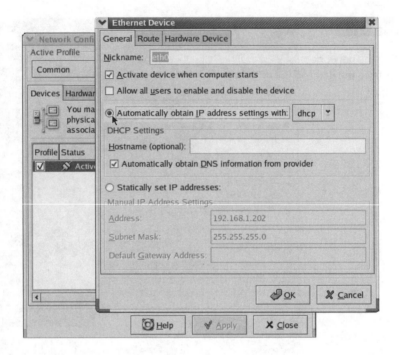

If you wish to configure the Linux machine as a DHCP client so that its address information
is obtained automatically, you will need to bring the Network Configuration dialog box up
again, select the Automatically Obtain IP Address Settings With option, and ensure that
DHCP is selected (as shown in Figure 4-10). You will most likely want to ensure that the
Automatically Obtain DNS Information From Provider option is selected too. This setting
allows you to configure Linux to obtain the address of the DNS server from DHCP as well.

Once you have configured TCP/IP on the Linux system, you may want to verify the settings
by viewing your IP address information. You will look at TCP/IP utilities in Chapter 6, but to
make our Linux walkthrough complete, let's take a look at how to view the TCP/IP settings
in Linux. To view your IP address information in Linux, you need to bring up a command
prompt, known as a terminal session. To start a terminal session, right-click the desktop in
Linux and choose New Terminal, as shown in Figure 4-11.

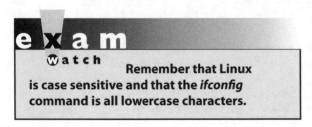

Once the new terminal starts up, you can type
ifconfig (case sensitive) to view your TCP/IP
settings, or you can use the Ping utility to test
connectivity to another system. Figure 4-12
demonstrates ifconfig being used to view the
TCP/IP settings of the network interface. You
may type **exit** at the prompt to exit out of the
terminal.

**Remember that Linux
is case sensitive and that the *ifconfig*
command is all lowercase characters.**

FIGURE 4-11

Starting a terminal
session in Linux

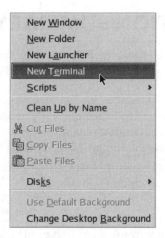

FIGURE 4-12   Viewing your TCP/IP settings with ifconfig in Linux

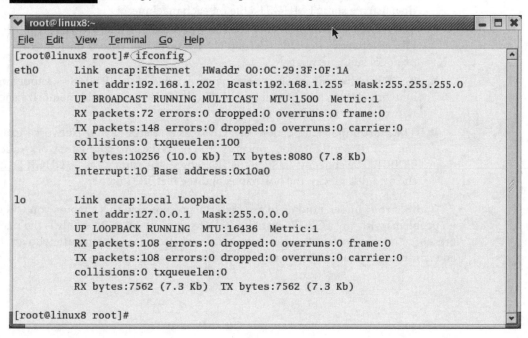

CERTIFICATION SUMMARY

In this chapter you learned about the fundamentals of TCP/IP and what makes this protocol so common in today's networking market. The following list summarizes what you learned:

- The IP address and subnet mask are the most important configuration settings and must be specified correctly in order to communicate on the TCP/IP-based network. Next in importance is the default gateway, which specifies where to route packets if you are communicating outside the local network.

- The Dynamic Host Configuration Protocol (DHCP) automatically configures a workstation with the correct TCP/IP settings, relieving you of the burden of manually configuring every workstation.

- The Domain Name System (DNS) is essential for Internet-based machines and company intranets that use DNS for hostname resolution. You learned about the hostname, domain name, resolution, and Internet domain name server hierarchies.

- The Windows Internet Naming Service (WINS), which ironically has little to do with the Internet, enables workstations to resolve NetBIOS names to IP addresses rather than using a static LMHOSTS file on each machine.

- TCP/IP is a suite of protocols, the most popular of which are TCP, UDP, IP, and ARP. (Your Network+ exam will definitely have several questions on some of these TCP/IP protocol suite members.)

- TCP/IP addressing involves a strong knowledge of the IP address, subnet mask, network classes, and special reserved addresses. (You should memorize each network class for the exam.)

- The most important portions of TCP/IP as it relates to your Network+ exam are the TCP/IP configuration concepts. You need these to configure workstations with TCP/IP. The concepts include the IP address, the subnet mask, DHCP, DNS, WINS, the default gateway, the hostname, and the NetBIOS name.

With a strong understanding of the material presented in this chapter, you will have no problems with any TCP/IP-related questions on your exam. Not only is the material presented here important for the exam, but it will also be important after you ace the exam and continue on to a career as a networking professional.

✓ TWO-MINUTE DRILL

TCP/IP Fundamentals

❑ TCP/IP addresses are 32-bit addresses.

❑ The IP address is a unique value assigned to the system that identifies the system on the network.

❑ The subnet mask is used to determine the network ID portion of an IP address.

❑ The network ID is used to determine whether the destination system exists on the same network or not. If the two systems have the same network ID, then they are on the same network.

❑ The host ID identifies the system within the network.

❑ The default gateway refers to the IP address of the router and is used to send data from the local network.

TCP/IP Addressing

❑ Class A addresses have a first octet ranging from 0 to 127 and have a default subnet mask of 255.0.0.0.

❑ Class B addresses have a first octet ranging from 128 to 191 and have a default subnet mask of 255.255.0.0.

❑ Class C addresses have a first octet ranging from 192 to 223 and have a default subnet mask of 255.255.255.0.

❑ Class D addresses are used for multicasting.

❑ An application or process uses a TCP/IP port to communicate between client and server computers.

❑ The most popular, and therefore most likely, exam choices to remember are the FTP ports (20 and 21), SMTP port (25), HTTP port (80), and HTTPS port (443).

TCP/IP Configuration Concepts

❑ You have two options for configuring a workstation: You can configure it manually, or you can use a DHCP server.

❑ DHCP is responsible for assigning IP addresses to clients automatically and reduces the network administration load.

❑ DNS is used to resolve FQDNs (www.gleneclarke.com) to IP addresses.

❑ WINS is used to convert NetBIOS names (computer names) to IP addresses.

❑ Hosts is a text file on the client that performs the same role as DNS, but is configured on each system manually.

❑ LMHOSTS is a text file on the client that performs the same role as WINS, but is configured on each system manually.

SELF TEST

The following questions will help you measure your understanding of the material presented in this chapter. Read all the choices carefully because there might be more than one correct answer. Choose all correct answers for each question.

TCP/IP Fundamentals

1. Which TCP/IP setting is not required if you want to communicate on the LAN only?
   A. IP address
   B. Subnet mask
   C. Default gateway
   D. DNS

2. How many bits in an IP address?
   A. 8 bits
   B. 32 bits
   C. 48 bits
   D. 96 bits

3. How many octets in an IP address?
   A. 1
   B. 2
   C. 3
   D. 4

4. A computer with a subnet mask of 255.255.255.0 has how many octets for the network ID?
   A. 1
   B. 2
   C. 3
   D. 4

5. A computer with the IP address of 134.67.89.12 and a subnet mask of 255.255.0.0 is on the same network with which of the following systems?
   A. 134.76.89.11
   B. 134.67.112.23
   C. 13.4.67.34
   D. 109.67.45.10

TCP/IP Addressing

6. Which network address class supports 65,534 hosts?
   A. Class A
   B. Class B
   C. Class C
   D. Class D

7. What is the default subnet mask for a class C network?
   A. 255.0.0.0
   B. 225.225.0.0
   C. 255.255.255.0
   D. 225.255.255.255

8. Which address is reserved for internal loopback functions?
   A. 0.0.0.0
   B. 1.0.0.1
   C. 121.0.0.1
   D. 127.0.0.1

9. What is the well-known port number for the HTTP service?
   A. 20
   B. 21
   C. 80
   D. 25

10. Which of the following addresses is a private IP address? (Select all that apply.)
    A. 10.0.0.34
    B. 191.167.34.5
    C. 172.16.7.99
    D. 12.108.56.7

11. Which port is used by SMTP?
    A. 23
    B. 25
    C. 443
    D. 110

12. What is the subnet mask for 171.103.2.30?
    A. 255.0.0.0
    B. 255.255.0.0
    C. 255.255.255.0
    D. 255.255.255.255

TCP/IP Configuration Concepts

13. Which network service is responsible for assigning IP addresses to systems on the network when they boot up?
    A. DNS
    B. WINS
    C. DHCP
    D. Server

14. Which network service is responsible for resolving (or converting) FQDNs to IP addresses?
    A. DNS
    B. WINS
    C. DHCP
    D. Server

15. Bob is having trouble pinging addresses by their FQDN, but he can seem to ping them by their IP address. What should you do to help Bob?
    A. Verify Bob's WINS setting in TCP/IP.
    B. Verify Bob's DNS setting in TCP/IP.
    C. Make sure that the system Bob is trying to connect to is in the LMHOSTS file.
    D. Make sure that the system Bob is trying to connect to is on the network.

Performance-Based Question Review: See the performance-based question sample from the author included with the accompanying media.

A SELF TEST ANSWERS

TCP/IP Fundamentals

1. ☑ **C.** If you want to communicate with systems on the local network, you will not need to configure a default gateway.
   ☒ **A, B,** and **D** are incorrect. An IP address and a subnet mask are always needed when configuring TCP/IP. DNS is needed only if you want to communicate by FQDN, not by IP address.

2. ☑ **B.** An IP address is made up of four 8-bit octets, which gives a total of 32 bits.
   ☒ **A, C,** and **D** are incorrect because an IP address is made up of 32 bits.

3. ☑ **D.** An IP address is made up of four 8-bit octets.
   ☒ **A, B,** and **C** are incorrect because an IP address is made up of four octets.

4. ☑ **C.** A subnet mask of 255.255.255.0 means that the first three octets are part of the network ID and the last octet is the host ID portion of the address.
   ☒ **A, B,** and **D** are incorrect because a subnet mask of 255.255.255.0 has three octets that map to the network ID.

5. ☑ **B.** Because the subnet mask is 255.255.0.0, the network ID of the IP address is 134.67.*x.y*—which means that anyone else with the same first two octets is on the same network.
   ☒ **A, C,** and **D** are incorrect because they have different network IDs.

TCP/IP Addressing

6. ☑ **B.** Class B networks support 65,534 hosts because the last two octets are the host ID and each octet supports 256 possible values. 256 × 256 = 65,536—but don't forget there are two addresses that are unusable (the network ID and the broadcast address).
   ☒ **A, C,** and **D** are incorrect. Class A addresses support 16,777,214 hosts, whereas class C addresses support 254 hosts on the network. Class D addresses are used for multicast and not used for unicast communication.

7. ☑ **C.** The default subnet mask of a class C network is 255.255.255.0, which means that the first three octets are the network ID and the last octet is the host ID.
   ☒ **A, B,** and **D** are incorrect because they are not the default subnet mask of a class C address.

8. ☑ **D.** The loopback address is typically known as the 127.0.0.1 address, but it could be any address starting with 127.*x.y.z*.
   ☒ **A, B,** and **C** are incorrect because they are not reserved for the loopback address.

9. ☑ **C.** The port used by HTTP is port 80.

☒ **A, B,** and **D** are incorrect because 20 and 21 are used by FTP, while 25 is used by SMTP.

10. ☑ **A** and **C.** 10.0.0.34 and 172.16.7.99 are examples of addresses that fall into the private IP address ranges, which are not routable on the Internet.

☒ **B** and **D** are incorrect because they are not private ranges.

11. ☑ **B.** Port 25 is used by SMTP to send e-mail over a TCP/IP network.

☒ **A, C,** and **D** are incorrect. Port 23 is used by Telnet, port 443 is used by Secure HTTP (HTTPS), and port 110 is used by POP3 for reading e-mail on the Internet.

12. ☑ **B.** 171.103.2.30 is a class B address, so it has a subnet mask of 255.255.0.0.

☒ **A, C,** and **D** are incorrect because they are not the subnet mask of 171.103.2.30.

TCP/IP Configuration Concepts

13. ☑ **C.** DHCP is responsible for assigning IP addresses to systems automatically so that the network administrator does not have to perform that job manually.

☒ **A, B,** and **D** are incorrect. DNS is used to resolve FQDNs to IP addresses, WINS is used to resolve NetBIOS names to IP addresses, and the Server service is used to connect to files on the server.

14. ☑ **A.** DNS is used to resolve FQDNs to IP addresses.

☒ **B, C,** and **D** are incorrect because WINS is used to resolve NetBIOS names to IP addresses, DHCP is used to automatically assign IP addresses, and the Server service is used to connect to files on the server.

15. ☑ **B.** If you are having trouble resolving FQDNs to IP addresses, you would make sure that the client is pointing to a valid DNS server in its TCP/IP settings.

☒ **A, C,** and **D** are incorrect because they do not deal with troubleshooting name resolution for FQDNs.

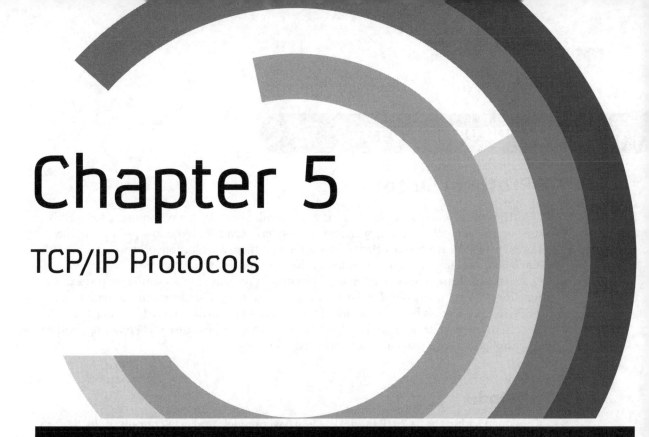

Chapter 5

TCP/IP Protocols

N ow that you know the basics of TCP/IP addressing, it is time to move forward and learn some of the advanced topics such as the different protocols that exist in the protocol suite. In this chapter, you will also learn about the new version of TCP/IP known as IPv6 and some of the network services that are offered as TCP/IP services. Using the information presented in this chapter, along with the knowledge already obtained on IP addressing, you will be able to answer easily any TCP/IP-related questions presented to you on the exam.

TCP/IP Protocol Suite

TCP/IP is the protocol suite used by most, if not all, networking environments today. It is used on small, medium, and large networks and has been adopted as the protocol of the Internet. TCP/IP is a protocol suite—meaning that there are multiple protocols within it. You will be required to know a number of these protocols for the Network+ exam.

As you will learn in this chapter, each protocol in the suite has a specific purpose and function. It is not important for the Network+ exam that you understand the evolution of TCP/IP, so we discuss here the details of the protocol on which you are likely to be tested. Be sure to spend your time on the TCP/IP-related chapters, because this knowledge will help you throughout your years as a networking professional.

The TCP/IP Model

Contained within the TCP/IP model is a four-layer model similar in concept to the seven-layer OSI model. The four layers of the TCP/IP model map to the seven layers of the OSI, but you may find that one layer of the TCP/IP model combines multiple layers of the OSI model, as shown in Figure 5-1. There are several protocols that direct how computers connect and communicate using TCP/IP within the TCP/IP protocol suite, and each protocol runs on different layers of the Internet model.

Application Layer

Let's start at the top of this model, which is the application layer. The application layer is responsible for making the network request (sending computer) or servicing the request (receiving computer). For example, when a user submits a request from a web browser, the web browser is responsible for the submission of the request and is running at this layer. When that web request reaches the web server, the web server, running at the application layer, accepts that request. The following are popular application-layer protocols; for more information, see the section "Application-Layer Protocols" in this chapter:

- Hypertext Transfer Protocol (HTTP)
- Simple Mail Transfer Protocol (SMTP)
- Network News Transport Protocol (NNTP)
- File Transfer Protocol (FTP)

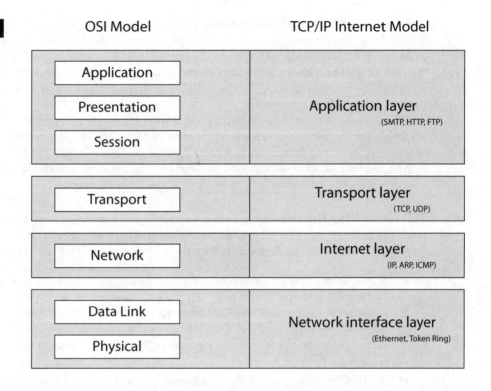

FIGURE 5-1

The TCP/IP Internet model versus the OSI model

OSI Model

TCP/IP Internet Model

OSI Model	TCP/IP Internet Model
Application	Application layer
Presentation	(SMTP, HTTP, FTP)
Session	
Transport	Transport layer (TCP, UDP)
Network	Internet layer (IP, ARP, ICMP)
Data Link	Network interface layer
Physical	(Ethernet, Token Ring)

Transport Layer

The next layer under the application layer is the transport layer. The transport layer is responsible for both connection-oriented communication (a session is established) and connectionless communication (a session is not established). When the request comes down from the higher (application) layer, a transport protocol is then chosen. The two transport protocols in TCP/IP are the Transmission Control Protocol (TCP) and the User Datagram Protocol (UDP).

Transmission Control Protocol   TCP is responsible for providing connection-oriented communication and for ensuring delivery of the data (known as reliable delivery). Connection-oriented communication involves first establishing a connection between two systems and then ensuring that data sent across the connection reaches the destination. TCP will make sure that the data reaches its destination by retransmitting any data that is lost or corrupt. TCP is used by applications that require a reliable transport, but this transport has more overhead than a connectionless protocol because of the construction of the session and the monitoring and retransmission of any data across that session.

Another factor to remember about TCP is that the protocol requires that the recipient acknowledge the successful receipt of data. Of course, all the acknowledgments, known as ACKs, generate additional traffic on the network, which reduces the amount of data that can be passed within a given time frame. The extra overhead involved in the creation, monitoring, and ending of the TCP session is worth the certainty that TCP will ensure that the data will reach its destination.

TCP ensures that data is delivered by using what is known as sequence numbers and acknowledgment numbers. A *sequence number* is a number assigned to each piece of data that is sent. After a system receives a piece of data, it acknowledges that it has received the data by sending an acknowledgment message back to the sender, with the original sequence number being the acknowledgment number of the reply message.

TCP Three-Way Handshake   Before a system can communicate over TCP, it must first establish a connection to the remote system. It does this through what is called the TCP three-way handshake (see Figure 5-2). The three phases to the TCP three-way handshake are

- **SYN**   In the first phase, the sending system sends a SYN message to the receiving system. Each packet sent is assigned a sequence number, which is a unique number assigned to the packet. The SYN message contains the *initial sequence number (ISN)*, which is the first sequence number to be used. In this example, Computer A is connecting to the website on Computer B, so a SYN message is sent to port 80 on Computer B.

- **ACK/SYN**   The second phase is known as the ACK/SYN phase because this message is acknowledging the first message, but at the same time is indicating its initial sequence number. In this example, Computer B sends back the ACK/SYN message that is acknowledging that it has received packet 123 (by acknowledging that 124 is the next sequence number), but it has also specified that its ISN is 326.

- **ACK**   The final phase of the three-way handshake is the acknowledgment message that acknowledges that the packet sent in the second phase has been received. In this example, Computer A sends the ACK to acknowledge that it has received packet 326 by acknowledging that the next packet will be sequence number 327.

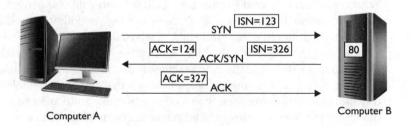

FIGURE 5-2

The TCP three-way handshake

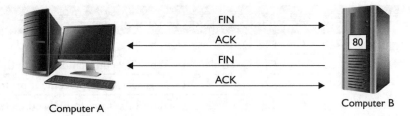

FIGURE 5-3

Terminating a TCP
connection

Disconnecting from a TCP Session   Just as TCP has a three-way handshake to create a connection between two systems that wish to communicate, TCP also has a process to have a participant disconnect from the conversation. Looking at Figure 5-3 you can see that if Computer A wants to disconnect from a TCP session, it must first send a FIN flag to signal that it wants to end the conversation.

When Computer B receives the FIN message, it replies with an acknowledgment and then sends its own FIN message back to Computer A. As a final step to this process, Computer A must acknowledge that it has received the FIN message from Computer B. This is similar to talking to someone on the phone—to end the conversation, you say goodbye and then wait for the other person to say goodbye before hanging up. I describe this as ending the conversation in a "polite" way.

There is also a way to end a conversation in an "impolite" manner. Back to the telephone analogy: You can end the conversation impolitely by hanging up the phone without saying goodbye. In the TCP world, you can "hang up" by sending a TCP message with the RST (reset) flag set.

TCP Ports   When applications use TCP to communicate over the network, each application must be uniquely identified by using a unique port number on the system. A port is an address assigned to the application. When a client wants to communicate with one of those applications (also known as a service), it must send the request to the appropriate port number on the system.

As a networking professional, it is critical that you know some of the port numbers used by popular services. Table 5-1 identifies common TCP port numbers you should know for the Network+ certification exam.

TCP Flags   The TCP protocol uses what is known as TCP flags to identify important types of packets. The following are the common TCP flags you should be familiar with for the Network+ certification exam. Figure 5-4 displays the flags in a packet capture. Note that instead of showing the actual flag, the value is interpreted by Network Monitor and a description is shown. For example, instead of seeing the URG flag set to zero, you can see the first flag set to zero with a description of "No urgent data."

Port	Service	Description
20	FTP Data	Used by FTP to send data to a client.
21	FTP Control	Used by FTP commands sent to the server.
22	SSH	Used as a secure replacement protocol for Telnet.
23	Telnet	Used by Telnet to remotely connect to a system such as a server or router.
25	SMTP	Used to send Internet e-mail.
53	DNS	Used for DNS zone transfers.
80	HTTP	Internet protocol for delivering webpages to the browser.
110	POP3	Used by POP3, which is the Internet protocol to read e-mail.
143	IMAP	Used by IMAP, which is a newer Internet protocol to read e-mail.
443	HTTPS	Used for secure web traffic.
3389	RDP	Remote Desktop is used to remotely manage a Windows system and uses TCP port 3389.

TABLE 5-1 Popular TCP Ports

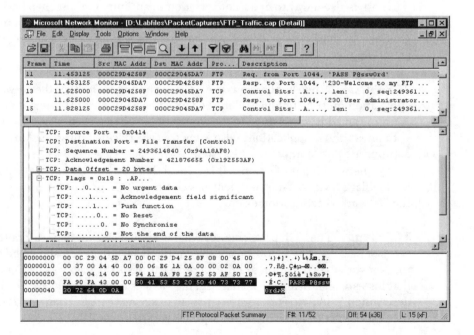

FIGURE 5-4 TCP flags in the TCP header

- **SYN**   The SYN flag is assigned to any packets that are part of the SYN phases of the three-way handshake.
- **ACK**   The acknowledgment flag acknowledges that a previous packet has been received.
- **PSH**   The push flag is designed to force data on an application.
- **URG**   The urgent flag specifies that a packet is urgent.
- **FIN**   The finish flag specifies that you would like to finalize, or end, the connection. This is how a TCP connection is ended the polite way—it is like saying goodbye to end a phone conversation.
- **RST**   The reset flag is used to end a TCP conversation impolitely. This is like hanging up the phone without saying goodbye.

TCP Header   Every packet that is sent using the TCP protocol has a TCP header assigned to it, which contains TCP-related information such as the source port, destination port, and the TCP flags. Figure 5-5 displays the different fields in the TCP header. A quick description of each field follows.

- **Source Port**   This 16-bit field identifies the port number of the sending system.
- **Destination Port**   This 16-bit field identifies the port number the packet is destined for on the destination system.
- **Sequence Number**   This 32-bit field identifies the sequence number of the packet.
- **Acknowledgment Number**   This 32-bit field identifies the packet that this packet is acknowledging.

FIGURE 5-5

The TCP header

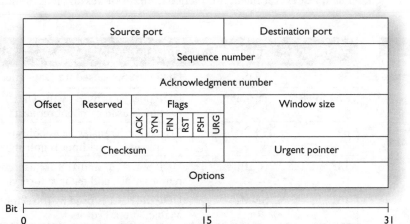

- **Offset**   This 4-bit field indicates where the data begins.
- **Reserved**   This 6-bit field is always set to 0 and was designed for future use.
- **Flags**   This 6-bit field is where the TCP flags are stored. There is a 1-bit field for each of the flags mentioned earlier in this section.
- **Window Size**   This 16-bit field determines the amount of information that can be sent before an acknowledgment is expected.
- **Checksum**   This 16-bit field is used to verify the integrity of the TCP header.

- **Urgent Pointer**   This 16-bit field is used only if the URG flag is set, and is a reference to the last piece of information that was urgent.
- **Options**   This is a variable-length field that specifies any additional settings that may be needed in the TCP header.

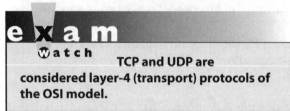

TCP and UDP are considered layer-4 (transport) protocols of the OSI model.

User Datagram Protocol   UDP is used by applications that are not concerned with ensuring the data reaches the destination system. UDP is used for connectionless communication (unreliable), which means that data is sent to the destination and no effort is made to track the progress of the packet and whether it has reached the destination.

UDP Ports   Like TCP, the UDP protocol uses port numbers to identify different types of UDP traffic. Table 5-2 identifies a few examples of UDP traffic and the ports used.

UDP Header   Because the UDP protocol does not have to acknowledge the receipt of a packet, the structure of the UDP header is much simpler than the TCP header. For example, the UDP header does not need a sequence number or acknowledgment number; it also

TABLE 5-2	Port	Service	Description
Popular UDP Ports	53	DNS	UDP port 53 is used for DNS queries.
	67 and 68	DHCP	UDP port 67 is used by the DHCP service, and UDP port 68 is used by client requests.
	69	TFTP	Trivial File Transfer Protocol is used to upload or download files without requiring authentication.
	137 and 138	NetBIOS	UDP ports 137 and 138 are used by the NetBIOS name service and datagram service.
	161	SNMP	UDP port 161 is used by the Simple Network Management Protocol.

FIGURE 5-6

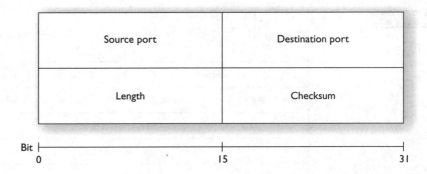

The UDP header

does not need flags to indicate special packets such as a SYN message because there is no three-way handshake (UDP is connectionless). Figure 5-6 displays the UDP header with a listing of the following fields:

- **Source Port**   A 16-bit field that indicates the port used by the sending application on the sending system.
- **Destination Port**   A 16-bit field that indicates the port used by the application on the destination system.
- **Length**   A 16-bit field that specifies the size of the UDP header in bytes.
- **Checksum**   A 16-bit field used to verify the integrity of the UDP header.

Internet Layer

After a transport protocol has been selected, which is based on whether the communication should be connection oriented or connectionless, the information is passed to the Internet layer to determine who is responsible for its delivery. There are a few protocols that run at the Internet layer; IP, ICMP, and ARP are examples.

Internet Protocol   The Internet Protocol (IP) provides packet delivery for protocols higher in the model. It is a connectionless delivery system that makes a "best-effort" attempt to deliver the packets to the correct destination. IP does not guarantee delivery of the packets—that is the responsibility of transport protocols; IP simply sends the data.

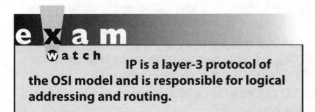

The IP protocol is also responsible for the logical addressing and routing of TCP/IP and, therefore, is considered a layer-3 protocol of the OSI model. The IP protocol on the router is responsible for decrementing (usually by a value of 1) the TTL (time to live) of the packet to prevent it from running in a "network loop." Once the TTL of the packet is decremented to 0,

exam

ⓦatch   IP is a layer-3 protocol of the OSI model and is responsible for logical addressing and routing.

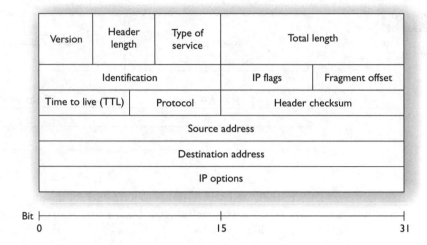

FIGURE 5-7

The IP header

the router removes the packet from the network and sends a status message to the sender (using ICMP as the protocol); this prevents loops. Windows operating systems have a default TTL of 128, whereas most Linux operating systems have a TTL of 64 by default.

IP Header   The IP header in the packet contains information that helps the packet make its way from the source to the destination. The following is a listing of the fields and their meaning, while Figure 5-7 displays the IP header structure:

- **Version**   A 4-bit field that identifies the version of IP being used, for example, 4 or 6.
- **Header Length**   A 4-bit field that indicates the size of the IP header.
- **Type of Service**   An 8-bit field that indicates how the packet should be handled by the system. For example, if the low delay option is specified here, it means that the system should deal with the packet right away.
- **Total Length**   A 16-bit field that indicates the size of the IP packet.
- **Identification**   A 16-bit field. Networks can only handle packets of a specific maximum size—known as a *maximum transmission unit (MTU)*—so the system may break the data being sent into multiple fragments. This field uniquely identifies the fragment.
- **IP Flags**   A 3-bit field that specifies how fragments are going to be dealt with. For example, a More Fragments (MF) flag indicates more fragments are to come. Also, a bit known as Don't Fragment (DF) specifies not to fragment the packet.
- **Fragment Offset**   A 13-bit field that specifies the order in which the fragments are to be put back together when the packet is assembled.

- **Time to Live (TTL)**   An 8-bit field that specifies when the packet is to expire. The TTL is a value that is decremented with every router the packet passes through. When the TTL reaches 0, the packet is discarded.
- **Protocol**   An 8-bit field that specifies what layer-4 protocol (TCP or UDP) the packet should use.
- **Header Checksum**   A 16-bit field that verifies the integrity of the IP header.
- **Source Address**   A 32-bit field that represents the IP address of the sending system. This is how the receiving system knows where to send the reply message.
- **Destination Address**   A 32-bit field that represents the IP address of the system the packet is destined for.
- **IP Options**   A variable-length field that is used to specify any other settings in the IP header.

Internet Control Message Protocol   Internet Control Message Protocol (ICMP) enables systems on a TCP/IP network to share status and error information. You can use the status information to detect network trouble. ICMP messages are encapsulated within IP datagrams so that they can be routed throughout a network. Two programs that use ICMP messages are Ping and Tracert.

You can use Ping to send ICMP echo requests to an IP address and wait for ICMP echo responses. Ping reports the time interval between sending the request and receiving the response. With Ping, you can determine whether a particular IP system on your network is functioning correctly. You can use many different options with the Ping utility.

Tracert traces the path taken to a particular host. This utility can be useful in troubleshooting internetworks. Tracert sends ICMP echo requests to an IP address while it increments the TTL field in the IP header by a count of 1, after starting at 1, and then analyzing the ICMP errors that are returned. Each succeeding echo request should get one unit further into the network before the TTL field reaches 0 and an "ICMP time exceeded" error message is returned by the router attempting to forward it.

exam

⚠ a t c h   **ICMP is the protocol in the TCP/IP protocol suite that is responsible for error and status reporting. Programs such as Ping and Tracert use ICMP.**

ICMP Types and Codes   ICMP does not use port numbers, but instead uses ICMP types and codes to identify the different types of messages. For example, an echo request message that is used by the Ping request uses ICMP type 8, while the Ping reply comes back with an ICMP type 0 message.

Some of the ICMP types are broken down to finer levels with different codes in the type. For example, ICMP type 3 is a "destination unreachable" message, but because there are

Type	Code	Description
0 – Echo Reply	0	Echo reply message
3 – Destination Unreachable	0	Destination network
	1	Destination host unreachable
	2	Destination protocol unreachable
	3	Destination port unreachable
8 – Echo Request	0	Echo request message

many reasons why a destination is unreachable, the type is subdivided into different codes. Each code is for a different message in the type (see Table 5-3).

ICMP Header   The ICMP header is a very small header compared to the IP header and the TCP header. Figure 5-8 displays the ICMP header, and a listing of the fields follows:

- **Type**   An 8-bit field that indicates the ICMP type being used.
- **Code**   An 8-bit field indicating the ICMP code being used.
- **Checksum**   A 16-bit field that is used to verify the integrity of the ICMP header.
- **Other**   A field that stores any data within the ICMP header. For example, Microsoft operating systems place part of the alphabet in this field for echo request messages.

Also note that Internet Group Management Protocol (IGMP) is another Internet-layer protocol and is used for multicast applications.

Address Resolution Protocol   The Address Resolution Protocol (ARP) provides IP address–to–physical address resolution on a TCP/IP network. To accomplish this feat, ARP sends out a broadcast message with an ARP request packet that contains the IP address of the system it is trying to find. All systems on the local network see the message, and the system that owns the IP address for which ARP is looking replies by sending its physical address to the originating system in an ARP reply packet. The physical/IP address combo is

FIGURE 5-8

The ICMP header

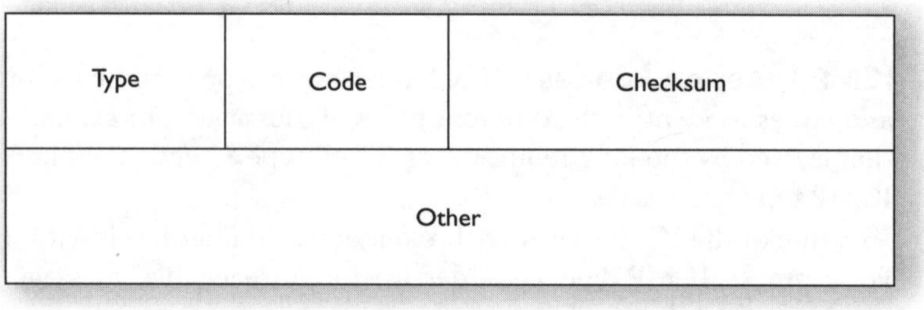

e x a m

w a t c h   ARP is responsible for converting an IP address (layer-3 address) to the physical Media Access Control (MAC) address (layer-2 address).

then stored in the ARP cache of the originating system for future use.

All systems maintain ARP caches that include IP address–to–physical address mappings. The ARP cache is always checked for an IP address–to–physical address mapping before initiating a broadcast. You can learn more about the ARP utility and other related TCP/IP utilities in Chapter 6.

EXERCISE 5-1

Identifying TCP/IP Protocols

In this exercise, you will review the TCP/IP protocols by matching the protocol to the correct description.

Protocol	Description
___ TCP	A. Converts the logical address to the physical address
___ SMTP	B. Responsible for logical addressing and routing
___ ICMP	C. Responsible for reliable delivery
___ ARP	D. Application-layer protocol used to download files
___ UDP	E. Responsible for error and status reporting
___ HTTPS	F. Internet protocol to send mail
___ FTP	G. Secure transmission of web traffic
___ IP	H. Unreliable delivery

Network Access Layer

The network access layer is sometimes referred to as the network interface layer or the link layer. The network access layer corresponds to layer 2 and layer 1 of the OSI model. Examples of network access–layer components are network architectures, physical addressing, cables, connectors, network media, and any other layer-2 and layer-1 network components.

Application-Layer Protocols

Now that you have learned about some of the core protocols such as TCP, UDP, and IP in the TCP/IP protocol suite, let's take a look at some of the protocols that run at the application layer of the TCP/IP Internet model.

HTTP and HTTPS The Hypertext Transfer Protocol (HTTP) is the protocol used on the Internet to allow clients to request webpages from web servers and to allow client interaction with those web servers. HTTP is a stateless protocol, meaning that the web servers are not aware of what a client has or has not requested and cannot track users who have requested specific content. This system does not allow for good interaction with the web server, but does allow for retrieving the HTML pages stored on websites. To aid in tracking client requests, we use cookies—small files stored on the client computer that allow the web server to store data on the client that the client will send back with each request to the server.

Hypertext Transfer Protocol, Secure (HTTPS) allows you to connect to a website and receive and send content in an encrypted format using SSL. HTTPS is most commonly used on e-commerce sites to allow you to send personal information without worrying that an Internet hacker is viewing this information, especially credit card numbers and other confidential data. You can determine when HTTPS is being used because the address of the website starts with https:// and not http://, which marks the regular HTTP protocol. Another sign that HTTPS is in use: In Internet Explorer, a lock appears in the status bar of a page; the lock is either closed when the communication is secure or open when the communication is not secure (as shown in Figure 5-9).

exam **ⓦatch** **For the exam, know that a newer protocol to secure traffic that is designed to be more secure than Secure Sockets Layer (SSL) is Transport Layer Security (TLS).**

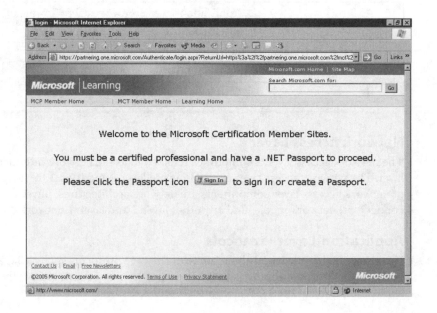

FIGURE 5-9

Identifying the use of secure traffic by the lock in Internet Explorer

Normally, HTTPS is not used for an entire e-commerce site because the encryption and decryption processes slow the connection time, so only the part of the site that requests personal information uses HTTPS.

Network Time Protocol   The Network Time Protocol (NTP) is used to synchronize the clocks of PCs on a network or the Internet. This is accomplished by configuring a server to be the time server, which then is the server from which all other PCs on the network synchronize their time.

On earlier Windows networks, you can manage time synchronization by placing a command in a logon script to synchronize the time on the client with the time server. Use the following command:

```
NET TIME \\computername /SET
```

Newer Microsoft networks, such as Active Directory networks, have the *Primary Domain Controller* (PDC) emulator provide the time to all servers and clients automatically, so there is no need to create a logon script for the clients to synchronize the time with the time server. PDC emulators can also retrieve their time from Internet NTP servers.

Time servers on the Internet allow you to synchronize your PC's clock with the exact time kept by atomic clocks. The time synchronization takes into account time zone settings of your operating system and allows you to synchronize with a time server even if it is not set for your local time zone.

Network News Transfer Protocol   News clients use Network News Transfer Protocol (NNTP) to send and retrieve news articles to a newsgroup. Newsgroups are typically used as a place for users to post questions and answers on a particular topic area (called a newsgroup). NNTP uses TCP to send and receive news articles. NNTP allows the submission and retrieval of only the news articles that have not previously been sent or retrieved.

Simple Mail Transfer Protocol   Simple Mail Transfer Protocol (SMTP) is used to send or route mail over a TCP/IP network such as the Internet. Most e-mail server products support SMTP in order to send e-mail out of the corporation and onto the Internet.

watch   **POP3 and IMAP4 are the Internet protocols for reading e-mail, whereas SMTP is the Internet protocol for sending e-mail.**

Post Office Protocol 3   Post Office Protocol, version 3 (POP3) is the Internet protocol used to retrieve e-mail from a mail server to the POP3 client. The e-mail is "popped," or downloaded, to the client after the client has been authenticated to its mailbox. POP3 has limited capabilities as far as folder support is concerned. A POP3 client program supports only an inbox, an outbox, sent items, and deleted items. If additional folder support is required, you would need to use an IMAP4 client.

Internet Message Access Protocol 4   Internet Message Access Protocol, version 4 (IMAP4) is another protocol similar to POP3 that allows clients to retrieve messages from a mail server. IMAP4 allows additional folders other than the four basic ones provided with POP3. For example, you can use an IMAP4 client to connect to public folders stored on an Exchange Server.

Simple Network Management Protocol   Simple Network Management Protocol (SNMP) is an Internet standard that provides a simple method for remotely managing or gathering statistics from virtually any network device that supports it. A network device can be a network card in a server; a program or service running on a server; or a network device such as a hub, switch, or router.

The SNMP standard defines a two-tiered approach to network device management: a central management system and the management information base (MIB) located on the managed device. The management system can monitor one or many MIBs, allowing for centralized management of a network. From a management system, you can see valuable performance and network device operation statistics, enabling you to diagnose network health without leaving your office.

The goal of a management system is to provide centralized network management. Any computer running SNMP management software is referred to as a management system. For a management system to be able to perform centralized network management, it must be able to collect and analyze many things, including the following:

- Network protocol identification and statistics
- Dynamic identification of computers attached to the network (referred to as discovery)
- Hardware and software configuration data
- Computer performance and usage statistics
- Computer event and error messages
- Program and application usage statistics

File Transfer Protocol   FTP is a TCP/IP protocol that exists to upload and download files between FTP servers and clients. Like Telnet and Ping, FTP can establish a connection to a remote computer using either the hostname or the IP address, and must resolve hostnames to IP addresses to establish communication with the remote computer.

When TCP/IP is installed on the system, an FTP utility is available, but there are also a number of third-party graphical user interface (GUI) FTP clients available for all operating systems. If you use FTP a great deal, a GUI FTP client could save you a lot of time and frustration in dealing with FTP commands.

Trivial File Transfer Protocol   Trivial File Transfer Protocol (TFTP) is a simple protocol compared to FTP that supports only reading and writing to files and does not support features such as listing directory contents and authentication. TFTP uses UDP as the transport protocol, as opposed to FTP, which uses TCP. TFTP is typically used to boot diskless workstations.

Secure File Transfer Protocol   Secure File Transfer Protocol (SFTP) is an interactive file transfer protocol similar to FTP, but it encrypts all traffic between the SFTP client and the SFTP server. SFTP supports additional features such as public key authentication and compression. Unlike TFTP, SFTP does support a number of commands in its interactive shell, such as listing directory contents, creating directories, downloading files, and uploading files.

Telnet   Telnet is a terminal emulation protocol that allows a client to run or emulate the program running on the server. A number of devices allow you to use Telnet to communicate with the device and perform remote administration using the command set available to the Telnet session.

Secure Shell   Secure Shell (SSH) is a program used to create a shell, or session, with a remote system. Once the remote session is established, the client can execute commands within this shell and copy files to the local system. SSH has a major purpose in life, and that is to support remote shells using secure authentication and encrypted communication. SSH runs over TCP port 22 and is a secure replacement for protocols such as Telnet.

exam
ⓦatch   LDAP is the industry-standard protocol for accessing a directory service and is supported by Active Directory and Novell's eDirectory.

Secure Copy Protocol   Secure Copy Protocol (SCP) is responsible for copying files from a remote server to the local system over a secure connection, ensuring that data in transit is kept confidential. A number of SCP products use an SSH connection to ensure the security of the SCP copy operation.

Lightweight Directory Access Protocol   Lightweight Directory Access Protocol (LDAP) is the TCP/IP protocol for directory service access that is supported by all the principal directory services, such as Novell's eDirectory and Microsoft's Active Directory. LDAP allows LDAP clients to connect to the network database, or directory, and query the database for information about its objects, such as user accounts and printers. For example, a user on the network could find out the phone number of another user by using the LDAP protocol.

Line Printer Daemon and Line Printer Remote Line Printer Daemon (LPD) is a printer protocol, or service, installed on the print server to allow Line Printer Remote (LPR) clients to send print requests to the print server. When LPD receives the print request, it stores the print request in a queue until the printer becomes available.

CERTIFICATION OBJECTIVE 5.02

IPv6 Fundamentals

Our entire discussion so far about TCP/IP is based on version 4, known as IPv4. The use of TCP/IP over the years has far exceeded expectations, and we are running out of IP addresses. Running out of addresses is only one of the reasons why TCP/IP has been redesigned to a new version known as IP version 6 (IPv6).

Some of the benefits of the new IPv6 protocol include

- **Minimized overhead** The IPv6 packet has been reformatted to create a simpler IP header that minimizes the overhead of systems and devices that process the packet.
- **Larger address space** IPv6 uses a 128-bit address scheme versus the 32-bit address scheme used by IPv4. This ensures that there are more than enough addresses to handle future needs.
- **Multicasting** IPv6 uses multicasting as a core communication method in IPv6. IPv6 does not have broadcast communication like IPv4 does, which is a misuse of network bandwidth.
- **IPSec** The IPv4 protocol did not include the industry standard Internet Protocol Security (IPSec) protocol, but did support it. IPv6 has IPSec built into the protocol suite, which can be used to encrypt all network communication.

IPv6 Addressing and Hexadecimal Addressing

There are major changes to IPv6 from what we know of IPv4. For starters, IPv4 uses a 32-bit address scheme, while IPv6 will use a 128-bit address scheme. This will give us an insane number of unique possible addresses—3.4×10^{38} to be exact (2^{128})! This is a huge improvement over $2^{32} = 4$ billion unique addresses with IPv4.

An IPv6 address will no longer use four octets. The IPv6 address is divided into eight hexadecimal blocks (16 bits each) that are separated by a colon (:) as shown in the following example:

```
65b3:b834:45a3:0000:0000:762e:0270:5224
```

There are a few facts about the IP address that you should be familiar with—the IP address is not case sensitive, and you do not need to specify leading zeros in the address. Also, you can compress the address by using a double colon (::) instead of a group of consecutive zeros when writing out the address. For example, the loopback address in IPv6 is as follows:

```
0000:0000:0000:0000:0000:0000:0000:0001
```

In IPv6 you can perform address compression by first removing leading zeros from each block to give you the following address:

```
0:0:0:0:0:0:0:1
```

After removing the leading zeros, you can compress the address by converting all the consecutive zeros with a ::, giving you a loopback address of ::1! This is something you can do with any IPv6 address that has multiple contiguous blocks of zeros.

The addressing scheme in IPv6 has totally changed, as there are three types of addresses in IPv6:

- **Unicast**   A unicast address is used for one-on-one communication.
- **Multicast**   A multicast address is used to send data to multiple systems at one time. Multicast addresses start with the FF01 prefix. For example FF01::1 is the multicast address to send data to all nodes on the network, while FF01::2 is the multicast address to send data to all routers on the network.
- **Anycast**   Refers to a group of systems providing a service.

Note that there is no broadcast address listed. To prepare for the Network+ exam, you should be familiar with these changes to the addressing scheme and be familiar with the different types of unicast addresses listed here:

- **Global unicast**   A global unicast address is a public address in IPv6 that is routable on the Internet. A global unicast address is equivalent to a public IP address in IPv4.
- **Site-local unicast**   The site-local unicast address is a private address and is similar to a private address in IPv4 and is used for local communication only. An IPv6 site-local unicast address always starts with FEC0.
- **Link-local unicast**   A link-local unicast address is similar to an Automatic Private Internet Protocol Addressing (APIPA) address in IPv4 and can only be used to communicate with other nodes on the link. A link-local address starts with FE80.

Calculating Hex Addresses

Let's take a look at how an IPv6 address is converted from binary to make the hexadecimal address. Figure 5-10 displays the structure of a typical IPv6 address and denotes the bit structure.

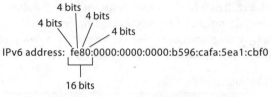

FIGURE 5-10

Converting hex to binary

Conversion Table (number 7)

Value	8	4	2	1
Bit	0	1	1	1

Decimal	Hex	Binary	Decimal	Hex	Binary
0	0	0000	8	8	1000
1	1	0001	9	9	1001
2	2	0010	10	A	1010
3	3	0011	11	B	1011
4	4	0100	12	C	1100
5	5	0101	13	D	1101
6	6	0110	14	E	1110
7	7	0111	15	F	1111

Let's break down the figure. At the top left of the figure you can see an IPv6 address that starts with FE80. Each character in the IPv6 address is made up of 4 bits. This means that each block in the address separated by a : is 16 bits in length. There are 8 blocks, so 8 × 16 bits = 128 bits.

The pattern of 4 bits that each character makes can be easily figured out using a quick conversion table shown in the top-right corner of Figure 5-10. You can see the values of each of the 4 bits are 8, 4, 2, and finally 1 on the far right side. Just like figuring out the value of an octet with IPv4, you can calculate the 4 bits used by taking the decimal number (7 is the example in the figure) and turning on (1) the 4-, 2-, and 1-bit placeholders. This will create a decimal value of 4 + 2 + 1 = 7. Looking at the chart in the figure, the decimal value of 7 is also the hex value of 7, which has a binary value of 0111. Knowing that each character is based off a 4-bit value, we could use a conversion table to help us figure out what each hex value is in binary.

To start the table I list 16 decimal numbers in order from 0 through 15 (because hexadecimal address is 16 based). I then list each hexadecimal value in order starting with 0 to 9 (that is only 10 numbers; we need 6 more), then the tenth hex value is A and continues to F to make the 16 values in the hex system. Finally, I create a third column, which is the binary value of each of those hex values—you can cheat and use the corresponding decimal number of a hex value to figure out what the binary should be. For example, the hex value of "C" corresponds to a decimal value of 12, and to calculate 12 in binary is 1100 (8 + 4 + 0 + 0).

This means that the first block in the IPv6 of FE80 has the 16-bit pattern of

```
1111 1110 1000 0000
```

Calculating Octal Addresses

The Network+ certification exam expects you to know the decimal numbering system, binary system, hexadecimal system, and the octal system. You have learned about decimal and binary systems (conversion) in Chapter 4, and this chapter has discussed hexadecimal addresses. I want to take a minute to discuss the octal numbering system.

The octal numbering system has values that range from 0 through 7. You can convert from binary to octal by using the following table:

Bit Value	4	2	1
	0	1	1

Let's look at an example. If I wanted to convert the number 3 to an octal value, it would be 011 because I need to turn on the second bit (to get 2) and then turn on the third bit (to get 1), which gives me 2 + 1 = 3. If I wanted to have the number 5 converted to octal, it would be 101 (4 + 1). Notice that this is similar to converting an octet to binary, which you learned in Chapter 4; the difference here is that the octal system only has 3 bits.

Address Breakdown

The other thing that should be noted is that IPv6 also uses the Classless Inter-Domain Routing (CIDR) notation that has become popular with IPv4 in recent years to denote the network ID portion of the address. For example, the address of 2001:0db8:a385::1/48 means that the first 48 bits make up the network ID.

Now that you have an understanding of how the 128 bits in an IPv6 address become a pattern of hexadecimal characters, let's talk about how the IPv6 address breaks down into three major parts:

- **Network ID** The network ID is typically made up of the first 48 bits of the IPv6 address. With global addresses, this would be assigned to your organization by the Internet service provider (ISP). For example, you may have a network ID of 2001:ab34:cd56 /48.

- **Subnet ID** The subnet ID is made up of 16 bits and is how you can divide the IPv6 network into multiple subnets. For example, I could create two subnets with the previously mentioned network ID of *2001:ab34:cd56:0001/64* and *2001:ab34:cd56:0002/64*.

- **Unique Identifier (EUI-64)** The last 64 bits is known as the unique identifier, and it is similar to the host ID portion of an IPv4 address—it uniquely identifies the system on the network. The unique identifier is made up of the system's MAC address (48 bits) divided into two parts, with the value of FFFE (16 bits) placed in the middle. The unique identifier portion is also known as the EUI-64 address.

Auto-configuration

IPv6 has the benefit of being able to leverage auto-configuration, which is the fact that IPv6 systems can generate their own IPv6 address and then check to see if that address is already in use on the network using a neighbor solicitation message to the IPv6 address it is attempting to use. If any other system is using the address, it will respond to the solicitation and the originating host will know not to use that address. It should be noted that it is rare for a duplicate address to be used because the MAC address makes up part of the auto-configured address and is typically unique.

IPv6 Protocols

The Network+ exam expects you to have a basic understanding of the addressing scheme for IPv6, but I also want to mention a few of the new protocols that come with IPv6. The following outlines a few of the changes to the protocols in IPv6:

- **IPv6**   The IPv6 protocol is a replacement to IPv4 and handles logical addressing and routing functions.
- **ICMPv6**   ICMPv6 handles error and status reporting. Similar to ICMPv4, ICMPv6 uses types to identify different messages. ICMPv6 types numbered 1 to 127 are error messages, while 128 to 255 are reserved for information messages. As an example, the echo request message with ICMPv6 is type 128, while the echo reply message is type 129.
- **Multicast Listener Discovery (MLD)**   MLD is a function of the ICMPv6 protocol that serves as the multicasting protocol and is a replacement for IGMP in IPv4, which handles multicast communication.
- **Neighboring Discovery (ND)**   The Neighboring Discovery function is a component of ICMPv6 and replaces the ARP protocol from IPv4. ND performs functions such as neighboring router discovery, automatic address assignment, and detecting duplicate addresses on the network.
- **DHCP6**   The IPv6 protocol supports automatic configuration of IPv6 on clients by using DHCPv6. Similar to DHCPv4, you can configure a Dynamic Host Configuration Protocol (DHCP) server to configure a DHCP client with an IPv6 address.

Tunneling Protocols

We are in a transitioning stage where most of the Internet is still using IPv4, but some companies are using IPv6 on their networks. To help with this transitioning phase, IPv6 was designed as a dual stack protocol, which means that it can run alongside of IPv4.

We also have tunneling protocols that will allow us to carry IPv6 traffic across an IPv4 network (such as the Internet) by encapsulating the IPv6 packet into an IPv4 packet. The following are tunneling protocols that can be used:

- **6to4** The most common tunneling protocol used today and an automatic tunneling protocol (routers determine the end points) that uses protocol ID 41 to indicate that the packet encapsulates an IPv6 packet.
- **Teredo** An automatic tunneling protocol (routers determine end points) that you use if you are sitting behind a Network Address Translation (NAT) device.
- **ISATAP** The 6to4 and Teredo tunneling protocols are designed to be used across sites, while Intra-Site Automatic Tunnel Addressing Protocol (ISATAP) is an automatic tunneling protocol used for intrasite communication.
- **Miredo** A Teredo tunneling client that you can use on Linux systems. This is important to mention, as most Linux systems implement 6to4 by default, so you can install Miredo for Teredo support.
- **4to6** All of the tunneling protocols discussed so far encapsulate IPv6 packets into an IPv4 packet so that the data can travel across an IPv4 network. If you are using IPv4 and need to carry that data across an IPv6 network, you can use a 4to6 tunnel!

EXERCISE 5-2

Exploring IPv6

In this exercise you will use the ipconfig command to determine your IPv6 address information.

1. Log on to the Windows 8 VM.
2. Start a command prompt and type **ipconfig**.
3. Locate your network card in the ipconfig output. Do you see an IPv6 address assigned to the network card? _____
4. Record the IPv6 address: _____
5. What type of address is it? _____

Network Services

This section is designed to introduce to you some common network services that are used in most networks today. Be sure to be familiar with all of these network services for the Network+ exam.

A network service is responsible for a specific function on the network. For example, the file and print services are responsible for providing files on the network, and the DHCP service is responsible for assigning IP addresses automatically to systems on the network. Let's identify popular network services found on the Network+ exam.

Web Services

Web services, or web servers, are designed to deliver webpages from the web server to your client machine's browser. The webpages located on the web server are created in a language known as HTML, but are delivered from the web server to the client browser using HTTP.

Network Controllers

Network controllers are network interfaces, or network cards, in a system or device. The network controller is responsible for sending and receiving data to and from the network. You can increase bandwidth of a network device by installing multiple network controllers and teaming the network controller together (also known as bonding). In this configuration, the device can use both network controllers at the same time to increase performance.

DHCP

DHCP is responsible for assigning IP address information automatically to systems on the network. The network administrator configures the DHCP server by configuring a scope (a range of addresses) that the server can assign addresses from. The DHCP service may configure a client with all the TCP/IP settings, including the subnet mask, the default gateway, and the addresses of both the DNS server and the WINS server.

DNS

DNS is a network service that is responsible for converting fully qualified domain names (FQDNs) to IP addresses so that communication can occur. Most networking applications allow users to type an FQDN (for example, www.gleneclarke.com) as the address of the

FIGURE 5-11

Looking at the DNS database in the DNS Management tool for Windows

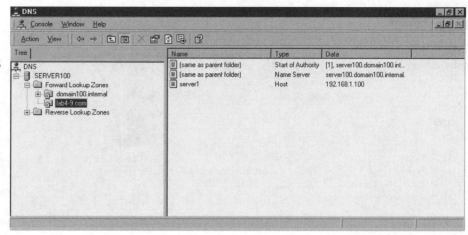

system they want to communicate with. The FQDN must be converted to an IP address, and DNS is responsible for this.

Linux, Novell, and Microsoft Windows servers all contain DNS server software that can be installed to create the database of FQDNs and matching IP addresses. The Windows Server DNS Management tool is shown in Figure 5-11.

RDP

The Remote Desktop Protocol (RDP) is a network service that allows you to remotely connect to a system across a TCP/IP network and manage the system as if you were sitting at it. Windows operating systems have a feature called Remote Desktop. Once enabled, the RDP port of TCP 3389 is open on the system, and the system awaits a connection from an RDP client for remote administration.

WINS

As you learned earlier in the chapter, Windows Internet Naming Service (WINS) is used to resolve, or convert, NetBIOS names (computer names) to IP addresses. NetBIOS applications use NetBIOS names as a way to identify the remote system that the application is to communicate with. The NetBIOS name will be converted to the IP address by a WINS server.

NAT/PAT/SNAT

Most networks today are connected to the Internet, and having an Internet connection presents a number of security concerns. For example, if you have your server connected

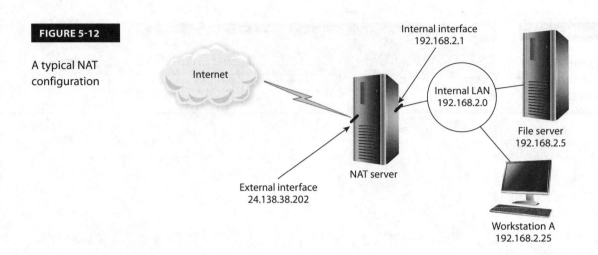

FIGURE 5-12

A typical NAT configuration

directly to the Internet, it will take no time at all for the system to be hacked. *Network Address Translation (NAT)* is a network service that is responsible for translating internal IP addresses from machines inside the network to a public address used by the NAT service—essentially hiding your internal network addresses. Figure 5-12 displays a typical NAT configuration.

In Figure 5-12, you can see that the NAT server has two network interfaces (cards): the internal interface and the external interface. The internal interface has an IP address within the range of the internal network, whereas the external interface uses an external address. Notice that the NAT server has two IP addresses assigned and that the internal interface uses the IP address of 192.168.2.1. This will be the default gateway address of all other systems on the network because the NAT server is the way off the network.

In Figure 5-12, when Workstation A wants to send information to the Internet, it submits the request to the NAT server. The NAT server then modifies or translates the source address of the packet to 24.138.38.202 so that the packet appears to have come from the external interface of the NAT server. This is beneficial, because anyone who intercepts the data on the Internet will believe that the packet came from the NAT server and not the internal computer on the local area network (LAN). As a result, anyone who decides to attack the source of the packets will be attacking the NAT server, which will typically be a firewall product as well; if the system is compromised, however, at least it was only the NAT server, and not one of the internal systems that holds the company data!

PAT and SNAT

When implementing your NAT solution, you have a few options. You could have each private address inside the network translated to a single public address that is associated

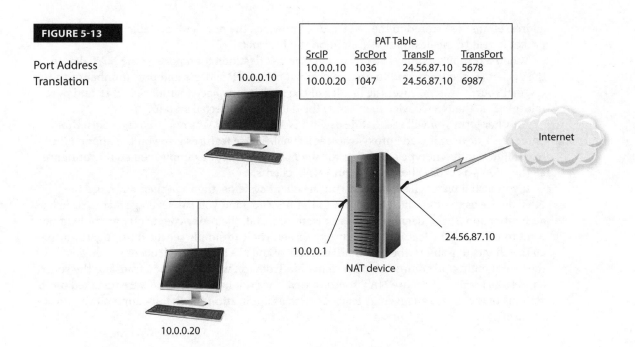

FIGURE 5-13

Port Address
Translation

with the public interface. This would mean that you need to have multiple public addresses in order to create the one-to-one mapping by which one private IP address translates to one public IP address. This is known as static NAT (SNAT) and is typically used if you want systems on the Internet to communicate with an internal system.

If you only have one public IP address on the NAT device and need to use that for all private addresses on the LAN, then you will need to *overload* the public address with multiple private addresses. NAT overloading is used when each of the private IP addresses is translated to the one public IP address, essentially overloading the poor public address.

With NAT overloading, the big question is "How does the NAT device know which internal system to send the response to when data is returned from the Internet?" This is an important question because all of the packets will be returned to whatever the public address is on the NAT device. This is where *Port Address Translation (PAT)* comes in. If you look at Figure 5-13, you will see that the NAT device using port addressing is keeping track of not only the IP address of the system sending outbound traffic, but also the port used by the application on the private system. The source address of the outbound packet is converted from the IP address of the private system to the IP address of the public interface on the NAT device. Also, the port used by the application on the sending computer is then converted to a unique port address used by the NAT device. All IP addresses and port addresses are then stored in the NAT table, known as the port address table, and then the packet is sent to the destination system on the Internet.

When a response comes back from the Internet destined for a port on the NAT device, the packet is then translated to use the original private IP address and port number of the original source system. After the header of the packet is replaced with original IP and port information, the NAT device then sends the data to the internal system.

Another term you will see that deals with NAT is *Secure Network Address Translation*. Some NAT devices include proxy features as well. These features give you the opportunity to configure different types of clients for the NAT device; for example, you could configure all the clients as proxy clients, or secure NAT clients.

If you install proxy client software on the client systems, then the clients can use the NAT device as their method to get out to the Internet, and you can leverage features such as authentication. If you decide you do not want to install the proxy client software but simply want to use the NAT features of the proxy server, you can simply set the default gateway of all the clients to point to the private IP address of the NAT device. All client systems will then send outbound communication to the NAT device, which will then translate the source address as normal. A secure NAT solution that does not have client software installed on the stations of the users can leverage features such as application filters but cannot authenticate the users.

ICS

Internet Connection Sharing (ICS) is a service built into Windows operating systems that allows you to share your Internet connection with other users on the network. ICS acts as a NAT server and a DHCP server at the same time. When you enable ICS in Windows, it automatically starts assigning IP addresses out on the network so that the DHCP clients use the ICS computer as their default gateway. When clients send information to the ICS machine to be sent on the Internet, the ICS machine translates the source address (the NAT feature) to use the external interface of the system.

To enable ICS, right-click your Internet LAN connection and choose Properties. On the Advanced page tab, select Allow Other Network Users To Connect Through This Computer's Internet Connection (shown in Figure 5-14) and then choose OK.

SMB/CIFS

The Server Message Block (SMB) protocol, used primarily by Microsoft operating systems, is responsible for sharing files and printers on a system and making those resources available to SMB clients on the network. SMB is an application-layer protocol that runs on top of TCP/IP, Internetwork Packet Exchange (IPX), and NetBEUI and relies on those protocols for transport functionality.

FIGURE 5-14

Enabling ICS in
Windows

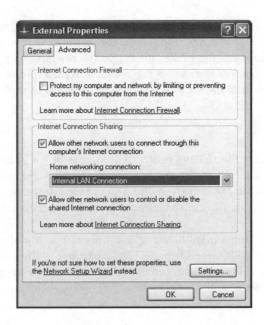

e**x**a m
wa t c h   **SMB is a term that is being**   **are protocols responsible for allowing**
phased out. Microsoft is now using the   **access to a remote file system as if it were**
term Common Internet File System (CIFS)   **stored on the local system in a Microsoft**
instead of SMB. Either way, SMB and CIFS   **environment.**

NFS

Microsoft environments use SMB; the Network File System (NFS) is a protocol developed
by Sun Microsystems that allows users to access
files stored on a remote system as if it were a
local resource.

NFS is the equivalent of SMB used in UNIX
and Linux environments and is platform
independent, meaning that the NFS client may
be accessing a file system resource from any type
of server that is an NFS server—not just a Linux
server.

e**x**a m
wa t c h   **NFS is a file-sharing**
protocol used in UNIX and Linux
environments; SMB is the file-sharing
protocol in Microsoft environments.

NFS uses an interface that runs on top of TCP/IP networks called the Virtual File System (VFS), which is responsible for making the resource available to a local application. The local application makes the call to the resource as if it were a local resource, and the application never learns that the resource is on a remote system—NFS makes the location and platform of the remote resource transparent to the application and users.

AFP

If SMB is the file-sharing protocol in Microsoft environments and NFS is the file-sharing protocol in UNIX environments, what is responsible for allowing access to files on remote systems in the Macintosh world? You guessed it; the AppleTalk Filing Protocol (AFP) is responsible for allowing Macintosh systems to access remote file systems on an AppleTalk network.

Original implementations of AFP only ran on top of AppleTalk networks, but newer versions of AFP run on top of TCP/IP because of the popularity of the protocol. Like SMB and NFS, AFP provides an environment that allows users to access files on a remote system as if they were on the local system. AFP also provides security as to who accesses the file.

Samba

Samba is an application environment that runs on Linux systems and uses SMB to allow Microsoft clients to access the Samba-enabled UNIX servers as if they were Microsoft servers. A Samba-enabled UNIX server may provide a number of services to Microsoft clients, including

- Sharing the file system of the UNIX server to Microsoft clients
- Sharing printer resources from the UNIX environment to Microsoft clients
- Performing authentication and authorization services to Microsoft clients

ⓦatch **Samba is a network service loaded on UNIX/Linux systems that implements SMB services so that Microsoft clients can access files and printers on the UNIX/Linux servers.**

This may not sound like a very exciting feature, but it has proven to be a very exciting technology because without it, the Microsoft clients would only be able to access the Microsoft servers in your organization and not the UNIX servers. The reason is that UNIX servers use NFS as a file-sharing protocol, while Microsoft uses SMB—so Samba gives you the best of both worlds because it allows the UNIX server to run its NFS protocol for UNIX clients while providing the SMB service for Microsoft clients. Both types of clients can now share resources with one another! Figure 5-15 shows an example of configuring Samba with Webmin tools in Linux.

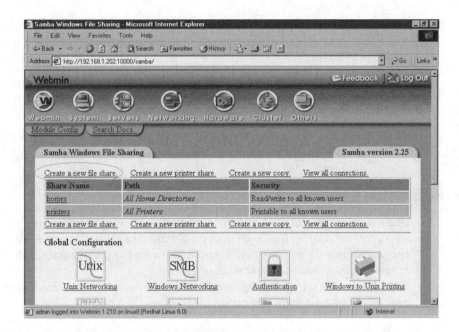

FIGURE 5-15

Creating Samba file shares with Webmin tools in Linux

UNIX uses two different services, called *daemons,* to provide Samba services:

■ **smbd daemon** This daemon provides the core services of Samba, offering file-and-print-services functionality from the UNIX server to Windows clients. The smbd daemon also provides authentication and authorization services to Windows clients.

■ **nmbd daemon** This daemon is loaded on the UNIX server to provide WINS services and network browsing functionality so that the Samba servers appear in My Network Places on Windows clients.

ZeroConfig

Zero Configuration Networking (ZeroConfig) is a service designed to minimize the configuration of clients by broadcasting services on the network to the clients. After the service has been discovered, the client is automatically configured to use it with no interaction from the network administrator.

VoIP

Voice over IP (VoIP) is a common technology found in network environments today. VoIP is the underlining protocol that allows companies to use the phone to make calls over an IP network and the Internet. This can dramatically cut down on long-distance calls, as the VoIP system sends the voice data as network packets.

In order to use VoIP you need special equipment, such as the VoIP phones, to connect to the network. VoIP uses a number of different protocols to handle the calls over the IP network, including

- **Session Initiation Protocol (SIP)** SIP is the protocol responsible for establishing the VoIP connection and managing that connection. This includes disconnecting from the session.
- **Real-time Transport Protocol (RTP)** RTP is responsible for delivering the data across the VoIP session once the session has been established.

Unified Voice Services

Unified voice services, also known as unified communications, allows the integration of all communication into a single system. Companies today are using VoIP to have phone conversations over an IP network, but are also looking to integrate features such as instant messaging into the communication offerings.

Unified voice services is the integration of all real-time communication employees will use. That real-time communication involves

- **Instant messaging** Employees can use an instant messaging client to quickly send an instant message to another employee.
- **Presence information** Before sending a message or making a call, you can see if the employee is available because their presence information is displayed (available or busy).
- **Video conferencing** You can quickly set up a video conference allowing you to have an online meeting with other employees.
- **Desktop sharing** In video conferences, you can share your desktop in order to display things like presentations or spreadsheets.
- **Voice mail and e-mail** Unified communications also allows the employee to access their voice mail and e-mail from a single client system.

CERTIFICATION SUMMARY

In this chapter you learned about the fundamentals of TCP/IP and what makes this protocol so common in today's networking market. The following list summarizes what you learned:

- The Dynamic Host Configuration Protocol (DHCP) automatically configures a workstation with the correct TCP/IP settings, relieving you of the burden of manually configuring every workstation.

- The Domain Name System (DNS) is essential for Internet-based machines and company intranets that use DNS for hostname resolution. You learned about the hostname, domain name, resolution, and Internet domain name server hierarchies.

- The Windows Internet Naming Service (WINS), which ironically has little to do with the Internet, enables workstations to resolve NetBIOS names to IP addresses rather than using a static LMHOSTS file on each machine.

- TCP/IP is a suite of protocols, the most popular of which are TCP, UDP, IP, and ARP. (Your Network+ exam will definitely have several questions on some of these TCP/IP protocol suite members.)

With a strong understanding of the material presented in this chapter, along with the previous chapter, you will have no problems with any TCP/IP-related questions on your exam. Not only is the material presented here important for the exam, but it will also be important after you ace the exam and continue on to a career as a networking professional.

 # TWO-MINUTE DRILL

TCP/IP Protocol Suite

- ❏ TCP/IP is a suite of protocols.
- ❏ TCP is used for connection-oriented communication and ensures delivery.
- ❏ UDP is used for connectionless communication and does not ensure delivery.
- ❏ The Internet Control Message Protocol (ICMP) enables systems on a TCP/IP network to share status and error information.
- ❏ IP provides packet routing and delivery for all other protocols within the suite.
- ❏ The Address Resolution Protocol (ARP) is used to provide IP address–to–physical address resolution.
- ❏ HTTP is used to deliver webpages from the web server to the web browser, while HTTPS is used to deliver the pages securely.
- ❏ The Simple Mail Transfer Protocol (SMTP) is used to send mail over the Internet.
- ❏ The Post Office Protocol (POP) is the Internet protocol for reading e-mail.
- ❏ The Internet Message Access Protocol (IMAP), a protocol similar to POP, is used to retrieve messages from a mail server.

❑ The Simple Network Management Protocol (SNMP) is an Internet standard that provides a simple method for remotely managing virtually any network device.

❑ The File Transfer Protocol (FTP) is a TCP/IP utility that exists solely to copy files from one computer to another.

IPv6 Fundamentals

❑ IPv6 uses a 128-bit address scheme versus the 32-bit scheme used by IPv4.

❑ The IPv6 address is represented as eight 16-bit hexadecimal blocks with each block separated by a colon (:).

❑ The loopback address in IPv6 is 0000:0000:0000:0000:0000:0000:0000:0001, or ::1 as a compressed address.

❑ IPv6 addresses that start with 2001 are global addresses (similar to IPv4 public IP addresses), while addresses that start with FE80 are known as link-local addresses.

Network Services

❑ DHCP is responsible for assigning IP address information to clients.

❑ DNS is a distributed database that is responsible for converting FQDNs to IP addresses.

❑ WINS is responsible for converting computer names to IP addresses.

❑ NAT is responsible for hiding internal network addresses by configuring all systems to use the NAT system as the default gateway. The NAT server will then change the source address of outgoing packets to its own external address, ensuring that all requests look as though they are coming from the NAT server. The NAT server will receive any responses and then send the response to the internal client—ensuring that no external system can communicate with internal systems.

❑ SMB is the file-sharing protocol on Microsoft networks that allows clients to access file systems on remote Microsoft systems.

❑ NFS is the file-sharing protocol on UNIX networks that allows UNIX clients to access file systems on NFS servers.

❑ AFP is the file-sharing protocol for Macintosh systems, allowing Macs to access remote file systems on Macintosh systems.

❑ Samba is a service that implements SMB on UNIX servers, allowing Microsoft clients to access file systems on the UNIX server.

SELF TEST

The following questions will help you measure your understanding of the material presented in this chapter. Read all the choices carefully because there might be more than one correct answer. Choose all correct answers for each question.

TCP/IP Protocol Suite

1. Which layer of the OSI model does the IP protocol run at?
    A. Layer 2
    B. Layer 3
    C. Layer 4
    D. Layer 5

2. Which of the following protocols are layer-4 protocols? (Select all that apply.)
    A. TCP
    B. IP
    C. ARP
    D. UDP

3. Which protocol is responsible for converting the IP address to a MAC address?
    A. IP
    B. TCP
    C. ARP
    D. ICMP

4. Which protocol is responsible for sending e-mail across the Internet?
    A. POP3
    B. IMAP4
    C. HTTP
    D. SMTP

5. Which protocol is responsible for connection-oriented communication?
    A. TCP
    B. IP
    C. UDP
    D. ICMP

6. Which protocol is responsible for error reporting and status information?
   A.   ICMP
   B.   TCP
   C.   UDP
   D.   IP

7. Which protocol is responsible for logical addressing and delivery of packets?
   A.   ICMP
   B.   TCP
   C.   IP
   D.   UDP

IPv6 Fundamentals

8. Jeff is one of the network administrators in your office and he says that he noticed his Windows 8 desktop has a link-local address assigned. Which of the following addresses is his Windows 8 system using?
   A.   ::1
   B.   fe80::b596:cafa:5ea1:cbf0
   C.   2001::b596:cafa:5ea1:cbf0
   D.   FF01:0:0:0:0:0:0:2

9. How many bits in an IPv6 address?
   A.   128 bits
   B.   32 bits
   C.   48 bits
   D.   256 bits

10. Which of the following represents an IPv6 global address?
   A.   ::1
   B.   fe80::b596:cafa:5ea1:cbf0
   C.   2001::b596:cafa:5ea1:cbf0
   D.   FF01:0:0:0:0:0:0:2

11. Which of the following tunneling protocols would you use to tunnel IPv6 packets in an IPv4 packet when sitting behind a NAT device?
   A.   6to4
   B.   ISATAP
   C.   4to6
   D.   Teredo

12. Which of the following identify benefits of IPv6 over IPv4? (Select three.)
   A. Auto-configuration
   B. Decreased address space
   C. No broadcast messages
   D. Increased address space
   E. More broadcast messages

Network Services

13. Which network service is responsible for allowing Microsoft clients access to the file system on a UNIX server?
   A. NAT
   B. NFS
   C. SMB
   D. Samba

14. Which network service is responsible for assigning IP addresses to clients on the network?
   A. NAT
   B. WINS
   C. DHCP
   D. NFS

15. Which network service is responsible for allowing Microsoft clients to access the file system on Microsoft servers?
   A. SMB
   B. NFS
   C. NAT
   D. Samba

16. Which network service is responsible for hiding internal network resources by changing the source address of every outbound packet?
   A. NAT
   B. NFS
   C. SMB
   D. Samba

Performance-Based Question Review: See the performance-based question sample from the author included with the accompanying media.

SELF TEST ANSWERS

TCP/IP Protocol Suite

1. ☑ **B.** The IP protocol is responsible for logical addressing and routing, which is a function of layer 3 of the OSI model.
   ☒ **A, C,** and **D** are incorrect. The IP protocol does not run at those layers or perform their functions.

2. ☑ **A** and **D.** TCP and UDP are transport protocols. TCP is responsible for connection-oriented communication and error-free delivery, whereas UDP is responsible for connectionless communication.
   ☒ **B** and **C** are incorrect. IP is a network-layer protocol, and ARP is a layer-2 protocol.

3. ☑ **C.** The Address Resolution Protocol (ARP) is responsible for converting an IP address to a MAC address so that communication can occur.
   ☒ **A, B,** and **D** are incorrect. IP is used for packet delivery, TCP is used for ensuring packet delivery, and ICMP is used for error reporting and status reporting.

4. ☑ **D.** The Simple Mail Transport Protocol (SMTP) is responsible for sending mail across the Internet.
   ☒ **A, B,** and **C** are incorrect. POP3 and IMAP are e-mail protocols, but they are standards for reading e-mail, not sending e-mail. HTTP is the protocol used by web browsers to receive webpages from the web server.

5. ☑ **A.** TCP is responsible for connection-oriented communication in the TCP/IP protocol suite.
   ☒ **B, C,** and **D** are incorrect. IP is used for packet delivery, UDP is used for connectionless communication, and ICMP is used for error reporting and status display.

6. ☑ **A.** ICMP is responsible for reporting errors and sending back status information when communicating over TCP/IP.
   ☒ **B, C,** and **D** are incorrect. TCP is used for connection-oriented communication, UDP is used for connectionless communication, and the IP protocol is used to deliver the packets.

7. ☑ **C.** IP is responsible for packet delivery and logical addressing.
   ☒ **A, B,** and **D** are incorrect. ICMP is used for error reporting, TCP is used to ensure that the packet reaches the destination, and UDP is used for connectionless communication.

IPv6 Fundamentals

8. ☑ **B.** A link-local address is automatically assigned to a Windows 8 system and is an address that starts with FE80.

☒ **A, C,** and **D** are incorrect. ::1 is the loopback address in IPv6, while addresses that start with 2001 are global addresses. An address that starts with FF01 is a multicast address in IPv6.

9. ☑ **A.** An IPv6 address is made up of 128 bits that are organized into 16-bit blocks separated by a colon (:). Each 16-bit block is made up of a 4-bit hexadecimal character. An example IPv6 address is fe80:0000:0000:0000:b596:cafa:5ea1:cbf0.

☒ **B, C,** and **D** are incorrect, as they are not the length of an IPv6 address.

10. ☑ **C.** A global address in IPv6 is equivalent to an IPv4 public address and has 2001 as a prefix.

☒ **A, B,** and **D** are incorrect. ::1 is the compressed version of a loopback address, link-local addresses start with FE80, and addresses that start with FF01 are multicast addresses.

11. ☑ **D.** Teredo is a tunneling protocol that works behind a NAT device when tunneling IPv6 packets inside IPv4 packets.

☒ **A, B,** and **C** are incorrect, as they are tunneling protocols but do not work behind a NAT device.

12. ☑ **A, C,** and **D.** There are a number of benefits to IPv6, such as increased number of addresses, auto-configuration, and no broadcast messages.

☒ **B** and **E** are incorrect, as IPv6 has not decreased the address space or increased the number of broadcast messages.

Network Services

13. ☑ **D.** Samba is responsible for allowing Microsoft clients to access resources on the UNIX system because Samba implements the SMB protocol.

☒ **A, B,** and **C** are incorrect. NAT is used to translate the source address of an outgoing packet to that of the external interface of the NAT server. NFS is the file-sharing protocol on UNIX systems, and SMB is the file-sharing protocol used between Microsoft operating systems.

14. ☑ **C.** DHCP is responsible for assigning IP addresses to clients on the network.

☒ **A, B,** and **D** are incorrect. NAT is used to translate the source address of an outgoing packet to that of the external interface of the NAT server. WINS is used to convert computer names (NetBIOS names) to IP addresses. NFS is the protocol that allows UNIX clients to connect to the remote file system of other UNIX (NFS) systems.

15. ☑ **A.** SMB is the protocol in Microsoft environments that allows Microsoft clients to connect to the file system of other Microsoft systems.

☒ **B, C,** and **D** are incorrect. NFS is the protocol that allows UNIX clients to connect to the remote file system of other UNIX (NFS) systems. NAT is used to translate the source address of an outgoing packet to that of the external interface of the NAT server. Samba is the service loaded on UNIX systems to allow Microsoft clients to access resources of the UNIX server.

16. ☑ **A.** NAT is used to translate the source address of an outgoing packet to that of the external interface of the NAT server.

☒ **B, C,** and **D** are incorrect. NFS is the protocol that allows UNIX clients to connect to the remote file system of other UNIX (NFS) systems. SMB is the protocol in Microsoft environments that allows Microsoft clients to connect to the file system of other Microsoft systems. Samba is the service loaded on UNIX systems to allow Microsoft clients to access resources of the UNIX server.

Chapter 6

TCP/IP Utilities and Troubleshooting

Many utilities are available to troubleshoot TCP/IP connectivity problems. Most utilities are in the public domain and are included with the TCP/IP protocol stack provided with the operating system that you are using. This also means that the utilities may vary slightly, depending on the operating system being used. For example, to view the TCP/IP settings on a Windows server, you would use IPCONFIG, whereas on a Linux box, you would use ifconfig—each of which may support different command-line switches. Although these utilities generally provide very basic functionality, they will prove to be invaluable when troubleshooting network problems.

In the first part of this chapter, we discuss the most commonly used TCP/IP troubleshooting tools, and in the final section, we look at how these tools can be used to help troubleshoot common networking problems. The following list provides a brief description of each utility discussed in this chapter along with its core functions—be sure to know these for the exam:

- **ARP**   Displays and modifies the local ARP cache.
- **IPCONFIG and ifconfig**   Displays current IP configuration information.
- **Ping**   Verifies hostname, host IP address, and physical connectivity to a remote TCP/IP computer.
- **Tracert**   Traces and reports on the route to a remote computer.
- **Netstat**   Displays statistics for current TCP/IP connections.
- **Telnet**   Remote terminal emulation, administration, and troubleshooting.
- **FTP**   Enables file transfers between remote computers.
- **NBTSTAT**   Used to troubleshoot NetBIOS over TCP/IP connections.

CERTIFICATION OBJECTIVE 6.01

Communication Requires ARP

As discussed in Chapter 3, network interface cards (NICs) have a hardware address, or Media Access Control (MAC) address, burned into the network card itself. When you communicate from one system to another, you normally are familiar with the IP address of the host with which you want to communicate, but underneath the hood, the systems must use the physical MAC address to send and receive data—the problem being, how does one system find out the MAC address of the other system so that it can send the data across the network? The answer—ARP. The Address Resolution Protocol (ARP) was designed to provide a mapping from the logical TCP/IP addresses to the physical MAC addresses.

Address resolution is the process of resolving addresses or converting from one type of address to another. In the case of ARP, the logical address (layer-3 address) is being converted to the MAC address (layer-2 address) by a broadcast out on the network. With ARP, the sending computer yells out on the network, "Whoever has this IP address, I need your MAC address!" This broadcast is sent out on the wire, and every host looks at the broadcast data. The host with that IP address will reply with its MAC address. The address resolution process is complete once the original computer has received the MAC address information of the destination system, and is then able to send data, as shown in Figure 6-1.

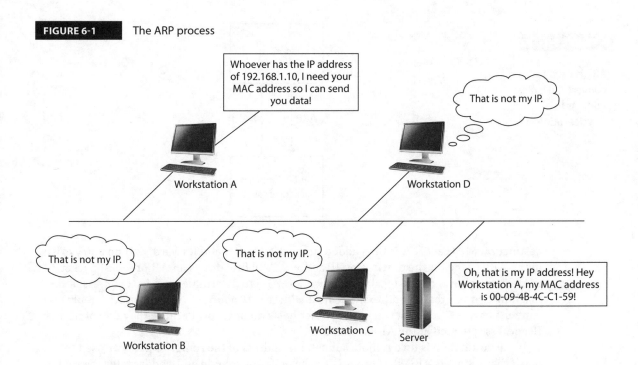

FIGURE 6-1 The ARP process

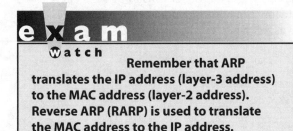

Remember that ARP translates the IP address (layer-3 address) to the MAC address (layer-2 address). Reverse ARP (RARP) is used to translate the MAC address to the IP address.

ARP maintains the protocol rules for making this translation and providing address conversion in both directions, from a layer-3 address to a layer-2 address (ARP), and from a layer-2 address to a layer-3 address (Reverse ARP), as shown in Figure 6-2. A utility by the same name is available for Windows- and Linux-based operating systems. This utility is used to display and modify entries within the ARP cache, which is where the addresses that have been resolved are stored for future reference. ARP is defined in depth in RFC 826.

How ARP Works

When a host wants to send data out on the network, the ARP protocol is tasked with finding a MAC address that matches the IP address for the destination computer. The ARP protocol first looks inside its ARP cache table for the appropriate address. If the address is found, the

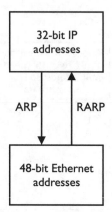

FIGURE 6-2

ARP is used to convert the logical address to a physical address.

destination MAC address is then added to the data packet and forwarded. If no entry exists in the ARP cache for the destination IP address, ARP broadcasts an ARP request packet to all the machines on the local area network (LAN) to determine the MAC address of the machine that has that IP address. The host with that IP address will send an ARP reply that contains its MAC address, whereas all other hosts do not reply because they do not have the IP address specified in the ARP request.

If the destination is on a remote subnet, the address of the router or gateway used to reach that subnet is ARPed. If the ARP cache does not contain an IP address for the router or gateway, the sending computer will ARP the IP address of the router.

Once the MAC address is determined by the ARP reply, the IP and MAC addresses of the destination system are stored in the ARP cache (stored in memory) so that next time, the address will be resolved from the cache and a broadcast will not be needed.

As protocols go, ARP provides very basic functionality; only four types of messages can be sent out by the ARP protocol, which are as follows:

- ARP request
- ARP reply
- RARP request
- RARP reply

ARP Cache

To reduce the number of address resolution broadcasts, thereby minimizing network utilization, a client caches resolved addresses for a short time in a table in memory. This table, known as the ARP cache, is used to maintain the mappings between each MAC address and its corresponding IP address locally. This is the most important part of this protocol. Since the size of the ARP cache is limited, entries need to be purged periodically. If they are not, the cache could become huge in size and could contain quite a few obsolete

FIGURE 6-3

Viewing the ARP
cache with **arp -a**

```
C:\>arp -a
Interface: 207.222.234.73
    Internet Address        Physical Address        Type
    10.37.14.92             00-60-08-72-43-d6        static
    198.70.146.70           20-53-52-43-00-00        dynamic
    199.182.120.2           20-53-52-43-00-00        dynamic
    199.182.120.202         20-53-52-43-00-00        dynamic
    206.246.150.88          20-53-52-43-00-00        dynamic
    207.211.106.40          20-53-52-43-00-00        dynamic
    207.211.106.90          20-53-52-43-00-00        dynamic
    208.223.32.77           20-53-52-43-00-00        dynamic
```

entries. Therefore, ARP cache entries are removed at predefined intervals. This process also removes any unsuccessful attempts to contact computers that are not currently running.

Entries in the ARP cache can be viewed, added, or deleted by using the ARP utility. Entries that are added with this utility manually are called *static* entries and will not expire out of cache, whereas the entries that are added automatically through broadcast are known as *dynamic* entries and will expire from the cache. Being able to view the ARP cache can be helpful in trying to resolve address resolution problems. By displaying the current cache, you can determine whether a host's MAC address is being resolved correctly.

To view the ARP cache, type the following command in a command-prompt window and press ENTER:

```
arp -a
```

Figure 6-3 shows an example of an ARP cache.

Customizing the ARP Cache

Additional options are available to customize the information found in the ARP cache. For example, you can filter the entries displayed when you list them with ARP. When you append the appropriate IP address after the **-a** switch, the table will list entries only for that particular IP address, as shown in Figure 6-4. This can be useful when trying to isolate specific entries in a large table.

FIGURE 6-4

Filtering the
ARP cache by IP
address

```
C:\>arp -a 10.37.14.92

Interface: 207.222.234.73
    Internet Address        Physical Address        Type
    10.37.14.92             00-60-08-72-43-d6        static
```

Displaying the
ARP cache by
interface

```
C:\>arp -a -n 207.222.234.73

Interface: 207.222.234.73
    Internet Address         Physical Address        Type
    10.37.14.92              00-60-08-72-43-d6        static
    32.97.105.123           20-53-52-43-00-00        dynamic
    198.70.146.70           20-53-52-43-00-00        dynamic
    199.182.120.2           20-53-52-43-00-00        dynamic
    207.211.106.40          20-53-52-43-00-00        dynamic
    207.211.106.90          20-53-52-43-00-00        dynamic
```

Type the following command, and press ENTER to view the ARP cache for a specific IP
address:

```
arp -a <IP address>
```

Computers that contain multiple NICs, or multihomed computers, have more than
one network interface listed, and the ARP cache maintains addresses for each interface
independently. When you use the ARP **-a** option, all network interfaces will be listed. To
filter the display by a specific interface, use the **-n** option. This enables you to specify which
interface to display addresses for, as shown in Figure 6-5.

Type the following command, and press ENTER to view the ARP cache for a specific
interface:

```
arp -a -n <interface>
```

To learn more about ARP, check out Exercise 6-1 and the training video for Exercise 6-1.

EXERCISE 6-1

Video

Using ARP to See Your Local ARP Cache

In this exercise, you will view your ARP cache to view the MAC addresses of systems that
you have communicated with. You will then ping the IP address of a system that does not
appear in your ARP cache and verify that it was added to the cache. After viewing the ARP
cache, you will analyze Ping traffic from a capture file and view the ARP request being sent
on the network.

1. Go to the Windows 8 virtual machine (VM).
2. Go to the command prompt by selecting Start and then type **cmd**.
3. At the command prompt, type **arp -a** and press ENTER.

4. Make a note of any entries that are in your ARP cache.

5. To delete all entries from your ARP cache, type **arp -d** and press ENTER.

6. To verify the ARP cache has been cleared, type **arp -a** and press ENTER.

7. Ping 2012SERVERA by typing **ping 10.0.0.1**.

8. At the command prompt, type **arp -a**.

9. Notice that the system that you have pinged is in the cache. This is because in order for any data to be sent to the target system, the Windows 8 system needs to know the MAC address of the target system. To learn the MAC address of the SERVER2012A system, the Windows 8 system sent an ARP request and then stored the reply in the ARP cache.

View ARP Traffic with Network Monitor

In this part of the exercise, you will open a packet capture made with Network Monitor, and you will analyze the traffic that occurs when you ping another system. Understand that Ping is just one example of communication between two systems and that no matter what type of communication occurs, the MAC address must be determined.

10. Start Network Monitor.

11. Open the packet capture called ping.cap from the Lab Files\PacketCaptures folder.

12. Once you have the packet capture open, notice that there are 13 frames in the capture. Further, by looking at the protocol column in the capture, you can see that there are two ARP frames (frames 3 and 4). You can also see that frame 3 is the ARP request going out to the network, and frame 4 is the ARP reply coming back to the system.

13. Frame 3 is the ARP request; we need to find out whom the request is for. Double-click frame 3 and expand the Ethernet section in the Frame Details pane to determine the destination MAC address of the frame (shown in the following illustration). Record the MAC address information in the space provided:

Destination MAC Address: _____

Source MAC Address: _____

Ethernet Type: _____

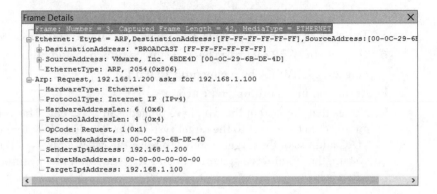

14. Double-click the last line in the Frame Details pane (the ARP: Request line). Notice that you have the sender's hardware address, the sender's protocol address, and the target computer's IP address, and that the target computer's hardware address is set to all 0s—because it is unknown. That is what ARP is trying to figure out.

15. Highlight frame 4 in the summary pane. This is the ARP reply. Double-click the ARP reply section of the frame in the details pane to expand it. Notice that in the ARP section of the reply, you have the sender's IP address and MAC address, along with the destination's MAC address and IP address. The sender's MAC address is what the initial system will use to send data to this host.

16. Record the following information:

    Source MAC Address: _____

    Source IP Address: _____

    Destination MAC Address: _____

    Destination IP Address: _____

17. What is the MAC address of the system that was pinged (192.168.1.100)?

    _____

18. Close Network Monitor.

Adding Static Entries

When ARP broadcasts out on the network to resolve an address and then adds that entry to the ARP cache, it creates a dynamic entry. A dynamic entry is added and removed from the cache automatically. The systems administrator can add static entries to the ARP cache manually when necessary. This can be especially helpful when you have a computer that transfers large amounts of data to a remote host continually. By adding a static entry for the remote host into the computer's ARP cache table, you determine that ARP broadcasts do not need to occur periodically, which minimizes network traffic. This option can also be used to test whether the local computer is receiving updates correctly.

Suppose that you are trying to connect to another computer on the same network. You are unable to find the remote computer; however, the other machines around you seem to work fine. First, display the local ARP cache to determine whether the target host has an entry present in the ARP cache. If not, you can add a static entry into the ARP cache to determine whether the computer is properly receiving updates. If, with the new static entry placed in the cache, you notice that you can now connect to the remote computer, the problem was probably that the cache was not being updated correctly with the appropriate MAC address. Adding a static entry bypassed that problem because you have forced the entry into the cache, which is checked first for ARP resolution.

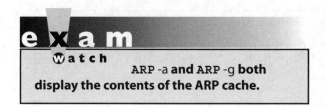

ARP -a and ARP -g both display the contents of the ARP cache.

You can manually add entries with the following command:

```
ARP -s <IP address> <MAC address>
```

Deleting Static Entries

You might need to delete entries that you have manually added or manually remove any entries that have been dynamically added to the ARP cache. Use the following command to delete an entry from the ARP cache:

```
ARP -d <IP Address>
```

ARP Cache Aging

Unlike static addresses, which never age out, dynamic addresses remain for only a predetermined amount of time. The initial cache lifetime of entries is two minutes on Windows systems, but Windows adjusts the size of the ARP cache automatically. If entries are reused within two minutes, they remain for ten minutes. A Registry parameter within Windows is also available to allow for more control over the aging parameters. The Registry parameter is located in the following location:

```
Hkey_Local_Machine\System\CurrentControlSet\Services\Tcpip\
Parameters\ArpCacheLife
```

If the ArpCacheLife entry is not found in the Tcpip\Parameters portion of the Registry, the default lifetime of two minutes (120 seconds) will be used. If you want to create the ArpCacheLife Registry entry, create a dword value named ArpCacheLife and set its value in seconds.

TABLE 6-1	ARP Switch	Definition
ARP Switches	-a	Displays the entire current ARP cache or a single entry by allowing you to specify the IP address of an adapter.
	-g	Same as -a.
	-N	Shows the ARP entries for a specified IP address and allows for modification.
	-d	Deletes a specified entry or, when used by itself, will clear the entire ARP cache.
	-s	Adds an entry to the ARP cache by specifying a MAC address and an IP address.

RARP

A little-known protocol exists to facilitate the reverse function of ARP. The *Reverse Address Resolution Protocol (RARP)* enables a machine to learn its own IP address by broadcasting to resolve its own MAC address. A RARP server containing these mappings can respond with the IP address for the requesting host. In most cases, a machine knows its own IP address; therefore, RARP is primarily used in situations such as diskless workstations or machines without hard disks. Dumb terminals and NetPCs are good examples of diskless workstations.

To summarize, although ARP is a simple protocol compared to most other protocols, it is just as important as any other to TCP/IP for proper functionality. The utility included with this protocol (ARP) will enable you to display and modify the ARP cache as needed. This enables you to effectively troubleshoot any issues that might arise with ARP. Table 6-1 details the ARP switches and their corresponding definitions.

CERTIFICATION OBJECTIVE 6.02

Common TCP/IP Commands

In this section you will learn about common TCP/IP commands that are used every day when troubleshooting networking environments. Be sure to know these commands for the exam and their output!

IPCONFIG and ifconfig

IPCONFIG and ifconfig are utilities used to display the current TCP/IP configuration. IPCONFIG is a command-line utility for Windows-based systems, and ifconfig is a command-line utility for UNIX and Linux systems. Mac OS X is based on Berkeley Software Distribution (BSD) UNIX, so ifconfig also works on Apple computers running that operating system. By default, IPCONFIG displays the IP address, the subnet mask, and the default gateway. The **ifconfig** command in Linux does not display the default gateway—use the **ip route** command instead. On newer versions of Linux, you can also use the **ip addr** command to display IP address information.

IPCONFIG

IPCONFIG is used in Windows to display TCP/IP information from a command prompt. With this utility, you can also display other related IP settings, such as who your Domain Name System (DNS) and Windows Internet Naming Service (WINS) servers are. You can also view the network interface's physical MAC address with IPCONFIG. If you have more than one network interface, statistics are displayed about each one individually or can be filtered to a particular one.

If you use the IPCONFIG command by itself with no command-line switches, it will display your IP address, subnet mask, and default gateway, but if you use the /ALL switch with it, it will display all TCP/IP information available. To view all your TCP/IP settings, type the following in a command prompt:

```
ipconfig /all
```

The following output will be displayed. Notice that you can see the hostname, IPv4 address, IPv6 address, physical address (MAC address), DNS server, and IP address of the Dynamic Host Configuration Protocol (DHCP) server that gave your system its IP address.

```
C:\Users\gclarke>ipconfig /all
Windows IP Configuration

        Host Name . . . . . . . . . . . . : SONY1
        Primary Dns Suffix  . . . . . . . :
        Node Type . . . . . . . . . . . . : Hybrid
        IP Routing Enabled. . . . . . . . : No
        WINS Proxy Enabled. . . . . . . . : No
        DNS Suffix Search List. . . . . . : eastlink.ca
Ethernet adapter Ethernet:
        Connection-specific DNS Suffix  . : eastlink.ca
        Description . . . . . . . . . . . : Realtek PCIe GBE Family Controller
        Physical Address. . . . . . . . . : 54-53-ED-BC-12-B4
        DHCP Enabled. . . . . . . . . . . : Yes
        Autoconfiguration Enabled . . . . : Yes
        Link-local IPv6 Address . : fe80::b596:cafa:5ea1:cbf0%13(Preferred)
        IPv4 Address. . . . . . . . . . . : 192.168.1.179(Preferred)
```

```
Subnet Mask . . . . . . . . . . . : 255.255.255.0
Lease Obtained. . . . . . . . : Tuesday, September 2, 2014 8:02:10 AM
Lease Expires . . . . . . . . : Friday, September 5, 2014 10:00:04 AM
Default Gateway . . . . . . . . : 192.168.1.1
DHCP Server . . . . . . . . . . : 192.168.1.1
DHCPv6 IAID . . . . . . . . . . : 357848045
DHCPv6 Client DUID. . . : 00-01-00-01-1A-CA-5A-4A-60-36-DD-6A-1A-D0

DNS Servers . . . . . . . . . . : 192.168.1.1
NetBIOS over Tcpip. . . . . . . : Enabled
Connection-specific DNS Suffix Search List :
                                  eastlink.ca
```

IPCONFIG DHCP Parameters   The IPCONFIG command-line utility enables you to control DHCP functions with command-line switches such as **/release** and **/renew**.

The **/release** option removes the assigned IP address from your system. By default, **/release** removes the assigned IP address from all adapters configured for DHCP use. By specifying the adapter name after the switch, only that adapter will be affected by the command. The **/release** option can be useful if you are experiencing problems associated with DHCP, such as realizing that you received an address from the wrong DHCP server. It can also be used to release the address if an IP conflict occurs.

The **/renew** option sends a request to the DHCP server asking for an address. It takes the last address DHCP assigned to your system if it is available. If not, the computer is given the next available address in the pool. As with the **/release** option, you can specify a particular adapter after the switch to renew the address. This will only work if the adapter has been set up to receive its IP address from a DHCP server.

The IPCONFIG utility also supports switches for troubleshooting DNS name resolution. Windows has a DNS resolver cache that stores responses from the DNS server in memory so that the client will not need to query DNS a second time for an address already stored in the cache—the name is resolved from the cache. If you want to display the DNS resolver cache, you may use the **/displaydns** switch with IPCONFIG. If you want to clear, or flush, the DNS resolver cache, you may use the **/flushdns** switch. Flushing the cache will ensure that the client system will query DNS and get up-to-date records.

on the job

A number of times I have modified a record in DNS and had trouble communicating with the host for which the DNS change was made. The reason was that the machine I was sitting at had the old DNS data in the resolver cache, and I ended up needing to flush the cache.

To display the DNS resolver cache on your system, type the following at a command prompt:

```
ipconfig /displaydns
```

To clear the entries from the DNS resolver cache, type the following at a command prompt:

```
ipconfig /flushdns
```

EXERCISE 6-2

Using IPCONFIG

In this exercise, you will experiment with the IPCONFIG command-line utility to view your TCP/IP settings.

1. Go to the Windows 8 VM and ensure that it is a DHCP client.
2. Go to Start | Run and type **CMD**.
3. Type **ipconfig** and record your current TCP/IP settings in the space provided:
   - IP Address: _____
   - Subnet Mask: _____
   - Default Gateway: _____
4. At the command prompt, type **ipconfig /all** to view all of your TCP/IP settings. Record your findings in the space provided:
   - Your MAC Address: _____
   - Your DHCP Server: _____
   - Your DNS Server: _____
   - Lease Renew Date/Time_____
5. At the command prompt, renew your IP address by typing **ipconfig /renew**.
6. Type **ipconfig /all** and record your settings in the space provided:
   - Lease Obtain Date/Time: _____
   - Lease Renew Date/Time: _____
7. Type **exit**.

ifconfig

UNIX and Linux operating systems have a command similar to IPCONFIG, and it is **ifconfig** (case sensitive). The **ifconfig** command stands for Interface Config and is used to control the network interface, which is most commonly referred to as the network card. Let's look at a few **ifconfig** commands.

Using **ifconfig** in Linux to display IP address information

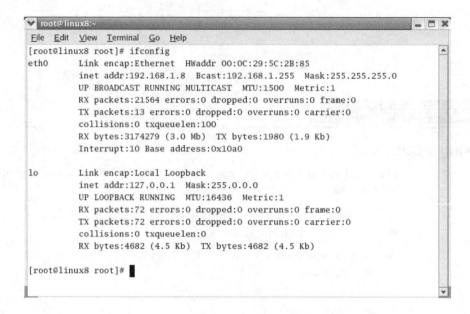

```
[root@linux8 root]# ifconfig
eth0      Link encap:Ethernet  HWaddr 00:0C:29:5C:2B:85
          inet addr:192.168.1.8  Bcast:192.168.1.255  Mask:255.255.255.0
          UP BROADCAST RUNNING MULTICAST  MTU:1500  Metric:1
          RX packets:21564 errors:0 dropped:0 overruns:0 frame:0
          TX packets:13 errors:0 dropped:0 overruns:0 carrier:0
          collisions:0 txqueuelen:100
          RX bytes:3174279 (3.0 Mb)  TX bytes:1980 (1.9 Kb)
          Interrupt:10 Base address:0x10a0

lo        Link encap:Local Loopback
          inet addr:127.0.0.1  Mask:255.0.0.0
          UP LOOPBACK RUNNING  MTU:16436  Metric:1
          RX packets:72 errors:0 dropped:0 overruns:0 frame:0
          TX packets:72 errors:0 dropped:0 overruns:0 carrier:0
          collisions:0 txqueuelen:0
          RX bytes:4682 (4.5 Kb)  TX bytes:4682 (4.5 Kb)

[root@linux8 root]#
```

The first example is to use **ifconfig** by itself without any additional switches. When you type **ifconfig** in Linux, you will get a list of network cards and the IP address and MAC addresses associated with each card (shown in Figure 6-6).

In Windows, we can enable and disable a network card by right-clicking the LAN Connection and choosing Enable or Disable. In Linux, if you wish to disable the network card, you will use the **ifconfig** command as follows:

```
ifconfig eth0 up
```

The eth0 part of the command is how you specify the network card you wish to work with. If you had two network cards in the Linux computer, they might be known as eth0 and eth1. This is very similar to how a Cisco router refers to the different network interfaces. The **up** switch means that you wish to bring the card up, or enable it. If you wish to disable the card, you would use the keyword **down**.

In many Linux distributions, if you wish to renew your IP address, you can use the **dhclient** command (shown in Figure 6-7), which is the equivalent to the Windows **ipconfig /renew** command.

exam

ⓦatch   For the Network+ exam, know that ifconfig **is the command to display your IP address settings in Linux. Also, remember that Linux is case sensitive.**

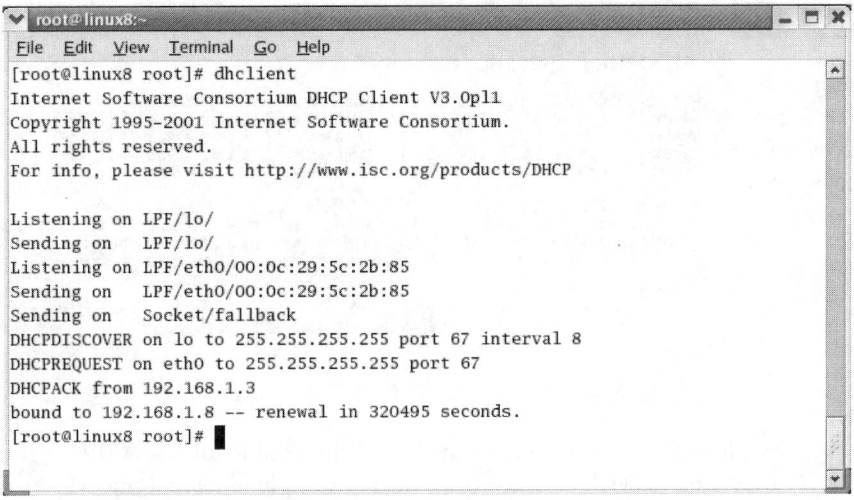

FIGURE 6-7

Using **dhclient**
to renew the IP
address in Linux

```
root@linux8:~                                                          _ ☐ ✕
File  Edit  View  Terminal  Go  Help
[root@linux8 root]# dhclient
Internet Software Consortium DHCP Client V3.0pl1
Copyright 1995-2001 Internet Software Consortium.
All rights reserved.
For info, please visit http://www.isc.org/products/DHCP

Listening on LPF/lo/
Sending on   LPF/lo/
Listening on LPF/eth0/00:0c:29:5c:2b:85
Sending on   LPF/eth0/00:0c:29:5c:2b:85
Sending on   Socket/fallback
DHCPDISCOVER on lo to 255.255.255.255 port 67 interval 8
DHCPREQUEST on eth0 to 255.255.255.255 port 67
DHCPACK from 192.168.1.3
bound to 192.168.1.8 -- renewal in 320495 seconds.
[root@linux8 root]# ▮
```

FIGURE 6-7

Using **dhclient** to renew the IP address in Linux

Looking at Figure 6-7, you can see that the **dhclient** command was typed in. You will also notice at the bottom of the output that a DHCPACK came from 192.168.1.3. This means that the Linux machine has received an IP address from the DHCP server running on 192.168.1.3. You will also notice that the Linux network card is bound to address 192.168.1.8.

Ping and Hping2

The Ping (Packet Internet Groper) command is the most-used TCP/IP troubleshooting tool available. This command is used to test a machine's connectivity to another system and to verify that the target system is active.

Usually, using this command is the first step to any troubleshooting if a connectivity problem is occurring between two computers. This can quickly help you determine whether a remote host is available and responsive.

How Ping Works

Ping uses the Internet Control Message Protocol (ICMP) protocol to verify connections to remote hosts by sending *echo request* packets and listening for *echo reply* packets. Ping sends

FIGURE 6-8

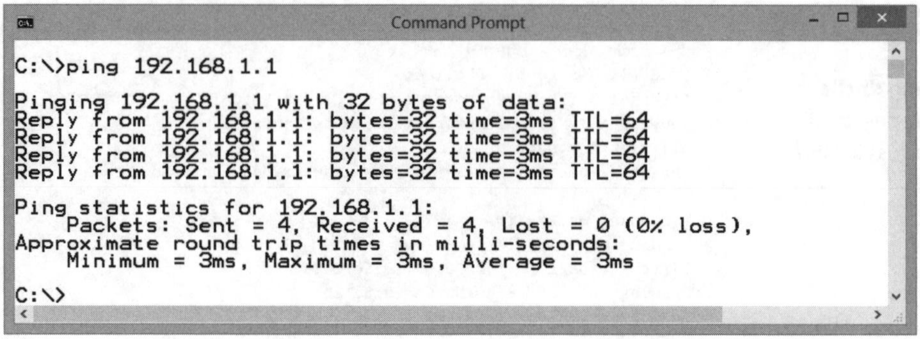

The **ping** command tests connectivity to another system.

```
C:\>ping 192.168.1.1

Pinging 192.168.1.1 with 32 bytes of data:
Reply from 192.168.1.1: bytes=32 time=3ms TTL=64
Reply from 192.168.1.1: bytes=32 time=3ms TTL=64
Reply from 192.168.1.1: bytes=32 time=3ms TTL=64
Reply from 192.168.1.1: bytes=32 time=3ms TTL=64

Ping statistics for 192.168.1.1:
    Packets: Sent = 4, Received = 4, Lost = 0 (0% loss),
Approximate round trip times in milli-seconds:
    Minimum = 3ms, Maximum = 3ms, Average = 3ms

C:\>
```

out four different echo messages and prints out feedback of the replies on the screen when they are received. Figure 6-8 shows an example of using Ping.

To use the **ping** command and see the results, perform Exercise 6-3 or watch the training video for this book.

EXERCISE 6-3

Video

Using Ping

In this exercise, you will ping a system on your network and then ping your own software stack by pinging the loopback address.

1. Ensure that you have the 2012SERVERA and Windows 8 VMs running.
2. Go to the Windows 8 VM and log on.
3. Go to the command prompt by selecting Start and then type **CMD**.
4. At the command prompt, type **ping 10.0.0.1**. In this example, you are pinging the 2012SERVERA system by its IP address.
5. You will get four replies back from the ping message if the system you have pinged is up and running.
6. To test your TCP/IP software stack, you can ping the loopback address by typing **ping 127.0.0.1**.
7. If you receive four lines of information showing successes, the TCP/IP protocol is initialized and functioning. Four lines of failed transmissions will show that TCP/IP is not initialized and cannot be used to perform network transmissions.

Ping Options

Additional options are available to customize the output that Ping provides. Options include changing packet length, type of service, and time to live (TTL) settings. You can append the **-a** option to resolve an IP address to its hostname. The **-f** option ensures the packets are not allowed to be fragmented by a router or gateway. The **-l <size>** parameter is used to set the size of the Ping packet. Together, the **-f** and **-l** can be used to further stress connections to determine whether they are failing.

The TTL settings can be specified with the **-i** option. In addition, the type of service option is available via the **-v** switch.

Setting the Length Option   By default, packets are sent in 32-byte chunks. You can modify the packet size to further test the response time. When larger packets are involved, you can see what larger loads will do to response time. To change the packet size, use the **-l** option followed by the packet length. The maximum packet length that can be specified is 65,500 bytes.

Setting the Number of Echo Packets   You can specify the number of packets to send to the remote host. By default, only four packets are sent. You can specify any number of packets to send with the **-n** option. You can also use the **-t** option to specify a continuous stream of packets, and to continuously ping the remote host until you stop the command with a CTRL-BREAK. This functionality is useful in monitoring trends in data transfers.

Timeout Intervals   Timeout intervals are used to interpret the time to travel between hops. A normal LAN usually lists devices as being less than 10 milliseconds away. By default, two seconds is the timeout before a "reply timed out" message is generated. You can use the **-w** option to raise this value for troubleshooting.

Loose-Source Routing   Use Ping to specify intermediate gateways to test against. You can route packets through particular IP addresses or hostnames. The **-j** option enables you to specify the hosts to route through. The **-k** option enables you to exclude hosts from this route list. The maximum number of hosts you can specify with both options is nine.

ping -4 versus ping -6   Because Windows systems today are running both IPv4 and IPv6 at the same time, the **ping** command now has options for you to specify whether you want to use IPv4 or IPv6 to perform the Ping operation. To use IPv4, you would use the following command:

```
C:\>ping -4 SONY1
Pinging SONY1 [192.168.114.1] with 32 bytes of data:
Reply from 192.168.114.1: bytes=32 time<1ms TTL=128
Reply from 192.168.114.1: bytes=32 time<1ms TTL=128
```

```
Reply from 192.168.114.1: bytes=32 time<1ms TTL=128
Reply from 192.168.114.1: bytes=32 time<1ms TTL=128
Ping statistics for 192.168.114.1:
    Packets: Sent = 4, Received = 4, Lost = 0 (0% loss),
Approximate round trip times in milli-seconds:
    Minimum = 0ms, Maximum = 0ms, Average = 0ms
```

Notice in the output the IPv4 address of 192.168.114.1 when I ping a system called SONY1. If I wanted to use IPv6 to ping the same system, I would use the following command:

```
C:\>ping -6 SONY1

Pinging SONY1 [fe80::81f2:cdf4:71b:93cb%25] with 32 bytes of data:
Reply from fe80::81f2:cdf4:71b:93cb%25: time<1ms
Reply from fe80::81f2:cdf4:71b:93cb%25: time<1ms
Reply from fe80::81f2:cdf4:71b:93cb%25: time<1ms
Reply from fe80::81f2:cdf4:71b:93cb%25: time<1ms

Ping statistics for fe80::81f2:cdf4:71b:93cb%25:
    Packets: Sent = 4, Received = 4, Lost = 0 (0% loss),
Approximate round trip times in milli-seconds:
    Minimum = 0ms, Maximum = 0ms, Average = 0ms
```

Notice this time that the IPv6 address of fe80::81f2:cdf4:71b:93cb is being tested.

Troubleshooting with Ping

Use the Ping utility to verify connectivity by IP address or hostname. You must be able to resolve the hostname to use this functionality. If you are unable to ping by hostname but you can ping by IP address, you most likely have a name-resolution problem.

If you are receiving "reply timed out" messages, you might try bumping up the timeout value with the **-w** option. Maybe the packets are arriving but are timing out before two seconds. After bumping up the value, if the replies are returning, a bandwidth problem might be present. Contact the network administrator when the numbers seem to rise. Table 6-2 details the Ping command-line switches.

	Ping Switch	Definition
TABLE 6-2	-t	Specifies to perform the **ping** command until interrupted.
	-a	Resolves addresses to computer names.
Ping Command-Line Switches	-n	Specifies the number of echo packets; the default is 4.
	-l	Specifies the amount of data to send in an echo packet. The default is 32 bytes; the maximum is 65,500 bytes.
	-f	Specifies to not fragment packets.
	-I	Sets TTL value for packets.
	-v	Sets TOS (type of service).
	-r	Records routes of packets.
	-s	Specifies timestamp for number of hops.
	-j	Specifies route for packets (loose-source route).
	-k	Specifies route for packets (strict-source route).
	-w	Specifies timeout interval in milliseconds.
	-destination-list	Specifies remote PC to ping.

watch   The Ping utility uses the ICMP protocol instead of TCP, which is used by File Transfer Protocol (FTP) and Telnet. ICMP has different types of messages that can be sent; ICMP Type 8 is the message type of an echo request, while echo replies come back as ICMP Type 0.

Hping2

The Ping utility that ships with most operating systems uses ICMP as the underlining protocol. There are other Ping-type utilities out there that give you more flexibility, such as Hping or the newer version, Hping2. Hping2 is popular because instead of using ICMP, it uses TCP as the underlying protocol and allows you to craft the packets to use whatever port you wish. This allows you to ping through firewalls that may be blocking ICMP traffic. The following is a typical **hping2** command:

```
hping2 -c 3 -s 53 -p 80 -S 10.0.0.25
```

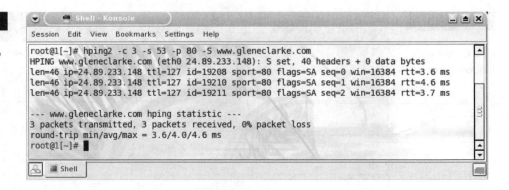

FIGURE 6-9

Using Hping2 to craft a TCP Ping message

In this code example, the **-c** switch is used to specify how many Ping messages you wish to send. In this example, I have specified to send three messages. The **-s** switch is used to specify the source port, and the **-p** is used to specify the destination port of the packet. In this example, I have made the traffic look as if it is coming from a DNS server but is destined for the web server. The **-S** specifies that I want to send a TCP SYN message, while the 10.0.0.25 is the target IP address of the system to ping. Figure 6-9 displays the Hping2 utility being used to bypass my firewall, which is blocking ICMP traffic.

exam
watch

Hping2 is a Ping-style program that allows you to craft your own TCP packet used in the ping operation. This gives you the flexibility of being able to bypass firewalls, because you can create a packet that uses port numbers open on the firewall.

Tracert/traceroute

Tracert in Windows, or traceroute as it is known in Linux, is a command-line utility that was designed to perform a very basic task: to determine the path taken by a data packet to reach its destination. This is different from using the Ping utility. The Ping utility will give you a response if the address you have pinged is up and running. Tracert will send you a response with each router that is hit on the way. This will help you understand the number of networks, or hops, between you and the destination.

This could be useful in a scenario where you know that from the Boston office to the New York office there are 13 hops normally, but one day, users start complaining that the

exam
watch

For the exam, know that the Tracert (Windows) and traceroute (Linux) utilities use ICMP as their underlying protocol.

```
C:\WINDOWS\System32\cmd.exe

C:\Documents and Settings\gclarke>tracert www.novell.com
Tracing route to www.novell.com [130.57.4.27]
over a maximum of 30 hops:

  1     2 ms     2 ms     1 ms  192.168.14.254
  2     8 ms     3 ms     3 ms  142.176.245.137
  3    16 ms     *       20 ms  142.176.203.101
  4    15 ms    21 ms     9 ms  alns-dr01-ge-6-0.aliant.net [142.166.182.130]
  5    16 ms    15 ms    12 ms  alns-dr02-g5-0.aliant.net [142.166.181.22]
  6    77 ms    28 ms    37 ms  69.156.255.45
  7    31 ms    37 ms    33 ms  core1-montrealak-pos5-2.in.bellnexxia.net [64.23
0.240.1]
  8    37 ms    25 ms    27 ms  bx1-montrealak-pos1-0.in.bellnexxia.net [64.230.
240.50]
  9    34 ms    28 ms    25 ms  if-1-0.core1.mtt-montreal.teleglobe.net [207.45.
204.1]
 10    46 ms    49 ms    53 ms  if-5-0.core2.mtt-montreal.teleglobe.net [64.86.8
1.162]
 11    49 ms    54 ms    46 ms  if-3-0.core2.ttt-scarborough.teleglobe.net [66.1
98.82.10]
 12    53 ms    49 ms    54 ms  if-3-0.core2.cqw-chicago.teleglobe.net [207.45.2
22.182]
 13    48 ms    46 ms    46 ms  if-7-0.core2.ct8-chicago.teleglobe.net [66.110.1
4.165]
 14    45 ms    50 ms    53 ms  if-4-1.core1.ct8-chicago.teleglobe.net [66.110.2
7.189]
 15    55 ms    52 ms    55 ms  ix-6-3.core1.ct8-chicago.teleglobe.net [66.110.2
7.30]
 16    68 ms    53 ms    55 ms  tbr1-p010401.cgcil.ip.att.net [12.123.6.66]
 17   108 ms   104 ms   103 ms  gbr4-p10.dvmco.ip.att.net [12.122.10.118]
 18   109 ms    99 ms   104 ms  12.122.10.141
 19    99 ms    99 ms    99 ms  gar1-p360.slkut.ip.att.net [12.122.2.237]
 20   108 ms   107 ms    99 ms  12.127.106.34
 21   104 ms   100 ms   108 ms  192.94.118.221
 22   103 ms   103 ms   103 ms  www.novell.com [130.57.4.27]

Trace complete.

C:\Documents and Settings\gclarke>^@
```

network is slow, and when you do a Tracert, you notice that there are 19 hops. This means that your packets are taking a different route than usual, and it could be because networks along the usual route are down and your packets are taking a roundabout route to get to the destination.

When using the utility, you will notice several numbers in the display. Figure 6-10 shows an example of the **tracert** command used to display the routing path to www.novell.com.

Although a Tracert might look rather confusing at first, it is fairly easy to understand. Each row gathers information about that hop three times. The first column shows the number of hops away that router is. The next three columns show the time it took for the router to respond to each attempt. The last column lists the fully qualified domain name (FQDN) of that router, which typically gives you an indication of where the router is. For example, looking at Figure 6-10 again, you can see that hop number 12 looks like it is in Chicago!

Using Tracert

Suppose you cannot access a particular website on the Internet. Your company is directly connected to the Internet via an Integrated Services Digital Network (ISDN) line, which is used by approximately 35 people. You are able to hit certain websites consistently, but others are available only sporadically. Other users begin to notice that they are unable to connect to the same websites with which you are having a problem.

Tracert fits in well here to begin isolating where the problem is. Although you might have a good idea of what network equipment and options are used within your company, once packets enter the Internet, there is no telling what they might come across. Because routes can be so dynamic, this is a great tool for figuring out where the data is traveling to reach its destination.

You can begin troubleshooting this problem by typing one of the following commands:

```
TRACERT <hostname>
```

or

```
TRACERT <ipaddress>
```

After the utility has run, you might notice the following entry on one of the routers along the way:

```
Destination Net Unreachable
```

Although this utility is unable to determine why the error is occurring, it has effectively found at what point the problem exists. Armed with this information, the owner can then examine that router to resolve the issue.

Maximum Number of Hops   One function of the Tracert utility is to provide the number of hops, or networks, that the data is crossing. You may want to limit the number of hops the program will make to search for the remote host; if you don't, Tracert will continue for 30 hops by default. In the unusual case that you must surpass 30 hops, you can also specify a greater interval.

By using the **-h** option with Tracert, you can specify the maximum number of hops to trace a route to. Figure 6-11 shows an example of limiting the number of hops returned.

FIGURE 6-11

Specifying
the maximum
number of hops
with Tracert

```
C:\>tracert -d -h 15 www.syngress.com
Tracing route to www.syngress.com [146.115.28.75]
over a maximum of 15 hops:

  1     *         *         *       Request timed out.
  2   312 ms    325 ms    381 ms   165.236.51.1
  3   383 ms    272 ms    354 ms   163.179.232.194
  4   396 ms    354 ms    408 ms   163.179.220.182
  5   301 ms    354 ms    258 ms   192.41.177.74
  6   384 ms    325 ms     *       204.152.42.2
  7   366 ms    422 ms    353 ms   207.152.148.41
  8   301 ms    272 ms    299 ms   207.152.148.30
  9   268 ms    270 ms    268 ms   207.152.148.34
 10   383 ms   2030 ms    409 ms   207.152.148.37
 11   410 ms    382 ms    271 ms   198.32.178.13
 12   439 ms    272 ms    368 ms   146.115.17.125
 13   384 ms    381 ms    410 ms   199.232.56.39
 14   274 ms    382 ms    271 ms   146.115.28.75

Trace complete.

C:\>_
```

Adjusting Timeout Values   Another option associated with Tracert is to adjust the timeout value using the **-w** switch. This value determines the amount of time in milliseconds the program will wait for a response before moving on. Using this option will enable you to understand a little more about the problem that is occurring. For example, if you notice that many responses are timing out, you can raise this value. If, after raising this value, remote devices are responding, this could be a good indication that you have a bandwidth problem.

Loose-Source Routing Options   An additional option is loose-source routing. The **-j** option can be used to force the outbound datagram to pass through a specific router and back. This enables you to trace the round-trip route for a destination. A normal Tracert follows the route until it reaches its destination or times out. When you specify this option, Tracert follows the path to the router specified and returns to your computer. To use loose-source routing, enter the following command:

```
TRACERT -j <hop list>
```

tracert -4 versus tracert -6   Just as the **ping** command has an IPv4 mode and an IPv6 mode, the **tracert** command does as well. If you would like to use IPv4 to perform the trace (which is the default), then you can use the following command:

```
TRACERT -4 www.google.ca
```

If you would like to use IPv6 to perform the trace, then you can use the following command:

```
TRACERT -6 www.google.ca
```

Tracert Switch	Definition
-d	Does not resolve address to computer names.
-h	Specifies maximum number of hops.
-j	Specifies loose-source route along host list.
-w	Specifies time in milliseconds to wait for reply.
-target_name	Specifies target computer.

w a t c h
It is important to note that the tracert **command is used in Windows. The equivalent command in the Linux world is** traceroute**. Also, know how to perform an IPv4 trace route and an IPv6 trace route.**

It should also be noted that Linux systems have a **traceroute6** command, which performs an IPv6 trace route. Linux systems also have a **traceroute -6** command to perform the same function.

Tracert can be a useful tool in determining why a remote host can't be reached. It can also be a good tool to notice other issues, such as bandwidth utilization problems. Its additional options and functionality make it a powerful tool. Table 6-3 lists the Tracert switches and the corresponding definitions.

Netstat

Now that you've learned how to trace data packets throughout the network, another utility useful for troubleshooting TCP/IP-specific issues is Netstat. Netstat displays protocol statistics and current TCP/IP network connections. This utility can be used to display in-depth detail about protocol status and statistics for the different network interfaces, as well as viewing the current listening ports and the routing table.

How Netstat Works

TCP-based connections use a three-step handshake method for establishing sessions. This forms the basis for TCP and its reliable data transfer methodology. This enables it to act as a message-validation protocol to provide reliable communication between two hosts. A session is created via this handshake to appropriately handle the transport messages. Netstat displays information about these sessions, the network interfaces, and how they are being used.

By default, Netstat lists the protocol type, local address and port information, remote address and port information, and current state. The information provided explains what connections are open or in progress, through what ports, and what their current states are. Figure 6-12 shows an example of the Netstat utility.

FIGURE 6-12

Viewing current
connections with
Netstat

```
C:\>netstat

Active Connections

   Proto  Local Address          Foreign Address        State
   TCP    workstation2:1192      207.211.106.40:80      TIME_WAIT
   TCP    workstation2:1201      207.211.106.90:80      TIME_WAIT
   TCP    workstation2:1218      www.syngress.com:80    ESTABLISHED
   TCP    workstation2:1219      www.syngress.com:80    ESTABLISHED

C:\>
```

In Figure 6-12 you can see that the local address column references the local system and the ports on the local system that are being used as connection points to a remote system. Let's use the last entry in the output as the example to be analyzed. You can see in the last entry of the output that I have a connection to the www.syngress.com website. How do you know this? If you look at the foreign address column, you will notice the FQDN of www. syngress.com (most times, you will see an IP address here), and you will notice that the address shows an :80 at the end, which is the default port of a web server. This means that I am connected to port 80 of that FQDN. You will also notice that port 1219 is the port used by my local system—this would be the port used by my web browser, and it is what the web server at www.syngress.com uses to sends its webpages back to my system.

The state column displays the current status of TCP connections only. You can determine from the state column whether the connection is currently established or if the application running on that port is in listening mode (waiting for a connection). Table 6-4 lists the available states.

TABLE 6-4

A Look at the
Different Netstat
States

State	Explanation
SYN_SEND	Indicates an active open.
SYN_RECEIVED	Server just received a SYN from the remote client.
ESTABLISHED	Client received SYN, and the connection is complete.
LISTEN	Server is waiting for a connection.
FIN_WAIT_1	Indicates an active close.
TIMED_WAIT	Clients enter this state after an active close.
CLOSE_WAIT	Indicates a passive close; the server has just received the first FIN from the client.
FIN_WAIT_2	Client just received acknowledgment of its first FIN from the server.
LAST+ACK	Server enters this state when it sends its own FIN.
CLOSED	Server received the ACK from the client, and the connection is closed.

Netstat Options

Different types of statistics are available depending on the command-line switches used with Netstat. You can display all connections and listening ports because server connections are not displayed in the standard output. You can also display Ethernet statistics and per-protocol statistics. The routing table can also be displayed with this command.

You can use the **-n** option to display addresses and port numbers without resolving the names. Resolving names could incur additional overhead if the listing is long, and it might not work properly if you have no form of name resolution set up. Another cool switch is the interval switch—suppose you want the information that is displayed to continually update. By default, the information is displayed once. You can specify an interval in seconds appended to the end of the command to have the utility update itself. The following is an example of the command line:

```
netstat -a 5
```

This command will display the active connections every five seconds. Use CTRL-C to stop this program. This can be helpful when trying to actively monitor connections and their statistics.

Displaying Server Connections and Listening Ports   With the standard output, Netstat does not display your computer's connections and listening ports. This information might be necessary to understand what the computer is communicating with and whether a port is open and ready to receive data. Hackers can plant a number of Trojans on systems that open ports so that the hacker can connect to the open port later and send malicious data to that port. A good example is the old Netbus program. When a user ran Netbus, it would do nothing but open port 12345 so that the hacker could connect and do things like eject your CD-ROM, run a program on your system, navigate your system to a URL, and switch your left and right mouse buttons. It is important that you are able to identify whether a system has been hit with such a program, and one way is to monitor the listening ports with Netstat. To view a list of listening ports, type the following command:

```
netstat -a
```

Displaying Interface Statistics   Another option enables you to display the Ethernet interface statistics of your system. The information available with the **-e** option includes the number of bytes received and sent, the number of discards and errors, and unknown protocols. By understanding what this information means, you can monitor the amount of traffic that is being used in communications. Since this option also displays errors, you can check here to see if communication-related problems are occurring. Figure 6-13 shows an example of the Netstat utility with this option.

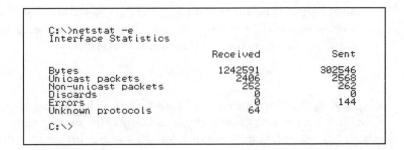

FIGURE 6-13

Viewing network
interface statistics
with Netstat

Displaying Per-Protocol Statistics Although the previous option shows Ethernet interface–specific information, protocol-specific information is also available. With the **-s** option, you can display statistics for all the communications protocols used by TCP/IP. The protocols include TCP, UDP (User Datagram Protocol), ICMP, and IP. Detailed information can be obtained with this option that can help you isolate TCP/IP communications issues.

You can also filter the list of statistics by protocol to focus on a specific area. The **-p** option can be used alone to display connection information by TCP or UDP, or you can use it with the protocol statistics option (**-s**) to filter the statistics by TCP, UDP, ICMP, or IP. Figure 6-14 shows an example of this filtering.

FIGURE 6-14

Viewing specific
protocol
information
with Netstat

```
C:\>netstat -s -p IP

IP Statistics

    Packets Received            = 2564
    Received Header Errors      = 0
    Received Address Errors     = 28
    Datagrams Forwarded         = 0
    Unknown Protocols Received  = 0
    Received Packets Discarded  = 0
    Received Packets Delivered  = 2564
    Output Requests             = 2801
    Routing Discards            = 4194332
    Discarded Output Packets    = 0
    Output Packet No Route      = 0
    Reassembly Required         = 0
    Reassembly Successful       = 0
    Reassembly Failures         = 0
    Datagrams Successfully Fragmented = 0
    Datagrams Failing Fragmentation   = 0
    Fragments Created           = 0

C:\>_
```

One of my favorite switches for Netstat is the **-p** switch; I can pass it the argument of TCP to view all the TCP-based connections that my system has. If you type the following command, you can view your TCP connection information:

```
netstat -p TCP
```

Displaying the Current Route Table   You will learn more about routing tables in Chapter 8, but for now, know that you can display the routing table on a system with two commands—the **netstat –r** command or the **route print** command..

Troubleshooting with Netstat

Using Netstat to monitor TCP protocol activity can enable you to troubleshoot TCP/IP-based connections. Netstat can be used in a variety of ways. You can use the **-a** option to monitor active connections. I use this a lot to monitor systems connected to my website. From a security point of view, you can use **netstat -a** to view a list of listening ports—useful if you suspect that someone has planted a Trojan on your system. Newer versions of Windows now support the **-o** switch with Netstat to display the process ID number of the program that is responsible for opening the port! Very useful when trying to close down open ports and you need to know what program has opened the port so you know which program to end. Figure 6-15 displays the **netstat** command with the **-o** switch.

Notice in Figure 6-15 that the **-na** option was used, which shows all ports in numerical format. The **-o** is the reason there is a column for the process ID number (PID). Once you know the process ID number, you can then use the Windows **tasklist** command to display which executable is associated with that process ID (shown in Figure 6-16).

FIGURE 6-15

The **-o** switch of Netstat displays the process ID.

```
Microsoft Windows [Version 5.2.3790]
(C) Copyright 1985-2003 Microsoft Corp.

H:\>netstat -na -o

Active Connections

  Proto  Local Address          Foreign Address        State           PID
  TCP    0.0.0.0:25             0.0.0.0:0              LISTENING       1668
  TCP    0.0.0.0:53             0.0.0.0:0              LISTENING       1544
  TCP    0.0.0.0:80             0.0.0.0:0              LISTENING       4
  TCP    0.0.0.0:88             0.0.0.0:0              LISTENING       400
  TCP    0.0.0.0:110            0.0.0.0:0              LISTENING       1668
  TCP    0.0.0.0:135            0.0.0.0:0              LISTENING       752
  TCP    0.0.0.0:389            0.0.0.0:0              LISTENING       400
  TCP    0.0.0.0:445            0.0.0.0:0              LISTENING       4
  TCP    0.0.0.0:464            0.0.0.0:0              LISTENING       400
  TCP    0.0.0.0:593            0.0.0.0:0              LISTENING       752
  TCP    0.0.0.0:636            0.0.0.0:0              LISTENING       400
  TCP    0.0.0.0:691            0.0.0.0:0              LISTENING       1668
  TCP    0.0.0.0:995            0.0.0.0:0              LISTENING       1668
  TCP    0.0.0.0:1026           0.0.0.0:0              LISTENING       400
  TCP    0.0.0.0:1027           0.0.0.0:0              LISTENING       400
  TCP    0.0.0.0:1053           0.0.0.0:0              LISTENING       1544
  TCP    0.0.0.0:1168           0.0.0.0:0              LISTENING       1668
```

FIGURE 6-16

The **tasklist** command will allow you to match the .exe file with the process ID.

```
Command Prompt                                                    _ □ X

H:\>tasklist

Image Name                     PID Session Name      Session#   Mem Usage
========================= ======== ================ ============ ============
System Idle Process              0 Console                    0        16 K
System                           4 Console                    0       216 K
smss.exe                       268 Console                    0       460 K
csrss.exe                      316 Console                    0     1,632 K
winlogon.exe                   340 Console                    0    11,808 K
services.exe                   388 Console                    0    48,712 K
lsass.exe                      400 Console                    0    34,592 K
svchost.exe                    592 Console                    0     2,688 K
svchost.exe                    752 Console                    0     3,628 K
svchost.exe                    820 Console                    0     4,588 K
svchost.exe                    840 Console                    0     3,276 K
svchost.exe                    856 Console                    0    22,360 K
spoolsv.exe                   1208 Console                    0    14,452 K
BRSS01A.EXE                   1216 Console                    0     2,036 K
msdtc.exe                     1272 Console                    0     4,200 K
certsrv.exe                   1428 Console                    0     9,120 K
defwatch.exe                  1472 Console                    0     2,212 K
dfssvc.exe                    1488 Console                    0     4,288 K
dns.exe                       1544 Console                    0     6,056 K
svchost.exe                   1620 Console                    0     2,148 K
```

Table 6-5 displays popular Netstat command-line switches and the corresponding definitions.

TABLE 6-5

Netstat Command-Line Switches

Netstat Switch	Definition
-a	Displays all connections and ports.
-e	Displays Ethernet statistics.
-n	Lists addresses and ports in numerical form.
-s	Lists per-protocol statistics.
-p	Allows specification of protocol; can be TCP, UDP, ICMP, or IP.
-r	Lists routing table.
-o	Displays the process ID number of the process that opened the port.
interval	Specifies interval to pause display.

EXERCISE 6-4

Video

Using Netstat to Determine Open Connections to a System

In this exercise, you will connect to an internal website from the Windows 8 client system and then view who is connected to your web server using the **netstat -n** utility.

1. Be sure to start the 2012SERVERA and the Windows 8 VM.
2. Go to the 2012SERVERA VM.

3. Before connecting to your server from your clients, view the TCP connections on the server by going to a command prompt and typing **netstat -n**.

4. You have no results because no one is connected to your system. If you do have entries in the **netstat -n** results, verify that in the local address column you have no entries with an :80. These entries would be someone connected to your web server.

5. Once you have verified that there is no one connected to your web server, go to the Windows 8 VM and connect to your web server by typing **http://10.0.0.1** in Internet Explorer.

6. Now, go to the 2012SERVERA VM and verify that you can see the Windows 8 client system connected to your website by typing **netstat -n**. You are looking for an entry with an :80 at the end of the address in the local address column. If you don't get any results from **netstat -n**, you may need to go to the Windows 8 VM and refresh the page and then come back to 2012SERVERA, type **netstat -n** again, and press ENTER.

7. From the **netstat -n** output, you can see the Windows 8 system (in the foreign address column) is connected to your web server (local address).

8. Fill in the information that follows while looking at the **netstat -a** output:

   ■ What is the IP address of the system connected to your web server?
   _____

   ■ What is the port number used on the client system? _____

   ■ What is the IP address of the server? _____

   ■ What is the port number on the server the client is connected to?
   _____

9. Type **exit** from the command prompt.

Telnet

Another utility commonly used is Telnet, a terminal emulation program. This utility was designed to provide a virtual terminal or remote login across the network to a Telnet-based application. This enables the user to execute commands on a remote machine from anywhere on the network as if he or she were sitting in front of the console. The term Telnet refers to both the protocol and the application used to create the remote session.

Telnet was originally designed to allow for a single universal interface in a world that was very diverse. It was an efficient method of simulating a console session when very little else was available. It is still widely used for remotely administering devices such as network equipment and UNIX servers. It can also be a great troubleshooting tool when used correctly.

Using Telnet

A Telnet client utility is included with most operating systems, such as Windows and Linux. You can run the Telnet utility by typing **telnet.exe** at a command prompt in most operating systems. When connecting to a remote system using Telnet, you can enter either an IP address or a hostname. To connect via a hostname, the client must be able to resolve the name to an IP address. Optionally, you can specify the port to connect to. By default, Telnet will try to connect to the Telnet port (port 23) on the remote server. For example, to telnet into a router whose IP address is 12.0.0.1, you would enter the following command:

```
TELNET 12.0.0.1
```

Telnet uses TCP port 23.

When connecting to the remote system using Telnet, you may be required to enter a user name and password. After logging in to the remote system, you can use a number of commands to administer the remote system or device. These commands depend on what system or device you are connected to. Many external devices also offer Telnet capability, such as uninterruptible power supplies (UPSs), remote control server administration cards, and most networking equipment, such as routers and switches.

Troubleshooting with Telnet

The primary use of Telnet is remote administration. If you are unable to connect to a remote server by other methods, depending upon the problem, Telnet might still work as long as the telnet service or daemon was installed on the server. This will enable you to troubleshoot and work with a remote server without being in front of it. If a server is inaccessible, you might still be able to contact its peripherals.

Suppose a Windows server has crashed and is displaying a blue screen. Some servers include an option to have remote administration cards plugged in. In this case, you could telnet to this card and possibly determine whether there is a hardware failure, or you could reboot the server. Suppose you have a UPS attached to the server. This peripheral might have telnet capability to enable you to power-cycle the server. Both cases enable you to remotely troubleshoot the server without local interaction.

Another example of troubleshooting with Telnet is to connect to an application's service port (e.g., FTP, SMTP [Simple Mail Transport Protocol], or HTTP) to verify that it is functioning properly. As discussed earlier, every TCP/IP service uses a specific TCP or UDP port. You can specify a particular port to connect to and test the connectivity and functionality of a service by issuing the type of commands for that service. For example, if you have a user who is having trouble sending e-mail, you could connect to your SMTP server from the Telnet utility and issue the SMTP command to try to send an e-mail.

The purpose of going to the Telnet utility and not the e-mail client is that you want to verify whether the issue is server based or client based. If you can connect through Telnet and send an e-mail, then the problem is probably with the client. Exercise 6-2 shows how to telnet into a Cisco router.

EXERCISE 6-5

Video

Using Telnet to Remotely Administer a Cisco Router

In this exercise, use Telnet to remotely connect to a Cisco router and administer the device. Note that the device will need to be configured to allow someone to telnet into the router.

1. Navigate to a Windows command prompt.
2. To telnet into the router, type **telnet <IP_Of_Router>**.
3. When asked for a user name and password, enter them in.
4. Once logged in to the router, note the name of the router.
5. As an example of a configuration change, you will change the name of the router. To change the name of the router, type the following commands:

   Enable

   Config term

   Hostname R6
6. Type **exit** two times to exit out of global configuration mode.
7. Type **exit** to end the Telnet session.
8. Type **exit** to close the command prompt.

FTP

The File Transfer Protocol (FTP) is the TCP/IP protocol designed primarily for transferring files from one computer to another. FTP is the name of both a protocol and a utility used for the purpose of connecting to an FTP server and downloading a file. FTP was created to transfer data files from one host to another quickly and efficiently, either by allowing a user to do the download anonymously or by authenticating to the server.

How FTP Works

FTP is unusual in that it uses two TCP channels to operate: TCP port 20 is used as the data transfer channel, and TCP port 21 is used for control commands. The data transfer

FIGURE 6-17

An FTP session

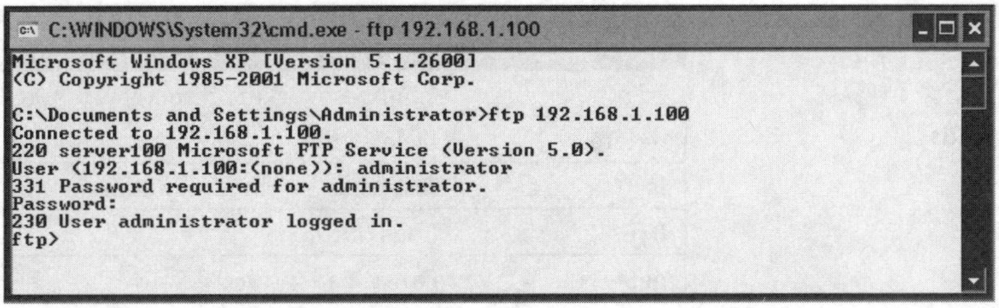

channel is known as the DTP, or Data Transfer Process, and the command channel is known as the PI, or Protocol Interpreter. The two channels enable you to transfer data and execute commands at the same time, providing a more efficient and faster data transfer.

Like Telnet, FTP requires a server-based program to answer the client requests for file download. An FTP service is available on most network operating systems today, including Windows Server 2012, UNIX, and Linux.

FTP enables file transfers in several formats based on the type of remote system being used. Most systems have two modes of transfer: text and binary. Text transfers are ASCII based and use characters separated by carriage returns and newline characters, while binary transfer mode is used to download binary files such as executables or non-ASCII data. Most systems default to text mode and require you to switch to binary mode for a binary transfer. Figure 6-17 shows an example of an FTP session.

You will notice in Figure 6-17 that to connect to the FTP server, you type

```
ftp 192.168.1.100
```

The server will then ask you for a user name and password. Once you type a valid user name and password, you will be logged on and placed at the FTP prompt, where you can type FTP commands to potentially view, upload, and download files.

Using FTP   A command-line client utility is included with many versions of Windows and Linux, and many third-party FTP server and client applications are available for connecting to an FTP server and downloading files. Some third-party utilities are Windows-based utilities, adding a graphical interface to the download functionality.

FTP is started by typing **ftp** at a command prompt, followed by the FQDN or IP address of the target machine. As with Telnet, the client computer must be able to resolve the remote computer's name into an IP address for the command to succeed. Once logged on, users can browse through directories, download and upload files, and log out.

TABLE 6-6	Command	Description
	cd	Changes working directory.
Popular FTP Commands	**delete**	Deletes file.
	ls	Lists current directory contents.
	bye	Logs out.
	get	Downloads a file.
	put	Uploads a file.
	verbose	Turns verbose mode on and off.

A wide array of commands is available in the FTP utility. These commands are used to control the FTP application and its functions. Table 6-6 lists some of the more common FTP commands that are available in an FTP session. Bear in mind that FTP commands on a Windows machine are not case sensitive, but FTP commands on a UNIX/Linux machine are.

EXERCISE 6-6

Video

Configuring and Using FTP

In this exercise, you will create two folders on a Windows Server 2012 FTP server and place a file into one of those folders. After you have placed the files on the FTP server, you will connect to the FTP server from the Windows 8 client. Make sure that you have the FTP server software installed on the 2012SERVERA VM before starting this exercise.

1. Ensure that the 2012SERVERA and the Windows 8 VMs are running.
2. On 2012SERVERA, navigate to the C: drive (use the folder list button on the task bar).
3. Double-click the Inetpub folder to open it.
4. Double-click the ftproot folder to open it.
5. To create a folder for the Marketing team, right-click and then choose File | New | Folder.
6. Type **Marketing** as the name of the new folder.
7. To create a folder for the Engineering team, right-click and then choose File | New | Folder.

8. Type **Engineering** as the name of the new folder. You should have two folders in the ftproot folder.

9. Double-click the Marketing folder.

10. To create a file in this folder, right-click and choose File | New | Text Document.

11. Type **MarketingTrends** as the filename.

12. Close all windows.

Using FTP on the Windows 8 Client to Download the MarketingTrends File

13. On the Windows 8 client, chose Start and then type **CMD**. This will place you in the Windows command prompt.

14. At the command prompt, type **ftp 10.0.0.1**.

15. You will be asked to log in. To log in with the anonymous account, type **ftp** as the user name and press ENTER.

16. You will then be prompted for a password. Because you are logging in with the anonymous account (ftp), you can simply press ENTER for the password, because there is no password.

17. You will then be notified that you have been logged in and will be presented with the ftp prompt.

18. Type **ls** and press ENTER to get a listing of files and directories available on the FTP server. Notice the Marketing and Engineering folders in the output.

19. To change to the Marketing directory, type **cd Marketing**, and press ENTER.

20. Type **ls** again to see the contents of the Marketing directory. Notice the MarketingTrends.txt file in the output.

21. To download the MarketingTrends.txt file, type **get marketingtrends.txt**.

22. The file is downloaded and confirmed with a transfer complete statement.

23. Type **Quit** to close the FTP session.

24. Type **exit** to close the command prompt.

Configuring FTP

Users require a login ID to access FTP services if anonymous access is disabled. Most systems today enable an anonymous login, but these users should not possess full rights to the system. Common problems with connecting via FTP are an invalid login or insufficient access rights. If you are having problems connecting to an FTP server, contact your FTP server administrator to verify that your login ID is set up correctly.

FTP Options Several switches are available for the command-line FTP utility. These options enable you to further customize the use of FTP to meet your needs. The **-v** option suppresses the display of remote server responses. This provides a more user-friendly interface to the utility. By default, when you start FTP, it attempts to log on automatically. You can disable this function by using the **-n** option.

The **-I** option turns off the interactive prompting that occurs during multiple transfers, which makes for a more automated approach to FTP. The **-d** option enables you to turn on the debugging functions. This feature displays all FTP commands that are passed between the client and server.

Another option included with the FTP command-line utility is the capability to run a script of commands after the program is started. The script file is used instead of redirection and can include any standard command. You must append the **-s:** switch followed by the path and filename of the script.

One of my favorite switches for FTP is **-a**, which will automatically log on as the anonymous account; this saves you the hassle of having to type the anonymous account name for a logon. Table 6-7 lists the FTP command-line switches. Bear in mind that while commands are not case sensitive, the command-line switches are.

Troubleshooting with FTP

When it comes to FTP, one of the biggest problems you may hit is with logging on to the FTP server. Make sure that you know the user name and password of an account that is allowed to access the FTP server. If you are interested in uploading files to the FTP server,

	FTP Switch	Definition
TABLE 6-7	-v	Does not list remote server responses.
	-n	Does not autologin on initial connection.
FTP Command-	-i	Disables interactive prompting for multiple file transfers.
Line Switches	-d	Enables debugging.
	-g	Allows use of wildcard characters.
	-s:filename	Specifies a text file of FTP commands to execute after FTP starts.
	-a	Allows use of any local interface when binding data connections.
	-w	Allows specification of transfer buffer size; the default is 4096.
	computer	Specifies FQDN or IP address of remote PC with which to connect.

you will need to ensure that you have the appropriate permission to do this. Typically, users who log on to the FTP server are granted only read permissions.

The other problem you may have with FTP sessions is understanding the commands that you can type during the session. This is just a matter of practice and getting familiar with the command set.

For the Network+ exam, remember that FTP uses two different TCP ports. Port 21 is used as a control port to send the commands, while port 20 is the data port used to transfer the data between the client and server.

TFTP

The Trivial File Transfer Protocol (TFTP) is a slight variation on FTP. TFTP differs from FTP in two ways: It uses the UDP connectionless transport instead of TCP, and you do not log on to the remote machine. The port that TFTP uses is different as well—TFTP uses UDP port 69. Because it uses UDP, TFTP does not provide error-correcting services as TCP does. This has advantages, but it does have to use more complex algorithms to guarantee data integrity. Because users do not log on, user-access and file-permission problems are avoided.

TFTP is generally not used for file transfers as FTP is; instead, it is used in situations such as diskless terminals or workstations. Typically, TFTP is used to load applications or for bootstrapping. Because the operating systems are not loaded at this point, the diskless machines cannot execute FTP. TFTP handles access and file permissions by imposing restraints from within the host operating system. For example, by setting the file permissions on the TFTP server, you can limit the security to areas inside the TFTP server.

TFTP is commonly employed when using Cisco routers. TFTP servers allow you to save the router configuration information to the TFTP server and be able to reload the configuration information from the TFTP server. You can also back up the Cisco Internetwork Operating System (IOS) to a TFTP server. TFTP is also often used in Preboot Execution Environments (PXE) to download a mini operating system from a network server that runs locally. TFTP is also used to back up device configuration to a server. For example, you can upload your Cisco router configuration to a TFTP server so that you can restore it at a later time.

CERTIFICATION OBJECTIVE 6.03

Name Resolution Commands

Now that you have seen some of the TCP/IP commands that are used day in and day out by network administrators, let us take a look at some common commands for troubleshooting name resolution.

NBTSTAT

The Microsoft TCP/IP stack uses an additional subprotocol for its services, NetBIOS over TCP/IP (NetBT). The purpose of NetBIOS over TCP/IP is to allow you to connect to servers and workstations by their NetBIOS name, also known as the computer name, and behind the scenes that name will be converted to an IP address. Because this is a Microsoft addition to the TCP/IP protocol, Microsoft created the NBTSTAT utility to troubleshoot problems that can arise with NetBIOS over TCP/IP, or NetBIOS name resolution problems.

Make sure that you are comfortable with the output of each of the TCP/IP utilities discussed in this chapter. On the Network+ exam, you will be shown output and have to indicate which command and command switch were used to create it.

How NetBIOS over TCP/IP Works

NetBIOS is a software interface and naming convention used in Microsoft networking environments. NetBIOS was built in to NetBEUI and is also a major part of the Microsoft TCP/IP protocol stack. NetBIOS over TCP/IP uses the NetBIOS application programming interface over the TCP/IP protocol—using NetBIOS as a method of referencing systems across the network with NetBIOS names. These NetBIOS names need to be resolved to IP addresses for communication to happen on the network.

NetBT Naming   The NetBIOS namespace is a flat structure and is used to give unique NetBIOS names (computer names) to all systems on the network. This means that all computers within a workgroup or domain must have unique names. You will receive

TABLE 6-8

Popular NetBIOS
Name Suffixes

Suffix	Usage
00	Workstation Service
20	Server Service or File and Print Services
03	Messenger Service
1C	Domain Controller
06	Remote Access Server

a duplicate computer name error if two systems are using the same name. Names are composed of 16 bytes; 15 bytes are used by the actual computer name, and the last byte is used by the NetBIOS name suffix. The administrator or user can set the first 15 bytes, representing the computer name, but the 16th byte is created automatically based on a service running on the system. The NetBIOS name suffix is a code that represents a service running on the system. Table 6-8 lists some common NetBIOS name suffix codes.

Let's look at an example: Assume I had a server named SERVER1 and you noticed that there was a name registered on the network (more on this later) that looked like

```
SERVER1      <20>
```

You would know that I have a computer running named SERVER1 and that it is running the server service, which allows clients to connect to it for the purpose of file and print sharing. How do you know that SERVER1 is running the server service? That is what the <20> NetBIOS suffix means. To summarize, the NetBIOS suffix is used to "advertise" which services a system offers.

NetBT Sessions   Because NetBT runs on top of TCP/IP, sessions are set up the same way as though you were connecting through TCP/IP directly. There is additional overhead associated with this due to name resolution, but it is usually very small. When an application attempts to connect to a resource using NetBT, it first resolves the name to an IP address. Next, a TCP connection is established to port 139, designated for the NetBIOS session service. When connected, the computer sends a NetBIOS session request to the server name over the TCP connection. If the server is listening, it will respond with the requested information.

Using NBTSTAT

NBTSTAT is used to troubleshoot connectivity between two computers trying to communicate via NetBT. It displays the protocol statistics and the current connections to each remote host. You can also display the information about a remote host and the names stored in its local name cache.

Displaying the Local Cache Every NetBIOS name that has been resolved is stored in memory, known as the NetBIOS name cache, so that the name resolution process will not need to go out to the network again. You can display the local cache by using the **NBTSTAT -c** option. When it comes to name resolution, the goal is to have a computer name that needs to be resolved in cache as quickly as possible so that the name resolves from memory and not through broadcast, or by contacting a WINS server. To have NetBIOS names referenced frequently loaded in cache automatically, you can use the #PRE tag in your lmhosts file so that those entries are loaded in cache on boot-up or by using the **-R** switch.

By using the **-n** option, you can display the services the local machine is advertising. This lists the registered names for the local machine as well.

Connecting to Remote Machines When a system boots up, it registers its NetBIOS names in the NetBIOS name table stored in memory on the machine. This NetBIOS name table can be queried by anyone on the network at any point in time by using either the **-a** switch if you are passing in the hostname or the **-A** switch if you are passing in the remote system's IP address. These options enable you to determine what services the remote machine is offering. Core operating system services such as the Server service or the Computer Browser service are listed here. Applications such as Microsoft Exchange or Microsoft Internet Information Server (IIS) might also list entries here as well. Figure 6-18 shows an example of a remote machine's name table.

NBTSTAT -A **is used to query the NetBIOS name table of a remote IP address.**

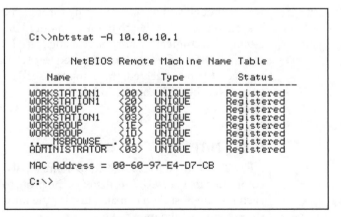

FIGURE 6-18

Viewing the NETBIOS name table of a remote system

```
C:\>nbtstat -A 10.10.10.1

        NetBIOS Remote Machine Name Table

    Name               Type         Status
    ---------------------------------------------
    WORKSTATION1   <00>  UNIQUE    Registered
    WORKSTATION1   <20>  UNIQUE    Registered
    WORKGROUP      <00>  GROUP     Registered
    WORKSTATION1   <03>  UNIQUE    Registered
    WORKGROUP      <1E>  GROUP     Registered
    WORKGROUP      <1D>  UNIQUE    Registered
    ..__MSBROWSE__.<01>  GROUP     Registered
    ADMINISTRATOR  <03>  UNIQUE    Registered

MAC Address = 00-60-97-E4-D7-CB

C:\>
```

Let's analyze the output in Figure 6-18. NetBIOS is exposing some pretty lethal information that can be used against you by a hacker. If I were to view your NetBIOS name table and get the results shown in Figure 6-18, I could probably guess that you are running a Microsoft operating system because of the 00 (Workstation service) and the 20 (Server service). You will also notice that there is a 03 code (Messenger service) registered twice—once for the locally logged-on user and the other for the computer name. In Windows, we can send messages to users or computers; therefore, both names need to be registered on the network so that the message being sent can find the user and computer. Because the Server service and the Workstation service are registered with a name of WORKSTATION1, we know that WORKSTATION1 with the 03 code is the computer, so ADMINISTRATOR with the 03 code must be the locally logged-on user. Pretty scary! As a best practice, you should be renaming the administrator account; if you don't control who has access to the NetBIOS name table information, someone can find out a user name very quickly.

on the **Job**

Any time you have the IP address of a system (maybe by viewing a log file), you can use NBTSTAT -A <ip address> **to find out the computer name of that IP address.**

Displaying Registration Statistics   Services can register on the network in two ways—via broadcast or with the WINS service. You can display the statistics of how many times you have registered and with what method. You can also display information on how remote NetBIOS names are being resolved. This can help you to determine whether you are using a WINS service correctly or are broadcasting to discover services. Broadcasting can consume a lot of bandwidth and is generally not recommended except in the smallest networks. To view the registration statistics, use the **-r** option with NBTSTAT.

on the **Job**

The NBTSTAT utility can be crucial in defining problems with Microsoft computers. Since they use the NetBIOS naming standard, this utility is good at finding and isolating connectivity problems. It provides the extra information on NetBIOS statistics that you can't get from regular TCP/IP utilities such as Tracert.

Displaying Session Information   Another option with NBTSTAT is to list the sessions that are currently open. You can see what you are connected to and list the open sessions that other computers have with your machine. Use the **-S** (uppercase) option to list names by IP address only. When you use the **-s** (lowercase) option, NBTSTAT will attempt to resolve the IP addresses to hostnames.

| FIGURE 6-19 | Viewing NetBIOS session information |

```
C:\>nbtstat -s

              NetBIOS Connection Table

Local Name           State    In/Out  Remote Host           Input   Output
------------------------------------------------------------------------------
WORKSTATION2  <03>  Listening
WORKSTATION2        Listening
ADMINISTRATOR <03>  Listening

C:\>
```

Statistics available with this option include number of bytes in, number of bytes out, current state, and whether the connection is inbound or outbound. Figure 6-19 shows an example of the sessions displayed with this option.

Table 6-9 details the NBTSTAT command-line switches and their definitions.

TABLE 6-9	**NBTSTAT Switch**	**Definition**
NBTSTAT Command -Line Switches	-a	Lists a remote PC's name table by specifying a remote PC's name.
	-A	Lists a remote PC's name table by specifying a remote PC's IP address.
	-c	Displays contents of the name cache, giving the IP address of each name.
	-n	Displays local names.
	-R	Deletes the name cache and reloads entries from the lmhosts file that contains the #PRE tag.
	-r	Displays name resolution statistics.
	-S	Lists client and server sessions, listing the remote computers by IP address.
	-s	Displays both client and server sessions, attempting to convert the remote computer IP address to a name using the hosts file.
	Interval	Specifies the interval to pause display.

EXERCISE 6-7

Using NBTSTAT to View NetBIOS Name Tables

In this exercise, you will view the NetBIOS name table of your local system and of a remote system on the network to determine what names are registered on the network. It is important to note that current Windows operating systems do not expose as much information through the NetBIOS name table because the systems have been locked down.

1. Go to the command prompt by selecting Start | Run, and then type **cmd**.
2. At the command prompt, type **nbtstat -n**.
3. You will get a list of NetBIOS names registered on the local computer.

```
C:\WINDOWS\System32\cmd.exe                                    _ □ ×

C:\Documents and Settings\Administrator>nbtstat -n

Local Area Connection 3:
Node IpAddress: [192.168.1.200] Scope Id: []

              NetBIOS Local Name Table

       Name             Type          Status
    ---------------------------------------------
    CLIENT100      <00>  UNIQUE      Registered
    WORKGROUP      <00>  GROUP       Registered
    CLIENT100      <03>  UNIQUE      Registered
    CLIENT100      <20>  UNIQUE      Registered
    WORKGROUP      <1E>  GROUP       Registered
    WORKGROUP      <1D>  UNIQUE      Registered
    ..__MSBROWSE__.<01>  GROUP       Registered
    ADMINISTRATOR  <03>  UNIQUE      Registered

C:\Documents and Settings\Administrator>
```

4. Record the following information about your system:

    Computer name: _____

    Locally logged-on user name: _____

    Is your system running the server service? _____

    How do you know? _____

5. The following answers are coming from the output that was shown in the preceding illustration:

    Computer name: **client100**

    Locally logged-on user name: **Administrator**

    Is your system running the Server service? **Yes**

    How do you know? **<20> code—server service**

View a Remote System's Name Table with NBTSTAT

1. At the command prompt, type **nbtstat -A <ip address>** to view the name table of another system on your network. In my example, I am viewing the name table of a system that is using the IP address of 192.168.1.100 (shown in the accompanying illustration).

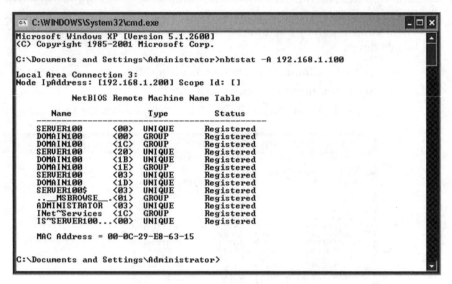

```
C:\WINDOWS\System32\cmd.exe

Microsoft Windows XP [Version 5.1.2600]
(C) Copyright 1985-2001 Microsoft Corp.

C:\Documents and Settings\Administrator>nbtstat -A 192.168.1.100

Local Area Connection 3:
Node IpAddress: [192.168.1.200] Scope Id: []

            NetBIOS Remote Machine Name Table

       Name               Type         Status
    ---------------------------------------------
    SERVER100      <00>  UNIQUE      Registered
    DOMAIN100      <00>  GROUP       Registered
    DOMAIN100      <1C>  GROUP       Registered
    SERVER100      <20>  UNIQUE      Registered
    DOMAIN100      <1B>  UNIQUE      Registered
    DOMAIN100      <1E>  GROUP       Registered
    SERVER100      <03>  UNIQUE      Registered
    DOMAIN100      <1D>  UNIQUE      Registered
    SERVER100$     <03>  UNIQUE      Registered
    .._MSBROWSE__.<01>  GROUP       Registered
    ADMINISTRATOR  <03>  UNIQUE      Registered
    INet~Services  <1C>  GROUP       Registered
    IS~SERVER100...<00>  UNIQUE      Registered

    MAC Address = 00-0C-29-E8-63-15

C:\Documents and Settings\Administrator>
```

2. Analyzing the preceding output, you can see the <00> and <20> codes, which means that the Workstation and Server services are running. You can see the <03> code registered twice, once for the computer name of server100 and once for the locally logged-on user name of administrator. You can also see that this is a domain controller. You know this because of the <1C> code for the domain named domain100. You also know that the server we hit is running IIS because of the <1C> code for INet Services.

3. Compare my findings with the findings of a computer on your network, and record the information in the space provided. You may not have all the answers, depending on the type of system you are analyzing.

   Computer name: _____

   Locally logged-on user name: _____

   Is the system running the Server service? _____

   Is the system running the Workstation service? _____

   Is the system running the Messenger service? _____

   Is the system running IIS? _____

4. Type **exit** to close the command prompt.

NSLOOKUP and DIG

The NSLOOKUP command is used to verify DNS name resolution from a DNS server. This is very useful for a Windows network, which depends immensely on the use of DNS. If DNS should fail or return improper information, network communication can slow due to name resolution. If DNS fails, the client systems could have trouble authenticating, and domain controllers could have trouble communicating with one another, because locating a domain controller on the network is a function of DNS. In a Windows network, Active Directory needs DNS, or both Active Directory and the domain will fail.

How NSLOOKUP Works

NSLOOKUP will query a DNS server (not the local DNS client cache) for specific types of records, and can be used to troubleshoot why a system cannot connect to another remote system. If there is an incorrect record in DNS, or no record at all, you will be able to determine this with NSLOOKUP.

These items can be verified fairly quickly if you are located at the client PC. You can ping the server by the server IP address. If you can ping the server by IP address and not by the server DNS name, there is a DNS name-resolution issue. You can then pursue the issue further by using NSLOOKUP to verify that the DNS server is operational and that a record exists for the host in the DNS database.

It is possible, but unlikely, that the name-to-IP-address resolution is incorrect. The DNS name could be matched to an improper IP address. This can cause the data packets to be sent to a PC or network device other than the correct system, or even to a nonexistent IP address.

NSLOOKUP Options

There are two modes in which you can use NSLOOKUP: interactive and noninteractive.

FIGURE 6-20

Using NSLOOKUP
in interactive
mode

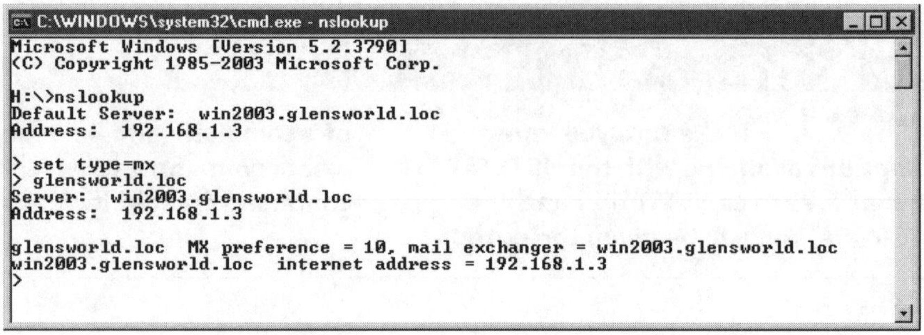

```
C:\WINDOWS\system32\cmd.exe - nslookup

Microsoft Windows [Version 5.2.3790]
(C) Copyright 1985-2003 Microsoft Corp.

H:\>nslookup
Default Server:  win2003.glensworld.loc
Address:  192.168.1.3

> set type=mx
> glensworld.loc
Server:  win2003.glensworld.loc
Address:  192.168.1.3

glensworld.loc  MX preference = 10, mail exchanger = win2003.glensworld.loc
win2003.glensworld.loc  internet address = 192.168.1.3
>
```

Interactive Mode In *interactive* mode, you simply type the NSLOOKUP command; you are then placed at the NSLOOKUP prompt, where you type one NSLOOKUP command after another. Figure 6-20 displays the interactive prompt. Notice that one command is typed after the other and they all work together to obtain a result.

Interactive mode is used when you have more than one item in the DNS database you will be querying. Interactive mode will allow you to enter a command-line state that will keep prompting you for more commands until you type **exit** at the NSLOOKUP command prompt to return to a standard DOS command prompt and exit the NSLOOKUP utility.

Notice in Figure 6-20 that the command **nslookup** was typed to go to interactive mode. In interactive mode, you would then type the different NSLOOKUP commands at the prompt that displays with a >. Notice that **set type=mx** was typed next—this tells **nslookup** that I want to find MX records for whatever domain I specify next. MX records point to the mail servers for a company, which is what is specified in the next line—glensworld.loc—my fictitious company. Notice in the figure that **nslookup** returns the address of the MX record, which is equal to win2003.glensworld.loc, which has the Internet address of 192.168.1.3. Bear in mind that NSLOOKUP interactive mode commands are case sensitive. For example, SET TYPE=MX fails while set type=mx succeeds.

Table 6-10 lists the commands available in the NSLOOKUP prompt.

Noninteractive Mode When using noninteractive mode, you will type the NSLOOKUP command followed by the command options. You are not placed at an interactive prompt where you type many commands. Figure 6-21 displays the noninteractive use of NSLOOKUP. In this example, you are simply trying to resolve a single host to an IP address. You can see from Figure 6-21 that the address www.gleneclarke.com has the IP address of 24.89.233.148.

| TABLE 6-10 | NSLOOKUP Commands |

Command	Description
help	Displays a brief summary of NSLOOKUP commands.
exit	Exits the NSLOOKUP utility.
ls (-t, -a, -d, -h, -s)	Lists information for a DNS domain: **-t** lists all records of a specified type. **-a** lists aliases in the DNS domain. **-d** lists all DNS domain records. **-h** lists CPU and OS information for the DNS domain. **-s** lists well-known services in the DNS domain.
server	Changes the server to a specified DNS domain.
set	Changes configuration settings for the NSLOOKUP utility.
set all	Lists current NSLOOKUP configuration values.
set cl[ass] = **(in, chaos, hesiod, any)**	Sets Query class as specified by the option setting: IN: Internet class CHAOS: Chaos class HESIOD: MIT Athena Hesiod class ANY: Any of the previously listed wildcards
set po[rt]	Changes port used by DNS name server.
set q[uerytype] = **(a, any, cname, gid, hinfo,** **mb, mg, minfo, mr, mx,** **ns, ptr, soa, txt, uid, uinfo,** **wks)**	Changes type of query: A: Computer's IP address ANY: All types of data CNAME: Canonical name for an alias GID: Group name's group identifier HINFO: CPU and operating system type of computer MB: Mailbox domain name MG: Mail group member MINFO: Mailbox or mail list information MR: Mail rename domain name MX: Mail exchanger NS: DNS name server for the zone PTR: Computer name if the query is an IP address SOA: DNS domain's start-of-authority record TXT: Text information UID: User identifier UINFO: User information WKS: Well-known service description
set [no] rec[urse]	Allows you to specify whether to recurse a query to other servers.
set ret[ry]	Sets the number of retries.
set ty[pe]	Changes type of information queried.

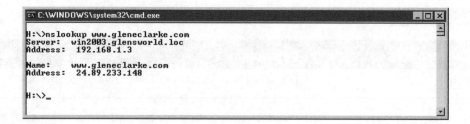

FIGURE 6-21

Using NSLOOKUP
in noninteractive
mode

EXERCISE 6-8

Video

Using NSLOOKUP

In this exercise, you will use NSLOOKUP to view a list of DNS entries for a particular company. You will also switch the record type to MX and view a list of mail servers for Microsoft.com on the Internet.

1. Switch to the Windows 8 VM.

2. Go to Start and then type **CMD** and press ENTER.

3. First, let's find out the IP address of www.certworld.loc by typing **nslookup www .certworld.loc**—you are then returned the IP address of that system.

4. To use the interactive prompt of NSLOOKUP, type NSLOOKUP and press ENTER.

5. NSLOOKUP will display two lines of information: the first specifies your default DNS server name to which you are connected, and the second is the IP address of that DNS server. The default DNS server is the one configured in your TCP/IP properties. The prompt will be blinking next to a ">" symbol.

6. The first thing you want to do is switch to a different DNS server to send your queries to. You can do this by typing **server 10.0.0.2** (the IP address of a different DNS server) and pressing ENTER.

7. You can see that NSLOOKUP reports the new server you are connected to, and you can now send queries to the server for specific records. You actually want to use 10.0.0.1 as your DNS server, so type **server 10.0.0.1** and press ENTER.

8. To transfer a zone on the server, type **ls certworld.loc** and press ENTER (if zone transfers are disabled on the DNS server, you may receive an error).

9. You can see in the output that the certworld.loc company has www and ftp servers and you see their associated IP addresses.
10. Next you will see a list of e-mail servers for the certworld.loc fictitious company. Type **set type=mx** and press ENTER. This tells NSLOOKUP that you want to view the mail exchange records. Mail exchange records are the records in DNS that point to a company's mail servers.
11. To view the mail exchange records, type the domain name of the company and press ENTER. In our example, you type **certworld.loc** and press ENTER.
12. Type **exit** and press ENTER to quit the NSLOOKUP prompt.
13. Type **exit** and press ENTER to quit the command prompt.

DIG

DIG is a very popular TCP/IP utility that is available on most Linux systems and is used to query DNS. DIG will give you much the same information as NSLOOKUP, but is much more flexible. Let's look at some examples. If you want to find out the IP address for an FQDN, you simply type the **dig** command followed by the FQDN, as shown in Figure 6-22.

FIGURE 6-22

Using **dig** to query DNS

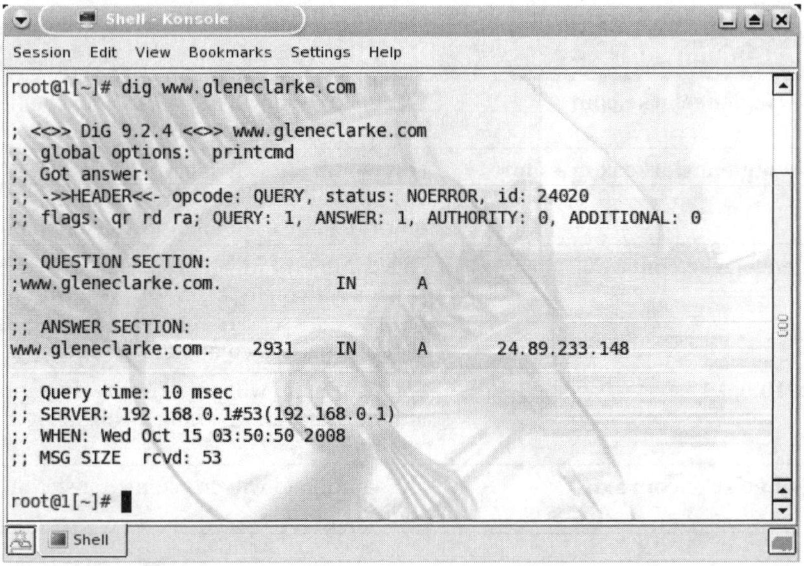
Shell - Konsole
Session Edit View Bookmarks Settings Help
root@1[~]# dig www.gleneclarke.com
; <<>> DiG 9.2.4 <<>> www.gleneclarke.com
;; global options: printcmd
;; Got answer:
;; ->>HEADER<<- opcode: QUERY, status: NOERROR, id: 24020
;; flags: qr rd ra; QUERY: 1, ANSWER: 1, AUTHORITY: 0, ADDITIONAL: 0
;; QUESTION SECTION:
;www.gleneclarke.com. IN A
;; ANSWER SECTION:
www.gleneclarke.com. 2931 IN A 24.89.233.148
;; Query time: 10 msec
;; SERVER: 192.168.0.1#53(192.168.0.1)
;; WHEN: Wed Oct 15 03:50:50 2008
;; MSG SIZE rcvd: 53
root@1[~]#
Shell

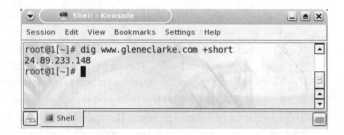

FIGURE 6-23

Using the **+short** option with **dig**

What I love about the **dig** command is that as you learn the commands, you can place the **+short** switch on the command to see the "short" version of the results. Looking back to Figure 6-22, you can see that when you typed the command in, it came back and summarized the question and gave us the answer—I don't want all that! Just give me the answer, which is what the **+short** switch does. Figure 6-23 displays the **+short** switch being used.

We can use a wealth of example commands with DIG. I have summarized the commands I use most in Table 6-11.

TABLE 6-11   Example **dig** Commands

Example Command	Definition
dig www.gleneclarke.com	This command will query DNS for the IP address associated with www.gleneclarke.com.
dig www.gleneclarke.com +short	This command will query DNS for the IP address associated with www.gleneclarke.com, but give the "short answer" version. **+short** can be used on most **dig** commands.
dig gleneclarke.com MX	This command will query DNS for all the MX records for the gleneclarke.com domain. MX records are special records that point to mail servers. This command is used to find out what the IP addresses of a company's mail servers are.
dig -x 10.0.0.1	This command will perform a reverse query. If you know the IP address and want to know the name of the host, you can use this command.
dig gleneclarke.com axfr	This command will do a zone transfer of all DNS data for the domain specified.

TCP/IP Utilities

This chapter is such a big chapter because there are so many TCP/IP utilities and options with each utility. You need to be familiar with a few more utilities for the Network+ exam—they are the **hostname, MTR,** and **route** commands.

Hostname and Host

There is a popular utility in Windows and Linux that you can use to find out the computer name, or hostname, of your system—the **hostname** command, which is shown in Figure 6-24.

Another useful utility that is available on Linux systems to query DNS is the host utility. There are a number of switches that go along with the host utility, but in its simplest form you could type:

```
host www.gleneclarke.com
```

This will return the IP address of the FQDN www.gleneclarke.com. You can also perform tasks such as finding all the mail servers for the company, as you can with DIG or NSLOOKUP. To do this with the **host** command, type the following:

```
host -t MX glensworld.loc
```

In this code example, the **-t** switch allows you to specify the type of records you wish to query for; in my example, I am looking for the MX records from the domain glensworld.loc. Figure 6-25 displays the output of the two **host** commands discussed.

FIGURE 6-24
 	
Display your
system name
with the
hostname
command.
	
	`C:\WINDOWS\system32\cmd.exe`
	`H:\>hostname`
	`win2003`
	`H:\>`

FIGURE 6-25

Using the **host** command in Linux

```
root@linux8:~                                                    _ □ ✗
File  Edit  View  Terminal  Go  Help

[root@linux8 root]# host www.gleneclarke.com
www.gleneclarke.com has address 24.89.233.148
[root@linux8 root]#
[root@linux8 root]# host -t MX glensworld.loc
glensworld.loc mail is handled by 10 win2003.glensworld.loc.
[root@linux8 root]#
```

MTR

MTR is a network diagnostics program available in Linux that combines features of Tracert and Ping. It is a glorified traceroute tool that sends multiple Ping messages to each router between the source and the destination. To use MTR, you simply type **mtr** and then specify your destination, as shown in Figure 6-26.

You can see in the figure that there are five hops between my system and the destination. With each destination, you can see the packets sent and the packets that have been received as replies, along with the percentage of packets lost.

Route

The **route** command is a very popular TCP/IP utility that is used to manage the routing table of the local system. You will learn more about the **route** command in Chapter 8, but just as a primer, Table 6-12 is a listing of popular options with the **route** command.

FIGURE 6-26

MTR is a Linux utility that combines Tracert with Ping.

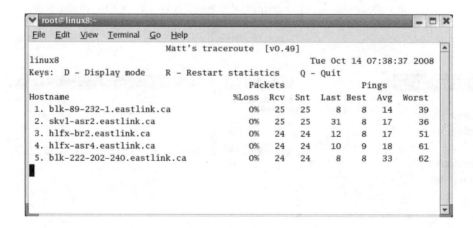

```
root@linux8:~                                                    _ □ ✗
File  Edit  View  Terminal  Go  Help
                      Matt's traceroute   [v0.49]
linux8                                      Tue Oct 14 07:38:37 2008
Keys:  D - Display mode    R - Restart statistics   Q - Quit
                                   Packets              Pings
Hostname                      %Loss  Rcv  Snt  Last Best  Avg  Worst
 1. blk-89-232-1.eastlink.ca    0%   25   25     8    8   14    39
 2. skvl-asr2.eastlink.ca       0%   25   25    31    8   17    36
 3. hlfx-br2.eastlink.ca        0%   24   24    12    8   17    51
 4. hlfx-asr4.eastlink.ca       0%   24   24    10    9   18    61
 5. blk-222-202-240.eastlink.ca 0%   24   24     8    8   33    62
```

TABLE 6-12	Route Command	Description
Popular **route** Commands	route print	Displays the local routing table.
	route add 192.168.2.0 MASK 255.255.255.0 192.168.1.2	Adds a route to the local routing table for destination network 192.168.2.0 via 192.168.1.2.
	route delete 192.168.2.0	Deletes the route from the routing table.

To see an example of the **route** command in use, check out the video.

Video

Arping

Arping is a popular Linux utility that combines the **ping** command with the concept of ARP. Remember that ARP is a protocol used to convert the IP address to a MAC address—so when you use arping, you will be sending out Ping messages, but you will get replies that include the MAC address of the IP address you pinged. Very cool! Figure 6-27 displays the output of the Arping utility.

Now that you have an understanding of some of the popular TCP/IP utilities, let's look at some common troubleshooting situations that can be solved with these utilities.

FIGURE 6-27	
The Linux Arping utility returns the MAC address with Ping responses.	

```
root@linux8:~                                                    _ □ ✕
 File  Edit  View  Terminal  Go  Help
[root@linux8 root]# arping 192.168.1.3
ARPING 192.168.1.3 from 192.168.1.8 eth0
Unicast reply from 192.168.1.3 [00:01:80:35:00:7B]   0.977ms
Unicast reply from 192.168.1.3 [00:01:80:35:00:7B]   0.745ms
Unicast reply from 192.168.1.3 [00:01:80:35:00:7B]   0.772ms
Sent 3 probes (1 broadcast(s))
Received 3 response(s)
[root@linux8 root]# ▐
```

Pathping

Pathping is a command-line utility that combines Ping with Tracert functionality. Pathping is different from Tracert in the sense that it reports statistic information at the end of the ping, summarizing information such as percent packet loss so that you can identify the hop that is causing problems along the pathway of communication.

```
C:\Users\gclarke>pathping www.google.ca
Tracing route to www.google.ca [74.125.226.183]
over a maximum of 30 hops:
  0   SONY1.eastlink.ca [192.168.1.179]
  1   Linksys04306 [192.168.1.1]
  2   blk-137-88-1.eastlink.ca [24.137.88.1]
  3   ns-skvl-asr002.eastlink.ca [24.222.226.49]
  4   ns-hlfx-dr002.ns.eastlink.ca [24.215.102.133]
  5   ns-hlfx-br002.ns.eastlink.ca [24.215.102.221]
  6   te-9-1.car2.Montreal2.Level3.net [4.59.178.77]
  7   ae-11-11.car1.Montreal2.Level3.net [4.69.141.2]
  8      *          *          *
Computing statistics for 175 seconds...
              Source to Here   This Node/Link
Hop   RTT     Lost/Sent = Pct  Lost/Sent = Pct  Address
  0                                             SONY1.eastlink.ca
[192.168.1.179]


                                 0/ 100 =  0%   |
  1    0ms      0/ 100 =  0%     0/ 100 =  0%   Linksys04306
[192.168.1.1]
                                 0/ 100 =  0%   |
  2   12ms      0/ 100 =  0%     0/ 100 =  0%   blk-137-88-1.eastlink.
ca [24.137.88.1]
                                 0/ 100 =  0%   |
  3    9ms      0/ 100 =  0%     0/ 100 =  0%   ns-skvl-asr002.
eastlink.ca [24.222.226.49]
                                 0/ 100 =  0%   |
  4   10ms      0/ 100 =  0%     0/ 100 =  0%   ns-hlfx-dr002.
ns.eastlink.ca [24.215.102.133]
                                 0/ 100 =  0%   |
  5   10ms      0/ 100 =  0%     0/ 100 =  0%   ns-hlfx-br002.
ns.eastlink.ca [24.215.102.221]
                                 0/ 100 =  0%   |
  6   56ms      0/ 100 =  0%     0/ 100 =  0%   te-9-1.car2.Montreal2.
Level3.net [4.59.178.77]
```

```
                                      0/ 100 =  0%   |
   7    63ms      0/ 100 =  0%      0/ 100 =  0%  ae-11-11.car1.
Montreal2.Level3.net [4.69.141.2]

Trace complete.
```

MAC Address Lookup Table

When troubleshooting network issues, you can use a MAC address lookup tool to help you identify the vendor of a network card using the vendor ID portion of the MAC address. The vendor ID portion of the MAC address is the first half of the MAC address (24 bits).

A reason you might wish to look up a MAC address is that, as the network administrator, you may be looking at the MAC address table of a network switch and notice one of the MAC addresses is unlike any of the others. Entering the number into a MAC address lookup table can help identify the type of device on the network that is using the MAC address.

An example of a MAC address lookup table website is *www.macaddresslookup.org*. When I enter my MAC address into the site, it comes back with the name of the manufacturer that created my network card (Sony Corporation).

CERTIFICATION OBJECTIVE 6.05

Troubleshooting with TCP/IP Utilities

The two most common TCP/IP problems are network connectivity and name resolution. In this section, you will learn how to troubleshoot these problems and how to determine where the problems truly reside.

Given the following scenario, how do you troubleshoot the problem?

Scenario   You are trying to use a third-party application to access a remote computer via TCP/IP. You are unable to connect to the remote server.

To properly troubleshoot this problem, you must know where to begin. Most communication problems with TCP/IP can be categorized as one of the following:

■ Basic network connectivity problem
■ Name-resolution problem

It is very easy to determine which problem is occurring in a given situation. Start by trying to access the resource via the IP address rather than the hostname by pinging the IP address. For example, if the problem is related to name resolution, pinging the hostname might not work, but pinging the IP address will. This indicates that because you can communicate with the IP address but not the hostname, you are having name-resolution problems. If you cannot access the resource via the IP address, this indicates a connectivity problem—the system does not exist or it is turned off, or you have a network problem.

Connectivity Problems

Connectivity problems can be difficult to isolate and resolve quickly, especially in complex networks. Let's use some of the tools you've learned about to troubleshoot the earlier problem of using a third-party application to access a remote computer via TCP/IP and being unable to connect to the remote server. You cannot ping the remote host by its IP address.

Check Your TCP/IP Configuration

Start by checking your TCP/IP configuration. TCP/IP requires several settings to be complete and accurate. When you use TCP/IP as your network protocol, an incorrect setting, such as a mistyped subnet mask, can keep your computer from talking with other hosts on the network. For example, if you have an incorrect default gateway setup, you might not be able to communicate with anyone on a remote network.

Use the IPCONFIG utility or the ifconfig utility on Linux or UNIX to determine your computer's basic TCP/IP settings. Verify that the IP address and subnet mask displayed by the IPCONFIG command are the correct values for your computer. Verify that your default gateway is set up with the correct address of the router on the network.

Ping the Loopback Address

Try pinging the loopback address by pinging "localhost," "loopback," or the address 127.0.0.1. To test your loopback address in an IPv6 environment, ping ::1. You can use the **ping** command to verify that TCP/IP is working properly. By pinging the loopback address, which is 127.0.0.1, you are actually verifying that the protocol stack is functioning properly. You should receive a reply like the one shown in Figure 6-28.

An error while pinging the loopback address usually indicates a problem with the TCP/IP protocol installed locally. If you do receive an error at this point, you should try uninstalling and reinstalling TCP/IP. You can remove and install TCP/IP from your LAN connection properties.

Ping the Local IP Address

If you can successfully ping the loopback address, try pinging your local computer's IP address. If you do not know what your IP address is, remember that IPCONFIG/ifconfig will

FIGURE 6-28

Pinging the
loopback address

```
C:\WINDOWS\System32\cmd.exe                                    _ □ ✕

Microsoft Windows XP [Version 5.1.2600]
(C) Copyright 1985-2001 Microsoft Corp.

C:\Documents and Settings\Administrator>ping localhost

Pinging CLIENT100 [127.0.0.1] with 32 bytes of data:

Reply from 127.0.0.1: bytes=32 time=31ms TTL=128
Reply from 127.0.0.1: bytes=32 time<1ms TTL=128
Reply from 127.0.0.1: bytes=32 time<1ms TTL=128
Reply from 127.0.0.1: bytes=32 time<1ms TTL=128

Ping statistics for 127.0.0.1:
    Packets: Sent = 4, Received = 4, Lost = 0 (0% loss),
Approximate round trip times in milli-seconds:
    Minimum = 0ms, Maximum = 31ms, Average = 7ms

C:\Documents and Settings\Administrator>█
```

display this information for you. By typing the following at a command prompt, you should receive a response similar to the one shown in Figure 6-28:

```
PING <local IP address>
```

If an error occurs at this point, there might be a problem communicating with the NIC. You can first try reinstalling the adapter driver for the card. If that doesn't work, try removing and reseating the card. This error might only be resolved by completely replacing the NIC.

Clear the ARP Cache Table

If the local IP address responds correctly, try clearing the ARP cache. If an IP address was stored here by mistake, it could cause the client to attempt to contact the wrong computer.

Start by displaying the ARP cache. You can then see if there is an entry located for the remote IP address. If an incorrect entry exists, try deleting it with the **-d** option.

Verify the Default Gateway

After removing any errant entries from the ARP cache, the next step is to ping the default gateway that your system is using. By pinging the default gateway, you are verifying two items in one step: You are verifying whether or not your system can communicate on the network with another host, and you are verifying that the default gateway is available. The default gateway will be involved in communication only if you are trying to communicate with a host on a remote network. If the gateway does not respond, the packets will not be able to get to the remote host.

on the
job

You can use IPCONFIG or ip route **(in Linux) to display your default gateway. Once you have that address, try pinging it to verify that the gateway is up and running.**

Trace the Route to the Remote Host

After a packet leaves the default gateway, any route can be taken to reach a remote computer. The next step is to try to trace the route to the remote computer.

A wide array of problems could show up here. You may notice that when the utility gets to a certain point, it responds with "Request timed out." If this occurs, it could indicate a route problem or a device failure. It could also indicate bandwidth issues. Try raising the timeout value. If it responds but with high values, your data transfers could be failing because the application does not wait long enough. Try reconfiguring your application or adding more bandwidth to your network.

Another error message you might receive is "Destination Net Unreachable." This usually indicates a network routing problem. Contact the network administrator responsible for that network segment.

Check the TCP/IP Port on the Server

The next thing to try is to verify that you are sending data to the correct port. For example, your web browser automatically tries to connect to port 80 on a server; if the administrator of that server changes the port value, you will need to specify the port when you make the connection. Table 6-13 lists the standard port settings for commonly used protocols.

You can use the Telnet tool to verify that the other computer is configured to permit connections on the same port you are using. If you do not receive an error message, the other computer is configured to enable connections. If you do receive an error, try looking at the settings on the remote computer to verify that they are set up properly.

Name-Resolution Problems

Suppose you are able to connect to a remote host by IP address but are unable to connect via its hostname. This indicates a name-resolution problem. In the Microsoft world, there

TABLE 6-13		
	Port	**Protocol**
Common Ports Used by Network Services	80	HTTP
	443	HTTPS
	21	FTP
	23	TELNET
	25	SMTP
	110	POP3
	3389	Remote Desktop

are two types of computer names: FQDNs used by socket-based applications and NetBIOS names (computer names) used by NetBIOS applications. These names can be resolved in several ways, including using DNS, WINS, a hosts file, or an lmhosts file. Each method has its advantages and disadvantages.

atch **Although many techniques can be used to resolve the two different style names, for the exam, understand**	**that DNS resolves FQDNs to IP addresses, whereas WINS resolves NetBIOS names to IP addresses.**

Name-Resolution Order

The two types of Microsoft computer names each work a little differently. They can use the other's services; however, they use their own resolution methods first. When communicating with an FQDN, the name is resolved by the following resolution methods (in order):

1. Checking the local name
2. Checking the local hosts file
3. Checking DNS servers
4. Checking the local NetBIOS cache
5. Checking WINS servers
6. Broadcasts

NetBIOS name resolution works in a similar way. The NetBIOS name is resolved by using the following methods:

1. Checking its local NetBIOS cache
2. Checking the WINS server
3. Broadcasting for a computer
4. Checking the lmhosts file
5. Checking the local hostname
6. Checking the TCP/IP hosts file
7. Checking DNS servers

By knowing the order of name resolution, you can better understand how these services work and effectively troubleshoot them.

Check the Hosts File

You can start by checking the hosts file. A hosts file is a text file that can be configured with any standard text editor. It contains static mappings for remote TCP/IP hosts by using an IP address column and a hostname column. Each computer has its own hosts file, HOSTS, located in %SystemRoot%\System32\Drivers\Etc on Windows systems.

Because every machine maintains its own hosts file, these files are not generally used in medium or large environments. If a modification or addition has to be made, each machine needs to receive this update by receiving a new version of the hosts file. When you are talking about four or five machines, it's not that bad. When you have to keep 150 machines up to date, it can become very difficult. Figure 6-29 shows an example of a hosts file.

To check your hosts file, open it and scan for the entry of the remote host. If your computer resolves addresses using this file, verify that the entry exists and that it contains the correct information. If this is not the resolution method you are using, try checking your DNS configuration.

Check Your DNS Configuration

DNS provides TCP/IP name-resolution services. DNS is a central server that systems can use to query for name resolution. For example, if any system on your network were to try to

FIGURE 6-29

The hosts file used for FQDN name resolution

```
# Copyright (c) 1993-1999 Microsoft Corp.
#
# This is a sample HOSTS file used by Microsoft TCP/IP for Windows.
#
# This file contains the mappings of IP addresses to host names. Each
# entry should be kept on an individual line. The IP address should
# be placed in the first column followed by the corresponding host name.
# The IP address and the host name should be separated by at least one
# space.
#
# Additionally, comments (such as these) may be inserted on individual
# lines or following the machine name denoted by a '#' symbol.
#
# For example:
#
#      102.54.94.97     rhino.acme.com        # source server
#      38.25.63.10      x.acme.com            # x client host

127.0.0.1              localhost
192.168.1.100          glenserver.glensworld.loc
```

contact server1.yourdomain.com, any system could query DNS and have the name resolved. In addition, if an entry is added to the DNS server, all systems know about the change right away, because DNS is a central database that everyone uses (versus the HOSTS file, which all users have their own copy of).

If you use DNS for name resolution, first verify that you have the DNS client set up correctly on the workstation. From a command prompt, type **ipconfig /all** to list the DNS servers configured on a client. If they exist and are correct, try pinging the DNS server to see if it is online. If it responds, try changing your DNS server to another DNS server, if you have multiple DNS servers. It is possible that one DNS server might have information that is different from what another has. You also might need to contact your DNS administrator to verify that the name exists in DNS and has the correct information.

It is possible that name resolution is a problem because your DNS resolver cache is incorrect. When troubleshooting DNS problems, always flush the DNS resolver cache on the client by typing ipconfig /flushdns.

Check the LMHOSTS File

The LMHOSTS file is similar to the HOSTS file, but is used primarily for NetBIOS name resolution, as opposed to FQDN resolution. It can be used to handle TCP/IP hostname resolution, but it is not recommended, because it is low in the name-resolution techniques order.

Like the HOSTS file, LMHOSTS is a text file that can be edited using any standard text editor. If your network uses LMHOSTS files for NetBIOS name resolution and you cannot connect to the remote computer using its NetBIOS name, there could be an invalid entry in your LMHOSTS file. Try scanning this file for the name of the remote machine. Verify that it exists and that it contains the correct information. If you are not using LMHOSTS, try checking your WINS server configuration settings.

The LMHOSTS file that comes with Windows has a hidden file extension of .sam (for sample). You will not see this file extension unless you turn off the hiding of known file extensions in Windows, and the file will not work with a .sam extension—you will need to rename the file so that it is called simply LMHOSTS, not LMHOSTS.sam.

Check Your WINS Configuration

A WINS server provides NetBIOS name resolution much the way DNS servers provide TCP/IP hostname resolution. If you use WINS for NetBIOS name resolution and you cannot connect to the other machine with its NetBIOS name, there might be a problem with your computer's WINS configuration.

Start by verifying that your system is configured to use a WINS server. From a command prompt, type **ipconfig /all**. This will display the current WINS servers configured for your computer. If the correct servers are listed, try pinging the WINS server. If you cannot ping the WINS server address, contact your WINS administrator to correct the problem. You might also need to verify that the remote host you are trying to connect to is registered with WINS correctly.

Check Your DNS Database

A DNS will provide the DNS domain name–to–IP address resolution when trying to connect to services using domain names, such as on the Internet. If the name and IP address are not matched correctly in the database, you will be unable to access the proper PC for the services you are requesting.

For example, if you were on the Internet and wanted to access an FTP site but the company had changed the IP address of the FTP server, you would type in the DNS name of the FTP server in the address bar, and this name would be matched to the old FTP IP address. The FTP utility would try to query the old IP address for the FTP service. If no FTP service existed on the old IP address, or if a server were not currently using the old IP address, you would receive an error message. Until the company updated the DNS servers on the Internet, the FTP server would be unreachable unless you could find the new IP address of the FTP server.

After querying the DNS server and getting an IP address for the DNS name, you should try to ping the IP address returned to verify that the server at the IP address is functioning.

It is also possible that the DNS server might be unavailable and you will receive no response to your request for the DNS name resolution. If this occurs, you will need to change your DNS server setting on the client to a server that is functioning, or contact someone about the DNS server and report that it is not functioning.

CERTIFICATION SUMMARY

This chapter has introduced you to a number of TCP/IP utilities that are popular for everyday troubleshooting and for the Network+ exam. Be sure that you are familiar with each command-line tool before you book the exam. Also make sure you understand the output shown by the different commands and the command-line switches—you will most definitely be tested in this area.

The ARP utility is used to troubleshoot the ARP process, including the display and modification of the ARP cache. This protocol maintains the mappings between the layer-3 TCP/IP addresses and the layer-2 Ethernet addresses. Each time you access a remote computer, its IP address/MAC address entry is updated in the ARP cache, if need be. Entries can also be manually added and deleted. By default, the ARP cache maintains unused entries for two minutes, and it can contain a frequently used entry for up to ten minutes. RARP works in reverse to provide Ethernet address–to–TCP/IP address mappings.

The Telnet utility provides a virtual terminal to execute remote console commands. Telnet uses a TCP protocol connection to port 23. The default line buffer size is 25, and it can be configured to a maximum of 399 lines. The default terminal emulation for Telnet is VT100.

NBTSTAT displays NetBIOS over TCP/IP (NetBT) protocol statistics. NetBT is a software standard and naming convention used to connect to remote systems. Each workstation in a domain or workgroup must have a unique NetBIOS name. NetBIOS names are 16 bytes, with the last byte reserved for the NetBIOS name suffix. You can display the name table of a host by using **nbtstat -A <ip address>**.

Tracert is used to determine the route that data travels to reach its destination. It uses the ICMP protocol to display status information such as hop count and timeout values. You can specify the maximum number of hops and timeout values to further customize the utility.

Netstat displays TCP/IP protocol statistics and session information. You can also display the local IP routing table with Netstat. Netstat can display Ethernet-specific statistics, protocol statistics, and session information, including listening ports.

IPCONFIG displays the current TCP/IP configuration for a Windows system. ifconfig is a command-line tool used on UNIX and Linux computers to display TCP/IP configuration information such as the IP address and subnet mask. IPCONFIG can display the IP address, subnet mask, DNS servers, WINS servers, and default gateway. IPCONFIG can be used to release or renew DHCP addresses assigned to a system.

The File Transfer Protocol (FTP) is used for file transfers between two computers. FTP requires two TCP port connections: port 20 for data and port 21 for control commands. Using the two ports allows for faster transfer speeds than sending both types of data over the one port. A server-based FTP program, called a service or daemon, is used to store files and process commands.

Ping is used to verify a remote computer's connectivity to the network. Additional options for troubleshooting include setting packet lengths, changing the TTL values, and specifying host lists to return routing statistics for.

NSLOOKUP and DIG are used to query a DNS server for information in its database to verify that name resolution is working with DNS names.

TWO-MINUTE DRILL

Communication Requires ARP

❑ The Address Resolution Protocol (ARP) was designed to provide a mapping from the logical 32-bit TCP/IP addresses to the physical 48-bit MAC addresses.

❑ Address resolution is the process of finding the address of a host within a network.

❑ Remember that ARP translates IP addresses (layer 3) into MAC addresses (layer 2). The Reverse Address Resolution Protocol (RARP) is used to find a TCP/IP address from a MAC address.

❑ Only four types of messages can be sent by the ARP protocol on any machine:
  ❑ ARP request
  ❑ ARP reply
  ❑ RARP request
  ❑ RARP reply

❑ RARP enables a machine to learn its own IP address by broadcasting to resolve its own MAC address.

Common TCP/IP Commands

❑ IPCONFIG is used to display the current TCP/IP configurations on the local workstations and to modify the DHCP addresses assigned to each interface.

❑ IPCONFIG is used in Windows to display TCP/IP information from a command prompt.

❑ The **ifconfig** (lowercase) command is used to display TCP/IP settings on UNIX and Linux.

❑ The **ping** command is used to test a machine's connectivity to the network and to verify that it is active. You can use the **ping** command with an IP address or hostname.

❑ Ping uses the Internet Control Message Protocol (ICMP) to verify connections to remote hosts by sending ECHO packets and listening for reply packets.

❑ Make sure you understand the differences between hostname resolution and NetBIOS (machine) name resolution. The exam will quiz you on both scenarios.

❑ Tracert is a command-line utility that was designed to perform a very basic task: to determine the path taken by a data packet to reach its destination.

❑ You will use the trace route utility by typing **TRACERT <ip address>**.

❑ Netstat displays protocol statistics and current TCP/IP network connections.

❑ Using Netstat to monitor TCP protocol activity can enable you to troubleshoot TCP/IP-based connections.

❑ **Netstat -a** will display listening ports—useful if you need to monitor what applications are awaiting a connection.

❑ **Netstat -n** will display who is connected to your system along with port information.

❑ Telnet was designed to provide a virtual terminal or remote login across the network. It is connection based and handles its own session negotiation.

❑ The primary use of Telnet is for remote administration.

❑ Telnet uses TCP port 23.

❑ The File Transfer Protocol (FTP) is designed primarily for transferring data across a network.

❑ TFTP differs from FTP in two ways: It uses the User Datagram Protocol (UDP) connectionless transport instead of TCP, and it does not log on to the remote machine.

Name Resolution Commands

❑ The Microsoft TCP/IP stack uses an additional protocol for networking services: NetBIOS over TCP/IP (NetBT).

❑ NBTSTAT is used to troubleshoot NetBIOS over TCP/IP.

❑ **NBTSTAT -A <IP address>** will display the name table of the IP address supplied. This is a useful feature when you know the IP address of a system and want to know the computer name.

❑ **NBTSTAT -R** purges and reloads the NetBIOS name cache.

❑ **NBTSTAT -c** will display the NetBIOS name cache, which displays computer names that have been resolved to IP addresses.

❑ NSLOOKUP displays information in the DNS server database.

❑ You can use NSLOOKUP to troubleshoot name-resolution problems that may arise because of incorrect records on the server.

❑ DIG is a very popular Linux tool used to query and troubleshoot DNS.

Other TCP/IP Utilities

❑ The host and hostname utilities are used to display the local system name.

❑ The **route** command is used to manage the local routing table.

❑ The **MTR** command is a Linux command that combines features of Tracert and Ping.

Troubleshooting with TCP/IP Utilities

❑ When troubleshooting connectivity issues, first use IPCONFIG to display and verify your TCP/IP settings.

❑ Use the **ping** command to test and verify which systems you can communicate.

❑ Always remember that if you cannot communicate with a system by name, try to use the IP address. Most communication problems are due to name resolution issues.

SELF TEST

The following Self Test questions will help measure your understanding of the material presented in this chapter. Read all the choices carefully, as there may be more than one correct answer. Choose all correct answers for each question.

Communication Requires ARP

1. Which utility can be used to display and modify the table that maintains the TCP/IP address–to–MAC address translation?
   A. NBTSTAT
   B. Telnet
   C. ARP
   D. SNMP

2. Which are not valid message types for ARP? (Choose all that apply.)
   A. ARP reply
   B. ARP decline
   C. ARP response
   D. ARP request

3. How long will a dynamic ARP entry remain in cache if it has not been reused?
   A. 10 minutes
   B. 5 minutes

   C. 2 minutes

   D. None of the above

4. ARP is responsible for converting _____ addresses to _____ addresses.

   A. layer-3, layer-2

   B. layer-4, layer-3

   C. layer-2, layer-3

   D. layer-3, layer-4

5. Which command and command switch were used to generate the following output?

```
Interface: 10.10.10.101
Internet Address  Physical Address   Type
12.10.10.10       00-06-6b-8e-4e-e3  dynamic
12.10.10.19       00-c0-ae-d0-bb-f5  dynamic
```

   A. ARP -d

   B. IPCONFIG /DISPLAYMAC

   C. ARP -a

   D. IPCONFIG /ALL

Common TCP/IP Commands

6. Which utility enables you to execute console commands remotely through a terminal session?

   A. FTP

   B. Ping

   C. Telnet

   D. NBTSTAT

7. Which protocol is defined to use TCP port 23?

   A. Telnet

   B. FTP

   C. HTTP

   D. SMTP

8. Which utility is used to determine the path that data takes to a remote host?

   A. NBTSTAT

   B. ARP

   C. FTP

   D. Tracert

9. Which command was used to generate the following command output?

```
1 <10 ms <10 ms <10 ms 192.168.0.254
2 <10 ms <10 ms <10 ms 12.127.106.34
```

```
3 40 ms    40 ms   50 ms r04.nycmny01.us.bb.verio.net [129.250.10.37]
4 40 ms    40 ms   40 ms r20.nycmny01.us.bb.verio.net [129.250.2.36]
5 40 ms    40 ms   50 ms r00.nwrknj01.us.bb.verio.net [129.250.2.216]
6 110 ms 121 ms 120 ms 192.94.118.221
7 110 ms 130 ms 120 ms www.novell.com [130.57.4.27]
Trace complete.
```

   A. TRACERT www.novell.com

   B. Ping www.novell.com

   C. NSLOOKUP www.novell.com

   D. ROUTE PRINT www.novell.com

10. Which utility is used to display TCP/IP-specific protocol and interface statistics?

   A. NBTSTAT

   B. ARP

   C. Netstat

   D. None of the above

11. Which command and command switch were used to generate the following output?

```
Active Connections
Proto Local Address        Foreign Address          Stat
TCP comp1:smtp             2kpc1.domain5.net:0      LISTENING
TCP comp1:http             xppc2.domain5.net:1256   LISTENING
TCP comp1:epmap            2kpc1.domain5.net:0      LISTENING
TCP comp1:https            2kpc1.domain5.net:0      LISTENING
TCP comp1:microsoft-ds     2kpc1.domain5.net:0      LISTENING
TCP comp1:1025             2kpc1.domain5.net:0      LISTENING
TCP comp1:1245             2kpc1.domain5.net:0      LISTENING
TCP comp1:1277             2kpc1.domain5.net:0      LISTENING
TCP comp1:1312             2kpc1.domain5.net:0      LISTENING
```

   A. NBTSTAT -c

   B. NETSTAT -a

   C. IPCONFIG /ALL

   D. ARP -g

12. Which items are not available for display in IPCONFIG?

   A. TCP/IP address

   B. MAC address

   C. DHCP lease information

   D. None of the above

13. Which option of IPCONFIG is used to receive a new lease on your IP address?

   A. /all

   B. /release

C. /obtain

D. /renew

14. You are troubleshooting to determine why Sue's computer cannot connect to the Internet. What command would you type to view all of Sue's TCP/IP settings in a Windows command prompt?

   A. IPCONFIG

   B. IPCONFIG /ALL

   C. IPCONFIG /SHOWITALL

   D. IPCONFIG /DISPLAYALL

15. Which utility is used to facilitate file transfers between two remote hosts?

   A. FTP

   B. Telnet

   C. Ping

   D. None of the above

16. What TCP ports are used by FTP services? (Choose two.)

   A. TCP port 20

   B. TCP port 25

   C. TCP port 21

   D. TCP port 80

17. Which utility is used to verify network connectivity of a remote host?

   A. Route

   B. ARP

   C. Ping

   D. None of the above

18. You are having trouble connecting to resources on the Internet, so you use the IPCONFIG utility to verify your TCP/IP configuration. The configuration is shown.

   ```
   Ethernet adapter Lan Connection:
   Connection-specific DNS Suffix . : glensworld.loc
   IP Address. . . . . . . . . . . : 192.168.1.100
   Subnet Mask . . . . . . . . . . : 255.255.255.0
   Default Gateway . . . . . . . . : 192.168.1.1
   ```

   Your configuration seems to be accurate. Which command would you type next to help determine what the problem is?

   A. Ping glensworld.loc

   B. Ping 192.168.1.100

   C. Ping 192.168.1.1

   D. Ping 127.0.0.1

19. The following output was generated from which command?

```
Reply from 10.10.10.1: bytes>32 time<1ms TTL>128
Reply from 10.10.10.1: bytes>32 time<1ms TTL>128
Reply from 10.10.10.1: bytes>32 time<1ms TTL>128
Reply from 10.10.10.1: bytes>32 time<1ms TTL>128
Ping statistics for 10.10.10.1:
Packets: Sent > 4, Received > 4, Lost > 0 (0% loss),
Approximate round trip times in milli-seconds:
Minimum > 0ms, Maximum > 0ms, Average > 0ms
```

   A. TRACERT 10.10.10.1
   B. ROUTE 10.10.10.1
   C. Ping 127.0.0.1
   D. Ping 10.10.10.1

Name Resolution Commands

20. Which protocol uses a 16-byte name, with the last digit reserved as a resource identifier?
   A. TCP/IP
   B. IPX
   C. NetBIOS
   D. NBTSTAT

21. Which utility can be used to troubleshoot NetBIOS over TCP/IP connectivity issues?
   A. NetBT
   B. NetBEUI
   C. NBTSTAT
   D. NetBIOS

22. Which NBTSTAT switch enables you to display the computer's NetBIOS name cache?
   A. -R
   B. -c
   C. -a
   D. -A

23. Which command-line utility and command switch were used to generate the following command output?

```
Lan Connection:
Node IpAddress: [192.168.1.100] Scope Id: []
NetBIOS Local Name Table
Name       Type Status
```

```
SERVER100 <00> UNIQUE Registered
DOMAIN100 <00> GROUP Registered
SERVER100 <20> UNIQUE Registered
DOMAIN100 <1E> GROUP Registered
```

    A. IPCONFIG /ALL

    B. NBTSTAT -A

    C. NETSTAT -n

    D. NBTSTAT -n

24. Which utility is used to verify the DNS database on a DNS server?

    A. Route

    B. ARP

    C. Ping

    D. NSLOOKUP

25. What **dig** command is used to perform a reverse name query?

    A. Dig www.gleneclarke.com

    B. Dig www.gleneclarke.com +short

    C. Dig -x 192.168.2.200

    D. Dig gleneclarke.com axfr

Other TCP/IP Utilities

26. Which TCP/IP utility is used to manage the routing table on the local system?

    A. Route

    B. ARP

    C. Ping

    D. NSLOOKUP

27. You wish to find out what your system name is. What utility would you use?

    A. Route

    B. hostname

    C. Ping

    D. NSLOOKUP

Troubleshooting with TCP/IP Utilities

28. What command would you use to verify that TCP/IP is running successfully on your system?

    A. arp

    B. ping 127.0.0.1

    C. telnet

    D. NSLOOKUP

29. What service is used to convert an FQDN to an IP address?
    A. WINS
    B. Telnet
    C. FTP
    D. DNS

Performance-Based Question Review: See the performance-based question sample from the author included with the accompanying media.

SELF TEST ANSWERS

Communication Requires ARP

1. ☑ **C.** ARP is responsible for converting a layer-3 address (IP address) to a layer-2 address (MAC address). A utility by the same name is available in most operating systems and is responsible for modifying entries within the ARP cache.
   ☒ **A, B,** and **D** are incorrect. NBTSTAT is used to view the NetBIOS name table of a system, Telnet is used to open a terminal emulation session with a terminal server, and SNMP is used to monitor devices.

2. ☑ **B** and **C.** ARP decline and ARP response are not valid ARP messages. Only four types of messages can be sent out by the ARP protocol: ARP request, ARP reply, RARP request, and RARP reply.
   ☒ **A** and **D** are incorrect because they are valid ARP messages.

3. ☑ **C.** Two minutes. Unlike static addresses, which never age out, dynamic addresses remain for only a predetermined amount of time. Windows adjusts the size of the ARP cache automatically. Entries not used after two minutes are removed. If entries are used frequently, they remain in the ARP cache for ten minutes.
   ☒ **A, B,** and **D** are incorrect because a dynamic ARP entry remains in cache for two minutes by default.

4. ☑ **A.** ARP is responsible for converting IP addresses (layer-3 addresses) to MAC addresses (layer-2 addresses).

☒ **B, C,** and **D** are incorrect because they are not the layered addresses that ARP is responsible for resolving.

5. ☑ **C. ARP -a** will display the ARP cache, which is what the output for this question is showing. Be sure you can identify the output for the exam.

☒ **A, B,** and **D** are incorrect because they are the wrong commands or switches to generate this output.

Common TCP/IP Commands

6. ☑ **C.** Telnet (telecommunications network) was designed to provide a virtual terminal or remote login across the network. This enables the user to execute commands on a remote machine anywhere on the network as if he or she were sitting in front of the console. The term Telnet refers to both the protocol and the application used for remote management.

☒ **A, B,** and **D** are incorrect because FTP allows for file transfers between two PCs; Ping is used to verify that connectivity can be established between two PCs; and NBTSTAT will allow you to view the NetBIOS name table available on a PC.

7. ☑ **A.** Telnet uses TCP port 23 by default.

☒ **B, C,** and **D** are incorrect because FTP uses ports 20 and 21, HTTP uses port 80, and SMTP uses port 25.

8. ☑ **D.** Tracert is a command-line utility that was designed to determine the path taken by a data packet to reach its destination. This can be very helpful in determining at what point a network connection is no longer active. It can also be helpful in troubleshooting issues with network response times.

☒ **A, B,** and **C** are incorrect. NBTSTAT is used to troubleshoot NetBIOS over TCP/IP. ARP is used to view or modify the ARP cache. FTP is used to transfer files between two PCs.

9. ☑ **A.** Tracert sends back multiple responses, one for each router that it hits on its way to the destination address. In this example, we are tracing the pathway to www.novell.com and getting a hop entry with each router on the way.

☒ **B, C,** and **D** are incorrect. Ping is used to send a test message to the destination, but does not send a response with each router it hits; NSLOOKUP is used to query DNS and troubleshoot DNS problems; and the **route print** command is used to view the routing table of a system.

10. ☑ **C.** Netstat displays protocol statistics and current TCP/IP network connections. This utility can be used to display in-depth detail about protocol status, statistics for the different network interfaces, and the current routing table.

☒ **A** and **B** are incorrect. NBTSTAT is used to troubleshoot NetBIOS over TCP/IP. ARP is used to troubleshoot the ARP cache.

11. ☑ **B.** The Netstat utility is used to view TCP/IP connection information and listening ports.
☒ **A, C,** and **D** are incorrect. NBTSTAT is used to troubleshoot NetBIOS over TCP/IP, IPCONFIG is used to view your TCP/IP settings, and ARP is used to view or modify your ARP cache.

12. ☑ **D.** All of the options listed can be displayed in IPCONFIG by using the /**ALL** option.
☒ **A, B,** and **C** are incorrect because all are available for display in IPCONFIG.

13. ☑ **D.** The /**renew** switch is used to renew the IP address that you have obtained from the DHCP server.
☒ **A, B,** and **C** are incorrect. /**ALL** will display all of your TCP/IP settings, and /**RELEASE** will allow your system to give up its IP address. /**OBTAIN** is not a switch of IPCONFIG.

14. ☑ **B. IPCONFIG** /**ALL** is used to view all of the TCP/IP settings on a system.
☒ **A, C,** and **D** are incorrect. /**SHOWITALL** and /**DISPLAYALL** are not switches of IPCONFIG, and **IPCONFIG** by itself shows only basic settings, not all the settings.

15. ☑ **A.** FTP (File Transfer Protocol) is designed primarily for transferring data across a network. FTP denotes both a protocol and a utility used for this purpose.
☒ **B, C,** and **D** are incorrect. Ping is used to verify communication between two PCs, and Telnet is used to create a remote session with a Telnet server.

16. ☑ **A** and **C.** FTP uses two TCP channels to operate. It uses TCP port 20 as the data transfer channel and TCP port 21 for control commands. The data transfer channel is known as the DTP, or Data Transfer Process, and the command channel is known as the PI, or Protocol Interpreter. The two channels enable you to transfer data and execute commands at the same time, and they provide a more efficient and faster data transfer. FTP also works in real time. It does not queue up requests as most other utilities do; it transfers data while you watch.
☒ **B** and **D** are incorrect. Port 25 is used by SMTP, and port 80 is used by HTTP.

17. ☑ **C.** The Ping (Packet Internet Groper) command is the most-used TCP/IP troubleshooting tool available. This command is used to test a machine's connectivity to the network and to verify that it is active. Usually, using this command is one of the first steps to any troubleshooting if a connectivity problem is occurring between two computers. This can quickly help you to determine whether a remote host is available and responsive.
☒ **A** and **B** are incorrect. **Route** is a command that we can use to view or modify the routing table in Windows. ARP is used to view or modify the ARP cache.

18. ☑ **C.** When troubleshooting connectivity to the Internet, you first check your TCP/IP settings and then ping the IP address of the default gateway to verify that the router is up and running.
☒ **A, B,** and **D** are incorrect. Although you may start pinging addresses, given that you are having trouble connecting to the Internet, you may want to start by pinging the router.

19. ☑ **D.** In the output you can see that the address of 10.10.10.1 is sending responses back. There are four responses that are the four ping response messages.
☒ **A, B,** and **C** are incorrect. The output is coming from a **ping** command to the IP address of 10.10.10.1.

Name Resolution Commands

20. ☑ **C.** NetBIOS uses unique 15-character names for each system, known as computer names. Each NetBIOS name is made up of 16 bytes; 15 are used for the computer name, and the 16th byte is used as the NetBIOS name suffix, which identifies a service running on the system.
☒ **A, B,** and **D** are incorrect because they do not use 16-byte names.

21. ☑ **C.** NBTSTAT is used to troubleshoot connectivity between two computers trying to communicate via NetBIOS over TCP/IP (NetBT). It displays the protocol statistics and the current connections to each remote host. You can also display the information about a remote host and the names stored in its NetBIOS name table.
☒ **A, B,** and **D** are incorrect. NetBT stands for NetBIOS over TCP/IP, NetBEUI is a nonroutable protocol, and NetBIOS is a software and naming convention. All of these are protocols, not utilities.

22. ☑ **B.** The **-c** option is correct. When a system resolves a NetBIOS name to an IP address, that information is stored in the NetBIOS name cache.
☒ **A, C,** and **D** are incorrect. The **-R** option will purge the cache and reload any entries in the cache that have the #PRE tag in the LMHOSTS file. The **-a** parameter is used to list a name table of a remote PC by specifying its name; **-A** does the same, but you must specify the remote PC by IP address. You should know all these switches for the exam.

23. ☑ **D.** The local NetBIOS name table can be viewed with **NBTSTAT -n**. This output shows the names that this system has registered on the network and indicates what services it runs. In this example you can see that the system runs the Server service and Workstation service.
☒ **A, B,** and **C** are incorrect. **IPCONFIG /ALL** is used to view all the TCP/IP settings on the host, **NBTSTAT -A** is used to view the NetBIOS name table of a remote system, and **NETSTAT -n** is used to view the active connections.

24. ☑ **D.** The NSLOOKUP utility is used to view and test the DNS database on the DNS server.
☒ **A, B,** and **C** are incorrect. Route is used to view or modify the routing table in Windows. ARP is used to view or modify the ARP cache. Ping is used to verify communications between two PCs.

25. ☑ **C.** To perform a reverse query with **dig**, you use the **-x** switch and then supply the IP address of the system you wish to know the name of.
☒ **A, B,** and **D** are incorrect because they are not the switches used to do a reverse query.

Other TCP/IP Utilities

26. ☑ **A.** The route utility is used to manage the local routing table. You can view the routing table with route print and add a route with route add.
☒ **B, C,** and **D** are incorrect because they do not manage the local routing table of a system.

27. ☑ **B.** The **hostname** command is used to display the system name.
☒ **A, C,** and **D** are incorrect because they are not used to display the local system name.

Troubleshooting with TCP/IP Utilities

28. ☑ **B.** You would ping the loopback address to verify that the TCP/IP software stack is installed and working.

☒ **A, C,** and **D** are incorrect because they are not used to test the local system. You would use ARP to troubleshoot MAC address resolution problems, Telnet to remotely connect to another system, and NSLOOKUP to troubleshoot DNS problems.

29. ☑ **D.** DNS is used to convert the FQDN—for example, www.gleneclarke.com—to an IP address.

☒ **A, B,** and **C** are incorrect because they are not used to convert the FQDN to an IP address. WINS is used to convert the NetBIOS (computer name) to an IP address, Telnet is used to remotely connect to another system, and FTP is a protocol to download files from a remote system.

Chapter 7

Configuring Routers and Switches

Routers and switches make up an important part of every network. The switch is used to connect all of your systems together to create the local area network (LAN), while the router is used to connect your LAN to the Internet or your company wide area network (WAN) environment.

In this chapter you will learn the basics of routers and switches, including basic configuration tasks of a Cisco router and switch. The new Network+ exam objectives expand on this area, so be familiar with it for the exam!

CERTIFICATION OBJECTIVE 7.01

Basic Router Configuration

In this section you will learn the basics of Cisco router configuration. This includes a quick primer on the different configuration modes and basic configuration, such as changing the name of the router and configuring its interfaces.

Configuration Modes

The trickiest part of learning how to manage a Cisco device is understanding the different configuration modes and how to navigate from one mode to another. When you first connect to a Cisco router, you are placed in what is known as *user exec* mode. User exec mode is a read-only mode where you can only look at the device settings, but not modify any settings. You know that you are in user exec mode because your prompt displays with a ">" as shown:

```
Router>
```

If you want to make changes to your Cisco device, you need to move into *privilege exec* mode, which allows you to make changes to the router's configuration. You can move to privilege exec mode by typing the **enable** command while in user exec mode. Once you enter privilege exec mode, your prompt changes by having a "#" sign in it:

```
Router>enable
Router#
```

The weird thing about privilege exec mode is that you actually cannot change any settings from there. You must move a level deeper, into *global configuration* mode, to make any changes. To move into global configuration mode, you type **config term** (for configure terminal), and then your prompt changes with the word "(config)" in it as shown:

```
Router>enable
Router#config term
Router(config)#
```

Once you are in global configuration mode, you can make changes to the router. There are configuration locations you need to navigate to after global configuration, which we will discuss later.

If you wanted to go back to privilege exec mode, also known as *priv exec* mode, from global configuration mode, you would type the **exit** command. This would take you back to privilege exec mode, where you could type **disable** to get back to user exec mode.

```
Router(config)#exit
Router#disable
Router>
```

The reason that you should know how to navigate back and forth between the different configuration modes is that commands are only available in certain modes. For example, if you want to change the name of the router, you must be in global configuration mode, but if you want to view the settings on the router, you go back to user exec mode.

Configuring the Hostname

The first configuration task most administrators perform on their router is to change the name. Changing the name of the router simply changes the prompt to display that name so that you know which device you are configuring. The default name on all routers is "router," while the default name on all switches is "switch." If you are managing a number of devices, it would be hard to know what device you are configuring with those names!

To change the name of the Cisco router, you simply move into priv exec mode and then global configuration mode. Once in global configuration mode, you can use the **hostname** command to change the name of the router. The **hostname** command expects you to specify the name of the router as a parameter. This is shown in the following code listing:

```
Router>enable
Router#config term
Router(config)#hostname VAN-R1
VAN-R1(config)#
```

Notice in the code listing that after the **hostname** command is used, the router's prompt changes to include the name of the device. Also note that the default name of the router is Router.

Configuring Interfaces

The next step to configuring your router is to configure each of the interfaces on the router with an IP address. Most routers will contain any number of interfaces, with each interface being of a different type:

- **Ethernet**   An Ethernet interface is a 10 Mbps network card in the router that is used to connect to a LAN environment. This interface could also connect to a high-speed Internet connection for home or small office use.
- **Fast Ethernet**   A Fast Ethernet interface is a 100 Mbps network card in the router that is used to connect to a LAN environment. The Fast Ethernet interface supports speed settings of 10 or 100 Mbps. This interface could also connect to a high-speed Internet connection for home or small office use.
- **Gigabit Ethernet**   A Gigabit Ethernet interface is a 1000 Mbps network card in the router that is used to connect to a LAN environment or a high-speed Internet connection for home or small office use. This interface supports speed settings of 10, 100, or 1000 Mbps.

■ **Serial**   A serial port is used to connect to your WAN environment by connecting to the channel service unit/data service unit (CSU/DSU) or another WAN interface. You can also use the serial port to connect one Cisco router directly to another using a back-to-back serial cable.

A number of other interfaces may exist on the router, such as wireless interfaces or interfaces to connect to the WAN environment, such as a built-in CSU/DSU, or an Integrated Services Digital Network (ISDN) interface. You will learn more about WAN technologies in Chapter 12.

Configuring Fast Ethernet Ports

It doesn't matter what type of interface you have in your routers; the general concept in administering the interfaces is the same, although there may be a few extra settings. I will use the Fast Ethernet interface as my example in this section.

The first setting you want to configure on your Fast Ethernet port is the IP address of the network interface. To configure the Fast Ethernet interface, you must first navigate to global configuration mode with the following commands:

```
VAN-R1>enable
VAN-R1#config term
```

Once in global configuration mode, you need to move into the interface subprompt by using the **interface** <ID> command. The ID of the interface is based on the type of interface, plus an index number representing the interface. For example, the first Ethernet interface on a router is known as Eth0, while the second interface is known as Eth1. To specify a Fast Ethernet port, you use F0/0 or F0/1. In this example, there are two numbers: the first number represents the card, or module, in the router, while the second number represents the port on the module. A module can have many ports. The following is your command to move to the first Fast Ethernet port on the router:

```
VAN-R1(config)#interface f0/0
```

Once you navigate to the interface prompt (shown with an "if" in the prompt), you can then specify settings on the interface, such as the IP address and a description of the interface. The description has no technical benefit, but is a great way to remember what the interface is connecting to when viewing the configuration.

```
VAN-R1(config-if)#ip address 14.0.0.1 255.0.0.0
VAN-R1(config-if)#description Private LAN
```

Once you configure the IP address on the interface, you can specify settings such as the speed of the interface (10, 100, or 1000 Mbps) and the duplex setting of half duplex, full duplex, or auto. Remember from Chapter 3 that half duplex means the interface can send and receive, but only in one direction at a time. Full duplex means that the interface can send and receive at the same time. Setting the duplex setting to auto means that the interface will detect what is supported by the network and automatically configure itself for that. The following commands are used to configure the duplex setting on the interface and the speed:

```
VAN-R1(config-if)#duplex full
VAN-R1(config-if)#speed 100
```

For the Network+ exam, know how to configure the IP address, the duplex setting, and speed on an interface.

Once you have the IP address and other interface settings configured, you can then enable the card. Because Cisco has already used the command "enable" to move to priv exec mode, you must use the **no shutdown** command to enable the card. Conversely, the **shutdown** command is how you disable the interface.

```
VAN-R1(config-if)#no shutdown
```

Configuring Serial Ports

The other type of interface that I want to talk about in this chapter is the serial interface on the router. As mentioned earlier, serial interfaces are used to connect to WAN environments or to connect two routers directly together. The following commands are used to navigate to the serial interface on a Cisco router:

```
VAN-R1>enable
VAN-R1#config term
VAN-R1(config)#interface serial 0/0
VAN-R1(config-if)#
```

The first thing you want to do once you are at the interface prompt is assign an IP address to the serial interface. You can either assign the address manually or you can specify that you wish to obtain the address from a Dynamic Host Configuration Protocol (DHCP) server using the **ip address dhcp** command. In this example I will assign the IP address manually:

```
VAN-R1(config-if)#ip address 24.138.2.5 255.0.0.0
```

Once you have configured the IP address on the interface, you then specify the serial link encapsulation protocol that will carry the data across the link. There are two common serial link encapsulation protocols:

- **HDLC** The High Data Link Control protocol is a Cisco-proprietary protocol that you can use to connect to another Cisco device at the other end of the serial link.

- **PPP** The Point-To-Point Protocol is an industry-standard serial link protocol that supports authentication. This protocol can be used to connect to any equipment that supports PPP.

Once you set the encapsulation protocol, you then must specify the clock rate of the link if you are at the data communication equipment (DCE) end of the link. You will typically only need to do this if you are using a back-to-back serial cable to connect two routers together, because normally the serial port connects to your Internet service provider (ISP) and they will set the clock rate on the link. To configure the encapsulation protocol and the clock rate on the link, type the following commands:

```
VAN-R1(config-if)#encapsulation hdlc
VAN-R1(config-if)#clock rate 64000
```

Like the Fast Ethernet port, you then need to enable the interface by typing the **no shutdown** command:

```
VAN-R1(config-if)#no shutdown
```

Once you have the network interfaces configured, you are ready to configure the routing tables on the routers. This chapter is designed to give you a quick primer on router configuration. Chapter 8 discusses routing and how to manage the routing table on a Cisco router.

It is important to note that when making changes to your router configuration, the changes are stored in temporary memory (known as the running configuration). You will need to copy the running configuration to the startup configuration for permanent storage of the configuration—meaning if you want to retain the changes after a reboot, you need to store the configuration in the startup configuration. To do this you use the **copy running-config startup-config** command. You can also look at your changes with the **show running-config** command.

EXERCISE 7-1

Video

Performing Basic Configuration of Cisco Routers

In this exercise you will practice configuring the hostname and interfaces on two Cisco routers. You will need two Cisco routers with serial ports, and a back-to-back serial cable. You could also use a router simulator.

1. Connect the two routers together through the serial ports with a back-to-back serial cable. Ensure you know which router has the end of the cable that is labeled with DCE.
2. The router with the DCE end of the cable is going to be known as ExerR1, while the other router is known as ExerR2.
3. Connect one of the Fast Ethernet ports on each router to a switch.
4. Connect a console cable from the serial port on your workstation to the console port on router ExerR1, and then launch a HyperTerminal application. Within the HyperTerminal application, name the connection Cisco and choose COM1 as your connection type.

5. Once at the router's screen, press ENTER to display a prompt and then type the following commands to configure the hostname and interface:

```
Router>enable
Router#config term
Router(config)#hostname ExerR1
ExerR1(config)#interface f0/0
ExerR1(config-if)#ip address 24.0.0.1 255.0.0.0
ExerR1(config-if)#description Private LAN
ExerR1(config-if)#duplex full
ExerR1(config-if)#speed 100
ExerR1(config-if)#no shutdown
ExerR1(config-if)#interface serial 0/0
ExerR1(config-if)#ip address 25.0.0.1 255.0.0.0
ExerR1(config-if)#encapsulation hdlc
ExerR1(config-if)#clock rate 64000
ExerR1(config-if)#no shutdown
```

6. Connect to the console port on router ExerR2, and type the following commands to configure the hostname and interface:

```
Router>enable
Router#config term
Router(config)#hostname ExerR2
ExerR2(config)#interface f0/0
ExerR2(config-if)#ip address 26.0.0.1 255.0.0.0
ExerR2(config-if)#description Private LAN
ExerR2(config-if)#duplex full
ExerR2(config-if)#speed 100
ExerR2(config-if)#no shutdown
ExerR2(config-if)#interface serial 0/0
ExerR2(config-if)#ip address 25.0.0.2 255.0.0.0
ExerR2(config-if)#encapsulation hdlc
ExerR2(config-if)#no shutdown
```

7. From router ExerR2, try to ping router ExerR1 with the following commands. If you receive five exclamation points (!), then you have received five replies:

```
ExerR2(config-if)#exit
ExerR2(config)#exit
ExerR2#ping 25.0.0.1
```

CERTIFICATION OBJECTIVE 7.02

Basic Switch Configuration

In Chapter 3 you learned about different network devices and the purpose of a network switch. You learned that a switch filters network traffic by only sending data to the port on the switch that is associated with the destination Media Access Control (MAC) address of the frame.

For the Network+ exam, understand that a switch offers three core services:

- **Addressing learning** The switch learns the MAC addresses of all systems connected to ports on it.
- **Filtering** Once the switch knows what systems are connected to each port (by MAC address), it can then filter traffic by only sending data to the port that is associated with the destination MAC address in the frame.
- **Loop avoidance** A network loop is when you connect the switches in such a way that there are multiple pathways to a destination system. Having a network loop can bring down the network, so switches have loop avoidance protocols that disable the loop. Switches use the Spanning Tree Protocol (STP) to prevent loops on the network.

The idea behind the STP loop avoidance protocol is that when you connect the switches in such a way that they create a network loop, the loop avoidance protocol will place one of the ports involved in the loop in a blocking state. The switch knows that the port is in a blocking state and, therefore, does not try to send data through that pathway. The benefit of having multiple pathways is that if one of the links goes down, the loop avoidance protocol will detect this and then change the secondary pathway from a blocking state to a forwarding state again.

There are a number of different terms you should be familiar with in regard to how a switch deals with frames it receives. The following list identifies actions that a switch can perform on a frame (data it receives):

- **Flooding** A switch will flood a frame it receives when it does not know the port that the destination MAC address (of the frame) is connected to. Flooding means that the switch sends the frame to all ports on it in hopes that the destination system will receive the frame.
- **Forwarding** Forwarding is what the switch does when it knows the port that the destination system is connected to. The switch forwards the frame to the appropriate port so that it can be received by the destination system.
- **Blocking** A port is placed in a blocking state by STP to prevent a layer-2 loop.
- **Filtering** Switches filter traffic by only sending the data to the port that the destination system is connected to.

The STP protocol has been around for many years, and it does have its problems. STP uses an algorithm to determine which port out of all the ports creating the loop on the network should be placed in a blocking state. The algorithm uses a process that takes time (up to 52 seconds) before the port transitions from a blocking state to a forwarding state when needed. In today's networking environments, this is quite a large convergence time when we could be talking about voice data being transmitted over the network (imagine your business call pausing for 52 seconds).

This is where Rapid Spanning Tree Protocol (RSTP) comes in. RSTP is known as the IEEE 802.1w standard and is an improvement on STP. With STP, the ports move through four different states (blocking, listening, learning, and then forwarding), which is why it could take 52 seconds before the port moves to a forwarding state. RSTP reduces these states to three, but also introduces an alternative port feature. The alternative port is used as a backup link when RSTP originally determines which ports go into a forwarding state. When a port goes down, RSTP simply activates the alternative port instead of going through a voting process that STP would do (which takes time).

For the Network+ exam, know that STP is responsible for preventing loops on the network and is defined as the IEEE 802.1d standard. Also know that RSTP is an improvement on STP and uses alternative ports. RSTP is defined as the IEEE 802.1w standard.

Configuring Interfaces

The benefit of a Cisco network switch is that it is considered a managed switch. A *managed* switch allows you to fully configure settings on the switch, such as the interface settings for each port, security settings, and virtual LANs (VLANs). An *unmanaged* switch refers to a relatively cheap switch that does not offer the capabilities to configure the switch to suit your needs.

One of the common tasks you can perform with a network switch is to manage the ports, or interfaces, on the switch. You have already learned some common settings on interfaces with the Cisco router discussion. Know that those settings can be configured for each port on the switch. For example, the following commands are used to configure port 3 on the switch:

```
VAN-SW1>enable
VAN-SW1#config term
VAN-SW1(config)#interface f0/3
VAN-SW1(config-if)#description Mail Server Port
VAN-SW1(config-if)#speed 100
VAN-SW1(config-if)#duplex full
```

Note that in this example you are administering port number 3 and that the description of the port is set to Mail Server Port. Notice that you configure the speed on the port to 100 Mbps and set the port to full duplex. The speed command accepts speed associated with the interface such as 10, 100, or 1000. The duplex command supports parameters such as full, half, or auto for auto detect.

For security reasons, you may also decide to disable ports that are not being used. The following commands are used to disable port 4 on the switch. Notice that the commands you used in the router discussion apply to switches as well.

```
VAN-SW1>enable
VAN-SW1#config term
VAN-SW1(config)#interface f0/4
VAN-SW1(config-if)#shutdown
```

Because routers and switches have different default shutdown states for interfaces, it is important to always explicitly specify whether you want to disable a port with a **shutdown** command, or enable it with a **no shutdown** command.

Other Interface Settings

There are a number of other interface features you need to be familiar with for the new Network+ certification exam.

Port Bonding (LACP)   Port bonding, also known as link aggregation, is a feature that allows you to link multiple ports together on a switch to combine the bandwidth of the ports together as one. Port bonding is supported by the industry-standard protocol known as *Link Aggregation Control Protocol (LACP)* and is supported by many vendors.

The following commands are used on a Cisco switch to configure the link aggregation feature known as EtherChannel on Gigabit Ethernet ports 11 and 12. Note that the ports are placed in VLAN 2 and assigned to the EtherChannel 5 (that is a link aggregation grouping number). Each switch can have up to 48 EtherChannels with up to 16 ports in each channel aggregated.

```
VAN-SW1# configure terminal
VAN-SW1(config)# interface range gigabitethernet0/11 - 12
VAN-SW1(config-if-range)# switchport mode access
VAN-SW1(config-if-range)# switchport access vlan 2
VAN-SW1(config-if-range)# channel-group 5 mode active
```

IP Address Assignment   In order to remotely manage the switch, you can assign an IP address to the switch by configuring VLAN 1 (known as the management VLAN) with an

IP address and subnet mask. The following commands are used to assign an IP address to a switch:

```
VAN-SW1> enable
VAN-SW1# configure terminal
VAN-SW1(config)# interface vlan1
VAN-SW1(config-if)# ip address 14.0.0.25 255.0.0.0
VAN-SW1(config-if)# no shutdown
VAN-SW1(config-if)# exit
```

Keep in mind that the switch does not need to have an IP address assigned to it in order to function properly. The only reason to add an IP address to a switch is so that you can remotely connect to it to manage the device.

Default Gateway Assignment   If you are going to remotely connect to the switch from a different network, you are going to have to configure the switch for a default gateway so that it can send data off the network. The following commands are used to configure a default gateway on the switch:

```
VAN-SW1> enable
VAN-SW1# configure terminal
VAN-SW1(config)# ip default-gateway 14.0.0.1
```

PoE and PoE+ (802.3af, 802.3at)   Switches today support a feature known as *Power Over Ethernet (PoE)*, or IEEE 802.3af. PoE is a technology supported by newer switches that allows a device to receive power through the Ethernet cable as well as network traffic. This is an important technology when you look at the fact that companies are deploying Voice over IP (VoIP) phones to everyone's desk. The VoIP phone will connect to the port on the switch and will be powered by the switch—using PoE, there is no additional power cable for the phone itself. In this configuration the employee's computer would then connect to the phone—so the one port on the switch is used for voice and data communication.

Like any technology, PoE has been enhanced to become PoE+ (or PoE Plus), which is defined as IEEE 802.3at. One of the major enhancements is the power that is supplied through a single port—with PoE, 15.4 watts of direct current (DC) power are supplied to each device through a single port, while PoE+ provides 25.5 watts of power. This is important to note so that when you purchase your VoIP phones, you know which standard they require and ensure that your switch supports that standard (to ensure enough power is supplied through the port to the phone).

One last note that I wanted to make here is that most network switches also have the capability of providing Quality of Service (QoS) features, which involves the network administrator controlling how much bandwidth certain types of traffic can use.

Configuring VLANs

One of the great security benefits of switches is the capabilities to create and manage VLANs. You learned in Chapter 3 that VLANs are a way to create a communication boundary, because systems in one VLAN cannot communicate with systems in another VLAN by default. For example, if you wanted to ensure that no systems can communicate with the accounting systems and server, you could create an accounting VLAN and then associate a number of ports on the switch with the accounting VLAN. When you connect systems to those ports, they will be able to communicate with one another, but not with systems not in the VLAN.

By default, all ports are in the default VLAN, and you can create additional VLANs. The following code listing is used to create two VLANs named Marketing and Engineering. Notice that you first navigate to the VLAN database, and your prompt changes to indicate this with (vlan).

```
VAN-SW1>enable
VAN-SW1#vlan database
VAN-SW1(vlan)#vlan 2 name Marketing
VLAN 2 added:
    Name: Marketing
VAN-SW1(vlan)#vlan 3 name Engineering
VLAN 3 added:
    Name: Engineering
VAN-SW1(vlan)#exit
APPLY completed.
Exiting....
```

Once you have created the two new VLANs, you can then place the different ports on the switch in the appropriate VLAN. To place ports in a VLAN, you navigate to the appropriate port with the **interface** command and then use the **switchport access vlan #** command to place a port in a particular VLAN. Notice in the following code listing that I am using the **interface range** command to modify multiple ports at one time.

```
VAN-SW1>enable
VAN-SW1#config term
VAN-SW1(config)#interface range f0/2 - 4
VAN-SW1(config-if-range)#switchport access vlan 2
VAN-SW1(config-if-range)#interface range f0/9 - 12
VAN-SW1(config-if-range)#switchport access vlan 3
VAN-SW1(config-if-range)#exit
VAN-SW1(config)#exit
```

To verify that the ports have been placed in the correct VLAN, you can use the **show vlan** command:

```
VAN-SW1#show vlan
VLAN Name        Status    Ports
---- ----------  ------    ------
1    default     active    Fa0/1,Fa0/5, Fa0/6, Fa0/7,
                           Fa0/8, Fa0/13, Fa0/14, Fa0/15,
                           Fa0/16, Fa0/17, Fa0/18, Fa0/19
                           Fa0/20, Fa0/21, Fa0/22, Fa0/23
                           Fa0/24, Gig1/1, Gig1/2
2    Marketing   active    Fa0/2, Fa0/3, Fa0/4
3    Engineering active    Fa0/9, Fa0/10, Fa0/11, Fa0/12
```

Be sure you know how to create a VLAN and how to place ports into a VLAN for the Network+ exam. You can also **view the list of VLANs with the** show vlan **command.**

ISL and 802.1Q

You learned in Chapter 3 that switches support a trunking feature that allows you to connect one switch to another switch and then assign the ports responsible for that connection as trunking ports. A trunk port carries the VLAN packets from one switch to another. For example, if there were three ports on two different switches that were part of the Engineering VLAN, when the frame is received from a client at the first switch, that switch then tags the frame for the VLAN that the client port is a member of. The switch then sends the frame to all other ports in the VLAN and the trunking port, where the frame then follows the link on the trunk port to the second switch. When the second switch receives the frame, it reads the VLAN identification information (known as a tag) and then sends the frame to any ports that are a part of that VLAN.

In order for VLAN traffic to make its way from one switch to another, the switch must tag the frame to include the VLAN ID. Two different protocols can be used for VLAN tagging:

- **ISL** The *InterSwitch Link (ISL)* is the Cisco-proprietary protocol for tagging packets and associating them with a particular VLAN on older switches.
- **802.1Q** 802.1Q is the IEEE standard for VLAN trunking. Newer Cisco switches and Juniper Networks switches use 802.1Q as the tagging method.

VTP

The *VLAN Trunking Protocol (VTP)* is a protocol developed by Cisco that allows a network administrator to create a list of VLANs on one switch and then have the list of VLANs delivered to other switches within the VTP domain, which is a logical grouping of switches that is organized by the administrator. The benefit of VTP is that in a large network environment with dozens or even hundreds of switches, the network administrator does not have to create the same list of VLANs on each individual switch!

e x a m

ⓦ a t c h　　　**For the Network+ exam, be sure to know the difference between ISL, 802.1Q, and the VTP protocol. ISL and 802.1Q** **are VLAN tagging protocols, while VTP is a VLAN management protocol.**

Native VLAN/Default VLAN

The native VLAN is also known as the default VLAN. When a switch receives a frame from a trunk port that is not tagged with a VLAN, the receiving switch automatically assumes the frame is for the default VLAN, or native VLAN, and tags it as such.

As a switch administrator, it is important to consider what VLAN you would like untagged frames to be part of and then configure the native VLAN setting of the switch to that VLAN. The following code listing configures port 12 on the switch for native VLAN 1:

```
VAN-SW1> enable
VAN-SW1# configure terminal
VAN-SW1(config)# interface gigabitethernet0/12
VAN-SW1(config-if)# switchport trunk native vlan 1
```

Port Mirroring

Port mirroring, also known as port monitoring, is a feature that allows the switch to send a copy of data that reaches certain ports to a mirrored port. Port monitoring allows an administrator to plug his or her workstation into the mirrored port and monitor the network traffic.

Port mirroring is an important feature of a switch because, by default, the switch filters traffic by only sending the data to the port that the destination system resides on. The switch's filtering feature will prevent the monitoring of traffic, and as a result, the administrator will have to enable port mirroring (monitoring) and specify the port that receives the copy of data.

EXERCISE 7-2

Configuring VLANs on Cisco Switches

In this exercise you will practice configuring VLANs on a Cisco 2950 switch.

1. Create two VLANs called Exer62a and Exer62b.
2. Place ports 5 and 6 in VLAN Exer62a.
3. Place ports 7 and 8 in VLAN Exer62b.
4. The following are the commands you should have used:

```
VAN-SW1>enable
VAN-SW1#vlan database
VAN-SW1(vlan)#vlan 2 name Exer62a
VAN-SW1(vlan)#vlan 3 name Exer62b
VAN-SW1(vlan)#exit
VAN-SW1#config term
VAN-SW1(config)#interface range f0/5 - 6
VAN-SW1(config-if-range)#switchport access vlan 2
VAN-SW1(config-if-range)#interface range f0/7 - 8
VAN-SW1(config-if-range)#switchport access vlan 3
VAN-SW1(config-if-range)#exit
VAN-SW1(config)#exit
```

5. Display your VLAN configuration with the **show vlan** command to verify that the ports are in the correct VLAN.

Configuring Port Security

Another great feature of switches is the capability to associate a particular MAC address with a port so that an unauthorized system cannot be connected to the network. In the following code example you are modifying interface 7 and placing the port in access mode, which allows stations to be connected to the port. You then enable the port security feature on the switch and specify the MAC address of the system. You then specify the maximum number of addresses for the port to 1 so that the switch does not learn additional addresses that may connect to the port. Finally, you specify what happens if there is an address violation. In this example, you are setting the port to shutdown, which means it is disabled until the administrator enables the port again.

```
VAN-SW1>enable
VAN-SW1#config term
VAN-SW1(config)#interface f0/7
```

```
VAN-SW1(config-if)#switchport mode access
VAN-SW1(config-if)#switchport port-security
VAN-SW1(config-if)#switchport port-security mac-address 000b.0c2b.4c6a
VAN-SW1(config-if)#switchport port-security maximum 1
VAN-SW1(config-if)#switchport port-security violation shutdown
```

Port security is a critical feature of a switch, as it allows you to control what systems can connect to a port on a switch by MAC address.

Switch Management

A number of best practices should be followed when configuring switches on the network. In this section you are introduced to common switch management concepts that should be followed in all implementations!

User Names and Passwords

The first thing you want to do is create user names and passwords on the switch so that administrators can connect to the switch and either view settings or change the settings. Keep in mind that you are only creating user names and passwords for network administrators—users connecting their workstations to the switch do not need user names and passwords.

To create a user name called GlenEClarke with a password of P@ssw0rd, perform the following:

```
VAN-SW1>enable
VAN-SW1#config term
VAN-SW1(config)#username GlenEClarke password P@ssw0rd
```

Console and Virtual Terminal Password

Once you have configured the user name you can then configure the console port and telnet ports (known as virtual terminal) to use that user name and password in order for someone to get access to those configuration ports. In order to configure the console port to force login with that user name, use the following commands:

```
VAN-SW1>enable
VAN-SW1#config term
VAN-SW1(config)#line con 0
VAN-SW1(config-line)#login local
```

Note that the **login local** command is used to force someone to log on with the locally created user name. In order to force login access to the telnet ports, you can use the following commands:

```
VAN-SW1>enable
VAN-SW1#config term
VAN-SW1(config)#line vty 0 4
VAN-SW1(config-line)#login local
```

In these commands, the **line vty 0 4** command is used to navigate to the first five telnet ports on the device. Each virtual port is numbered from 0 to the maximum number of Telnet ports for that device.

AAA Configuration

The term *AAA* stands for *authentication, authorization, and accounting* and is an important technology used with networks today to ensure that the authentication and authorization are handled centrally on the network. AAA technologies typically use a central authentication server known as a Remote Authentication Dial-In User Server (RADIUS) server, or in the Cisco world using Terminal Access Controller Access Control System+ (TACACS+). You will learn more about RADIUS and TACACS+ in Chapter 15.

In-Band/Out-of-Band Management

When configuring network devices, you can perform the management of those devices using in-band management or out-of-band management.

In-band management means that you configure the device using regular network protocols such as Telnet or Simple Network Management Protocol (SNMP) and manage the device remotely using a regular network connection. In-band management is not something to rely on because if the network goes down, you have no way to connect to the device from across the network in order to change the configuration and fix the network problem.

Out-of-band management involves creating an alternative method of connecting to the device for management purposes. This could involve using local ports on the device to connect to it or installing network controllers for a dedicated management network connection to the device. Many companies will have a separate management network that only network administrators can access in order to remotely connect to network devices and manage their configuration.

Managed vs. Unmanaged Switches

The final terms that I want to address before moving into some troubleshooting with routers and switches is what is known as a managed switch and an unmanaged switch. A managed switch allows the network administrator to configure a lot of the cool features we discussed in this chapter such as port mirroring, port security, VLANs, and configuration of the ports. An unmanaged switch does not allow you to configure the switch—it simply acts as a connection point for your clients to connect to the network.

CERTIFICATION OBJECTIVE 7.03

Troubleshooting Connectivity

Now that you understand some of the basic configuration tasks related to managing a Cisco router and switch, let's take a look at some common reasons why you may experience communication problems on the network.

When experiencing communication problems, whether it be with a client talking to a server, a system not being able to establish a connection, or unpredictable traffic due to a network issue, you can normally break down your troubleshooting to physical or logical problems. Physical problems deal with troubleshooting layer-1 and layer-2 components, while logical troubleshooting deals with troubleshooting layer-3 components of the OSI model.

Layer-1 and Layer-2 Troubleshooting

A number of communication problems are a result of physical- or data link–layer component failure or misconfiguration. The following is a breakdown of some common troubleshooting issues related to layer 1 and layer 2:

- **Switching loop** If you are connecting a large network together, you cannot connect your switches in such a way that it creates a loop on the network. If you do, the network will fail. To help prevent this problem, most high-end switches, including Cisco switches, have a protocol known as STP to disable the loop by placing a port in a blocking state.

- **Bad cables/improper cable types** A common problem with connecting to the network is when you grab a cable from the server room and find that the system cannot connect to the network. Always double-check that the cable you are using is the correct type (straight-through or crossover) and that the cable is crimped properly.

- **Port configuration** If you are having trouble making a connection (getting a green link light on the switch), ensure that the port has not been disabled or attempt to determine whether port security has been configured so that it prevents your system from connecting.

- **VLAN assignment** You may experience communication problems because the port was placed in a VLAN and the system you are trying to communicate with is not in that VLAN. You may need to connect your system to another port.

- **Mismatched MTU/MTU black hole** You may experience network issues when the maximum transmission unit (MTU) of the system does not match that of the network. You may also encounter a black hole, which involves the system losing a connection within a certain area of the network. This could be the result of a network attack.

■ **Power failure**   You may experience communication issues because the power supply in the network device fails. For example, the power supply in the switch may fail.

■ **Bad modules**   You may experience connectivity issues due to a bad module placed in the switch. A module is a card that has different ports on it and is placed in the switch. Modules may contain serial ports and Fast Ethernet ports. You may also have a bad small form factor pluggable module (SFPS) or gigabit interface converter (GBIC), which are hot-swappable modules allowing you to connect to Gigabit networks.

Layer-3 Troubleshooting

After you have verified the physical connections and links on the network, you can then look to dealing with the logical aspect. The logical aspect of the network deals with the software configuration and layer-3 addressing issues. The following should be verified to help diagnose the problem:

■ **Bad/missing routes**   You may have missing routes in the routing table on your routers, which causes communication issues. In Chapter 8 you will learn about managing the routing table.

■ **Wrong subnet masks**   You may have configured the wrong subnet mask on a system, which causes the system to use the wrong network ID.

■ **Wrong gateway**   You may have configured a system with the wrong IP address for the default gateway. Verify the IP address, subnet mask, and default gateway settings on any system with communication problems.

■ **Duplicate IP address**   If you have a duplicate IP address, you will be unable to communicate on the network. Verify that your IP address is not already in use.

■ **Wrong DNS**   If you are experiencing name resolution problems, verify that you are referencing the correct Domain Name System (DNS) server on the network.

To learn more about troubleshooting network problems, check out Chapter 18.

CERTIFICATION SUMMARY

In this chapter you learned how to configure the basic settings on a Cisco router and switch. You first learned about the different configuration modes and how to change basic settings on the router, such as the hostname. Those router basics also apply to Cisco switches, as the switches have the same configuration modes.

You learned how to configure settings on a Cisco device interface, such as the duplex setting and the speed of the interface. You also learned how to configure features on the switch such as port security and VLANs.

With a strong understanding of the material presented in this chapter, you will have no problems with any router- or switch-related questions on your exam. Not only is the material presented here important for the exam, but it will also be important after you ace the exam and continue on to a career as a networking professional.

TWO-MINUTE DRILL

Basic Router Configuration

❑ Cisco devices support three major configuration modes: user exec, priv exec, and global configuration.

❑ You can configure an interface on the router by using the **interface** command to navigate to the interface subprompt. You can then assign an IP address to the interface with the **IP address** command.

❑ You can enable the interface with the **no shutdown** command, or disable it with the **shutdown** command.

Basic Switch Configuration

❑ You can configure settings such as the duplex, speed, and description on an interface.

❑ Port security allows you to control which systems can connect to a port on the switch, while port mirroring allows you to send all traffic to a port, where you typically would have a monitoring station set up.

❑ VLANs are a great way to create communication boundaries on the switch.

Troubleshooting Connectivity

❑ Always check the physical aspect of the connection first. Verify the correct cable type is being used and the connector is crimped properly.

❑ After checking the physical aspect of the connection, check the logical aspect. This includes the IP address configuration and items such as the routing table.

SELF TEST

The following questions will help you measure your understanding of the material presented in this chapter. Read all the choices carefully because there might be more than one correct answer. Choose all correct answers for each question.

Basic Router Configuration

1. Which of the following symbols indicates that you are in priv exec mode?
   A. >
   B. #
   C. $
   D. &

2. You wish to enable the interface on the Cisco router; what command would you use?
   A. Shutdown
   B. Enable
   C. Disable
   D. No shutdown

3. Which of the following commands would you use to assign an IP address to an interface?
   A. Router(config-if)#ip address 10.0.0.1 255.0.0.0
   B. Router(config)#ip address 10.0.0.1 255.0.0.0
   C. Router#ip address 10.0.0.1 255.0.0.0
   D. Router>ip address 10.0.0.1 255.0.0.0

4. You want to ensure that the network interface on the router is using full duplex. What command would you use?
   A. Router(config)#duplex full
   B. Router(config-if)#duplex half
   C. Router(config-if)#duplex full
   D. Router(config-if)#full duplex

Basic Switch Configuration

5. Your manager is concerned about unauthorized systems being able to connect to the network. What feature of a switch can settle her concerns?

   A. STP

   B. Port security

   C. Port mirroring

   D. VLANs

6. Which of the following protocols is responsible for preventing loops on the network?

   A. 802.1Q

   B. TCP

   C. VTP

   D. STP

7. Which of the following protocols are responsible for VLAN tagging? (Select two.)

   A. 802.1Q

   B. TCP

   C. ISL

   D. STP

Troubleshooting Connectivity

8. You are troubleshooting a system that cannot communicate with SERVER1 when connected to ports 1 through 6, but can when you connect the system to ports 8 through 12. What may be the reason?

   A. Ports 1 through 6 may be using the wrong subnet mask.

   B. Ports 1 through 6 may have the wrong IP address.

   C. Ports 1 through 6 may be in a different VLAN than SERVER1.

   D. Ports 1 through 6 may have the wrong default gateway set.

9. You are a router administrator, and clients on your network are having trouble communicating with a system that has the IP address of 122.34.5.4. You have verified that the IP configuration of your clients, including the default gateway setting, is correct. You can communicate with systems on your network and other networks. What should you check?

   A. Verify the routes in the routing table.

   B. Change the subnet mask.

   C. Change the IP address to match the IP address of the system you are connecting to.

   D. Verify the VLAN settings.

10. Your company policy is to have all network traffic sent to port 24 on the switch so that the administrator can have monitoring software check all network activity. What is the name of this switch feature?
   A. Port security
   B. Security monitoring
   C. Packet sniffer
   D. Port mirroring

Performance-Based Question Review: See the performance-based question sample from the author included with the accompanying media.

SELF TEST ANSWERS

Basic Router Configuration

1. ☑ **B.** The # symbol is used in the prompt to indicate privilege exec mode.
   ☒ **A, C,** and **D** are incorrect. The > is used to identify user exec mode, while the $ and & are not used as symbols in a Cisco prompt.

2. ☑ **D.** The **no shutdown** command is used to enable an interface on a Cisco device.
   ☒ **A, B,** and **C** are incorrect. The **shutdown** command is used to disable an interface, the **enable** command is used to move from user exec mode to priv exec mode, and the **disable** command is used to move from priv exec to user exec.

3. ☑ **A.** To assign an IP address to an interface, you use the **IP address** command at an interface prompt.
   ☒ **B, C,** and **D** are incorrect because they are not at the interface prompt.

4. ☑ **C.** To configure the interface for full-duplex mode, you use the **duplex full** command at an interface prompt.
   ☒ **A, B,** and **D** are incorrect because they are not at the interface prompt or are using the wrong command.

Basic Switch Configuration

5. ☑ **B.** The port security feature allows you to specify the MAC addresses of systems that can connect to each port.
    ☒ **A, C,** and **D** are incorrect. The STP protocol is a loop avoidance protocol, port mirroring is a method to monitor traffic on the switch, and VLANs are a method to create communication boundaries.

6. ☑ **D.** The Spanning Tree Protocol (STP) is designed to prevent loops on the network.
    ☒ **A, B,** and **C** are incorrect. 802.1Q and VTP are VLAN tagging protocols, while TCP is a connection-oriented protocol that runs at the transport layer and has nothing to do with switch configuration or communication.

7. ☑ **A** and **C.** 802.1Q is the IEEE standard for VLAN tagging, while ISL is a Cisco protocol for VLAN tagging.
    ☒ **B** and **D** are incorrect. TCP is a transport-layer protocol, while STP is a loop avoidance protocol that runs on the switch.

Troubleshooting Connectivity

8. ☑ **C.** If you are having trouble communicating with systems when connecting to a specific port on the switch, it could be because the port is part of a specific VLAN. Remember that you can only communicate with systems in the same VLAN.
    ☒ **A, B,** and **D** are incorrect, as the question indicates that you have verified the logical addressing, so the problem must exist in the switch configuration.

9. ☑ **A.** If you are having trouble communicating with a specific network, you should verify that there is a route to that network in the routing table on the router.
    ☒ **B, C,** and **D** are incorrect because you have verified the IP address configuration already, so now the focus must be on the configuration of the router or switch. Since it seems to be a problem communicating with a network, you focus on the router, as it is a network-layer device.

10. ☑ **D.** Port mirroring is the feature on the switch that allows you to send a copy of all traffic to a specified port and monitor the traffic from that port.
    ☒ **A, B,** and **C** are incorrect. Port security is a switch feature that allows you to limit which systems can connect to the switch by MAC address, and packet sniffer is a software application used to monitor the traffic.

Chapter 8

Subnetting and Routing

I n Chapter 4 you learned the basics of TCP/IP addressing. In this chapter you learn how to take one network address range and break it into multiple network ranges called subnets. Subnetting is one of those topics that most IT professionals tend to avoid because of how tedious it is to sit down and calculate the required information to configure your newly created subnets.

The purpose of subnetting is take one address range and break it down into multiple address ranges so that you can assign each address range to a separate network (subnet) in your internetwork (network made up of multiple networks). You may have multiple networks due to physical locations, or maybe you have one location, but because you want to cut down on traffic, you have decided to segment your one network into multiple segments by placing a router in between each network segment.

Each segment will need its own network address range so that the router can route (send) the data from one network to another. If you were to have two physical networks but kept the one IP range without subnetting, the router would "logically" think that all systems are on the same network and would never try to route data from one side to the other.

If you do not subnet a network range that is divided into multiple physical network segments, the IP protocol will "logically" think that all systems are on the same network, and it will not try to route the data across the router separating the network segments. As a result, you will be able to communicate with hosts on your segment, but not the other segments.

CERTIFICATION OBJECTIVE 8.01

Understanding Subnetting

In this section you will walk through a subnetting example using a class A address. In this example, you have an address range of 10.0.0.0 and you will subnet, or divide, the network into four subnetworks known as *subnets*. The physical network structure is shown in Figure 8-1. The concept of subnetting takes some of the host bits from the subnet mask and uses them

FIGURE 8-1

Subnetting to match this physical network structure

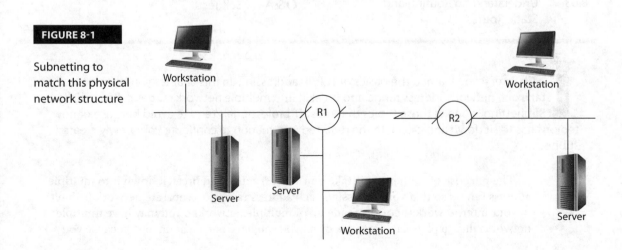

as additional network bits, which will give you more networks. With subnetting, you are taking additional host bits and "masking" them (flagging them as network bits) by setting the bits to a "1" so that they are no longer representing the host ID portion of the subnet mask. This creates additional networks, but results in fewer hosts on the network.

To begin, you need to know how many host bits are required to make the desired number of networks. To calculate how many bits are needed to subnet into four networks (subnets), you use the formula:

$$2^{\text{Masked bits}} = \text{\# of Subnets}$$

For example, if you are looking for four subnets, the formula would be $2^2 = 4$. So you would steal, or mask, two of the host bits in the subnet mask and make them network bits. Actually, we call them subnet bits.

Now that you know that two bits must be masked to create the four subnets, the next step is to look at your IP range of 10.0.0.0 and ask yourself, "What is the default subnet mask of this address?" You should come up with 255.0.0.0, because it is a class A address. Once you know the default subnet mask, the next step is to break the subnet mask down into binary. A default class A subnet mask in binary looks like the following:

Decimal	255	0	0	0
Binary	11111111	00000000	00000000	00000000

Once the subnet mask has been written out in binary, this will be the work area to calculate the new addresses of the four subnets. The first thing you need to do is steal, or "mask," two bits from the host ID portion of the subnet mask and make them subnet bits by setting them to a "1" state. Remember, the reason for taking two bits is because of your calculation earlier. Because the last three octets of this subnet mask represent the host bits of a class A address, work from left to right and mask two additional bits to get the new binary table that follows:

Decimal	255	0	0	0
Binary	11111111	**11**000000	00000000	00000000

Notice that the two bits that are now enabled are in the second octet. Also notice that you always work from left to right in the subnet mask.

The next thing you want to do is convert the subnet mask back to decimal; then you will have the new subnet mask that will be configured on each of the four networks (subnets) we are building. If you convert the new binary value in the preceding table of 11111111.11000000.00000000.00000000, you should get 255.192.0.0 as the new subnet mask of your four new subnets. Write that number down, because it will be needed later.

The next step is to calculate the IP ranges for the four different networks, but before that, there are five pieces of information you should know about each of the new subnets you are designing:

■ **New subnet mask**   After subnetting a network, you will have a new subnet mask that is used by all subnets you have created.

■ **Network ID**   All host bits are set to 0.

■ **First valid address**   The least significant host bit is set to 1; all other host bits are 0.

■ **Broadcast address**   All host bits are set to 1.

■ **Last valid address**   The least significant host bit is set to 0; all other host bits are 1.

You know that the new subnet mask is 255.192.0.0, so you can start by calculating the network ID of each of the four subnets. To determine each piece of information listed previously, you need to determine all of the on/off states of the number of bits that you have stolen. For example, two bits were stolen to create more networks, so there are four possible on/off states with two bits: 00, 01, 10, and 11. As calculated in your binary work area, it would look like the following table:

	First Octet (Decimal)	Second Octet (Binary)	Third Octet (Binary)	Fourth Octet (Binary)
Original IP	10	0	0	0
	10	00000000	00000000	00000000
	10	01000000	00000000	00000000
	10	10000000	00000000	00000000
	10	11000000	00000000	00000000

The next thing to do after calculating all of the on/off state combinations of two bits is to add in the remaining 0s to the bits that represent the host ID portion. Remember that the original network ID was 10.0.0.0, so the first octet will start with 10, no matter what you change in the binary, because you are starting your work with the second octet.

The next step is to bring the 10 down to the first octet; each network ID will start with 10 because that is what it was originally. After bringing the 10 down in the first octet, you then calculate the network ID of each of the two networks by leaving all host bits set to 0 (the nonbolded bits), as shown in the following table:

	First Octet (Decimal)	Second Octet (Binary)	Third Octet (Binary)	Fourth Octet (Binary)	Calculation
Original IP	10	0	0	0	
Subnet #1	10	**00**000000	00000000	00000000	10.0.0.0
Subnet #2	10	**01**000000	00000000	00000000	10.64.0.0
Subnet #3	10	**10**000000	00000000	00000000	10.128.0.0
Subnet #4	10	**11**000000	00000000	00000000	10.192.0.0

In this example, because the two subnet bits are being manipulated, and because all host bits are set to zero, the four new network IDs of 10.0.0.0, 10.64.0.0, 10.128.0.0, and 10.192.0.0 are created. Now that you have calculated the network ID of each subnet, the next number to calculate is the first valid address that can be assigned to a host on each of these networks. To calculate the first valid address, you simply enable the least significant bit, which will be the bit on the far right side. The work area is shown in the following table, and you can see that with the four subnets you have a first valid address for each network of 10.0.0.1, 10.64.0.1, 10.128.0.1, and 10.192.0.1:

	First Octet (Decimal)	Second Octet (Binary)	Third Octet (Binary)	Fourth Octet (Binary)	Calculation
Original IP	10	0	0	0	
Subnet #1	10	**00**000000	00000000	00000001	10.0.0.1
Subnet #2	10	**01**000000	00000000	00000001	10.64.0.1
Subnet #3	10	**10**000000	00000000	00000001	10.128.0.1
Subnet #4	10	**11**000000	00000000	00000001	10.192.0.1

Now that you have calculated the first valid address for each of the four networks, you will need to calculate the broadcast address. The broadcast address is the address that any system will send data to in order to ensure that each system on the network receives the data.

To calculate the broadcast address, you will enable all of the host bits and get the outcome in the following table:

	First Octet (Decimal)	Second Octet (Binary)	Third Octet (Binary)	Fourth Octet (Binary)	Calculation
Original IP	10	0	0	0	
Subnet #1	10	00111111	11111111	11111111	10.63.255.255
Subnet #2	10	01111111	11111111	11111111	10.127.255.255
Subnet #3	10	10111111	11111111	11111111	10.191.255.255
Subnet #4	10	11111111	11111111	11111111	10.255.255.255

As you can see, with all of the host bits enabled, if you convert that to decimal, you get 10.63.255.255, 10.127.255.255, 10.191.255.255, and 10.255.255.255 for the broadcast addresses of your four networks. Notice that the first two bits from the left in the second octet have not been changed in this entire process, but they are used in the conversion of that octet from binary to decimal.

on the **Job**

Remember that a host address that has all host bits set to 0 (which is reserved for the network ID) or all host bits set to 1 (which is reserved for the broadcast address) is considered an invalid address.

Now that you have calculated the new subnet mask, the network ID, the first valid address, and the broadcast address for your two new subnets, the only additional information you need is the last valid address that may be assigned to hosts on each subnet. To calculate the last valid host address of each subnet, simply subtract one from the broadcast address by disabling the least significant bit (the far-right host bit). To view what the binary and decimal representations look like for our last valid address of each network, take a look at the following table:

	First Octet (Decimal)	Second Octet (Binary)	Third Octet (Binary)	Fourth Octet (Binary)	Calculation
Original IP	10	0	0	0	
Subnet #1	10	00111111	11111111	11111110	10.63.255.254
Subnet #2	10	01111111	11111111	11111110	10.127.255.254
Subnet #3	10	10111111	11111111	11111110	10.191.255.254
Subnet #4	10	11111111	11111111	11111110	10.255.255.254

| FIGURE 8-2 | Subnetting a Class A network into four network segments |

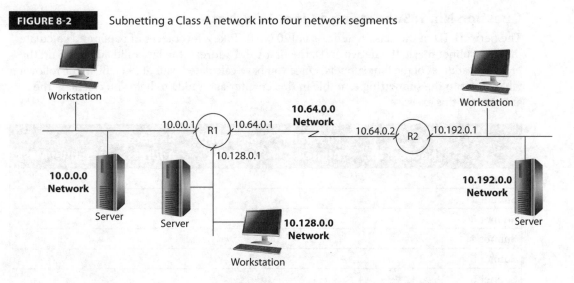

You have now calculated all of the information required to configure the four physical network segments that you have created. The following table summarizes the configuration for each of the four network segments, and Figure 8-2 displays how these two network segments will be configured.

	Network ID	First Valid Address	Last Valid Address	Broadcast Address	Subnet Mask
Subnet 1	10.0.0.0	10.0.0.1	10.63.255.254	10.63.255.255	255.192.0.0
Subnet 2	10.64.0.0	10.64.0.1	10.127.255.254	10.127.255.255	255.192.0.0
Subnet 3	10.128.0.0	10.128.0.1	10.191.255.254	10.191.255.255	255.192.0.0
Subnet 4	10.192.0.0	10.192.0.1	10.255.255.254	10.255.255.255	255.192.0.0

EXERCISE 8-1

Subnetting IP Addresses

In this exercise you will determine the five pieces of information needed for a class A network that is being divided into six network segments.

Question No. 1: Subnetting a Class A Address

The network ID of the class A address is 120.0.0.0. Take a few pieces of paper and calculate the new subnet mask, the network ID, the first valid address, the last valid address, and the broadcast address of the four subnets. Once you have calculated your answer, fill in the following table. Refer to the subnetting example in this chapter as a guide to help you calculate the answers for this exercise.

	Network ID	First Valid Address	Last Valid Address	Broadcast Address	Subnet Mask
Subnet 1					
Subnet 2					
Subnet 3					
Subnet 4					
Subnet 5					
Subnet 6					
Subnet 7					
Subnet 8					

Once you have your answers, check your work against the table under "Answer No. 1."

The Work   Given that we want to have six subnets, we will need to take three bits; to determine how many bits we need to steal from the host ID portion of the address to subnet into six networks, we can use our formula of $2^{\text{masked bits}}$ = # of subnets. In this example, you will need to use the formula of $2^3 = 8$. Although we only need six subnets, if we would have masked only two bits instead of three, we would only get four subnets, which is not enough! In this example, using three bits, we will have two extra subnets for future growth.

The next thing to calculate is the new subnet mask used by these six new networks. The new subnet mask is determined by masking additional bits in the original subnet mask. The original subnet mask was 11111111.00000000.00000000.00000000, and by masking three additional bits, we get the following:

Binary	11111111	11100000	00000000	00000000
Decimal	255	224	0	0

So your new subnet mask used by all six networks is 255.224.0.0. Now that we have determined that we have to take three bits, we then figure out all the on/off states of three bits. The following should be the on/off states of three bits. (I have also filled in all the host bits.)

	First Octet (Decimal)	Second Octet (Binary)	Third Octet (Binary)	Fourth Octet (Binary)
Original IP	120	0	0	0
	120	00000000	00000000	00000000
	120	00100000	00000000	00000000
	120	01000000	00000000	00000000
	120	01100000	00000000	00000000
	120	10000000	00000000	00000000
	120	10100000	00000000	00000000
	120	11000000	00000000	00000000
	120	11100000	00000000	00000000

Once you have figured out each of the on/off states of three bits and have filled in the host bits of all 0s, you have the network ID for each of the six networks. If you convert the binary to decimal, you should have the following as the network ID of each subnet:

	First Octet (Decimal)	Second Octet (Binary)	Third Octet (Binary)	Fourth Octet (Binary)	Decimal Value
Original IP	120	0	0	0	
Subnet #1	120	00000000	00000000	00000000	120.0.0.0
Subnet #2	120	00100000	00000000	00000000	120.32.0.0
Subnet #3	120	01000000	00000000	00000000	120.64.0.0
Subnet #4	120	01100000	00000000	00000000	120.96.0.0
Subnet #5	120	10000000	00000000	00000000	120.128.0.0
Subnet #6	120	10100000	00000000	00000000	120.160.0.0
Subnet #7	120	11000000	00000000	00000000	120.192.0.0
Subnet #8	120	11100000	00000000	00000000	120.224.0.0

Once you have calculated the network IDs, continue with figuring out the first valid address by turning on the low-order bit to get the following result:

	First Octet (Decimal)	Second Octet (Binary)	Third Octet (Binary)	Fourth Octet (Binary)	Decimal Value
Original IP	120	0	0	0	
Subnet #1	120	00000000	00000000	00000001	120.0.0.1
Subnet #2	120	00100000	00000000	00000001	120.32.0.1
Subnet #3	120	01000000	00000000	00000001	120.64.0.1
Subnet #4	120	01100000	00000000	00000001	120.96.0.1
Subnet #5	120	10000000	00000000	00000001	120.128.0.1
Subnet #6	120	10100000	00000000	00000001	120.160.0.1
Subnet #7	120	11000000	00000000	00000001	120.192.0.1
Subnet #8	120	11100000	00000000	00000001	120.224.0.1

To calculate the broadcast address, you should have enabled all of the host bits to get the list of addresses shown in the following table:

	First Octet (Decimal)	Second Octet (Binary)	Third Octet (Binary)	Fourth Octet (Binary)	Decimal Value
Original IP	120	0	0	0	
Subnet #1	120	00011111	11111111	11111111	120.31.255.255
Subnet #2	120	00111111	11111111	11111111	120.63.255.255
Subnet #3	120	01011111	11111111	11111111	120.95.255.255
Subnet #4	120	01111111	11111111	11111111	120.127.255.255
Subnet #5	120	10011111	11111111	11111111	120.159.255.255
Subnet #6	120	10111111	11111111	11111111	120.191.255.255
Subnet #7	120	11011111	11111111	11111111	120.223.255.255
Subnet #8	120	11111111	11111111	11111111	120.255.255.255

Finally, calculate the last valid address used by each of these six subnets (remember there are eight, but you only need six) by turning off the least significant host bit and leaving all other host bits enabled, as shown in the following table:

	First Octet (Decimal)	Second Octet (Binary)	Third Octet (Binary)	Fourth Octet (Binary)	Decimal Value
Original IP	120	0	0	0	
Subnet #1	120	00011111	11111111	11111110	120.31.255.254
Subnet #2	120	00111111	11111111	11111110	120.63.255.254
Subnet #3	120	01011111	11111111	11111110	120.95.255.254
Subnet #4	120	01111111	11111111	11111110	120.127.255.254
Subnet #5	120	10011111	11111111	11111110	120.159.255.254
Subnet #6	120	10111111	11111111	11111110	120.191.255.254
Subnet #7	120	11011111	11111111	11111110	120.223.255.254
Subnet #8	120	11111111	11111111	11111110	120.255.255.254

Now that you have done all the paperwork, you should have come up with the following answer for the eight subnets in the 120.0.0.0 network.

Answer No. 1

	Network ID	First Valid Address	Last Valid Address	Broadcast Address
Subnet 1	120.0.0.0	120.0.0.1	120.31.255.254	120.31.255.255
Subnet 2	120.32.0.0	120.32.0.1	120.63.255.254	120.63.255.255
Subnet 3	120.64.0.0	120.64.0.1	120.95.255.254	120.95.255.255
Subnet 4	120.96.0.0	120.96.0.1	120.127.255.254	120.127.255.255
Subnet 5	120.128.0.0	120.128.0.1	120.159.255.254	120.159.255.255
Subnet 6	120.160.0.0	120.160.0.1	120.191.255.254	120.191.255.255
Subnet 7	120.192.0.0	120.192.0.1	120.223.255.254	120.223.255.255
Subnet 8	120.224.0.0	120.224.0.1	120.255.255.254	120.255.255.255

The subnet mask for each of the four networks is 255.224.0.0.

Question No. 2: Subnet a Class B Address

You are responsible for subnetting the network ID of 190.34.0.0 into four subnets. Take some paper and walk through your binary work of subnetting this class B network into four subnets. Once you have calculated the information on paper, fill in the following table:

	Network ID	First Valid Address	Last Valid Address	Broadcast Address	Subnet Mask
Subnet 1					
Subnet 2					
Subnet 3					
Subnet 4					

Check your answer with the lab answer key found in the accompanying material for this book.

Question No. 3

Your manager has purchased a class C network range and has asked that you subnet this class C network into two subnets for the two network segments that are going to be built. One network segment will host client machines used by customers to do online ordering, and the other segment will host the corporate machines used by your employees.

The class C network ID that you have purchased is 216.83.11.0. Once again, take a piece of paper and start by writing out the default subnet mask of this class C address and then start manipulating the host bits to get the network ID, first valid host ID, last valid host ID, broadcast address, and new subnet mask. Once you have calculated all the required information, fill in the following table:

	Network ID	First Valid Address	Last Valid Address	Broadcast Address
Subnet 1				
Subnet 2				

The new subnet mask for all subnets is_____.

Check your answer with the lab answer key found in the accompanying material for this book.

This section has introduced you to the concept of subnetting, which you will need to know for the Network+ exam. So make sure you are familiar with identifying the class addresses and then have a solid understanding of subnetting!

CERTIFICATION OBJECTIVE 8.02

Classful vs. Classless Addressing

Chapter 4 focused on introducing you to the different class IP addresses: class A, class B, and class C. Each IP address that you use on a system falls into one of these three classes—this is known as classful addressing. Table 8-1 summarizes the three major address classes. Everything that you have learned about the different address classes, including network IDs, host IDs, and default subnet masks, is based on classful addressing.

Classful IP addressing divides the network ID and host ID portions of an IP address at an octet. For example, **a class B address uses the first two octets as the network ID and the last two octets as the host ID.**

CIDR

Classless Inter-Domain Routing (CIDR), or classless addressing, does not follow the default concepts of classful addressing. For example, if you wish to break your class A address down into more than one network and subnet the network, then you are breaking the "classful" part of the addressing and using classless addressing. Subnetting is part of CIDR.

TABLE 8-1				
Reviewing Classful IP Addressing	**Address Class**	**Value of First Octet**	**Octet Setup**	**Number of Hosts**
	Class A	1–127	N.H.H.H	16,777,214
	Class B	128–191	N.N.H.H	65,534
	Class C	192–223	N.N.N.H	254

Another feature of CIDR is the capability of using a different subnet mask in each of the subnets when you subnet the network. This allows you to have different size networks for each of the different subnets. For example, you may have a small branch office that only needs 14 addresses, while the head office needs over 100 addresses. With a feature known as a *variable-length subnet mask (VLSM)* you may have different size subnets with different subnet masks. This is all part of CIDR.

With CIDR, there needed to be a standard method of indicating how many bits in the IP address were network bits, so the concept of CIDR notation was created. With CIDR notation, you specify the IP address and a forward slash (/) followed by the number of bits that make up the network ID. For example, 10.0.0.0/8 specifies that the network ID is the first eight bits (which would mean the subnet mask is 255.0.0.0). Likewise, 131.107.64.0/18 indicates that this network ID is a result of subnetting a class B address.

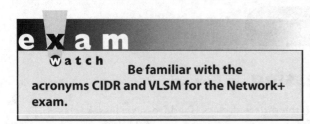

Be familiar with the acronyms CIDR and VLSM for the Network+ exam.

EXERCISE 8-2

Subnetting Networks

Subnetting a Class B Network

You have the class B network ID of 150.87.0.0, and you need to divide this network into 16 subnets. Use some paper and calculate the network ID, first valid address, last valid address, and broadcast address of each of the *first six subnets of the 16*. Don't forget to determine the new subnet mask of these networks as well. Fill in the following table when you have completed your work on paper:

	Network ID	First Valid Address	Last Valid Address	Broadcast Address
Subnet 1				
Subnet 2				
Subnet 3				
Subnet 4				
Subnet 5				
Subnet 6				

New Subnet Mask: _____

Subnetting a Class A Network

You have the class A network ID of 14.0.0.0, and you need to divide this network into eight subnets. Use some paper and calculate the network ID, first valid address, last valid address, and broadcast address of each of the eight subnets. Don't forget to determine the new subnet mask of these networks as well. Fill in the following table when you have completed your work on paper:

	Network ID	First Valid Address	Last Valid Address	Broadcast Address
Subnet 1				
Subnet 2				
Subnet 3				
Subnet 4				
Subnet 5				
Subnet 6				
Subnet 7				
Subnet 8				

New Subnet Mask: _____

Subnetting a Class C Network

You have the class C network ID of 202.15.67.0, and you need to divide this network into four subnets. Use some paper and calculate the network ID, first valid address, last valid address, and broadcast address of each of the four subnets. Don't forget to determine the new subnet mask of these networks as well. Fill in the following table when you have completed your work on paper:

	Network ID	First Valid Address	Last Valid Address	Broadcast Address
Subnet 1				
Subnet 2				
Subnet 3				
Subnet 4				

New Subnet Mask: _____

Supernetting

Supernetting, like subnetting, is part of the CIDR concept where we are altering the default way the IP address scheme works. You learned earlier that the goal of subnetting was to take bits from the host ID portion of an address to create more networks (subnets). Supernetting works the opposite way: You take bits away from the network ID to combine networks. The goal of supernetting is to combine multiple smaller networks into one big network ID.

CERTIFICATION OBJECTIVE 8.03

Understanding Routing and Static Routes

Now that you have an understanding of subnetting, the next topic to discuss is routing. *Routing* involves sending data from one network to another. Once we have the network broken into segments, it is up to the routers to move the data from one network segment to another, as shown in Figure 8-3.

The router is responsible for routing information to the destination network, and it does this by using what is known as a routing table. A routing table is a list of destination networks that resides in memory on the router, and the router uses this to identify where to send data to reach the destination. If the destination is not in the routing table, the router will not be able to send the information to the destination, as shown in Figure 8-3.

| FIGURE 8-3 | A router depends on its routing table for knowledge of destination networks. |

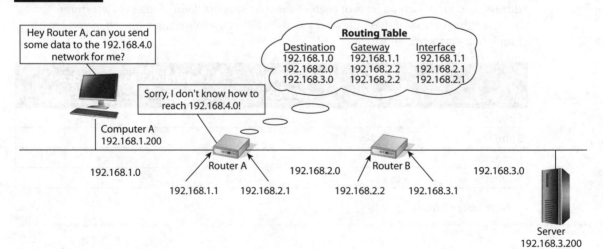

If you take a look at Figure 8-3, you can see that COMPUTERA is trying to send data off the network by sending it to ROUTERA. ROUTERA looks in its routing table to see whether the destination of 192.168.4.0 is listed, and as you can see in the figure, the router does not know how to reach that destination, so it returns an error.

Let's look at the routing table in the figure and learn how to read it. If you take a look at the third entry in the routing table, you can see that ROUTERA has an entry for the 192.168.3.0 network. If any systems on the 192.168.1.0 network send data to the 192.168.3.0 network, the router will send the information to the next hop value for that entry (shown as the "gateway" column in the figure). The next hop is where the router needs to send the data to reach that particular destination. In this case, it will send the data to 192.168.2.2, and it will get to 192.168.2.2 by sending the data out the interface of 192.168.2.1 on ROUTERA. The interface column is important because it lets the router know how that gateway can be reached from ROUTERA.

Routing Concepts

Before looking at how to configure a router, it is important that we take a few minutes to learn some routing concepts and terminology. The following are some key routing terms you should be familiar with for the Network+ certification exam:

- **Loopback interface**   Routers have network interface cards connecting to different networks in order to send data (route the data) from one network to another. The router can also have a loopback interface, which is a virtual network interface card configured on the router. A reason to do this may be for testing purposes or because a router feature may use the loopback interface. For example, the routing protocol Open Shortest Path First (OSPF) will use the IP address of the loopback interface as its router ID. To control the router ID, you can configure a loopback interface and assign an IP address to the loopback interface.

- **Routing loops**   A routing loop is when you have two routers sending the packet back and forth to one another because they believe the packet belongs on the other network (because of the destination IP of the packet and the route on the router). Routers use the time to live (TTL) field as a method to prevent infinite loops by decreasing the TTL every time the packet hits a router. Once the TTL reaches 0, the packet is removed from the network.

- **Routing tables**   The routing table on a router is used to determine where the router needs to send a packet when it reaches the router. The router compares the destination IP address of the packet against the destination networks in the routing table. If there is a match, then the router sends the packet to the IP address specified with that entry in the routing table.

■ **Static vs. dynamic routes** Routes are either manually added to a routing table by the network administrator (known as static routes) or they are automatically learned from other routers (known as dynamic routes) using a routing protocol. You will learn more about static routes and dynamic routes as the chapter progresses.

■ **Default route** A default route can be added to the router and will be used if there is no entry in the routing table that matches the destination IP address of the packet. When the router does not know where to send a packet, it will use the default route if one has been configured. An interesting point to make is that when you configure a default gateway on a computer, it adds a default route to the routing table of the system. Configuring a default route on a router is like telling the router, "When you have no idea where to send a packet, send it to this IP address."

Cisco Routers

The most popular vendor that supplies routers is Cisco. Routers are used to connect networks together and route data between these networks. A router connects to different networks by having network cards, known as interfaces, built into the router. Each interface is assigned an IP address and is connected to a network (as shown back in Figure 8-3).

Let's assume that ROUTERA and ROUTERB in Figure 8-3 are Cisco routers. Also, we will assume that on ROUTERA the interface assigned the IP address of 192.168.1.1 is an Ethernet interface (which connects to an Ethernet network). We will also assume that the interface on ROUTERA that is assigned the IP address of 192.168.2.1 is a serial interface. Serial interfaces are used either to connect to your wide area network (WAN) or to serve as a point-to-point link (a direct connection between two routers).

Assigning IP Addresses to Cisco Routers

Let's review your Cisco router commands. To assign an IP address to the Ethernet interface on ROUTERA, you will need to type the following commands (excluding what appears before > or #—those are the prompts):

```
ROUTERA> enable
ROUTERA# configure terminal
ROUTERA(config)# interface fastethernet0/0
ROUTERA(config-if)# ip address 192.168.1.1 255.255.255.0
ROUTERA(config-if)# no shutdown
```

Let's take a look at what each of these commands does. The first command, **enable**, is used to move from user exec mode of the router to privilege exec mode. In user exec mode, you are unable to make changes, so you had to go to privilege exec mode.

In order to change the settings of the Ethernet interface, you need to go to the interface prompt, which is in global configuration mode, where most changes are made. To move to global configuration mode, you type **configure terminal**, and to move to the interface prompt, you type **interface fastethernet0/0**. FastEthernet0/0 is the first Fast Ethernet interface on the router; the second Fast Ethernet interface would be FastEthernet0/1 (if you had a second Ethernet interface).

Once at the Ethernet interface prompt, you assign the IP address using the **ip address** command. The last command, **no shutdown**, is used to enable the interface. You can also disable the interface at any time using the **shutdown** command.

To assign the IP address to the Serial 0 port on ROUTERA, you would type the following commands:

```
ROUTERA> enable
ROUTERA# configure terminal
ROUTERA(config)# interface serial0
ROUTERA(config-if)# ip address 192.168.2.1 255.255.255.0
ROUTERA(config-if)# encapsulation hdlc
ROUTERA(config-if)# no shutdown
```

Note that the commands are basically the same, except for the fact that we navigate to the Serial0 interface instead of the Ethernet0 interface. After the IP address is assigned with the **ip address** command, you then set the encapsulation protocol for the serial link. Popular encapsulation protocols over a serial link are High-Level Data Link Control (HDLC) or Point-to-Point Protocol (PPP). You need to ensure you are using the same protocol that is on the other end of the serial link.

Viewing the Routing Table on Cisco Routers

Once you have the IP addresses assigned to each interface, you will need to ensure that routing is enabled on the router by typing the following commands:

```
ROUTERA> enable
ROUTERA# configure terminal
ROUTERA(config)# ip routing
```

The **ip routing** command is used to enable routing. Should you wish to disable routing, you would type the **no ip routing** command.

Once routing has been enabled, the router will automatically add a route for each of the networks it is directly connected to. To view the routing table and verify that the routes are added, type

```
ROUTERA> show ip route
```

If you have a look at Figure 8-4, you will notice that the **show ip route** command was typed and the routing table displayed. Notice in the figure that the route to the 192.168.1.0 and 192.168.2.0 networks is automatically added because the router is connected to those networks. You will also notice a letter *C* to the left of each route entry, which means that the route is there because the router is directly connected to the network.

| FIGURE 8-4 | Looking at the routing table of a Cisco router |

```
Cisco - HyperTerminal
File  Edit  View  Call  Transfer  Help

ROUTERA>show ip route
Codes: C - connected, S - static, I - IGRP, R - RIP, M - mobile, B - BGP
       D - EIGRP, EX - EIGRP external, O - OSPF, IA - OSPF inter area
       N1 - OSPF NSSA external type 1, N2 - OSPF NSSA external type 2
       E1 - OSPF external type 1, E2 - OSPF external type 2, E - EGP
       i - IS-IS, L1 - IS-IS level-1, L2 - IS-IS level-2, ia - IS-IS inter area
       * - candidate default, U - per-user static route, o - ODR
       P - periodic downloaded static route

Gateway of last resort is not set

C    192.168.1.0/24 is directly connected, Ethernet0
C    192.168.2.0/24 is directly connected, Serial0
ROUTERA>_

Connected 0:15:32    Auto detect    9600 8-N-1    SCROLL    CAPS    NUM    Capture    Print echo
```

Adding a Static Route to Cisco Routers

When administering a Cisco router, you will need to add any routes that do not exist in the routing table. For example, looking back to Figure 8-4, ROUTERA knows about the 192.168.1.0 and 192.168.2.0 networks but not the 192.168.3.0 network. If you want to configure ROUTERA so that it knows about the 192.168.3.0 network, you will need to add the route manually by typing

```
ROUTERA> enable
ROUTERA# configure terminal
ROUTERA(config)# ip route 192.168.3.0 255.255.255.0 192.168.2.2
```

In this code listing, the command **ip route** (shown in Figure 8-5) adds a route to the routing table. The 192.168.3.0 is the address of the destination network you are adding, and its subnet mask, 192.168.2.2, is known as the *next hop*—the address that ROUTERA is to send information to in order to have data reach the 192.168.3.0 network. Notice that

FIGURE 8-5   Adding a static route to a Cisco router

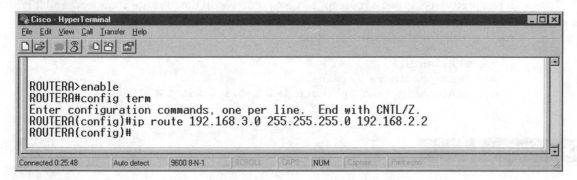

192.168.2.2 is the address of an interface on ROUTERB that ROUTERA can communicate directly with. The idea here is that in order for ROUTERA to send data to the 192.168.3.0 network, it will pass the data to ROUTERB via the interface at 192.168.2.2, which will then send the data on to the 192.168.3.0 network.

If you view the routing table with the **show ip route** command, you will notice that certain routes in the routing table are there because the router is connected to that network, and you will notice the static routes, which are indicated with a letter *S*. Figure 8-6 displays the new routing table with the static route added.

FIGURE 8-6   Displaying the routing table after the static route has been added

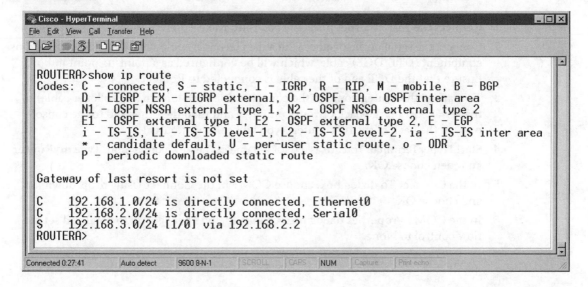

Deleting a Static Route on a Cisco Router

It was pretty easy to add a route to the Cisco router with the **ip route** command, and it is just as easy to delete a route with the **no ip route** command. To delete a route from the routing table, use the following syntax:

```
ROUTERA> enable
ROUTERA# configure terminal
ROUTERA(config)# no ip route 192.168.3.0 255.255.255.0
```

EXERCISE 8-3

Video

Configuring Cisco Routers

In this exercise, you will configure two Cisco 2600 series routers by changing the names of the routers and configuring the interfaces so that they route data between the three different networks shown next. To see how to configure a Cisco router, check out the video for this exercise found in the accompanying material.

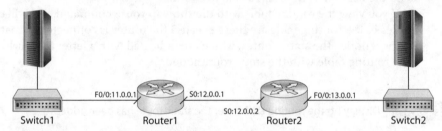

1. Connect the Fast Ethernet ports of each router to a different switch.

2. Connect the serial ports together with a data terminal equipment/data communications equipment (DTE/DCE) cable, which will be configured as a point-to-point link. Ensure that the DCE end of the cable is connected to Router1.

3. To manage the router, connect the console cable (also known as a rollover cable) to the serial port on the back of your computer and then the other end to the console port on the back of the first router—you will call this Router1.

4. Start HyperTerminal. You are asked for a name of the new connection. Type **myRouter** and then choose OK.

5. In the Connect To dialog box, choose COM1 in the Connect Using drop-down list and choose OK.

6. In the COM1 Properties dialog box, change the bits per second to 9600 and set the flow control to None.

7. Click OK.

8. Power on the router. You should see the output of the switch booting up that includes the make and model of the switch and the version of the Cisco Internetwork Operating System (IOS).

Configuring Router1

1. To configure the name of the router, type the following commands:

```
Enable
Config term
Hostname Router1
```

2. To configure the IP address on the Fast Ethernet interface and enable the interface, type the following:

```
Interface fastethernet0/0
Ip address 11.0.0.1 255.0.0.0
No shutdown
```

3. To configure the Serial 0 port on Router1, type the following:

```
Interface serial0
Ip address 12.0.0.1 255.0.0.0
Encapsulation hdlc
Clock rate 64000
No shutdown
```

The previous commands assign an IP address to the serial port, but also set the encapsulation protocol. Setting the encapsulation protocol is something that must be done on the serial link. Also, because Router1 is the data communication equipment, you need to set the speed of the link with the **clock rate** command.

Configuring Router2

1. Connect your console cable to the back of Router2 and power on Router2.

2. To configure the name of the router, type the following commands:

```
Enable
Config term
Hostname Router2
```

3. To configure the IP address on the Fast Ethernet interface and enable the interface, type the following:

```
Interface fastethernet0/0
Ip address 13.0.0.1 255.0.0.0
No shutdown
```

4. To configure the Serial 0 port on Router1, type the following:

```
Interface serial0
Ip address 12.0.0.2 255.0.0.0
Encapsulation hdlc
No shutdown
```

Adding a Route on Router1 to the 13.0.0.0 Network

1. Connect to the console port of Router1, and press ENTER to refresh the screen.

2. Type **exit** twice to navigate back to the Router1 # prompt.

3. Type **ping 13.0.0.1**—do you get replies? _____ The answer should be no because Router1 does not have a route to the 13.0.0.0 network.

4. To view the routing table on Router1, type **show ip route**—notice that you have a route to the 11.0.0.0 and 12.0.0.0 networks because the router is connected to those networks.

5. To add a route to the 13.0.0.0 network, type the following:

```
Config term
Ip route 13.0.0.0 255.0.0.0 12.0.0.2
```

6. Type **exit** and then **show ip route** to verify that the new route has been added.

Adding a Route on Router2 to the 11.0.0.0 Network

1. Connect to the console port of Router2, and press ENTER to refresh the screen.

2. Type **exit** twice to navigate back to the Router2 prompt.

3. Type **ping 11.0.0.1**—do you get replies? _____ The answer should be no because Router2 does not have a route to the 11.0.0.0 network.

4. To view the routing table on Router2, type **show ip route**—notice that you have a route to the 13.0.0.0 and 12.0.0.0 networks because the router is connected to those networks.

5. To add a route to the 11.0.0.0 network, type the following:

```
Config term
Ip route 11.0.0.0 255.0.0.0 12.0.0.1
```

6. Type **exit** and then **show ip route** to verify that the new route has been added.

Windows Routers

It is important to understand that because the IP protocol is running on your Windows computer, it has a built-in routing table as well. Windows uses this built-in routing table to determine how to send data.

It is also important to note that it is possible to take a Windows server and install routing features on it so that it routes data from one network to another. In order to do this, you will need to have at least two network cards, each acting like an interface on a real router.

Once you have all network cards installed and have assigned IP addresses to them, you will need to install the routing functionality in Windows Server 2012 by installing the Remote Access role within Server Manager. Once you have the Remote Access role installed, you can then enable the Windows Routing feature by going to Server Manager on a Windows Server 2012 system and choosing Tools | Routing And Remote Access. Once the *Routing and Remote Access (RRAS)* console is started, you then must enable it by right-clicking your server in the left side of the window and choosing Configure And Enable Routing And Remote Access. This will launch a wizard that will allow you to enable the routing feature of a Windows server. In the RRAS Setup Wizard, you will need to choose Custom Configuration and then choose Next. When you reach the screen asking which services you wish to install, select LAN Routing (shown in Figure 8-7); then click Next and then Finish to end the wizard. When informed you need to start the Routing and Remote Access service, choose the Start Service button.

FIGURE 8-7	
Enabling LAN routing on a Windows server	

FIGURE 8-7

Enabling LAN routing on a Windows server

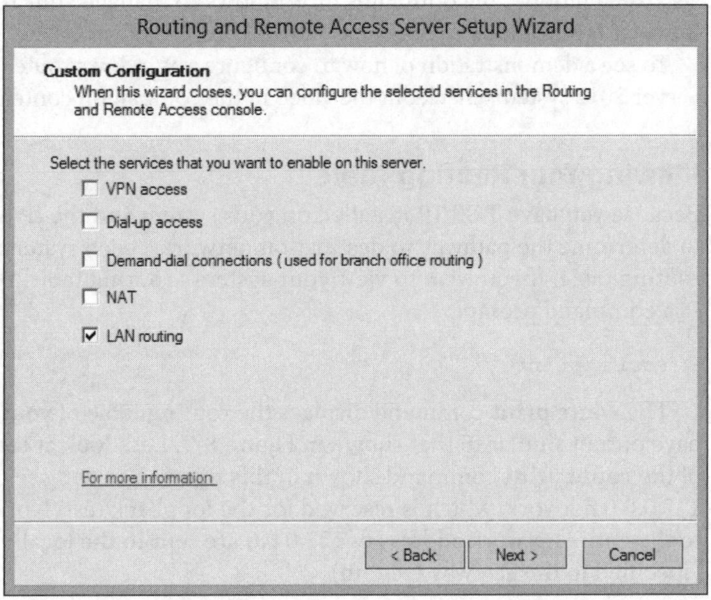

FIGURE 8-8

Displaying the
Windows server
routing table or
adding a new
static route

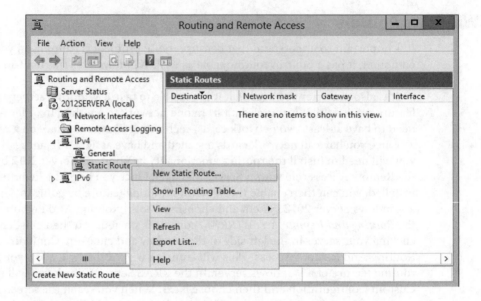

Once you have enabled LAN routing in Routing and Remote Access, you can then
perform tasks such as viewing your routing table, adding routes, or deleting routes by right-
clicking Static Routes and choosing the appropriate command shown in Figure 8-8. You can
also use a number of commands in Windows to manage your routing table, which is what
the next few sections cover.

To see a demonstration of how to configure a Windows router on a Windows
Server 2012 system, check out the video in the companion content for this book.

Viewing Your Routing Table

Because you have TCP/IP installed on your system and the IP protocol uses a routing table
to determine the pathway to destination networks, each system running TCP/IP has a
routing table. If you wish to view your system's routing table, type the following command
in a command prompt:

```
route print
```

The **route print** command displays the routing table of your local system, and you should
have output similar to that shown in Figure 8-9. Let's look at the contents of the output
of the **route print** command shown in this figure. You can see that there is a route for the
127.0.0.0 network, which is reserved for the loopback test. Notice that any messages sent
to the entire network address of 127.0.0.0 are sent to the localhost address of 127.0.0.1
(specified in the gateway column).

FIGURE 8-9

Displaying the routing table on a Windows server

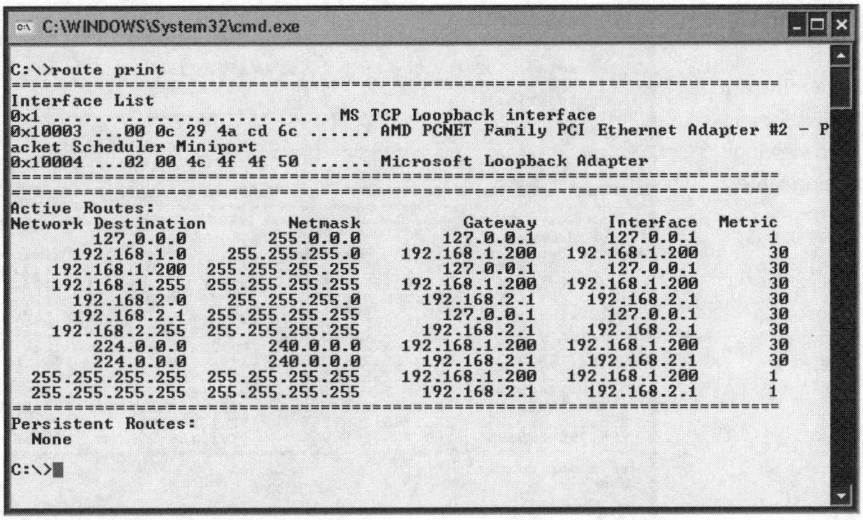

```
C:\WINDOWS\System32\cmd.exe

C:\>route print
===========================================================================
Interface List
0x1 ........................... MS TCP Loopback interface
0x10003 ...00 0c 29 4a cd 6c ...... AMD PCNET Family PCI Ethernet Adapter #2 - P
acket Scheduler Miniport
0x10004 ...02 00 4c 4f 4f 50 ...... Microsoft Loopback Adapter
===========================================================================
===========================================================================
Active Routes:
Network Destination        Netmask          Gateway       Interface  Metric
          127.0.0.0        255.0.0.0        127.0.0.1      127.0.0.1       1
        192.168.1.0    255.255.255.0    192.168.1.200  192.168.1.200      30
      192.168.1.200  255.255.255.255      127.0.0.1      127.0.0.1       30
      192.168.1.255  255.255.255.255  192.168.1.200  192.168.1.200      30
        192.168.2.0    255.255.255.0    192.168.2.1    192.168.2.1       30
        192.168.2.1  255.255.255.255      127.0.0.1      127.0.0.1       30
      192.168.2.255  255.255.255.255  192.168.2.1    192.168.2.1       30
          224.0.0.0        240.0.0.0  192.168.1.200  192.168.1.200      30
          224.0.0.0        240.0.0.0  192.168.2.1    192.168.2.1       30
    255.255.255.255  255.255.255.255  192.168.1.200  192.168.1.200       1
    255.255.255.255  255.255.255.255  192.168.2.1    192.168.2.1        1
===========================================================================
Persistent Routes:
  None

C:\>
```

You will also notice that there is a route for the 192.168.1.0 network. This is actually the network that my system is plugged into. Therefore, in order for this system to send data to the network, it simply sends data to the 192.168.1.200 address (which is its own network card). You will also notice that there is a route for the 224.0.0.0 network address range, which is the class D range used by multicasting applications.

Looking at Figure 8-9, you will also notice that there are two entries for broadcast addresses. The first entry is 192.168.1.255, which is the broadcast address for the 192.168.1.0 network segment; there is also a broadcast address for all network segments, which is known as the 255.255.255.255 address. The 255.255.255.255 address is known as an internetwork broadcast address, and clients can use it to send data to all systems on all subnets, not just their own subnets. Bear in mind that routers do not normally forward broadcast traffic.

Adding a Static Route

Let's assume that Figure 8-9 is displaying the routing table of ROUTERA, which was shown in the network diagram of Figure 8-3. In this routing table, we don't have a route for the 192.168.3.0 network, so you will learn how to add a route to the routing table using the **route add** command. The syntax to use the **route add** command is as follows:

```
route add <destination IP> MASK <subnet mask> <next_hop>
```

In our example, you would like to add a route for the destination address of 192.168.3.0 with a subnet mask of 255.255.255.0. The next hop address is where your system will send the data so that it can reach the desired destination network. If you were adding the route to

FIGURE 8-10

Adding a route on
a Windows server
and then viewing
the routing table

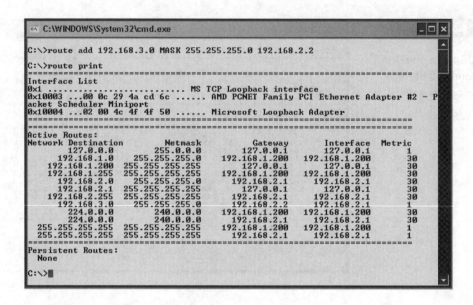

```
 C:\WINDOWS\System32\cmd.exe

C:\>route add 192.168.3.0 MASK 255.255.255.0 192.168.2.2

C:\>route print
===========================================================================
Interface List
0x1 .......................... MS TCP Loopback interface
0x10003 ...00 0c 29 4a cd 6c ...... AMD PCNET Family PCI Ethernet Adapter #2 - P
acket Scheduler Miniport
0x10004 ...02 00 4c 4f 4f 50 ...... Microsoft Loopback Adapter
===========================================================================
===========================================================================
Active Routes:
Network Destination        Netmask          Gateway       Interface  Metric
          127.0.0.0        255.0.0.0        127.0.0.1       127.0.0.1       1
        192.168.1.0    255.255.255.0    192.168.1.200   192.168.1.200      30
      192.168.1.200  255.255.255.255      127.0.0.1       127.0.0.1       30
      192.168.1.255  255.255.255.255    192.168.1.200   192.168.1.200      30
        192.168.2.0    255.255.255.0    192.168.2.1     192.168.2.1       30
        192.168.2.1  255.255.255.255      127.0.0.1       127.0.0.1       30
      192.168.2.255  255.255.255.255    192.168.2.1     192.168.2.1       30
        192.168.3.0    255.255.255.0    192.168.2.2     192.168.2.1        1
          224.0.0.0        240.0.0.0    192.168.1.200   192.168.1.200      30
          224.0.0.0        240.0.0.0    192.168.2.1     192.168.2.1       30
    255.255.255.255  255.255.255.255    192.168.1.200   192.168.1.200       1
    255.255.255.255  255.255.255.255    192.168.2.1     192.168.2.1        1
===========================================================================
Persistent Routes:
  None

C:\>
```

ROUTERA found in Figure 8-3, you would send it to the next hop of 192.168.2.2. To add the
route to a Windows router, you would type the following:

```
route add 192.168.3.0 MASK 255.255.255.0 192.168.2.2
```

Once you have typed this command into ROUTERA, you can verify that the route has
been added by typing the **route print** command again at the command prompt. Figure 8-10
displays both the addition of the route and the routing table after the route has been added.

e x a m

w a t c h　　　**For the Network+ exam, know**　　route add **command and to view your routing**
that in Windows, to add a route you use the　　　**table you use the** route print **command.**

Deleting a Static Route

You may delete a route from the routing table at any time by using the **route delete** command.
The **route delete** command uses one parameter—the destination route that you wish to
delete from the routing table. For example, if you wanted to delete the 192.168.3.0 network
from your routing table, the syntax for the **route delete** command is as follows:

```
route delete 192.168.3.0
```

CERTIFICATION OBJECTIVE 8.04

Dynamic Routing Protocols

Managing the entries in routing tables on a large internetwork could be a time-consuming task. To help administrators with this, *dynamic* routing protocols are enabled. These protocols allow the routers to share information contained within their routing tables with one another. As a result, routes that are known by one router will be shared with the other routers, thus saving the administrator from having to manually add all the routes!

When preparing for the Network+ certification exam, you need to be familiar with the two major categories of routing protocols:

- **Interior gateway protocols (IGP)**   An interior gateway protocol shares routing table information with other routers located inside your network, known as an *autonomous system (AS)*. An example of an IGP protocol is Routing Information Protocol (RIP) or Enhanced Interior Gateway Routing Protocol (EIGRP).

- **Exterior gateway protocols (EGP)**   An exterior gateway protocol that is loaded on a router will share routing table information to other routers outside your network. An example of an EGP protocol is Border Gateway Protocol (BGP).

Convergence, also known as steady state, is when the routes on each	**router are shared with all other routers and merged into each router's routing table.**

Another term the Network+ exam expects you to be familiar with is convergence. *Convergence* occurs when all routing tables have been shared with all other routers and all routers have updated their routing table with that new information.

Routing Metrics

A routing protocol decides on the best route to a network by analyzing the routing table and choosing the route with the lowest metric value. The routing protocol uses the metric value to determine which route is the best one, and it can mean different things depending on the routing protocol. The following are common values used to measure the metric value of a route:

- **Hop count**   Some routing protocols use hop count as a metric value, which means that the best route is determined based on how many hops away the network is. Every router that data must pass through is considered a hop, and the lowest hop count is the best route to take with this metric.

- **MTU or bandwidth** Some routing protocols determine the best route to take based on the maximum transmission unit (MTU), or bandwidth of the link. Routes with more bandwidth would be preferred over lower-bandwidth routes.

- **Costs** Some routing protocols choose the best route based on the one with the lowest cost. A cost value is considered a preference value on the link, and the link with the lowest cost value will be selected as the route to the destination. For example, a link to a destination with a cost of three is chosen over a different link to the same destination with a cost value of five.

- **Latency** Another value that routing protocols could use as the metric value is the latency of the link. Latency refers to how long it takes a packet to travel from one place to another. Lower-latency routes are preferred over higher-latency routes with this metric criterion.

- **Administrative distance** The administrative distance is the "trustworthiness" of the route that is in the routing table. Each different method of adding a route to a routing table has an administrative distance value—if the router was to learn about a route two or more different ways, then the route with the lower administrative distance is the one the router would use. For example, a static route has an administrative distance of 0, while a route learned via RIP has an administrative distance of 120. In this case, if the routes were for the same destination network, the router would use the static route as it is considered to be more trustworthy information.

- **SPB** Shortest Path Bridging (SPB) is a replacement protocol for the older Spanning Tree Protocol (STP). STP is a layer-2 protocol that prevents loops on a switched network, while SPB allows multiple pathways between switches that are active using the same cost value. The benefit of SPB is that it increases bandwidth and redundancy between switches while having a fast convergence time.

It is important to note that some routing protocols combine some of these different metric values to determine the best route possible.

When discussing the different routing protocols, it is important to note that there are two major classes: distance vector and link state. Each routing protocol is either a distance vector protocol or a link state protocol.

Distance Vector

Distance vector routing protocols measure the best route to use based on the lowest hop count. The hop count is increased by one for every router between the source and the destination. With distance vector routing protocols, the route with the lowest hop count is typically selected as the destination path for the data.

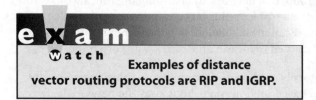

RIP/RIPv2

The *Routing Information Protocol (RIP)* is a distance vector protocol and is responsible for sharing its routing table information with neighboring routers by broadcasting the information over User Datagram Protocol (UDP) every 30 seconds. This broadcasting of the routing table is known as advertising, and advertising the routing table information with neighboring routers exempts the network administrator from having to add the routes manually.

RIP is an industry-standard routing protocol, which means that it is supported by many different vendors, so you could use it as a routing protocol to share routing table information between routers from different manufacturers. RIP will choose the route with the lowest hop count, but if two different routes have the same hop count, RIP will load-balance the traffic over those two routes. Know that RIP is limited to 15 hops, so it is used only on small networks.

RIPv1 only works with classful addresses because it doesn't send subnet mask information with the routing table. RIPv2 is an update to RIPv1 and does support classless addressing and variable-length subnet masks because it sends the subnet mask information with the routing table.

Let's assume you are the administrator for ROUTERA shown back in Figure 8-3. ROUTERA will have routes to the 192.168.1.0 and 192.168.2.0 networks by default. If you wanted to configure RIP on ROUTERA to advertise knowledge of those two networks, you would type the following commands on ROUTERA (remember not to type what is before the > and # because they are the prompts that would appear on the screen):

```
ROUTERA> enable
ROUTERA# configure terminal
ROUTERA(config)# router rip
ROUTERA(config-router)# network 192.168.1.0
ROUTERA(config-router)# network 192.168.2.0
```

Once RIP, or any other routing protocol, has been enabled on both ROUTERA and ROUTERB, the two routers will then share knowledge of any networks they know about. When ROUTERA receives knowledge of the 192.168.3.0 network and builds the new network into its routing table, this is known as convergence. Figure 8-11 displays the routing table on ROUTERA after RIP has been enabled on both routers. Notice the letter *R* beside the 192.168.3.0 route, meaning that the route was learned about through RIP.

IGRP

Another example of a distance vector routing protocol is the *Interior Gateway Routing Protocol (IGRP)*. IGRP is a classful routing protocol that was built by Cisco, so you will only use it on networks where you have only Cisco routers.

FIGURE 8-11 **FIGURE 8-11** The routing table displays the new route learned through RIP.

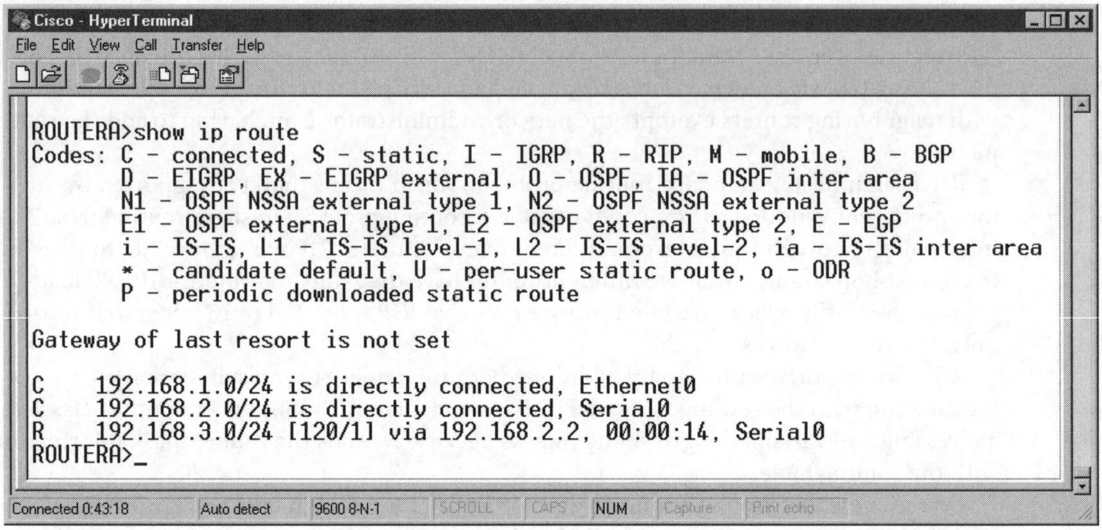

```
Cisco - HyperTerminal                                                    _ □ ×
File  Edit  View  Call  Transfer  Help

ROUTERA>show ip route
Codes: C - connected, S - static, I - IGRP, R - RIP, M - mobile, B - BGP
       D - EIGRP, EX - EIGRP external, O - OSPF, IA - OSPF inter area
       N1 - OSPF NSSA external type 1, N2 - OSPF NSSA external type 2
       E1 - OSPF external type 1, E2 - OSPF external type 2, E - EGP
       i - IS-IS, L1 - IS-IS level-1, L2 - IS-IS level-2, ia - IS-IS inter area
       * - candidate default, U - per-user static route, o - ODR
       P - periodic downloaded static route

Gateway of last resort is not set

C    192.168.1.0/24 is directly connected, Ethernet0
C    192.168.2.0/24 is directly connected, Serial0
R    192.168.3.0/24 [120/1] via 192.168.2.2, 00:00:14, Serial0
ROUTERA>_

Connected 0:43:18      Auto detect      9600 8-N-1      SCROLL    CAPS    NUM    Capture   Print echo
```

IGRP was designed to improve on RIP limitations; it has a maximum hop count of 255 and uses the concepts of an *autonomous system (AS)*. An autonomous system is a grouping of routers that share routing table information. Routers using IGRP will only share the routes with other routers in the AS. Another improvement is that the full routing table is advertised every 90 seconds instead of 30 seconds, as is the case with RIP.

To enable IGRP on your Cisco router, type the following commands:

```
ROUTERA> enable
ROUTERA# configure terminal
ROUTERA(config)# router igrp 10
ROUTERA(config-router)# network 192.168.1.0
ROUTERA(config-router)# network 192.168.2.0
```

In this code listing, you will notice that enabling IGRP on a Cisco router is similar to enabling RIP. The difference is that when you enable IGRP, you specify the AS number for the router. In this case, I have used 10, so any other router with an AS number of 10 will receive routing information for the 192.168.1.0 and 192.168.2.0 networks.

Link State

Link state routing protocols are a little more advanced than distance vector routing protocols in the sense that a link state routing protocol knows about the entire network topology. A link state protocol is responsible for monitoring the state of the link between the routers. This link state information is then used to determine the optimal route to a destination network. Although protocols such as RIP have knowledge of neighboring routers, link state protocols have knowledge of the entire network topology and multicast the routing table information to the entire network.

One of the benefits of the link state routing protocols is that if a link is down, that information is stored in the routing table and that pathway will not be used. Because a distance vector routing protocol does not store link state information, it is possible that it will not know that a link is unavailable for some time and it could still send traffic through that pathway.

OSPF

Open Shortest Path First (OSPF) is an example of a link state protocol. OSPF is an industry-standard protocol, which means that it is available to routers built by different manufacturers, and you can use it to share routing information between dissimilar routers.

Like IGRP, OSPF uses autonomous systems, but it also has the capability of dividing the AS into logical groups called areas. OSPF supports VLSMs and has an unlimited hop count.

e x a m
ⓦ a t c h **OSPF and IS-IS are examples of link state routing protocols.**

IS-IS

The intermediate system–to–intermediate system (IS-IS) routing protocol competes with OSPF by being a link state routing protocol for inside the network (interior gateway). IS-IS was developed by Digital Equipment Corporation (DEC) and has become an industry-standard protocol, although not as popular as OSPF.

Like OSPF, IS-IS uses a link state algorithm to maintain status information on all the links and routes on the network so that each router running the IS-IS protocol will have knowledge of the entire network topology.

Hybrid

Hybrid routing protocols combine the features of distance vector and link state.

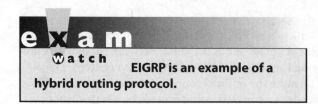

EIGRP

A popular hybrid routing protocol that was built by Cisco is the *Enhanced Interior Gateway Routing Protocol (EIGRP)*, which improves upon IGRP by being a classless routing protocol that supports VLSM and supports both IPv4 and IPv6. EIGRP also has a maximum hop count of 255 hops.

BGP

The *Border Gateway Protocol (BGP)* is an EGP that is responsible for sharing routing table information with routers outside your autonomous system. The protocols discussed before this are known as interior gateway protocols, which are responsible for sharing routing tables within your autonomous system (or network).

BGP is designed to send changes made to the routing table when they occur, versus at a regular interval like RIP. BGP only sends the change, while other routing protocols such as RIP send the entire table. BGP is also a classless routing protocol that supports CIDR.

BGP is a newer version of the exterior gateway protocol (EGP).

Advanced Concepts

Now that you understand the basics of routing and how to configure a router, it is important to know some of the advanced concepts related to routing that the Network+ certification exam is sure to test you on.

Route Redistribution, Aggregation, and AS Numbers

The routing terms and concepts you should be familiar with that are covered on the new Network+ exam include the following:

- **Autonomous system numbers**   An autonomous system (AS) number is a number assigned to a group of routers running the same routing protocol such as IGRP. The autonomous system number is a way to control which routes a router shares with other routers, as it only shares routes with other routers with the same AS number.
- **Route redistribution**   Route redistribution is an advanced routing feature that allows you to share routes between routers running different routing protocols. Normally, routes are only shared with other routers running the same routing protocol, but with route redistribution you can have one of your OSPF routes shared with a RIP router, for example.
- **Route aggregation**   Route aggregation is also known as route summarization and is a method to summarize routes in the routing table to keep the routing table

small. This will save resources on the router by reducing processing and memory requirements. For example, a router may have routes for multiple subnets, such as 10.1.0.0/24, 10.1.1.0/24, 10.1.2.0/24, 10.1.3.0/24, and so on, and these may be routed to the same destination; instead of having each route listed in the routing table, you could summarize them all by having a route for 10.1.0.0/16. Route summarization is essentially supernetting, but know that router vendors and protocols refer to the term route summarization quite often.

High Availability

When you configure a LAN environment, you typically have a router connected to the Internet and to your LAN. The IP address of the router's interface that is connected to the LAN is the default gateway of all systems on the network, which allows the systems to send packets to the router for delivery out to the Internet. What if the router crashes and becomes unavailable? All systems will lose Internet access, or even WAN access to the rest of the corporate network. This is a huge problem and one that can be solved by using a high-availability protocol on the router to ensure that multiple routers are working together as the default gateway.

Figure 8-12 displays a typical high-availability setup with Cisco routers. Notice that there are two routers known as NY-R1 and NY-R2. These two routers are configured with an IP address as normal on the LAN interface. Notice in the figure that the routers are connected to a switch and that the clients on the network are also connected to the switch. The goal is have the NY-R1 router as the active router, while the NY-R2 router is to act as a standby router and is to take over (and become the new active router) when the NY-R1 router fails. Because the client is to use whichever router is currently the active router as the gateway, you are unable to configure either router as the actual default gateway. The high-availability protocol will create what is known as a virtual router, which is not a physical device on the network, but is a virtual device using a *virtual IP address*. You configure the clients to use the virtual router as their default gateway, and the virtual router will forward the packets to whichever router is the active router.

There are a number of different high-availability protocols that can be used to create a high-availability environment for your routers. Two common protocols are

■ **Hot Standby Router Protocol (HSRP)** This is a Cisco-proprietary protocol that involves having one router as an active router and the other router as a standby router. HSRP also creates a virtual router with a virtual IP address that is to be used as the default gateway of hosts on the subnet. Figure 8-12 shows a typical HSRP setup.

■ **Virtual Router Redundancy Protocol (VRRP)** This is an Institute of Electrical and Electronics Engineers (IEEE) protocol that provides high availability to your routers. Because it is an IEEE standard, it is not specific to one router vendor. With VRRP, you create a virtual router group, and each router performs a role in that group. The active router is known as the master router with VRRP, and one of the benefits of VRRP is that you can have multiple backup routers in the group (HSRP only has one standby router).

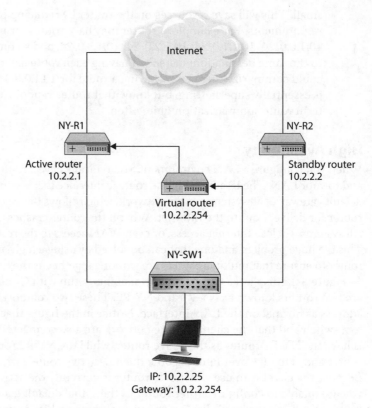

FIGURE 8-12

High-availability
routers

CERTIFICATION SUMMARY

In this chapter you have learned more about the TCP/IP protocol and some of its functionality, such as subnetting and routing. You have learned that from time to time you may need to divide a network range into multiple network blocks (subnets) to follow the physical structure of the network. You have also learned that the IP protocol uses a routing table to determine how to deliver data to its destination.

This chapter has also discussed routing protocols, and you have learned the difference between a distance vector routing protocol and a link state routing protocol.

TWO-MINUTE DRILL

Understanding Subnetting

❑ The purpose of subnetting is to break one network ID into multiple subnetworks (subnets) so that you can follow the physical structure of the network.

❑ With subnetting, you take host bits from the subnet mask and turn them into network bits—thus creating more networks but fewer machines per network.

❑ To determine how many bits to take from the host ID portion of the subnet mask, use the formula $2^{\text{masked bits}} - 2 = \#$ of Subnets.

❑ Remember to calculate the network ID, first valid address, last valid address, broadcast address, and new subnet mask of each subnet created.

Classful vs. Classless Addressing

❑ Classful addressing is when the network ID falls into one of the default network IDs of a class A, class B, or class C address.

❑ Classless addressing is when the network ID is altered from a normal classful address.

Understanding Routing and Static Routes

❑ The IP protocol is responsible for routing data to its destination.

❑ You can view your routing table in Windows with **route print**.

❑ You may add a route to a routing table in Windows with **route add**.

❑ You may delete a route from the routing table in Windows with **route delete**.

❑ You may use a dynamic routing protocol such as RIP or OSPF so that the routers share routing table information with one another, eliminating the need to manually configure the routes individually.

Dynamic Routing Protocols

❑ There are two major types of routing protocols: distance vector and link state.

❑ Distance vector routing protocols share routing information with neighboring routers and measure the best route by how many hops away a destination is.

❑ Link state routing protocols share routing information with all routers on the network and include information on the state of the link.

❑ RIP and IGRP are examples of distance vector routing protocols.

❑ OSPF and IS-IS are examples of link state routing protocols.

SELF TEST

The following questions will help you measure your understanding of the material presented in this chapter. Read all the choices carefully, because there may appear to be more than one correct answer, but you will need to choose the best answer.

Understanding Subnetting

1. You have a network ID of 131.107.0.0 and you would like to subnet your network into six networks. What is your new subnet mask?
   A. 255.224.0.0
   B. 255.255.224.0
   C. 255.192.0.0
   D. 255.255.192.0

2. You want to divide your network into eight networks. How many bits will you need to take from the host ID portion of the subnet mask?
   A. 2
   B. 3
   C. 4
   D. 6

3. In binary, how do you calculate the broadcast address of a network range?
   A. All host bits set to 0
   B. All host bits set to 0, except for the low-order bit
   C. All host bits set to 1, except for the low-order bit
   D. All host bits set to 1

4. In binary, how do you calculate the network ID of a network range?
   A. All host bits set to 0
   B. All host bits set to 0, except for the low-order bit
   C. All host bits set to 1, except for the low-order bit
   D. All host bits set to 1

5. The last valid address of a subnet is always
   A. One more than the broadcast address
   B. One less than the broadcast address
   C. One more than the network ID
   D. One less than the network ID

Classful vs. Classless Addressing

6. Which of the following is an example of CIDR notation?
    A. 16/10.34.56.78
    B. 10.34.56.78
    C. 10.34.56.0
    D. 10.34.56.78/16

7. Your router has the IP address of 216.83.11.65/27. You wish to connect a new system on the network. Which of the following addresses would you assign to that new system?
    A. 216.83.11.45
    B. 216.83.11.87
    C. 216.83.11.95
    D. 216.83.11.96

Understanding Routing and Static Routes

8. You want to add a new route to your Windows router. Which of the following is the correct syntax to add a route to the routing table?
    A. routetable add 12.0.0.0 255.0.0.0 11.0.0.254
    B. routetable add 12.0.0.0 MASK 255.0.0.0 11.0.0.254
    C. route add 12.0.0.0 MASK 255.0.0.0 11.0.0.254
    D. route add 12.0.0.0 255.0.0.0 11.0.0.254

9. You wish to view the routing table on the router. Which command can you use?
    A. routetable view
    B. routetable print
    C. route view
    D. route print

10. You wish to remove a route from the routing table. Which command would you use?
    A. router remove
    B. route delete
    C. remove route
    D. delete route

Dynamic Routing Protocols

11. Which dynamic routing protocol is a distance vector protocol?
    A. OSPF
    B. DIP
    C. RIP
    D. NIP

12. Which dynamic routing protocol monitors the state of the links?
    A. OSPF
    B. SIP
    C. RIP
    D. SLIP

13. Which high-availability routing protocol is a Cisco-proprietary protocol that uses a standby router?
    A. OSPF
    B. HSRP
    C. RIP
    D. VRRP

 Performance-Based Question Review: See the performance-based question sample from the author included with the accompanying media.

SELF TEST ANSWERS

Understanding Subnetting

1. ☑ **B.** Given that we are dealing with a class B address, the default subnet mask is 255.255.0.0. Therefore, if you take three bits (needed for six networks) from the host ID, you will get a new subnet mask of 255.255.224.0.
    ☒ **A, C,** and **D** are incorrect because they don't have the correct subnet mask for the six new subnets.

2. ☑ **B.** The formula to calculate how many bits you wish to take from the host ID portion of the subnet mask is $2^{masked\ bits}$ = # of Subnets. We need to mask three bits to get a minimum of eight networks.
    ☒ **A, C,** and **D** are incorrect because they will not give us the correct number of networks.

3. ☑ **D.** The broadcast address is calculated by converting all host bits to 1.

☒ **A, B,** and **C** are incorrect. All host bits set to 0 is the network ID, all host bits set to 0 except the low-order bit would be used by the first valid address, and all host bits set to 1 except the low-order bit would be used by the last valid address.

4. ☑ **A.** The network ID is determined by setting all host bits to 0.

☒ **B, C,** and **D** are incorrect. All host bits set to 1 is the broadcast address, all host bits set to 0 except the low-order bit would be used by the first valid address, and all host bits set to 1 except the low-order bit would be used by the last valid address.

5. ☑ **B.** The last valid address is always one less than the broadcast address.

☒ **A, C,** and **D** are incorrect because they are not used to determine the last valid address.

Classful vs. Classless Addressing

6. ☑ **D.** CIDR notation is used to identify how many bits make up the network ID in the IP address. With CIDR notation, you specify the number of bits that make up the network ID by placing a forward slash (/) after the IP address and then the number of bits that make up the network ID: for example, 10.34.56.78/16.

☒ **A, B,** and **C** are incorrect because they do not resemble CIDR notation.

7. ☑ **B.** Because /27 is being used to identify the number of bits that make up the subnet mask, you know the network is subnetted (class C has a /24 by default). In this example, the network that the router is on is the 216.83.11.64 network and 216.83.11.87 is the only valid address on that network listed.

☒ **A, C,** and **D** are incorrect. 216.83.11.45 is incorrect because it is not on the same network. 216.83.11.95 is incorrect because although it is part of the correct network, it is the broadcast address for that network. 216.83.11.96 is incorrect because it is the network ID of the next network.

Understanding Routing and Static Routes

8. ☑ **C.** The command to add a route to a router is **route add**, and you must supply the MASK keyword when supplying the subnet mask.

☒ **A, B,** and **D** are incorrect because they are not the correct commands to add a route to the routing table.

9. ☑ **D.** The command to view a routing table is **route print**.

☒ **A, B,** and **C** are incorrect because they are not used to view the routing table.

10. ☑ **B.** To delete a route from the routing table, we use **route delete**.

☒ **A, C,** and **D** are incorrect because they are not commands used to delete a route from the routing table.

Dynamic Routing Protocols

11. ☑ **C.** The RIP routing protocol is a distance vector protocol, meaning that it measures how far a destination is in hops.
☒ **A, B,** and **D** are incorrect because they are not routing protocols except for OSPF. OSPF is a routing protocol, but it is not vector based—it is a link state protocol.

12. ☑ **A.** OSPF is a link state protocol, meaning that it monitors the link between the routers and shares that link state information with other OSPF-enabled devices. The preferred route is always selected based on the link state.
☒ **B, C,** and **D** are incorrect because they are not link state protocols. RIP is a distance vector protocol.

13. ☑ **B.** The Hot Standby Router Protocol (HSRP) is a Cisco-proprietary protocol that offers high availability of a router by configuring an active router, standby router, and a virtual router with a virtual IP address.
☒ **A, C,** and **D** are incorrect. OSPF is a link state routing protocol and is not a high-availability protocol. RIP is a distance vector routing protocol and not a high-availability routing protocol. Virtual Router Redundancy Protocol (VRRP) is an IEEE high-availability protocol for routers that uses a router group, a master router, and multiple backup routers in the group.

Chapter 9

Configuring Network Services

One of the major improvements in the objectives of the new Network+ certification is the fact that they expect you to not only understand what the purpose of different network services are, but they also expect you to know the basic steps to configure a service. In this chapter you will learn the details of DNS, DHCP, and NAT, including basic configuration requirements to get these services to work.

CERTIFICATION OBJECTIVE 9.01

Understanding DNS

You learned in Chapter 4 that the Domain Name System (DNS) is a hierarchy of servers that are designed to resolve fully qualified domain names (FQDNs) to IP addresses. For example, looking at Figure 9-1, if you try to connect to my website at www.gleneclarke.com, your system first sends a query to the DNS server on your network asking for the IP address of www.gleneclarke.com. If your local DNS server does not know the IP address of the site, it then sends the query to the DNS root servers. They then forward the request on to the .com name servers, and then on to my DNS server. My DNS server has the IP address of my website in its database, so my server sends that back to your DNS server in the office. Your DNS server then sends the IP address to your client system that wishes to surf the website.

In this section you will learn more about installing and configuring a DNS server so that it can participate in name resolution.

FIGURE 9-1   DNS resolves FQDNs to IP addresses.

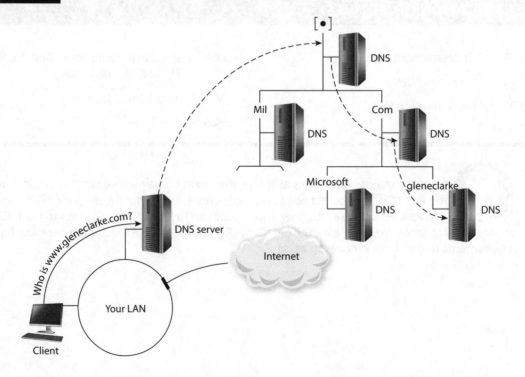

DNS Overview

When configuring DNS there are a number of things to consider. You need to think about whether you want to configure a primary or secondary DNS server and what types of DNS records need to be configured.

Primary and Secondary DNS Servers

When configuring DNS on the network, it is recommended that you have two DNS servers—a primary DNS server and a secondary DNS server. The primary DNS server has the writable copy of the DNS database, while the secondary DNS server has a read-only copy of the database that it receives from the primary DNS server. The purpose of the secondary DNS server is to hold a copy of your DNS data in case the primary DNS server fails.

Installing DNS

To have a functioning primary or secondary DNS server, you must first install the DNS service on your server. The following outlines the steps for installing DNS on a Windows Server 2012.

1. Log on to 2012ServerA as administrator.
2. If Server Manager is not running, launch it by clicking the button in the task bar.
3. Choose Manage | Add Roles And Features.
4. On the Before You Begin page, choose Next.
5. Ensure Role-Based or Feature-Based Installation is selected and then choose Next.
6. Ensure 2012ServerA is selected and then choose Next.
7. From the Select Server Roles screen, choose DNS Server (select the check box). You are prompted to add the DNS Server Tools; choose Add Feature and then choose Next.
8. Choose Next two more times and then choose Install.

Once you have the DNS service installed on your systems, you are ready to configure DNS records.

Configuring DNS Records

Now that you have the DNS server installed, your next step is to configure the DNS service. You first create a DNS zone. A DNS zone is the area of the DNS hierarchy that you are responsible for managing. For example, I am responsible for managing the gleneclarke.com DNS zone. There are different types of DNS zones that you can create, with the two common types being

■ **Primary DNS zone**   The primary DNS zone is a read/write copy of the zone data and is where you create the DNS records.

■ **Secondary DNS zone**   The secondary DNS zone is a read-only copy of the DNS data. You create secondary DNS zones to have a backup in case the server holding the primary zone fails.

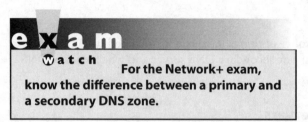

To create the primary or secondary zone on a Windows Server 2012 system, follow these steps.

1. If Server Manager is not already running, start it by clicking the Server Manager button on the task bar.

2. Choose Tools | DNS.

3. Once the DNS management console launches, expand the server and then select Forward Lookup Zones. A forward lookup zone will convert FQDNs to IP addresses, while a reverse lookup zone translates IP addresses to FQDNs.

4. To create a new primary zone, right-click Forward Lookup Zones and choose New Zone.

5. In the New Zone Wizard, choose Next.

6. On the Zone Type page, choose Primary Zone as the type of zone you wish to create and then disable the option to create an Active Directory–integrated zone. Note the other zone types in the list, and then choose Next.

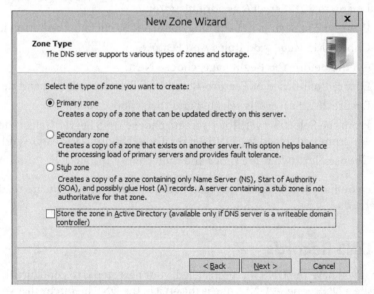

7. Type **chapter9.com** as the zone name and then choose Next.

8. Choose Next to accept the default filename where the DNS records are going to be stored.

9. Select Do Not Allow Dynamic Updates and then choose Next (we will talk about dynamic updates in the next section).

10. Choose Finish.

Once you have created the primary zone for the DNS namespace that you are authorized for, you need to create DNS records. The DNS records are stored in DNS and match a friendly FQDN to the corresponding IP address of that system. Actually, that is a bit of a lie, because it really depends on what type of DNS record you create. If you create a hosts record, then my previous statement is true, but it is important to understand that there are different types of DNS records:

- ■ **Hosts (A)**   The host record is one of the most common types of records and is used to resolve an FQDN to an IPv4 address.

- ■ **Hosts (AAAA)**   The AAAA record is also known as a host record, but is used to resolve an FQDN to an IPv6 address.

- ■ **Alias (CNAME)**   The CNAME record is known as the alias record and is a way to create a record that has a name and points to another host record. It allows you to create many records with different names, with all the names referencing the one IP address.

- ■ **Mail Exchange (MX)**   The MX record is known as the mail exchange record and is used to point to your inbound e-mail server. For example, when you send an e-mail to bob@mycompany.com, a DNS query is sent to the mycompany.com DNS server asking where the e-mail server is for mycompany.com by asking for the MX record.

- ■ **Name Server (NS)**   The NS record specifies who the DNS servers are for the zone.

- ■ **Start Of Authority (SOA)**   The SOA record stores the settings for the DNS zone, such as the increment number, which acts as a version number and increments any time the zone changes. If the secondary DNS server has a different increment number, then the secondary DNS knows that it needs to copy the zone from the primary DNS server to be up to date.

- ■ **Pointer (PTR)**   A PTR record is created in a reverse lookup zone and associates the IP address with a DNS name for reverse lookups.

For the Network+ exam, know the different types of DNS records presented in this section, such as A, MX, PTR, CNAME, NS, SOA, and AAAA.

FIGURE 9-2   Looking at the default zone records

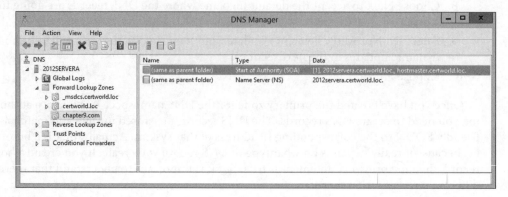

Once the zone is created, you will notice that the SOA record and the NS record are created automatically. In Figure 9-2, you can see that the increment is set to [1] and the primary DNS server for the zone is 2012serverA.certworld.loc. In addition, notice that the NS record reference for the DNS server is also 2012serverA.

Creating additional DNS records is fairly straightforward once you have the zone created. In order to create a host record, you right-click the zone and choose the type of record you wish to create. For example, as shown in Figure 9-3, when you right-click chapter9.com, you see that you can create a new host record by choosing New Host (A or AAAA).

FIGURE 9-3

Creating new DNS
records

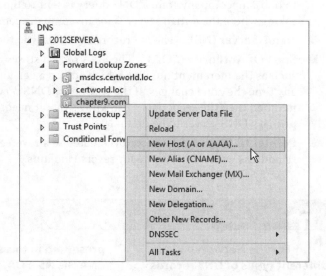

FIGURE 9-4

Creating a host
record in DNS

Once you choose to create a new host record, you then need to fill in the details by specifying
a name for the record (such as www). Notice that once you fill in the name, the FQDN is
generated by the name, plus the zone name, to give you www.chapter9.com in this case
(see Figure 9-4). You then specify the IP address of that record.

Dynamic DNS

Years ago, DNS name resolution was only used for Internet resources such as websites and
e-mail servers. But today, most networking environments use DNS to resolve the FQDN
of internal resources to IP addresses. The problem was that administrators did not want to
create DNS records for all the internal systems on the network. The solution was to create
a protocol, known as dynamic DNS, that allows the systems to contact the DNS server and
create and update their own records.

Configuring Dynamic DNS

To enable dynamic DNS on your DNS zone, follow these steps.

1. From Server Manager, choose Tools | DNS.
2. Expand the server and then expand Forward Lookup Zones.
3. Right-click your DNS zone, such as chapter9.com, and choose Properties.

4. On the general page, choose Nonsecure And Secure from the Dynamic Updates drop-down list to enable dynamic updates on this zone.

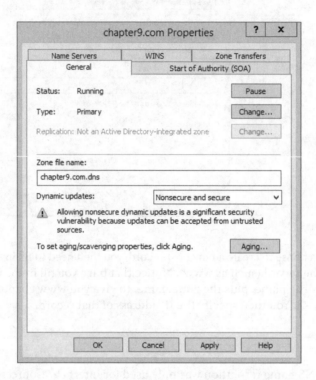

Once dynamic updates have been enabled, you can configure all clients' and servers' TCP/IP settings to point to this server for DNS and they will automatically add a host record for themselves.

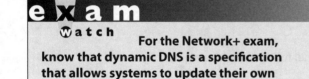

For the Network+ exam, know that dynamic DNS is a specification that allows systems to update their own DNS records instead of requiring the administrator to update all the DNS records.

EXERCISE 9-1

Video

Installing and Configuring DNS

Using the steps demonstrated in this chapter, install DNS on a Windows Server 2012 system and configure the records discussed in step 1. Check out the video of the author performing these steps.

1. Create a DNS zone with the following information:
   - Zone type: Primary
   - Zone name: Exer91.com
2. Create the following DNS records:
   - Create a host record (A) called www that references 10.0.0.1.
   - Create an alias (CNAME) record called ftp that references www.exer91.com.
   - Create an alias (CNAME) record called mail that references www.exer91.com.
   - Create an MX record that references mail.exer91.com.
3. Go to a command prompt and ping www.exer91.com. Do you receive a reply?

Public Dynamic DNS Solutions

Dynamic DNS solutions are available to the public that you can subscribe to. The benefit of public dynamic DNS solutions is that they can be used to update DNS dynamically for a system that is configured with a dynamic IP address (a DHCP client) from their Internet service provider. If you had a dynamic IP address (which most of us have) and you wanted to host services such as a website, you would constantly have to update the DNS record as your IP address changed daily. With dynamic DNS, an agent is installed on your system that is responsible for updating DNS automatically for you! An example of a public dynamic DNS provider is noip.com.

CERTIFICATION OBJECTIVE 9.02

Deploying DHCP

You learned in Chapter 4 about IP addressing and the fact that addressing can be assigned either statically, meaning you manually configure the IP address information on each system, or dynamically through Dynamic Host Configuration Protocol (DHCP). The downfall of static addressing is the time it takes to configure all systems on the network with the TCP/IP-related settings, and the fact that there is ample opportunity to make a mistake with all that typing.

FIGURE 9-5

Looking at
DHCP traffic

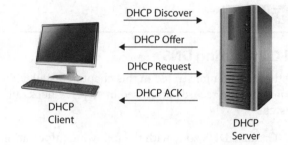

DHCP Overview

DHCP is an application-layer protocol that can automatically configure each system on the network with IP address information. You first install the DHCP service on a server and then configure a scope. A *scope* is the range of IP addresses that DHCP gives out on the network, as well as any additional settings like the router address (known as the default gateway), the DNS server, and how long the system is to have the IP address.

Figure 9-5 displays the four phases that a DHCP client goes through to obtain an IP address from the DHCP server. They are the following:

- **DHCP Discover**   The DHCP discover message is sent by a client to all systems on the network using the destination broadcast address (FF-FF-FF-FF-FF-FF). This message is basically saying, "If you are a DHCP server, I need an IP address." Note that all phases use this broadcast address for communication because the client does not have an IP address yet.

- **DHCP Offer**   Any DHCP servers on the network that receive the discover message will send an offer to the client basically stating, "I am a DHCP server and you can have this IP address."

- **DHCP Request**   The client sends out a DHCP request message stating which offer (IP address) it wishes to receive. Keep in mind that the client may receive many offers, so when the client sends out the DHCP request message confirming which offer it is taking, all other DHCP servers retract their offers.

- **DHCP Acknowledgment**   After the DHCP server receives the DHCP request message from the client requesting to have the IP address that was offered, the DHCP server then sends a final acknowledgment message indicating to the client that the address is theirs and how long they are to have the address (known as a lease time). The DHCP acknowledgment message also contains any additional IP address options for the client, such as the router address and the DNS server address.

w a t c h   **For the Network+ exam, know the four phases a client goes through to obtain an IP address.**

Configuring DHCP

In order to configure a DHCP server, you must first install the DHCP service similar to how you install the DNS server in Windows. The following outlines the steps to install the DHCP service on a Windows Server 2012.

1. Log on to 2012ServerA as administrator.
2. If Server Manager is not running, launch it by clicking the button in the task bar.
3. Choose Manage | Add Roles And Features.
4. On the Before You Begin page, choose Next.
5. Ensure Role-Based or Feature-Based Installation is selected and then choose Next.
6. Ensure 2012ServerA is selected and then choose Next.
7. From the Select Server Roles screen, choose DHCP Server (select the check box). You are prompted to add the DHCP Server Tools; choose Add Feature and then choose Next.
8. Choose Next three times and then choose Install.
9. Choose Close to finish the installation.

Configuring a Scope

Once you have installed DHCP, you are ready to create a DHCP scope, which is a range of addresses that the DHCP server is allowed to give out to the network. To create the DHCP scope:

1. From Server Manager, choose Tools | DHCP.
2. Once in the DHCP management console, expand your server, expand IPv4, right-click IPv4, and choose New Scope.
3. Choose Next in the New Scope Wizard.
4. Type **Chapter9 Scope** for the name of the scope, and leave the description blank. Choose Next.

5. Type **14.0.0.1** for the starting IP address and **14.0.0.20** for the ending address. Leave the subnet mask of 255.0.0.0, which is a length of 8 bits enabled in the subnet mask. Choose Next.

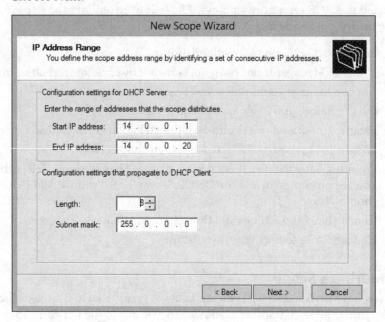

6. You are next asked if you want to exclude any addresses. The reason to exclude an address is you may have already statically assigned an address to a server or printer on the network and you do not want the DHCP server to give that address out. To exclude the first five addresses, type **14.0.0.1** and **14.0.0.5**, the starting and

ending addresses of the range, and then click the Add button to add the range to the
exclusion list.

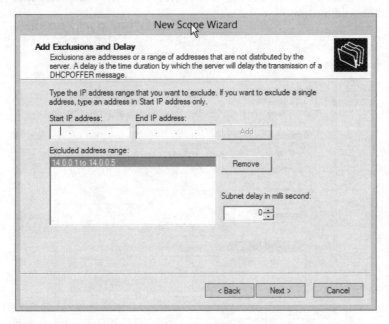

7. Choose Next.
8. You are then asked how long the client will lease an address from the DHCP server.
   Type **3 days** as the lease duration, and choose Next.
9. On the Configure DHCP Option dialog, choose No, I Will Configure These Options
   Later, and then choose Next.
10. Choose Finish to complete creating the DHCP scope.

Configuring Scope Options

When you configure your DHCP scope, you will most likely want the DHCP server to give
out more than just the IP address and subnet mask. You can configure DHCP scope options,
which allow you to specify additional settings such as the router address, DNS server, and
DNS domain name (also known as the DNS suffix), which all should be deployed to clients
along with the IP address. To configure these options:

1. Launch the DHCP management console.
2. Expand the server by clicking the arrow on the left side, expand IPv4, and then expand
   your newly created scope.
3. Select the Scope Options folder, and notice that no scope options are configured.

4. To configure the scope options, right-click Scope Options and choose Configure Options.

5. Select the 003 Router check box. Then type the IP address for your router and click the Add button.

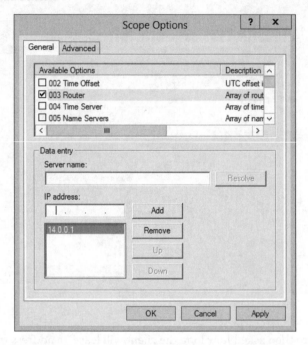

6. Select the 006 DNS Servers check box. Then type the IP address for your DNS server and click the Add button.

7. Select the 015 DNS Domain Name check box. Then type your domain name in the String Value field. Note that I am configuring the domain name to deploy certworld.loc.

8. Once you have finished, you will notice each of the DHCP scope options you configured on the right side of the screen.

Activating the Scope and Authorizing the Server

Once you have configured your scope options, you are ready to put the DHCP server in production. Before the DHCP server hands out addresses on your network, you must first activate the scope and authorize the server (for Windows DHCP servers). This helps prevent rogue DHCP servers from handing out addresses on the network. The following demonstrates how to activate the scope and authorize the server.

1. Launch the DHCP management console, if it is not already running.

2. To authorize your DHCP server, right-click the server and choose Authorize.

3. To activate the scope, right-click it and choose Activate.

Configuring Reservations

In environments that need more control over the allocation of IP addresses using DHCP, you can use a feature called DHCP reservations. Reservations are addresses configured in DHCP that are assigned to a specific Media Access Control (MAC) address and are only given out to the computer on the network that has that MAC address. The following steps can be used to configure a reservation in DHCP.

1. Launch the DHCP management console.
2. Expand the server by clicking the arrow on the left side, expand IPv4, and then expand your scope.
3. Right-click the Reservations folder found under the Scope, and choose New Reservation.
4. In the New Reservation dialog box, type the name of the system the reservation is for, the IP address you would like to reserve, and the MAC address of the system the address is reserved for.

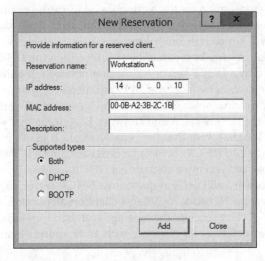

5. Choose Add to add the reservation and then choose Close.

EXERCISE 9-2

Installing and Configuring DHCP

Using the steps demonstrated in this chapter, install DHCP on a Windows Server 2012 system and configure a DHCP scope. Check out the video of the author performing these steps.

1. Install DHCP on the system.
2. Create a DHCP scope with the following information:
   - Name: Exer9-2 Scope
   - IP address range: 18.0.0.1 to 18.0.0.200
   - Subnet mask: 255.0.0.0
   - Exclusion: 18.0.0.1 to 18.0.0.5
3. Configure the scope options as follows:
   - DNS server: 18.0.0.1
   - Router: 18.0.0.1
   - DNS name: exer92.com
4. Be sure to activate the scope and then authorize your server if it has not already been done.

DHCP Relay and IP Helper

It is important to understand for the Network+ certification exam and for the real world the role of a DHCP relay on a network. Remember that DHCP messages are broadcast messages, which normally will not pass through a router. So the problem is if you have an enterprise made up of multiple networks separated by routers, then the DHCP clients on one network cannot be serviced by a DHCP server on another network. A quick solution is to configure a DHCP server on each network to assign IP addresses for that network. But you could also use a DHCP relay. For example, let's assume you have two networks separated by a single router—we'll call them Network A and Network B. Assume that you configure a DHCP server on Network A, but want the clients on Network B to use it as well (because you do not want to manage two DHCP servers). In order for the DHCP clients on Network B to reach the DHCP server, you must configure a DHCP relay on Network B. The DHCP relay is configured to forward all DHCP requests to a DHCP server, so you specify the IP address of the DHCP server on Network A. When a client on Network B sends out a DHCP discover message, the DHCP relay receives the message and then forwards it to the DHCP server that is configured. The DHCP server responds with an IP address to assign to the client.

The same feature can be configured on a Cisco router and is known as an IP Helper. To configure the IP Helper feature on a Cisco router to forward traffic to the DHCP server, you can use the following commands:

```
VAN-R1>Enable
VAN-R1#config term
VAN-R1(config)#interface FastEthernet0/0
VAN-R1(config-if)#ip helper-address global 10.0.0.1
VAN-R1(config-if)#exit
VAN-R1(config)#exit
```

Keep in mind that this will forward all User Datagram Protocol (UDP) traffic to the IP address of 10.0.0.1 and you only want to forward DHCP messages that use UDP 67 and 68. So you will need to disable all forwarding of non-DHCP messages by using the **no ip forward-protocol udp <port_number>** command, where the port number represents the port number of other UDP protocols such as TFTP (port 69) and DNS (port 53).

CERTIFICATION OBJECTIVE 9.03

Implementing NAT

Another common network service today is Network Address Translation (NAT). NAT is a network service that is running by default on your home routers and allows you to have multiple computers using private addresses on your local area network (LAN) and surf the Internet using the one public address. In this section you will learn about NAT and how to install a NAT server in Windows.

NAT Overview

NAT is a common network service that is supported by most wireless routers, home routers, enterprise-class routers, and most server operating systems such as Windows Server 2012/2008.

As mentioned earlier, the purpose of NAT is to translate the private address that is in the source address fields of the packet to a public address being used by the NAT device. There are two major reasons why NAT is an important technology today:

- **Sharing of a public IP address**   Instead of purchasing multiple public IP addresses so employees can surf the Internet, NAT allows you to have all users on the network surf the Internet with the one public IP address.
- **Hiding internal address scheme**   A security benefit of NAT is that you are hiding the internal addresses of your network because all packets sent out through the NAT device have the public address of the NAT device as the source address.

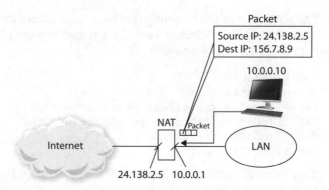

FIGURE 9-6

NAT rebuilds the header of a packet and replaces the source address with a public address.

This is how it works. When you configure the TCP/IP settings on the client, you configure their default gateway setting to point to the internal IP address of the NAT device. This means that all traffic sent by the client to the Internet will pass through the NAT device. Looking at Figure 9-6 you can see that when the NAT device receives the packet, it strips out the source IP address from the IP header of the packet and then replaces it with the public IP address used by the NAT device. Before the NAT device sends the packet on its way, it records the original source IP address and destination IP address in the NAT translation table so that when a reply comes back from the destination address, the NAT device can make the reverse translation and send the reply to the system on the internal network.

For the Network+ exam, know that NAT is responsible for translating the source IP address of an outbound packet to use the public IP address on the NAT device.

There are two major types of NAT that you should be familiar with for the Network+ certification exam: static NAT and NAT overloading.

Static NAT

With static NAT your company will use multiple public IP addresses, with each public IP address mapping to a single internal address, as shown in Figure 9-7. This is a common solution if you want to publish an internal server out to the Internet and allow Internet users to access the server.

The NAT device may have multiple public IP addresses assigned to a single network card, or it may have multiple network cards with each network card bound to a single IP address.

FIGURE 9-7

Static NAT has one public address per internal address.

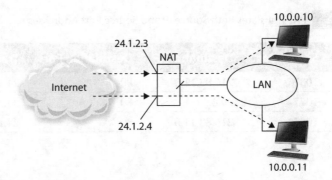

Remember that static NAT is useful when you need to allow clients on the Internet to access an internal server. NAT overloading is more common, but don't underestimate the usefulness of static NAT.

NAT Overloading

Most implementations of NAT use what is known as *NAT overloading,* which involves all internal systems accessing the Internet through the NAT device using a single public IP address. This is possible with a feature of NAT known as *Port Address Translation,* or *PAT.* With NAT overloading using PAT, the NAT device translates not only the source IP address to track the request, but also the source port address. PAT is used to ensure that when multiple users on the network connect to the same Internet resource, the NAT device knows which system to send the reply to (Figure 9-8).

Looking at Table 9-1 you can see what the NAT table would look like on the device. Notice that the source IP address and original source port address are recorded with each packet being sent. The NAT device also records the destination IP address and the destination port for the request. Finally, the NAT device strips out the source IP address

FIGURE 9-8

Looking at NAT overloading

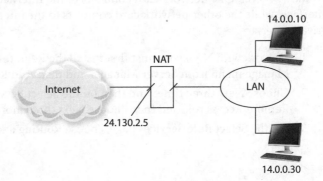

TABLE 9-1	PAT Translates Both Source IP and Source Port Addresses

Source IP	Source Port	Destination IP	Destination Port	Translated IP	Translated Port
14.0.0.10	1037	216.83.11.5	80	24.138.2.5	50001
14.0.0.25	1077	29.4.5.6	80	24.138.2.5	50002
14.0.0.30	1087	216.83.11.5	80	24.138.2.5	50003

and source port address from the packet header and replaces them with what we will call the translated IP address and translated port number. Notice that with NAT overloading, the translated IP address is the same for all outbound requests, so the only way the NAT device knows where to send the reply to when it comes back from the destination site is by looking at each message's translated port address. For example, when the NAT device receives a message from the 216.83.11.5 website with a destination port of 50003, it knows to rebuild the reply with 14.0.0.30 as the destination address and 1087 as the destination port (remember that reply messages have the source and destination fields reversed).

Configuring NAT

Now that you understand the types of NAT and the benefit of NAT as a network service, let's take a look at how to configure NAT on a Windows server and then a Cisco router. Keep in mind that the home routers and wireless routers you use also support NAT and have it enabled by default.

Configuring NAT on a Windows Server

The first step to configuring NAT on a Windows server is to have two network cards in the Windows server. One network card connects to the Internet and is known as the public interface, while the other network card connects to the internal LAN and is known as the private interface.

1. To work with NAT you must first install the Remote Access role by choosing the Manage menu from Server Manager and then Add Roles And Features.
2. Choose Next three times and then on the Select Server Roles page, choose the Remote Access role and then choose Next three more times.
3. On the Select Role Services page, choose Routing and then choose Next and Install.

4. To configure NAT on a Windows Server 2012 system, launch Routing And Remote Access (RRAS) from the Tools menu in Server Manager.

5. Once in RRAS, right-click your server and choose Configure And Enable Routing And Remote Access.

6. The RRAS Setup Wizard launches. Choose Next.

7. A number of different services can be configured with RRAS, including virtual private network (VPN), Remote Access Services (RAS), and a Windows router. Choose Network Address Translation (NAT) and then choose Next.

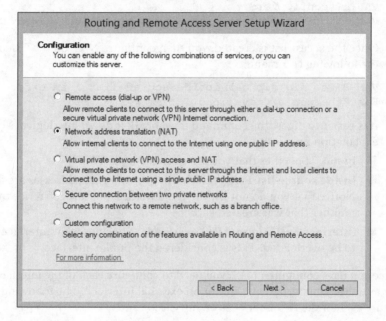

8. You are then asked which network interface will be used for the public interface of the NAT device; select the public interface and then choose Next. The public interface will typically be the interface that has Internet access. This interface will be overloaded.

9. All other interfaces will be considered private interfaces. Choose Finish to complete configuring NAT.

Once NAT has been configured, you can view the translation table on the NAT-enabled server. To view the translation table, make sure you are in the RRAS tool, expand IPv4, and then select General. Right-click the public interface and choose Show Address Translations.

Configuring NAT on a Cisco Router

Although you are not required to know how to configure NAT on a Cisco router for the Network+ certification exam, I wanted to show you the commands to do so and then review them with you.

1. The first step is to create an access list, which is a group of addresses that are to be permitted (in this case) to perform an action.

```
VAN-R1>enable
VAN-R1#config term
VAN-R1(config)#Access-list 1 permit 14.0.0.0 0.255.255.255
```

2. Once the access list is created, you then configure NAT on the Cisco router by typing the following command:

```
VAN-R1(config)#ip nat inside source list 1 interface
FastEthernet 0/0 overload
```

3. It is easier to digest the command if we break it down into logical sections for explanation purposes:

   ■ **ip nat** Specifies that you are configuring NAT.

   ■ **inside source list 1** Specifies what the internal addresses are for your network. Notice that you do not list the IP addresses, but just reference the access list number that was created earlier.

   ■ **interface FastEthernet 0/0 overload** Specifies what interface on the router is to be overloaded. This is considered the public interface.

Once you have configured NAT, you need to configure each of the interfaces on your Cisco router as either an internal interface or an external interface. The following commands configure each of the two interfaces on my Cisco router:

```
VAN-R1(config)#interface FastEthernet0/0
VAN-R1(config-if)#ip nat outside
VAN-R1(config-if)#interface FastEthernet0/1
VAN-R1(config-if)#ip nat inside
```

EXERCISE 9-3

Video

Configuring NAT on Windows Server

Using the steps demonstrated in this chapter, configure your Windows server for NAT using RRAS. To see the author performing these steps, check out the video.

1. Ensure you have two network cards installed in the system.

2. Assign one network card the address of 24.138.2.5.

3. Assign the other network card the address of 10.0.0.1.

4. Launch RRAS from the Administrative Tools menu and run the Configuration wizard as shown earlier to configure NAT on your system. Be sure to configure the network interface that is using 24.138.2.5 as the public interface.

Port Forwarding, Proxy Servers, and Unified Communications

The new Network+ certification exam has added exam objectives on port forwarding and proxy servers. In this section you will learn about port forwarding and proxy servers and what they offer as network features.

Port Forwarding

Port forwarding is the concept of configuring your router or firewall to forward specific packets to systems on the demilitarized zone (DMZ) or the internal network. The benefit of port forwarding is that you typically block packets from the Internet from entering into your network, but when you wish to host your own server, such as a web server or File Transfer Protocol (FTP) server that you can access from the Internet, then you need to configure the router/firewall to forward those specific packets to a specific system on your network while still blocking all other traffic.

When configuring port forwarding, you will do so using a port-forwarding rule, which allows you to specify which type of traffic you wish to forward by specifying characteristics such as the destination IP address and destination port of the packet. You then specify the IP address of where you want the router or firewall to forward the packet on to (see Figure 9-9).

Many products can have port forwarding enabled, with the most common example being the home router or wireless router that connects your home network to the Internet. If you check the configuration of the home router, you will notice a port-forwarding option that allows you to specify traffic that is forwarded into the network. Linux uses the Destination Network Address Translation (DNAT) feature of IPTables to implement port forwarding.

FIGURE 9-9

The role of port
forwarding

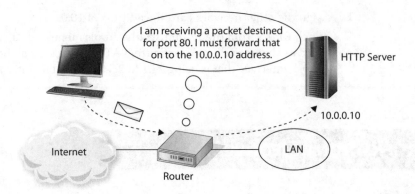

EXERCISE 9-4

Configuring Port Forwarding

In this exercise you will configure port forwarding on a wireless home router. It is important
to note that each router has the settings located in different places of the router configuration.
I am using a Linksys Smart Wi-Fi router for this exercise. To see a demonstration of port
forwarding, check out the video on this book's accompanying material.

1. Log on to your wireless router as administrator.
2. From the Router Settings menu on the left, choose Security.
3. Choose the Apps And Gaming tab and then the Single Port Forwarding link.
4. Choose Add A New Single Port Forwarding. Then fill in the rule as follows: the
   application name is **FTP Server**, the external and internal ports are **21**, the protocol
   is **TCP**, and the device IP address to forward the packet to is 192.168.**1**.**3**. Ensure the
   Enabled check box for the rule is set.

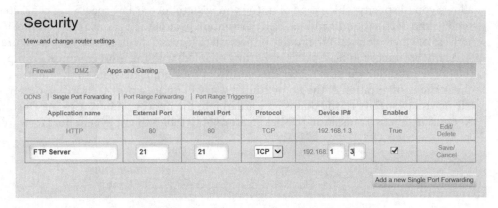

5. Choose OK.

Proxy Servers

Proxy servers have been around for many years; these are network devices that implement a number of network and security features. Proxy servers are configured as the default gateway for your clients so that all clients pass data destined to the Internet through the proxy server. The following are some benefits of proxy servers:

- **NAT**   Proxy servers implement NAT so that all requests coming from clients are translated to use the public IP address of the NAT device.
- **Authentication/authorization**   The proxy server can ensure that the user is authenticated to the network before being allowed to surf the Internet. Once the user is authenticated, the proxy server can allow or disallow users access to the Internet.
- **Restrict site**   The proxy server can be configured to restrict access to certain sites. For example, if the company does not want employees surfing facebook.com from work, then that site can be disabled by the proxy server.
- **Protocol rules**   The proxy server has rules that allow or disallow different Internet protocols. For example, you may be able to surf the Internet using Hypertext Transfer Protocol (HTTP), but the proxy server may block access to FTP as a protocol.
- **Content filters**   The proxy server can have content filters that block access to certain sites based on their content.
- **Caching**   The proxy server can cache webpages on its disk. This means that when a second employee requests a page, the page is returned from cache instead of retrieved from the Internet.
- **Reverse proxy**   Reverse proxy is a feature that allows an Internet user to send a request to one of your internal web servers, but the request goes to the proxy server, who then verifies the request and forwards it to the internal web server on behalf of the Internet user.

It is important to note that when the client sends the request for a webpage to the proxy server, the proxy server retrieves the page from the Internet for the user—in this example, the user is not accessing Internet resources, which helps protect the client from attack.

Unified Communications

Unified communications is a set of technologies that allows employees to communicate with one another in real time. Examples of technologies used for this real-time communication are

- **VoIP**   Unified communications integrates telephone systems into the solution by using Voice over IP (VoIP)—a protocol suite used to allow voice communication to run over an IP network.
- **Video**   Unified communications involves having users participate in video-conferencing sessions, which allows users to host meetings online and have voice and video capabilities with users at remote offices.

- **Desktop sharing**   Unified communications allows an employee to share their desktop with others so that others can view things like a presentation being shared by the employee as a meeting takes place.
- **Instant messaging**   Unified communications allows the usage of real-time chat to allow employees to text one another within a meeting session.

Real-Time Services

There are some other real-time services offered by unified communications solutions, such as presence information and the ability to multicast the communication. The following outlines these two services:

- **Presence**   Presence information provided by unified communications solutions allows users to see the availability of other users in real time. The benefit of this is that you are not trying to call someone who has their presence set to "Busy" or "Unavailable."
- **Multicast vs. unicast**   With unified communications, telephone systems using VoIP can use unicast communication (one-to-one communication) or multicast communication (one-to-many communication). It is important to properly configure the system for multicast where applicable, as you can conserve network bandwidth. For example, most VoIP communication is unicast, as there is one sender and one receiver, but a feature such as playing music while on hold should be using multicast communication, as that music is being sent to multiple phones at different times.

QoS

When implementing a unified communications solution, you should be concerned with the Quality of Service (QoS) of the VoIP traffic. QoS is ensuring that users are experiencing good performance with the technology—in this case, the phone systems and computer network that are using VoIP traffic. You would not want packets to be lost when a phone conversation is occurring and you are using the network to carry the voice communication in VoIP. QoS solutions can place priority on different types of traffic by using the following:

- **DSCP**   Differentiated Services Code Point (DSCP) is a field within the IPv4 and IPv6 header known as the DS field that is designed to identify the type of traffic that the IP packet is carrying. For example, it can be used to identify voice traffic or streaming audio so that QoS can be provided. DSCP does this by assigning traffic to a class (using the DS field) and then configuring devices to manage or prioritize that traffic based on its class.

■ **COS** Class of Service (CoS) is another method of providing QoS, but it is done at layer 2. This QoS technique uses a field known as the Priority Code Point (PCP) within the Ethernet frame to specify a priority value from 0 (lowest priority) to 7 (highest priority). This QoS technique is known as IEEE 802.1p and is part of the IEEE 802.1q standard.

Devices

A number of different devices can participate in a unified communications solution. The following are some of those key devices:

■ **UC servers** The unified communication server is the component that provides all the UC features, such as voice features, document sharing, meeting rooms, presence information, and video and audio conferencing. An example of a UC server is Microsoft's Lync Server.

■ **UC devices** Unified communication devices are devices such as VoIP phones and devices running soft phones (software running on a system that emulates a phone). Users can use mobile devices such as smart phones running the UC client software to participate in conference calls.

■ **UC gateways** Unified communication gateways are components that allow you to extend the unified communications feature to external environments. For example, to integrate with the existing phone system, a private branch exchange (PBX) gateway is required.

CERTIFICATION SUMMARY

In this chapter you learned about core network services such as DNS, DHCP, and NAT. You learned the theory behind each of the services and learned how to install and configure each service.

TWO-MINUTE DRILL

Understanding DNS

❑ DNS is used to resolve FQDNs to IP addresses.

❑ There are two main types of DNS servers: a primary DNS server and a secondary DNS server. You create the DNS records on the primary server while a copy is sent to a secondary server.

❑ A host record is known as an A record for IPv4, but is known as an AAAA record for IPv6.

❑ Be familiar with the other DNS records, such as NS, CNAME, and MX.

Deploying DHCP

❑ DHCP is a protocol used to automatically configure systems on the network with IP configuration.

❑ When configuring the DHCP server, you must configure a scope, which is a range of addresses that the server will hand out. The DHCP scope must also be activated.

❑ You can configure scope options, which are additional settings outside the IP address that the DHCP server should give out. For example, you should configure the scope to hand out the address of the router as well.

Implementing NAT

❑ NAT is a network service used to share a single IP address with the rest of the network so that all internal systems can gain Internet access with the one public IP address.

❑ There are two types of NAT: static NAT and NAT overloading. Static NAT is when one public address is mapped to one internal address, while NAT overloading maps all internal addresses to the one public address.

❑ You can configure NAT on a Windows server through Routing and Remote Access.

Port Forwarding, Proxy Servers, and Unified Communications

❑ Port forwarding allows you to publish servers out to the Internet while minimizing the traffic that can reach the server.

❑ Port forwarding is configured using rules on a router or firewall.

❑ Proxy servers are devices that can request resources such as webpages on behalf of the client.

❑ Unified communications is a set of technologies that allows employees to communicate with one another in real time, combining voice, video conferencing, presence, and real-time chat.

SELF TEST

The following questions will help you measure your understanding of the material presented in this chapter. Read all the choices carefully because there might be more than one correct answer. Choose all correct answers for each question.

Understanding DNS

1. Your manager is concerned that if your existing DNS server fails, your company's fully qualified DNS names will not be resolvable. What should you do?
   A. Create a primary zone.
   B. Create a secondary zone.
   C. Create a host record.
   D. Create an MX record.

2. Which of the following DNS record types resolves to an IPv6 address?
   A. A
   B. MX
   C. CNAME
   D. AAAA

3. You would like to ensure that if anyone sends an e-mail message to employees at the gleneclarke.com domain, it is sent to mail.gleneclarke.com. What type of DNS record should you create?
   A. MX
   B. CNAME
   C. A
   D. AAAA

Deploying DHCP

4. You have installed DHCP on your Windows server and authorized the server. You have created a DHCP scope on the server, but systems on the network are not receiving addresses from your DHCP server. What should you do?
   A. Delete and re-create the scope.
   B. Unauthorize the server.
   C. Authorize the server.
   D. Activate the scope.

5. You wish to configure your DHCP server to assign the address of the router as the default gateway when assigning an IP address to clients. What should you do?
   A. Create an A record.
   B. Create an AAAA record.
   C. Configure the scope options.
   D. Activate the scope.

6. DHCP communication is a four-phase process. What is the term associated with the first DHCP message?
   A. DHCP ACK
   B. DHCP Discover
   C. DHCP Request
   D. DHCP Offer

Implementing NAT

7. What type of NAT allows a number of internal systems to use the same public IP address?
   A. Static NAT
   B. SNAT
   C. TNAT
   D. NAT overloading

8. What mechanism does NAT use to allow multiple systems on the network to use the same public IP address when connecting to the Internet?
   A. SNAT
   B. PAT
   C. TNAT
   D. JNAT

9. What type of NAT involves having a single public IP address mapped to a single private address?
   A. Static NAT
   B. PAT
   C. TNAT
   D. NAT overloading

Port Forwarding, Proxy Servers, and Unified Communications

10. Using the following exhibit, which type of traffic is not allowed to enter the network?

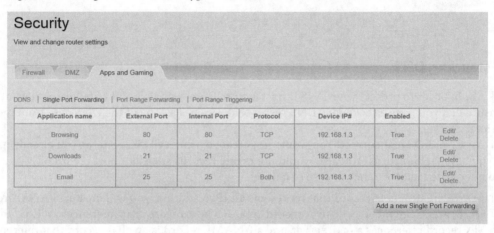

Application name	External Port	Internal Port	Protocol	Device IP#	Enabled	
Browsing	80	80	TCP	192.168.1.3	True	Edit/Delete
Downloads	21	21	TCP	192.168.1.3	True	Edit/Delete
Email	25	25	Both	192.168.1.3	True	Edit/Delete

A. SMTP
B. Telnet
C. FTP
D. HTTP

Performance-Based Question Review: See the performance-based question sample from the author included with the accompanying media.

SELF TEST ANSWERS

Understanding DNS

1. ☑ **B.** In order to protect your DNS infrastructure from a single point of failure, you want to ensure that you have a secondary DNS server that receives a copy of the DNS data from the primary server.
    ☒ **A, C,** and **D** are incorrect. You would not create a primary DNS zone, as you already have one if you have DNS records. You also would not create records such as a host record or MX, as they do not create fault tolerance in case of failure.

2. ☑ **D.** To create a host record that represents an IPv6 address, you will create an AAAA record.
    ☒ **A, B,** and **C** are incorrect. An A record creates a host record that references an IPv4 address, an MX record references a mail server, and a CNAME record is an alias record that references another host record.

3. ☑ **A.** An MX record is a mail exchange record that is used to reference the mail server for a given domain.
    ☒ **B, C,** and **D** are incorrect. A CNAME record is an alias record that references another host record. An A record creates a host record that references an IPv4 address, and an AAAA is a host record that references an IPv6 address.

Deploying DHCP

4. ☑ **D.** Once you create the DHCP scope, you need to ensure you activate the scope.
    ☒ **A, B,** and **C** are incorrect. There would be no need to delete and re-create the DHCP scope or unauthorize the server. You would not need to authorize the server, as the question states that has already been done.

5. ☑ **C.** In order to have the DHCP server give out the address of the router as well, you would configure the scope options.
    ☒ **A, B,** and **D** are incorrect. A and B are incorrect, as they are DNS record types and have nothing to do with DHCP. D is incorrect because activating the scope will not help if you have not configured the scope options.

6. ☑ **B.** The first DHCP message sent by a DHCP client is the DHCP discover message.
    ☒ **A, C,** and **D** are incorrect, as they do not represent the first DHCP message.

Implementing NAT

7. ☑   **D.** NAT overloading allows a number of internal systems to surf the Internet using the one public address on the NAT device.
☒   **A, B,** and **C** are incorrect. Static NAT, or SNAT, maps a single public address to a single private address. There is no such thing as TNAT.

8. ☑   **B.** Port Address Translation is the mechanism used by NAT overloading to allow multiple internal systems to surf the Internet through the one public address.
☒   **A, C,** and **D** are incorrect, as they are not used by NAT overloading.

9. ☑   **A.** Static NAT is when a single public IP address is mapped to a single private address.
☒   **B, C,** and **D** are incorrect. NAT overloading allows a single public address to be used by multiple internal systems, and PAT is the method that NAT overloading uses to allow the use of the one public address.

Port Forwarding, Proxy Servers, and Unified Communications

10. ☑   **B.** Telnet uses port 23 and is the only port not listed in the port-forwarding rules, so it will be blocked from entering the network.
☒   **A, C,** and **D** are incorrect because the three port-forwarding rules shown in the exhibit will allow HTTP (port 80), SMTP (port 25), and FTP (port 21) traffic to enter the network.

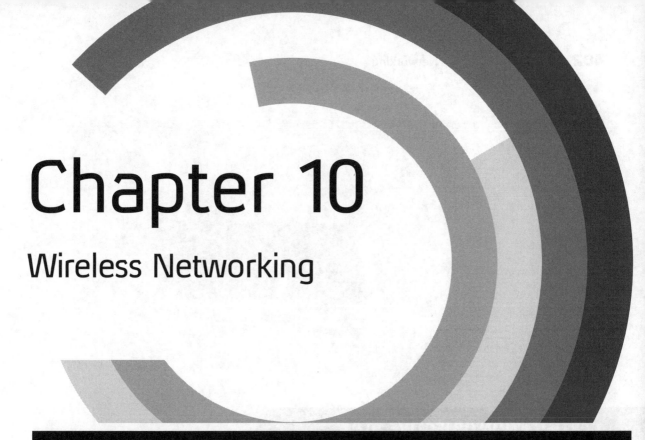

Chapter 10

Wireless Networking

Today's networks are no longer limited to using cabled, or wired, devices. Today's networks have a mix of wired systems along with wireless systems that use radio frequencies to send data to a wireless access point (as shown in Figure 10-1). The wireless access point may have a connection to the wired network, allowing the wireless devices to communicate with the entire network.

This chapter introduces you to the world of wireless networks! It is a very popular topic to know for the Network+ certification exam, so be sure to study this well. This chapter will introduce you to wireless basics, show you how to set up the wireless network, and then discuss some security concerns around wireless.

FIGURE 10-1

A wireless router acts as a wireless access point.

CERTIFICATION OBJECTIVE 10.01

Wireless Basics

As mentioned, the wireless network uses radio frequencies to transmit data through the air. This means that if you have a laptop user who wishes to be mobile within the office, you can allow her to access the network through a wireless access point as long as she has a wireless network card in her laptop.

Wireless Concepts

The typical wireless network environment involves using a *wireless access point (WAP)* that has antennas connected to it in order to transmit the radio signal through the air. The new Network+ exam expects you to understand the different types of wireless antennas that are used by wireless technologies. The different types of wireless antennas include

- **Omni-directional** An omni-directional antenna sends the radio signals in all directions to cover a broad range or area in all directions of the antenna.
- **Semi-directional** A semi-directional antenna sends radio signals in a single direction, but the signal has a wide range of coverage in that direction. You can compare this to a streetlight that shines downward but covers a wide area in that direction. An example of a semi-directional antenna is a hallway wireless antenna in a facility.

- **Highly directional**   A highly directional antenna, also known as unidirectional, sends radio signals in a single direction covering a very small area. Back to the light analogy, you can compare this to the way that a spotlight covers a small area when the light shines. An example of a highly directional antenna is a building-to-building antenna that is placed on the top of the buildings.

There are a few common practices that help control connections to your wireless network. Note the following as methods of helping to secure your wireless network by manipulating characteristics of the antenna:

- **WAP/antenna placement**   The first thing you want to do to help control who is connecting to your wireless network is place the wireless access point (and its antennas) in the center of the building. If you place the access point close to the outer wall of the building, it is possible that someone outside the building could connect to the wireless network.
- **Power levels**   You can also change the power levels on the access point to control how strong the signal is. The goal here is to lower the power levels so that the range of the signal does not go beyond the building walls.

Note that in order to connect your wireless clients to a wireless network, you need to have a WAP. The wireless access point has antennas that send and receive the wireless signal between the wireless client and access point, but the access point also has a connection to the wired network so that wireless clients can access resources on the wired network. Note that most home users have a wireless router, which performs the function of an access point, but also includes other features such as Network Address Translation (NAT), a network firewall, and Dynamic Host Configuration Protocol (DHCP) services. Although most IT folks interchange the two terms, they are technically different devices.

Wireless Network Types

There are two major types of wireless networks you can create: ad hoc mode or infrastructure mode. Each of these is known as a wireless mode, and each has its advantages.

With *ad hoc mode*, the wireless device, such as a laptop, is connected to other wireless devices in a peer-to-peer environment without the need for a wireless access point. With *infrastructure mode*, the wireless clients are connected to a central device, also known as a wireless access point. The wireless client sends data to the access point, which then sends the data on to the destination (as shown in Figure 10-2). As mentioned previously, the wireless client can access network resources on the wired network once connected to the access point because the access point has a connection to the wired network.

FIGURE 10-2

A typical wireless network running in infrastructure mode

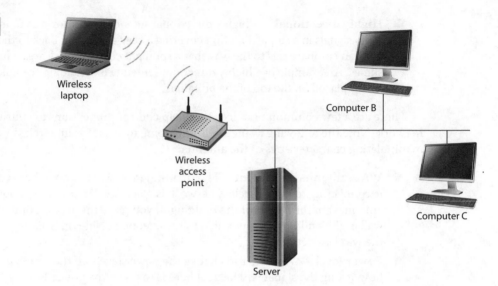

Wireless laptop

Wireless access point

Computer B

Computer C

Server

The advantage of ad hoc mode is that you don't need to purchase the access point; the benefit of infrastructure mode is that when you use the wireless access point, you get to control who can connect to the wireless network and filter out types of network traffic. For example, if you use a wireless access point to allow wireless clients to connect to the Internet, you can control which websites the users can connect to. This type of centralized control makes infrastructure mode extremely popular.

I mentioned that ad hoc and infrastructure mode were the two major types of wireless networks, known as topologies, but a third wireless topology you should be familiar with is a mesh topology. A *mesh topology*, also known as a *wireless mesh network (WMN)*, is made up of wireless clients connecting to wireless routers, which are all connected to one another in a mesh topology (each router has a connection to each other router) in order to create fault tolerance in the network.

Wireless Standards

The Institute of Electrical and Electronics Engineers (IEEE) committee has developed wireless standards in the 802 project models for wireless networking. Wireless is defined by the 802.11 project model and has several standards defined.

802.11a

The 802.11a wireless standard is an older one that runs at the 5 GHz frequency. 802.11a devices can transmit data at 54 Mbps and are incompatible with 802.11b and 802.11g devices.

For the exam, remember that 802.11a was an early wireless standard that ran at a different frequency than 80211.b and 802.11g. This makes it incompatible with 802.11b/g. Remember that 802.11a defines wireless environments running at 54 Mbps while using a frequency of 5 GHz.

Note that 802.11b runs at 11 Mbps, and 802.11g runs at 54 Mbps. The 802.11n standard is designed to reach up to 600 Mbps!

Wireless networks today are called Wi-Fi, which stands for *wireless fidelity*. 802.11b, 802.11g, and 802.11n are all part of the Wi-Fi standard and, as a result, are compatible with one another.

802.11b

The 802.11b wireless standard has a transfer rate of 11 Mbps while using a frequency of 2.4 GHz. These devices are compatible with 802.11g/n devices because they run at the same frequency and follow the Wi-Fi standard.

802.11g

The 802.11g wireless standard is a newer one that was designed to be compatible with 802.11b, but also increases the transfer rate. The transfer rate of 802.11g devices is 54 Mbps using a frequency of 2.4 GHz.

All 802.11g devices are compatible with 802.11b/n devices because they all follow the Wi-Fi standard and run at the same frequency of 2.4 GHz.

802.11n

The 802.11n wireless standard is a new standard that came out in late 2009. The goal of 802.11n is to increase the transfer rate beyond what current standards such as 802.11g support. 802.11n supports transfer rates up to 600 Mbps!

To help accomplish this, 802.11n uses two new features: multiple input multiple output (MIMO) and channel bonding. *MIMO* uses multiple antennas to achieve more throughput than can be accomplished with only a single antenna. *Channel bonding* allows 802.11n to transmit data over two nonoverlapping channels to achieve more throughput. 802.11n is designed to be backward compatible with 802.11a, 802.11b, and 802.11g and can run at the 2.4 GHz or 5 GHz frequency.

Table 10-1 summarizes key points you need to be familiar with about the different wireless standards for the Network+ certification exam.

It is important to note that 802.11a was an early implementation of wireless networking and is not compatible with early Wi-Fi networks such as 802.11b and 802.11g. As an example of the compatibility, my wireless network at my home has an access point that is an 802.11g device, but one of my old laptops has an 802.11b wireless network card. I am

TABLE 10-1		802.11a	802.11b	802.11g	802.11n
	Frequency	5 GHz	2.4 GHz	2.4 GHz	5/2.4 GHz
Comparing the	Transfer Rate	54 Mbps	11 Mbps	54 Mbps	Up to 600 Mbps
Different Wireless	Range	150 feet	300 feet	300 feet	300 feet
Standards	Compatibility	802.11a	802.11b/g/n	802.11b/g/n	802.11a/b/g

watch Wireless transmission speeds decrease as your distance from the wireless access point increases.

still able to have my old laptop communicate on the network because the two standards are 100 percent compatible with one another. In this example, the laptop with the 802.11b card only connects at 11 Mbps, while my new laptop with the 802.11g card is connecting at 54 Mbps.

802.11ac

The 802.11ac wireless standard was approved in 2014 and is considered a high-throughput wireless standard that runs on the 5 GHz frequency range. The 802.11ac standard offers throughput of potentially 1 Gbps by increasing the channel width and offering similar features to the 802.11n standard such as MIMO and *multi-user MIMO (MUMIMO),* which involves allowing multiple transmitters to send separate signals and multiple receivers to receive separate signals at the same time.

Most 802.11ac wireless routers have a universal serial bus (USB) 3.0 port that allows you to connect an external hard drive to the wireless router and stream high-definition video to clients.

Channels

It was stated that 802.11b/g/n all run at the 2.4 GHz frequency, but it is important to understand that 2.4 GHz is a frequency range. Each frequency in the range is known as a *channel*. Note that this discussion focuses on the 2.4 GHz frequency. The 5 GHz frequency also uses channels, but because they are not overlapping channels, they are not discussed as much.

Most wireless devices allow you to specify which channel you would like to use. The reason this is important is that if you find you are having trouble with your wireless network failing a lot, it could be that the wireless devices are conflicting or interfering with other wireless devices in your area. A good example of this is cordless phones; they can run at the

To avoid interference on the wireless network from other household items, try to purchase items like cordless phones that run on a different frequency than 2.4 GHz. If you are experiencing problems on the wireless network, you could try changing the channel on the wireless equipment and see if a different channel is more reliable. Also note there are other non-wireless devices such as a microwave that can cause interference by generating noise signals in the 2.4 GHz frequency range.

2.4 GHz range as well and could cause issues with your wireless network. As a solution, you could change the channel on your wireless access point and clients, which changes the frequency—hopefully preventing any conflicts with other household items!

Table 10-2 lists the different frequencies used by the different channels.

Remember when troubleshooting wireless networks that you could be getting interference from other wireless devices and household devices such as cordless phones or Bluetooth devices running on the same channel. To resolve this, experiment by changing the channel your wireless network uses to reduce the amount of interference received. As noted in Table 10-2, adjacent channels have overlapping frequencies and will interfere with one another, so changing from channel 2 to channel 1 will not solve interference problems, but changing from channel 2 to channel 6 might.

TABLE 10-2	Channel	Frequency Range
	1	2.3995 GHz–2.4245 GHz
Different Wi-Fi Channels and Their Operating Frequency Ranges	2	2.4045 GHz–2.4295 GHz
	3	2.4095 GHz–2.4345 GHz
	4	2.4145 GHz–2.4395 GHz
	5	2.4195 GHz–2.4445 GHz
	6	2.4245 GHz–2.4495 GHz
	7	2.4295 GHz–2.4545 GHz
	8	2.4345 GHz–2.4595 GHz
	9	2.4395 GHz–2.4645 GHz
	10	2.4445 GHz–2.4695 GHz
	11	2.4495 GHz–2.4745 GHz
	12	2.4545 GHz–2.4795 GHz
	13	2.4595 GHz–2.4845 GHz

Authentication and Encryption

A number of wireless authentication and encryption protocols have been developed over the years. The purpose of these protocols is to help secure your wireless network, and you should consider them for implementation on your wireless network.

WEP

Wired Equivalent Privacy (WEP) was designed to give the wireless world a level of security that could equate to what the wired networking world has. In the wired world, someone would have to be in your office to connect a cable to your network, but with wireless networking, this is not the case. Someone could sit outside your building in a parked car and connect to your wireless network.

To configure your wireless network with WEP, you simply specify a shared key, or passphrase, on the wireless access point. The theory is that if anyone wants to connect to your wireless network, they need to know the shared key and need to configure their workstation with that key.

When you configure the shared key on the access point and client, any data sent between the client and the access point is encrypted with WEP. This will prevent unauthorized individuals from capturing data in transit and reading it.

It is important to understand that there were huge flaws in how WEP implemented its encryption and key usage, and as a result, both 64-bit and 128-bit WEP are easily cracked. For security reasons, you should not use WEP unless you have older access points that do not support WPA or WPA2.

WPA

Wi-Fi Protected Access (WPA) was designed to improve upon wireless security and fix some of the flaws found in WEP. WPA uses a 128-bit key and the *Temporal Key Integrity Protocol (TKIP)*, which is a protocol that is used to change the encryption keys for every packet that is sent. This will make it much harder for hackers to crack the key, which is very easy to do with WEP.

WPA has a number of other improvements over WEP; for example, it has improved integrity checking and it supports authentication using the *Extensible Authentication Protocol (EAP)*, a very secure authentication protocol.

WPA operates in two different modes: WPA-Personal and WPA-Enterprise:

■ **WPA-Personal**   WPA-Personal is also known as WPA-PSK, which means WPA preshared key. With WPA-Personal you will configure the access point with a starting key value, known as the preshared key, which is then used to encrypt the traffic. This mode is used most by home users and small businesses.

- **WPA-Enterprise**   WPA-Enterprise, also known as WPA-802.1x, is a WPA implementation that uses a central authentication server such as a Remote Authentication Dial-In User Service (RADIUS) server for authentication and auditing features. WPA-Enterprise is used by larger companies so that they can use their existing authentication server to control who has access to the wireless network and to log network access.

WPA2

WPA2 improves upon the security of WPA and should be used instead of WPA if you have the choice. WPA2 uses *Counter Mode with Cipher Block Chaining Message Authentication Code Protocol (CCMP or CCM Mode Protocol)* for data privacy, integrity, and authentication on a WPA2 wireless network. WPA2 uses CCMP with the *Advanced Encryption Standard (AES)* protocol for the encryption of wireless traffic instead of TKIP and supports additional features, such as added protection for ad hoc networks and key caching.

Because WPA2 uses AES as its encryption protocol, it supports 128-bit, 192-bit, and 256-bit encryption.

WPA2 also supports the *Transport Layer Security (TLS)* and the *Tunneled Transport Layer Security (TTLS)* protocols through the use of the Extensible Authentication Protocol (EAP). Known as EAP-TLS and EAP-TTLS, these protocols offer secure methods of performing authentication on a wireless network.

e x a m

ⓦ a t c h   **Be sure to be familiar with the different wireless authentication and encryption protocols for the Network+ exam.**

CERTIFICATION OBJECTIVE 10.02

Securing Wireless

Years ago when I purchased my first wireless router, I knew nothing about wireless and was concerned that I would not be able to set up the wireless network. Well, my concerns were quickly dismissed when I took the wireless router (access point) out of the box and gave it power. My laptop connected almost immediately! I was amazed at how easy it was to connect to the wireless network—there was *no* configuration required. Then it dawned on me—if my laptop connected with no configuration, what is stopping the rest of the world from connecting to my wireless network? The answer, of course, is that nothing is stopping someone from sitting outside my yard and connecting to my wireless network. I needed to figure out how to stop unauthorized access to my wireless access point.

Security Best Practices

There are a number of different techniques that you can use to prevent unauthorized persons from connecting to your wireless network. You may want to implement some or all of these features. To help secure your wireless infrastructure, you should consider changing settings on the router, such as the admin password, the Service Set Identifier (SSID), and Media Access Control (MAC) filtering, to name a few. The following are some basic best practices that you should follow to secure your wireless router. You can see the steps to configure these features in the later section "Implementing a Wireless Network."

Change the Admin Password

The first thing you should do when you take the wireless router out of the box and plug it in is change the admin password. The admin password is needed to connect to the web administration pages and change the settings of the router. All routers have a default admin password, so you want to be sure to change the password from the default.

Figure 10-3 displays how to change the admin password on a D-Link router by going to the Tools link at the top and then choosing the Admin link on the left.

FIGURE 10-3   Changing the admin password on a D-Link router

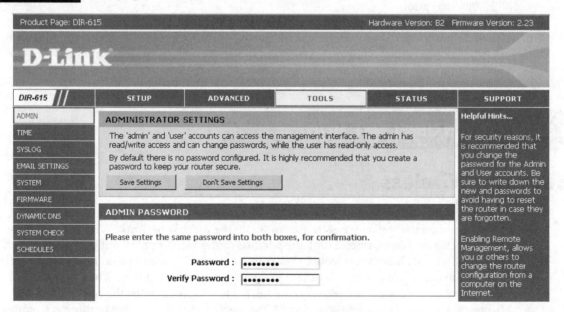

Service Set Identifier

The *Service Set Identifier (SSID)* is a name that you give the wireless network, and in order for someone to connect to your wireless network, that person needs to know the SSID. When a client connects to the wireless network, they will need to specify the SSID, either in their wireless network card settings or when prompted by the operating system. It is important that you change the SSID from the default so that anyone wishing to connect to your wireless network needs to know the name, or SSID.

The problem is that wireless routers are configured to advertise this SSID automatically, so even if you change the SSID to something hard to guess, the router advertises the name. This means an individual can connect to your network by name without really knowing the name of the network because the router is advertising it. Proof of this is shown when you choose the option in Windows XP or Windows 7 to connect to a network and a dialog box displays (shown in Figure 10-4), showing you all the wireless networks close to you.

To fix this, you should disable SSID broadcasting. In order to disable SSID broadcasting, you should see a setting in the router configuration to not advertise the SSID. This will prevent Windows users from displaying a list of wireless networks and having your network display in the list. Figure 10-5 displays how to disable SSID broadcasting on a D-Link wireless router (set the Visibility Status to Invisible). Most routers have this as a setting

FIGURE 10-4

Displaying wireless networks close to you. Notice the D-Link network.

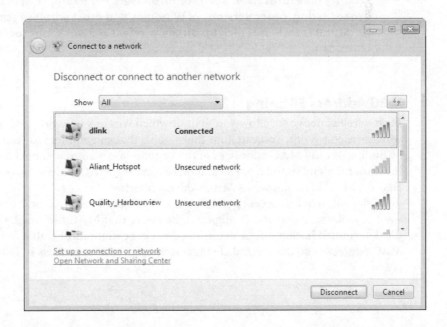

Disabling SSID
broadcasting on a
D-Link router

WIRELESS NETWORK SETTINGS

Enable Wireless :	☑ Always ▾ [Add New]
Wireless Network Name :	dlink (Also called the SSID)
802.11 Mode :	Mixed 802.11n, 802.11g and 802.11b ▾
Enable Auto Channel Scan :	☑
Wireless Channel :	2.437 GHz - CH 6 ▾
Transmission Rate :	Best (automatic) ▾ (Mbit/s)
Channel Width :	20 MHz ▾
Visibility Status :	⊙ Visible ○ Invisible

called "Disable SSID Broadcasting." When viewing wireless networks to connect to, newer operating systems such as Windows 7 will display nonbroadcasting SSIDs labeled as "Other Network." In order to connect to the wireless network with SSID broadcasting disabled with Windows 7, choose the Other Network option and then enter the SSID for the wireless network. If the wireless network is configured for encryption, you will be prompted for the encryption key in order to complete the connection.

So to summarize the SSID issue, be sure to change the SSID to something hard to guess (don't use your company name if you are setting up the wireless network for the company), and be sure to disable SSID broadcasting on the router.

on the job

Although this chapter is giving you a number of best practices to make it harder for someone to compromise your wireless network, know that most of the security measures have been compromised. For example, when you disable SSID broadcasting, older versions of Windows and most wireless scanners such as NetStumbler will not pick up on the wireless network, but tools such as Kismet in Linux can.

MAC Address Filtering

Most wireless networks allow you to limit which wireless network cards can connect to the wireless access point. You can limit the systems that can connect to your wireless network by finding out the MAC addresses of the systems you want to connect and then configuring the router to deny traffic from all systems except the MAC addresses you input (see Figure 10-6). This is known as MAC address filtering.

By default, wireless access points are not configured for MAC address filtering, so you want to make sure that you configure it. Be aware that MAC filtering by itself will not keep the determined hacker out. A determined hacker can monitor traffic in the air, see the MAC address of an authorized client, and then spoof that address so that the hacker's traffic is allowed.

FIGURE 10-6   Configuring MAC filtering

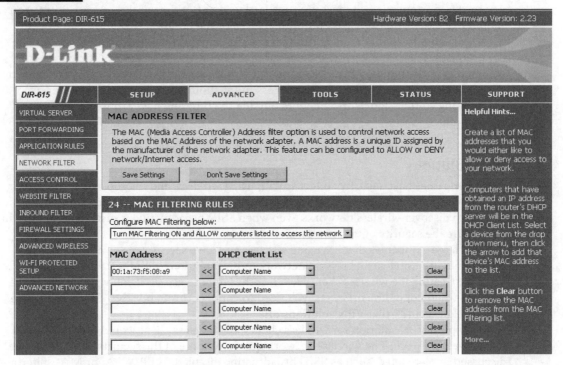

Encrypt Wireless Traffic

You want to ensure that you are encrypting any traffic from the wireless clients to the access point. You can use WEP, WPA, or WPA2 to encrypt traffic. Remember to use the more secure WPA or WPA2 if you can. To stress the importance of implementing some level of encryption, let's review WEP.

WEP is a feature used to encrypt content between the wireless client and the access point. When configuring WEP, you must configure the wireless access point with an encryption key and then make sure that each wireless client is using the same key. Be aware that WEP encryption has been cracked with products such as AirSnort, so if your devices support WPA or WPA2, use one of those encryption methods. Always use the largest encryption cipher strength your wireless access point and wireless cards support (for example, 128 bit versus 64 bit).

The other point to make about using WEP or WPA is that not only does it encrypt your traffic, but anyone who wishes to connect to your wireless network must know the key and input it into their wireless card configuration. This helps ensure that people not authorized to use the wireless network cannot connect to it.

Antenna Placement and Power Levels

Another important security best practice is placement of the wireless access point. You should place the wireless access point in an area of the building that allows all of your wireless clients to connect but minimizes the exposure of the wireless network outside the premises. For example, you should not place the wireless access point close to the outer walls of the building because it may allow someone outside the facility to connect to the wireless network. The wireless access point should be placed in the center of the building so that signals from clients outside the building have trouble reaching the access point.

VPN Solutions

Most companies have security concerns with using wireless, and for good reason. Hackers can bypass the MAC filtering, they can crack the WEP key, and they can use tools such as Kismet to discover wireless networks even when SSID broadcasting is disabled—so how do you ensure the security of the wireless network?

Most large companies that are using wireless and have security needs of the utmost importance are using virtual private network (VPN) solutions with their wireless clients. They are treating the wireless client like any other remote user—"if you want access to the network when not on the premises, you need to connect through VPN." This is due to the high level of security that VPN solutions offer.

In a typical VPN solution for wireless clients, the wireless client would first connect to the wireless network. The wireless network may have some of the security precautions we discussed implemented, such as SSID broadcasting disabled, WEP/WPA, or MAC filtering. After connecting to the wireless network and getting an IP address, the wireless client will then create a VPN into the network with the VPN software. The software will authenticate the user and create an encrypted tunnel to secure data transmission from the client to the corporate network.

on the **job**

If securing wireless access is a concern in your organization, look to using a VPN solution.

Threats Against Wireless

The Network+ certification exam expects you to understand some of the different threats that exist against wireless networks. In order to protect yourself from some of these threats, you want to ensure that you are following the wireless security best practices discussed in this chapter. Some of the wireless threats to be familiar with are war driving, war chalking, WEP/WPA cracking, evil twin, and rogue access points.

Data Emanation, Interference, and Packet Sniffing

Because wireless network traffic is traveling through the air, it is susceptible to interference and packet sniffing. The following are considerations with regard to wireless vulnerabilities:

- **Data emanation**   Electronic components always release emissions, and someone could collect emissions from electrical components and piece them together into readable data.
- **Interference**   As mentioned earlier, you could experience interference on the wireless network from components such as cordless phones. This is a security issue because interference can make the wireless network go down, resulting in the network becoming unavailable.
- **Packet sniffing**   Anyone with a wireless network card and a sniffer can easily capture wireless data. Be sure to encrypt all wireless communication to protect confidential data.

War Driving

A common vulnerability with wireless networks is war driving. *War driving* is when someone drives around with a laptop and tries to locate wireless networks that they can connect to. It is critical that you place wireless access points in the middle of the building and control the power levels so that the signal cannot be reached from outside the building. Also, to help prevent an untrusted party from connecting to the wireless network, implement security features such as WPA2 encryption, MAC filtering, changing the SSID, and disabling SSID broadcasting.

War Chalking

Another term you should know that is associated with war driving is *war chalking.* With war chalking, when someone discovers a wireless network, they chalk a symbol outside the building notifying the rest of the war-driving community that a wireless network is inside. With war chalking, different symbols represent the configuration of the wireless network that was discovered. For example, Figure 10-7 displays three different symbols: an open network, which allows anyone to connect; a closed network with the SSID; and a secure network using WEP. With each symbol, the hacker puts the SSID above the symbol and the bandwidth below it.

WPA/WEP/WPS Cracking

Wireless networks that use a weak encryption method such as WEP, or even a weak encryption key, are also vulnerable. WEP, WPA, and WPA2 have been cracked, but WEP encryption can be cracked in minutes due to the repeating 24-bit IV found in the header of the wireless packet.

FIGURE 10-7 War-chalking symbols

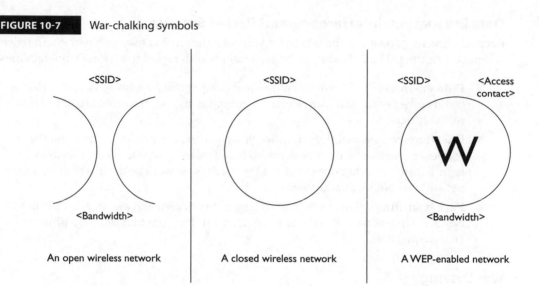

An open wireless network   A closed wireless network   A WEP-enabled network

Because it is possible for the hacker to crack the encryption key if he or she captures enough traffic, it is critical that you limit the range of your wireless network by lowering the power levels on the access point. Figure 10-8 displays a screenshot of me cracking 128-bit WEP encryption. Notice that the key has been cracked and it is ethicalhackme!

Wi-Fi- Protected Setup (WPS) is a wireless security feature that involves using a personal identification number (PIN) to access the wireless router. WPS was developed as a method to allow users with little knowledge of wireless security to easily configure a

FIGURE 10-8

Cracking WEP

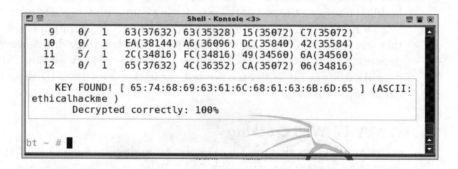

router and connect clients to the wireless router. The wireless router would have a PIN number on the router that would need to be entered by the client in order to access the wireless network.

It has been found that a malicious hacker can figure out the WPS PIN within a few hours using a brute-force attack where the hacker uses a program to automate and attempt every possible PIN number.

Hackers use a number of different methods to crack wireless protocols such as WEP, WPA, WPA2, and WPS:

- **Brute force**   With brute force, the hacker uses a program that mathematically attempts every possible key to break into the wireless network.
- **Session hijacking**   With session hijacking, the hacker can monitor the wireless network for valid clients and then take over the session by spoofing the MAC address of the client.
- **Man-in-the-middle**   With a man-in-the-middle (MiTM) attack, the hacker can capture wireless traffic that is destined for the wireless router and then use that traffic as a workload to crack wireless encryption or simply monitor the traffic for sensitive data.

Rogue Access Point

Rogue access points are a serious vulnerability to organizations and one that you need to be familiar with for the Network+ certification exam. For example, you have secured your network environment, but the security can be easily compromised when an employee connects a wireless access point or router to the network so that he can connect to it and access the Internet while eating lunch in the company cafeteria.

Also keep in mind that the hacker can place an access point unknown to you on your network through an unsecured network jack, like those in reception areas of a lot of offices. To protect against such actions, be sure to limit the MAC addresses that can connect to the network jack, or even disable it if it is not being used.

What the employee is not aware of in this example is the risk he has placed on the company assets by connecting a wireless router to the network. This is considered a rogue access point to the network because it is an unauthorized device that the network administrator is unaware of.

watch   For the exam, remember that a rogue access point is a huge vulnerability to the network. You should perform regular wireless scans with software such as NetStumbler or Kismet to locate any rogue wireless access points. Also note that enterprise networks using wireless controller–based systems using Lightweight Access Point Protocol (LWAPP) will have rogue detection built into the system.

Evil Twin

A hacker can install a rogue access point from their wireless connection on a laptop and make the laptop device appear to be a valid access point. This is known as an *evil twin*, with the benefit to the hacker being that clients will connect to the hacker's fake access point, thinking it is a valid wireless network. All data sent on this wireless network will be sent to the hacker's laptop, where they can capture and read the data.

Now that you have an understanding of some of the basic concepts of wireless configuration, let's take a look at how to configure a wireless network.

CERTIFICATION OBJECTIVE 10.03

Implementing a Wireless Network

In this section you will learn the steps to configure your wireless access point and the wireless client. Be sure to familiarize yourself with the types of settings that exist, but be aware that the screens and steps will be different depending on the make and model of your wireless router.

Configuring the Wireless Router/Access Point

This discussion demonstrates how to configure a wireless router for wireless access, but you can also use a wireless access point. A *wireless router* is an all-in-one device that is a router, switch, firewall, wireless access point, and VPN end point. A *wireless access point* is a device that you connect to the network that simply allows wireless access to the network. The wireless access point has a number of wireless security features that can be enabled and has methods of managing multiple access points centrally from a single location. Part of the technologies used to allow central management are the wireless controllers—the wireless controller can automatically manage channel selection and power-level settings. The LWAPP is a protocol used to deploy the configuration to the wireless local area network (LAN) controllers over a network.

The Network+ exam has a number of new networking terms you should be familiar with. Some other wireless LAN technologies you should be familiar with are

- **VLAN pooling** This is a method to make configuration of wireless networks for large enterprises easier. When a client connects to an access point, they are assigned to a VLAN pool, which is responsible for allocating an IP address to the client.
- **Wireless bridge** A wireless bridge is a method to connect two wired networks together that span a certain distance and you do not want to run a network cable. This is a great solution for building-to-building connectivity.

- **Site surveys (heat maps)** A wireless site survey is when you assess a business location for wireless capabilities and potential interference. The goal of the site survey is to determine the best place to install the access points in order to get optimal wireless coverage and data rates. Many surveying tools such as AirMagnet generate a heat map diagram showing you optimal placement and coverage of access points.

- **Goodput** Goodput is a network characteristic that represents the amount of data (in bits) that can be delivered at one time. This number represents actual data bits and not protocol data, header information, or retransmitted data.

- **Connection types (802.11g-ht/802.11a-ht)** When working with wireless controllers, you can see the types of connections clients have. If the connection shows as either 802.11g-ht or 802.11a-ht, it means that the client is connected via a wireless "g" or "a" frequency but with "high throughput" (the ht), meaning that the client is connected with wireless 802.11n either at the 2.4 GHz (802.11g-ht) or 5 GHz (802.11a-ht) frequency.

- **Device density** The number of clients connecting to the wireless network. In larger organizations you will need to plan for large device density, which is planning for a large number of client devices connecting to the wireless network. This means that you will likely need to plan for more access points and roaming capabilities.

When you take the wireless access point or wireless router out of the box, you will first connect your Internet modem to the wide area network (WAN) port on the wireless router. You can then connect any wired systems on the network to any of the four ports that exist on the switch part of the router, as shown in Figure 10-9.

FIGURE 10-9

Looking at the physical ports on a D-Link wireless router

LAN ports   Internet port

Once you have everything connected and the router has power, you will need to go through some basic configuration steps to ensure the security of the device. I want to stress that just by plugging everything in, the wireless router is working and allowing wireless clients to access the network. You want to control who can connect to the wireless network! It should be noted that it is best to configure the wireless router before connecting it to the Internet or allowing clients to connect to it. This way you can ensure that it is secure before connecting to the outside world or having clients access the wireless router. The following section outlines some basic settings you can change.

Admin Password

The first thing you want to do is change the wireless router's administrative password. This password is set by default by the manufacturer, and anyone who has the same router will know the password. In order to change the admin password, you will need to start a web browser and type the IP address of the wireless router. The IP address is normally 192.168.1.1 or 192.168.0.1, depending on the manufacturer.

Once you type in the IP address, you will be asked to log on. In my example, I am using a D-Link DIR-615 wireless router, so the password is blank when you take it out of the box. To log on to the router, ensure that admin is chosen as the user name and type your password, or leave it blank if you don't know the password. Click the Log In button, as shown in Figure 10-10, and you will be logged on.

Once logged on, you will change the admin password by going to the Tools link at the top of the page and then selecting the Admin link on the left side of the page (shown in Figure 10-11). In the Admin Password section of the page, you will type the password you

FIGURE 10-10   Logging on to the administration pages of a wireless router

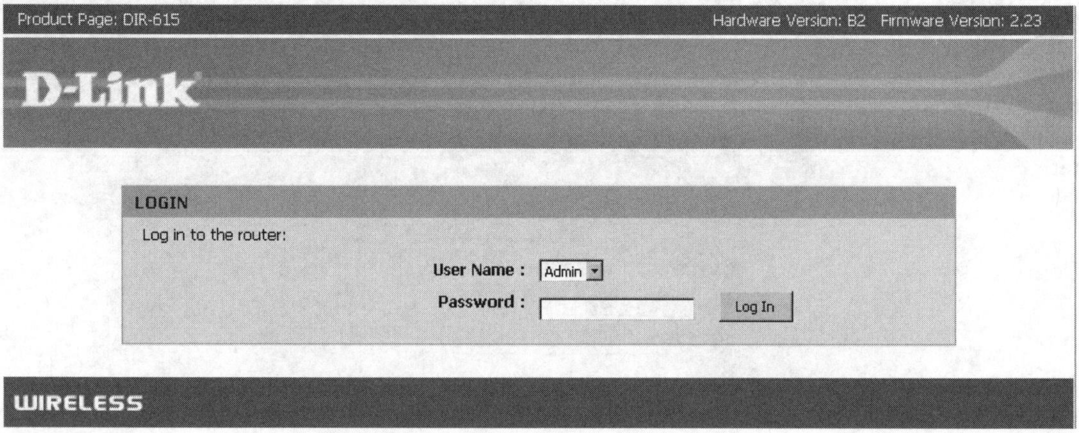

FIGURE 10-11   Changing the admin password on a D-Link router

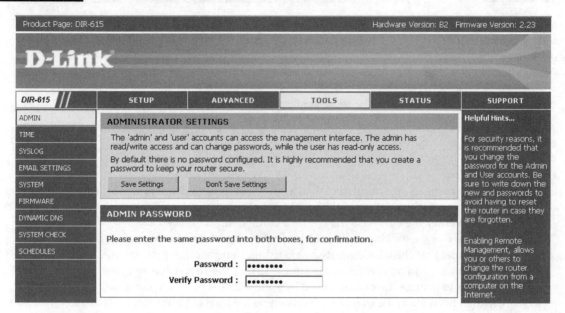

would like to use for the admin account and then retype it in the verify box. Once you have both password boxes filled in, you can click the Save Settings button at the top of the page.

Service Set Identifier

After changing your router admin password, you want to change the name of the wireless network, known as the SSID. Remember that in order to connect to your wireless network, clients have to know the value of the SSID. To change the SSID on the D-Link router, click the Setup link at the top of the page and then choose the Wireless Settings link on the left. You can then choose to configure the wireless network settings manually by scrolling to the bottom of the page and choosing the Manual Wireless Network Setup button.

You are then taken to the wireless networking setup screen (shown in Figure 10-12), where you can change most wireless network settings. To change the SSID name, type the name you would like to use in the Wireless Network Name box, and then click Save Settings.

After changing the value of the SSID, disable SSID broadcasting so that your router does not broadcast the name out on the network to anyone who wants to connect to it. To disable SSID broadcasting on the D-Link wireless router, set the Visibility Status to Invisible and then click Save Settings (see Figure 10-12).

Now that you have SSID broadcasting disabled, users who want to connect to your network will not see the wireless network through Windows unless they manually input

Changing the
channel and name
of the wireless
network (SSID)

WIRELESS NETWORK SETTINGS

Enable Wireless :	☑ Always ▾ Add New
Wireless Network Name :	dlink (Also called the SSID)
802.11 Mode :	Mixed 802.11n, 802.11g and 802.11b ▾
Enable Auto Channel Scan :	☐
Wireless Channel :	2.462 GHz - CH 11 ▾
Transmission Rate :	Best (automatic) ▾ (Mbit/s)
Channel Width :	20 MHz ▾
Visibility Status :	⦿ Visible ○ Invisible

the SSID name. As mentioned earlier, a Windows system displays nonbroadcasting wireless networks as "Other Network" within the list of networks. Users must select Other Network and then enter the correct SSID before a connection is allowed.

While you are looking at the wireless network settings on the router, take a look at the channel that the wireless network is using. In my example, the router is auto-picking the channel, and you can see in Figure 10-12 that the router has selected channel 11. If you wish to change the channel used by your wireless network, disable the Enable Auto Channel Scan check box and then you can pick which channel you wish to use.

It should be noted that most enterprise-class access points allow you to configure multiple SSIDs on the access point and have them map to virtual LANs (VLANs). This allows you to easily create corporate and guest wireless networks using the same access point for both networks, and then separating traffic with VLANs so that someone on the guest network cannot communicate with systems on the corporate network.

MAC Filtering

The next step to help secure the wireless network is to enable MAC filtering. Remember that MAC filtering allows you to input the MAC addresses of the wireless network cards you want to connect to your wireless network. Systems using any other MAC addresses will not be able to connect to the wireless network.

To configure MAC filtering on a D-Link DIR-615 router, you simply click the Advanced link at the top of the page and then choose the Network Filter link on the left. Turn on MAC filtering from the drop-down list (as shown in Figure 10-13), and then list the MAC addresses that are allowed to connect to the network.

Wireless Security

As part of securing a wireless router, the first thing you may decide to do is disable the wireless aspect of the router if you are not using wireless. A number of people purchase a

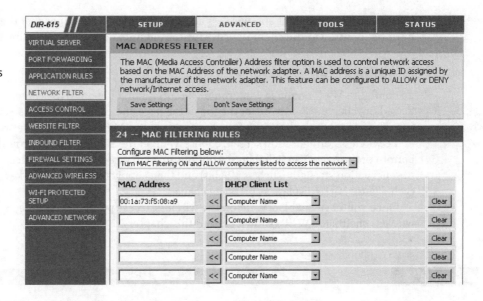

FIGURE 10-13

Filtering which systems can access the network by MAC addresses

wireless router and don't actually have any wireless clients at the time—the best thing to do in this case is disable wireless functionality until you need it.

To disable the wireless features on the D-Link router, go to the Setup link at the top of the page and then choose Wireless Settings on the left. At the bottom of the page choose Manual Wireless Network Setup. Once in the wireless settings, turn off the Enable Wireless option, as shown in Figure 10-14. Also notice that there is an Add New button to the right. This allows you to create a schedule, specifying the times during the day that the wireless is allowed if you want to control the wireless by time instead of disabling the feature entirely.

As mentioned earlier, you will want to configure some form of encryption on the wireless router. Most wireless routers will allow you to configure WEP, WPA, or WPA2 to encrypt

FIGURE 10-14

Disable the wireless functions entirely if you don't use wireless.

WIRELESS NETWORK SETTINGS		
Enable Wireless :	☑ Always ▾	Add New
Wireless Network Name :	dlink	(Also called the SSID)
802.11 Mode :	Mixed 802.11n, 802.11g and 802.11b ▾	
Enable Auto Channel Scan :	☑	
Wireless Channel :	2.437 GHz - CH 6 ▾	
Transmission Rate :	Best (automatic) ▾	(Mbit/s)
Channel Width :	20 MHz ▾	
Visibility Status :	⊙ Visible ○ Invisible	

traffic between the client and wireless access point. Also remember that the encryption key must be inputted at the client in order for the client to connect to the wireless network.

Configure WEP

To configure WEP on the D-Link router, be sure to first log on to the router. Once you have logged on, click the Setup link at the top of the page and then the Wireless Settings link on the left. Then scroll to the bottom of the page and choose Manual Wireless Network Setup. Once in the wireless configuration screen, choose WEP in the Security Mode drop-down list at the bottom of the page. You will then see options to configure WEP; for instance, you can specify the encryption strength (such as 128 bit) and then supply four encryption keys of 13 characters each. Figure 10-15 displays WEP being enabled.

Once you have enabled WEP on the wireless access point, you will need to configure the wireless clients for WEP (shown later in this chapter).

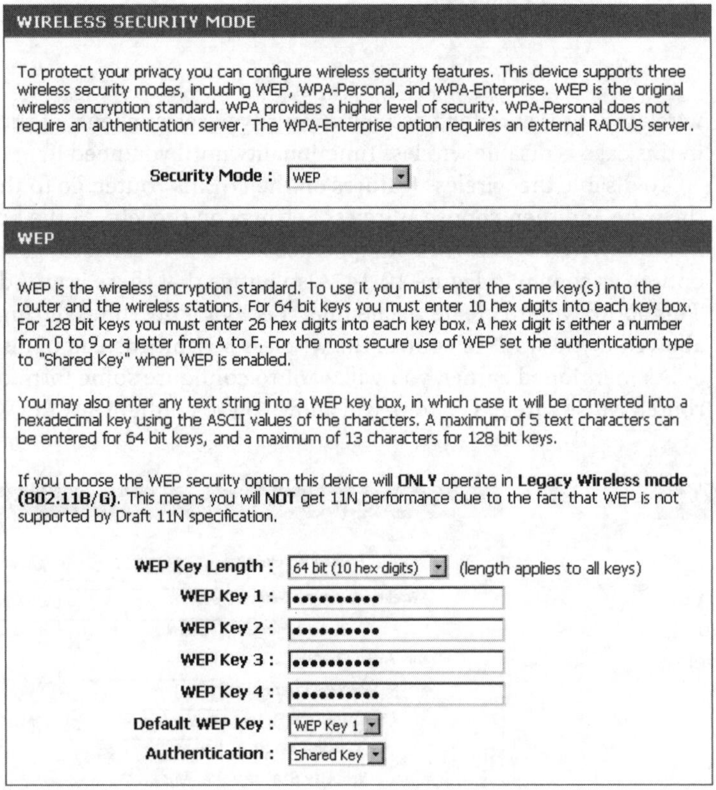

FIGURE 10-15

Enabling WEP
security on a
wireless router

WIRELESS SECURITY MODE

To protect your privacy you can configure wireless security features. This device supports three wireless security modes, including WEP, WPA-Personal, and WPA-Enterprise. WEP is the original wireless encryption standard. WPA provides a higher level of security. WPA-Personal does not require an authentication server. The WPA-Enterprise option requires an external RADIUS server.

Security Mode : [WEP ▼]

WEP

WEP is the wireless encryption standard. To use it you must enter the same key(s) into the router and the wireless stations. For 64 bit keys you must enter 10 hex digits into each key box. For 128 bit keys you must enter 26 hex digits into each key box. A hex digit is either a number from 0 to 9 or a letter from A to F. For the most secure use of WEP set the authentication type to "Shared Key" when WEP is enabled.

You may also enter any text string into a WEP key box, in which case it will be converted into a hexadecimal key using the ASCII values of the characters. A maximum of 5 text characters can be entered for 64 bit keys, and a maximum of 13 characters for 128 bit keys.

If you choose the WEP security option this device will **ONLY** operate in **Legacy Wireless mode (802.11B/G)**. This means you will **NOT** get 11N performance due to the fact that WEP is not supported by Draft 11N specification.

WEP Key Length : [64 bit (10 hex digits) ▼] (length applies to all keys)
WEP Key 1 : [••••••••••]
WEP Key 2 : [••••••••••]
WEP Key 3 : [••••••••••]
WEP Key 4 : [••••••••••]
Default WEP Key : [WEP Key 1 ▼]
Authentication : [Shared Key ▼]

Configure WPA

To configure WPA on the D-Link wireless router, you will follow similar steps. Once you have logged on to the router, click the Setup link at the top of the page and then the Wireless Settings link on the left. Then scroll to the bottom of the page and choose Manual Wireless Network Setup.

Once in the wireless configuration screen, choose WPA-Personal in the Security Mode drop-down list at the bottom of the page. If you are using a central RADIUS server for authentication with WPA, choose WPA-Enterprise in the Security Mode drop-down list.

Once you choose WPA-Personal (shown in Figure 10-16), you can then choose whether you want to support WPA, WPA2, or both. You can also choose which encryption protocol you wish to use, with AES being the most secure. With WPA you can also specify how often the key changes with the group key interval.

FIGURE 10-16

Enabling WPA-
Personal on a
wireless router

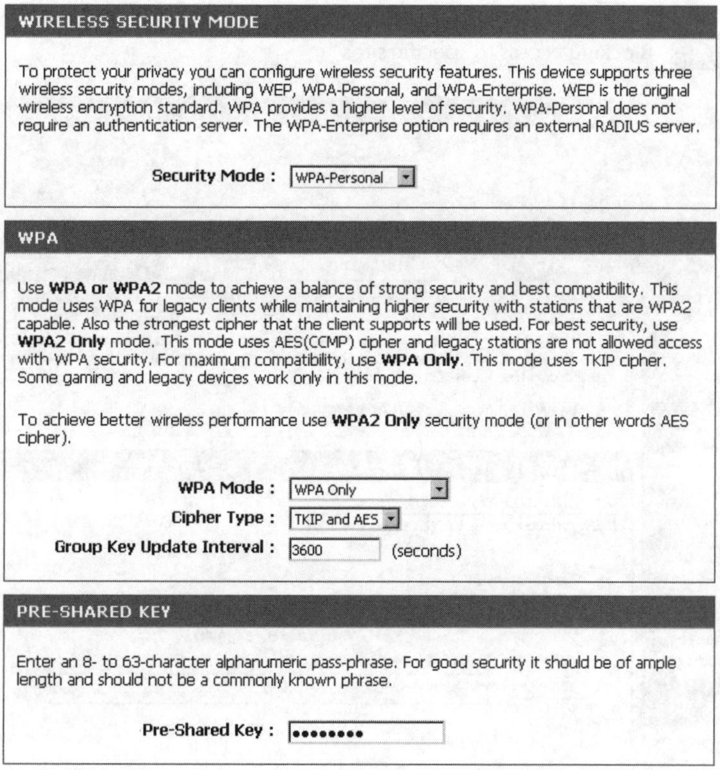

WIRELESS SECURITY MODE

To protect your privacy you can configure wireless security features. This device supports three wireless security modes, including WEP, WPA-Personal, and WPA-Enterprise. WEP is the original wireless encryption standard. WPA provides a higher level of security. WPA-Personal does not require an authentication server. The WPA-Enterprise option requires an external RADIUS server.

Security Mode : WPA-Personal

WPA

Use **WPA or WPA2** mode to achieve a balance of strong security and best compatibility. This mode uses WPA for legacy clients while maintaining higher security with stations that are WPA2 capable. Also the strongest cipher that the client supports will be used. For best security, use **WPA2 Only** mode. This mode uses AES(CCMP) cipher and legacy stations are not allowed access with WPA security. For maximum compatibility, use **WPA Only**. This mode uses TKIP cipher. Some gaming and legacy devices work only in this mode.

To achieve better wireless performance use **WPA2 Only** security mode (or in other words AES cipher).

WPA Mode : WPA Only
Cipher Type : TKIP and AES
Group Key Update Interval : 3600   (seconds)

PRE-SHARED KEY

Enter an 8- to 63-character alphanumeric pass-phrase. For good security it should be of ample length and should not be a commonly known phrase.

Pre-Shared Key : ••••••••

Controlling Internet Sites

Most wireless routers today allow you to control Internet activity, such as what times of the day the Internet is allowed to be used and what Internet sites are allowed to be visited.

You may want to block a number of sites from your users. It may be something as simple as a small company not wanting its employees wasting company time on a site such as facebook.com, or you may want to block inappropriate sites.

The following steps will guide you through blocking a specific website on the router so that users cannot visit it.

1. Log on to the router.
2. Go to the Advanced menu at the top of the page.
3. Click the Website Filter link on the left side of the page.
4. Type the URL you would like to block (shown in Figure 10-17). This will prevent users on your network from accessing this site.

FIGURE 10-17   Blocking access to specific sites

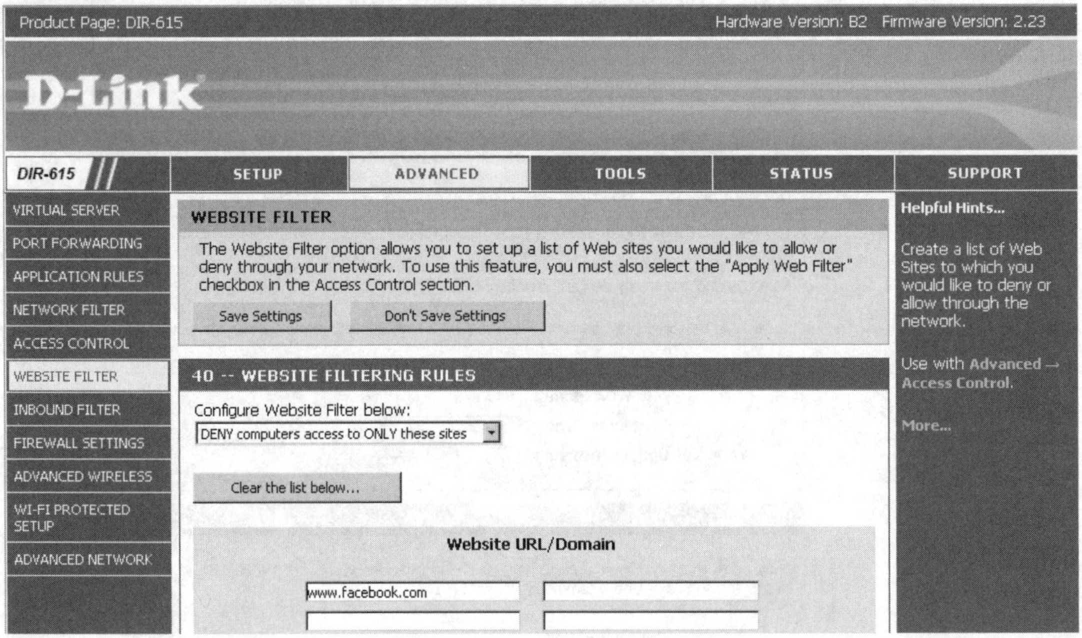

Enabling the Web
Filter policy

STEP 4: SELECT FILTERING METHOD

Select the method for filtering.

Method : ○ Log Web Access Only ○ Block All Access ◉ Block Some Access

Apply Web Filter : ☑
Apply Advanced Port Filters : ☐

Prev   Next   Save   Cancel

5. Now you will have to create a policy that enforces your website filter at all hours of the day. To do this, click the Advanced link at the top and then choose the Access Control link on the left.

6. Turn on the Enable Access Control option.

7. Click Add Policy to create a policy that enforces the web filter.

8. Click Next.

9. Type the name of the policy (I called mine "FilterSites"), and then click Next.

10. Choose Always for when this policy applies, and then click Next.

11. Choose Other Machines so that the policy applies to all systems, and then click OK.

12. Click Next.

13. Choose Block Some Access and then ensure the Web Filter option is selected so that the web filter is applied (shown in Figure 10-18).

14. Click Next.

15. Ensure that Web Access Logging is enabled. This will allow you to log what sites your users are visiting. After you enable logging, you can view the log at any time to see what sites are being visited.

16. Click Save to save the access policy.

View Web Activity

Once you have enabled logging of web activity, you will want to check the logs once in a while. Most routers allow you to view a list of sites that your users have been visiting, or in the case of the D-Link DIR-615 router, you can have the log e-mailed to you if you configure the e-mail settings.

To view the log on the router, go to the Status link at the top of the page and then click the Log link on the left. You will see the logged activity for your router in the middle of the screen (shown in Figure 10-19).

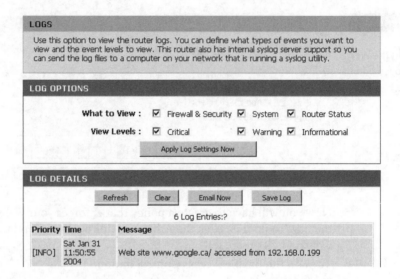

View websites
visited by users in
the router's log.

Configuring the Client

Once your wireless router has been configured, you are now ready to connect the wireless clients to the network. Ensure you have the following information before you get started:

- **SSID name** Because you have most likely disabled SSID broadcasting, you need to know the clients' SSID so that you can manually input it into the client.
- **WEP or WPA key** If you have protected the wireless network with WEP or WPA, you will need to know the key.
- **MAC address** If you are filtering by MAC addresses, you will need to know the MAC of your client and then input that into the router.

Once you have all the information in the bulleted list, you are ready to connect the clients to the wireless network. This section will outline the steps needed to allow your client systems to connect to the wireless network.

Connecting a Windows 8 Client

If you are using Windows 8, you can connect to the wireless network by choosing the network icon in the system tray. When you choose the network icon a list of available networks appears. Click the network you wish to connect to, choose the Connect button (seen in Figure 10-20), and then type the wireless encryption key to gain access.

FIGURE 10-20

Connecting to a
wireless network

EXERCISE 10-1

Configuring a Wireless Network

In this exercise, you will configure a D-Link DIR-615 wireless router. You will perform tasks such as changing the admin password, implementing MAC filtering, and implementing WEP.

1. Take the wireless router out of the box and connect the WAN port to your Internet connection. Plug your workstation network cable into an available port on the wireless router, or if using a workstation with wireless capabilities, connect to the wireless network. Keep in mind that when configuring wireless, it's a best practice to have a wired connection as changes to the configuration could cause you to lose your wireless connection.

2. To administer the wireless router, start Internet Explorer, type **http://192.168.0.1**, and then press ENTER.

3. You are asked to log on. There is no password on the admin account by default, so click Logon.

4. Once logged on, you want to change the admin password. To set a password for the admin account so that others cannot log on, click the Tools link at the top and then in the Admin Password section, type the password **Pa$$w0rd** and confirm the password by typing the same thing again. Click Save Settings at the top of the page.

5. Choose Reboot Now to have the changes take effect. Wait 30 seconds and then type **http://192.168.0.1** in the browser again.

6. Try to log on with no password. Were you successful? _____

7. Now log on with the admin password Pa$$w0rd that you set earlier.

Implementing MAC Filtering

1. To implement MAC filtering on this router, click the Advanced link at the top.

2. Choose the Network Filter option on the left.

3. You will notice that MAC filtering is disabled by default. To enable MAC filtering, from the Configure MAC Filtering drop-down list, choose Turn MAC Filtering On And Allow Computers Listed To Access The Network.

4. Now you are able to add the MAC addresses of people who may connect to the network by typing them or choosing them from the client list and then clicking the << button.

5. Once you have added all of the MAC addresses, click Save Settings.

Changing the SSID and Implementing WEP

1. To implement WEP security on the wireless router, choose the Setup link at the top of the page and then click the Wireless Settings link on the left.

2. Choose Manual Wireless Setup.

3. For the wireless network name, type **NetPlus**.

4. If you wanted to disable SSID broadcasting, you would set the Visibility Status to Invisible. I am going to leave it at Visible.

5. To enable WEP encryption, from the Security Mode drop-down list, select WEP.

6. Then below that set the key strength to 128 bit and set each WEP key (in all four places) to **NetPlus123456**.

7. Choose Save Settings at the top of the page. You will lose your connection if you are connected to the router via wireless because now you have to configure the wireless client settings the same as the router.

Configuring a Windows 8 Client

1. On the Windows 8 client with a wireless network card, click the network icon in the system tray.
2. You should see the NetPlus network. Select it and choose Connect.
3. When prompted for the key, type **NetPlus123456**.
4. Once connected, you should be able to surf the Internet.

Configuring Roaming Wireless

When configuring a wireless network, you may need to cover a larger area than possible with a single wireless access point. When you place multiple access points at your office location with the goal of having each access point as part of the same wireless network, you are creating what is known as a *roaming wireless network*. With a roaming wireless network, clients would transparently connect to whichever wireless access point was closer to the client, and if the employee moves to a different area of the building, they may connect to a different wireless access point.

Certain rules need to be followed when creating a roaming wireless network:

- **Same SSID**   All access points will use the same SSID value in order to create a single wireless network made up of all access points.
- **Different channels**   Each access point should be configured with a different channel that does not have an overlapping frequency with other channels.
- **Overlapping coverage**   The access points must overlap coverage areas by at least 10 percent in order for roaming clients to not lose a network connection.

Understanding Mobile Devices

Wireless networks are one of the more complex networks, as the types of network clients that connect to it vary. The following identifies some of the types of devices that may connect to your wireless network:

- **Cell phones**   Many employees have personal or business cell phones they may wish to connect to the wireless network. Consider having a guest wireless network for employees to connect their personal cell phones, laptops, or tablets. Also, if you have a home network, configure a guest wireless network for your kid's friends to connect their cell phone to!

- **Laptops and tablets** One of the more common types of devices to connect to the wireless network is the laptop or even tablets. For personal devices, ensure that you have a guest wireless network.

- **Gaming devices** Gaming consoles are very common network devices today! You can game online, but also use the gaming console as a full entertainment device by watching movies on it. Gaming consoles can be configured to connect to a wired or wireless network.

- **Media devices** Media devices allow you to stream audio or video files across the networks and are great examples of wireless devices.

Troubleshooting Wireless

When troubleshooting why a client will not connect to wireless networks, there are a number of issues to consider. The following is a list of common problems when connecting to wireless:

- **Signal strength/signal loss** If you are too far from the wireless network, you may not have a strong enough signal to connect. Try moving closer to the access point.

- **Interference** You could be getting interference from other home equipment, such as a cordless phone. Try changing the channel on the wireless network. When monitoring wireless networks to diagnose the issue, be sure to watch for *wireless channel utilization*—which is when many wireless networks are using the same channel. You want to ensure that wireless routers configured in the same area are using different channels to prevent interference.

- **Overlapping channels/mismatched channels** You could be using the wrong channel to connect to the wireless network. Verify the channel settings. Also, you may have wireless access points or devices using the same channel, which will cause interference, so verify each access point is configured for a unique channel.

- **Signal-to-noise ratio** Monitor the signal-to-noise ratio, which is the measure of useful information (the signal) being delivered to bad data (noise signals) being delivered.

- **Device saturation** If having issues with connectivity to wireless networks, ensure that you have not exceeded the maximum number of clients for the particular access point you are using.

- **Bandwidth saturation** Another common issue with larger wireless environments is bandwidth saturation, which is when all the available bandwidth is being utilized. Look to installing additional access points.

- **Untested updates** Ensure that any updates are tested before they are applied to client systems or devices. Updates could cause issues with existing features, so be sure to test!

■ **Wrong SSID**   You must input the correct SSID name in order to connect to the wireless network. If you are having trouble connecting, verify that you are using the correct SSID.

■ **Power levels**   You can increase the power levels on the wireless router/access point to ensure that the signal is strong enough to cover the distance required to reach the client.

■ **Open networks**   An open network is a network in which no authentication is being performed. Your wireless implementation should have at least a WPA2 wireless key, which is needed in order to access the network.

■ **Rogue access point**   If having trouble connecting to systems on the wireless network, ensure that you are connected to the correct wireless network. If there is an unauthorized access point connected to the network, it could cause communication issues as clients connect to the rogue access point.

■ **Wrong antenna type**   Ensure that your wireless network is using the correct type of antenna and that the wireless configuration is set to the type that is actually being used.

■ **Incompatibilities**   Be sure that the wireless device you are connecting to the wireless network is compatible with it. For example, know that a wireless 802.11a device is not compatible with an 802.11g wireless access point.

■ **Wrong encryption**   You could be using the wrong encryption type or even the wrong encryption key. Verify all encryption settings.

■ **Bounce**   The term *bouncing* refers to the signal reflecting off an object instead of passing through it. Bouncing can cause performance problems, as the signal is dispersed in different directions with some of the signal passing through the object and other parts reflecting (bouncing).

■ **MIMO**   Multiple input multiple output is the capability of 802.11n and 802.11ac to divide the signal into multiple streams and have each stream delivered from a different antenna to increase performance. This is known as spatial multiplexing, and you may need to verify the configuration of the router to support it.

■ **Access point placement**   Be sure to place the wireless access point in an open area that will get the best coverage. Try placing it up high, such as on a bookshelf, and in the middle of the building in order to limit persons outside the facility from connecting to the wireless network.

■ **Access point configuration**   Ensure that the configuration of the wireless device is not preventing you from connecting to it. For example, in order for a client to connect to a wireless network that has MAC filtering enabled, you will need to add the MAC address of the client to the filter list on the access point. To aid in the configuration of access points, you can use LWAPP. Access points using LWAPP require a controller to manage the configuration. This is part of the ease of configuration, as you can simply add/register an access point on the controller, and the controller takes care of the actual configuration of the access point for you. A stand-alone access point is known as a thick AP, whereas you can use LWAPP to configure what is known as a thin AP.

■ **Environmental factors**   A number of environmental factors can degrade your wireless signal, such as concrete walls, window film, and metal studs. It is important to perform a site survey in order to plan for such interference.

■ **Wireless standard–related issues**   One of the more common issues related to wireless is due to the configuration of the wireless network. You should verify configuration such as the throughput, frequency being used, distance being covered, and the channels being used.

■ **Latency**   Wireless networks may experience latency (delay in response) due to interference from other wireless components such as microwaves or cordless phones. To reduce the interference, change the channel on the wireless access point.

When troubleshooting wireless networking, a number of tools can be used to help diagnose problems with the network or wireless access point/router. You can use the following tools to troubleshoot wireless issues:

■ **Wireless survey tools**   You can use a wireless survey tool to scan a site and help identity the wireless topology that is needed. These tools can document radio frequency (RF) coverage, along with connection speeds, before actual implementation.

■ **Wireless analyzers**   A wireless analyzer can be used to discover wireless networks and their characteristics such as power levels and channels. Wireless analyzers are great tools to use to help troubleshoot network issues.

CERTIFICATION OBJECTIVE 10.04

PAN Networking

Today's wireless network environments are not limited only to 802.11 wireless LAN equipment. As a Network+ professional, you should be familiar with other popular wireless standards that are used to create a personal area network (PAN).

Infrared (IR)

Infrared wireless is the type of wireless communication that is used by VCR and TV remote controls, along with some computer peripherals. Infrared is typically a line-of-sight technology, which means that the signal is lost if anything blocks the pathway between the two devices. With infrared, the two devices will need to be within one meter of each other.

Infrared devices contain a transceiver that sends and receives light signals as on-off patterns to create the data that travels at transfer rates up to 4 Mbps. Because line of sight is required, you may need to use a radio frequency solution such as Bluetooth if line of sight becomes an issue.

Bluetooth

Bluetooth is a radio frequency wireless technology that allows systems to connect to peripherals over a distance of up to 10 meters away. Bluetooth is more flexible than infrared because it will automatically connect to other Bluetooth devices and does not depend on line of sight. This is a popular technology used by handheld devices to connect to other networking components.

Bluetooth is less susceptible to interference because it uses spread-spectrum frequency hopping, which means that it can hop between any of 79 frequencies in the 2.4 GHz range. Bluetooth hops between frequencies 1600 times per second and provides a transfer rate of up to 1 Mbps.

Bluetooth is a popular technology with handheld devices such as personal digital assistants (PDAs) and cell phones because users can use their wireless headsets with their cell phones and talk "hands free."

There are potential security risks with Bluetooth, however, as it is possible for a hacker to connect to your cell phone remotely and steal data off your phone. In order to secure your Bluetooth-enabled device, follow these best practices:

- **Disable Bluetooth**   If you are not using the Bluetooth feature on your phone, disable it through the phone's menu system.
- **Phone visibility**   If you are using Bluetooth, set the phone's visibility setting to invisible so that hackers cannot pick up on your phone with a Bluetooth scanner.
- **Pair security**   Ensure you are using a Bluetooth phone that uses *pair security*, which allows people to connect to your phone only if they know the PIN code you have set on it.

Earlier in the chapter we talked about threats against wireless networking. Now we want to talk about threats against Bluetooth-enabled devices. There are a number of threats against Bluetooth; the two main threats the Network+ exam expects you to know are

- **Bluejacking**   Sending unsolicited messages using the Bluetooth wireless protocol over Bluetooth-enabled devices such as phones or tablets.
- **Bluesnarfing**   Exploiting a Bluetooth-enabled device and copying data off the device.

NFC

Another common wireless technology today is known as near field communication (NFC). NFC is a short-range wireless technology that allows devices to conveniently communicate with one another. NFC is commonly found in mobile devices and can be a quick way to share contact information between those devices by moving them close to one another (a few centimeters). We are also seeing NFC now as a payment method for merchandise—you simply move your payment card (debit or credit card) close to the merchant in order to pay. Mobile devices are now supporting emulation of a payment card so that you can use your mobile device with NFC to make a payment!

CERTIFICATION SUMMARY

In this chapter you have learned about wireless basics and the security issues surrounding wireless. You have learned that wireless networks come in two forms: infrastructure mode and ad hoc mode. Infrastructure mode uses a wireless access point, whereas ad hoc mode allows clients to connect to one another.

You have also learned about wireless standards, such as 802.11b, 802.11g, and 802.11n. 802.11b is an old wireless standard that runs at 11 Mbps, whereas 802.11g runs at 54 Mbps and 802.11n runs at 600 Mbps.

You have learned that there are many steps to securing a wireless network, such as limiting which systems can connect through MAC filtering, encrypting traffic with WEP or WPA, and making sure to change the SSID and disable SSID broadcasting. You have learned that all these measures have been compromised by hackers, so if security is a concern, you should look to using a VPN solution with your wireless network.

 TWO-MINUTE DRILL

This chapter has introduced you to a number of concepts related to wireless networking and has shown you how to configure a wireless network. Be sure to remember the following points when preparing for the Network+ exam.

Wireless Basics

❑ Be familiar with the wireless standards such as 802.11a, 802.11b, 802.11g, and 802.11n.

❑ Know that 802.11b, 802.11g, and 802.11n are all compatible because they all run at the 2.4 GHz frequency range.

❏ Know that 802.11a and 802.11n are compatible because they run at the 5 GHz frequency range.

❏ If you are experiencing problems with your wireless clients connecting to the wireless access point, it could be because of interference from other household devices. Try changing the channel on your wireless devices.

Securing Wireless

❏ WEP is a simple form of encryption that uses a passphrase or shared key to secure communications.

❏ You can set up a central authentication server with WPA-Enterprise. This is known as the 802.1x standard.

❏ Be sure to change the SSID and disable SSID broadcasting.

❏ Limit which systems can connect to your wireless network using MAC filtering.

❏ Configure wireless encryption through WEP or WPA.

❏ For the highest level of security, use VPN solutions to secure your wireless infrastructure.

Implementing a Wireless Network

❏ Make sure that you set the admin password on your router.

❏ Configure logging on your router so that you can monitor websites accessed.

❏ You can implement website filters to control what sites can be accessed by users on your network.

❏ A wireless roaming network can be created by having multiple wireless access points using the same SSID but different non-overlapping channels (such as 1, 6, 11).

PAN Networking

❏ Bluetooth has a transfer rate of approximately 1 Mbps and is used by a number of handheld devices.

❏ Infrared is used by some devices and is a line-of-sight technology.

SELF TEST

Wireless Basics

1. Which wireless mode involves two laptops connecting directly to one another?
   A. Infrastructure mode
   B. Ad hoc mode
   C. Laptop mode
   D. Enterprise mode

2. Which of the following wireless standards does not fall into the Wi-Fi standard?
   A. 802.11n
   B. 802.11g
   C. 802.11b
   D. 802.11a

3. Which wireless standard runs at 54 Mbps per second at the 2.4 GHz frequency?
   A. 802.11n
   B. 802.11a
   C. 802.11g
   D. 802.11b

4. Which wireless standard can reach transfer rates of up to 600 Mbps?
   A. 802.11n
   B. 802.11a
   C. 802.11g
   D. 802.11b

5. Which wireless security protocol changes the key using TKIP?
   A. WEP
   B. WPA
   C. WEP2
   D. WPA5

Securing Wireless

6. Which of the following is the name you assign to your wireless network?
   A. MAC address
   B. Service Set Identifier (SSID)
   C. WEP key
   D. IP address

7. What should you do with the wireless router to help hide the wireless network from unauthorized users?
   A. Turn it off when it is not being used.
   B. Enable WEP.
   C. Disable SSID broadcasting.
   D. Unplug the network cable from the router.

8. You wish to encrypt traffic between the wireless client and the access point, but you don't have a wireless access point that supports WPA or WPA2. What would you do to secure the traffic?
   A. Use a third-party program to encrypt the traffic.
   B. Use WPA on the client but WEP on the router.
   C. Use WPA2 on the client but WEP on the router.
   D. Use WEP on both the client and the router.

Implementing a Wireless Network

9. What is the first thing you should change on the wireless router when it is powered on?
   A. Configure WEP.
   B. Change the admin password.
   C. Change the IP address.
   D. Change the DHCP server scope.

10. You have purchased a wireless router but do not intend on having any wireless clients for the first six months. What should you do to help secure the router?
   A. Enable WEP.
   B. Disable SSID broadcasting.
   C. Enable WPA2.
   D. Disable the wireless feature.

11. What program could be used to do a survey of your area and discover wireless networks?
   A. MBSA
   B. Device Manager
   C. NetStumbler
   D. Routing and Remote Access

PAN Networking

12. What is the transfer rate of Bluetooth?
    A. 10 Mbps
    B. 1 Mbps
    C. 4 Mbps
    D. 8 Mbps

Performance-Based Question Review: See the performance-based question sample from the author included with the accompanying media.

SELF TEST ANSWERS

Wireless Basics

1. ☑ **B.** Ad hoc mode is when two laptops connect directly together through a wireless connection.
   ☒ **A, C,** and **D** are incorrect. Infrastructure mode is the other wireless topology, which involves having the wireless clients connect to an access point. There are no such things as laptop or enterprise wireless modes.

2. ☑ **D.** 802.11a was created before the Wi-Fi standard was created and runs at the 5 GHz frequency. 802.11b/g/n all run within the 2.4 GHz frequency range.
   ☒ **A, B,** and **C** are incorrect. 802.11b/g/n are all part of the Wi-Fi standard and are compatible with one another.

3. ☑ **C.** 802.11g runs at 54 Mbps and within the 2.4 GHz range.
   ☒ **A, B,** and **D** are incorrect. 802.11n supports speeds of 600 Mbps, whereas 802.11b only supports 11 Mbps. 802.11a supports 54 Mbps, but runs at the 5 GHz range.

4. ☑ **A.** 802.11n is one of the newer wireless standards that supports transfer rates of 600 Mbps!
    ☒ **B, C,** and **D** are incorrect. 802.11a supports a transfer rate of 54 Mbps, 802.11b supports a transfer rate of 11 Mbps, and 802.11g supports a transfer rate of 54 Mbps.

5. ☑ **B.** WPA uses the TKIP protocol to change the key used to secure the wireless network at regular intervals.
    ☒ **A, C,** and **D** are incorrect. WEP has static keys configured, and there is no such thing as WEP2 or WPA5.

Securing Wireless

6. ☑ **B.** The SSID is the name of your wireless network. This name should not be easy to guess, and you should also have SSID broadcasting disabled.
    ☒ **A, C,** and **D** are incorrect because they are not the name of the wireless network.

7. ☑ **C.** When configuring your wireless router, be sure to disable SSID broadcasting so that the wireless router does not advertise itself.
    ☒ **A, B,** and **D** are incorrect. You should enable some form of encryption, such as WEP or WPA, but that will not hide the network.

8. ☑ **D.** You will need to use WEP if you have an older router that does not support WPA or WPA2. If you are using WEP on the router, you will need to configure WEP on the client.
    ☒ **A, B,** and **C** are incorrect because WPA and WPA2 are not supported on the router, so you cannot use them on the client.

Implementing a Wireless Network

9. ☑ **B.** When you first purchase the router, you should set the admin password to prevent others from logging on and changing your router's settings.
    ☒ **A, C,** and **D** are incorrect. Although you will want to change a number of settings on the router, the admin password should be the first.

10. ☑ **D.** If you do not have a need for the wireless features of the router, then you should disable them.
    ☒ **A, B,** and **C** are incorrect because they are all settings you would set if you had wireless clients.

11. ☑ **C.** NetStumbler is a wireless scanner that can detect wireless networks that are close to you.
    ☒ **A, B,** and **D** are incorrect because they are not wireless scanners.

PAN Networking

12. ☑ **B.** Approximately 1 Mbps is the transfer rate of Bluetooth.
    ☒ **A, C,** and **D** are incorrect because they are not the transfer rate of Bluetooth.

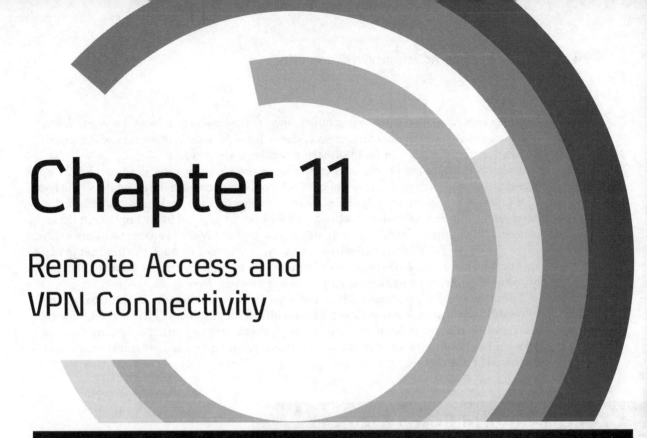

Chapter 11

Remote Access and VPN Connectivity

B ecause of the expansion of networks in the world today, user demands for connectivity are increasing dramatically. Users require the ability to connect to network resources from remote locations, at home, and across the Internet. This chapter will introduce you to a number of methods that allow remote users to connect to the network.

As companies expanded and joined an increasingly global market, the need to interconnect offices became crucial to business operations. The Internet is now based on this concept: making information accessible to anyone in the world, from any location. To enable remote installations to communicate with each other and to provide redundancy in case of war, the U.S. government created ARPANET, the first truly remote network. As ARPANET began its transformation into what is now known as the Internet, universities began using it to interconnect and share information and resources. Now, a large portion of the world population uses the Internet for information exchange and research.

Today, companies use networks to interconnect remote sites. They also provide dial-up access to their users to enable them to connect from home or from hotels while on the road. This increased connectivity helps increase productivity and allows the use of additional communication channels. Many technologies we take for granted today implement these concepts. For example, telephone systems use complex networks to enable us to call almost anyone in the world. E-mail is used to send messages and files through the Internet to reach anyone who has access to these services. As with any technology that we come to depend on, remote connectivity has become a part of our everyday lives.

Companies also use features such as Terminal Services and Remote Desktop to connect to systems over a Transmission Control Protocol/Internet Protocol (TCP/IP) connection and remotely manage those systems or run applications from a particular system. Terminal Services has become a core network service that is required by most organizations, and is discussed in this chapter.

CERTIFICATION OBJECTIVE 11.01

Remote Connectivity Concepts

Many technologies and functions are used for remote connectivity. One of the first networks—the telephone system—is still used today by almost everyone in the world. The concept of the telephone system was based on the idea of enabling two people in different physical locations to speak with each other. The same basic idea is used today for many different applications. Global networks have been created by corporations and institutions alike to enable remote communication and information sharing.

The basic functionality of remote connectivity is available in many different protocols and devices. For example, companies use network links such as Frame Relay and Asynchronous Transfer Mode (ATM), which encompass many different technologies. More common applications include Remote Access Service (RAS), which allows a remote user to use a protocol such as the Point-to-Point Protocol (PPP) to dial in to the RAS server over the public switched telephone network (PSTN).

This chapter will first introduce you to types of connections, such as PSTN and Integrated Services Digital Network (ISDN), and then talk about RAS services and protocols for dial-up using those connection types. The chapter will then focus on virtual private network (VPN)–type connections and protocols as an alternative way to connect to a remote network.

Public Switched Telephone Network

Almost everyone in the world has used a telephone at least once. Today, you can call anywhere in the world and get a direct connection almost instantly using this technology. The PSTN was originally designed as an analog switching system for routing voice calls. Because it has existed for several decades and has been used by so many, it has come to be known as plain old telephone service (POTS). Because PSTN is considered the first wide area network (WAN), it was the basis for many of the WAN technologies that exist today and has been instrumental in their evolution.

A History of PSTN

During the initial years of PSTN, digital technologies had not even been considered. The telephone network was based purely on analog signals traveling across copper wire to transport a human voice. The only repetitions of the signal that might have occurred were through one or two repeater devices. The term *via net loss* (VNL) was coined to calculate the signal degradation that occurred. This degradation was measured in decibels (dB). The only metering equipment needed to test connections consisted of test tones, decibel meters, and volume unit (VU) meters. VU meters were used to measure complex signals such as the human voice. These meters simply measure the loss or gain of a specific circuit.

Prior to the 1960s, PSTN lines could handle nothing more than what they were originally designed for—voice communication. Since then, many great technology leaps have helped the network progress. The beginning of this era was marked by the advent of the Bell T1 transmission system. As T1s became more frequently used in the telephone network, bandwidth and quality increased. This advent also began the true migration from using human operators to route calls to switching these functions electronically.

In the 1970s and 1980s, the phone companies began to invest more resources in improving the quality of the PSTN backbone. This backbone, also known as the digital access cross-connect system (DACCS), was a combination of all the T1 and T3 lines. Although many problems were associated with DACCS at that time, it provided a technology upgrade to help improve services all the way around. Soon, companies started looking at PSTN lines as an alternative to the dedicated point-to-point links they were using.

As the industry started to move in the direction of PSTN lines, manufacturers began to market modems for this purpose. As modems became more commonplace, the manufacturers began mass-marketing them for everyday users. Today, although using a modem to dial in to a remote network is not as common as connecting through a broadband connection, it is still an important option for persons who don't have broadband technologies available. People in rural areas may still need to rely on PSTN, and some companies may still rely on PSTN lines to enable remote users to dial in to private networks, as well as to back up data links for computer systems that require remote connectivity.

How PSTN Works

The POTS network originally began with human operators sitting at a switch, manually routing calls. The original concept of the Bell Telephone system was a series of PSTN trunks connecting the major U.S. cities. This was an analog-based system that met its requirements for human voice transmissions at the time. Since the inception of the telephone, the world has changed. PSTN systems still use analog from the end node to the first switch. Once the signal is received, the switch converts the signal to a digital format and then routes the call on. Once the call is received on the other end, the last switch in the loop converts the signal back to analog, and the call is initiated. Because the end node is still analog, modems are used in most homes to facilitate dial-up access. Faster technologies such as ISDN or T1s use a dedicated point-to-point link through a completely digital path, making higher bandwidths attainable. Currently, analog lines can reach only a maximum speed of 56 Kbps. Using digital lines, speeds in excess of 2 Gbps (gigabits per second) can be reached.

Remember that the maximum available speed with an analog modem is 56 Kbps.

The telephone network works much like the TCP transport protocol. It is connection based, and the connection is maintained until the call is terminated. This enables you to hear the other person almost instantaneously. Telephone networks use two copper wires in most homes, but the switching medium is mainly fiber. This allows for the high-speed switching in the back end but slow response in data communications because of the modem device connected to the system.

Modem Types

Analog modems are used to connect to a remote network via a PSTN line. Although there are many different types and makes of modems, they can be categorized into three classes: single external, single internal, and multiline rack or shelf mounted.

The *external modem* is the modem most commonly used today. Many Internet service providers (ISPs) use pools of external modems to enable dial-in access. These modems are also common in server hardware. Many IT workers include modems in production systems to allow for a backup communications link or for remote access.

The *internal modem* belongs to the same device type as the external modem. The only real difference is that it is located inside the computer chassis. Most companies no longer use these modems because externals are easier to replace and troubleshoot. For example, internal modems do not have the light-emitting diodes (LEDs) that external modems have. This translates into a headache if you have to figure out why the modem won't connect to a remote host via the dial-up connection. Some modem manufacturers provide software interfaces, but they are generally not as full featured as those in external modems. A common use for internal modems is in laptop computers using PC (PCMCIA) cards. Many laptop vendors still integrate phone jacks into the chassis of their computers. In addition,

PC cards can technically be classified as internal modems. These are used widely and do not include the LEDs or lamps an external modem offers. Quite a few businesses use external modems, and home users use internal modems. The cost difference is almost negligible, but home users usually opt for the cheaper of the two.

These solutions are becoming increasingly popular. Many vendors offer solutions that have a single chassis containing a certain number of modem cards that can be connected directly to the network. The modularity and size of these devices make them much more efficient than trying to maintain a shelf with a stack of external modems sitting on it. These solutions have also been included in some new networking equipment. Manufacturers place analog modems in their equipment to facilitate redundancy features such as a backup network link.

Integrated Services Digital Network

In the past, the phone network consisted of an interconnection of wires that directly connected telephone users via an analog-based system. This system was very inefficient because it did not work well for long-distance connections and was very prone to "noise." In the 1960s, the telephone company began converting this system to a packet-based, digital switching network. Today, nearly all voice switching in the United States is digital; however, the customer connection to the switching office is primarily still analog.

The *Integrated Services Digital Network (ISDN)* is a system of digital telephone connections that enables data to be transmitted simultaneously end to end. This technology has been available for more than two decades and is designed to enable faster, clearer communications for small offices and home users. It came about as the standard telephone system began its migration from an analog format to digital. ISDN is the format portion of the digital telephone system now being used to replace analog systems.

A History of ISDN

The concept of ISDN was introduced in 1972. It was based on moving the analog-to-digital conversion equipment onto the customer's premises to enable voice and data services to be sent through a single line. Telephone companies also began using a new kind of digital communications link between each central office. A T1 link could carry twenty-four 64 Kbps voice channels, and it used the same amount of copper wire as only two analog voice calls. Throughout the 1970s, the telephone companies continued to upgrade their switching offices. They began rolling out T1 links directly to customers to provide high-speed access. The need for an efficient solution was greater than ever.

In the early 1990s, an effort was begun to establish a standard implementation for ISDN in the United States. The National ISDN 1 (NI-1) standard was defined by the industry so that users would not have to know the type of switch they were connected to in order to buy equipment and software compatible with it.

Because some major office switches were incompatible with this standard, some major telephone companies had trouble switching to the NI-1 standard. This caused a number of problems in trying to communicate between these nonstandard systems and everyone else. Eventually, all the systems were brought up to standard. A set of core services was defined in all basic rate interfaces (BRIs) of the NI-1 standard. The services include data-call services, voice-call services, call forwarding, and call waiting. Most devices today conform to the NI-1 standard.

A more comprehensive standardization initiative, National ISDN 2 (NI-2), was recently adopted. Now, several major manufacturers of networking equipment have become involved to help set the standard and make ISDN a more economical solution. The NI-2 standard had two goals: to standardize the primary rate interface (PRI), as NI-1 did for BRI, and to simplify the identification process. Until this point, PRIs were mainly vendor dependent, which made it difficult to interconnect them. Furthermore, a standard was created for NI-2 for identifiers.

ISDN Channels

An ISDN transmission circuit consists of a logical grouping of data channels. With ISDN, voice and data are carried by these channels. Two types of channels, a B channel and a D channel, are used for a single ISDN connection. Each channel has a specific function and bandwidth associated with it. The bearer channels, or B channels, transfer data. They offer a bandwidth of 64 Kbps per channel.

The data channel, or D channel, handles signaling at 16 Kbps or 64 Kbps. This includes the session setup and teardown using a communications language known as DSS1. The purpose of the D channel is to enable the B channels to strictly pass data and not have to worry about signaling information. You remove the administrative overhead from B channels using the D channel. The bandwidth available for the D channel depends on the type of ISDN service; BRIs usually require 16 Kbps, and PRIs use 64 Kbps. Typically, ISDN service contains two B channels and a single D channel.

ISDN supports what are known as high-speed channels (H channels), which are made up of a number of B channels. The following list shows the implementations of H channels:

- **H0** 384 Kbps (6 B channels)
- **H10** 1472 Kbps (23 B channels)
- **H11** 1536 Kbps (24 B channels)
- **H12** 1920 Kbps (30 B channels, the European standard)

ISDN Interfaces

Although B channels and D channels can be combined in any number of ways, the phone companies created two standard configurations. There are two basic types of ISDN service: BRI and PRI.

- **Basic Rate Interface (BRI)** BRI consists of two 64 Kbps B channels and one 16 Kbps D channel, for a total of 144 Kbps. With BRI, only 128 Kbps is used for data transfers, while the remaining 16 Kbps is used for signaling information. BRIs were designed to enable customers to use their existing wiring. Because this provided a low-cost solution for customers, it is the most basic type of service intended for small business or home use.
- **Primary Rate Interface (PRI)** PRI is intended for users who need greater bandwidth. It requires T1 carriers to facilitate communications. Normally, the channel structure contains twenty-three B channels plus one 64 Kbps D channel, for a total of 1536 Kbps. This standard is used only in North America and Japan. European countries support a different kind of ISDN standard for PRI. It consists of thirty B channels and one 64 Kbps D channel, for a total of 1984 Kbps. A technology known as non-facility associated signaling (NFAS) is available to enable support of multiple PRI lines with one 64 Kbps D channel.

exam

watch　　　**For the exam, know that BRI uses two 64 Kbps B channels for data and one 16 Kbps D channel for signaling. Also know that PRI uses twenty-three 64 Kbps B channels for data and one 64 Kbps D channel for signaling.**

To use BRI services, you must subscribe to ISDN services through a local telephone company or provider. By default, you must be within 18,000 feet (about 3.4 miles) of the telephone company's central office to use BRI services. Repeater devices are available for the ISDN service to extend this distance, but these devices can be very expensive. Special types of equipment are required to communicate with the ISDN provider switch and with other ISDN devices. You must have an ISDN terminal adapter and an ISDN router.

ISDN Devices

The phrase *ISDN standard* refers to the devices that are required to connect the end node to the network. Although some vendors provide devices that include several functions, a separate device defines each function within the standard. The protocols that each device uses are also defined and are associated with a specific letter. Also known as reference points, these letters are R, S, T, and U. ISDN standards also define the device types. They are NT1, NT2, TE1, TE2, and TA. The architecture for these devices and the reference points are shown in Figure 11-1 and are explained in the following section.

ISDN Reference Points

Reference points are used to define logical interfaces. They are, in effect, a type of protocol used in communications. The following list contains the reference points:

- **R** Defines the reference point between a TE2 device and a TA device.
- **S** Defines the reference point between TE1 devices and NT1 or NT2 devices.

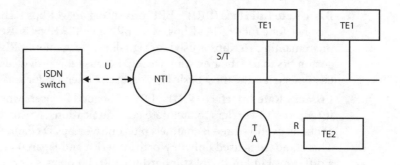

FIGURE 11-1

ISDN device
architecture

- **T**   Defines the reference point between NT1 and NT2 devices.
- **U**   Defines the reference point between NT1 devices and line termination
equipment. This is usually the central switch.

Network terminator 1 (NT1) is the device that communicates directly with the central office switch. The NT1 receives a U-interface connection from the telephone company and puts out a T-interface connection for the NT2. NT1 handles the physical-layer portions of the connection, such as physical and electrical termination, line monitoring, and multiplexing.

Network terminator 2 (NT2) is placed between an NT1 device and any adapters or terminal equipment. Many devices provide the NT1 and NT2 devices in the same physical hardware. Larger installations generally separate these devices. An example of an NT2 device is a digital private branch exchange (PBX) or ISDN router. An NT2 device provides an S interface and accepts a T interface from an NT1. NT2 usually handles data link– and network-layer functions, such as contention monitoring and routing, in networks with multiple devices.

Terminal equipment 1 (TE1) is a local device that speaks via an S interface. It can be directly connected to the NT1 or NT2 devices. An ISDN telephone and an ISDN fax are good examples of TE1 devices.

Terminal equipment 2 (TE2) devices are common, everyday devices that can be used for ISDN connectivity. Any telecommunications device that is not in the TE1 category is classified as a TE2 device. A terminal adapter is used to connect these devices to an ISDN and attaches through an R interface. Examples of TE2 devices include standard fax machines, PCs, and regular telephones.

A *terminal adapter (TA)* connects TE2 devices to an ISDN. A TA connects through the R interface to the TE2 device and through the S interface to the ISDN. The peripheral required for personal computers often includes an NT1 device, better known as an ISDN modem.

on the job **ISDN modems are used in PCs to connect them to an ISDN network. The term "modem" is used incorrectly here. ISDN passes data in a digital format, so there is no need to convert the digital data from the computer the way a traditional modem converts the digital data to analog so that it can travel. Conventional modems convert analog to digital and vice versa.**

Identifiers

Standard telephone lines use a ten-digit identifier, better known as a telephone number, which is permanently assigned. ISDN uses similar types of identifiers, but they are not as easily used as a telephone number. ISDN uses five separate identifiers to make a connection. When the connection is first set up, the provider assigns two of these: the service profile identifier (SPID) and the directory number (DN). These are the most common numbers used because the other three are dynamically set up each time a connection is made. The three dynamic identifiers are the terminal endpoint identifier (TEI), the service address point identifier (SAPI), and the bearer code (BC).

The *directory number (DN)* is the ten-digit phone number the telephone company assigns to any analog line. ISDN services enable a greater degree of flexibility in using this number than analog services do. Unlike an analog line, where a one-to-one relationship exists, the DN is only a logical mapping. A single DN can be used for multiple channels or devices. In addition, up to eight DNs can be assigned to one device. Because a single BRI can have up to eight devices, it can support up to 64 directory numbers. This is how offices are able to have multiple numbers assigned to them. Most standard BRI installations include only two directory numbers, one for each B channel.

The *service profile identifier (SPID)* is the most important number needed when you are using ISDN. The provider statically assigns the SPID when the ISDN service is set up. It usually includes the DN plus a few extra digits. The SPID usually contains between 10 and 14 characters and varies from region to region. SPIDs can be assigned for every ISDN device, for the entire line, or for each B channel.

The SPID is unique throughout the entire switch and must be set up correctly. If it is incorrect, the result is like dialing the wrong phone number—you will not be able to contact the person you are trying to reach. When an ISDN device is connected to the network, it sends the SPID to the switch. If the SPID is correct, the switch uses the stored information about your service profile to set up the data link. The ISDN device will not send the SPID again unless the device is disconnected from the network.

A *terminal endpoint identifier (TEI)* identifies the particular ISDN device to the switch. This identifier changes each time a device is connected to the ISDN. Unlike the SPID or the DN, the TEI is dynamically allocated by the central switch.

The *service address point identifier (SAPI)* identifies the particular interface on the switch to which your devices are connected. This identifier is used by the switch and is also dynamically updated each time a device connects to the network.

The *bearer code (BC)* is an identifier made up of the combination of TEI and SAPI. It is used as the call reference and is dynamic, like the two identifiers included within it. It changes each time a connection is established.

Advantages of ISDN

ISDN offers several major advantages over conventional analog methods. First, it has a speed advantage over normal dial-up lines. Normal dial-up lines use a modem to convert the digital signals from a PC into analog. This enables data to be transferred over public phone lines. This technology does, however, have speed limitations. The fastest standard modem connection that is currently available is 56 Kbps. Given that this is an analog connection, many modems cannot reach this speed, because they are limited by the quality of the connection. This fact accounts for your connecting at different speeds each time you dial in to a remote network. Because phone lines cannot actually transmit at 56 Kbps, a special kind of compression is used to enable these speeds.

ISDN enables you to use multiple digital channels at the same time to pass data through regular phone lines. The connection made from your computer, however, is completely digital; it is not converted to analog. You can use other protocols that enable you to bind channels together to get a higher bandwidth rate. In addition, ISDN makes a connection in half the time of an analog line.

In addition to speed, ISDN supports multiple devices set up in one link. In an analog system, a single line is required for each device that is attached. For example, a separate phone line is needed for a normal phone, a fax machine, or a computer modem. Since ISDN supports multiple devices, you can use each one of these items on a single line. The connection will also be clearer because the data is being passed in digital format.

Because ISDN uses a separate channel—the D channel for signaling information—it removes the administrative overhead from the B channel so that it can focus on carrying just the data signals. This means that the data is not hindered by the session setups and the signaling information that maintains the session that is required by the devices for communication. The D channel keeps all this information off the data streams (also known as "out-of-band signaling"). Because of this separation, the setup and takedown of each session is much faster. In addition, ISDN equipment is able to handle calls more efficiently.

CERTIFICATION OBJECTIVE 11.02

Remote Access Service (RAS)

RAS has become a major part of network solutions, using the telephone lines as the physical medium to transfer data. RAS allows remote clients to connect to the server over a modem using a RAS-based protocol, such as the Serial Line Internet Protocol (SLIP) or the newer Point-to-Point Protocol (PPP).

PPP can run with network protocols such as TCP/IP, Internetwork Packet Exchange/ Sequenced Packet Exchange (IPX/SPX), and NetBEUI; SLIP only supports TCP/IP. This means that you will need to ensure that the client has the same network protocol as the destination network installed and that the RAS protocol (SLIP or PPP) can run with that network protocol. For example, if the remote network is running IPX/SPX, you will need to ensure that the user who wishes to dial up to that network is running IPX/SPX and that the RAS protocol supports IPX/SPX (which the PPP protocol does).

SLIP and PPP are two communications protocols that are used by RAS to connect a computer to a remote network through a serial connection using a device such as a modem. When the computer dials up to the remote network, it is treated as an actual node on the network like any other networking device. This setup enables users to run network applications from home as though they were on the network.

SLIP and PPP are fairly similar protocols as far as the overall goal, but they differ in their implementation. They use some of the same underlying technologies, but PPP is newer and better suited for today's expanding networks. The following sections discuss each protocol—how it works and some of its advantages.

Serial Line Internet Protocol

The *Serial Line Internet Protocol (SLIP)* is an old communications protocol used for making a TCP/IP connection over a serial interface to a remote network. SLIP was designed for connecting to remote UNIX servers across a standard phone line. This protocol was one of the first of its kind, enabling a remote network connection to be established over a standard phone line. The SLIP protocol was used for dial-in over a TCP/IP network, but has been replaced by PPP.

SLIP is a very simple serial-based protocol. It does not provide the complexity that others, such as PPP, do. Although that can be an advantage, SLIP unfortunately does not include the feature set of other protocols. For example, it does not support option negotiation or error detection during the session setup. It cannot be assigned an address from a Dynamic Host Configuration Protocol (DHCP) server—it must use static addresses. It also cannot negotiate the authentication method. Issues such as these have helped define the new protocols that are emerging because a given functionality does not exist in SLIP.

The following list summarizes the characteristics of SLIP:

- Runs only with TCP/IP.
- Does not support DHCP functionality.
- Does not support compression or password encryption.
- Used to connect to older UNIX or Linux SLIP servers.

Point-to-Point Protocol

The *Point-to-Point Protocol (PPP)* is the default RAS protocol in Windows and is a data link–layer protocol used to encapsulate higher network-layer protocols to pass over synchronous and asynchronous communication lines. PPP was originally designed as an encapsulation protocol for transporting traffic from different network-based protocols over point-to-point links. PPP also established other standards, including asynchronous and bit-oriented synchronous encapsulation, network protocol multiplexing, session negotiation, and data-compression negotiation. Although everyone is using TCP/IP today, one of the original benefits of PPP was it supported protocols other than TCP/IP, such as IPX/SPX and DECnet.

For PPP to transmit data over a serial point-to-point link, it uses three components. Each component has its own separate function, but requires the use of the other two to complete its tasks. The following list explains the three components and their purposes:

- PPP uses the *High-Level Data-Link Control (HDLC)* protocol as the basis to encapsulate its data during transmission.
- PPP uses the *Link Control Protocol (LCP)* to establish, test, and configure the data link connection.
- Various *network control protocols (NCPs)* are used to configure the different communications protocols. This system enables the use of different protocols, such as TCP/IP and IPX, over the same line simultaneously.

Network Control Protocols

Although multiple network protocols are available, Microsoft products use three main protocols for PPP. Each NCP is specific to a particular network-layer protocol, such as IP or IPX/SPX. The following is a list of network control protocols:

- The *Internet Protocol Control Protocol (IPCP)* is used to enable, configure, and disable the IP protocol modules at each end of the link.
- The *Internet Packet Exchange Control Protocol (IPXCP)* is used to enable, configure, and disable IPX protocol modules at each end of the link. Although multiple versions of this NCP are available, IPXCP is the most common and is overtaking the other IPX NCPs in popularity.
- The *NetBIOS Frames Control Protocol (NBFCP)* is used to enable, configure, and disable NetBEUI protocol modules at each end of the link.

How PPP Works

PPP uses these three components together to communicate. It starts by sending LCP frames to test and configure the data link. Next, the authentication protocols are negotiated. Although numerous authentication protocols are available, the most common are the Challenge Handshake Authentication Protocol (CHAP) and the Password Authentication Protocol (PAP). They determine the type of validation performed for security. The client then sends NCP frames to configure and set up the network-layer protocols to be used during this session. When this step is complete, each network protocol can pass data through this connection. HDLC is used to encapsulate the data stream as it passes through the PPP connection. The link remains active until an LCP or NCP frame closes the link or until an error or external event occurs, such as a user disconnecting the link.

A control mechanism is included in PPP to enable each protocol to communicate with the others. Finite-state automation (FSA) processes status messages between each layer to coordinate communications. FSA does not actually participate in data flows; it works with the other protocols to keep them in sync and enables them to concentrate on their own jobs.

PPP Framing

PPP framing defines the format in which data is encapsulated before it crosses the network. PPP offers a standard framing solution that enables connections to any standard PPP server because all vendors use the same format. PPP uses HDLC as the basis for its encapsulation framing for serial connections. HDLC is widely used in other implementations and has been slightly modified for use with PPP to facilitate multiplexing NCP layers.

PPP Devices

PPP is capable of operating across any data terminal equipment or data circuit terminating equipment (DTE/DCE) device. Many examples of these devices are available, including the most common: those following the EIA/TIA-232 standard—better known as modems. PPP is able to use any DTE/DCE devices as long as they support full-duplex circuits. These can be dedicated or switched and can operate in an asynchronous or synchronous bit-serial mode. In addition, the limit on transmission rates is specified by the interfaces and is not controlled by PPP.

You should remember that the DTE is the terminal or PC used to communicate with other systems and the DCE is the modem that actually does the communicating.

Authentication Protocols

With PPP, each system could be required to authenticate itself. This can be done using an authentication protocol. The most common authentication protocols are PAP, CHAP, and the Microsoft adaptation of CHAP, MS-CHAP. When a connection is being established, either end node can require the other to authenticate itself, whether it is the remote host or the originator of the call. The LCP can be used to send information to the other node to specify the authentication type. Using the authentication protocols, you enable the capability to offer a level of security by requiring authentication to make a remote connection; you also have control over the level of security used.

PAP works much like a regular network login. The client authenticates itself to a server by passing the user name and password to it. The server then compares this information to its password store. Because the password is passed in clear text, this system would not work well in an environment in which security concerns are an issue. The system opens the door for anyone "listening" to the line, such as with a network sniffer.

Alternatively, CHAP uses an encryption algorithm to pass the authentication data to protect it from hackers. The server sends the client a randomly generated challenge request with its hostname. The client then uses the hostname to look up the appropriate secret password and returns a response using a one-way hash with the client's hostname. The host now compares the result and acknowledges the client if it matches. CHAP also sends challenges at regular intervals to verify that the correct client is still using this connection. The challenge values change during each interval. Because CHAP is so much more secure than PAP, it is used widely on the Internet. PAP is usually used only in public FTP sites or other public areas.

MS-CHAP is a Microsoft adaptation of CHAP. It uses the same type of encryption methodology, but is slightly more secure. The server sends a challenge to the originating host, which must return the user name and an MD-4 hash of the challenge string, the session ID, and the MD-4 hashed password. This system enables the authenticator to store the passwords in an encrypted format instead of plain text. Figure 11-2 shows the authentication protocol selections when using PPP as the dial-in protocol for Windows. To obtain a list of the supported protocols, go to your dial-in connection properties and select the Security tab. Once on the Security tab, you can select the Advanced security option and then click Settings to view the authentication protocols.

FIGURE 11-2

Authentication protocols supported with PPP in Windows

RAS and VPN Authentication Protocols

The Network+ certification exam expects you to remember some of the common authentication protocols used when connecting to a remote system over RAS or a secure VPN tunnel. Both RAS and VPN support authentication before allowing someone to remotely connect with any of the following protocols:

- **Kerberos**   Kerberos is a mutual authentication protocol that is used to authenticate not just the user connecting to a server, but authenticates the server as well. Kerberos is based on a ticket-granting service where the client is granted a ticket to access a server (or service) for a certain amount of time. The ticket is granted by the *Key Distribution Center (KDC)*. Active Directory is an example of a network environment that uses Kerberos.

- **Password Authentication Protocol (PAP)**   The Password Authentication Protocol sends the user's credentials in plain text and is very unsecure because of how easy it is for someone to analyze and interpret the logon traffic. This is the authentication protocol used by the basic authentication method mentioned previously.

- **Challenge Handshake Authentication Protocol (CHAP)**   With CHAP, the server sends a challenge to the client that is then used in the authentication process. The following steps are performed by CHAP:

  1. The server sends the client a challenge (a key).

  2. The client then combines the challenge with the password. Both the user's password and the

challenge are run through the MD5 hashing algorithm (a formula), which generates a hash value, or mathematical answer. The hash value is sent to the server for authentication.

  3. The server uses the same key to create a hash value with the password stored on the server and then compares the resulting value with the hash value sent by the client. If the two hash values are the same, the client has supplied the correct password. The benefit is that the user's credentials have not been passed across the network at all.

- **Microsoft Challenge Handshake Authentication Protocol (MS-CHAP)**   MS-CHAP is a variation of the CHAP authentication protocol and uses MD4 as the hashing algorithm versus MD5 used by CHAP. MS-CHAP also uses the Microsoft Point-to-Point Encryption (MPPE) protocol along with MS-CHAP to encrypt all traffic from the client to the server.

- **MS-CHAPv2**   With MS-CHAP version 2, the authentication method has been extended to authenticate both the client and the server. MS-CHAPv2 also uses stronger encryption keys than CHAP and MS-CHAP.

- **Extensible Authentication Protocol (EAP)**   EAP allows for multiple logon methods, such as smartcard logon, certificates, Kerberos, and public-key authentication. EAP is also frequently used with Remote Authentication Dial-In User Service (RADIUS), which is a central authentication service that can be used by RAS, wireless, or VPN solutions.

Multifactor Authentication

Along with authentication protocols, you can use multifactor authentication models. Multifactor authentication is when we use more than one of the following authentication factors together:

- **Something you know**   User is authenticated by something they can type like a password or PIN number.
- **Something you have**   Authentication occurs by having an item in your possession such as a smartcard or authentication token.
- **Something you are**   You are authenticated to a system or network by one of your characteristics such as a fingerprint or retina scan.

An example of multifactor authentication is using a debit card (something you have) and providing the PIN number for that debit card (something you know). It should be stressed that when two of the previous factors are used together, we call that *two-factor authentication,* while if we are using more than two, we simply call it multifactor authentication. Note that the most common method of logging onto a system is knowing the user name and password and that is only *single-factor authentication,* and is not considered a strong authentication method.

One last authentication term you should know for the Network+ exam is *single sign-on (SSO).* SSO is the concept that when you log on with your user name and password to the network, that authentication should allow you to access all the network resources you are allowed to access, such as files, folders, printers, the database server, and your e-mail. In an SSO environment, you would not need to log on each time you tried to access one of those resources—including resources on different servers.

Troubleshooting PPP

When you use PPP to connect to a remote network, you may encounter problems. These problems can range from no dial tone to a modem misconfiguration or connectivity problems with the remote PPP server. A log is included with your communication device to enable you to monitor the steps in opening a PPP connection and to troubleshoot where the breakdown might have occurred. To enable modem logging in Windows, go to the properties of the modem device in Device Manager and click the Diagnostics tab. On the Diagnostics tab, choose the Append To Log option as shown in Figure 11-3.

When logging has been enabled, you can see the log file after the next attempt to connect to a PPP server. The log file, modemlog_modemname.txt, is stored in the Windows directory by default. It can be viewed using any standard text editor and is appended each time a new connection is attempted.

FIGURE 11-3

Enabling modem
logging in
Windows

Figure 11-4 shows the beginning of a PPP connection to a remote network. It demonstrates the layout of the log file and how detailed it can become. Understanding how to read these log files enables you to troubleshoot almost any PPP problem that could occur.

FIGURE 11-4

Viewing the
modem log

```
05-18-1998 20:10:30.83 - Remote access driver log opened.
05-18-1998 20:10:30.83 - Installable CP VxD SPAP     is loaded
05-18-1998 20:10:30.83 - Server type is  PPP (Point to Point
Protocol).
05-18-1998 20:10:30.83 - FSA : Adding Control Protocol 80fd (CCP) to
control protocol chain.
05-18-1998 20:10:30.83 - FSA : Protocol not bound - skipping control
protocol 803f (NBFCP).
05-18-1998 20:10:30.83 - FSA : Adding Control Protocol 8021 (IPCP) to
control protocol chain.
05-18-1998 20:10:30.83 - FSA : Protocol not bound - skipping control
protocol 802b (IPXCP).
05-18-1998 20:10:30.83 - FSA : Adding Control Protocol c029
(CallbackCP) to control protocol chain.
05-18-1998 20:10:30.83 - FSA : Adding Control Protocol c027 (no
description) to control protocol chain.
05-18-1998 20:10:30.83 - FSA : Adding Control Protocol c023 (PAP) to
control protocol chain.
```

EXERCISE 11-1

Enabling Modem Logging in Windows

In this exercise, you will enable logging on the modem to aid in the troubleshooting of communication problems with RAS-based protocols. In this exercise you will need a Windows 8 system that has a modem installed. You can see this exercise in action in video 11-1.

1. Switch to the Windows 8 virtual machine (VM).
2. Go to Device Manager.
3. In Device Manager, locate your modem in the modems category. Right-click your modem and choose Properties.
4. In the modem properties dialog box, click the Diagnostics tab and at the bottom choose the Append To Log option. Notice that you can also do a diagnostics check on the modem with the Query Modem button.
5. Click OK and close all windows.

Advantages of PPP over SLIP

PPP offers several advantages over the older SLIP protocol. First, PPP offers multinetwork protocol support, meaning that it can run with IPX/SPX, TCP/IP, NetBEUI, and AppleTalk, while SLIP can be used only with TCP/IP. Any of these protocols can be used, which enables you to connect to multiple types of systems on the remote network through dial-up. The addition of NCPs allows for this functionality in PPP.

In addition, PPP offers the capability to use DHCP, which was made possible through the use of LCP. Furthermore, PPP handles higher-speed links better than SLIP does. This is due to the error-checking capability within the protocol. SLIP does not check datagrams for errors as they pass through the connection.

The following list summarizes the characteristics of PPP:

For the exam, know that PPP and SLIP are RAS protocols.

- PPP can run with TCP/IP, IPX/SPX, NetBEUI, AppleTalk, or DECnet.
- PPP can use DHCP.
- PPP performs error checking and supports compression.

Understanding PPPoE

Another PPP technology you should be familiar with for the Network+ certification exam is Point-to-Point Protocol over Ethernet, or PPPoE for short. PPPoE is a network protocol that is responsible for placing PPP packets into an Ethernet frame to carry the data from one point to another. PPPoE is a common protocol in high-speed Internet solutions such as Digital Subscriber Line (DSL), the high-speed Internet solution offered by many phone companies. You will learn more about DSL in Chapter 12.

CERTIFICATION OBJECTIVE 11.03

Dial-Up Networking

Remote connectivity has had a huge impact on the world market. Many businesses everywhere use remote connectivity to interconnect sites to a single network. It is also used to connect users to the public Internet and to private corporate networks. The New Connection Wizard in Windows allows you to connect to several different remote servers or to act as a server, depending on how you answer the questions in the wizard. Figure 11-5 shows the various connections that can be built with the New Connection Wizard in Windows 8.

FIGURE 11-5

Creating network connections with the New Connection Wizard

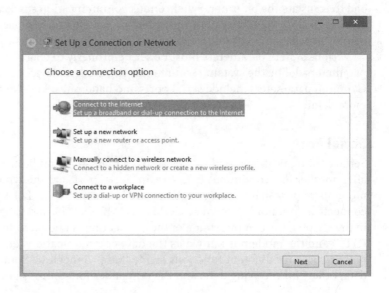

The following list summarizes the options found in the New Connection Wizard that are used to connect to a remote system in one form or another:

- **Connect to the Internet**   This option is used to create a dial-in client that is set up by the wizard asking you questions about your connection to your ISP.
- **Set up a new network**   This option helps you configure a detected wireless router or access point with the Network Setup Wizard.
- **Manually connect to a wireless network**   This option will allow you to connect to a wireless network by manually configuring settings such as the Service Set Identifier (SSID).
- **Connect to a workplace**   This option is used to create a dial-in client to a RAS server; it also allows you to create a VPN client that connects to a VPN server.

Modem Configuration Parameters

Modems are data communication devices that are used to pass data through the PSTN from node to node. A modem—the word combines modulator with demodulator—is used to convert a digital signal to an analog format to transmit data across the network. It reverses the conversion process on the other end node to receive the data. Typically, the EIA/TIA-232 serial standard is used to connect the modem to a computer.

Modem communication can be of several types: asynchronous, synchronous, or both. In asynchronous communication, all data is sent separately, relying on the node on the other end to translate the bit order. Synchronous communication sends all data in a steady stream and uses a clock signal to interpret the beginning and end of a packet. Most users today employ synchronous communication in the modems that they buy.

Various system parameters must be set up properly to enable a modem to work. These parameters define the system resources for the modem device to use during its operations. Common parameters include serial ports and baud rates. Let's look at these parameters in more detail.

Serial Port

Serial communications send signals across a point-to-point link. Bits are transmitted one after another in a continuous data stream. Serial ports are the typical means for connecting modems to personal computers. They are based on 9-pin (DB-9) and 25-pin (DB-25) connectors commonly known as COM1, COM2, COM3, and COM4. As mentioned earlier in the chapter, the computer side of the connection is known as the data terminal equipment (DTE) and the modem is known as the data communications equipment (DCE). Various pins are used for different functions inside these connectors. Some are used for transmitting data, others for receiving data, and the remainder for control signals.

You must specify the appropriate serial port settings when you set up a modem. Most modems attempt to use COM1 by default. Each COM port is assigned a specific set of address variables by default when you set up connections. To change the modem COM port after the setup is complete, select Start | Control Panel | Printers And Other Hardware | Phone And Modem Options. Highlight the appropriate modem on the Modem page and click Properties.

Maximum Port Speed

The maximum port speed is defined by the kilobits per second that the modem can support. Maximum rates are defined primarily by the modem hardware; however, the current public telephone network has an upper limit of 56 Kbps through an analog modem. Port speeds are defined by the standards and features available to them.

on the Job

Note that the terms baud and port speed are not identical. Port speed defines how fast data is traveling; baud measures the signal change per second. With encoding, 2 bits look like 1; therefore, the two terms will not match.

Multiple modem standards exist to define the various features and bandwidths available. Various models provide different standards levels. Before you purchase any modem, you should verify that it fits your current needs and meets the appropriate standard. Table 11-1 illustrates the standards.

To configure the port speed in Windows 8, select the Settings charm and then choose Control Panel | Hardware And Sound. Choose the Device Manager link in the Devices And Printers category. In Device Manager, right-click your modem and choose Properties.

TABLE 11-1

Modem Standards That Define Speeds and Features

Standard	Feature Set
V.22	1200 bps, full duplex
V.22bis	2400 bps, full duplex
V.32	Async/sync, 4800 bps/9600 bps
V.32bis	Async/sync, 14,400 bps
V.35	Defines high transfer rates over dedicated circuits
V.42	Defines error-checking standards
V.42bis	Defines modem compression
V.34	28,800 bps
V.34+	33,600 bps

FIGURE 11-6

Setting the
modem speed

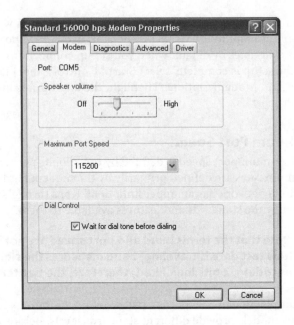

When the properties dialog box of the modem appears, click the Modem tab. Select the
appropriate port speed from the Maximum Port Speed list, as shown in Figure 11-6.

Unimodem

With Windows operating systems, an additional subsystem is available to simplify dial-up
networking. Unimodem provides an easy, centralized mechanism for installing and
configuring modems, as shown in Figure 11-7. When installing the modem, the wizard
enables you to specify configurations included with Windows or to obtain the configuration
from disk. Windows ships with over 600 modem configurations included. The information
obtained by this process is then accessible to any other application. Many applications
written today that run on Windows specifically request information from this process if
a modem is required. To get to the Phone And Modems dialog in Windows 8, choose the
Start charm and type **Phone And Modem**.

Telephony API

The Microsoft Telephony API (TAPI) is an application interface used for accessing
communications features such as connection monitoring. This API is used to provide
services such as these without relying on the hardware to set them up. It ties in heavily to

FIGURE 11-7

The Unimodem process enables one interface for configuring modems.

the Unimodem mechanism. TAPI functions completely independently from the device hardware. It is now used for modem data transfers; the COMM.API is used for these operations.

When modems were first becoming popular, they could be difficult to configure. You had to understand the settings to use, such as which COM port to set up; the system resources, such as IRQs and DMA channels; and modem baud rates. Each application that was to use this device had to be set up separately. This process could take a great deal of time and quickly became complex when you attempted to use advanced modem initialization strings. TAPI replaced this requirement by providing a standard interface with which the modem would communicate so that the interface could be set up once and all applications could use it.

TAPI also provides other features, such as multiple calling locations. You can set up connection profiles for different dial-up access numbers. You can also customize how the number is dialed. For example, suppose you set up two separate connection profiles, one with call waiting enabled and the second without it. This setup enables you to manage multiple connections without having to reconfigure your modem setup every time you need a variation.

To access the TAPI options, select the Start charm and then type **Phone And Modem**. Choose the Phone And Modem option from the search results. On the Dialing Rules tab, ensure My Location is selected and choose the Edit button. Figure 11-8 displays some of the options available for customization.

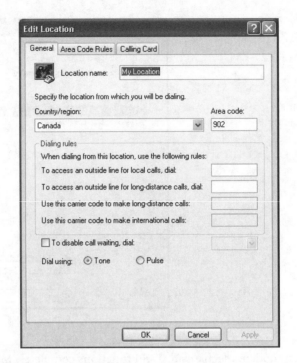

FIGURE 11-8

TAPI interface in
Windows

Requirements for a Remote Connection

Over the course of this chapter, we have addressed several types of remote connectivity technologies. Each has its strengths and weaknesses along with its core functions. Some technologies provide features or functionality that you might not need or want. Understanding how each one works and its benefits and disadvantages enables you to recommend solutions to fit business needs. It is now time to pull all the information together to figure out what is required to make your remote connection work.

To provide access to a remote server or network, you must properly set up and configure several items. Each item depends on other items, and this connection will not work without them all. The following list contains the common components required to connect to remote resources:

- **Dial-up networking client**   This client must be set up with the appropriate parameters defined.
- **Remote access server**   You must have a remote access server to dial in to reach a remote network.
- **User account (PPP, SLIP, RAS)**   You must have a valid ID and password on the remote server or network that has been granted dial-in permission.

- **Modem/ISDN**   You must have a hardware device that enables you to communicate with the remote host.
- **Access protocol**   A network-layer protocol must be set up and configured properly to access resources on the remote server or network. Examples could include TCP/IP, IPX, and NetBEUI, but realistically, TCP/IP will be the underlining protocol.

EXERCISE 11-2

Video

Creating a PPP Dial-Up Connection

In this exercise, you will use the New Connection Wizard in Windows 8 to create a RAS connection that will dial up a corporate RAS server that resides at the phone number 555-5555.

1. Switch to your Windows 8 VM.
2. Go to your Settings charm and choose Control Panel | Network And Internet | Network And Sharing Center.
3. In the Network And Sharing Center, click the Set Up A New Connection Or Network link.
4. Select the type of connection you want to build. In this example, you are dialing in to a RAS server over a phone line, so choose the Connect To A Workplace option. You will notice that the description of this option specifies that you are using the dial-up feature or VPN. Also note that the option says that you are connecting to the workplace, but you would use this option any time you are dialing into a RAS server or a VPN server. Click Next.
5. Now you specify whether you want to use the dial-up or VPN feature. In this example, you are going to dial up the server; choose Dial Directly.
6. You are then asked for the phone number of the server you wish to connect to. You will need to include the area code and maybe a 1 if the call is long distance. Enter **555-555-5555** as the phone number and specify a name for this destination as **Workplace In Toronto** and then choose Next.
7. Type the user name and password and, optionally, the domain name of the user account that you will use to authenticate to this remote network and then choose Connect.
8. The connection will be attempted, but because it is a fake number, choose Skip and then choose Close.
9. To change settings of the connection, such as the phone number being dialed or the authentication protocol to use, choose the Change Adapter Settings link on the left side and then you can right-click the connection and choose Properties.

10. In the properties dialog box of the connection, you can change a number of settings, including the phone number you are dialing on the General page, your dialing option on the Option tab, the authentication protocols on the Security tab, and the protocols to use on the Networking tab.

11. Once you have browsed through the options, click Cancel and then close all Windows.

12. To connect to the server by dialing the phone number of the connection, choose the Settings charm and then choose Network. A list of connections appears; choose the connection and then click the Connect button. Type the user name and password of someone who has permission to dial into that server and then choose the Dial button.

13. Close all windows to end the exercise.

CERTIFICATION OBJECTIVE 11.04

Virtual Private Networks (VPNs)

This chapter has so far discussed how to connect to a remote network using RAS, which typically involves a connection across the PSTN from one system to another. RAS is a great solution to remotely connect to a system, but it does mean that we are incurring long-distance phone calls. The solution to cut down on long-distance calls was to use the Internet as the physical connection. In order to use the public Internet as a physical medium to carry data between a client and the remote network, you first want to create an encrypted tunnel between you and the remote network; then the data is delivered in the encrypted tunnel. This will ensure that no one can intercept the data and read it because it is transmitted in an encrypted format—the purpose of the VPN.

VPN Overview

Once the Internet became popular, it was an obvious solution to allow users in remote locations to communicate with distant networks. For example, if we had an office in New York and a user in a hotel room in Boston who wanted to access the network in New York, what better solution than to use the Internet? The problem, of course, is the security issues that surround sending data across the Internet for the entire world to tap into!

Virtual private networks (VPNs) offer a solution. The idea of a VPN is that the user in Boston who is in the hotel will dial up to the Internet using the ISP in Boston provided by the hotel. Once the user in the hotel has the Internet connection, he or she will then dial the IP address of the VPN server in New York to create a "secure tunnel" between the client system and the VPN server in New York. Any data that travels between the two systems will be encrypted and therefore will be considered secure.

Two of the major benefits of VPN are secure communication across an unsecure medium and the lack of long-distance costs incurred to communicate between the two locations. Once all systems have an Internet connection, VPN solutions leverage that Internet connection and add security to it.

Just as there are two primary RAS protocols (SLIP and PPP), there are three primary VPN protocols that provide this tunneling security; they are the Point-to-Point Tunneling Protocol (PPTP), Layer 2 Tunneling Protocol (L2TP), and Secure Socket Transport Protocol (SSTP).

VPN Protocols

The *Point-to-Point Tunneling Protocol (PPTP),* sometimes referred to as the *Point to Point (PTP)* protocol, provides for the secure transfer of data from a remote client to a private server by creating a multiprotocol virtual private network, or VPN. PPTP is used in TCP/IP networks as an alternative to conventional dial-up networking methods. This system enables multiprotocol secure communication over a public TCP/IP network such as the Internet. PPTP takes advantage of an additional level of security that is not currently available in other standard implementations.

e x a m
ⓦ a t c h　　　**Both PPTP and L2TP are** **VPN protocols used to create a secure tunnel across an unsecured network such as the Internet. PPTP is actually an extension of PPP. It encapsulates PPP packets into IP datagrams for transmission** **across a network. This system enables the functionality of PPP while taking advantage of the security features offered by the VPN technology. Using both options tied into one protocol, you get the best of both worlds.**

A Brief History of PPTP

PPTP was recognized by the IETF (a standards committee) in June 1996. Although many tunneling protocols have been created and implemented, this was the first standard tunneling protocol to become available. Many vendors have adopted it in an attempt to provide a secure method to connect across the public Internet into a corporate internal network.

How PPTP Works

VPNs are used to provide tunneling through a public network with a secure communications channel. Users can employ PPTP to dial into a public network, such as PSTN, to use the

Internet to connect to their corporate offices. This system enables users to use the network infrastructure that is already in place and eliminates the need for dedicated modem banks for users.

PPTP tunneling can be defined as the process of routing packets through an intermediate public network to reach a private network. Only the PPTP-enabled client can access the remote network; other clients on the same segment cannot. The interesting thing about this process is that you can dial into a standard PPP server and use it to establish a PPTP connection to the remote network. No additional setup or option choices are required of your ISP; most offer PPP access already. You could also set up a PPTP server to dial into; this setup would enable you to only require PPP to be set up on the clients.

INSIDE THE EXAM

Securing Communication with VPNs

The Network+ certification exam expects you to understand the purpose of a VPN and the two main protocols to encrypt communication with a VPN. Remember that a VPN is designed to establish a secure (encrypted) tunnel over an untrusted network, such as the Internet, and is used to encrypt traffic that travels across that untrusted network.

The following are three common protocols used to secure VPN traffic:

- **Point-to-Point Tunneling Protocol (PPTP)** PPTP is an older VPN protocol used to encrypt PPP traffic and is common in Microsoft environments. PPTP uses the Generic Routing Encapsulation (GRE) protocol to transport the PPP packets, but the Microsoft Point-to-Point Encryption (MPPE) protocol to encrypt the traffic. To allow PPTP traffic to pass through the firewall, you will need to open TCP port 1723 (control port) and protocol ID 47 (carries the data) on the firewall.

- **Layer 2 Tunneling Protocol (L2TP)** L2TP has been around for quite a few years now, but is a newer VPN protocol than PPTP. L2TP uses the more secure IPSec (Internet Protocol Security) for encryption of traffic instead of MPPE. To allow L2TP traffic through your firewall, you will need to open UDP port 500 (for key exchange), UDP port 5500 (for IPSec NAT), and UDP port 1701 on the firewall.

- **Secure Socket Transport Protocol (SSTP)** The SSTP protocol is a common VPN protocol today and is the newest of the three protocols listed here. SSTP has the benefit that it uses Secure Sockets Layer (SSL) to encrypt the VPN traffic so it is easy to configure the firewall to allow VPN traffic to pass through—you simply need to open the SSL port of 443!

Once the PPTP server receives the packet from the client connection, it routes the data to the appropriate resource. The PPTP and PPP overhead is stripped off to obtain the addressing information originally applied to it. The PPTP server must be configured with TCP/IP to communicate with PPTP and whatever other protocols are being passed through this VPN tunnel.

A VPN works by encapsulating the data within IP packets to transport it through PPP. This enables the data to pass through the Internet and use the standards already in place. No configuration changes are required to your existing network stacks; they can be used as-is over the PPTP connection. Other protocols, such as NetBEUI and IPX, can also pass through this secure connection.

VPNs are virtual devices set up as though they were regular devices such as modems. In addition, PPTP must be set up on the client and the server. Host computers in the route between these two computers do not need to be PPTP aware, since the packet's IP header is not encrypted. They need only provide an IP route to the remote server. Figure 11-9 shows the layout of a VPN solution.

PPTP mainly involves three processes to set up a secure communications channel. Each process must be completed before beginning the next process. The following list identifies the processes involved:

- **PPP connection and communication** PPTP uses PPP to connect to a remote network. When connected, PPP is also used to encrypt the data packets being passed between the remote host and the local machine.

FIGURE 11-9 PPTP connections create a secure tunnel over an unsecured network.

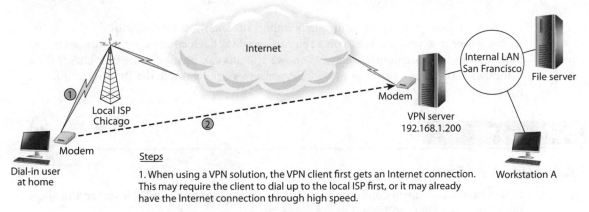

Steps

1. When using a VPN solution, the VPN client first gets an Internet connection. This may require the client to dial up to the local ISP first, or it may already have the Internet connection through high speed.

2. The VPN client dials the IP address or FQDN of the VPN server. When authenticated, a secure tunnel is created by the VPN protocol such as PPTP or L2TP. All traffic between the VPN client and VPN server is encrypted.

■ **PPTP control connection** When the PPP session is established, PPTP creates a control connection between the client and the remote PPTP server. This process is referred to as tunneling.

■ **PPTP data tunneling** PPTP creates the IP datagrams for PPP to send. PPP encrypts the data portion of packets, which are sent through the tunnel to the PPTP server. The PPTP server is then used to decrypt the PPP-encrypted packets, disassemble the IP datagram, and route to the appropriate host.

PPTP relies heavily on PPP to perform its job. PPP is used to enable multiple network-layer protocols to be used within the connection. It is also used to perform other functions, such as establishing and maintaining a connection, authenticating users, and encrypting data packets.

Be sure that you know the three processes involved with PPTP and how PPP applies to each one.

Setting Up PPTP

There are three main components to setting up a PPTP connection:

■ **PPTP client** This is a client system that connects to the PPTP server by IP address or fully qualified domain name (FQDN).

■ **PPTP server** This is the VPN server that allows for PPTP connections.

■ **Network access server (NAS)** This is the server that connects to the network you will use to call the PPTP server. Typically, this is the ISP that is responsible for connecting you to the Internet.

These various components are equally important and must be configured properly to enable a user to access resources on a remote network. Each component has its specified functions and requirements. Today, Windows systems can be used as a PPTP client, while Windows 2003 Server also supports PPTP server services through the Routing and Remote Access Service (RRAS).

EXERCISE 11-3

Setting Up a VPN Server

In this exercise, you will configure your 2012SERVERA system as a VPN server and allow the Windows 8 client to VPN into the network.

Setting Up the VMs

1. Ensure that all VMs are stopped.
2. Add a second network card to 2012SERVERA, and choose Private as the type of connection for the card.
3. Start the 2012SERVERA and the Windows 8 VMs.
4. Change the IP address on the newly added card for the 2012SERVERA VM to 14.0.0.1 with a subnet mask of 255.0.0.0. You will pretend that the 14.0.0.0 network is on the Internet.
5. Change the IP address of the Windows 8 VM to 14.0.0.2 with a subnet mask of 255.0.0.0. This will place the Windows 8 client on the "Internet" with the 2012SERVERA.
6. From the Windows 8 client, can you ping 14.0.0.1? _____
7. On the 2012SERVERA VM, create a user named Bob with a password of Pa$$w0rd in Active Directory. This will be the user who can VPN into the network. Create a group called MyVPNUsers and place Bob in that group.

Configuring the VPN Server

1. To configure 2012SERVERA as the VPN server, choose the Server Manager button on the task bar to add VPN capabilities to the system.
2. Choose Manage | Add Roles And Features.
3. Choose Next.
4. Choose Role-Based Or Feature-Based Installation and then choose Next.
5. Ensure your server is selected and then choose Next.
6. Choose the Network Policy And Access Services role and the Remote Access role.
7. Choose Add Features and then choose Next.
8. Choose Next three times to pass by the Features list and the Network Policy and Access Services overview, and to select the default service of Network Policy Server.
9. Choose Install.
10. After installation, choose Close.
11. In Server Manager, choose Tools | Routing And Remote Access.
12. Right-click the 2012SERVERA icon and choose Configure And Enable Routing And Remote Access.
13. The Routing and Remote Access Wizard starts. Click Next.

14. In the Configuration screen, choose Remote Access (Dial-up Or VPN) and then choose Next.

15. For the connection type, choose VPN and then click Next.

16. In the VPN connection screen, choose the interface that clients will connect to from the Internet. This is the interface with the IP address of 14.0.0.1. Choose that interface and then click Next. Notice that there is an option selected stating that packet filtering is enabled on this interface. This will configure packet-filtering rules so that only VPN traffic can pass through the interface.

17. You will let DHCP assign an IP address to the client when the client connects, so ensure Automatically is selected and then click Next.

18. Choose Next to not use RADIUS.

19. Click Finish.

20. Read the message that appears. You have to configure the 2012SERVERA system as the DHCP relay agent to allow VPN clients to obtain an IP address from DHCP. Click OK.

21. To configure the DHCP relay agent, select the DHCP Relay Agent node on the left (found under IPv4). Now right-click the DHCP relay agent and choose Properties.

22. Type the IP address of the DHCP server, which is **10.0.0.1**, and then click Add.

23. To allow users to VPN into the network, you will have to change the RAS policy because by default no one is allowed to RAS or VPN into the network. To change the RAS policy, go to Server Manager and choose Tools | Network Policy Server.

24. In the Network Policy Server, expand Policies and select Network Policies. Notice the two default policies on the right are to deny access. Right-click Network Policies and choose New.

25. Specify a policy name of **Allow_VPNUsers** and then choose Remote Access Server (VPN-Dial Up) as the type of network access server. Choose Next.

26. In the Specify Conditions window, click Add. Choose Windows Group as the condition and then choose Add.

27. Choose Add Group, type **MyVPNUsers**, and click the Check Name button to verify that the group exists. Choose OK twice and then choose Next.

28. Choose the Access Granted option to ensure the rule allows this group to VPN into the network.

29. Click Next four times and then choose Finish.

Understand that in this day and age, the VPN client will typically not need to dial up to the ISP to get an Internet connection before dialing into the VPN server. With the widespread use of high-speed Internet, today's VPN client will most likely already have an Internet connection and, therefore, simply needs to connect to the IP address of the VPN server to make a VPN connection.

EXERCISE 11-4

Setting Up a VPN Client

In this exercise you will use the New Connection Wizard to configure your Windows 8 system as a VPN client to connect to the VPN server using PPTP as the VPN protocol.

1. Switch to your Windows 8 VM.

2. Go to your Settings charm and choose Control Panel | Network And Internet | Network And Sharing Center.

3. In the Network and Sharing Center, click the Set Up A New Connection Or Network link.

4. Select the type of connection you want to build. In this example, you are connecting to a VPN server, so choose the Connect To A Workplace option. Click Next.

5. Now you specify whether you want to use the dial-up or VPN feature. In this example, you are going to dial up the server; choose Use My Internet Connection (VPN).

6. You will now specify whether you want to automatically dial up to the Internet when this VPN connection is used. We will assume that you will already have the Internet connection when you use the VPN connection, so choose the Let Me Decide Later option and choose Next.

7. You will now provide the IP address or FQDN of the VPN server. This will act as the "phone number" for the VPN server that you will dial once you have a connection to the Internet. Type **14.0.0.1** as the Internet address and set the destination name to **VPN Server In New York**. Choose Create.

8. To force the VPN client to use a specific protocol such as PPTP, go to the Settings charm | Control Panel | Network And Internet | Network And Sharing Center | Change Adapter Settings.

9. Right-click the VPN Server In New York connection and choose Properties.

10. In the properties dialog box of the connection, go to the Security tab and click the drop-down list to set the type of VPN you want to use. Select PPTP VPN from the list. Then choose OK.

11. Close all windows.

12. To connect to the VPN server at any time, you can navigate to the Settings charm and then choose Network. A list of connections appears; choose the **VPN Server In New York** connection and then click the Connect button. Type the user name and password of someone who has permission to VPN into that server and then choose the OK button.

13. Close all windows to end the exercise.

Because of the popularity of PPP and the Internet, a more secure dial-in solution is needed. PPTP grants you the capability to have a user log in to a remote, private, corporate network via any ISP and maintain a secure, encrypted connection. This concept is being implemented by more and more companies every year; its popularity has exploded since its first draft was proposed in 1996.

Other Tunneling and Encryption Protocols

The Network+ certification exam is sure to ask you about VPN technologies and expects you to know PPTP, L2TP, and SSTP, but the exam objectives also make reference to other encryption technologies you should be familiar with:

■ **SSL VPN** As mentioned earlier in this chapter, a newer approach to encrypting VPN traffic is to use an SSL VPN solution, which secures communication over SSL traffic. The benefit of using SSL VPN is that it is based on common Internet protocols (SSL), so your company may already have the SSL port open on the firewall (TCP port 443). The problem with PPTP and L2TP is that you must open a number of ports on the firewall.

■ **IPSec** The *IP Security (IPSec) protocol* is used to encrypt all IP traffic once IPSec has been enabled on the system or device. The IPSec protocol uses Encapsulation Security Payload (ESP) to encrypt traffic, Authentication Header (AH) protocol for message integrity and authentication, and Internet Key Exchange (IKE) to exchange encryption keys between systems.

■ **ISAKMP** The *Internet Security Association and Key Management protocol (ISAKMP)* is responsible for setting up a secure channel (known as a security association) and exchanging keys. ISAKMP is used by IKE for authentication before key exchange.

■ **TLS and TLS 1.2** Transport Layer Security (TLS) and TLS 1.2 are encryption protocols designed to replace SSL to encrypt Internet traffic. TLS can be used to encrypt different types of network traffic, such as HTTP, FTP, VoIP, and VPN.

■ **TACACS/RADIUS** *Remote Authentication Dial-In User Service (RADIUS)* is a central authentication service that you can use to control who can connect to the network via VPN solutions, wireless, and wired network connections. *Terminal Access Controller Access-Control System (TACACS)* is similar to RADIUS, but is an older authentication service that was common with UNIX environments.

■ **SSH** *Secure Shell (SSH)* is a common security protocol that is responsible for encrypting communication between a client and the SSH host. SSH is a secure replacement for unsecure Internet protocols such as Telnet and uses TCP port 22.

There are different topologies for VPN, or ways to configure your VPN environment. The following are the most common VPN topologies:

- **Site to site** A common term used when discussing VPN solutions is site to site. A site-to-site VPN means that there is a VPN appliance at each location that is used to create the encrypted tunnel from one location to another. In this example, the clients are not establishing the tunnel and, as such, do not need a configured VPN connection to the remote location; they will go through a network device such as a router that will create the VPN tunnel to the other location.

- **Host to site** The opposite of site to site is host to site, which means that the client (which is the host) creates the secure VPN tunnel to the remote location. In this example, if you wanted five users to transmit the data to a remote site securely, each client would create their own VPN tunnel, whereas with site to site, the tunnel is established once by the VPN appliance and all users send information securely through the one tunnel.

- **Host to host** You can also use VPN technology to create an encrypted tunnel between two computers in a host-to-host topology. In this case, a client computer is creating a VPN connection to another client computer and all communication between the two is encrypted.

Most larger companies now have employees traveling for training, seminars, and conventions. Companies require a means for these traveling employees to be able to access the company network securely. Remote access is becoming widely used, whether via direct connections with modems or a VPN connection through the Internet.

CERTIFICATION SUMMARY

The concept behind remote connectivity is to provide access to a network from a remote location. Originally, the U.S. government used ARPANET to connect remote sites. From there, networks have drastically expanded in size during the past several decades. Many technologies have been spawned from the growing need for remote access.

The Point-to-Point Protocol (PPP) and Serial Line Internet Protocol (SLIP) are communications protocols used to communicate with remote networks through a serial device such as an analog modem. SLIP was originally designed to connect to remote UNIX computers. SLIP supports only the TCP/IP network-layer protocol. It has been replaced by PPP.

PPP is a more robust protocol than SLIP. It was designed to handle multiple network-layer protocols, such as TCP/IP, IPX, and NetBEUI. It includes additional features, such as encapsulation, network protocol multiplexing, session negotiation, and data-compression negotiation. PPP uses three subprotocols: the High-Level Data-Link Control (HDLC), network control protocol (NCP), and Link Control Protocol (LCP). HDLC handles data encapsulation, NCP handles network-layer protocols, and LCP handles connection maintenance and testing. PPP uses three different NCPs: IPCP for TCP/IP, IPXCP for IPX, and NBFCP for NetBEUI. PPP uses authentication protocols such as CHAP, PAP, and MS-CHAP. The file ppplog.txt is located in the Windows directory, which by default is C:\Windows, and is used to troubleshoot PPP issues.

The Point-to-Point Tunneling Protocol (PPTP) provides a secure communications channel through a public TCP/IP network such as the Internet. It provides multiple network-layer protocol support using PPP as the underlying structure. PPTP uses a technology called virtual private networks (VPNs) to create the encrypted channel through which data is transmitted. You can use a PPTP client to connect to a standard PPP server and create a tunnel to another PPTP server across the network. You can also use a PPP client to connect to a PPTP server and enable it to handle the tunneling. VPN devices are created to facilitate PPTP connectivity following a three-step process: PPP connection and communication, PPTP control connection, and PPTP data tunneling.

The Integrated Services Digital Network (ISDN) is a system of digital telephone connections that enables data to be transmitted simultaneously end to end. ISDN developed as the standard telephone network progressed. It uses channels to make up a logical circuit. Two types of channels are used: a B channel for data transfer and a D channel for circuit-control functions. Each B channel equals 64 Kbps; each D channel represents either 16 Kbps or 64 Kbps. H channels are used to specify a number of B channels. A basic rate interface (BRI) consists of two B channels and one 16 Kbps D channel, totaling 144 Kbps. A primary rate interface (PRI) consists of twenty-three B channels and one 64 Kbps D channel, totaling 1536 Kbps. ISDN device types define the type of hardware used and include NT1, NT2, TE1, TE2, and TA. Reference points are used to define logical interfaces. Identifiers label the connection, and include the service profile identifier (SPID), the directory number (DN), the terminal endpoint identifier (TEI), the service address point identifier (SAPI), and the bearer code (BC).

The public switched telephone network (PSTN) facilitates voice communications globally. Also known as plain old telephone system (POTS), the PSTN was the first telecommunications network of its size in existence. WAN technologies are all based to some degree on this network. Various analog device types, including external modems, internal modems, and modem banks, are available to enable data communications.

Dial-up networking functionality is included with all Windows versions since Windows 95. It enables users to connect to their internal networks or the Internet from remote locations. Two major RAS protocols have been used over the years: SLIP and PPP, with PPP being the protocol used for dial-up networking today. Three methods exist to invoke a dial-up session: explicit, implicit, or application invoked. Because modems are used to connect to remote networks, you must know how to configure them. Modems have a maximum port speed defined by the standards they meet. The Unimodem subsystem provides one interface for all applications to tie into the modem. The Telephony API (TAPI) provides additional features such as connection monitoring and multiple-location support. Specific items are required to use dial-up networking; you must have the appropriate network protocol set up, a line protocol set up, a server to dial into, and a properly set-up modem.

TWO-MINUTE DRILL

Remote Connectivity Concepts

❏ The basic functionality that remote connectivity uses is available in many different protocols and devices.

❏ Companies use links such as POTS and ISDN to make remote connections.

❏ Common applications include PPP dial-up and the PSTN.

❏ ISDN is a system of digital telephone connections that enables data to be transmitted simultaneously end to end.

❏ There are two basic types of ISDN services: the basic rate interface (BRI) and the primary rate interface (PRI).

❏ Be sure to know the device types and where each type is used. In addition, know the number of channels and speeds associated with BRI and PRI.

❏ PSTN was originally designed as an analog switching system for routing voice calls.

Remote Access Service (RAS)

❏ SLIP and PPP are two communication protocols that are used to connect a computer to a remote network through a serial connection using a device such as a modem.

❏ SLIP is a communications protocol used to make a TCP/IP connection over a serial interface to a remote network.

❏ PPP is a data link–layer protocol used to encapsulate higher network-layer protocols to pass over synchronous and asynchronous communication lines.

❏ The most common authentication protocols include the Password Authentication Protocol (PAP), the Challenge Handshake Authentication Protocol (CHAP), and the Microsoft adaptation of CHAP, MS-CHAP.

Dial-Up Networking

❏ Remember that the maximum available speed with an analog modem is 56 Kbps.

❏ Windows includes a dial-up networking client.

❏ Dial-up networking provides support for four types of line protocols.

❏ Modems are asynchronous, synchronous, or both.

Virtual Private Networks (VPNs)

❑ The Point-to-Point Tunneling Protocol (PPTP) is a network protocol that provides for the secure transfer of data from a remote client to a private server by creating a multiprotocol virtual private network (VPN). PPTP is used in TCP/IP networks as an alternative to conventional dial-up networking methods. Be sure to know the three processes involved with PPTP and how PPP applies to each one.

❑ A VPN works by encapsulating the data within IP packets to transport it through PPP. VPNs are virtual devices set up as though they were regular devices such as a modem.

SELF TEST

The following questions will help you measure your understanding of the material presented in this chapter. Read all the choices carefully, because there might be more than one correct answer. Choose all correct answers for each question.

Remote Connectivity Concepts

1. Which of the following is the standard that was defined by the industry so that users would not have to know the type of ISDN switch they are connected to in order to buy equipment?
   A. ISDN-1
   B. ISDN-NI
   C. NI
   D. NI-1

2. How many B channels are available in a typical ISDN PRI?
   A. 2
   B. 20
   C. 23
   D. 30

Remote Access Service (RAS)

3. Which network-layer protocols can the Serial Line Internet Protocol use during a dial-up session?
   A. TCP/IP
   B. IPX/SPX

   C. PPP

   D. NetBEUI

4. Which remote protocol supports running many different types of network protocols over a serial link?

   A. SLIP

   B. PPP

   C. IPX

   D. NetBEUI

5. Which components are part of the Point-to-Point Protocol?

   A. Network control protocol

   B. Link Control Protocol

   C. Internet Protocol

   D. Internet Packet Exchange Protocol

6. Which network control protocol is used in PPP to facilitate the transport of TCP/IP?

   A. IPNP

   B. IPCP

   C. IPXCP

   D. None of the above

7. Which forms of validation can PPP use to authenticate a remote server?

   A. CHAP

   B. Domain account

   C. PAP

   D. KPA

8. How many incoming RAS connections does Windows XP support?

   A. 1

   B. 10

   C. 256

   D. 1024

Dial-Up Networking

9. Where is the logging information for a connection appended when modem logging is enabled?

   A. modemlog.txt

   B. ppp.log

   C. modemlog_modemname.txt

   D. ppp.txt

10. Which Windows feature can create a dial-up connection in Windows XP?
    A. Device Manager
    B. Control Panel
    C. Accessories
    D. New Connection Wizard

11. Which application programming interface is used to include features such as call monitoring and multiple localities?
    A. Unimodem
    B. COMM
    C. TAPI
    D. None of the above

Virtual Private Networks (VPNs)

12. What technology do virtual private networks offer to provide a more secure communications channel?
    A. IP header compression
    B. Tunneling
    C. Multiple network protocol support
    D. None of the above

13. Which of the following are protocols used for VPN solutions?
    A. PPTP
    B. PPP
    C. L2TP
    D. SLIP

14. Which of the following is the process for setting up a "tunnel" for PPTP?
    A. PPP connection and communication
    B. PPTP control connection
    C. PPTP data tunneling
    D. PPTP data transfer

Performance-Based Question Review: See the performance-based question sample from the author included with the accompanying media.

SELF TEST ANSWERS

Remote Connectivity Concepts

1. ☑ **D.** The National ISDN 1 (NI-1) standard was defined by the industry so that users would not have to know the type of switch to which they are connected in order to buy equipment and software compatible with it.

   ☒ **A, B,** and **C** are incorrect because NI-1 is the term used for ISDN.

2. ☑ **C.** PRI is intended for users with greater bandwidth requirements. It requires T1 carriers to facilitate communications. Normally, the channel structure contains twenty-three B channels plus one 64 Kbps D channel, for a total of 1536 Kbps.

   ☒ **A, B,** and **D** are incorrect because these are incorrect numbers of B channels.

Remote Access Service (RAS)

3. ☑ **A.** The Serial Line Internet Protocol, or SLIP, is a communications protocol used for making a TCP/IP connection over a serial interface to a remote network. SLIP was designed for connecting to remote UNIX servers across a standard phone line. This protocol was one of the first of its kind, enabling a remote network connection to be established over a standard phone line.

   ☒ **B, C,** and **D** are incorrect because IPX/SPX and NetBEUI cannot run over SLIP. PPP is incorrect because it is not a network protocol, but rather a RAS protocol that competes with SLIP.

4. ☑ **B.** PPP established other standards, including asynchronous and bit-oriented synchronous encapsulation, network protocol multiplexing, session negotiation, and data-compression negotiation. PPP also supports protocols other than TCP/IP, such as IPX/SPX and DECnet.

   ☒ **A, C,** and **D** are incorrect because SLIP is limited to running on TCP/IP networks. IPX and NetBEUI are standard network protocols, not protocols for RAS.

5. ☑ **A** and **B.** PPP uses the High-Level Data-Link Control (HDLC) protocol as the basis to encapsulate its data during transmission; PPP uses the Link Control Protocol (LCP) to establish, test, and configure the data link connection; various network control protocols (NCPs) are used to configure the different communications protocols. This enables you to use different protocols, such as TCP/IP and IPX, over the same line simultaneously.

   ☒ **C** and **D** are incorrect because they are not a part of the Point-to-Point Protocol.

6. ☑ **B.** The Internet Protocol Control Protocol (IPCP) is the NCP used to configure, enable, and disable the IP protocol modules at each end of the link.

   ☒ **A** and **C** are incorrect because these items do not exist.

7. ☑ **A** and **C.** With PPP, each system could be required to authenticate itself. This can be done using an authentication protocol. The most common authentication protocols include the Password Authentication Protocol (PAP), the Challenge Handshake Authentication Protocol (CHAP), and the Microsoft adaptation of CHAP, MS-CHAP.
    ☒ **B** and **D** are incorrect because domain authentication is used to validate a user, not the connection, and KPA does not exist.

8. ☑ **A.** Windows XP allows you to create a VPN server or RAS server that allows one connection. You may create these servers through the New Connection Wizard.
    ☒ **B, C,** and **D** are incorrect as Windows XP only supports one incoming RAS connection.

Dial-Up Networking

9. ☑ **C.** When logging has been enabled, you can see the log file after the next attempt to connect to a PPP server. The log file, modemlog_modemname.txt, is stored in the Windows directory by default. It can be viewed by any standard text editor and is appended to each time a new connection is attempted.
    ☒ **A, B,** and **D** are incorrect because none of them is the name of the log file that modem logging appends logging information to.

10. ☑ **D.** The New Connection Wizard found in your network connections window allows you to create new connections that connect to a RAS or VPN server.
    ☒ **A, B,** and **C** are incorrect because you do not create new connections that way.

11. ☑ **C.** TAPI also provides other features, such as multiple calling locations. You can set up different connection profiles for different dial-up access numbers. You can also customize how the number is dialed. For example, if you set up two separate connection profiles, one with call waiting enabled and the second without it, you can manage multiple connections without having to reconfigure your modem setup every time you need a variation.
    ☒ **A** is incorrect because Unimodem is a part of Windows that allows for a single installation and configuration of a modem. **B** is incorrect because COMM is not a valid choice, since it is not a common program name with Windows; it is a driver name.

Virtual Private Networks (VPNs)

12. ☑ **B.** PPTP tunneling is used in TCP/IP networks as an alternative to conventional dial-up networking methods. This enables multiprotocol secure communications over a public TCP/IP network such as the Internet. PPTP takes advantage of an additional level of security that is not currently available in other standard implementations.
    ☒ **A, C,** and **D** are incorrect because none of the other choices provides a secure link.

13. ☑ **A** and **C.** VPNs establish tunnels by using VPN protocols such as PPTP and L2TP.
    ☒ **B** and **D** are incorrect because they are RAS protocols, not VPN protocols.

14. ☑ **B.** When the PPP session is established, PPTP creates a control connection between the client and the remote PPTP server. This process is referred to as tunneling.

☒ **A** is incorrect because PPTP uses PPP to connect to a remote network. When connected, PPP is also used to encrypt the data packets being passed between the remote host and the local machine. **C** is incorrect because PPTP creates the IP datagrams for PPP to send. The packets are encrypted by PPP and sent through the tunnel to the PPTP server. The PPTP server is then used to decrypt the PPP-encrypted packets, disassemble the IP datagram, and route to the appropriate host. **D** is incorrect because the transfer of data is not started until the tunnel has been established.

Chapter 12

Wide Area Network Technologies

With companies becoming larger and more geographically diverse, wide area
networks (WANs) have become increasingly the norm for networks these days.
Connecting two different local area networks (LANs) found at different locations
within a company is a typical scenario for a WAN environment. For example, Company ABC may have
two locations: one in New York and the other in Boston. The company wants the two locations to be
able to communicate with one another without using the Internet. You, as the network administrator,
will need to choose a WAN technology that connects these two LANs together, basing your decision
on the performance and cost of the technology.

This chapter identifies some of the popular technologies that are used in WAN environments—be sure to be familiar with them for the Network+ exam. Also, note that organizations may connect their different offices together using Remote Access Services (RAS) or Integrated Services Digital Network (ISDN) technologies as discussed in Chapter 11—be sure to review those for the exam as well.

CERTIFICATION OBJECTIVE 12.01

Packet-Switching vs. Circuit-Switching Networks

This section introduces the concepts of packet-switching networking and circuit-switching networking technologies. Be sure to know these two terms for the Network+ exam.

Packet Switching

Packet switching is used by the Internet and routed networks. The path that is used to send data packets from one point to another through routers is not predetermined, meaning that each packet can take a different pathway to the destination. Packet-switched networks are efficient in that they consume bandwidth only when there is something to send. If you look at the routed network in Figure 12-1, you can see that from point A to point B, many paths exist for packets to travel.

When a user at PC A wants to copy a shared file from PC B, the data path is not a set path between specific routers. Packets are sent from router to router by the quickest or shortest path. If a router is extremely busy, it will not be used, and a different path will be chosen if one exists. Remember that other users are also sending data packets over the same media and routers.

FIGURE 12-1

A routed network

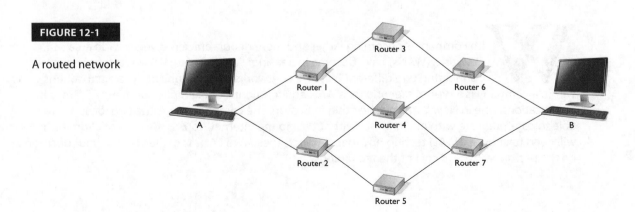

Referring to Figure 12-1, let's now look at an example of how packet switching works. PC B sends its data to the router that is the least busy. For the first data packet, let us assume that it is Router 6. Now that Router 6 has the data packet, it looks at its routing table and determines that Router 3 might be the best way for it to reach PC A. Router 6 sends the data packet to Router 3, which in turn decides that the best path is to forward the packet on to Router 1. Router 1 then sends the packet to PC A. Now, the second packet might be sent to Router 7 because Router 6 has suddenly become very busy. Router 7 receives the data packet and forwards it to Router 4. Router 4 sends the packet to Router 2. Router 2 checks its routing table and sends the packet on to PC A. PC A then starts assembling the entire data file from the packets received. For the third data packet, let's say that it is also sent to Router 7, which sends it to Router 5. Now let's say that Router 2 has suddenly gone offline. Router 5 waits to contact Router 2, but eventually it is timed out and sends the data packet back to Router 7, which then tries to send the data packet to Router 4. Router 4 has since determined that Router 2 is offline and sends the data packet to Router 1. Router 1 sends the data packet to PC A. The fourth data packet is sent to Router 6, on to Router 3, then to Router 1, and finally is delivered to PC A.

Let's look more closely at packets 3 and 4: While packet 3 was detained at Router 5 because of the failure of Router 2, packet 4 was delivered to PC A before the arrival of packet 3. This shows that a packet-switched network does not depend on packets being delivered in the order in which they were sent. Actually, if there are enough data paths, it is very common for packets to be received out of order. With routable protocols, data packets are numbered so they can be placed back in the proper order to create the original block of data that existed at the sending PC. It would be counterproductive to receive a jumbled database or an unreadable document.

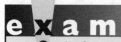

Packet switching is the process of breaking a transmission down into multiple packets, each potentially taking a different route to the destination network. The packets can be received out of order and are assembled at the destination.

Data packets are sent out of order on the Internet constantly. The only time this presents a problem is when the data being sent is streaming voice or video. If you have ever tried to use the Internet as a medium for making telephone calls, you know that the sound quality is not very good on slow network links, such as a 56 Kbps modem.

There are a number of packet-switched networking technologies; a few examples of WAN technologies that employ packet-switched networks are Asynchronous Transfer Mode (ATM) and Frame Relay.

Circuit Switching

Circuit switching, on the other hand, is the foundation for the telephone system, but it is also widely used for data communications. When you make a telephone call from your home to someone next door or even 1000 miles away, a circuit is opened between your telephone and the telephone to which you are calling. The circuit is a dedicated 64 Kbps pathway used by the communication and is not usable by others, so it is 100 percent dedicated for your use. As you speak, your voice is sent over the media to the other telephone and is not broken up or rerouted. Generally speaking, circuit switching is less efficient than packet switching, in that the bandwidth is consumed whether or not there is data to transmit; however, this allows service providers to offer customers a guaranteed bandwidth.

One of the major problems with circuit switching occurs when a circuit fails—the circuit is a permanent path, and there is no redirection of data through another path unless a new circuit is created. For example, if you are speaking with someone on the phone and the line you're using is brought down by a fallen tree, your circuit will be broken and the line will go dead. You will have to hang up and place the call again. When you place the call again, a different circuit will be established and you will use that circuit for the duration of the communication.

Know the differences between packet-switching and circuit-switching networks. In addition, remember that data networks are usually packet switched, whereas telephone connections are normally circuit switched.

X.25 and Frame Relay

This section will introduce you to two popular packet-switched WAN technologies: X.25 and Frame Relay. The two technologies have been around for many years, and you may be asked a question or two about them on the exam.

X.25

X.25 is a packet-switched network that uses a device called a Packet Assembler/Dissembler (PAD) to connect a system to the X.25 network. The PAD connects to serial ports of a device and is therefore considered RS-232 compliant.

X.25 runs at layers 1, 2, and 3 of the OSI model and has transfer rates of 2 Mbps. Overall, this technology is fairly old and slow compared with some of today's standards. Most X.25 implementations communicate over analog lines.

X.25 uses a PAD to connect to the X.25 network.

Frame Relay

Frame Relay is the digital version of X.25 and is much faster than it. Frame Relay runs at layers 1 and 2 of the OSI model and supports transfer rates as high as 50 Mbps along with features such as Quality of Service (QoS). It is a choice for WAN networking along with ATM, Broadcast ISDN (BISDN), and Cell Relay.

Frame Relay transmission speeds are not always constant. The data packets, or frames, are sent through a packet-switching network with higher-level protocols managing error checking, such as Internetwork Packet Exchange/Sequenced Packet Exchange (IPX/SPX) or Transmission Control Protocol/Internet Protocol (TCP/IP).

Frame Relay is a highly efficient method of transmitting data using bandwidth at an optimal level, allowing for bandwidths well over X.25's 2 Mbps. The nodes, which are used to route the frames in the packet-switching network, each use a routing algorithm that can help determine the efficiency of the Frame Relay network. Frame Relay sends frames as variable-length packets, which are not all set at the same size before transmission.

If the bandwidth becomes too congested, Frame Relay will drop any frames that it cannot handle. This can include corrupted frames, as well as those that are unable to be delivered because the destination cannot be reached. Any dropped frames must be requested for retransmission by the protocols being used. When the available bandwidth is at a minimum, the source or destination can be notified to slow the transmissions to avoid overutilization of the bandwidth, which will keep packets from being dropped due to congestion. Although the source or destination is requested to slow the transmissions, the transmissions do not necessarily have to be slow.

To determine which packets are dropped, we must first be aware of who is transmitting over the Frame Relay network. Multiple companies can share a Frame Relay backbone to the Internet or between office buildings. Each company pays for a specific amount of the bandwidth on the Frame Relay medium. If the bandwidth is available, a company can use more bandwidth than that for which they have paid. Once other companies start using their bandwidth, all the companies will be limited to the bandwidth that has been committed to them. The bandwidth that each company pays for is noted by its Committed Information Rate (CIR). The CIR helps determine whether frames can be dropped when the bandwidth becomes congested. It is included in all frames sent by any company on the Frame Relay network. The Frame Relay nodes will keep statistics on network bandwidth and usage by all companies. If a company is using less bandwidth than what it paid for, its frames will be sent on through the node. If the company is using more bandwidth than the CIR designates, the frames are likely to be dropped.

exam

ⓌＡＴＣＨ X.25 supports transfer rates of 2 Mbps and uses a serial device known as a PAD, whereas Frame Relay supports speeds as high as 50 Mbps and is a digital version of X.25.

CERTIFICATION OBJECTIVE 12.02

Fiber-Optic WAN Technologies

You can use a number of fiber-optic technologies to connect your WAN environment over high speed. In this section, you will learn about high-speed WAN technologies such as SONET, optical carriers, the FDDI network architecture, and ATM technology. Know these technologies for the exam!

Synchronous Optical Network/Synchronous Digital Hierarchy

The *Synchronous Optical Network (SONET)* is a North American standard that allows the uniting of unlike transmissions into one single data stream. The *Synchronous Digital Hierarchy (SDH)* is the European standard designed for the same purpose as SONET. Basically, SONET allows multiple companies to transmit the packets on their networks onto a SONET backbone to be transmitted to a remote location using fiber-optic cabling. Because many companies might be using different network topologies and protocols, the data streams from each company would most likely differ. These companies can transmit their information over SONET without having to conform to a network standard. For example, one company might have a 10 Mbps Category-5 Ethernet network using IPX/SPX, while another is using fiber-optic cable with TCP/IP. These can be combined into a single data stream (this is called *multiplexing*) for transmission over one cable. More companies can be added for transmission over the SONET medium without making any changes to any of the company networks.

This architecture allows for different media types and transmission types to be combined into one stream and sent over a fiber-optic cable. It is measured by optical carrier (OC) speed, which is the standard for fiber-optic transmission. SONET runs at the lowest OC rate, which is a minimum speed of 54.84 Mbps, known as SONET-1.

SONET is divided into electrical levels that have varying speeds, termed synchronous transport signals (STSs). The highest level is SONET-192, with a speed of 9953.280 Mbps. SDH has no equivalent for SONET-1 at the speed of 51.84 Mbps, but has a low speed of 155.520 Mbps, which maps to SONET-3. The different SDH levels are termed synchronous transfer modes (STMs). Table 12-1, shown in the following section, lists the various levels.

The format for SONET is created by multiplexing all data signals into a single data stream called an STS. The multiplexer is managed by the path-terminating equipment (PTE) from various media and transmission types, as shown in Figure 12-2. Now that the STS signal has been created, it must be transmitted on the SONET media. The STS transmission is managed by the line-terminating equipment (LTE), also shown in Figure 12-2.

FIGURE 12-2

Components of a SONET architecture

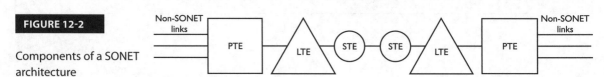

The LTE will send and receive the STS signal on both ends of the SONET media. Remember that the STS signal is in the form of electrical pulses. The SONET link might not be a single connection from one point to another, and entire segments might be composed of sections of SONET media. Therefore, to create the sections and have the entire segment appear as one physical link, section-terminating equipment (STE) is used to begin and end a section, as shown in Figure 12-2.

Remember the characteristics and speeds of SONET/SDH.

There is also a device that allows transmissions to be scrambled. The scrambling device must exist at both ends of the transmission to be able to descramble the stream back into usable data.

ATM (OSI layers 2 and 3) signals can be sent over a SONET/SDH link (OSI layer 1), as was discussed in the preceding section. In addition, Point-to-Point Protocol (PPP) (OSI layers 2 and 3) can be transmitted over SONET/SDH.

Optical Carrier Level-X

The *optical carrier (OC)* standard is used to specify bandwidth for transmissions that are sent over fiber-optic cables. These standards are used to rate the SONET standards and will correlate to the bandwidths available for SONET/SDH.

One OC channel (OC-1) is 51.84 Mbps, as is STS-1. When multiple channels are used, the bandwidth increases by 51.84 Mbps per channel. For example, nine OC channels (OC-9) are composed of nine OC-1 channels at 51.84 Mbps each. This results in a total bandwidth of 466.56 Mbps. The OC levels can be matched to the SONET levels and to the SDH levels, as shown in Table 12-1.

TABLE 12-1	Optical Carrier Level	SONET Electrical Level	SDH Level	Bandwidth
OC Levels and How They Relate to the SONET/SDH Transfer Rate	OC-1	STS-1	None	51.84 Mbps
	OC-3	STS-3	STM-1	155.52 Mbps
	OC-9	STS-9	STM-3	466.56 Mbps
	OC-12	STS-12	STM-4	622.08 Mbps
	OC-18	STS-18	STM-6	933.15 Mbps
	OC-24	STS-24	STM-8	1244.16 Mbps
	OC-36	STS-36	STM-12	1866.24 Mbps
	OC-48	STS-48	STM-16	2488.32 Mbps
	OC-96	STS-96	STM-32	4976.64 Mbps
	OC-192	STS-192	STM-64	9953.28 Mbps

The Network+ exam expects you to be familiar with a few other technologies that relate to fiber-optic networking. Be sure to know the following technologies when preparing for the exam:

- **DWDM**   *Dense Wavelength Division Multiplexing (DWDM)* is a technology used to increase the bandwidth over existing fiber-optic cabling. With DWDM, multiple signals are delivered at different frequencies in the fiber, which allows you to send more data through the fiber cable. DWDM can be used with ATM, SONET/SDH, and Ethernet networks.

- **CWDM**   *Coarse Wavelength Division Multiplexing (CWDM)* is a multiplexing approach to carrying data across fiber-optic cables. CWDM can have up to 16 wavelengths (channels) in a single fiber pair that are spaced apart (allowing the use of cost-effective lasers) enabling data to reach 120 KM.

- **PON**   *Passive Optical Network (PON)* is a technology wherein the service provider installs a splitter at their location to split a single-fiber link to multiple customer locations.

Fiber Distributed Data Interface

The *Fiber Distributed Data Interface (FDDI)* is a network architecture that uses token passing as the access method, with two rings instead of one, so that there is a fault-tolerant ring in case the first ring goes down. FDDI uses fiber-optic cable operating at 100 Mbps or greater that can cover distances of up to 200 KM. If copper cable is used, such as Category 5 at 100 Mbps, the topology is termed a *Copper Distributed Data Interface (CDDI)*.

As mentioned, two rings are used in the FDDI architecture—the primary ring and the secondary ring. The primary ring is used at all times, and the secondary ring is used only if the primary ring fails. The token is passed on each ring in opposite directions.

FDDI can be used in both LAN and campus area network (CAN) solutions. Each building or office would have either a dual-attachment concentrator (DAC) that allows both rings to be connected to the DAC or two single-attachment concentrators (SAC). The SAC connects to a single ring, allowing it to be powered down without affecting the ring.

Now let's examine the FDDI redundancy and find out why the two rings operate in opposite directions. If any ring should break or if a SAC should be shut down, as shown in Figure 12-3 part A, the network will still operate. Operation will continue because the broken section will be bypassed, using the secondary ring to allow the network to go back on itself and function as a continual ring. In Figure 12-3 part B, you can see that part of the ring is broken, so part of the secondary ring will be used to create a complete ring. The reason that the rings must operate in opposite directions is to continue passing the token from one ring to another without causing the direction to change. This allows for continuity if both rings are broken or if a DAC goes offline.

FIGURE 12-3

FDDI redundant rings

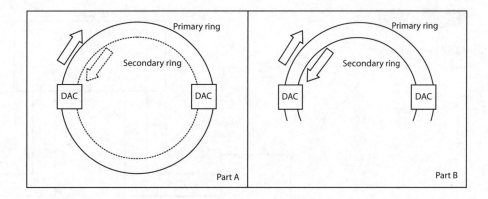

Each DAC will have two sets of connectors—one set for both rings coming in and one set for both rings going out. Now consider an example where a company has three office buildings set up with FDDI and how redundancy works to keep them online.

Figure 12-4 shows the three DACs or SACs, depending on which they use. The three locations are all connected with dual rings.

The grayed (inside) areas show the secondary ring, which is not in use. Now, assume that the fiber-optic cable is broken between Location 2 and Location 3. Figure 12-5 shows

FIGURE 12-4

Functional FDDI example

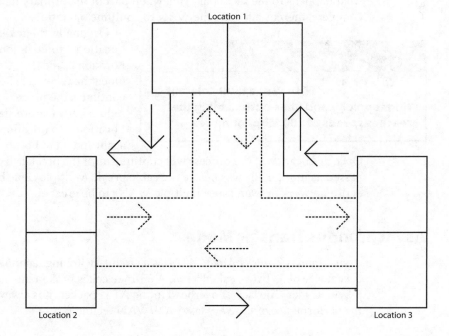

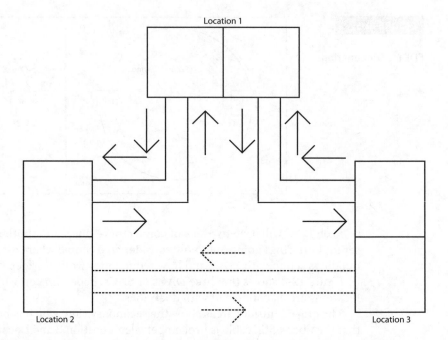

FIGURE 12-5

FDDI redundancy
example

what happens to the secondary ring when part of the primary fails and how the ring is still complete, thereby allowing the WAN to continue operating.

FDDI uses a fault-tolerant ring topology and fiber-optic cabling that reaches speeds of 100 Mbps or more.

Originally, the token is transferred from Location 1 to Location 2, from Location 2 to Location 3, and then from Location 3 to Location 1. Once the token reaches Location 1 again, it continues the process. After the break and the redundancy feature starts, the token will go from Location 1 to Location 2, then to Location 1 again and on to Location 3, and back to Location 1.

Once at Location 1, the process will continue until the break is fixed, and the token will be passed as it originally was before the cable break. Multiple cable breaks can take down the entire network or even cause multiple WANs to be created.

Asynchronous Transfer Mode

Asynchronous Transfer Mode (ATM) is a circuit-switching technology that uses a consistent packet size of 53 bytes, called a *cell*. A 53-byte cell is broken into a 48-byte payload and a 5-byte header. The lack of overhead in the ATM packet (it is always 53 bytes) helps promote the performance of this very fast LAN/WAN technology.

ATM can be used to enhance broadband ISDN to allow for the transmission of voice, data, and multimedia packets over the same media simultaneously. Broadband media use frequencies to manage many "circuits" over one cable. Digital transmissions are electrical or light pulses of "on" or "off," depending on the physical medium over which it is transferred. Broadband is how cable TV works, with multiple channels on one cable using different frequencies for each channel.

ATM will provide for high bandwidth as needed if enough users are requesting it. ATM bandwidth ranges from slow speeds (around 12.96 to 25 Mbps using copper media such as Category-3 UTP cable) to high speeds (around 622 Mbps using fiber-optic cable). With advances in technology, ATM speeds can reach 2.488 Gbps.

e x a m

ⓦ a t c h **ATM is a WAN technology that allows for speeds of 622 Mbps or more. This fast, reliable WAN technology is great for sending voice or video across great distances.**

ATM can be used with physical interfaces such as FDDI and SONET/SDH. This means that in an FDDI or SONET/SDH network, ATM can be used on the network topology for data transmissions. When setting up a packet-switched network similar to that shown in Figure 12-1, ATM can allow for parallel transmissions between nodes. This means that if data is being passed to and from PC A and PC B, the data packets can be passed between two routers (nodes) simultaneously. Remember that with ATM, data packets are referred to as cells, and each cell has a fixed length of 53 bytes. There are no variable-length cells as with some transmission standards. This allows all of the devices to be optimized for the specified cell size, thereby providing better performance. Once in place, an ATM network is transparent to users and provides for high data transmission speeds that can grow into a WAN when needed.

e x a m

ⓦ a t c h **ATM uses a fixed-size packet of 53 bytes, known as a cell, to send data.**

ATM can be used in LAN environments, but its use is uncommon due to the high price of ATM networking equipment, such as ATM network cards and ATM hubs or switches. ATM also supports QOS, which allows bandwidth to be allocated to different types of traffic.

CERTIFICATION OBJECTIVE 12.03

Internet Access Technologies

A number of technologies are used to connect to the Internet, including leased lines and high-speed Internet technologies that are used by small businesses or home users. This section is designed to introduce you to leased lines and includes Asymmetric Digital

TABLE 12-2	T-Carrier	Bandwidth
	T1	1.544 Mbps
Tx-Carriers and Bandwidth	T1C	3.152 Mbps
	T2	6.312 Mbps
	T3	44.736 Mbps
	T4	274.176 Mbps

Subscriber Line (ADSL) and cable modem Internet connections used by small businesses and home users.

Leased Lines with Tx-/Ex-Carriers

The *T-carrier* and *E-carrier* are both dedicated digital leased lines used to transmit voice, data, or images. The T-carrier is used in the United States, Japan, and Australia, whereas the E-carrier is used in Europe, Mexico, and South America. There are different categories of each carrier that indicate the speed of the line. T1 is composed of 24 channels that are made up of 64 Kbps bandwidth each, for a total of 1.544 Mbps. Each 64 Kbps channel is referred to as digital signal level 0 (DS0), with the 24 DS0 channels making a digital signal level 1 (DS1). These lines can be multiplexed into faster links, as shown in Table 12-2.

Most companies cannot afford a T-carrier line, so it is best for some companies to look into other means of connecting to the Internet or creating a WAN. If necessary, a company can lease a partial T1 line, which is called a Fractional T1, at a lower price. A Fractional T1 will also provide only a fraction of the bandwidth.

Remember the characteristics and speeds of the T- and E-carriers and where they are used. Also remember that these are examples of *leased lines* where a company pays a monthly fee to have access to their bandwidth.

The E-carrier is similar to the T-carrier, but differs in bandwidth. An E1-carrier is composed of thirty 64 Kbps data channels with two 64 Kbps channels for signaling. The E1-carrier has a total bandwidth of 2.048 Mbps. The E3-carrier is composed of 16 T1-carrier channels for a total bandwidth of 34.368 Mbps. The Ex-carriers are listed in Table 12-3 with their total bandwidth.

CSU/DSU

The *Channel Service Unit/Data Service Unit (CSU/DSU)* is a device that allows a business to connect a high-speed data link from the telephone company to the business's router for

TABLE 12-3	E-Carrier	Bandwidth
Ex-Carriers and Bandwidth	E1	2.048 Mbps
	E2	8.448 Mbps
	E3	34.368 Mbps
	E4	139.264 Mbps
	E5	565.148 Mbps

access to and from the LAN or WAN. The high-speed connections are usually T1 or T3 connections or their European counterparts, E1 and E3. The CSU/DSU used will be specific to the speed of the line being connected to and from the telephone company.

The CSU/DSU is a device that handles signaling over the T1/T3 link, sending data between your router and the service provider. The CSU/DSU performs other functions such as protecting against electrical interference from either side of the link. You may have an *external CSU/DSU* device that connects to the serial port on your company router and then is used to connect the T1 line from your service provider (see Figure 12-6).

Many routers today come with an internal CSU/DSU module installed, which allows you to connect the router to the T1 line without the use of an external CSU/DSU. Figure 12-7 displays an internal CSU/DSU built into a Cisco router.

DSL/ADSL

Digital Subscriber Lines (DSL) is a high-speed Internet service that allows the transfer of data over phone lines. DSL is typically referred to as *Asymmetric Digital Subscriber Line (ADSL)* and is provided by telecom providers and allows the ADSL subscriber to use the

FIGURE 12-6
Using an external CSU/DSU

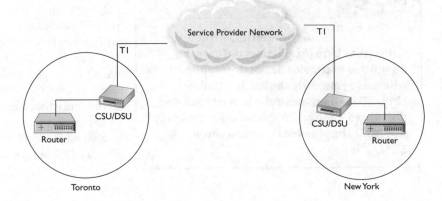

FIGURE 12-7

An integrated CSU/DSU
on a router

phone and the Internet simultaneously, with download speeds as high as 9 Mbps and upload speeds around 1 Mbps (hence asymmetric). The transfer rates differ for each service provider.

An ADSL subscriber connects his or her PC to the larger telephone network by connecting to a central office (CO) that must be located within a 5-KM distance of the subscriber. A special modem, known as an ADSL modem, is used to connect the ADSL user to a local CO. If there is not a CO close to a user's location, that user would be unable to subscribe to the service.

ADSL Hardware

In order for the ADSL subscriber to connect to the local CO, a splitter will be connected to the phone jack in the wall. The splitter will then connect to the phone and to the ADSL modem, as shown in Figure 12-8. This splitter is essentially a frequency filter. The human voice falls between 0 and 3.4 KHz, so the splitter sends transmissions below 3.4 KHz to the telephone, and transmissions above 3.4 KHz are sent to and from the ADSL modem. The ADSL modem has an RJ-45 jack that is used to connect to the network card in the PC. It is not really a modem, in the sense that a modem converts digital signals to analog signs; this modem is really just acting as a terminal adapter. Figure 12-9 displays an actual ADSL modem and splitter.

exam

⊕atch Asymmetric Digital Subscriber Line (ADSL) uses different download and upload speeds (asymmetric), whereas Symmetric Digital Subscriber Line (SDSL) uses an equivalent upload and download bandwidth; home users typically use ADSL, but businesses most often use SDSL.

FIGURE 12-8

A typical ADSL setup

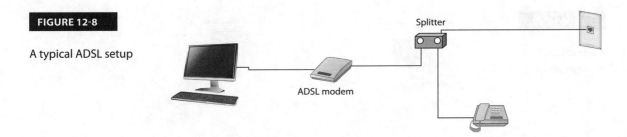

on the
job

A number of ADSL modems have the filter built in, so the filter wall plate may not be needed. Also know that Very High Bitrate DSL (VDSL) is a new high-speed Internet technology that, for short distances, can offer a transfer rate of 52 Mbps and is deployed over copper lines.

Broadband Cable

If the phone companies are going to offer high-speed Internet service through the phone lines, you can bet that the cable companies would come up with a broadband, high-speed Internet solution using the coaxial cable TV lines. The cable companies connect you to

FIGURE 12-9

An ADSL frequency filter and an ADSL modem

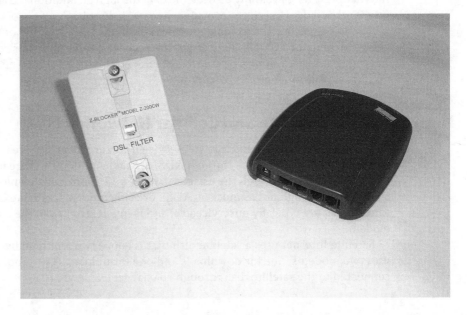

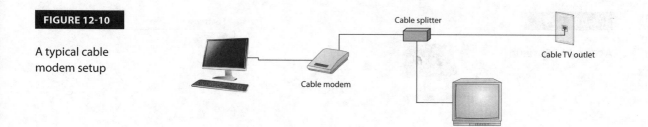

FIGURE 12-10

A typical cable
modem setup

the Internet over their lines using a cable modem that connects to the workstation using twisted-pair cabling, but then the modem connects to the cable jack in the wall using coaxial cable (as shown in Figure 12-10).

The cable provider supplies each channel on the cable in its own 6 MHz frequency range, and the signal for a particular channel is sent to you in that range. Cable companies supply the Internet data as its own channel, with a 6 MHz frequency range being used to send data to your cable modem. Download speeds of cable modems can reach 10 Mbps, but may differ with different providers.

One of the drawbacks of the cable modem is that you are sharing this bandwidth with your neighbors if they have subscribed to this Internet service as well. If you have a neighbor who constantly downloads large amounts of data, you may find that times are slow on the occasions when your neighbor uses the precious bandwidth. Keep in mind that the Internet provider can simply provide the data through an additional channel to keep up with neighborhood demands if the provider chooses to do so!

There is an advantage to cable modems—unlike ADSL, you do not need to be within close proximity of a CO. As long as you are receiving cable and your cable provider supplies Internet access, you should be able to subscribe to high-speed Internet service. Figure 12-11 displays a cable modem.

High Speed via Satellite and Cellular Networks

How can you get high-speed Internet service if you are in a rural area that does not have access to high-speed service through ADSL or cable modems? There is an option for getting high-speed service through the use of satellites, which provide download speeds as high as 500 Kbps. Although not as quick as ADSL or cable modems, satellite can provide service to areas that are typically unserviceable, and is much faster than the conventional 56 Kbps modem.

Satellite Internet uses a satellite dish that is about two feet high by three feet wide and uses two modems, one for downloads and one for uploads. The modems are typically connected to the satellite dish through coaxial cable.

FIGURE 12-11

A cable modem

GSM/CDMA

Cellular networking has been around for years and offers connectivity via radio waves. The radio network is made up of different cells (areas), with each cell containing a tower that allows coverage in that area. There are a number of cellular standards, with the following being the main ones:

- **Global System for Mobile Communications (GSM)** *GSM* is a cellular standard for 2G digital cellular networks that was developed to replace the 1G analog network. GSM allows full-duplex communication of data and voice over the digital cellular network. Cell phones connect to the network by locating GSM cells in close proximity and use Subscriber Identity Modules (SIM), also known as SIM cards, which contain the users' phone book and subscription information.

- **Code Division Multiple Access (CDMA)** *CDMA* is a multiaccess channel method used by radio communications such as CDMA2000. CDMA2000 is a 3G mobile technology used to send voice and data between mobile devices such as cell phones.

The Network+ exam expects you to know the following cellular terms:

- **2G** *Second Generation* mobile networks improve over the 1G networks by being a digital network (1G networks are analog), phone conversations are digitally encrypted, and data services such as text messaging are provided. GSM is an example of a 2G network provider.

- **3G** *Third Generation* mobile networks have the benefit of providing more bandwidth than 2G networks to support voice, data (including Internet access), and video (such as mobile TV). CDMA is a 3G network provider.

- **LTE/4G** *Long-Term Evolution (LTE)* is a 4G wireless technology designed to give broadband service to mobile users through the phone. LTE reports a speed of 300 Mbps in theory, but a practical speed of 100 Mbps is the current speed reached for downloads.

- **HSPA+** *Evolved High-Speed Packet Access (HSPA+)* is a broadband solution based on wireless technology. HSPA+ offers broadband speeds of 84 Mbps for downloads and 22 Mbps for uploads.

- **Edge** *Enhanced Data rates for GSM Evolution (EDGE)* is a cellular technology that is backward compatible with GSM that allows for enhanced transmission rates (approximately three times the transmission rate of GSM).

Other Methods of Internet Access

There are a variety of other methods to connect to the Internet if you don't have access to an ADSL or cable modem connection. The following is a list of potential methods to connect to the Internet in addition to those mentioned previously:

- **Dial-up/POTS/PSTN** One of the original ways of accessing the Internet was to dial up using the phone line and a modem to the Internet service provider (ISP) to get Internet access. The *plain old telephone service (POTS)/public-switched telephone network (PSTN)* provides access through conventional telephone lines, using a modem to receive transfer rates as high as 56 Kbps.

- **ISDN** You learned about Integrated Services Digital Network (ISDN) in the last chapter—it is a method of obtaining Internet or WAN access by a BRI or PRI subscription.

- **PPP/Multilink PPP** *PPP* is an encapsulation protocol that carries data across a serial link. *Multilink PPP* is a method of spreading traffic across multiple PPP links to gain greater bandwidth.

- **MPLS** *Multiprotocol Label Switching (MPLS)* is a technique to direct traffic from one network node to another using short labels instead of long network addresses. This allows for faster network access as complex lookups in routing tables are avoided.

- **WiMax** *Worldwide Interoperability for Microwave Access (WiMax)* is a technology that provides Internet access using microwave technology. It is a common solution in areas where the service provider does not have the wiring infrastructure (cable or DSL) to reach your home. Older versions of WiMax run at 40 Mbps, while newer versions offer speeds of 1 Gbps and above.

■ **Metro-Ethernet** *Metro-Ethernet* is a metropolitan area network (MAN) created based on Ethernet standards. Customers can use a Metro-Ethernet as a method to gain Internet access or to connect multiple offices together.

CERTIFICATION SUMMARY

Networks have become such an important element in the business world that most businesses could not survive the loss of their network. Wide area networks (WANs) have evolved to allow the connection of multiple local area networks (LANs) that are not within close proximity. WANs allow the multiple LANs to operate as a single large network for growing companies.

The different WAN technologies include Asynchronous Transfer Mode (ATM), which can also be used to create a LAN. ATM provides bandwidth on demand for users using an optical network. It can provide transfer rates as high as 622 Mbps.

Another WAN technology is SONET/SDH, which uses optical carrier (OC) levels. These use fiber-optic cables to transfer data from different media. Data streams can be taken from different media and combined (multiplexed) into one data stream, allowing for transmission speeds from 51.84 Mbps to 9953.28 Mbps. The non-SONET media are connected to a physical-terminating equipment (PTE) device, which converts the electrical signals into optical signals. The optical signal is sent to the line-terminating equipment (LTE), which transmits the signal over different sections of fiber-optic cable. The many different sections of fiber-optic cable making up the SONET network are terminated by section-terminating equipment (STE). The OC levels are standards used to specify bandwidth over fiber-optic cable.

Frame Relay is a leased-line solution whereby a company can share the medium and the cost with other companies. The amount of bandwidth available to a company is determined by the amount for which it pays.

FDDI is another WAN technology based on the Token Ring topology. It operates at 100 Mbps over fiber-optic or Category-5 cables. A setup using Category-5 cables is known as a Copper Distributed Data Interface (CDDI). FDDI is composed of two rings operating in different directions. The second ring is used only if the first ring fails.

Popular transmission methods are T-carriers and E-carriers. Each carrier is used in different countries with different bandwidths. The T- and E-carriers are completely digital and operate at speeds as high as 565.148 Mbps.

High-speed Internet services can be provided through ADSL or a cable modem. ADSL provides download speeds at approximately 9 Mbps and runs the voice and data services over the copper telephone wires at various frequencies. Cable companies provide high-speed Internet services with download speeds of about 10 Mbps; they supply this data to your home using a different channel on the coaxial cable.

TWO-MINUTE DRILL

Packet-Switching vs. Circuit-Switching Networks

❑ Packet-switching networks use whatever pathway is best at the time to reach the destination network, whereas circuit switching uses a dedicated pathway for the duration of the communication.

❑ Packet switching is a more efficient use of bandwidth than circuit switching.

❑ Packet-switching networks might not deliver packets in the order they were sent.

❑ X.25 uses a PAD to connect the client to the X.25 network.

❑ X.25 supports speeds of 2 Mbps.

❑ Frame Relay is the digital version of X.25 and runs at speeds up to 50 Mbps.

❑ Error correction used by Frame Relay is monitored by higher-layer protocols.

❑ Frame Relay supports QoS.

Fiber-Optic WAN Technologies

❑ SONET is used to unify unlike transmissions into one transmission data stream.

❑ SONET uses fiber-optic cable for transmissions.

❑ SDH is the European standard for SONET.

❑ Bandwidth ranges from 51.84 Mbps to 9953.28 Mbps.

❑ OC is used to specify bandwidth standards over fiber-optic media.

❑ The OC levels are used by SONET and SDH levels.

❑ OC-1 is 51.84 Mbps.

❑ OC-3 is 155.52 Mbps.

❑ OC-48 is 2.488 Gbps.

❑ FDDI uses token passing and the ring topology over fiber-optic cabling.

❑ There are two rings operating in opposite directions.

❑ FDDI is a local area network (LAN) or campus area network (CAN) technology that creates a high-speed, fault-tolerant network.

❑ Two rings allow for redundancy.

❑ ATM is used by applications that require high amounts of bandwidth.

❑ ATM has a transfer rate of 622 Mbps.

❑ Data packets are referred to as cells and are a consistent 53 bytes in size.

Internet Access Technologies

❑ T*x*/E*x*-carriers are widely used and very popular.

    ❑ They are used as a backbone by telephone companies.

    ❑ They are expensive.

❑ Two popular Internet access methods currently in use are ADSL and cable modems.

❑ ADSL provides high-speed Internet service over the phone lines, whereas a cable modem uses the coaxial television cable.

❑ ADSL provides voice and data over the same wire at the same time while running both at different frequencies.

❑ The cable company supplies the Internet data as another channel. Just as you can receive signals for channel 4, you can receive the "Internet channel."

SELF TEST

The following self-test questions will help you measure your understanding of the material presented in this chapter. Read all the choices carefully, as there may be more than one correct answer. Choose all correct answers for each question.

Packet-Switching vs. Circuit-Switching Networks

1. Which switching technology is used by the telephone company?

A. Packet

B. Circuit

C. WAN

D. Hub

2. Which switching method allows for data transmissions even when part of the network fails?

A. Packet

B. Circuit

C. WAN

D. Hub

3. How is error checking managed on a Frame Relay network?
   A. By network devices
   B. By the user at the sending PC
   C. By the user at the receiving PC
   D. By the protocol used

4. If the network is congested and the destination device requests that the source device slow its transmission, what will occur?
   A. The source will stop responding for 30 seconds and then continue transmitting.
   B. The source will find a different route to send the data.
   C. The destination will drop all packets for 30 seconds.
   D. Nothing will happen.

5. What happens if a company uses more bandwidth than it has paid for?
   A. Its packets will be dropped no matter the state of the network.
   B. Its packets will be delivered even if the network is busy.
   C. Its packets will be delivered if the bandwidth is available.
   D. Its packets will be delivered no matter the state of the network.

Fiber-Optic WAN Technologies

6. How many streams does the SONET network transfer?
   A. 1
   B. 2
   C. 3
   D. 4 or more

7. Which of the following consists of electrical pulses on a SONET network?
   A. STM
   B. STS
   C. PTE
   D. LTE

8. What can be used in a SONET network to allow a user's data to remain private?
   A. Multiplexer
   B. PTE
   C. LTE
   D. Scrambler

9. What is the speed of one SONET level?

    A. 32.24 Mbps

    B. 51.84 Mbps

    C. 64.08 Mbps

    D. 155.52 Mbps

10. What levels are the OC levels matched to?

    A. ATM

    B. SDH

    C. SONET

    D. T1

11. What is the highest OC level?

    A. 32

    B. 64

    C. 128

    D. 192

12. If the primary ring fails, what is used for redundancy?

    A. The entire secondary ring

    B. A portion of the primary ring that has not failed and a part of the secondary ring that is equal to the primary ring that failed

    C. A portion of the primary ring that has not failed and a part of the secondary ring that is equal to the primary ring that has not failed

    D. A portion of the primary ring that failed and a part of the secondary ring that is equal to the primary ring that has failed

13. How does the FDDI token pass on the rings when functioning normally?

    A. From one ring to the other

    B. Randomly

    C. In opposite directions

    D. In the same direction

14. At what speed does FDDI operate?

    A. 10 Mbps

    B. 100 Mbps

    C. 1 Gbps

    D. 2 Gbps

15. In which area networking environments is ATM usable?

    A. Dial-up

    B. Workgroup

    C. WAN

    D. LAN

16. What is the size of a cell in an ATM network?

    A. 48 bytes

    B. 5 bytes

    C. 53 bytes

    D. 512 bytes

Internet Access Technologies

17. In what countries do E-carriers operate? (Choose all that apply.)

    A. Japan

    B. Europe

    C. Mexico

    D. South America

18. How many channels make up a T1?

    A. 6

    B. 12

    C. 24

    D. 48

19. Which high-speed Internet service uses the phone lines?

    A. Cable modem

    B. T1

    C. T3

    D. ADSL

20. Which high-speed Internet service supplies the Internet data as its own channel over the television cable?

    A. Cable modem

    B. T1

    C. T3

    D. ADSL

21. At which frequency is the Internet data supplied with ADSL?
    A. 0 to 3.4 KHz
    B. Above 3.4 KHz
    C. 9 to 12 KHz
    D. 100 to 200 KHz

A
SELF TEST ANSWERS

Packet-Switching vs. Circuit-Switching Networks

1. ☑ **B.** Circuit switching is used by the telephone companies for the network of telephone users.
   ☒ **A, C,** and **D** are incorrect. Packet switching is used by most data networks. WANs and hubs are not types of switching technology.

2. ☑ **A.** With a packet-switching network, the failed portion will be routed around the point of failure to continue to deliver packets.
   ☒ **B, C,** and **D** are incorrect. In a circuit-switched network, the connection will be terminated. For example, if you are speaking with someone on the telephone and a telephone line breaks, the call is terminated and must be made again. WANs and hubs are not types of switching technology.

3. ☑ **D.** Frame Relay depends on the protocols used to manage error checking.
   ☒ **A, B,** and **C** are incorrect because Frame Relay depends on the protocols used to manage error checking.

4. ☑ **D.** Just because a device is requested to slow transmissions, that does not mean the device will perform the action.
   ☒ **A, B,** and **C** are incorrect; they are not valid choices.

5. ☑ **C.** The packets will be delivered if the bandwidth is available; if it is not, they will be dropped.
   ☒ **A, B,** and **D** are incorrect. The state of the network must be taken into account.

Fiber-Optic WAN Technologies

6. ☑ **A.** The SONET network will multiplex multiple streams into one stream and transmit this single stream over the SONET network. Multiple streams can be combined to form the single SONET data stream.
   ☒ **B, C,** and **D** are incorrect, as these are incorrect values.

7. ☑ **B.** The synchronous transport signal (STS) is in the form of electrical pulses.
   ☒ **A, C,** and **D** are incorrect. The electrical pulses are converted by the PTE into one stream and are sent to the LTE as light pulses on fiber-optic cable. STM is a term used to denote the different levels of SDH.

8. ☑ **D.** The scrambler is used to randomize the stream pattern to allow the data to be encrypted. This requires a descrambler on the other end of the connection to convert the data into a usable form.
   ☒ **A, B,** and **C** are incorrect. The multiplexer is used to generate one data stream from many data streams. The electrical pulses are converted by the PTE into one stream and are sent to the LTE as light pulses on fiber-optic cable.

9. ☑ **B.** One SONET level is 51.84 Mbps. If more are added, the value is multiplied by the number of levels.
   ☒ **A, C,** and **D** are incorrect, as these are incorrect speeds.

10. ☑ **B and C.** The OC levels are standards for transmitting over fiber-optic cable. The levels match those of SONET and SDH, which require fiber optics.
    ☒ **A and D** are incorrect. ATM and T1 do not have the same standards.

11. ☑ **D.** 192 is the highest level currently set for OC.
    ☒ **A, B,** and **C** are incorrect; they are not the highest OC levels.

12. ☑ **C.** The part that is used for redundancy is the portion of the primary ring that has not failed, as well as the same part of the secondary ring that has not failed.
    ☒ **A, B,** and **D** are incorrect. No part of the failed portion of the primary ring can be used, and neither can the same portion of the secondary ring.

13. ☑ **C.** The token is circulated in opposite directions. This helps to keep the flow of the token the same on both rings even after a failure.
    ☒ **A, B,** and **D** are incorrect. The token passes only from one ring to the other when a failure has occurred. The token is not randomly moved, nor does it move in the same direction on both rings.

14. ☑ **B.** FDDI operates at 100 Mbps, whether it is fiber-optic or copper cabling.
    ☒ **A, C,** and **D** are incorrect, as these are incorrect speeds.

15. ☑ **C and D.** ATM technology can be used to create LANs and connect them to a WAN.
    ☒ **A and B** are incorrect. Dial-up is a type of connection made from one PC to another, or even possibly a LAN to a LAN. A workgroup is a group of ten or fewer PCs that are connected together in order to share resources with no centralized administration point.

16. ☑ **C.** ATM uses consistent 53-byte cells.
     ☒ **A, B,** and **D** are incorrect. The payload in the cell is 48 bytes, and the header is 5 bytes, totaling 53 bytes.

Internet Access Technologies

17. ☑ **B, C,** and **D.** E-carriers are found in Europe, Mexico, and South America.
     ☒ **A** is incorrect. T-carriers are found in the United States, Japan, and Australia.

18. ☑ **C.** There are 24 channels that are 64 Kbps each to make one T1 for a total of 1.544 Mbps.
     ☒ **A, B,** and **D** are incorrect, as these are incorrect channel amounts.

19. ☑ **D.** ADSL is the high-speed Internet service provided by the phone companies that runs over the phone lines.
     ☒ **A, B,** and **C** are incorrect because they are not Internet services provided over the phone lines.

20. ☑ **A.** The cable modem receives data over the television cable as its own 6 MHz channel.
     ☒ **B, C,** and **D** are incorrect because they are not Internet services provided as their own channel over the television cable. ADSL is an Internet service, but it uses the phone lines.

21. ☑ **B.** ADSL supplies the Internet data over the phone line by using frequencies above 3.4 KHz.
     ☒ **A, C,** and **D** are incorrect because they are not the frequencies used to send Internet data. Voice travels over the phone lines at frequencies from 0 to 3 KHz.

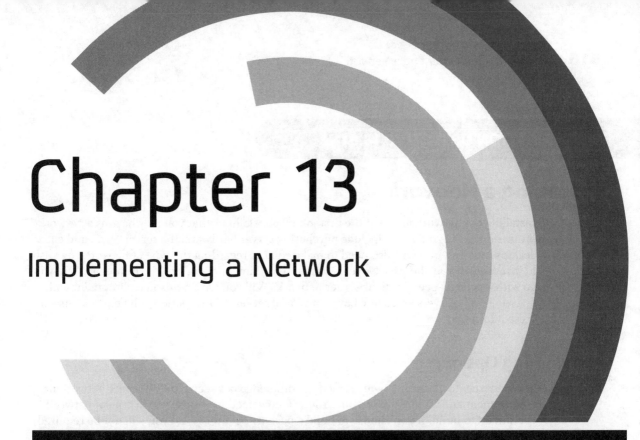

Chapter 13

Implementing a Network

You have learned about networking hardware components such as routers, switches, hubs, and network cabling thus far in the book. Being able to identify these components and connect them together is just a small part of implementing the network; you also need to install and configure the network operating system (NOS) on the server to publish resources out to the network.

In this chapter you will learn to implement a network by installing the network operating system, creating user accounts and groups, and subsequently assigning permissions to those user accounts for network resources such as files, folders, and printers.

Installing a Network

Installing the network is one of the first job responsibilities that you may have as a network professional. This duty may include purchasing server hardware, the server NOS, and client desktop systems. You will also need to make choices regarding the type of network you wish to install—will you choose a Novell, Microsoft, or Linux networking environment? Will you go with a peer-to-peer or client-server network? Will you have a mixed environment with a few Microsoft servers and a few Linux or Novell servers? This section will help you answer these questions.

Networking Options

Looking back to Chapter 1, you learned the difference between a peer-to-peer networking environment and a server-based one. You will now need to choose which type of network you intend to build. If you choose to build a peer-to-peer network, you will not be required to purchase server hardware and the network operating system, thereby reducing cost. The disadvantage of a peer-to-peer network is that it is typically limited to ten systems.

If you choose to go with a server-based network, you will need to purchase the server hardware and the server network operating system, so you can expect some additional cost. You will also need to obtain client access licenses. A client access license (CAL) is needed to allow the client to connect to the network operating system. It is important to understand that just because you have purchased the server operating system does not mean you can allow everyone to access data on the server. You will need to purchase a CAL for each client connecting.

Let us say that we have decided to go with a server-based network. When it comes to server-based networking environments, you have three popular types to choose from—Microsoft, Novell, and Linux.

Microsoft Networking

Microsoft networking environments have a big market share these days, with Windows Server 2012 being the most popular Windows server version on existing networks. When you install a Microsoft server, you will have to make a number of choices, such as deciding whether to install a stand-alone server, a member server, or a domain controller.

Stand-alone System

A stand-alone server has a local Security Accounts Manager (SAM) database, similar to a Windows 8 system. The SAM database is a database of accounts that resides on the local system and is used to access resources on the local system only. This is similar to having a number of Windows 8 systems in a workgroup (peer-to-peer) environment—the accounts are not "network" accounts; they are local accounts.

You may install a stand-alone server if this server is to act as your web server or firewall system. Typically, these systems are not part of the normal "Microsoft network," otherwise called a domain, because they are connected to the Internet.

Domain Controller

A domain controller (DC) is a server that has Microsoft's directory service installed, known as Active Directory. The Active Directory database is the term used by Microsoft for the network account database. If you are authenticated by or you log on to the Active Directory database, you can access resources across the network. The account is not used just to access resources on the local system, as is the case with the stand-alone system.

When a user logs on to the network, the logon request is sent to the domain controller on the network where the account information is verified. Once the domain controller has verified the information, the user can access network resources to which they have access anywhere on the network. The term for this Microsoft network is a *domain*.

When installing a Microsoft domain environment, you need to be familiar with a few more terms—trees and forests. A large organization may want to create a network environment that contains multiple domains. The following terms relate to Microsoft network environments:

- **Domain**   A logical grouping of computers and resources. Users log on to the domain and can be authenticated by any domain controller in the domain. A domain is a security boundary and a replication boundary.

- **Trees**   A hierarchy of domains that have a contiguous Domain Name System (DNS) namespace. For example, if you have a domain named companyabc.loc, you may have a child domain for each region, such as eastern, central, or western, or maybe for each country, such as the United States and Canada. Each domain will have a full domain name that includes the domain name joined by the parent domain (companyabc.loc), as shown in Figure 13-1.

- **Forest**   A forest is made up of one or more trees. In the Active Directory world, you will always have a domain, a tree, and a forest. It is just a question of how many domains make up this tree-and-forest structure. Each tree in the forest has its own DNS namespace and has a trust relationship to the forest root domain (the first domain installed in the forest).

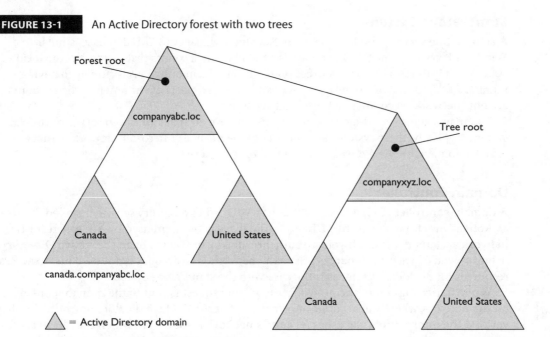

FIGURE 13-1   An Active Directory forest with two trees

Member Server

A member server is a machine that is part of a domain, or a member of the domain, and typically is a resource that users would access once they have been authenticated by a domain controller. A member server may be a server that is in the domain that performs any kind of function on the network, such as being a file and print server, a database server, or an e-mail server. The difference between a member server and a stand-alone server is simply that a stand-alone server is not part of a domain, so it cannot take advantage of the fact that a domain controller has authenticated the user. This means that the stand-alone server is responsible for authenticating the user when someone connects to the system. Figure 13-2 displays a typical domain environment in the Microsoft world.

Linux

Linux is starting to command a lot of attention in the IT industry because of its reliability and its secure architecture. Linux has a fairly limited directory service compared to Microsoft's Active Directory.

Linux (and UNIX) environments can store user account information in files (/etc/passwd holds user account information, /etc/shadow holds encrypted user passwords, and /etc/group holds group membership information). Without a directory service, this information

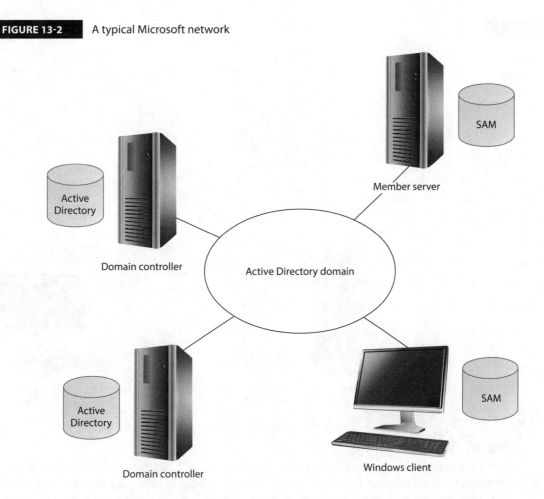

FIGURE 13-2   A typical Microsoft network

is specific to each server. Network Information Service (NIS) is commonly used to replicate user account information between servers, but many vendors, such as Sun and IBM, offer modified and enhanced versions of NIS for this purpose.

Network Requirements

This section introduces the hardware and software requirements for building a network. We will review the hardware that is required first and then discuss the software requirements. This section is in effect a summary of the network components you have already learned about in Chapter 3.

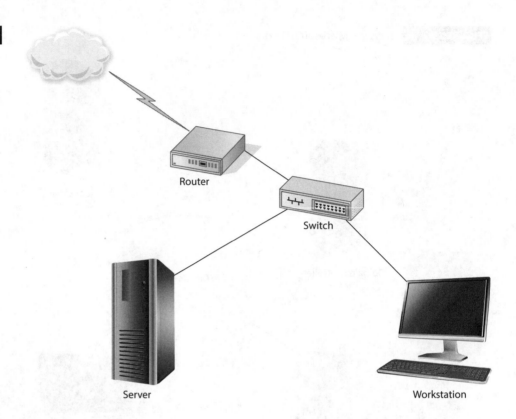

FIGURE 13-3

The networking
hardware used
to complete the
network

Router

Switch

Server

Workstation

Networking Hardware

The first thing that you will need in each of the systems or hosts that will participate on the network is a network interface card, which is the means the system uses to send and receive data on the network. You will also need to have a hub or a switch to act as a central connection point for all the systems. If your systems are going to send data to another network, you will need a router as well. Figure 13-3 displays the general setup of the networking hardware.

The networking server will also need to have its specs measured out. Today's servers will include a redundant array of independent disks (RAID) controller card that connects to and manages the RAID drives. There should be at least 4GB of RAM on the server, depending on its role. If the server is intended to act as a mail server or a database server, you may want more memory and multiple CPUs on the motherboard.

Networking components installed in Windows

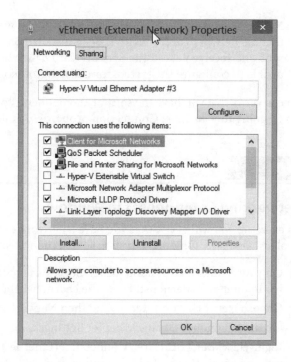

Networking Software

It is extremely important to understand what the network's software requirements are. Certainly, you will need all four of the following software components somewhere on the network:

- **Service** A *service* is what is being provided to clients on the network—it is typically the reason for the network. For example, most networks have a server that offers file and printer sharing services, or maybe web services that offer webpages to web clients on the network. Without a service, there is no purpose to the network.

- **Client** A *client* is a piece of software that connects to the service and makes the network request. For example, Internet Explorer is a client that makes requests to a web server (service) for different webpages on the web server. Another example is the Client for Microsoft Networks (shown in Figure 13-4), which allows users to connect to any Microsoft file and print server.

- **Protocol** A *protocol* is the networking language that a system uses to send the request from the client to the service. If you want two systems to communicate, they will need to speak the same language (protocol), such as TCP/IP or NetBEUI.

■ **Network card driver** In order for all of this to work, you will need to make sure that the network card driver has been installed on the system so that the system can send and receive data. If the network card driver has not been installed, you will be unable to configure the system for clients, protocols, or services.

You can verify that you have the software components to network the Microsoft operating system by going to your LAN Connection properties, as shown in Figure 13-4.

EXERCISE 13-1

Confirming Networking Components in Windows

In this exercise, you will verify that you have a network card driver, client software, and a protocol installed on a Windows 8 system so that the system can connect to a Microsoft server.

1. On your Windows 8 system, move your mouse to the bottom-right corner of the task bar to open the charm list. From the charm list choose Settings | Control Panel.

2. Choose Network And Internet and then Network And Sharing Center.

3. On the left choose Change Adapter Settings.

4. Right-click your Local Area Connection (Ethernet) and choose Properties. You will notice a listing that includes a number of pieces of software used by this network connection.

5. In the Local Area Connection Properties window, you can see the network card driver that is being used for this local area network (LAN) connection in the Connect Using option at the top of the dialog box.

6. You can also see that the Client for Microsoft Networks is loaded, which allows you to connect to shared folders on a system running Microsoft operating systems.

7. To view the protocol being used, scroll down until you see the protocols in the network components list. Do you see the TCP/IP v4 protocol (it displays as Internet Protocol Version 4)? _____

8. Notice that the system also has File and Print Sharing for Microsoft Networks—this is the network software that must be installed to allow Microsoft clients to connect to shared folders on your system.

9. Looking at the components in the list, answer yes or no to what is installed:

   a. TCP/IP? _____

   b. Client for Microsoft Networks? _____

   c. File and Print Sharing? _____

   d. IPX/SPX? _____

10. Close all windows.

Installing a Network Server

In this section you will learn to install a network server by installing Windows Server 2012 and then configure it as a domain controller for certworld2.loc. After installation of this server, you will learn to create users and groups on it.

When installing a Windows server, you want to make sure that you plan for installation by deciding on a number of settings and other issues, such as

- **Server name** You will need to decide what the name of the server will be. Clients will connect to the server by name when accessing folders and printers.

- **Domain name** If your server will be joining a domain, you will need to type in its name. If you are joining a domain, you will also need to know the user name and password of the administrator account that has permission to add servers to the domain. If the server is to be a domain controller for a domain, you will accomplish that by adding that role after installation, so you should have planned in advance what your domain name will be.

- **Server as domain controller** You will need to know before you start the installation whether or not the server will be a domain controller, because if the server is to be a domain controller, you will install it as a stand-alone server and then install the Active Directory role.

- **Hardware support** Make sure that your server hardware (network card, video card, and the like) will work with the server operating system by checking out the Windows Server Catalog at www.windowsservercatalog.com.

- **Partition setup** During installation, you will have the opportunity to create and delete the partitions on the hard disk of the server. Plan your partition strategy before the installation so that you are prepared for this step. By default, Windows Server 2012 creates a 100MB system-reserved partition (with no assigned drive letter) where the boot manager resides.

- **File system** After partitioning the disk, you will need to format the partition with a file system such as FAT32 or New Technology File System (NTFS). For security reasons, you should always go with the NTFS file system on Microsoft servers and desktop operating systems.

- **Licensing** When installing a Windows server, you will have to choose either per-seat or per-server licensing. With *per-server* licensing, you obtain a CAL for each connection to the server. During the installation of the server, you will need to specify how many simultaneous connections you expect. With *per-seat* licensing, you purchase a license for each individual client that will access the server. The difference between the two is illustrated in this example: If you have ten users accessing two different servers, with per-server licensing you need 20 licenses, whereas with per-seat licensing you only need 10 licenses, or one license for each client, no matter how many servers are being accessed.

In order to install the Windows Server operating system, you will first need to place your Windows Server 2012 DVD in the DVD drive and then power on the computer. The system boots off the DVD and then starts the installation.

To see how to install a Windows Server 2012 system, check out the "Installing Windows Server 2012" video found in the accompanying material.

Let's walk through the steps to install Windows Server 2012, and then you will create a domain controller that runs the Active Directory database. This domain controller will be referred to in all the remaining discussions and exercises in this chapter.

1. Place your Windows Server 2012 DVD in the drive and then power on the computer.
2. To install Windows Server 2012, on the Language And Preferences screen, choose Next to accept the defaults.
3. Choose Install Now to perform the installation.
4. Choose the edition of Windows Server 2012 you wish to install. In our example, we will install the Standard edition with GUI; select it and then choose Next.
5. Choose I Accept The License Terms and then choose Next.
6. To perform a new installation, choose Custom: Install Windows Only (Advanced).
7. Select Drive 0 as the drive to install Windows Server to and then choose Next.
8. The Windows Setup program informs you that it is installing Windows and it will take some time. After the system reboots, you will be asked for the password of the Administrator account—set the password to P@ssw0rd and then choose Finish.
9. Once the password is set, you can log in by pressing CTRL-ALT-DEL and then type the password of **P@ssw0rd** and press ENTER.

Once you have logged on, Server Manager launches so that you can perform initial configuration of the server, such as change the IP address and then change the computer name of the server. To change the IP address from Server Manager, choose Local Server on the left, and then on the right you will see your Ethernet card with a link specifying that it is using IPv4 assigned by Dynamic Host Configuration Protocol (DHCP). Choose that link to open your Network Connections. Right-click the Ethernet connection and go to Properties in order to change the IP address. You will want to ensure that you have statically assigned an IP address to your server. Go to your LAN Connection properties and change the IP address. I will use the IP address of 192.168.5.1 for this walkthrough and a subnet mask of 255.255.255.0. You may leave the default gateway entry empty, but set your primary DNS Server setting to 192.168.5.1 as well.

To change your computer name of the server, go back to the Local Server screen of Server Manager and then at the top of the list you can see the computer name of the server. Choose the link to go to System Properties, then choose the Change button to change the computer name to Server2012B, and then restart the system.

To see how to install Active Directory, check out the "Configuring Active Directory" video found in the accompanying material.

Creating a Domain Controller by Installing Active Directory

1. To install Active Directory, launch Server Manager from the task bar and choose Manage | Add Roles And Features.
2. Once the installation is completed, you can choose Close.
3. Choose Next three times to get to the roles list.
4. Choose the Active Directory Domain Services role and choose Next.
5. Choose Add Features when prompted to install the administrative tools as well.
6. Choose Next three times and then choose Install.
7. Once installation has completed, choose Close.
8. You next need to configure Active Directory. From Server Manager you should see a notification flag at the top of the screen. Choose the flag and a menu of tasks is displayed.
9. Choose Promote This Server To A Domain Controller to start the configuration of Active Directory.
10. Choose Add A New Forest and type the root domain of **certworld2.loc** and choose Next.
11. In the Domain Controller Options, accept all the defaults, but set the password for Directory Services Restore Mode to **P@ssw0rd** and then choose Next five times.
12. You will get a few warnings on the prerequisite checks. Choose Install.

Now that you have installed a Windows 2012 Server and Active Directory, you can start creating user accounts for individuals who will need to log on to the network and access network resources.

CERTIFICATION OBJECTIVE 13.02

Creating User Accounts

Now that you have the server installed, you will first need to make sure that each user who will access the network has a network user account to log on to the network with. A *user account* is a network object that users on the network use to prove their identity to the network. Once the user logs on with a valid user name and password, the user will be able to access resources on the network, such as files, folders, and printers, to which that user account has been granted permission.

Built-in Accounts

Before learning how to build a user account for each employee or individual who will access the network, it is important to understand that each operating system has built-in accounts. A built-in account comes already installed with the operating system and serves a specific purpose.

There are a few built-in accounts that you should be familiar with for the Network+ exam. Each of these accounts is typically used to perform the initial administrative tasks on the server, such as creating user accounts and groups. Table 13-1 displays some popular built-in accounts.

The password for these built-in administrative accounts is normally determined during the installation of the operating system. It is important to be sure that you know that password so that you can log on as that account. Therefore, be sure to make note of the password during the installation and be sure to use a strong password—one that is not easily guessed or cracked. It is also wise to rename the default administrative account for security reasons.

Creating User Accounts

Now that you have learned about built-in accounts, let's take a look at how to create and manage user accounts. To create a user account, first make sure that you are comfortable with the naming convention you will use for these accounts. The naming convention is

TABLE 13-1   Built-in Accounts Found with Different Operating Systems

Account Name	Operating System	Description
Administrator	Windows	This is an account, built during the installation of the operating system, that is used as the initial administration account. This account is used to build all other accounts and to configure the server. The Administrator account is disabled by default with Windows 7—you are asked to provide a user name during installation, and this supplied user name has administrative privileges.
Guest	Windows	This built-in account is used to allow individuals to access the network without requiring a user account. Anyone not authenticated with an account that connects to the system can connect as the Guest account. This account is disabled by default because of the security concerns involved in allowing individuals to connect to the server without requiring an account.
Root	Linux/UNIX	This is the main administrative account in the Linux and UNIX world. This account is used to create additional accounts and configure the server.

typically made up of the user's first and last name. A popular naming convention is to use the first initial of the first name and then use the entire last name. For example, for my user account you might use a user name of gclarke. Once you have decided on the naming convention, you are ready to create your user accounts.

Creating a Local SAM User Account

When creating a user account on a Windows machine in a workgroup environment, you are creating a local user account in the SAM database of that system. This user account will be able to access resources only on the local system; it is typically used where there is no Active Directory environment.

To create a local user account, go to the Computer Management console found in the Tools menu of Server Manager. Once in the Computer Management console, expand the Local Users And Groups folder on the left. Next, right-click the Users folder and choose New User to create a new user account.

Once the New User dialog box appears, type a user name and the user's full name. You can also type the description of the user account, such as Accounting Department. Once you have filled in the name information, you can fill in the password for the user account and confirm the password, as shown in Figure 13-5.

You will notice that there are four additional options at the bottom of the New User dialog box. They are listed with a description, as follows:

■ **User Must Change Password At Next Logon**   Select this option if you are planning on setting a temporary password for the account and you want to have users change the password once they log on with the account. If you select this option, Windows will force the user to change the password at logon.

FIGURE 13-5

Filling in the
user account
properties

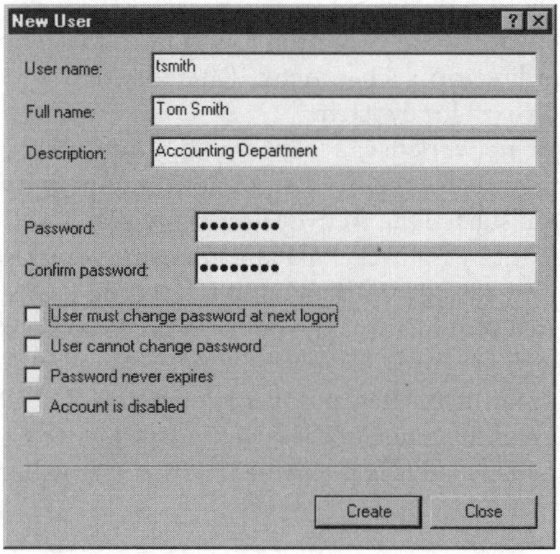

- **User Cannot Change Password**   Select this option if you want to control the user account password and you do not want users to change their own passwords. You may set this for a user account that is shared between employees if you want to ensure that one user does not change the password for another user.

- **Password Never Expires**   Select this option if you don't want this user account to have its password expire based on the time allowed by the company password policy. For whatever reason, you have decided that this account is an exception to the password-changing policy.

- **Account Is Disabled**   You may disable an account at any time. If a user goes on an extended leave (such as maternity or paternity leave), you may want to disable the account so that it cannot be used. When the employee comes back, you can simply enable the account by deselecting the check box.

Once you have your desired settings typed in and selected, you can create the account by clicking Create. Once you click Create, you should see the user account in the Users folder.

To see how to create a local user account, check out the "Creating a Local Account" video found in the accompanying material.

Creating a User Account in Active Directory

User accounts that are created in the local SAM database cannot be used to access other systems on the network. This becomes a huge problem in most networking environments, because you do not want to create the account on each system that the user will access. This is the purpose of creating an Active Directory account. An Active Directory account is a "network" account. When a user is authenticated by Active Directory, that user will have access to every system on the network, assuming that account has been given permission to access those systems.

As a network administrator in a Windows environment, you want to create your accounts in a central directory such as Active Directory so that you do not have to keep building network accounts on each local system.

To create network user accounts in the Active Directory database, go to Server Manager and launch Active Directory Users and Computers from the Tools menu.

Once you started the Active Directory Users and Computers console, you can now create a user account by right-clicking and choosing New User. Each user account can be placed in what is called an organizational unit (OU). The OU is designed to allow you to group user accounts that require the same policy settings or desktop restrictions. In Figure 13-6 you can see that a new user account is being created in the Halifax OU.

When creating the new user account, you will need to give details such as the first name, last name, and full name of the account (see Figure 13-7). You will also need to specify the user logon name—this is the name that the user will log on to the network with.

FIGURE 13-6

Creating a new
user account in
Active Directory

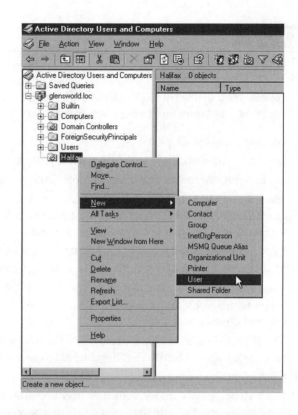

FIGURE 13-7

Filling in the user
account settings
for an Active
Directory account

EXERCISE 13-2

Creating Users in Active Directory

In this exercise, you will learn to create network user accounts in Active Directory by using the Active Directory Users and Computers console.

1. Go to the 2012SERVERA VM.
2. Log on as Administrator with a password of P@ssw0rd.
3. Go to Server Manager and choose Tools | Active Directory Users And Computers.
4. You may organize user accounts by OUs in any fashion you like. Some administrators organize users by department or by location. You will first create an OU to hold your user accounts. Right-click the certworld.loc domain and choose New | Organizational Unit.
5. Type **Chicago** as the name of the OU and choose OK.
6. Now create an organizational unit for New York.
7. You should now see the Chicago and New York OUs, each of which looks like a folder with a book on it. To create a user in the Chicago OU, right-click the Chicago OU and choose New | User.
8. The New User dialog box appears. Give the new user account the first name of **Bob** and a last name of **Smith**. Set the user logon name to **bsmith**.
9. Click Next.
10. Use a strong password for your new user account. You will use P@ssw0rd—not a great password, but one that uses a mix of uppercase and lowercase characters along with a symbol and number.
11. Click Next.
12. Click Finish.
13. You should see the Bob Smith user account in the Chicago OU.

Creating a User Account in Linux

If you have a Linux or a UNIX operating system, you may create users so that they can access resources on those systems. To create a user account in Red Hat Linux, click the Red Hat icon at the bottom-left corner of the screen and select System Settings | Users And Groups, as shown in Figure 13-8.

Once you are in the Red Hat User Manager tool, you may create a user account by clicking the Add User button in the top-left corner of the screen. Once you click Add User, you are presented with the Create New User dialog box, in which you will need to fill in the user account information, as shown in Figure 13-9.

FIGURE 13-8

Starting the Red
Hat User Manager
tool to create an
account in Linux

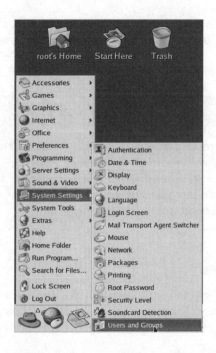

FIGURE 13-9

Supplying account
information for a
new user in Linux

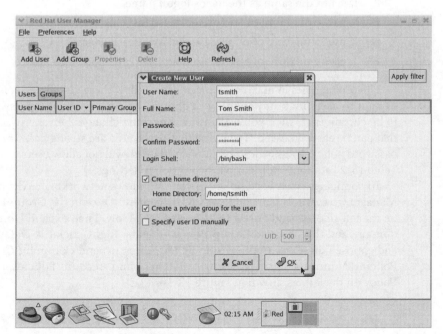

To see how to create an account in Linux, check out the "Create a User Account in Linux" video found in the accompanying material.

Password Policies

When creating your user accounts, make sure that you create strong passwords. Also make sure that when users change their passwords, they follow guidelines for strong passwords. What is a strong password? A strong, or complex, password is one that meets the following requirements:

- It is not the same as the user's logon name.
- It has a minimum of six (preferably eight) characters.
- It uses a mixture of uppercase and lowercase characters.
- It uses a mixture of letters, numbers, and symbols.

The problem lies in making sure that users follow these guidelines. It is extremely easy to explain to users that they should not choose their pet name as a password, but you need to be certain that when you walk away they don't change their password to a "weak" one that can be easily guessed. To ensure that passwords are strong passwords, you can build a password policy. A password policy, once enabled, will not allow users to have weak passwords. Table 13-2 lists some popular password policy settings.

To configure a password policy in your Windows networking environment, from Server Manager, go to Tools | Group Policy Management. Once in the Group Policy Management, on the left side, expand Forest by choosing the arrow. Then expand Domains, expand your domain, and then expand Group Policy Objects. Right-click the Default Domain Policy and choose Edit. Once in the Group Policy Editor, expand Computer Configuration; expand Policies, Windows Settings, Security Settings, and Account Policies; and select Password Policy on the left, as shown in Figure 13-10.

| TABLE 13-2 | Password Policy Settings |

Policy Settings	Description
Enforce password history	Enforcing password history means that the server maintains a given number of passwords previously chosen by a user and the user will not be able to choose a password that was already used within the duration of that history. For example, I normally configure my servers to remember at least 12 passwords, so users will not be able to reuse a password that they have chosen 12 times ago.
Maximum password age	This setting limits the user to having a password for a maximum amount of time. Normally, I set this to 30 days, which means that the user can keep a password for 30 days; after that it will expire, and the user will need to set a new one.
Minimum password age	Setting the minimum password age means that a user cannot change their password for the amount of time specified after it has been changed. For example, if you force users to change their passwords every 30 days, you may not want them to change it for a minimum of 2 days after that, so you can set the minimum password age to 2.
Minimum password length	The password must have a minimum number of characters. The more characters in a password, the harder it is to crack, because you have increased the number of potential characters. Eight characters or more is the recommendation for a minimum password length.
Need for password to meet complexity requirements	This is definitely a setting that should be enabled on any server that will hold the network accounts. Enabling complexity requirements means that the passwords must be strong and meet the conditions mentioned previously—a mixture of letters and numbers and employing uppercase and lowercase characters.

| FIGURE 13-10 |

Configuring a password policy on a Windows server

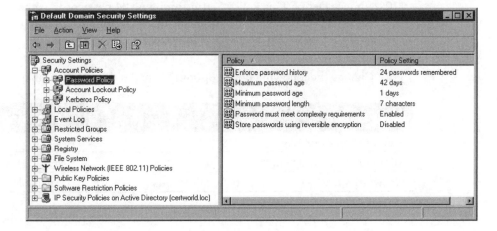

EXERCISE 13-3

Configuring a Password Policy

In this exercise, you will learn to create a password policy on a Windows Server 2012 domain controller so that the policy affects all domain accounts.

1. Go to the 2012SERVERA VM.

2. From Server Manager choose Tools | Group Policy Management. Once in Group Policy Management, on the left side, expand Forest by choosing the arrow. Then expand Domains, expand certworld.loc, and then expand Group Policy Objects.

3. To modify the password policy for the domain, right-click the Default Domain Policy and choose Edit.

4. Once in the Group Policy Editor, expand Computer Configuration; expand Policies, Windows Settings, Security Settings, and Account Policies; and select Password Policy on the left side.

5. Double-click Maximum Password Age on the right side of the screen to set the maximum number of days a user is allowed to keep his or her password.

6. Choose Define This Policy and type **30** days as the time when the password will expire.

7. Click OK.

8. Click OK.

9. Double-click the Enforce Password History option to specify how many passwords you want Windows to remember and not allow a user to reuse.

10. Choose Define This Policy Setting and type **24** passwords as the number of passwords to remember. This means that Windows will not allow a user to use a password he or she has used 24 times ago.

11. Click OK.

12. Change the following policy options to match those in the table.

Policy Option	Setting
Minimum Password Age	1
Minimum Password Length	8
Password Must Meet Complexity Requirements	Enabled

13. Now all users will need to follow those password requirements when they change their passwords. Close all windows.

CERTIFICATION OBJECTIVE 13.03

Managing Groups

Once you have created user accounts for your users, you are ready to organize those users into groups. The purpose of creating a group is to allow you to assign permissions or rights on the network to the group. This way, all the users who are members of that group will get the permission or right. For example, if you place all of the accountants in a group called Accountants, when you assign permissions to the accounting team, you can assign the permissions once—to the Accountants group; any user who is a member of the group will receive those permissions.

Groups are also a great way to facilitate role changes within the organization. For example, if you have a new accountant named Bob, you can create the Bob user account and place him in the Accountants group. You will not need to configure the permissions for Bob to access the accounting folder because the group already has the permission. This means that you are working smart as a network administrator and are using features of the network that facilitate change.

Built-in Groups

Before discussing how to create your own groups, it is important to understand that there are built-in groups within the network operating system. A built-in group is like a built-in user account in the sense that the group is installed with the operating system and has a predefined purpose within it. The following sections describe the popular built-in groups found in a Windows operating system.

Administrators

The Administrators local group is the most powerful of all the groups. As you might expect, users in this group have full control of the local system. This means that this group is responsible for managing the local system and has the capabilities to perform any action on the computer. For this reason, only trusted users should be members of this elite group. By default, the Domain Admins global group and the Administrator account are members of the Administrators local group for computers that are in a domain.

Users

The Users local group is a group that all users are members of, and this group has sufficient capabilities to log on to the desktop operating system and run applications that have been installed by the network administrator. The Domain Users global group is a member of the Users local group by default for computers in a domain.

Server Operators

The Server Operators group is intended to relieve the burden on the administrator by performing selected server administration tasks. Members of this group can shut down servers, format server hard disks, create and modify shares, lock and unlock the server, back up and restore files, and change the system time.

Printer Operators

Users in the Printer Operators local group have the capability to create, delete, and modify printers on a Windows system. Printing is one of the most common areas of troubleshooting on the network, and this group is used to alleviate the printing responsibility from the Administrators group.

Backup Operators

Members of the Backup Operators local group can back up and restore files and folders on a Windows system. This group is designed to take over the daily responsibility of doing backups from the Administrators group. Backup Operators can log on to and shut down the server, if needed.

Account Operators

Users in the Account Operators group have permissions to add, modify, and delete user and group accounts in the domain. The Account Operators group is used to create additional user accounts; however, it cannot change characteristics of Administrator accounts or modify members of any administrative group such as the Administrators, Server Operators, Backup Operators, or Print Operators groups.

Domain Admins

The Domain Admins global group is a member of the Administrators local group on every computer in the domain by default. To create a network administrator account (as opposed to creating a computer administrator), you should place the user account in the Domain Admins group; then the user can manage any system in the domain.

Domain Users

The Domain Users global group contains all user accounts created in the domain. The Domain Users global group is, by default, a member of the Users local group on every Windows system in the domain. If you need to assign permissions to all users on the network, it is recommended that you give permission to the Users group that contains the Domain Users group (which is all network users).

Placing users into these built-in groups gives them predefined administrative rights within the Windows operating system and Windows Server network operating systems. It is important to always place a user in the group that gives that user the minimum number of rights. For example, although the Administrators group and the Backup Operators group can perform backups, if you want a particular person to do backups, you should place that person in Backup Operators because administrators can perform any administrative tasks.

Creating Groups

You can also create your own groups within most network operating systems, which will allow you to assign permissions to groups of individuals in one action. To create a group within Active Directory, right-click an OU within Active Directory Users and Computers and choose New | Group, as shown in Figure 13-11. When you create a new group in Active Directory, you will need to choose one of two groups:

■ **Distribution**   A distribution group is used by e-mail applications to send an e-mail to a number of users at once. This is known as a distribution list in a number of e-mail systems.

■ **Security**   A security group is used to assign permissions to groups of people at a time. A security group is also used to e-mail a number of people at once.

FIGURE 13-11

Creating a new group in Active Directory

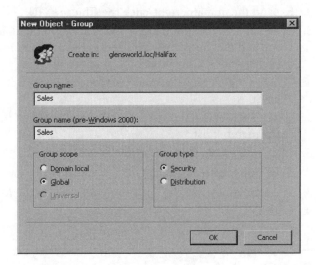

When creating a new group, you must also choose the group scope. The purpose of each group scope is as follows:

- **Global** A global group is used to organize users within an Active Directory domain. This group scope can contain any user or global group that exists within the same domain as the global group, and it can be used to assign permissions to resources in any domain.
- **Domain local** A domain local group is used to assign permissions or rights to resources within the domain. Domain local groups can contain users or groups from any domain in the enterprise.
- **Universal** A universal group is used to organize users across domains within the enterprise. For example, if you want to have a group called AllSales that contains the Sales group from all other domains, you will use a universal group to create the AllSales group. The Universal group can then have the Sales global groups from all other domains as a member.

EXERCISE 13-4

Creating Groups in Active Directory

In this exercise, you will learn to create a global group in Active Directory for the Sales team within your organization. You will then add the Bob Smith account to this Sales group.

1. From Server Manager, choose Tools | Active Directory Users And Computers.
2. Expand the domain, right-click the Chicago OU, and choose New | Group.
3. Type **Sales** as the group name and make sure that Global is selected to create a global group and that Security is selected as the group type so that you can use this group for permissions. Choose OK.
4. To add the Bob Smith account to the group, right-click the Sales group and choose Properties.
5. Select the Members tab to see who is a member of the group and to add a new user to the member list.
6. Click Add to add a member.
7. Type **Bob Smith** and click OK.
8. You should now see the Bob Smith account on the Members tab of the group.
9. Click OK.
10. Close all windows.

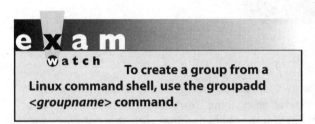

To create a group from a Linux command shell, use the groupadd *<groupname>* command.

Creating a Group in Linux

You can create groups within the Linux environment just as easily as you can within the Windows environment. To create a group within Linux, click the Red Hat icon located in the bottom-left corner and then choose System Settings | Users And Groups. Once the Red Hat User Manager tool appears, click the Groups tab at the top to see a list of existing groups.

To see how to create a group in Linux, check out the "Creating a Group in Linux" video found in the accompanying material.

To create a new group, click the Add Group button at the top of the Red Hat User Manager tool and specify a group name, as shown in Figure 13-12.

FIGURE 13-12

Creating a group in Linux

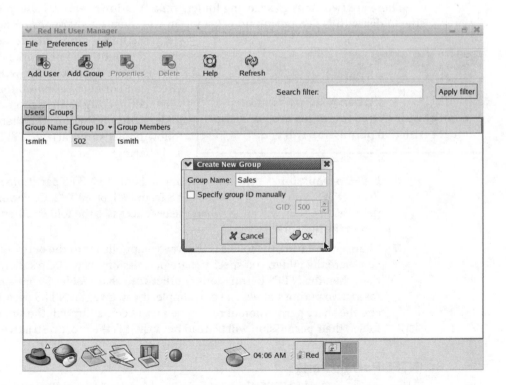

CERTIFICATION OBJECTIVE 13.04

Securing Files and Folders

In this section you will learn to secure folders and files by assigning permissions to users and groups within the various network operating systems. You will not be expected to be a security expert for the Network+ exam, but you should be familiar with some of the basic permissions found in the operating systems in current use.

Securing Files in Windows

In the Windows operating systems, once you have your users and groups built, you can then secure the folders and files on these systems so that only certain users can access certain folders. For example, you want to make sure that only accountants can get access to the accounting folder.

There are two steps to securing folders on a Windows server: First, you must secure the folder with NTFS permissions, and then you must set share permissions when you share the folder out to the network. Sharing the folder out to the network is the way you "publish" the folder to your Windows clients. Users can connect to shared folders only when connecting to the server and can access folders and files within the shared folder. The following list summarizes NTFS permissions and sharing:

When NTFS permissions conflict with shared folder permissions, the most restrictive permission will win.

- **NTFS permissions** These can be applied only to NTFS partitions. If you are not using NTFS, you can convert to NTFS from FAT or FAT32. Once you set the NTFS permissions, they will apply when the user accesses the folder either locally or from across the network.

- **Sharing** Sharing the folder is the way you publish it to the network clients. When you share the folder, you specify share permissions as well. Be sure to remember that when the NTFS permissions conflict with share folder permissions, the most restrictive permission wins. For example, if you give the NTFS permission of modify and the share permission of read, when users come through the share to access that folder, their permission will be read because it is the most restrictive.

NTFS Permissions

There are a number of NTFS permissions that you should be familiar with when it comes to securing folders; the popular NTFS permissions are listed in Table 13-3.

TABLE 13-3	Standard NTFS Permissions

NTFS Permission	Description
List Folder Contents	This is a permission assigned to a folder; it allows a user to view the contents of the folder but not necessarily to "read" the contents of files in the folder.
Read	This is a folder and file permission that enables a user to open and read the contents of files.
Read & Execute	This is a folder and file permission that allows users to read the contents of files and to run an executable file.
Write	This is a file and folder permission that allows a user to modify the contents of a file (write to it) or to create a new file or folder within that folder.
Modify	This is a folder and file permission that includes all the permissions mentioned previously. Having the Modify permission allows a user to read, execute, delete, list folder contents, and write to the contents of the folder or file.
Full Control	This is a folder and file permission that gives a user all permissions possible. If you assign the Full Control permission, the user will be able to modify the contents of the file and also change the permissions on the resource.

Shared Folder Permissions

Once you secure the folder with NTFS permissions, you will need to share the folder to publish it to the network. When sharing the folder, you will need to configure shared folder permissions. There are a few shared folder permissions that you should be familiar with when it comes to securing folders that are shared out on the network. Be aware that when a share permission is applied to a folder, it will be retained for all subfolders as well. For example, if you share the data folder and users have the change permission, when users connect to the data share, they will have the change share permission, and when they double-click a subfolder they will still have it. You will rely on NTFS to control the permissions at each subfolder level if needed. The share permissions are listed in Table 13-4.

Exercise 13-5 demonstrates how to configure a Windows server for NTFS permissions and publish the resource by sharing it and configuring share permissions.

EXERCISE 13-5

Video

Configuring Permissions in Windows Server 2012

In this exercise you will learn to set NTFS permissions and shared folder permissions to secure the data folder on your Windows Server 2012 system.

1. From the task bar choose the Folders button.
2. On the left, select Computer and then double-click drive C.

TABLE 13-4	Share Permissions in Windows
Share Permission	**Description**
Read	This share permission enables a user to open and read the contents of files within the share.
Change	This share permission enables a user to open and read the contents of files within the share, create new files, delete files, and change the contents of files within the share.
Full Control	This share permission enables a user to open and read the contents of files within the share, create new files, change the contents of files within the share, delete files, and change permissions on the share. This permission is typically not assigned to users on the network, but assigned to administrators so they have full access to the folder being shared.

3. Choose Home and then the New Folder button from the ribbon at the top of the screen.
4. Type **Data** as the name of the folder.
5. Right-click the data folder and choose Properties.
6. Select the Security tab and then click Advanced.
7. Choose Disable Inheritance and then choose Remove All Inherited Permissions From This Object.
8. Click OK and then Yes.
9. Click the Edit button, choose Add to add a user or group to the permission list, and then type **Sales** and choose OK.
10. Sales is added to the permission list. Select Sales and then choose the Modify permission.
11. Click OK.

Sharing the Data Folder

1. Right-click the Data folder, and choose Properties. Choose the Sharing tab and then the Advanced Sharing button.
2. Select Share This Folder. Notice that the share name is the same name as the folder—in this case, Data. Click Permissions to set the share permissions.
3. Click Remove to remove the default permission of Everyone having Read.
4. Click Add and type **administrators;sales** and then choose OK.
5. Select Administrators and then choose Full Control as the permission.

6. Select Sales and then choose Change as the permission.
7. Click OK.
8. Click OK again.

Connecting to a Shared Folder

Once you have configured the permissions on the Windows folder and have shared it out to the network, your clients will need to know how to connect to the shared folder. There are a number of ways to connect to the shared folder; two of my favorite methods are to use the run command and then connect to the UNC path of the shared folder, or to map a network drive to the shared folder.

■ **UNC path** The Universal Naming Convention (UNC) path is a standard naming convention to connect to network resources. A UNC path is made up of two backward slash (\) symbols followed by the name of the computer, another backward slash (\), and then the name of the share. For example, if you had a shared folder named DATA on a server called SERVER1, the UNC path would be \\SERVER1\DATA. The beautiful thing about UNC paths is that once you know the name of the server and the share, you can quickly connect by typing the UNC path in the run command or the Windows Explorer address bar.

■ **Mapped network drive** Some users are not comfortable with UNC paths and don't know what they are, let alone how to connect to one. To make your network easier to use, you would normally create mapped network drives on the user's computer. A mapped network drive is a logical drive under Computer (Windows 7) or This PC (Windows 8 and Server 2012) that does not connect to a drive on the local system but points to a folder on a server somewhere. You can always tell which drives are referring to a folder on a network server because the icon has a cable underneath the drive.

To map a network drive, right-click Computer (Windows 7) or This PC (Windows 8) and choose the Map Network Drive command.

In the Map Network Drive dialog box you specify the drive letter you would like to create and then specify the location of the shared folder that this drive will point to. You can also specify whether this mapped network drive should be created the next time the user logs on by selecting the Reconnect At Sign-in option, as shown in Figure 13-13. Note that in an Active Directory domain environment, mapping of drives is typically done by policies on the network.

To see how to map a network drive, check out the "Map a Network Drive" video found in the accompanying material.

FIGURE 13-13

Mapping a
network drive in
Windows

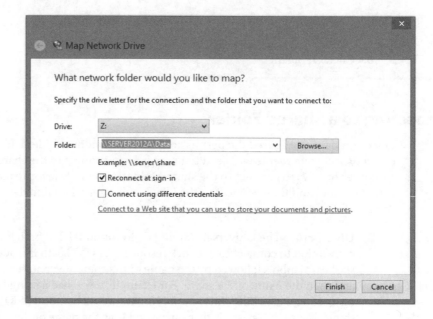

Securing Files in Linux

Securing files in Linux is a little bit different. Linux has three permissions for files and folders, and each permission has a numerical value associated with it:

- **Read (R):** 4
- **Write (W):** 2
- **Execute (X):** 1

Three entities can have these three permissions for a file or folder: the file owner, a group, and everyone else ("others"). To view the permissions assigned to a file, you can use the **ls -l** command in Linux to list files (see Figure 13-14).

Notice in the figure that the file called myfile.txt has the Read/Write permissions given to the owner, whereas the group and everyone have only the Read permission. If you want to change the permission, you can use the **chmod** (change mode) command and type a number to represent the desired permission for each of the three placeholders. The following code listing displays how to give the owner Read, Write, and Execute permission (adding up to seven) and also to give the group and everyone Read, Write, and Execute permission:

```
chmod 777 myfile.txt
```

FIGURE 13-14   Viewing permissions on a file in Linux

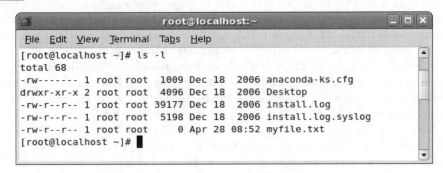

If you wanted to give the owner Read, Write, and Execute but ensure everyone else only has the Read permission to the myfile.txt, you would use the following command:

```
chmod 744 myfile.txt
```

Figure 13-15 displays the new permissions on the myfile.txt file. Notice that the owner has Read, Write, and Execute, and everyone else has just Read.

The **chmod** command supports a number of methods to change the permission on a file. For example, **chmod u=rwx /myfile.txt** would set Read, Write, and Execute for the file

FIGURE 13-15   Looking at the modified permissions

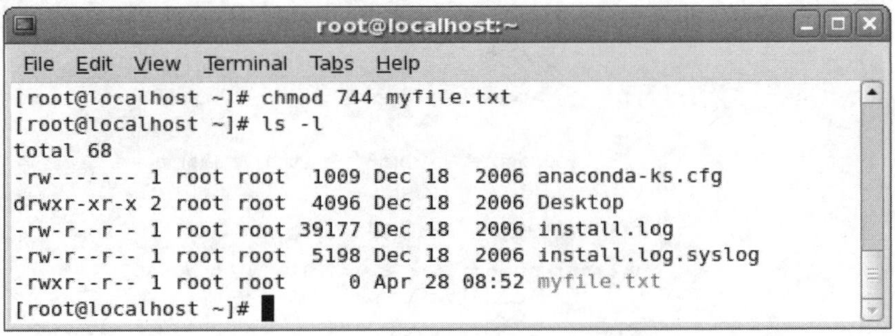

owner (u) to the file named myfile.txt. Another example, **chmod u=rwx,g=rw,o=r /myfile.txt**, grants the file owner (u) Read, Write, and Execute; allows a group (g) to read and write; and allows all others (o) only read access. Expressed numerically, the command would be **chmod 764 /myfile.txt**. Keep in mind that if you're using **chmod** to set permissions on a folder, you should use the **-R** switch to recursively change permissions for all subordinate files and folders. You can also use commands such as **chmod u+w /myfile.txt** to add the Write permission for the file owner to the existing permissions. You can also use **chmod u-w / myfile.txt** to remove the Write permission for the user. This same technique can be used to add or remove the Read and Execute permission for owner (u), group (g), and all others (o).

You can also modify the permissions on a file in Linux using the properties dialog box of the file. If you right-click a file and choose Properties, you can modify the permissions assigned to the owner, group, and others, as shown in Figure 13-16.

To see how to change permissions on a file in Linux, check out the "Change File Permissions in Linux" video found in the accompanying material.

FIGURE 13-16

Configuring permissions through file properties

Installing Printers

Another type of resource that appears on the network along with files and folders is printers. Being able to share a printer with other users on the network is one of the fundamental reasons for having a network. This section covers installing a printer and sharing it out to the network.

Before we get into the steps to configure a printer, let's take a look at some terminology that deals with printing. The following terms are used a lot in networking environments to describe the printing environment:

- **Print device**   The print device is the physical printer that takes paper and outputs the printout—in our terms, it is the "printer."
- **Printer**   The printer is the software interface to the print device. The printer is the little icon that appears in your printer folder and allows you to configure the settings through the properties of the printer. You can open the printer to see the print jobs that have been submitted. This is also termed the print queue in some environments.
- **Print server**   A print server is the machine that holds the shared printer. Remember that the printer is the icon and not the physical print device. The print server is where clients submit their print jobs. Figure 13-17 displays the relationship between the various printing terms.

Installing a Print Server

To install a print server in the Windows environment, run the Add Printer Wizard on the Windows Server 2012 machine. Clients connect to this shared printer to submit their print jobs.

When installing a printer on the server, run the Add Printer Wizard and select the option to install to a local printer. The term "local printer" means that the printer is a resource of the server and you will manage the printer on that system. Management of the printer could involve such things as adding drivers, configuring a schedule, or configuring permissions.

After specifying that you wish to install a local printer in the Add Printer Wizard, you will then need to specify the port the printer is connected to. The port could be a local port such as LPT1 or it could be a standard TCP/IP port. A standard TCP/IP port is the port type you use if the print device is connected directly to the network with a network card and has an IP address assigned to it.

After specifying the port type, you will then be asked for the manufacturer and model of the printer. After specifying the model, you will then need to specify a share name for the printer. The printer must be shared in order for clients to connect to it, and print to it, from across the network. The printer is shared in the same way that a folder is shared, but it is nice that the Add Printer Wizard gives the option to share the printer.

FIGURE 13-17 Identifying printing terminology

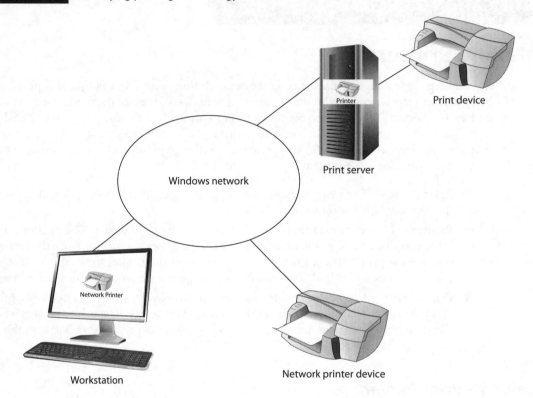

Changing Printer Permissions

Once the printer has been installed, you can then go to the properties of the printer to change its settings. One of the popular settings you may want to change is who has permission to print to the printer. To change the permissions on the printer, follow these steps:

1. Once the printer is installed, right-click the printer and choose Printer Properties.
2. Select the Security tab; then select the Everyone group and click Remove.
3. Click Add, type **sales**, and choose OK. In my example, I have added the Sales group to the permission list and given the print permission as shown in Figure 13-18.
4. Click OK.
5. Close all windows.

FIGURE 13-18

Giving the print permission to Sales

EXERCISE 13-6

Video

Installing a Printer on Windows Server 2012

In this exercise, you will learn to install a printer on a Windows Server 2012 machine, making the system a print server. Once you have installed the printer, you will configure the permissions so that only the Sales group can print to the printer.

1. Log on to 2012SERVERA as administrator.

2. Navigate to the Control Panel | Hardware | Devices And Printers and then choose the Add A Printer button on the toolbar.

3. Choose The Printer That I Want Isn't Listed option at the bottom of the Add Printer dialog box.

4. Choose Add A Local Or Network Printer With Manual Settings and then choose Next.

5. Choose an existing port of LPT1. Ensure that LPT1 is selected as the port for this demo, but note that you can print to a network print device (printer connected directly to the network) by choosing Create A New Port and then selecting Standard TCP/IP port. You will then be asked for the IP address of the device. I am assuming for this exercise there is no real print device, so simply choose LPT1.

6. Choose Next.

7. Choose the Brother Color Type3 Class Driver and then choose Next.

8. Type a Printer name of **Sales** and then choose Next.

9. Ensure that the printer is shared with the name Sales and then choose Next and then Finish.

Changing Printer Permissions

1. Once the printer is installed, right-click the Sales printer and choose Printer Properties.

2. Select the Security tab; then select the Everyone group and click Remove.

3. Click Add, type **sales**, and choose OK. The Sales group is added to the permission list and given the print permission.

4. Click OK.

5. Close all windows.

Configuring a Print Client

Once the printer has been installed on the server, which now makes the server a print server, you are ready to connect clients to the printer so they can print. You connect the clients to the printer by installing the printer on the client, but because the printer on the client references the share name of the printer on the server, we call it a *network printer* (from the client perspective). To install a printer on the client, run the Add Printer Wizard and, as shown in Figure 13-19, choose Select A Shared Printer By Name as the method to find the printer. You then type the share name of the printer. For example, in the preceding section you installed a shared printer on the Windows 2012 Server, and if a client wishes to reference it, the client will specify a UNC path of

```
\\SERVER2012A\sales
```

Any print jobs destined for the network printer will be redirected to the network print server to handle the print request. The printout will print to whatever device the print server is pointing to—in our case, LPT1.

To see how to install a network printer on a Windows client, check out the "Installing a Network Printer" video found in the accompanying material.

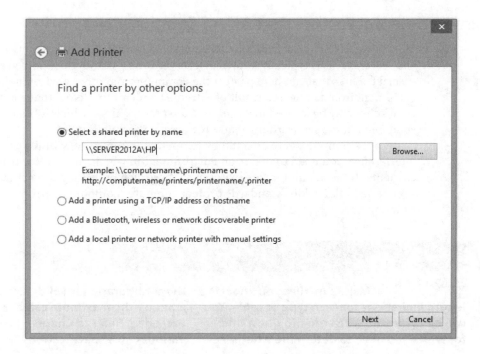

FIGURE 13-19

Installing a network printer

Printing in Linux

Common UNIX Printing System (CUPS) is the standard printing environment used in Linux. It includes support for the Internet Printing Protocol (IPP), Line Printer Daemon (LPD), and Line Printer Remote (LPR), among other standards.

LPD is a daemon (or service) that must be running on the Linux server; LPR refers to the Linux client. There are some basic Linux commands to control printing:

- **lp**   Sends print jobs to a Linux printer—for example, lp myfile.txt
- **lpstat**   Displays all configured printers and their print job status

CERTIFICATION OBJECTIVE 13.06

Working with Network Hardware

This section reviews the hardware that is required for the network to function and identifies potential issues surrounding networking hardware and networking equipment.

Environmental Factors that Affect Computer Networks

Most networks have a centrally located area that can safely house all network appliances and servers. This is typically known as a server room. Within this room are a multitude of special features that can help protect the computers and other environmentally "sensitive" equipment from failing as a result of extreme temperatures. Note that equipment such as switches may be located in a *Comms Closet* for the floor, which is then wired to the equipment in the server room at another area of the building.

Because computers are affected by temperature, moisture, vibrations, and electrical interference, you need to create an environment in which you can control each of these elements. If the computers are exposed to these elements, they can act irregularly and sometimes fail. Luckily, standards protect computer components from some of these situations.

Make sure that you know the length limitations for each type of cable. You will be presented with scenario questions for which you need to determine whether the configuration is valid; you must know whether the maximum cable length has been exceeded. Refer to Chapter 1 to review the various cable specifications.

Cables

Underneath the protection of most network cables lies a fragile layer of wire (or glass, in the case of fiber optics) that carries the data from one computer to another. Like most other computer components, this wire is not resistant to moisture, heat, or other electrical interference. A covering is placed over the wire to keep it from breaking or accidentally becoming wet. Some cable types have a layer of shielding that helps prevent crosstalk between cables and electromagnetic interference (EMI).

Cables that bring data to networks come in many different forms, from copper to fiber optic. The type of cable determines its feasible length. When a cable exceeds the recommended distance, the signal begins to fade and becomes unreadable. Be sure to verify that you have not exceeded the maximum distance of your cable types.

The Network Operations Center, Server Rooms, and Data Center

Your Network Operations Center (NOC) is the home base for all of the important servers on your network. The NOC enables you to centrally manage and keep a close eye on all your networked data.

The NOC is the control room used to monitor all network equipment in the server room or data center. This may be located inside the server room, but is often located outside of the room in a separate secure room. The NOC will have consoles and dashboards showing the health of the equipment in the server room.

exam

watch   **You will be asked to determine which environment of several scenarios is the most appropriate for a server room. Just remember that servers need an environment free of dust with plenty of** ventilation and reasonable temperature and humidity. Placing servers near a window on a sunny day or in a dusty warehouse would not create an ideal operating environment.

A server room or data center, above all else, needs to be secure and able to house all the data and servers. Normally, the server room is a secured room that is equipped with various types of fire suppression (halon, foam), raised floors to place the cabling, and temperature control. You can't put a value on your data, so this room should never be compromised in any way.

The server room should at all times be cool, dry, and temperature controlled. Computers and other electrical equipment do not like humidity, heat, or extreme cold, so you should be very careful to regulate the temperature of the server room. When a computer overheats, there is no guarantee that the data on your servers can be saved.

Because computer equipment is very sensitive to moisture, you need to use a form of fire suppression besides water. Putting out a fire in your server room or data center using a sprinkler system would ruin all your computer equipment. Many types of foam or halon are used to put out fires quickly and safely while minimizing the potential damage to your computer equipment. The laws of your geographical area could require that you not use certain types of fire control methods. Some states require older systems to be upgraded within a certain amount of time and consider older fire control methods dangerous.

exam

watch   **For the exam, remember to make sure that you should not expose computers or network equipment to any potential environmental hazards, such as moisture or extreme heat, or to electrical** interference, such as that created by generators and television sets. The exam might include questions pertaining to the location of equipment.

Minimizing Electrical Interference

Electromagnetic interference (EMI) can wreak great havoc on any type of computer equipment. You might be aware of certain types of speakers that are magnetically shielded to prevent electrical interference. However, magnets and computers don't mix, so unfortunately, this concept doesn't carry over to computer electronics. The alternative is to keep all your computer equipment away from any electrical device that could interrupt the computing power of your equipment.

Computer Chassis

With the rapid advances in today's technology, computers are faster than ever. Today there is more computing power on a single laptop computer than was used by NASA to place the first man on the moon. However, more computing power comes at a price, and the price that we pay is heat. As processors become faster and faster, they become hotter and hotter as they perform billions of calculations. The scenario is the same for disk drives. The larger the drives become, the more work that needs to be done to find the data on the drive. The result is that the temperature within the PC's chassis becomes too hot for the computer to operate. When this happens, the overheating part fails or destroys the PC altogether.

To combat this problem, a cooling fan (or multiple fans) is placed inside the PC to circulate the air and prevent the PC from overheating. Some of the more inventive computer chassis help circulate the air inside the PC to keep the computer cool. The room in which the servers are placed should also be air conditioned. The air in the PC chassis can only be as cool as the air it is circulating from the room in which it is placed.

One of the things that a number of organizations forget to do as part of their maintenance plan is to clean the inside of the computer. The collection of dust in the system can create problems with the cooling techniques used by the PC manufacturer. I remember trying to fix a client's computer that continued to crash. After trying everything, I opened the case and found that the cooling fan on the processor was jammed with dust. I reached for my can of compressed air and gave the system a good cleaning—problem fixed in five minutes!

Common Peripheral Ports and Network Components

What use is a computer without all the goodies that accompany it? There are literally hundreds of peripherals and network components to choose from in today's fun-filled world of computers. In this section, you will learn the basics about the companion pieces you will likely encounter in your day-to-day experience.

All these ports and network components are mainly used to make the experience of using a computer easier and more user friendly. If you want to be an expert in networking technology, you should know and understand each component in case you have to troubleshoot a problem someday.

Network Interface Cards

Your network interface card (NIC) should be auto-detected during setup, but if it is not, you must install the driver for the network card. The driver normally is shipped on a CD that comes with the card or system, and you should also be able to download the driver from the manufacturer's website. You must make sure that the network driver is installed before attempting any network communication activities.

Binding Protocols

When you install networking protocols on your system, the protocols are bound, or linked, to the network card through a feature called bindings. If you install multiple protocols, each protocol is bound to the network card so that if data leaves the network card, it could use either protocol that is installed. You can optimize network performance by changing the binding order, which specifies which protocol should be used first for communication.

Network Connection

Connecting to the Internet with a networked server requires a large amount of bandwidth to provide connectivity for all users. The amount of bandwidth determines the number of users that can access your site at once. A fast network connection enables easy access to your website, whereas a slow connection sometimes prohibits users from getting to your website. If you are on an intranet, you probably do not have to worry about the amount of bandwidth. A normal 100/1000 Mbps Ethernet network card should be sufficient for typical LAN traffic.

You will most likely have a router connected to the Internet using a WAN-type interface. The router will then connect your LAN using an internal network interface that will connect to a hub, or switch, where all other systems are connected. This router acts as the device that allows all users on the network to access the Internet.

Network-Attached Storage

Network-attached storage (NAS) units are stand-alone devices that have a group of hard drives providing storage to network clients. An NAS is a containment unit with a power supply, cooling fans, and bays to hold the hard drives. The unit usually can be locked to prevent anyone from opening it and removing its contents.

The NAS allows for a large point of mass storage, and it most likely includes a built-in RAID controller to allow all the hard disks to be fault tolerant and function as a single volume. You manage configuration of an NAS by telnetting to the system or connecting to its webpage and setting configuration options to allow sharing and setting up a unit name. The unit name allows you to use the UNC to connect to the unit and its devices.

Network-attached storage units are very useful in a network environment, as they provide lots of storage space and typically support RAID functions. In general, you will use an NAS device for sharing data and it can replace a file server.

Serial and Parallel Ports

Serial ports are a slow link that allows data flow, with the bits being sent one at a time. This is different from a parallel connection, which sends data eight bits at a time. A serial link typically transmits information at 128 Kbps. You may find a serial link on networking devices such as routers to connect to a WAN interface.

Serial ports are also known as COM ports, or communication ports.

As mentioned, parallel ports yield better performance by sending data eight bits at a time and offer transfer rates as high as 2 Mbps, depending on the parallel port mode. Printers are the most popular type of parallel port devices used on networks.

USB and SCSI

Universal serial bus (USB) is an innovation in computer peripheral technology that enables you to add devices such as audio players, scanners, printers, network cards, and external hard drives to your computer without having to add an adapter card, or even having to turn the computer off. USB comes in three flavors right now:

- **USB 1.0**   USB 1.0 has a transfer rate of 12 Mbps, which is a good speed, considering that serial ports and parallel ports offer only speeds up to 2 Mbps.
- **USB 2.0**   USB 2.0 has a transfer rate of 480 Mbps.
- **USB 3.0**   USB 3.0 has an amazing transfer rate of 5 Gbps!

Most systems today have USB ports on both the front and back of the computer. You can also purchase a USB hub device that will connect to your system and allow additional devices to be connected to it.

Small Computer System Interface/SAS

Small Computer System Interface (SCSI) is a standard interface that enables systems to communicate with peripheral hardware, such as disk drives, tape drives, CD-ROM drives, printers, and scanners. What makes SCSI devices so special is the improvement in data transfer over parallel devices. For example, Ultra-Wide SCSI 2 devices can transfer data up to 80 MBps compared to an Extended Integrated Drive Electronics device (EIDE), which has a transfer rate of 16 MBps. Another benefit of SCSI devices is the capability to daisy-chain as many as 7 or 15 devices (depending on the bus width). SCSI devices are more important for high-performance systems such as servers than they are for the home PC.

A special note should be made about a newer drive technology that is being used in servers and SANs; that drive technology is *Serial Attached SCSI (SAS)*. SAS is a technology that has replaced the older SCSI standard and uses the same SCSI command as its predecessor. SAS allows up to 65,535 devices to be connected and has a transfer rate of up to 12 Gbps depending on the implementation! SAS is backwards compatible with Serial Advanced Technology Attachment (SATA), allowing you to connect SATA drives to an SAS backplane.

Print Servers

Print servers either can be dedicated servers that are responsible for sending documents to various printer pools scattered around a corporation, or they can be used in tandem with file servers. These servers are used to send documents to the print device for printing. This system makes much more sense than having a separate printer for each computer, and it gives you more control over administering the documents that are sent to each network printer.

Hubs, Switches, and Bridges

Hubs enable you to connect systems together at a central point; they have been popular devices on networks for many years. Because hubs send data to all ports, they have been replaced by switches on networks today. A switch only sends data to the port where data needs to go, not to all the ports, like with a hub. The simple filtering features increase overall performance on the network but use less bandwidth, and also add to the security to the network because the traffic is being filtered (only sent to the port where the destination system resides).

on the job

Today's computer networks are using switches more than hubs because of both the performance benefits and the security benefits of switches.

Bridges are intelligent devices used to filter traffic on LANs by forwarding packets to specific network segments based on the packets' source and destination Media Access Control (MAC) addresses. Bridges have been popular in the past, but have been replaced by switches on today's networks.

Routers and Gateways

Routers route data packets from one network to another using the network address of the packet. Remember the OSI model that you learned about in Chapter 2? Routers essentially create broadcast and collision domains and route data destined for a particular network.

A gateway can link networks that have different protocols, such as TCP/IP to IPX/SPX. A gateway can change an entire protocol stack into another or provide protocol conversion and routing services between computer networks. Gateways examine the entire packet and then translate the incompatible protocols so that each network can understand the two different protocols. For example, protocol gateways can be used to convert Asynchronous Transfer Mode (ATM) cells to Frame Relay frames and vice versa.

Peripherals

With today's booming computer industry, you have many options when choosing peripherals for your computer. The standard I/O devices, such as keyboard and mouse, are the mainstays of computer peripherals, but you can choose many other peripherals to make your PC experience even better. Let's look at some now:

- **Keyboard**   A keyboard connects to the computer using a Personal System 2 (PS/2) or USB connection, and enables you to input data. Because the keyboard is the primary input device, you rely on the keyboard more than you realize. The keyboard contains certain standard function keys, such as the ESC key, the TAB key, cursor movement keys, the SHIFT and CTRL keys, and sometimes other manufacturer-customized keys, such as the WINDOWS key.

- **Mouse**   A mouse connects to the serial, PS/2, or USB port on your computer and enables you to move a cursor around the graphical user interface (GUI) of your desktop operating system or server.

- **Print device**   A print device outputs data from your computer to paper or other media, such as labels, transparencies, or envelopes. Sharing print devices is one of the more popular reasons to have a network, which allows multiple users to access a single print device.

- **Digital camera**   A digital camera is a fairly popular peripheral these days, which enables the user to take pictures and store them as files in memory on the camera instead of on film used by conventional cameras. The pictures that are saved as digital images on a memory card can be printed at a later time or e-mailed to friends, coworkers, or relatives.

- **Scanner**   Scanners are used to convert a photo already in print to a digital image on the computer. This digital image can then be manipulated after the fact. Scanners in the past have connected to a parallel port on the system, but today's scanners are connected to the USB port. Scanners today support Optical Character Recognition (OCR), which allows you to scan the text in an image and create a document and you can edit the text out of that scan. It should be noted that many people are replacing their scanner with digital photos of the item they need a digital copy of.

- **Modem**   A modem is a communications device that enables a computer to talk to another computer through a standard telephone line. The modem converts digital data from the computer into analog data for transmission over analog telephone lines. The analog signal is then converted back to digital data by the modem on the receiving computer.

Compatibility and Cabling Issues

All network cables are not created equal. There are three different types of commonly used network cables: coaxial, twisted pair, and fiber optic. For most of your networking needs, twisted pair is the cable of choice because it is relatively inexpensive and widely available. It is also easy to run in tight places, and many standards are adopted for its RJ-45 interface. The following outlines some issues you may come across when working with different types of cabling:

- **Incompatibilities with analog modems and a digital jack**   An analog modem and a digital jack will not work together because they use two different technologies. An analog modem works over a standard phone line, and a digital jack for Integrated Services Digital Network (ISDN) works with a digital Private Branch Exchange (PBX) switch, not an analog phone switch.

- **Uses of RJ-45 connectors with different cabling**   An RJ-45 connector is used to connect segments of twisted-pair cabling. To connect two different types of media cable, you need a media converter to convert from one cable type to another. For example, you cannot connect an unshielded twisted-pair (UTP) cable that plugs into a media converter that supports connectivity to fiber-optic cabling.

- **Patch cables and length of cabling segment**   A CAT 5 patch cable is normally a couple of feet long, or however long you need to connect the client to the network. Commonly, a patch cable is used to "patch" the length it takes to get from your network card to the digital jack on the floor of your office.

Implementing a SOHO Network

When discussing how to implement a network, it is important to discuss a small office/home office (SOHO) network. The Network+ exam expects you to be familiar with the equipment requirements and limitations of a SOHO network.

Equipment Requirements

In order to create a SOHO network, you will need the following equipment at a minimum:

- **A home router**   The first piece of equipment to purchase is a home router. The home router will give you a secure connection to the Internet (it is a firewall as well). The home router also has a network switch built in to allow you to connect a small number of systems to the network (usually four).

- **Printer**   Most small offices require that a printer be connected to the network and shared to all computers on the network. When purchasing your printer, double-check that it has network capability by either having a network card built in or having wireless capability.

- **Computers**   You will need a computer for each person connecting to the network.

- **NAS** You may look at purchasing a small network-attached storage (NAS) device so that all users are storing documents in a central location.
- **Cabling** You will also need to connect the computers, NAS, and printers to the network using cables. The most common type of cabling used today is CAT 5e or CAT 6. Be sure to not exceed the cable lengths that you learned of in Chapter 1. For example, UTP cabling has a maximum distance of 100 meters.

Equipment and Environmental Limitations

When designing your SOHO network, it is important to be aware of some of the limitations and compatibility requirements you will face. The following outlines some of the common equipment and environmental limitations you may be faced with:

- **Distance** One of the biggest problems with SOHO networks is if all devices are not within the same area of the building, you may have the problem of exceeding the maximum cable length. With today's networking technologies, you could look to wireless devices or even Ethernet over Powerline to accommodate for areas where it is difficult to run cables.
- **Environmental** One of the major environmental issues you are faced with regarding SOHO networks is the fact that the equipment such as the router, NAS, or maybe even the server is located in a room that has not been prepared to run computer equipment. You should ensure that you control humidity and temperature in any room that is holding servers, switches, and routers.
- **Compatibility** A final limitation you may be faced with is compatibility of the devices and systems you wish to connect to the network. For example, if you are running a wireless network for your SOHO network, you want to ensure that all of the wireless components support the same wireless standard, such as 802.11g or 802.11n. If you are using a wired network, ensure that all the devices support the same speed cards so that you can get the best performance out of your network. For example, there would be no benefit to purchasing the Gigabit Ethernet switch if all the systems and devices have 100 Mbps network cards in them.

Implement a Network Based on Requirements

All too often, network professionals install and implement networks based on what they would like to see being used versus what is actually needed by the customer. It is important to collect a list of requirements from your client and be sure to meet those requirements in a cost-effective manner. The following guidelines should be considered when implementing a basic network:

- **List of requirements** Ensure that you collect a list of business requirements for the network. Once you have identified what the company's goal of the network is, you can start designing the network.

- **Device types/requirements**   Based on the requirements you collected from a company for what they would like to be able to do on the network, you can then decide what types of devices and systems need to be used. For example, if the company has no need for wireless access, then you will not get a wireless access point, but if wireless is critical so employees can roam through the office with Internet access, then you will need to plan wireless access and devices.

- **Environmental limitations**   Computers are affected by temperature, moisture, vibrations, and electrical interference, so you need to assess the facility for these environmental factors and plan for corrective action. For example, if the area you plan to use for a server room is not able to control the temperature, you may need to plan for an HVAC system.

- **Equipment limitations**   When planning the equipment you will use, be sure to be aware of any limitations of that equipment. For example, if the company needs to allow employees to use a virtual private network (VPN) to access the network and you are looking at using a VPN appliance, be sure to know the maximum number of simultaneous connections of the device and ensure it is enough for that company.

- **Compatibility requirements**   When implementing a network, you need to ensure that all the hardware and software you are looking to use as a solution are compatible with one another. Also, if you are upgrading an existing network, you need to ensure that new components added to the network will work with the old components.

- **Wired/wireless considerations**   When implementing a wireless network, you will need to evaluate the distance that the wireless network needs to cover and ensure that your solution covers that distance. You also need to watch for interference from other wireless components and household devices. To learn more about wireless considerations, check out Chapter 10.

- **Security considerations**   When designing the network, security should always be in the forefront. You need to plan for how you are going to control who can get access to the different resources on the network and who can connect to the physical network itself. To learn more about security, check out Chapters 15 and 16.

CERTIFICATION SUMMARY

In this chapter you learned the basic elements that make up a network. You learned that clients connect to servers using client software. You also learned that each system will need a network card driver installed and a protocol if they are to communicate on this network.

You learned that each user who will access the network will need to have a user account. Users identify themselves to the network by user accounts; these are created by the network administrator. You learned how to create Active Directory accounts in Active Directory Users and Computers and to create Linux accounts in the Red Hat User Manager.

It is important that you create a strong password policy for your user accounts to ensure that the passwords are difficult for someone to guess or crack. A strong password has a minimum of six characters, has lowercase and uppercase characters, and uses symbols or numbers. You define your password policy within the Default Domain Policy.

You learned that you can organize your users into groups—this will allow you to assign permissions more easily because you can assign permissions to the groups instead of each user. Windows has two types of groups: a security group for permissions and e-mail, and a distribution group for just e-mail. You may use the Active Directory Users and Computers console to create groups with Active Directory, and you may use the Red Hat User Manager to create groups in Linux.

You learned how to set NTFS permissions to secure a folder and how to share that folder so that users on the network may access it. You learned of a number of permissions in NTFS; be sure to review those before the exam. You also learned how to create and share a printer on a Windows Server 2012 system.

Finally, we reviewed some of the different types of hardware you will encounter in your travels as a networking professional, and we discussed issues surrounding cabling and interference and compatibility.

✓ TWO-MINUTE DRILL

Installing a Network

- ❑ Microsoft has three types of servers: stand-alone, member, and domain controller.
- ❑ A stand-alone server is not part of a domain and sits on its own. It relies on its own security database, known as the SAM database, for user and group management and authentication services.
- ❑ A member server is a member of a domain but does not have the Active Directory database installed. A member server typically runs applications such as Exchange or SQL Server.
- ❑ A domain controller is a server that holds the Active Directory database.
- ❑ To have communication on a network, you need to have a network client, protocol, and network card driver installed.

Creating User Accounts

- ❑ There are two types of accounts: built in and administrator created.
- ❑ Built-in accounts are created during the installation of the operating system. There is typically an administrative account built in to the operating system and a guest account that is disabled by default.

❑ The built-in administrative account in Windows is called Administrator, and the one built into Linux/UNIX is called root.

❑ You can create a user account in Active Directory with the Active Directory Users and Computers console.

❑ You may create a user account in Linux with the Red Hat User Manager.

❑ You should create a password policy that enforces strong passwords.

❑ A strong password consists of uppercase and lowercase characters and has a minimum of six characters and a mix of letters, numbers, and symbols.

Managing Groups

❑ Groups are used to organize users into administrative units.

❑ There are built-in groups in Windows, such as Administrators, Backup Operators, Account Operators, and Printer Operators.

❑ Backup Operators can perform backups, Printer Operators can install and configure printers, and Account Operators can create and manage user accounts.

❑ Global groups are used to organize users within a domain, domain local groups are used for permissions or rights assignment, and universal groups are used to organize users across domains.

❑ Security groups are used for security or e-mail, and distribution groups are used only for e-mail.

Securing Files and Folders

❑ Use NTFS partitions so that you can configure NTFS permissions on folders.

❑ Use share permissions when creating the shared resource.

❑ When NTFS and share permissions conflict, the most restrictive wins.

❑ In Linux, you can configure permissions with the **chmod** command.

❑ The Full Control permission allows a user to modify the file contents and modify permissions, whereas the Modify permission only allows a user to modify the file contents—not permissions.

❑ You can connect to a folder with a UNC path. The UNC path has the following syntax: \\computername\sharename.

Installing Printers

❑ Microsoft considers the print device to be the machine that holds the paper and ink and prints the content on paper, whereas the printer is the software interface to the print device.

❑ A print server is a machine that has a shared printer and receives print requests from clients.

❑ A printer (or queue in other network environments) is where the print job is stored while trying to print.

Working with Network Hardware

❑ Because computers are affected by temperature, moisture, vibrations, and electrical interference, you need to create a controlled environment and be in control of each of these elements.

❑ Watch cable distance on the different cable types, and be familiar with the components that can create interference in your environment.

❑ Network-attached storage (NAS) is a popular choice for mass storage devices such as RAID drives and CD-ROMs.

SELF TEST

The following questions will help you measure your understanding of the material presented in this chapter. Read all the choices carefully and eliminate the ones you know are wrong; then figure out which one of the remaining choices is the correct answer.

Installing a Network

1. Which networking component is responsible for connecting to the server?

A. Client

B. Service

C. Protocol

D. Network card driver

2. Which type of Microsoft server holds the network account database known as Active Directory?
   A. Workstation
   B. Stand-alone
   C. Member server
   D. Domain controller

3. Which networking component is responsible for being the common language used by all systems that are communicating?
   A. Client
   B. Service
   C. Protocol
   D. Network card driver

Creating User Accounts

4. What is the built-in administrative account in Linux?
   A. Admin
   B. Administrator
   C. Root
   D. Guest

5. Which account in Windows Server 2012 is disabled by default?
   A. Admin
   B. Administrator
   C. Root
   D. Guest

6. Where are user accounts created on a Windows client system?
   A. SAM
   B. DNS
   C. Active Directory
   D. eDirectory

7. What shell command in Linux is used to create a user account?
   A. net use
   B. useradd
   C. perm
   D. chmod

Managing Groups

8. Which group scope is used to organize users within a Microsoft domain?
   A. Universal
   B. Global
   C. Domain local
   D. Distribution

9. Which group scope is used to assign permissions within a Microsoft domain?
   A. Universal
   B. Global
   C. Domain local
   D. Distribution

10. Which built-in group would you place Bob in to allow him to manage network user accounts in the domain?
    A. Administrators
    B. Printer Operators
    C. Backup Operators
    D. Account Operators

11. Which group would you place Sue in to allow her to manage your printing environment on the network?
    A. Administrators
    B. Printer Operators
    C. Backup Operators
    D. Account Operators

Securing Files and Folders

12. Which NTFS permission would you use to allow a user to delete a file?
    A. Read
    B. Modify
    C. Read and Execute
    D. Full Control

13. Which command in Linux/UNIX will allow you to change the permissions on a file?
    A. net use
    B. useradd
    C. perm
    D. chmod

14. When a share permission conflicts with an NTFS permission, which permission will be the effective one?

    A. Both

    B. The share permission

    C. The most restrictive

    D. The NTFS permission

Installing Printers

15. What is the name of the printer component that is the software interface to the print device?

    A. Print device

    B. Printer

    C. Print server

    D. Printout

16. In the Windows environment, which permission is needed to send a document to the printer?

    A. Print

    B. Manage Documents

    C. Full Control

    D. Modify

17. You want to install a printer on your Windows server to make it a print server. What would you do?

    A. Run the Add Printer Wizard, and then choose Network Printer.

    B. Go to the Registry and create the printer.

    C. Go to Active Directory Users and Computers.

    D. Run the Add Printer Wizard, and then choose Local Printer.

Working with Network Hardware

18. Which of the following will most likely create electromagnetic interference with your computer equipment?

    A. DVD player

    B. Generator

    C. TV

    D. Dining room table

19. What type of cable is used to connect the workstation to the network jack located in the wall?

    A. Crossover

    B. Thinnet

    C. Patch

    D. Thicknet

Performance-Based Question Review: See the performance-based question sample from the author included with the accompanying media.

SELF TEST ANSWERS

Installing a Network

1. ☑ **A.** Client software, also known as the redirector, is responsible for connecting to the server and sending the network request.
   ☒ **B, C,** and **D** are incorrect. A service is what the client connects to on the server, such as file and print services, and a protocol is the language the client and server use to communicate. The network card driver is the software that allows the operating system to communicate with the physical network card.

2. ☑ **D.** Domain controllers hold the user account database for the network when it comes to Microsoft networking environments. You create a domain controller by installing Active Directory with the **dcpromo** command.
   ☒ **A, B,** and **C** are incorrect because they all have a local SAM database.

3. ☑ **C.** A protocol is the language two systems use to communicate on the network.
   ☒ **A, B,** and **D** are incorrect. A service is what the client connects to on the server, such as file and print services. The network card driver is the software that allows the operating system to communicate with the physical network card. Client software, also known as the redirector, is responsible for connecting to the server and sending the network request.

Creating User Accounts

4. ☑ **C.** In Linux, the administrative account that configures the operating system is known as root.
   ☒ **A, B,** and **D** are incorrect. Admin is the administrative account in NetWare, whereas Administrator is used in Microsoft environments. The guest account is not an administrative account.

5. ☑ **D.** The guest account allows anonymous access to the network, meaning that individuals will not need a user account to authenticate—they will be authenticated as guest. This account is disabled by default.
    ☒ **A, B,** and **C** are incorrect. All of these accounts are administrative accounts, not guest accounts, and are not disabled by default.

6. ☑ **A.** The SAM database is the name of the local account database on a Windows client.
    ☒ **B, C,** and **D** are incorrect. DNS is a network service used for hostname resolution. Active Directory is Microsoft's network account database, and eDirectory is Novell NetWare's network account database.

7. ☑ **B.** The syntax in a shell command to create a new user account in Linux is useradd *<username>*.
    ☒ **A, C,** and **D** are incorrect. **Net use** is a Microsoft command to map drives and printer ports, perm is not a command, and **chmod** is a command to change file permissions in Linux.

Managing Groups

8. ☑ **B.** Global groups are used to organize users within a domain.
    ☒ **A, C,** and **D** are incorrect. Universal groups are used to organize users across domains, but domain local groups are used for permission assignment. Distribution groups are not a group scope, but a group type.

9. ☑ **C.** Domain local groups are used for permission assignment within the local domain.
    ☒ **A, B,** and **D** are incorrect. Global groups are used to organize users within a domain, and universal groups are used to organize users across domains, and they can also be used to assign permissions to resources in other domains. Distribution groups are not a group scope, but a group type.

10. ☑ **D.** Account Operators have permissions to create and manage user accounts throughout the domain.
    ☒ **A, B,** and **C** are incorrect. Administrators can perform any task, so you do not want to place Bob in this group. Printer Operators can manage the printing environment, and Backup Operators are allowed to perform backup and restore operations.

11. ☑ **B.** You would place Sue in the Printer Operators group so that she can perform any printing functions.
    ☒ **A, C,** and **D** are incorrect. Administrators can perform any task, so you do not want to place Sue in this group, Account Operators can manage user accounts, and Backup Operators are allowed to perform backup and restore operations.

Securing Files and Folders

12. ☑ **B.** The Modify permission allows users to read, create, delete, and modify the contents of files.
    ☒ **A, C,** and **D** are incorrect. The Read permission allows users only to read the file, whereas Read and Execute allows users to read the file and execute it if it is an .exe. Full Control allows the delete operation but also gives the ability to change permissions, which is what makes this a wrong choice.

13. ☑   **D.** The **chmod** command is used to change access permissions to a file in Linux.
☒   **A, B,** and **C** are incorrect. **Net use** is a Windows command to map network drives and printer ports, **useradd** is a Linux/UNIX command to create a user account, and perm is not a command.

14. ☑   **C.** When there is a conflict in combining NTFS permissions with shared folder permissions, the most restrictive one will win.
☒   **A, B,** and **D** are incorrect because the rule is that the most restrictive will win.

Installing Printers

15. ☑   **B.** The software interface to the print device is known as the printer in Microsoft terms.
☒   **A, C,** and **D** are incorrect. The print device is the physical hardware that outputs the printout, the print server is the Windows server on which the printer is installed, and the printout is the piece of paper you have in your hand when the print job completes.

16. ☑   **A.** You need to have the print permission to submit a document to a printer.
☒   **B, C,** and **D** are incorrect because they do not represent the permission needed. Full Control is given to individuals who need to modify the settings and permissions of a printer. Manage Documents is given to individuals who need to be able to manage the print queue, for example, cancelling print jobs sent to the printer.

17. ☑   **D.** You would run the Add Printer Wizard and choose to install a local printer and share it to create a print server.
☒   **A, B,** and **C** are incorrect because they are not the steps to install a printer on a print server.

Working with Network Hardware

18. ☑   **B.** A generator is the most likely to create electromagnetic interference with networking and computer equipment of the choices provided. You need to be aware of potential interference in your environment.
☒   **A, C,** and **D** are incorrect because they are not the most likely to create EMI. A TV may do so, but a generator will typically have greater potential.

19. ☑   **C.** A patch cable is used to connect the workstation to the RJ-45 jack in the wall.
☒   **A, B,** and **D** are incorrect because they are not used to connect the workstation to the wall jack.

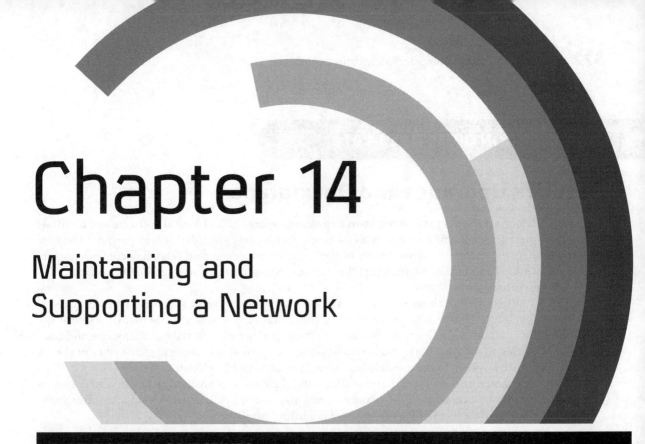

Chapter 14

Maintaining and Supporting a Network

CERTIFICATION OBJECTIVES

Installing and setting up the network is only the beginning of your job as a network professional. You are going to be required to maintain the network by performing some very common day-to-day tasks, such as updating the operating system with any new security patches and installing and maintaining antivirus software to protect your systems against virus attacks.

This chapter looks at these essential tasks along with other common critical tasks, such as backing up data and installing antispyware software. Each task is critical to the day-to-day maintenance of the network!

Network Upgrades and Downgrades

Before we discuss performing operating system upgrades, let's look at software and hardware upgrades and some best practices for dealing with these upgrades. It is important to be sure that before applying any software or hardware upgrade, you read related documentation and configure an environment to test the upgrade. Never perform an upgrade for the first time on production systems!

When we talk about network or system upgrades, it is critical that after planning the upgrade you ensure that you perform a configuration backup before actually performing the upgrade. A configuration backup is a backup of the current state of the system and can be used to roll back the upgrade should something go bad. It is important that you can always restore a system to its original state before you attempted a change.

It should also be noted that sometimes the change you are making is not an actual upgrade, but may be a downgrade. For example, you may be removing network equipment from one office to place in an office where there is a bigger need.

Safety Practices

It is important to follow safety best practices when performing network or system upgrades, specifically when working with hardware devices. In this section we will discuss common safety concepts and procedures.

MSDS

The *Material Safety Data Sheet (MSDS)* is a document that contains detailed information on hazardous chemicals found in different materials. This includes the ingredients that make up this material and their composition. The MSDS also includes information on the proper handling of this material and contains safety information such as lethal doses for each material, which can be helpful if the material is accidentally ingested.

Electrical Safety

When servicing networking and system equipment, it is important to ensure that you protect yourself and components such as memory and computer chips from electrical damage. The static electrical shock that we give to someone after scuffing our feet on the carpet and then touching the other person is enough to kill computer chips, memory modules, processors, or other components found in computers.

In order to protect your investment in computer components, it is important to properly ground yourself when upgrading systems. You can ground yourself by using an *electrostatic discharge (ESD)* wrist strap or by simply touching the metal chassis of a system before touching any computer parts. This will discharge any static electricity you have built up so that you are then safe to handle computer parts.

Installation Safety

When upgrading systems and networking components, it is important to follow safety best practices with regard to the handling and placement of those components:

- **Lifting equipment**   Ensure that you lift equipment with your legs and not your back. For any heavy equipment, ensure that you get two people to help lift it.
- **Rack installation**   Ensure that you have two or more people lift the server if the server is a 2U or more (this defines the vertical space being used by the server in the rack—1U is smaller and uses less space than 2U). If the server is heavier than 39 lbs, you should have two or more people involved in the installation of the server into the rack. Ensure that you have adequate airflow in the rack system, and do not block any air vents.
- **Placement**   Ensure that you place server and network equipment in a cool area that is controlled with a heating, ventilation, and air conditioning (HVAC) system.
- **Tool safety**   Ensure that you read documentation on proper usage of tools before using them. Take off your watch and jewelry before working on PC components. Be sure to unplug the power from components that you are servicing!

Emergency Procedures

Ensuring the safety of employees within the organization is of the utmost priority. It is imperative to ensure that you update emergency procedures to include the following:

- **Building layout**   Ensure that the emergency procedures contain an up-to-date building layout showing exits, entrances, and stairwells.
- **Fire escape plan**   Make sure that you have a current fire escape plan showing proper exit procedures for all locations within the facility.
- **Fail open/fail close**   Ensure that you properly plan the failsafe equipment in the office and ensure that the correct usage of fail open or fail close is used. Fail open means that when a failure occurs the device goes to an "open," or unlocked, state. This would be used for emergency exits to ensure employees can exit the building quickly and easily in case of emergency. If the exits were set to fail "close," then the doors would need to be unlocked before exiting, thus causing delays.
- **Emergency alert system**   You may look to having a security system installed with an emergency alert system that automates the signaling of emergency personnel.

■ **Fire suppression systems**   Ensure that you test fire suppression devices on a regular basis and document their location.

■ **HVAC**   It is important to ensure that you control the heat and humidity levels in the facility to ensure that servers and network equipment are kept cool. An HVAC system should be used to maintain these elements.

Software Upgrades

Software manufacturers release upgrades for their products to improve them and make them more powerful. You should always install an upgrade on a stand-alone machine before distributing it to the network. This enables you to test the application and go through the upgrade process in a nonproduction environment.

OS Updates

Many minor upgrades are free and require a simple download similar to a patch. Upgrading from one version of an application or operating system (OS) to another usually requires the purchaser to pay a fee for the new product. Sometimes an application can have a minor version change, such as version 5.01 to version 5.02, which may not require a fee due to the subtle changes contained in the upgrade. Other upgrades, meanwhile, can be ordered for free from the manufacturer, or may come at a minimal cost if you are a registered owner of the older version. Again, be sure to have a good backup before you install the upgrade in order to prevent data loss.

Be sure to have a test lab for any software or hardware upgrades so that you can thoroughly test the new changes with all of your existing hardware and software. Be sure that the upgrade has not caused another aspect of the network, including applications on the users' desktops, to stop working.

Driver Updates

After applying operating system updates, it is important to also check for driver updates, especially if you find the hardware is not working properly. You can perform some driver updates through Windows Update, but you should also look to the manufacturer's website for updates to drivers and firmware for your equipment.

Hardware Upgrades

Not only will you be responsible for replacing old devices with new ones, such as an old 10 Mbps hub with a new 10/100 Mbps network switch; you will also be responsible for updating the firmware that is contained in your servers and network devices. The firmware is a special type of read-only memory (ROM) chip that controls the functionality of the server or device; it is updated using a special software program called a ROM update or a flash program. It is recommended that you keep informed about the latest ROM updates for all the components on your network. If there is an update, there is a reason for it, and if you can avoid the problem before it happens, you'll save yourself a lot of headaches. Make sure that you have the correct update and that you have done sufficient research regarding what the update does.

Firmware Updates

Hardware manufacturers devote an area on their websites to their hardware products and allow you to download the latest firmware so that you can update the components in your servers, routers, switches, and workstations. Figure 14-1 shows how to download the latest Basic Input Output System (BIOS) updates from the Dell site for a PowerEdge 1800 server.

When downloading BIOS updates, be sure that you have the correct and most recent version. The Dell site shows the most recent version of the BIOS for this PowerEdge 1800, but also contains a link to view the previous versions. If you click the link for the current version, it will take you to a description of that version and to the file download you will be required to apply to the server.

FIGURE 14-1 Retrieving BIOS updates for a Dell PowerEdge 1800

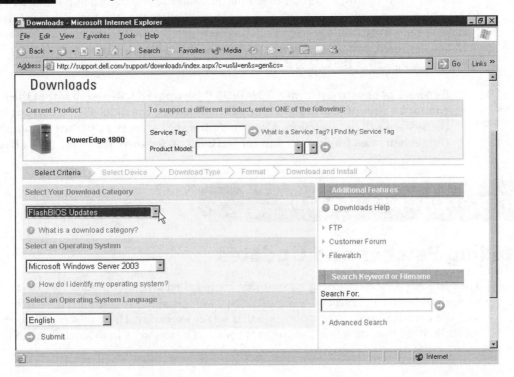

Viewing the
BIOS update
description and
download link

File Name	File Size	Download Time (56K)	File Format
▸ PE1800-BIOSA03.exe	757 KB	1.8 min	Floppy
Description			
This file contains a compressed (or zipped) set of files. Download the file to a folder on your hard drive, and then run (double-click) it to unzip the set of files. Follow the instructions to create a set of floppy diskettes, and then use the diskettes to complete the installation.			

If you click the link for the current BIOS update for the Dell PowerEdge 1800, you will see the description and download link of the BIOS update, as shown in Figure 14-2. When downloading the BIOS update, you should see the release date of the BIOS and the link for the BIOS update file that needs to be downloaded. Along with the file link, a description specifies what you will need to do with this file. In most cases, you will download the executable and then either run the update on the system directly or burn it to CD and then boot from the CD to perform the update. It is important to make sure that you read the directions first, because each vendor applies the update differently.

Some hardware items may not allow for ROM updates, and those that do may require a full hardware upgrade to meet the company's needs. For example, if a company upgrades its network from 10 Mbps to 100 Mbps Ethernet and the company had purchased only 10 Mbps Ethernet cards, there won't be a way to just update the ROM to allow for 100 Mbps transfer speeds. That would require a full hardware replacement of the network card.

When new hardware is purchased, you must verify that the hardware will work with your existing PCs, as well as the OSs and the network environment.

Be aware of how to perform a ROM BIOS flash upgrade. Remember that the power cannot be shut off during the upgrade; otherwise, the BIOS will be corrupt and the system will not function. Also remember that after the upgrade is complete, the system must be shut off and turned back on for the changes to take effect.

CERTIFICATION OBJECTIVE 14.02

Installing Patches and Updates

The applications and operating systems that are installed on our computers are developed by people like you and me, and will most likely have mistakes programmed into them along with the great features of the application that we see every day. These mistakes (known as vulnerabilities) that are left in the program code can be found by individuals, who then take over your system or network by exploiting that vulnerability! This is known as a network attack or system attack, depending on whether the entire network was taken over or just a single system.

A number of network attacks can be prevented because the manufacturers of the software and operating systems are always looking for the vulnerabilities in their code. They then fix those mistakes and ship the fixes in what is known as a fix or update. You will normally acquire these fixes and updates through the manufacturer's website. For example, Microsoft operating systems have a Windows Update program item in the Start menu to go to the company's update website and scan your system for any updates that need to be installed. This feature is known as Windows Update and may be run by going to the charm list (by moving your mouse to the right corner of the taskbar and then choosing Settings | Control Panel | System And Security | Windows Update). After Windows Update determines the updates, or fixes, that are needed on your system, your system will download the updates from the Windows Update site.

There are various types of updates that will be delivered to you through the Windows Update site. They are listed as follows:

- **Security hot-fix** A security hot-fix is a critical security update that should be applied to your system as quickly as possible because the vulnerability opens the system to serious security risks.

- **Patch** A patch is a fix to a particular problem in software or operating system code that does not create a security risk but does create problems with the system or the application.

- **Service pack** A service pack is all updates for a product, including patches and security hot-fixes, from the time the product was released up to the time of the service pack. If you install a service pack, you will not need to install each patch individually, because the service pack includes all updates up to that point in time. You will need to install patches and security fixes that come out after the service pack.

There are a number of other software updates that you should be checking for on a regular basis. These types of software updates include

- **Feature changes/updates** Look for feature changes or feature updates in your software or hardware. A good example of this was an older wireless router I had did not allow filtering by Media Access Control (MAC) address until I did a firmware update.

- **Major vs. minor updates** There are different levels of updates—major and minor updates. A major update would introduce new features, whereas minor updates are typically improvements on existing features.

- **Vulnerability patches** A huge type of update is a security update that patches a vulnerability that exists in a product. Once the vendor finds out about the vulnerability, they fix the issues and deploy the fix with a patch.

Consider now Exercise 14-1, which demonstrates how to configure Windows Update and patch a system with Windows Update. To see a video demonstration of how to configure Windows Update and patch a system, check out the corresponding video for this exercise that comes with the accompanying material.

EXERCISE 14-1

Configuring Windows Update

In this exercise you will configure Windows Update and then run Windows Update on a server in order to ensure that it is up to date with patches and fixes.

1. On the 2012SERVERA or Win8A, go to the charm list (by moving your mouse to the right corner of the taskbar and then choosing Settings | Control Panel | System And Security | Windows).

2. Choose Change Settings to ensure that Windows Update is enabled.

3. In the Important Updates drop-down list choose Install Updates Automatically (Recommended).

4. Choose OK. Windows will check for new updates to install.

5. To manually check for updates at any point in time, within the Windows Update screen click the Check For Updates link on the left side.

6. Notice in the Windows Update dialog box that you can see how many updates are available and the last time updates were installed.

7. Close all windows.

Windows Server Update Services (WSUS)

Running Windows Update on one system is no problem, but what if you have to manage 500 systems and ensure that each system is up to date with current patches and hot-fixes? Microsoft has created Windows Server Update Services (WSUS), which allows you to install a WSUS server and download the updates from the Internet to the WSUS server. You can then deploy the installation of those updates to some test systems to verify that the updates do not conflict with any applications on the systems; then you can send the updates out to the 500 systems.

When you send the updates to the 500 systems on the network, you can do it from a central point—the WSUS server. The WSUS server has a management tool that allows you to manually approve updates. Those updates are downloaded to the WSUS server so that they can then be distributed to systems on your network. Within WSUS you can create groups of computers and then send the updates out to the different groups on the network. An update that you have not approved will not be sent to the systems on the network. Figure 14-3 shows a WSUS structure.

FIGURE 14-3   Sending updates to clients with WSUS

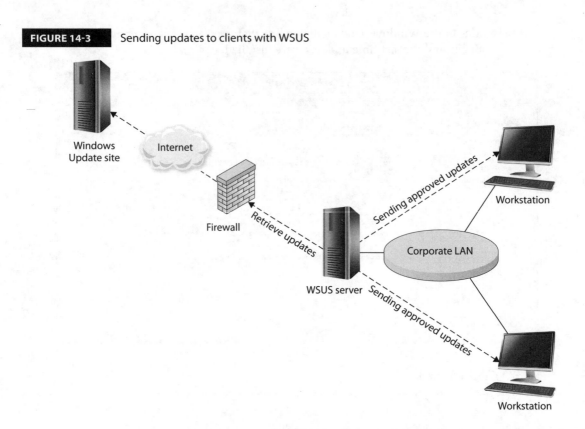

There are many benefits to a product like WSUS; for one thing, you can download the updates to one central machine from the Internet instead of having each system downloading from the Internet. This helps maintain available bandwidth by not having each person perform the download. Another benefit to WSUS is that clients are receiving only updates that you have approved. This happens because you will configure each client to retrieve the updates from the WSUS server and not the Internet. Once you have approved the update on the WSUS server, the client will get the update automatically through WSUS. Any updates that are not approved will not be downloaded by the clients on the network. It is also important to note that with WSUS the installation is performed by the system itself, not the user who has logged on. This is important because users typically do not have privileges to install software.

You can install WSUS on a Windows Server 2012 system by installing the role and then downloading the updates from Microsoft's website. After installing WSUS and downloading the updates from the Microsoft site, you then need to approve the updates. After approving the updates, the next step is to configure the clients to point to the WSUS server so that they download the updates from the WSUS server instead of the Windows Update site.

Configuring Clients to Use the WSUS Server for Updates

To configure the Windows clients on your network to use the WSUS server, you will set a domain policy that modifies each client in the domain to point to the WSUS server for the updates. If you are not in a domain environment, you may configure the clients through local policies. To change the default domain policy on a Windows Server 2012 network, follow these steps:

1. From Server Manager, choose Tools | Group Policy Management.

2. On the left side, expand the Certworld.loc forest, then expand Domains, then expand certworld.loc, and finally expand the folder called Group Policy Objects to view its contents.

3. Make sure that the Default Domain Policy is selected, right-click it, and choose Edit.

4. The Group Policy Management Editor appears. In the Computer Configuration section, expand Policies | Administrative Templates | Windows Components, and then highlight Windows Update.

5. To enable automatic updates on the clients in your domain, double-click Configure Automatic Updates.

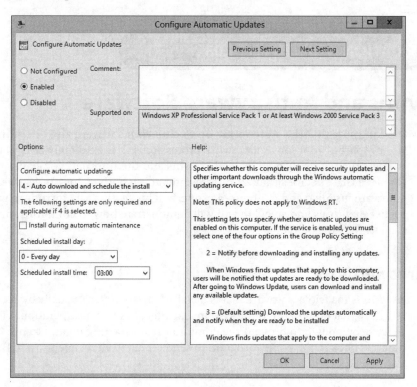

6. In the Configure Automatic Updates Properties, select Enable, choose Auto Download, and schedule the Install option. Specify a schedule of 3:00 A.M. for the automatic installation.

7. Click OK.

8. Double-click the Specify Intranet Microsoft Update Service Location policy and enable the policy setting. Set your intranet server to the name of the server that you installed WSUS on. For example, my server was called 2012SERVERA, so the intranet server address is http://2012SERVERA.

9. Close the Group Policy Object Editor window.

10. Click OK.

11. Close the Group Policy Management console.

Now that the policy is configured in Active Directory, the clients will automatically point to your WSUS server and install any updates that you approve in the WSUS administration site.

Watch "WSUS" to see a video demonstration of how to install a WSUS server and configure the client policies.

CERTIFICATION OBJECTIVE 14.03

Antivirus and Antispyware Software

Making sure that the systems are up to date with software and operating system patches is only part of your job as a network professional. It is extremely critical that, given today's threats that come through e-mail systems and the Internet, you have an antivirus policy in place that specifies that all systems, including both clients and servers, have antivirus software installed and configured properly. This section will introduce you to the differences between viruses and spyware and will demonstrate how to configure applications to protect you from malicious software.

Antivirus Software

A *virus* is malicious software that is installed on the system, usually by accident or through trickery, that does harm to the system and affects its normal operation. Viruses in the past have been known to prevent the computer from starting up and to use features like the address book in the e-mail program to send e-mail to all recipients in it. Bottom line—as a network professional you need to be familiar with installing antivirus software and keeping it up to date.

Antivirus software can be installed on systems automatically through software deployment features such as Group Policies in Active Directory or Microsoft's System Center Configuration Manager (SCCM).

There are a number of antivirus software products, the most popular of which appear in the following list:

- Norton AntiVirus
- McAfee Antivirus
- Panda Antivirus
- FProt Antivirus
- AVG Antivirus
- Microsoft Security Essentials (free download from Microsoft)

Each antivirus product offers pretty much the same type of functionality. Some of the features offered by antivirus products include

- **Scheduled scans** Each product should offer a scheduling feature that allows you to schedule a virus scan. A virus scan is what the virus protection software does—it scans the system to see whether it has been infected with a computer virus.

- **Scheduled definition updates** The virus protection software should allow the scheduling of a virus definition update. A virus definition is a list of all known viruses at the time the definition file was created. After you install the antivirus software, make sure that you are updating the virus definitions on a regular basis; this will ensure that your system is always being protected from the most current viruses. Figure 14-4 shows the option to update your antivirus definitions in Norton AntiVirus.

- **Real-time protection** Most antivirus products offer real-time protection, which is a feature that scans any file that you access, as you access it. This is an automatic feature—once it is enabled, you will not need to manually invoke the scan on a file before opening it. Figure 14-5 shows the enabling and disabling of real-time protection. In Figure 14-5 notice that you can enable the real-time protection features and specify what action the software should take when a virus is found. In this example, Norton will try to clean the virus (remove it); if that is not successful, it will quarantine the virus. You can also specify whether you want to see a message on the system and what file types are being protected.

FIGURE 14-4

Updating virus
definitions

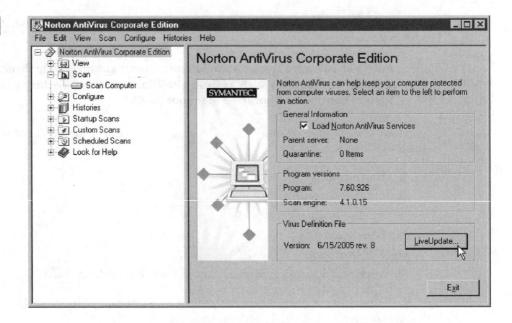

FIGURE 14-5 Enabling real-time antivirus protection

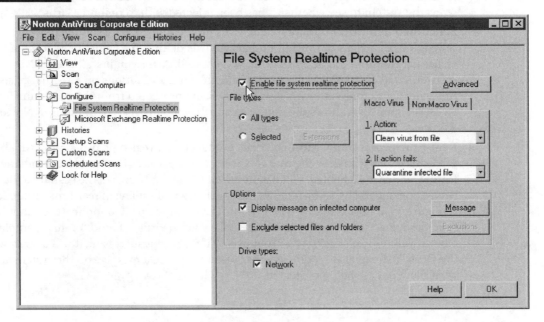

- **E-mail features**   A number of antivirus products integrate with your e-mail software so that they scan the contents of your e-mail and help protect your system from a virus that is received through e-mail. There are also server-class antivirus products that you can load on the e-mail server that scan the e-mail before depositing it in the user's mailbox. You most definitely want to load a server-based antivirus product on your e-mail server. Figure 14-6 shows a version of Norton AntiVirus that will scan e-mails going to your Exchange Server.

Antispyware/Adware

Spyware is software that is loaded on your system that monitors your Internet activity, and *adware* is software that is loaded on your system that will pop up with ads promoting different products and websites from time to time. Both pieces of software have become the "pain" of the Internet during the past few years. They are most often loaded on your system when you surf a malicious or hacked website.

Antispyware and anti-adware is software that you can use to remove these troublesome invaders from your system. It includes a number of products, such as Spybot, Ad-Aware, and Microsoft's Windows Defender. Antispyware has become as popular as antivirus software, and a lot of features in newer antispyware products are the same as those on antivirus software, such as real-time protection and scheduling of scans. Windows Defender includes such features as

- Antivirus and antispyware
- Real-time protection

FIGURE 14-6   Enabling real-time protection for e-mails

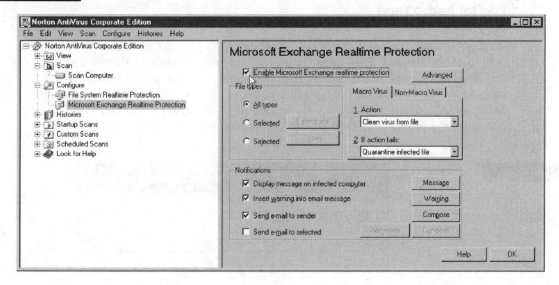

- Scheduled scans
- Browser hijack protection
- Automatic updates of malicious software definitions

In addition, you can view software that is running in memory with the Software Explorer feature!

CERTIFICATION OBJECTIVE 14.04

Backing Up Network Data

A critical task to help maintain the network and ensure that users have access to their data is to regularly back up data on the network to another location. You may back up the data to tape drives or to a backup file on another server, although tape drives are the more popular solution.

Tape Drives

The two most common types of tape drives are digital audio tape (DAT) and digital linear tape (DLT). This section looks at each drive in some detail. The exam will not delve into as many particulars, but understanding their characteristics will help you remember the information about the drives and ultimately help you on the test.

Digital Audio Tape

Digital audio tape (DAT) was developed in the mid-1980s by Sony and Philips to record music in a digital format, but it has now become very popular as a medium for computer data storage. The DAT drive uses a helical scan, which means that the read/write heads spin diagonally across the tape. DAT uses the digital data storage (DDS) format and a 4-mm tape. Although the speed isn't as good as that of a DLT drive, the capacity can be quite large. Different DDS formats allow for different amounts of storage on a tape. Table 14-1 lists different DDS formats and their storage capacities.

TABLE 14-1

Storage Capacities of DDS Formats

Type of Format	Storage Capacity
DDS	2GB
DDS-1	2–4GB
DDS-2	4–8GB
DDS-3	12–24GB

A DAT tape drive

As DDS-1 emerged, so did compression. That is why you'll notice that formats from DDS-1 to DDS-3 have a second number associated with them, which is always double the base storage capacity. Using this equation, standard 4-mm tapes for DAT drives can hold up to 24GB of data. Other technologies have also emerged with the appearance of 8-mm tapes, but you won't need to know these for the exam. Figure 14-7 shows a DAT tape drive.

Digital Linear Tape

Digital linear tape (DLT) was introduced by Digital Equipment Corporation in the mid-1980s, but Quantum Corporation owns the technology now. The DLT tape is a half-inch reel-to-reel magnetic tape, where the tape cartridge contains one reel and the DLT drive the other. The main advantages are fast data transfer rates, higher storage capacity, and higher reliability over DAT. All this, of course, comes at a price to the customer.

DLT drives store data on the tape differently than DAT drives do. The data path is made up of parallel tracks recorded in a serpentine pattern. What this means is that the first track is written from one end of the tape to the other and then the heads are repositioned and the next track goes the opposite direction (again for the entire length of the tape). The drive continues to go back and forth, writing until the tape is full.

Tape Rotation

When it comes to maintaining the network, you need to schedule a backup job and develop a backup schedule. Many companies do a tape rotation. They have daily, weekly, and monthly tapes, the rotation of which usually consists of 20 to 25 tapes, each with its purpose. Sometimes this is called an autopilot rotation. The backup software keeps a database and expects a certain tape on each day of the year. The most common is a 21-tape rotation consisting of 4 daily tapes for Monday through Thursday, 5 weekly tapes for each Friday (some months have 5 Fridays), and 12 monthly tapes for the last weekday of the month. There are no backups on Saturday or Sunday. It is a good idea to store the weekly or monthly tapes offsite to keep fire or some other major catastrophic event from ruining your data and your backups.

Offsite storage of tape backups is a critical part of your backup plan. If you have a fire in the office and it destroys your servers and tape backups, there wouldn't have been much point in having the backup at all. Make sure that copies of backups are stored offsite.

Along with tape rotations come tape libraries and tape arrays. Tape libraries are designed to contain a series of tapes in a holder that is inserted into the tape mechanism to automate the rotation of tapes throughout the week. If the amount of data is very large, the tape library may be used on a daily basis to rotate multiple tapes in and out of the various drives to make sure all data fits onto a tape. Tape arrays, on the other hand, are similar to redundant array of independent disks (RAID) technology with hard drives, wherein data is spread over a series of drives—for instance, there might be a parity drive to add fault tolerance. Manufacturers claim that tape arrays increase the throughput because multiple drives are writing simultaneously.

on the
job
It is extremely critical that you store copies of the backup offsite in case there is a disaster, such as fire or flooding in your building. If servers and backups are stored in the same location, the organization will be vulnerable to data loss.

Archives

Once the critical data to your business has been backed up, it is important to then archive a copy of the data offsite in case of a disaster such as a fire at the primary site. Most companies will store the current copy of the backup at the office, while the last backup is stored at an offsite storage location. If a disaster strikes at the company location, a new server can be installed and the data restored from the offsite archived data.

Full, Incremental, and Differential Backups

Backup software enables you to run three types of backups: full, incremental, and differential. These are the three you may see on the exam, so we will focus on them. The key to backing up data is to ensure that you can restore it in the event of a system failure. These three types of backups will function well if you use them together correctly.

Full Backup

A *full* backup backs up every file on the specified volume or volumes (or partitions). Many companies run a full backup every day, no matter what. Under such a system, the restore process requires only the most recent tape. However, a full backup necessitates a large storage capacity and a lot of time. If you have large amounts of data, running a daily full backup may not be practical because it may take too long to perform.

watch   **Full backups back up every file that is selected and then clear the archive bit. Note that there is also a copy backup that is similar to a full backup, only it does** **not clear the archive bit. Copy backups are useful if you need to send a copy of your data somewhere but you do not want to alter your backup cycle.**

Every file has an archive bit that flags whether or not the file needs to be backed up. When you change a file, this bit is flagged automatically, which means that the file needs to be backed up. In theory, any file that has been changed needs to be backed up because we want to be sure we can always bring the file to its most recent state.

To view the archive bit in Windows, right-click the file and go to the properties page. Once on the properties page, click the Advanced button on the General tab. You will see the File Is Ready For Archiving option, as shown in Figure 14-8.

The important thing to understand when a full backup is performed is that the backup backs up all the files that you select (whether the archive bit is set or not) and then clears the archive bit so that the operating system and applications know that the file has been backed up.

FIGURE 14-8

Looking at the archive bit in Windows

Advanced Attributes	? X
Choose the options you want for this file.	
Archive and Index attributes	
☑ File is ready for archiving	
☑ For fast searching, allow Indexing Service to index this file	
Compress or Encrypt attributes	
☐ Compress contents to save disk space	
☐ Encrypt contents to secure data	
OK	Cancel

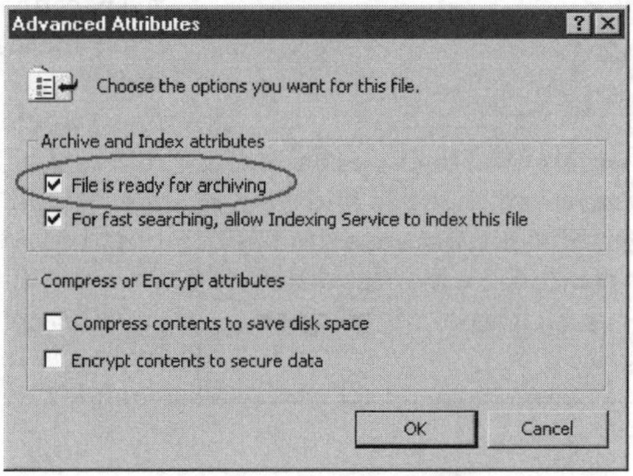

Incremental Backup

An *incremental* backup backs up the files that have changed or were added since the last incremental or full backup. It does this by backing up only files that have the archive bit set (meaning the file needs to be backed up). This is different from a full backup, in that a full backup will back up any file that is selected because it does not use the archive bit to determine whether to back up the file or not—it simply backs up whatever you tell it to. An incremental backup will back up whatever files you have selected that have the archive bit set.

Using a combination of the full backup and incremental backup is highly effective and less time consuming than running a full backup every day. A number of companies will set up a backup schedule that performs a full backup Friday night and then only backs up the changes each night through the week by performing an incremental backup. However, to restore, you will need the last full backup tape and every incremental backup tape made since the last full backup.

e x a m

ⓦ a t c h **Incremental backups back up any files that have changed and then clear the archive bit so that the next backup will not back up the file unless you do a full backup or unless the file is modified.**

An incremental backup clears the archive bit to report that the file has been backed up. If you were to perform an additional incremental backup the next day, the same file would not get backed up (unless it was changed) because the archive bit would not be set. Your restore strategy with incremental backups is to restore the full backup and then each incremental backup since the full backup. This will ensure that you get the buildup of changes since the full backup.

Differential Backup

A *differential* backup backs up the files that have changed or were added since the last full backup by looking for any files that have the archive bit set. The differential backup is different from the incremental, in that the differential does not clear the archive bit after the backup is done. This means that if you were to do another differential backup the next time you did a backup, the same files (and any new ones) would get backed up. As a result, every differential backup will have all changes since the last full backup. Your restore strategy would be to restore the last full backup and then restore your last differential backup.

e x a m

ⓦ a t c h **Differential backups back up any files that have had changes and do not clear the archive bit. Because the archive bit is not cleared, each differential backup will back up all files changed since the last full backup.**

Differential and incremental backups can make the restoration process a little more complex because you have to restore from the full backup first and then restore from the incremental or differential backups to make sure any files that have changed since the last full backup are restored. An important difference between differential and incremental backups is that incremental backups take less time to back up (because you are only getting changes since the last full or incremental backup) but more time to restore (because you restore multiple incremental backups). Differential backups take more time to back up but less time to restore.

If you decide to take a simpler approach by performing full backups each time, you can restore from the most recent full backup and get all the files restored in one session. The time it takes to perform the backup is a big factor when choosing your backup type. Most companies will go with full backups every night if the backup can complete between 11:00 P.M. and 7:00 A.M. To improve backup speed you can include using faster switches or network interface card (NIC) teaming (combining the bandwidth of multiple network cards) on the backup system.

It is important to understand the risks associated with the different types of backups, which is bad tapes and how they affect restore operations. When working with full backups, a bad tape for Tuesday means you lose a day's worth of data and need to go back to Monday's tape. With incremental backups, your issue is greater, as you need all the incremental tapes to be functional. With differential backups, the risk is reduced again, as you only need two working tapes: the full backup and the latest functional differential.

watch   You will definitely see a question or two on the exam about the different kinds of backups. Be sure to know the differences between full, incremental, and differential backups. You may be given a scenario where you have to choose the backup or restore strategy.

Scheduling Backups

Most network administrators would rather be at home late at night while the backup operation is being performed. That's why they schedule the backup operation so that they don't need to be in the office at night to start the backup after everyone else has gone home. Most backup software supports the scheduling of the backup operation, and that is definitely one of the features that you would look for in your backup software.

When scheduling your backup operations, you will need to create a backup plan. A backup plan will contain a listing of the data that will be backed up with each backup operation along with the type of backup that occurs (incremental, differential, or full). You should also make sure that the backup schedule is included in this plan.

For example, you may decide that every Saturday at midnight you will perform a full backup of your data files and your e-mail data. It is common to have in this backup plan an incremental backup of the same data files and e-mail servers that will be scheduled every morning at midnight. To restore any data that becomes corrupt, you would restore the last full backup and then apply the last differential backup on top of that. This will bring your data up to date to the point of the last differential.

When developing your backup plan, you should have a detailed plan of what resources on the server (such as folders, databases, or mail stores) will be backed up and what they will contain. You should also plot how often these items need to be backed up. This backup plan will serve as great documentation to go in your "Network Documentation" book in which you keep a collection of network diagrams, firewall rules, server configurations, and the like.

EXERCISE 14-2

Backing Up and Restoring Data on a Windows Server

In this exercise you will learn how to back up files on your Windows server using the Windows backup software and how to restore a file after it has been accidentally deleted. Check out the video for this exercise on this book's accompanying material to see a demonstration.

Installing Backup Software

1. From Server Manager choose Manage | Add Roles And Features.
2. Choose Next four times to get to the Select Features screen. Scroll down in the features list and choose the Windows Server Backup check box to install the Windows backup software.
3. Choose Next and then Install. The installation will take a minute, and then you can choose Close.

Performing a Backup

1. Now that the backup software is installed, you can launch it from Server Manager by choosing Tools | Windows Server Backup.

2. Select Local Backup on the left side to perform a backup on your system and store the backup locally on your network.

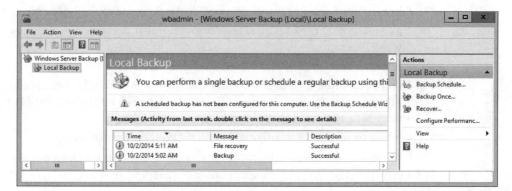

3. Notice in the action pane on the right side that you can set up a backup schedule to perform automatic backups on a regular basis (Backup Schedule option) or perform a one-time backup with the Backup Once option. Also notice the Recover option, which is used to do a restore action. Choose Backup Once.

4. Choose Different Options to specify your backup settings and then choose Next.

5. Notice you can back up the entire server (Full Server) or choose Custom to selectively choose which files to back up. Choose Custom and then choose Next.

6. Choose Add Item to choose a folder or file to back up.

7. To do a backup of the Labfiles\PacketCaptures folder, expand the C: drive, then expand Labfiles, choose the check box for PacketCaptures, and then choose OK.

8. Choose Next.

9. Choose to store the backup on a local drive, but notice that you could store the backup on a remote shared folder (a different server). Choose Next.

10. Choose a drive to store the backup on, then choose Next, and then choose Backup.

11. Once the backup is complete, choose Close.

Performing a Restore of a Deleted File

1. Open the folder list and choose Drive C | labfiles | PacketCaptures.

2. In the PacketCaptures folder, delete the HTTPTraffic.cap file by right-clicking it and choosing Delete.

3. Click Yes to confirm the deletion.

4. Close all windows.

5. To perform a restore of the deleted file, go to Server Manager (first button on the task bar) and then choose Tools | Windows Server Backup.

6. Choose Local Backup on the left side.

7. Choose Recover from the action pane on the right side in order to do a restore operation.

8. Choose This Server as the location of the backup and then choose Next.

9. Choose the date the backup was performed (most likely today's date) and then choose Next.

10. Choose to recover files and folders and then choose Next.

11. In the Select Items To Recover section, expand the server, C:, Labfiles, and select Packetcaptures to display a list of files. Select the HTTPTraffic.cap file on the right side to do a restore of that file and then choose Next.

12. Choose to restore to its original location and then choose Next.

13. Choose Recover. When the recovery has completed, choose Close.

14. Verify the file is back in the C:\Labfiles\Packetcaptures folder.

CERTIFICATION OBJECTIVE 14.05

Providing Fault Tolerance

Having a data backup is a great idea, and storing a copy of that backup offsite is a better idea to help ensure that you can recover from any type of disaster. One of the problems with relying only on a backup solution is that if a drive fails on the server, users will need to wait for you to replace the drive and then restore all the data—this could take hours, depending on the amount of data you are restoring.

To avoid having to replace the drive and restore the data in the middle of the day during business hours, you could take advantage of fault-tolerant solutions such as RAID. RAID is a technology that duplicates data across drives so that if a drive fails, the other drives in the solution can provide the data. The benefit is that if a drive fails, you can wait to fix the problem at the end of the business day, knowing that the redundancy of your solution will take care of the missing data.

There are different types of RAID, known as levels, and each level provides a different benefit with a different type of redundancy. The following sections describe the popular RAID levels supported by different network operating systems.

RAID Level 0

RAID level 0 is called striping or *striped volumes* in Windows. With RAID 0 multiple disks are used to create a volume; when data is saved to the volume, it is split up and spread across all disks in the volume. The benefit of striped volumes is that all disks are written to at the

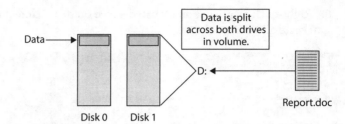

FIGURE 14-9

Looking at RAID 0

same time, giving you a performance benefit. For example, if you are saving a 12MB file to drive D and drive D is a striped volume made up of four disks, we can generalize the save operation by saying that each disk will save 3MB of data each and all disks will work at the same time to do the save operation that totals 12MB. If you only had one disk working for that 12MB save operation, it would take four times longer.

The disadvantage of RAID level 0 is that there is actually no duplication of data; therefore, if one of your hard drives fails within the volume, you can't read any of the data. RAID 0 is strictly for the performance benefit in the read and write operations. Figure 14-9 shows an example of a RAID 0 setup.

Configuring RAID 0 on a Windows Server

Windows Server offers a software RAID feature, which means that the operating system is responsible for the creation and management of the RAID volume. A hardware RAID solution would offer a better-performing solution, but it would be more expensive.

Before you can start creating fault-tolerant volumes, you must be sure to upgrade your disk to a dynamic disk. This is the disk type used in Windows to create RAID volumes. Take the following steps to convert your disk from a basic disk (which does not support volumes) to a dynamic disk and then create a RAID 0 volume.

Watch the "Striped Volumes" video on the accompanying material for this book to see a demonstration of how to create a striped volume (RAID 0).

1. From Server Manager (first button on the task bar) choose Tools | Computer Management.
2. In the Computer Management console, select Disk Management on the left side under the Storage category.
3. Right-click your disk on the right side and choose Convert To Dynamic Disk.
4. The Convert To Dynamic Disk dialog box appears, asking you to select which disk you want to make dynamic. Select all disks that you wish to convert.
5. Click OK.
6. Click Convert.
7. Click Yes.

8. Right-click an area of unallocated space on disk 1 and choose New Striped Volume to create a RAID 0 volume.

9. Choose Next to move past the welcome screen.
10. Select which disks of the available disk you would like to participate in the striped volume—for example, choose Disk 2—and then choose Add.
11. In the Select The Amount Of Space In MB field, type **1000** MB. Notice each drive will use 1000MB for a total volume size of 2000MB, and then choose Next.
12. Assign a drive letter of S for striped and then choose Next.
13. Type a volume label of **Striped** and choose the option to perform a quick format. Click Next to format for New Technology File System (NTFS).
14. Click Finish, and the new striped volume will be created. Notice that drive S shows multiple times because it is made up of multiple disks.
15. Close all windows.

e x a m
ⓦ a t c h

RAID 0, known as disk striping, splits the data across all disks in the volume. RAID 0 writes to all disks at the same time, decreasing the time it takes to read or write the data. There is no fault tolerance in RAID 0; it is strictly for performance benefits.

RAID Level 1

RAID level 1 is known as disk mirroring. Disk mirroring uses two hard drives and duplicates the data from one drive to another. The fact that RAID 1 does store a second copy of the data on another member of the volume means that this solution does offer fault tolerance. Fault tolerance is the concept that if one part of the solution fails, the other guy will pick up the workload and the solution will continue to function.

If one of the disks in the mirror fails, you can replace the failed disk by breaking the mirror, adding a new functioning disk, and then rebuilding the mirror from the existing disk that did not fail. Once you have reestablished the mirror, you have your fault tolerance back.

Figure 14-10 displays the concept of a mirror volume. When a user saves data to a mirrored volume, the data is written to both disks that make up the volume.

Creating a Mirrored Volume in Windows Server

In this step-by-step procedure, you will create a mirrored volume on a Windows server using two of the dynamic disks created in the preceding walk-through. Remember that a mirrored volume stores all the data on both members (disks) in the volume. To create a mirrored volume, follow these steps:

1. From Server Manager (first button on the task bar) choose Tools | Computer Management.
2. In the Computer Management console, select Disk Management on the left side under the Storage category.
3. Right-click an area of unallocated space on disk 1 and choose New Mirrored Volume.
4. The New Mirrored Volume Wizard appears. Click Next.

FIGURE 14-10

A mirrored volume stores a copy of the saved data on both disks.

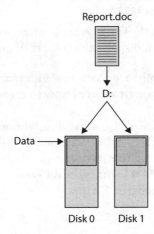

5. Add disk 2 as a selected disk for the mirrored volume, and type **2000** MB as the amount of space used on each disk. Notice that the total space used by the volume is 2000MB as well. Although there is 2000MB per disk, you can store only 2000MB of data on the volume—the other 2000MB stores a copy of the data in case of disaster.

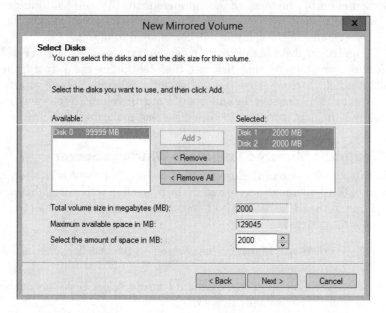

6. Click Next.
7. Assign drive M as the drive letter and choose Next.
8. Type a volume label of **Mirrored** and choose Perform A Quick Format. Choose Next to format for NTFS.
9. Choose Finish. The mirrored volume is created. Notice that the legend in disk management displays the color codes for each volume type.

Watch the "Mirrored Volume" video on the accompanying material for this book to see a demonstration of how to create a mirrored volume (RAID 1).

RAID 1 is known as disk mirroring, whereby the data is duplicated across two different disks, but using only one disk controller. When using two disk controllers, each one with a hard disk connected to it, we term the RAID 1 solution *disk duplexing* rather than disk mirroring. Figure 14-11 shows the difference between disk mirroring and disk duplexing. They are both considered RAID 1.

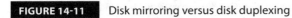

FIGURE 14-11 Disk mirroring versus disk duplexing

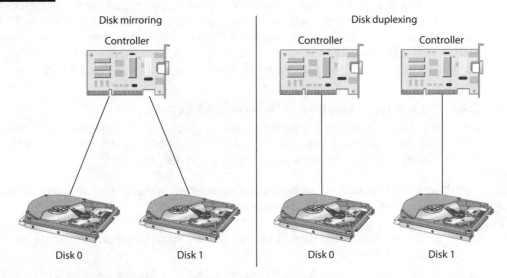

RAID 1 is known as disk mirroring, which "mirrors," or stores, a full copy of the data on a second disk in case **the first disk fails. RAID 1 gives great read performance, as data can be read from both drives at the same time.**

RAID 5

RAID level 5 is also known as striping with parity because a RAID 5 volume acts as a RAID 0 volume, but adds the parity information to create redundancy. RAID 5 volumes write data to all disks in the volume but store redundant information on one of the disks per stripe (a stripe is a row made up of 64KB chunks on each disk, as shown in Figure 14-12). For example, when you

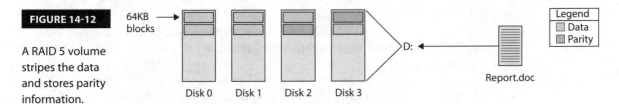

FIGURE 14-12

A RAID 5 volume stripes the data and stores parity information.

save data to a RAID 5 volume made up of four disks, the data is split up into 64KB data chunks (that may change, depending on the product or implementation) and written to each disk (let's say, disks 0, 1, and 2). But disk 3 will store redundant data (parity data) of the three 64KB blocks that have been saved already. If the three 64KB blocks are not sufficient to complete saving the file, the save operation will continue on to the next row. There will be parity information for that row as well, but the parity information is stored on a different disk for each row.

Creating a RAID 5 Volume with Windows Server

In the following walk-through you will see how to create a RAID 5 volume on a Windows server using three drives. Remember that a RAID 5 volume is similar to a striped volume, but also stores redundant information for each stripe that is written.

Watch the "RAID 5" video on the accompanying material for this book to see a demonstration of how to create a RAID 5 volume.

1. From Server Manager (first button on the task bar) choose Tools | Computer Management.
2. In the Computer Management console, select Disk Management on the left side under the Storage category.
3. Right-click an area of unallocated space on disk 1 and choose New RAID-5 Volume.
4. The New RAID-5 Volume Wizard appears. Click Next.
5. You will now need to choose the disks that will participate in the striped volume solution. Select disks 0 and 2 on the left, and click Add to add to the striped volume. Notice that the disk you started the volume on was already selected as a member of the volume. Because I started the volume on disk 1 and added disk 0 and disk 2, I will have three disks in this solution.
6. Once you have added each disk, at the bottom of the dialog box type the amount of space you want to use on each disk for the volume. Type **2000** and notice that each disk will use 2000MB, for a total of 4000MB for the entire volume, because a third of the space is used for parity and is not actual usable space.
7. Click Next.
8. Assign drive letter R for RAID 5 volume and then choose Next.
9. Type **RAID5** as the volume label and then choose Perform A Quick Format. Click Next to format for NTFS.
10. Click Finish; the new RAID 5 volume has been created. Notice that drive R shows multiple times because it is made up of multiple disks.
11. Close all windows.

If one of the disks fails, with a RAID 5 volume you can still access the data, but you may want to replace the faulty disk. To recover from a disk error with RAID 5, you simply replace the failed disk and regenerate the volume so that the data on the failed disk is created on the newly added disk. Note that while a failed disk is in the RAID 5 volume, you will notice a performance drop, as the RAID system must calculate the missing data from the parity information when you read data from the RAID array. The benefit of RAID 5 is you can still read the data when a disk fails, but it will be slower. Know that RAID 1 outperforms RAID 5 because with RAID 1 there is no overhead for calculating parity data—at the same time there is no redundancy either. Also note that most enterprises will use hardware RAID, which involves having a hardware controller perform all the RAID functions, which will outperform any software RAID offered by an operating system.

e x a m

ⓦ a t c h　　**RAID 5 volumes are known as striping with parity because this volume type splits the data across all disks but saves parity** **data on one of the disks per stripe. The parity information is used to calculate the missing data if a disk in the RAID 5 volume fails.**

EXERCISE 14-3

Video

Understanding and Configuring Fault Tolerance

In this exercise you will review the different RAID types and then configure fault tolerance on a Windows Server 2012 system.

Understanding RAID Types

In this exercise, you will read the description and then indicate what RAID type is being described.

Description	RAID Type
I am a volume that splits the data across each disk, but I do not store any redundant data. What level RAID volume am I?	
I duplicate data across two drives. What RAID level am I?	
I have two hard drive controllers and a drive on each hard drive controller. I am duplicating data across both drives. What type of RAID 1 solution am I?	
I am a RAID volume that stripes the data but also creates fault tolerance. What RAID level am I?	
I am a RAID level 1 solution that has only one controller. What type of RAID 1 solution am I?	

Configuring RAID

In this part of the exercise, you will configure different RAID volume types on a Windows server using the steps you have learned in this section. In this lab, you should have a server or virtual machine (VM) with four hard drives. Feel free to refer to the steps discussed earlier as you create each RAID volume.

1. Go to the 2012SERVERA VM.
2. If you have not already done so, convert all basic disks to dynamic disks.
3. Create a mirrored volume out of drive C: and mirror the volume to one of your other drives.
4. Using the unallocated space on three other drives, create a RAID 5 volume that is 300MB in size. Assign drive letter J to the volume, and format for NTFS.

CERTIFICATION OBJECTIVE 14.06

Network Documentation and Configuration Management

One of the duties that is often overlooked by most network professionals is the task of creating network documentation and maintaining that documentation. This section will outline different types of network documentation you should maintain.

Wiring Schematics

One of the hardest tasks to perform is to clean up or rewire the wiring closet because most administrators do not document or label the purpose of each cable coming out of a switch, router, or any cable present.

It is important to keep a wiring diagram, known as a wiring scheme, which outlines how all aspects of the network are connected. You want to be sure to document and label the purpose of each device, such as switches and routers, and what the device is connected to. For example, a number of companies will assign specific switches to specific departments or divisions within the company, so the purpose of those switches should be labeled and documented so that the wrong network cable does not get plugged into the switch.

Be sure to label and document the purpose of each wire, or at least group the related wires and then document their purpose.

Physical Network Diagrams

When preparing documentation of your network environment, be sure to include documentation of the physical aspect of the network. The physical components of the network are the networking hardware—the cables, switches, routers, and patch panels. Be sure to document each component of the physical network!

Network Map

The physical network diagram, also known as the network map, will document the physical network infrastructure, including the placement of switches, routers, servers, and workstations. The physical network diagram will display items such as wide area network (WAN) links and the speeds of these links.

A great piece of software to help create the network diagrams is Microsoft Visio. Visio has a number of graphical objects built in that represent routers, switches, and network links. You can create your network diagram with Visio and label each device and network link. Be sure to include information such as the make and model of the device and what the device is connected to.

To summarize, some of the physical network components that should be included in the network diagram are

- **Routers** The network diagram should include placement of routers and their make and model number.
- **Switches** The diagram should also include the placement of switches, including the make and model number of the switch.
- **WAN links** You should document the WAN links and what each WAN link is connecting to.
- **Cabling** Be sure to document all the cabling and how the network devices are connected. It is a good idea to use different color cables for different types of systems (for example, secret systems in a high-secure environment use a red cable). Also, be sure to put a label on each end of the cables indicating what the cable is for.
- **Servers** The network map should include the placement of servers on the network and the make and model of the server.

The Network+ exam objectives use the terms cable and asset management. Be aware that a big part of managing your assets, such as cables and other network assets (routers and switches), is to ensure that you fully document cable usage, wiring schemes, and placement of network devices.

Logical Network Diagrams

The logical components of your network are the software aspects of the network. This includes your domain controllers, Dynamic Host Configuration Protocol (DHCP) servers, Domain Name System (DNS) servers, and the IP configuration of the network. It is important to create documentation for the logical network components along with the physical network components.

The logical network diagram should document the location of these services and some of the core configuration, such as DHCP scopes, DNS domain names, organizational unit (OU) structure, and IP addresses. You should also document any virtual LANs (VLANs) that are being used on the network and which computers belong to which VLANs.

Asset Management

As part of your documentation, you want to ensure you document the company assets, their location, and who is responsible for those assets. This typically involves creating asset tag numbers for each piece of equipment and tracking those asset tag numbers with a description of the device and its characteristics (such as processor type, amount of RAM, and hard disk size).

The assets should be inventoried on a regular basis (typically once a year during a downtime) and compared to your documentation to ensure that the company investments are still present.

IP Address Utilization

You should also document your IP address ranges being used and track usage of IP addresses assigned on the network. When documenting IP addresses being used, be sure to record the static addresses assigned to servers, routers, switches, and printers, as well as any DHCP scopes being used.

Vendor Documentation

Ensure that you keep a copy of all vendor documentation in a central place and look at creating a summary document with key points on the configuration of each product. Also note any special situations that a technician should be aware of, for example, a special keystroke to get into the BIOS of a system.

Baselines

At some point you will end up troubleshooting performance problems with the network and the servers. You will use performance-monitoring tools to monitor the systems and network-monitoring tools to monitor the network. It is critical after the installation of the network that you use these tools to create a baseline. The baseline is a picture of what your systems and network look like from a performance point of view when life is normal.

Once you have saved and documented normal activity in a baseline, you can then refer to it when troubleshooting performance issues later on down the road. When there is a problem, you will use the monitoring tools again to capture activity on the poorly performing system or network and then compare the capture to the information in the baseline to determine the source of the problem. It would be really hard to determine what areas of the network are degrading without a baseline to refer to.

Internal Policies, Procedures, and Standards

When documenting aspects of the network, you want to be sure to document any network policy details.

Policies

There is a wide range of network policies that you want to be sure to document:

- **Password policy** The password policy will determine what are valid passwords on the network. It will allow you to configure settings such as maximum password length, password complexity, and how frequently passwords should change. Be sure to document all aspects of the password policy.

- **Account lockout** Be sure to document how many bad logon attempts are allowed before an account is locked. Also document how long the account is locked for.

- **User rights** Document any extra privileges that are given to users on the network. For example, if you allow Bob to back up files from the server, then you want to be sure to document those extra rights.

- **Audit policy** It is important to document your audit policy so that at any point in time you can determine what level of auditing is enabled on the network. Be sure to document what events are being audited and whether you are auditing the success or failure of a given event.

- **Firewall policy** An important network feature to document is the firewall policy. Document what the default rule is—either accept all traffic or deny all traffic—and then document each rule. You don't want to have to rebuild all those rules without any reference!

- **Software restriction policy** The software restriction policy will determine what applications are allowed to run on the computers. You want to be sure to document the rules in this policy so that if you have problems with an application running, you can refer to the policy to find out if there is a reason the application does not run.

Procedures

Along with documenting any policy settings on the network, you will want to make sure that you document all network procedures. Some examples of network procedures that should be documented are backup procedures, restore procedures, server recovery procedures, device replacement procedures such as for a router or switch, and hard drive replacement procedures.

Documenting the procedures to perform maintenance on the network will help when the time comes to perform those tasks. You will not need to scramble to figure out how to perform these tasks that were configured so long ago—you simply look at the documentation.

Standards

Standards are defined ways of performing an action that must be followed by all employees within the organization. A standards document defines any requirements or specifications needed in order to meet the standard. A good example of standards is provided by the International Standards Organization, which develops standards on a large number of technologies such as wireless (802.11) and Ethernet networks (802.3).

You may develop your own standards within the organization, such as a secure web server standard that specifies conditions and requirements that need to be met in order for the web server to be considered secure.

Change Management

While on the theme of policies and documenting your different policies, it is critical to ensure that you have a change management policy in place that specifies how changes are to be implemented within the network environment.

A change management policy should specify the steps to take to implement changes to any of the servers or network devices. An example of what your change management steps may be includes the following:

- *Determine the change that is needed.* The first step to making a change is identifying that the change is required.
- *Test the change in a test environment.* It is critical to have a test environment that is configured similar to your production environment so that you can test the change. Testing the change allows you to identify issues that arise when the change is made.
- *Prepare and test a backout plan.* Although the change worked in the test environment, always have a plan for how you are going to put the production system back to its original state should the change go bad.
- *Create a backup before implementing the change.* Back up the system or device before making a change on the production system.

■ *Schedule a time for the change.* Schedule an appropriate time for the change—this is typically during hours of low network utilization, such as the middle of the night or on the weekend. Notify your users that you have scheduled the change during that time.

■ *Implement the change.* During that scheduled time, implement the changes that have been planned and tested.

■ *Verify the state of the system after the change.* After the change has been implemented, make sure you verify that the system has not been negatively affected by it.

■ *Document the process and results.* Take time to document the process you followed during the change and document the results of the change (whether it was successful or failed).

Change Management Procedures

Change management is about defining a set of procedures that need to be followed in order to make a change. The following outlines the steps to implement change:

■ **Document reason for change**   The first step is to identify the need for the change and document the reason why the change is needed.

■ **Change request**   After documenting the need for the change, you can create the official request for change. In the change request include the configuration procedures for making the change. You should also include the rollback process you will take should something go wrong with the change. You want to document the potential impact that the change will have on a system or network (be sure to note positive impact and negative impact). Finally, you want to specify in the change request how employees will be notified of the change.

■ **Approval process**   After submitting the change request, the request will be reviewed and either approved or denied.

■ **Maintenance window**   Assuming the change has been approved, you will want to plan the maintenance window of when the change will occur. Make sure you are clear on your authorized downtime and ensure that you have the system or network operational again within that authorized downtime window. For example, management may say you can have the system down for three hours, so be sure that your change can be implemented and have things operational again within three hours—this takes great planning and testing (never perform the change the first time on a production system)!

■ **Notification of change**   It is a good idea to let the employees know when you are implementing a change and what they can expect to see after the change is made. For example, if you are deploying new software, be sure to warn them if the old software they are used to is being removed. After the change is made, you should follow up with a notification of what was changed and the status of the change.

■ **Documentation**   As mentioned earlier, it is important to update documentation after the change is completed. This includes any new or modified network configurations, additions to the network (maybe you added a new server), and any changes to the physical location.

watch   **Be sure to keep your network documentation up to date as the network environment changes, and store your network documentation in a secure location!**

I would like to make two last points about network documentation. The first is to be sure to maintain the documentation by keeping it up to date as changes to the network occur. Network documentation that is not kept up to date is just as bad as not having any.

The second point is that the network documentation includes critical private information about your network setup that a hacker would love to have! Be sure to store the current copy of your network documentation in a secure location and shred any old copies.

Configuration Management

Two important configuration management tasks that the Network+ exam expects you to be familiar with are on-boarding and off-boarding of mobile devices, and network access control (NAC).

On-boarding is a term we use to describe the process or steps that need to be taken when a company hires a new employee. For example, we need to ensure they have a card pass to get into the building, an e-mail address, a mobile phone, and a user account to access the network. *Off-boarding* is the term we use for the process or steps that need to be taken when an employee leaves the organization. For example, we should have an exit interview, collect their laptop and mobile phone, and review the confidentiality agreement with them.

On-boarding and off-boarding mobile devices is similar in concept—it represents the steps that need to be taken when a new mobile device is needed within the organization or when it is decommissioned. Examples of steps that should be taken when on-boarding a mobile device (introducing the device to the organization) are

■ *Add the device to the network management software.* Most network management software today can manage mobile devices and features of the device, but you first must add the device to the management software.

■ *Verify the functionality of the device.* Ensure that the device is working as expected and any unwanted features of the device are disabled.

■ *Verify security compliance.* Ensure that the device is configured in a secure manner. For example, ensure passwords are set on the device, the screen auto-locks, and wireless or Bluetooth functionality is disabled if not being used.

Network access control (NAC) is another configuration management technology that allows you to control which devices can access the network based on certain health requirements being met. An example health requirement is if the system has antivirus software installed, has Windows Update enabled, or has the firewall enabled on the system.

When the user connects to the network, the NAC feature checks to see if these health requirements are met before allowing the client to connect to the network. If the health requirements are not met, then the client could be sent to a remediation network where they can update the system or download new virus definitions.

CERTIFICATION SUMMARY

In this chapter you have learned a number of methods to maintain the network and ensure that it is in good operational order. This chapter has introduced you to a number of day-to-day tasks that must be performed to help maintain network integrity. When it comes to hardware and software upgrades, make sure that you have tested the upgrade in a lab first so that you do not find out about upgrade problems on production systems. It is critical to back up the system before applying any major upgrade so that if something does go wrong, you have a recent backup to rely on.

Make sure that you have installed antivirus software on all servers and desktop systems. You will also need to schedule a virus scan on the systems regularly and update the virus definitions often. The virus definitions list is a list of all the known viruses at the time the virus definition file was created.

You will most likely want to load antispyware software on computers on which users spend a lot of time surfing the Internet. Spyware and adware are malicious programs that can be installed on your system without your knowledge. This malicious software is a security risk because it can monitor your activity, and it can dramatically slow down system performance.

It is extremely critical that you back up data regularly. You should back up data provided by all services, including file and print services, database servers, and e-mail services. Further, you should make sure that you perform a backup of the operating system so that you can get it up and running quickly when presented with a system failure.

There are three major types of backups: a full backup, an incremental backup, and a differential backup. A full backup backs up any file that you select, whether the archive bit is set or not, and then clears the archive bit. An incremental backup only backs up a file that has the archive bit set and clears the archive bit when it is done. A differential backup backs up any files that have the archive bit set and does not clear the archive bit when it is done.

When restoring from an incremental backup, you will need to restore the last full backup and then each incremental since the last full backup. When restoring from a differential backup, you will need to restore the last full backup and then the last differential. If you perform full backups every night, you will need to restore only the last full backup.

Fault tolerance is the concept of trying to keep things running when there is a failure in a device. In this chapter you looked at disk fault tolerance and how to set up your server so that if a disk fails you can still have the server running. To implement disk fault tolerance, you implement a level of RAID.

RAID level 0 is known as striping. When a user saves a file to a RAID 0 volume, the file is split across all drives in the volume, which increases performance because you have multiple drives taking care of the save operation at the same time. There is no fault tolerance with RAID level 0. RAID level 1 is known as disk mirroring. Disk mirroring is responsible for duplicating all the data that is saved to the RAID 1 volume to the two drives that are mirrored. RAID level 5 stripes the data as RAID 0 does, but there is data redundancy, or parity information, stored with the data as well. If a drive fails in a RAID 5 volume, the system continues to run, reading the data from the RAID 5 volume.

As a network professional, always remember to set and follow strict policies that control use of software, passwords, account lockout, and auditing. Be sure to get management approval when designing the policies, and then implement the policies on the appropriate systems.

To help prepare for the day when you need them, make sure you are familiar with what level of logging your systems and software can perform. Also, know where the information is logged so that you can access the logs when you need to.

Always remember that a well-planned network design will always require documentation for the physical and logical aspects. Be sure to store the documentation in a secure location and update it as the network changes.

TWO-MINUTE DRILL

Network Upgrades and Downgrades

❑ Be sure to do an inventory on all your servers and verify that you have the most up-to-date ROMs on the device. Check for updates on the manufacturer's website for the device.

❑ Be sure to create a test lab to verify that any hardware or software upgrade is tested with all your existing hardware and software. You do not want to do the installation on production systems without testing them first.

Installing Patches and Updates

❑ Be sure to keep your systems up to date with patches and service packs. Most vulnerabilities are fixed with a software patch.

❑ A hot-fix is something that can't wait for the next service pack release. You should test and then apply any hot-fix as soon as possible.

❑ A service pack includes all updates since the release of the product. If you install a server and service pack 2 is the current service pack, you will not need to install service pack 1 and service pack 2—just service pack 2. You will need to get any updates released since service pack 2 in this example.

❑ You can use the Software Update Service in Microsoft environments to deploy updates across the network. This will simplify the management of the updates.

Antivirus and Antispyware Software

❑ After installing your antivirus software, make sure that you have scheduled regular virus scans.

❑ Make sure that you have the real-time protection enabled on your antivirus software so that any time you access a file, the virus protection software checks the file for viruses.

❑ Make sure that you keep your antivirus software up to date by downloading the most current virus definitions.

❑ Install server-based antivirus software on e-mail servers so that incoming mail is scanned before it is deposited into the user's mailbox.

Backing Up Network Data

❑ Make sure that you have a tape rotation schedule, and be sure to store a copy of backups offsite in case of disaster.

❑ Schedule backups to occur regularly.

❑ If the amount of data is too much to perform a full backup each night, create a backup plan that combines your full backup with an incremental or differential backup.

❑ A full backup backs up any selected file whether the archive bit is set or not and then clears the archive bit.

❑ An incremental backup backs up only the selected files that have the archive bit set and then clears the archive bit after the backup.

❑ A differential backup backs up only the selected files that have the archive bit set and does not clear the archive bit.

Providing Fault Tolerance

❑ Fault tolerance is the concept of ensuring that you can still have a solution running if part of the solution fails. For example, if you lose a power supply in a server, there would be a second one waiting to take over.

❑ RAID is a disk fault-tolerance technology that involves multiple drives storing the data. Depending on the RAID level you use, you can still get access to data if a disk fails because a copy of the data is stored on another disk.

❑ RAID level 0, known as disk striping, does not provide any fault tolerance. RAID 0 is used to increase performance with read and write operations because the data is split up and written to all disks in the solution at the same time.

❑ RAID level 1 is known as disk mirroring. RAID 1 stores a full copy of the data on both members of the mirrored volume so that if one disk fails, the other disk still has a copy.

❑ RAID level 5 is also known as disk striping with parity, whereby the data is striped across multiple disks. However, it does store parity information so that if a disk fails, the missing data can be recalculated.

Network Documentation and Configuration Management

❑ Be sure to document all aspects of the network, including the physical structure, such as the placement of routers and switches.

❑ You should document the link speeds between different branches and your routers.

❑ Document the logical structure, such as the VLAN configuration.

SELF TEST

The following questions will help you measure your understanding of the material presented in this chapter. Read all the choices carefully, because there may appear to be more than one correct answer.

Network Upgrades and Downgrades

1. You need to ensure that your server supports a new disk standard—what would you do?
    A. Purchase a new server that supports the new standard.
    B. Go to the server manufacturer's website and see if there is a BIOS update for that server that will update the BIOS code to make the server aware of the new standard.
    C. Format the hard drives and then restore the data.
    D. All of the above.

2. You are going to upgrade your e-mail server software to a new version. What should you do before the software upgrade?
    A. Perform the upgrade on a test system first.
    B. Delete the e-mails from the server—you need the space for the new software.
    C. Back up the server before attempting the upgrade.
    D. Both A and C.

Installing Patches and Updates

3. What is a hot-fix?
    A. An update that is noncritical
    B. A number of updates that are bundled and will bring your system up to date
    C. A critical update that should be applied to your system as soon as possible
    D. All of the above

4. What feature of Microsoft operating systems allows you to update the system fairly easily?
    A. System Restore
    B. Windows Messenger
    C. Backup
    D. Windows Update

5. What Microsoft feature can you use to deliver updates to all clients on the network from a central point?
    A. Windows Update
    B. Backup
    C. WSUS
    D. Active Directory

Antivirus and Antispyware Software

6. What is the name of malicious software that monitors Internet activity?
    A. Virus
    B. Worm
    C. Spyware
    D. Trojan

7. It is critical that you keep what part of your virus protection software up to date?
    A. Menu commands
    B. Version
    C. Viruses
    D. Virus definitions

8. What feature of virus protection software is responsible for protecting your system at the time a file with a virus is activated?
   A. Real-time protection
   B. At-the-time protection
   C. Active protection
   D. None of the above

Backing Up Network Data

9. What type of backup backs up files that have changed and then clears the archive bit?
   A. Full
   B. Incremental
   C. Differential
   D. Copy

10. You have been performing a full backup every Sunday night and have been doing incremental backups on Monday, Tuesday, Wednesday, and Thursday nights. Your server crashes during the day on Wednesday. What is your restore strategy?
    A. Restore only Tuesday night's backup.
    B. Restore the last full backup from Sunday and then restore the last incremental, which is Tuesday's.
    C. Restore the last full backup from Sunday and then restore the incremental backups from Monday and Tuesday.
    D. Restore only the full backup from Sunday.

11. Where should you make certain that you have stored a copy of your network backups?
    A. In a central cabinet in the server room
    B. In your manager's office
    C. On a different server for quick restores
    D. Offsite in a safe, trusted location

12. What type of backup backs up files that have changed and does not clear the archive bit?
    A. Full
    B. Incremental
    C. Differential
    D. Copy

13. You have been performing a full backup every Sunday night and have been doing differential backups on Monday, Tuesday, Wednesday, and Thursday nights. Your server crashes during the day on Thursday—what is your restore strategy?
    A. Restore only Wednesday night's backup.
    B. Restore the last full backup from Sunday and then restore the last differential backup, which is Wednesday's.

    C. Restore the last full backup from Sunday and then restore all of the differential backups from Monday and Tuesday.

    D. Restore only the full backup from Sunday.

14. How would you make sure that you do not forget to perform a backup each night?

    A. Create a backup plan.

    B. Schedule the backup software to do the backup automatically.

    C. Ask your manager to remind you to do the backup each night.

    D. Set a reminder in Outlook.

15. Before performing a backup operation, what should you have in place to ensure that everyone knows and understands the backup strategy?

    A. An assistant

    B. A backup plan

    C. A security document

    D. A tape

Providing Fault Tolerance

16. Which RAID level stores a full copy of the data on a second disk?

    A. RAID level 0

    B. RAID level 1

    C. RAID level 5

    D. All of the above

17. Which RAID level provides no duplication of data and therefore provides no fault tolerance?

    A. RAID level 0

    B. RAID level 1

    C. RAID level 5

    D. All of the above

18. Which RAID level writes the data across multiple disks and stores parity information for fault tolerance?

    A. RAID level 0

    B. RAID level 1

    C. RAID level 5

    D. All of the above

19. What tool in Windows is used to create RAID volumes?
   A.   Disk Management
   B.   Registry
   C.   Active Directory Users and Computers
   D.   Control Panel

20. A RAID level 1 solution that uses two hard disk controllers is called what?
   A.   Mirroring
   B.   Striping
   C.   Redundancy
   D.   Duplexing

Network Documentation and Configuration Management

21. Which of the following make up part of the physical structure documentation? (Select all that apply.)
   A.   Routers
   B.   Active Directory OUs
   C.   WAN links
   D.   VLAN configuration

22. What should you do with your documentation as changes are made to the network environment? (Select two.)
   A.   Throw the outdated documentation out.
   B.   Shred the outdated documentation.
   C.   Sell the outdated documentation.
   D.   Update the documentation.

Performance-Based Question Review: See the performance-based question sample from the author included with the accompanying media.

SELF TEST ANSWERS

Network Upgrades and Downgrades

1. ☑ **B.** It is important to remember that as your hardware gets older you can update the BIOS or ROM code on that server or device to bring it up to date with features or technologies that have come out since the manufacturer built the device.
    ☒ **A, C,** and **D** are incorrect. Purchasing a new server is a very expensive way to take advantage of new technologies. Simply flashing the BIOS would be a cheaper solution. Formatting the hard drive has nothing to do with the solution.

2. ☑ **D.** Before performing any kind of hardware or software upgrade, you should make sure that you have tested the upgrade first. After you have tested the upgrade, before performing the upgrade on a production server, make sure that you have backed up the production server in case something goes wrong.
    ☒ **B** is incorrect. You would never delete user data, because you will find yourself very busy restoring that data from the backup resource.

Installing Patches and Updates

3. ☑ **C.** A hot-fix is a critical update that cannot wait for the next service pack to be supplied. You should apply hot-fixes right away. Make sure that you have tested the hot-fix on a test system first.
    ☒ **A, B,** and **D** are incorrect because they all imply that the update should not be applied immediately.

4. ☑ **D.** Windows Update is a feature of Microsoft operating systems that allows the user to use Windows Update to connect to the Windows Update site, from which updates are downloaded for that operating system.
    ☒ **A, B,** and **C** are incorrect. System Restore is a feature of Windows client operating systems that brings the system back to the state of the last restore point. Windows Messenger is an online "chat" type of software, and Backup is the software used to perform a backup of the system.

5. ☑ **C.** Windows Software Update Service can be installed on a Windows server and allows you to manage deployment of patches and updates from a central point.
    ☒ **A, B,** and **D** are incorrect. Windows Update is where WSUS gets the updates from, but WSUS helps deploy the update to all your systems. Active Directory is the Microsoft directory service and is not really used to deploy updates.

Antivirus and Antispyware Software

6. ☑ **C.** Spyware is malicious software planted on your system that can monitor your Internet activity.
    ☒ **A, B,** and **D** are incorrect. A virus, a Trojan, and a worm are all malicious software that damages the system or slows it down.

7. ☑ **D.** It is critical that you keep your virus definitions up to date. The virus definitions are the part of the virus protection software that makes the software aware of what viruses exist. Virus protection software vendors are constantly updating their definitions, and you can download the updates from the Internet through the virus protection software.
    ☒ **A, B,** and **C** are incorrect because none of those are features of virus protection software.

8. ☑ **A.** Real-time protection saves you from needing to run a virus scan manually because as you open or access files, the virus protection software scans the file being accessed.
    ☒ **B, C,** and **D** are incorrect because these are not features of virus protection software.

Backing Up Network Data

9. ☑ **B.** Incremental backups clear the archive bit after backing up a file that has changed. Because the archive bit is cleared, the file will not be backed up with the next incremental backup unless it is changed again.
    ☒ **A, C,** and **D** are incorrect. A full backup backs up any file that is selected, whether it has changed or not. A differential backup backs up a file that has changed but does not clear the archive bit. A copy backup does not clear the archive bit; it is like a full backup in that it backs up any file you select.

10. ☑ **C.** You will need to restore the last full backup and each incremental backup up to the crash in this scenario. Each incremental backup applies the changes since the previous incremental, and all incrementals build on the full backup being performed, bringing the server up to date.
    ☒ **A, B,** and **D** are incorrect because they are all incorrect restore strategies when combining full backups with incremental backups.

11. ☑ **D.** You should make sure that you store a copy of your backups offsite in a safe, trusted location. The purpose of having the tapes stored offsite is to be able to recover from a disaster to your premises that would destroy servers and backups.
    ☒ **A, B,** and **C** are incorrect because they are all locations where a backup could be stored that will still make the backup media vulnerable to disaster along with the server.

12. ☑ **C.** A differential backup backs up any file that has changed, but does not clear the archive bit. This is useful because each differential backup includes all changes from the time of the last full backup to the time of the differential backup.
    ☒ **A, B,** and **D** are incorrect. Full backups back up any file that is selected, whether it has changed or not, and clears the archive bit. An incremental backup backs up only files that have changed and clears the archive bit, whereas a copy backup backs up any file that is selected and does not clear the archive bit.

13.   ☑   **B.** For this scenario you would restore Sunday's full backup to create a starting point and then apply the last differential backup to bring the server up to date to the time of the last differential.
☒   **A, C,** and **D** are incorrect because they are not restore strategies used with full backups and differential backups.

14.   ☑   **B.** The best thing to do is to schedule your backups so that you are not dependent on memory and they are performed automatically.
☒   **A, C,** and **D** are incorrect. Although you should create a backup plan, the plan does not actually ensure that the backups are performed. Make certain that you schedule the backups!

15.   ☑   **B.** Make sure that you have a backup plan and that it is up to date so that all systems administrators know what is being backed up and what the restore strategy is in case of failure.
☒   **A, C,** and **D** are incorrect because none of these options guarantees that all persons involved in the day-to-day network operations understand the backup strategy.

Providing Fault Tolerance

16.   ☑   **B.** RAID level 1 is disk mirroring; it mirrors, or duplicates, the data from one disk to another in case of a disk failure.
☒   **A, C,** and **D** are incorrect. RAID level 0 is known as disk striping and is responsible for saving the data across multiple disks but with no redundancy. RAID level 5 is disk striping but does store parity data as well, which provides fault tolerance.

17.   ☑   **A.** RAID level 0 is known as disk striping and is responsible for saving the data across multiple disks but with no redundancy. The benefit is strictly for performance—multiple disks working at saving your data at the same time.
☒   **B, C,** and **D** are incorrect. RAID level 1 is disk mirroring; it mirrors, or duplicates, the data from one disk to another in case of a disk failure. RAID level 5 is disk striping, but does store parity data as well, which provides fault tolerance.

18.   ☑   **C.** RAID level 5 is also known as striping with parity and stores parity data and writes the data across all disks.
☒   **A, B,** and **D** are incorrect. RAID level 0 is known as disk striping and is responsible for saving the data across multiple disks but with no redundancy. RAID level 1 is disk mirroring; it mirrors, or duplicates, the data from one disk to another in case of a disk failure. RAID level 5 is disk striping, but does store parity data as well, which provides fault tolerance.

19.   ☑   **A.** Disk Management is the tool used to create volumes on a Windows server.
☒   **B, C,** and **D** are incorrect because they are not used to create RAID volumes on a Windows server.

20.   ☑   **D.** Disk duplexing is the duplication of data on multiple disks, but the disks are connected to two different disk controllers.
☒   **A, B,** and **C** are incorrect. Disk mirroring stores copies of the data on multiple disks but uses only one disk controller. The other choices do not duplicate the data.

Network Documentation and Configuration Management

21. ☑ **A** and **C.** Routers and WAN links make up part of the physical structure of the network and therefore are part of that documentation.

☒ **B** and **D** are incorrect because they are part of documenting the logical structure of the network.

22. ☑ **B** and **D.** You need to ensure that you update the network documentation as changes are made to the network. For security reasons, you want to make sure that you shred any old copies and store the updated documentation in a secure location.

☒ **A** and **C** are incorrect. For security reasons, you should shred the documentation, not throw it out.

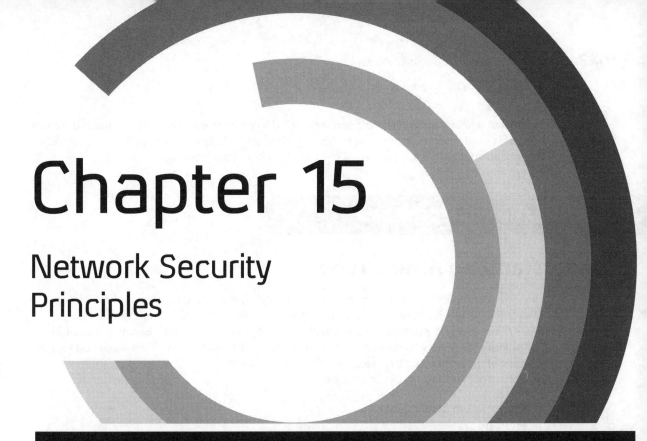

Chapter 15

Network Security Principles

Today's networks are becoming more dispersed and widespread, given the impact the Internet has had on extending the network to roaming users and business partners. It is extremely important that as you design the network, you consider the impact your design will have on the overall security of the organization and its resources. It is important to ensure that resources are protected and that data traveling on the wire or in the air is protected through encryption.

In this chapter you will be introduced to a number of security-related terms and learn what features of the operating system are used to help protect network resources. You will learn what a firewall is and the general steps used to configure it. You will also learn different protocols used to encrypt network traffic for wired and wireless networks. This chapter also lists some basic guidelines you could use to help secure your network.

CERTIFICATION OBJECTIVE 15.01

Understanding Attack Types

Due to the complexity of software and networks today, most systems and applications are susceptible to a number of different types of security attacks. Understanding the different types of attacks and methods that hackers are using to compromise systems is essential to understanding how to secure your environment. This section will introduce you to a number of different types of attacks.

There are two major types of attacks:

■ Social engineering attacks
■ Network attacks

Social Engineering

With a *social engineering* attack, the attacker compromises the network or system through social interaction with an individual, through an e-mail message or phone call, and tricks the individual into divulging information that can be used to compromise security. The information that the victim divulges to the hacker would most likely be used in a subsequent attack to gain unauthorized access to a system or network.

The key to protecting yourself and fellow employees from social engineering attacks is education! Keeping all personnel aware of the popularity of social engineering attacks and the different scenarios that could be examples of such attacks will help raise the security level of the organization.

There are a number of different examples of social engineering attacks. The following are some of the most common scenarios:

■ **Hacker impersonates administrator** In this example, the hacker may call the employee and impersonate the network administrator. The hacker will try to convince the employee to change their password or divulge password information.

■ **Hacker impersonates user** In this example, the hacker calls an unsuspecting network administrator and plays the role of a frustrated user who cannot log on to the network. The network administrator naturally helps the "user" by resetting the password and helping them log on—the problem is that it is actually the hacker!

■ **Hacker impersonates vendor**   In this example, the hacker may e-mail a customer and pretend to be the vendor of a piece of software. The hacker tries to get the user to install an update, but the user doesn't realize the update is really a Trojan virus that gives the hacker access to the system.

Phishing Attack

A common type of social engineering attack today is what is known as a phishing attack. A *phishing attack* is when the hacker creates a fake website that looks exactly like a popular website, such as a bank or eBay. The hacker then sends an e-mail message trying to trick the user into clicking a link that leads to the fake site (this is called "phishing"). When the user attempts to log on with their account information, the hacker records the user name and password and then tries that information on the real site.

Network-Based Attacks

Most types of attacks are considered network-based attacks, where the hacker performs the attack from a remote system. There are a number of different types of network attacks:

■ **Eavesdropping attack**   Also known as *packet sniffing,* eavesdropping involves the use of a network monitoring tool known as a sniffer, which is used to capture and analyze network traffic. If the traffic is not encrypted, the hacker could read confidential data, including user names and passwords.

■ **Spoof attack**   In a spoof attack, the hacker modifies the source address of the packets he or she is sending so that they appear to be coming from someone else. Hackers may spoof the IP address, Media Access Control (MAC) address, or e-mail address to make the message appear as if it is coming from someone else. Spoofing is a common method to bypass access controls placed on switches, routers, or firewalls.

■ **Man-in-the-middle (MITM) attack**   With an MITM attack, the hacker inserts himself in the middle of two systems that are communicating. He then passes the information back and forth between the two, with neither party knowing all the communication is passing through the hacker's system. The benefit of this is the hacker can then view any sensitive data sent between the two systems.

■ **Hijack attack**   A hacker takes over a session between you and another individual and disconnects the other individual from the communication. You still believe that you are talking to the original party and may send private information to the hacker unintentionally.

■ **Denial of service**   A denial of service (DOS) is a type of attack that causes the system or its services to crash. As a result, the system cannot fulfill its purpose and provide those services.

■ **Distributed denial of service (DDOS)**   The hacker uses multiple systems to attack a single target system. A good example is the *smurf attack,* in which the hacker pings a number of computers but modifies the source address of those packets so that they appear to come from another system (the victim, in this case). When all of these systems receive the ping request, they will reply to the same address, essentially overburdening that system with data.

■ **Buffer overflow**   A buffer overflow attack is when the attacker sends more data to an application than is expected. A buffer overflow attack usually results in the attacker gaining administrative access to the system in a command prompt or shell.

■ **Exploit attack**   In this type of attack, the attacker knows of a security problem within an operating system or a piece of software and leverages that knowledge by exploiting the vulnerability.

■ **Password attack**   An attacker tries to crack the passwords stored in a network account database or a password-protected file. There are three major types of password attacks: a dictionary attack, a brute-force attack, and a hybrid attack. A *dictionary attack* uses a word list file, which is a list of potential passwords. A *brute-force attack* is when the attacker tries every possible combination of characters. With brute force, a file is not read. A *hybrid attack* is similar to a dictionary attack in that it uses a word list file, but it also places numbers at the end of the word to catch passwords that are not dictionary words because the user placed a number at the end. For example, a dictionary attack would not find the password "pass1," but a hybrid attack would.

■ **FTP bounce**   An FTP bounce attack is when the hacker connects to a File Transfer Protocol (FTP) server and then, while in the FTP session with the server, sends commands to the FTP server to do a port scan. In this situation the hacker would normally not be able to do the port scan, but because a company had an FTP server that is vulnerable to a bounce attack, the hacker was able to do the port scan once connected to the FTP server.

■ **Botnet**   A botnet is a group of systems that a hacker takes over and uses in a DDoS attack.

■ **Traffic spike**   A traffic spike could be the result of an attacker sending malicious traffic on the network. For example, they could be trying to remotely crack passwords on your system.

■ **Coordinated attack**   Watch for attacks that are coordinated attacks, which are multiple security incidents that could be related and a result of the same attack.

■ **Reflective/amplified**   A reflective attack is a type of attack against challenge/response authentication protocols in order to try to get the other side to reveal the challenge.

■ **DNS**   There are number of attacks against Domain Name System (DNS). A hacker may try to poison your DNS data in order to redirect clients to the wrong server. Attackers may also try to do a zone transfer (copy your DNS data) in order to map out your network.

- **NTP** Attackers are now using the *Network Time Protocol (NTP),* which is a protocol used to synchronize time between clients and servers, to build a network profile. It has been discovered that hackers are now retrieving the list of systems an NTP server has sent the time to using the **monlist** command.

- **Smurfing** A smurf attack is when the hacker sends a ping message to a number of systems but spoofs the IP address so that it looks like the ping messages are coming from different systems. The result is that all the systems send ping replies to the victim, essentially performing a DDoS.

- **Friendly/unintentional DoS** Watch for scenarios that could lead to an unintentional DoS attack. For example, an account lockout policy could lead to a denial of service; the user cannot log on once the account is locked. Users may also unintentionally cause a denial of service if they are able to delete a file by accident.

- **Physical attack** Physical attacks are when the attacker gets physical access to your facility and is able to cause damage to your equipment or even the facility. Be sure to implement physical security controls, such as locking mechanisms and guards.

- **Permanent DoS** A permanent DoS attack involves the hacker making a change to the system or network that crashes a system or causes communication issues.

- **ARP cache poisoning** A hacker can insert him- or herself in the middle of communication by altering the Address Resolution Protocol (ARP) cache on a victim's system and causing all communication to pass through the hacker's system so he or she can capture all traffic. This is a common method to perform a man-in-the-middle attack.

- **Packet/protocol abuse** Packet or protocol abuse is when the hacker uses a protocol in an unsuspecting manner. For example, it was common years ago for a hacker to send Hypertext Transfer Protocol (HTTP) packets to a web server that would navigate the file system of the server and potentially access or delete files.

- **Spoofing** Spoofing is when the hacker alters the source address of a packet. MAC spoofing is altering the source MAC address, IP spoofing is altering the source IP address, and e-mail spoofing is altering the source e-mail address.

- **Wireless** There are a number of risks against wireless networks. Hackers can spoof their MAC address to get on a wireless network that has MAC filtering enabled, or crack the wireless encryption.

- **VLAN hopping** VLAN hopping is an exploit against virtual local area networks (VLANs) that allows an individual to gain access to a VLAN when they are not connected to it. Hackers accomplish this by double-tagging the frames for different VLANs, or the hacker can imitate a trunking port so that they receive all traffic.

- **Compromised system** A compromised system is a huge risk to the network, as it is a system that a hacker has exploited and has control of. You should ensure that systems are healthy before they connect to the network, which means they are fully patched, have a firewall enabled, and have antivirus software installed and up to date.

■ **Effect of malware on the network** Malware on the network is a huge risk, as it can destroy data, take control of systems, and infect other systems with malware. Be sure to have a malware protection strategy to prevent malware from entering the network.

■ **Insider threat/malicious employee** One of the hidden risks against our systems comes from an insider threat where a disgruntled employee can perform malicious actions against your data and systems. Be sure to limit permissions of users and educate the human resources (HR) department on the threat of a disgruntled employee.

■ **Zero-day attacks** A zero-day attack is an attack involving a vulnerability in software that is currently unknown. Companies can have a team in place to test software and identify vulnerabilities not yet known.

ⓦatch Be sure to know all of the different types of attacks before taking the Network+ exam. Be most familiar with buffer overflow, denial of service, spoofing, password attacks, and social engineering.

Common Vulnerabilities

There are a number of common vulnerabilities, or configuration settings that lead to vulnerabilities, that you should be aware of as a network administrator. The following is a list of common reasons systems are attacked:

■ **Unnecessary running services** Be sure to assess the services running on a computer and then disable any unnecessary ones. The more software running on a system, the more likely there are vulnerabilities the hacker can use to gain access to it.

■ **Open ports** A Transmission Control Protocol (TCP) or User Datagram Protocol (UDP) port open on the system is an open door for the hacker to gain access to the system. Close any open ports on the system that are not needed, and use a firewall to block access to ports that remain open.

■ **Unpatched/legacy systems** Be sure to keep your systems up to date with patches and security fixes. That way, any software on the system is less likely to have vulnerabilities that the hacker can take advantage of.

■ **Unencrypted channels** Ensure that any communication between systems is encrypted as much as possible. Using unencrypted communication allows hackers to capture the traffic and read the information.

■ **Clear-text credentials** Ensure that the authentication protocols being used are encrypting the passwords when users are authenticating to the systems. Replace any unsecure authentication protocols with a secure authentication protocol.

■ **Unsecure protocols** Be sure to encrypt all communication. Know that most Internet protocols we use daily, such as Telnet, HTTP, Serial Line Internet Protocol (SLIP), FTP, Trivial File Transfer Protocol (TFTP), Simple Network Management Protocol

(SNMPv1) and SNMPv2, send traffic in an unencrypted format. If a hacker captures traffic of you connecting to an FTP server, they will know your FTP user name and password. Each of these protocols has a secure replacement that should be used, which is discussed in Chapter 16.

- **TEMPEST/RF emanation**   Malicious persons can tap into radio or electrical signals, sounds, and vibrations coming from a system. A TEMPEST system protects a system by shielding it from someone tapping into those signals. *TEMPEST* is the standard for hiding such signals and the acronym stands for *Telecommunications Electronics Material Protected from Emanating Spurious Transmissions*.

Malicious Software

Another common form of attack by hackers is through malicious software. Malicious software is the term used for any software that is designed to harm a system, and this software comes in many forms! The following is a listing of some of the malicious software you should be familiar with for the Network+ exam:

- **Virus**   The traditional virus was attached to a file, and when you opened the file, the virus was activated and infected your system. These types of viruses could delete files from the system or modify the boot sector so that the computer no longer boots.

- **Worm virus**   Today we deal with worm viruses a lot. A worm virus is a self-replicating virus, which means that it can infect your system without you opening a file. A worm virus infects your system by spreading across the network or by infecting a flash drive and then infecting your system when you connect the flash drive to your computer.

- **Trojan virus**   A Trojan virus is a program that you are tricked into installing because you thought the application did something useful, but in reality, it is a virus that infects the system. The Trojan virus typically modifies the system by opening a TCP/IP port, which allows the hacker to connect to the system and take control of it.

- **Spyware**   Spyware is hidden software that monitors and collects information about you and your surfing habits. Spyware has also been known to do more than just monitor for information, such as making changes to the system through browser redirection (sending you to a different webpage) and slowing down the network connection.

- **Adware**   Adware is software that automatically loads advertisements on the screen, typically in the form of a pop-up window. The advertisement is designed to entice you into purchasing a product or subscribing to a site.

- **Logic bomb**   A logic bomb is a type of virus that is planted on the system, and the application you installed acts as it is supposed to until a certain event occurs. The event is usually tied to something like a specific date, where once that date occurs, the virus performs its malicious duty.

- **Keylogger** A keylogger is either a piece of software installed on the system or a hardware device that is designed to capture all of the keystrokes on a system.
- **Spam** Spam is the term used for any unsolicited commercial e-mails you receive. These e-mail messages typically are mass mailed, and they try to get you to purchase their products or services. The spammers (people who send the spam messages) usually get your e-mail address from a website or newsgroup after you have posted a comment to the group.

Mitigating Attacks

Later in this chapter you will learn how to protect your systems and networks from network attacks, but while we are on the topic of attacks, I wanted to take a minute to outline some security best practices to help protect your company assets. The following is a listing of common security best practices:

- **Patch systems** The first step you can take to protect your systems is to ensure that you have a patch management strategy in place. Make sure that you are keeping all systems up to date with patches, as a patch will remove a known vulnerability from the system. Most operating systems and applications have an automatic update feature that you can enable so that updates are downloaded and applied automatically.
- **Encrypt traffic** If you want to protect your data from prying eyes, then ensure that you are encrypting all network communication. This includes encrypting web, e-mail, and FTP traffic if need be.
- **Storage encryption** Ensure that you are encrypting data that is stored on laptops and other mobile devices. Employees will lose or have their mobile devices stolen at some point, so it is critical to have that data encrypted and the devices password protected.
- **Antivirus software** To protect your systems from malware, be sure to install antivirus software on all systems and keep the virus definitions up to date.
- **Strong passwords** Ensure that you are using strong passwords for all user accounts and devices.
- **Educate employees** It is important to educate your employees on security best practices and ensure they understand what can happen if they do not follow them.
- **Hashing** You can also verify the integrity of data by running it through a hashing algorithm, which generates an answer (known as a hash value). The theory behind it is that any changes to the data would cause a different hash value to calculate the next time you check the file by running it through the hash algorithm. Examples of hashing algorithms are Message Digest 5 (MD5) and Secure Hash Algorithm (SHA).

Understanding System Security

In this section you will be introduced to the differences between authentication and authorization and how those processes are used to allow or deny access to network resources. When securing network resources, you should first have users log on to the network with their own private user names and passwords; once logged on, they will be able to access network resources to which they have been given permission. The process of logging on to the network is known as authentication, whereas controlling what network resources users may access once they have logged on to the network is known as authorization.

Authentication

Authentication is the process whereby users or computers identify themselves to the network so that they can start accessing network resources or a network device (in the case of managing the device). The method used to authenticate a user depends on the network environment and can assume forms such as the following:

- **User name and password**   When the user starts the computer or connects to the network, they type a user name and password that are associated with their particular network user account.
- **Smartcard**   Using a smartcard for logon is similar to accessing your bank account at a teller machine. To log on to the network, you insert a device similar to a debit card, known as a smartcard, into a smartcard reader and then supply a personal identification number (PIN). To be authenticated, you must have the smartcard and know its password. These smartcards are also known as *PKI cards* and are used to authenticate the client in a public key infrastructure (PKI) environment because they contain the employee's private key.
- **Biometrics**   The user provides a retina scan or fingerprint as a credential. Biometrics is becoming a very popular solution in highly secure environments where special biometric devices are used.

Whatever method is used to provide the necessary credentials, the outcome is the same, in the sense that the credentials are sent to a directory service such as Microsoft Active Directory, where they are verified. For example, if the user name and password are correct, the user is authenticated and allowed to access network resources. Network servers also have the ability to authorize users to access different resources, depending on how they are authenticated—for example, authentication through biometrics might give a user access

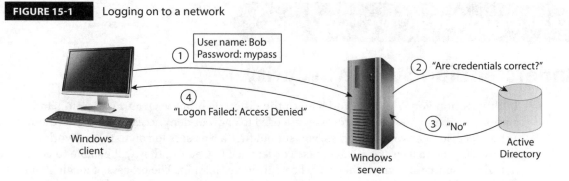

FIGURE 15-1 Logging on to a network

to more resources than simple user name and password authentication. If the credentials are incorrect, authentication fails and the user is denied access to the network, as shown in Figure 15-1.

When users provide credentials such as a user name and a password, the credentials are passed to the server using an authentication method. A number of authentication methods are used in the Microsoft world, as described in the following list:

■ **Anonymous authentication**   You are not required to log on. Windows uses an account for the actual service, and you are passed through as that account. Whatever permissions the anonymous account has are the permissions you will have while you are connected anonymously. This is a popular authentication method for websites or FTP servers.

■ **Basic authentication**   You are required to log on, and the user name and password are sent to the server in clear text. This means that if someone has a packet sniffer between you and the server, that person will be able to capture your password and view it because it is not encrypted.

■ **Integrated Windows authentication**   You are required to log on to the server, but your user name and password are sent to the server in an encrypted format. This authentication method is more secure than basic authentication if users are required to log on.

■ **Kerberos**   Kerberos is a popular mutual authentication protocol, and is used by default with Active Directory environments. Microsoft Active Directory adheres to the Lightweight Directory Access Protocol (LDAP) standard, which is the Internet protocol for accessing and querying a directory. Kerberos uses a Key Distribution Center (KDC) server that is responsible for issuing tickets. These tickets are needed in order for a client to request a service from any other server on the network (known as a realm). The Kerberos process starts when the client logs on to the network. The KDC has a component known as the authentication server (AS), which gives the client a ticket-granting ticket (TGT), which gives the client permission to request a service ticket. The service ticket is required to request service from a server on the network. When the client wants to connect to a specific server on the network, it must request a ticket from the ticket-granting service (TGS), which is another component of the KDC. The TGS grants the ticket to the client so the client can access the required server on the network.

These authentication methods are very "Microsoft-ish," but there are standard protocols used to perform authentication as well. The standard authentication protocols used by various network services, such as Remote Access Service (RAS) and Virtual Private Network (VPN), include the following:

- **Password Authentication Protocol (PAP)** PAP sends the user's credentials in plain text and is very insecure because it is easy for someone to analyze and interpret the logon traffic. This is the authentication protocol used by the basic authentication method mentioned previously.

- **Challenge Handshake Authentication Protocol (CHAP)** With CHAP, the server sends a client a challenge (a key), which is combined with the user's password. Both the user's password and the challenge are run through the MD5 hashing algorithm (a formula), which generates a hash value, or mathematical answer, and that hash value is sent to the server for authentication. The server uses the same key to create a hash value with the password stored on the server and then compares the resulting value with the hash value sent by the client. If the two hash values are the same, the client has supplied the correct password. The benefit is that the user's credentials have not been passed on the wire at all.

- **Microsoft Challenge Handshake Authentication Protocol (MS-CHAP)** MS-CHAP is a variation of the CHAP authentication protocol and uses MD4 as the hashing algorithm versus MD5, which is used by CHAP. MS-CHAP also uses the Microsoft Point-to-Point Encryption (MPPE) protocol along with MS-CHAP to encrypt all traffic from the client to the server.

- **MS-CHAPv2** With MS-CHAP version 2, the authentication method has been extended to authenticate both the client and the server. MS-CHAPv2 also uses stronger encryption keys than CHAP and MS-CHAP.

- **Extensible Authentication Protocol (EAP)** EAP allows for multiple logon methods, such as smartcard logon, certificates, Kerberos, and public-key authentication. EAP is also frequently used with *Remote Authentication Dial-In User Service (RADIUS),* which is a central authentication service that can be used by RAS, wireless, or VPN solutions.

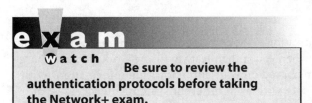

Authentication Factors

The Network+ exam expects you to know the different methods, or factors, of authentication. An individual can be authenticated using any of the following authentication factors:

- **Something they know**   This is the most common authentication factor, where the employee knows information to prove their identity. An example of this authentication factor is knowing a password or a PIN.
- **Something they have**   Also a common authentication factor, this is based on you having something in your possession to gain access to the environment. For example, you use a swipe card or physical token to enter a building.
- **Something they are**   Employees can gain access to a system by using a more advanced authentication factor known as something they are. With this authentication factor, employees use a characteristic of themselves, such as a retina scan, fingerprint, or voice recognition, to prove their identity. Authenticating to a system using this method is known as *biometrics* and is considered the most secure method of authentication.

The Network+ exam expects you to know these different authentication factors, but it also expects you to identify what are known as single-factor authentication, two-factor authentication, and three-factor authentication schemes. If you are authenticating to a system by using only one of the authentication factors, then you are using a single-factor authentication scheme. For example, knowing the user name and password is a single-factor authentication scheme because they are both examples of something you know.

A two-factor authentication scheme would be based on two authentication factors, such as something you know and something you have. For example, you have the bankcard (something you have) and you know the PIN for the bankcard. This authentication scheme is much stronger than simply needing to have the bankcard to gain access to the account. If that were the case, then anyone with the bankcard in their possession could withdraw money from the account.

For the exam, know that smartcards are an example of two-factor authentication because you need to have the smartcard and you need to know the PIN. Another example of two-factor authentication is doing a fingerprint scan and then typing a password. Notice that in this example, the two factors are something you are and something you know.

Single Sign-On (SSO)

An important concept regarding authentication is the concept of *single sign-on,* also known as *SSO.* Single sign-on is the principle that when you authenticate to the network, you then have the capability to access multiple systems based on your authentication information. With SSO, you are not required to authenticate with each different system you access—you authenticate once and then can gain access to multiple systems without authenticating again.

INSIDE THE EXAM

Multifactor Authentication Schemes

The Network+ certification exam is sure to test your knowledge of multifactor authentication schemes, so be sure that you are comfortable with identifying two-factor and three-factor authentication schemes.

The following are common examples of two-factor authentication schemes:

- **Physical token and password** This is an example of authenticating with something you have and something you know.

- **Smartcard and PIN** Again, this example is authenticating with something you have and something you know.

- **Biometrics and password** This example is an authentication scheme that uses something you are combined with something you know.

The reason SSO is so valuable is because many years ago, you would have to authenticate with each server individually. This meant that each system stored a separate user name and password database, and users had to remember various passwords to access more than one server. With SSO, the user logs on with one set of credentials and then accesses many different servers.

AAA

Now that you understand some of the different authentication methods and protocols you need to know for the exam, let's move on to authentication services. When thinking of authentication services, you should think of the following:

- **Authentication** The authentication service is responsible for validating the credentials presented by the user, and typically involves having an authentication database of criteria. For example, when a user logs on with a user name and password, that information is then verified against an account database.

- **Authorization** Once the account information has been verified, the user is granted access to the network. The authorization component may need other criteria besides account information before granting access. For example, the authorization service may require that the authentication request come from a specific subnet.

■ **Accounting** The third authentication service offered is accounting. Accounting deals with logging activity so that you can bill different departments for their usage of the different services.

It is important to note that the services of authentication, authorization, and accounting are collectively known in the industry as *AAA*. Many AAA services have come out over the years, such as RADIUS, Diameter, and TACACS+. These services offer the benefit of a central authentication system that can offer authentication, authorization, and accounting for many types of environments, such as wireless, RAS, or VPNs.

RADIUS

Remote Access Dial-In User Service (RADIUS) is a central authentication service that has been popular for many years. The client computer that needs access to the network connects to the network by dialing into a RAS server or by making a connection to a VPN server from across the Internet. This RAS or VPN server in this case is known as the RADIUS client because it sends the authentication request to the RADIUS server that is running in the background. This RADIUS server verifies the credentials and sends back a reply as to whether the network client is to be granted or denied access (see Figure 15-2).

Diameter

Diameter is a newer AAA protocol and is designed to replace RADIUS. Diameter provides more reliable communication than RADIUS because it is TCP based. Diameter has improved upon the services being offered over RADIUS by being a more secure, scalable protocol.

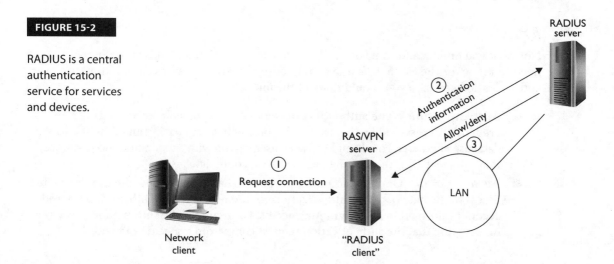

FIGURE 15-2

RADIUS is a central authentication service for services and devices.

TACACS and XTACACS

TACACS stands for *Terminal Access Controller Access-Control System* and originated as an authentication service that ran on UNIX systems. TACACS services ran over TCP and UDP port 49.

A few years after TACACS came out, Cisco created their own proprietary authentication service known as *Extended TACACS (XTACACS)* that worked as a central authentication service for Cisco devices.

TACACS+

The *Terminal Access Controller Access-Control System+ (TACACS+)* protocol is the AAA protocol used by Cisco networks and supersedes the original TACACS and XTACACS protocols. TACACS+ uses TCP for communication and uses the same topology as RADIUS in the sense that the client tries to connect to the network, and the network attached storage (NAS), which is the TACACS client in this case, sends the authentication request to the TACACS server.

TACACS+ has been improved over RADIUS from a security standpoint because it encrypts all information between the TACACS client and the TACACS server, whereas RADIUS encrypts only the password between the RADIUS client and the RADIUS server.

Authorization

Once you have been authenticated to the network, you will then be authorized to access network resources. There are various types of authorization, depending on what it is that you are trying to be authorized for. For example, if you are trying to access a file on the network, authorization is determined according to the permissions assigned to the file. If you are trying to change the time on the server, authorization is determined by your privileges or rights.

Permissions vs. Rights

In the Microsoft world, there is a difference between a permission and a right, so it is important to make that difference clear.

A *permission* is your level of access to a resource such as a file, folder, or object. The permission is a characteristic of the resource and not a characteristic of the user account. For example, if you would like to give Bob the read permission to a file, you would go to the properties of that file and set the permissions. Notice that you do not go to the user account to assign the permissions.

A *right* is your privilege within the operating system to perform a task. For example, when companies deploy Windows 8 to all client systems on the network, users are surprised that they cannot change the time on the computer if they want to. This is because they do not have the Change System Time right. In order to configure an aspect of the operating system, a person must have the appropriate right. This is a significant security feature of the Microsoft operating systems, and it is important to note that administrators can configure the operating system only because the group that they are a member of (Administrators) is assigned all the rights.

Be familiar with the difference between a right and a permission for the exam. A permission is the level of access to a resource, and a right is a privilege to perform an operating system task.

At times, a right can override a permission because the privilege you have been assigned takes precedence over everything else. For example, when configuring a server, I typically configure folders that contain sensitive data with permissions that do not allow administrators access to the folder. It is extremely important to understand that when configuring security, I cannot prevent people from performing their jobs, so the question is, can the administrator still perform backups of the folder if he does not have permissions to read the contents of the folder? The answer is yes, because the administrator has the right to back up files; although he has no permission to the folder, he can read from the folder when running backup software.

Windows Security Subsystem

To help you understand more about authentication and authorization, we will discuss the underlying architecture of Windows and its security subsystem. In this section we review the logon process and discuss different core services that take part in the authentication and authorization process.

A number of components make up the security subsystem in Windows, each playing an integral part in the security functions provided by the operating system. Table 15-1 lists the security subsystems and gives a brief description of them.

The logon process varies depending on whether you are logging on to the local SAM database or to the Active Directory database. The general steps of logging on to a SAM database are as follows:

1. The user presses CTRL-ALT-DEL to log on to the local system. The WinLogon process presents the user with the logon dialog box.
2. The user enters a user name and password and then presses ENTER.
3. The LSA makes a call to an authentication package and then passes the logon information to the NetLogon service.
4. The NetLogon service then compares the user name and password to the local SAM database.
5. Once verified, the NetLogon service returns the user's Security Identifier (SID) and any groups the user is a member of to the LSA.

| TABLE 15-1 | Components of the Windows Security Model |

Security Subsystem Component	Description
WinLogon	User interface provided for interactive logon. The WinLogon presents the logon screen when the user presses CTRL-ALT-DEL.
Local security authority (LSA)	Manages local security policies and user authentication. The LSA is also responsible for generating the access token during the authentication process and writing events to the audit log when an alert is fired by the security reference monitor, based on the audit policy.
Security reference monitor	Verifies that a user has the appropriate permissions or rights to access an object. It also enforces the audit policy provided by the LSA.
NetLogon	A service that verifies the credentials used during logon against the SAM database.
Security accounts manager (SAM)	Handles authentication services for LSA on a local Windows system. The SAM is the database of user and group machine accounts on a local Windows system, such as Windows client computers. The SAM is typically used in a peer-to-peer Windows network.
Active Directory	Microsoft's Directory Service in Windows 2008 and 2012 Server. Active Directory is the name given to the network account database used to store all user accounts and groups that may access network resources. The Active Directory database resides on domain controllers and is kept synchronized.

6. The local LSA generates an "access token," which contains the user account, any groups the user is a member of, and any rights the user might have.

7. The access token is associated with the user, and the Windows Explorer interface is started. The access token is assigned to any programs that are started by the user. This is important because if the user is not allowed to access a resource, she will not be able to sneak past the security of the system by starting an application to access the resource. Each application has the same security context as the user because the access token is applied to the running program. Figure 15-3 displays this logon process.

ⓦatch **The SAM database is the name of the local database of user accounts on a Windows system that is not a domain controller. A domain controller uses the network-wide database, known as Active Directory.**

Logging on
to a local SAM
database

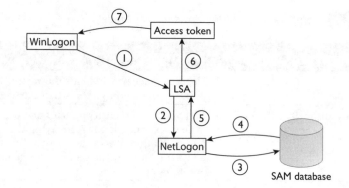

Kerberos

When logging on to the network, the logon process differs dramatically because users are authenticated by the Active Directory database, not the SAM database. Active Directory uses an authentication service known as Kerberos to log a user on to the network. The following is a general outline of the steps involved when logging on to the network using an Active Directory account and Kerberos authentication:

1. The user presses CTRL-ALT-DEL. The WinLogon process displays the user name and password dialog.
2. The user enters a user name, password, and a domain to log on to.
3. The logon credentials are passed to the LSA, which then queries DNS for a domain controller that can authenticate the user.
4. The LSA then contacts the KDC on the domain controller and requests a session ticket.
5. Kerberos contacts Active Directory to authenticate the user.
6. Upon authentication, Kerberos retrieves the user's universal group membership from the global catalog server.

7. After the user has been authenticated against Active Directory and every group membership has been determined, Kerberos sends a session ticket to the client that contains the user account's SID and any group memberships.
8. The LSA then sends that session ticket to the KDC and requests a session ticket for the local workstation.

e x a m

ⓦatch **You will not be required to know all the steps during the logon process, but be aware that Kerberos is a ticket-granting service.**

9. Kerberos sends a session ticket for the local system and the LSA; it then constructs an access token, which is assigned to any processes that the user starts.

Access Tokens

When a user logs on to a system or network, as part of the logon process, an access token is created for the user and is used to determine whether a user should be allowed to access a resource or perform an operating system task. The token maintains all the information required for resource validation and includes the following information:

- **Security Identifier (SID)**   An SID is a unique number assigned to the user. The SID is what Windows uses to identify the user instead of the actual user name. We know Bob as the bsmith user account, but Windows knows Bob as his SID, which looks something like S-1-5-21-2752813485-788270693-1974236881-116.

- **Group Security Identifiers**   The access token contains a list of any groups that the user is a member of. This is important, because when a user double-clicks a resource, the resource is normally configured with permissions assigned to groups. Windows checks to see which groups the user is a member of through the access token and then checks to see if one of those groups has permission to the resource being accessed. If a group that is contained in the access token is allowed access to the resource, the user will gain access to the resource.

- **Primary Group Security Identifier**   For *Portable Operating System Interface for UniX (POSIX)* compliance, you can specify your primary group—this is the group that becomes the owner of files and directories in POSIX environments.

- **Access Rights**   During the logon process, Windows determines the rights you have within the operating system and stores the list of your rights within the access token. For example, if you have the Change System Time right, that information will be stored in the access token during the logon process. If you try to change the time on the computer, your access token is checked for that right; if the right is in the access token, you will be allowed to change the system time.

It is important to note that the access token is re-created only at logon, so if you add a user to a new group while that user is logged on, the user would need to log off and log on again for the access token to contain the new group in the group membership list. After logging on again, the user should be able to access any resources that the newly added group can access because the access token has been updated.

on the job

To see a list of well-known SIDs used by the Windows operating systems, visit http://support.microsoft.com/default.aspx?scid=kb;EN-US;Q243330.

Security Descriptors and Access Control Lists

Most networking environments base their security model on objects. Everything is an object in the network world. For example, users, groups, computers, folders, and files are all examples of objects that you will work with as a network administrator. Every object has security-related information associated with it, known as a security descriptor, which includes a very important piece of information—the access control list (ACL). In general, the ACL is a list of users and/or groups allowed to access the object, as well as the level of permissions those users and groups have. The ACL of an object will have many entries, with each entry representing a security principal (a user or group) that has been given a permission to that resource. Each entry that is contained in the ACL is known as an access control entry (ACE). For example, a folder may be set up to allow the Sales team read-only access, whereas the Marketing group may have the Modify permission. In this example, which is shown in Figure 15-4, the folder (which is the object) has two entries (ACEs) in the ACL: one for the Sales group and one for the Marketing group.

There are two types of ACLs within the security descriptor of an object: the system access control list (SACL) and the discretionary access control list (DACL). The security descriptor

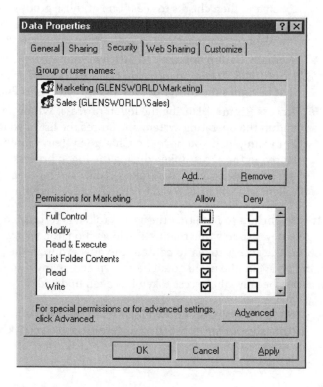

FIGURE 15-4

Looking at an ACL with ACEs in Windows

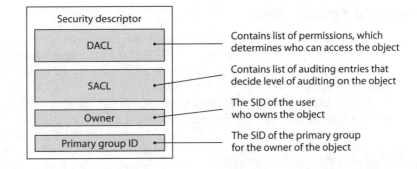

FIGURE 15-5

The security descriptor of an object contains attributes that describe the security of that object.

Security descriptor

DACL — Contains list of permissions, which determines who can access the object

SACL — Contains list of auditing entries that decide level of auditing on the object

Owner — The SID of the user who owns the object

Primary group ID — The SID of the primary group for the owner of the object

also contains attributes specifying who the owner of the object is and the primary group for that owner. Table 15-2 gives a summary of the security descriptor attributes that describe the security of an object. Figure 15-5 displays the common attributes contained in the security descriptor of an object.

In configuring security in a Windows environment, you use user-level security as the method of securing resources. With user-level security, when you configure security for the resource, you will use a DACL and pick which users have access to the resource.

TABLE 15-2   Attributes Contained in the Security Descriptor

Security Descriptor Attribute	Description
System access control list (SACL)	Contains auditing entries for the object if auditing has been enabled for it. For example, if you decide to audit everyone who fails to read the folder, the folder's SACL will have an entry for the Everyone group with the Failure to Read permission.
Discretionary access control list (DACL)	Determines which users and groups have access to this object and what their level of access will be. For example, you may want the Accountants group to be able to modify the contents of a file. The DACL will then have an entry for Accounts Allowed to Modify.
Owner	Maintains a record of the user who owns the resource. In the Microsoft world, the creator of the object is the person who owns it. The owner of the object can change its permissions at any time. This means that the owner of the object is determined by the security descriptor of the object.
Primary group	This attribute specifies the primary group ID of the owner of the resource.

Configuring Permissions

Windows operating systems use user-level security, which gives you the opportunity to choose a list of users or groups who can access the resources when configuring the DACL. Users who are not in the DACL will not be able to access the resource. Figure 15-6 shows a DACL on the security page of a Windows server.

When configuring the user-level security, you will need to first choose which users or groups (known as security principals) will get access to the resource. In Figure 15-6 you can see that Marketing and Sales have access to the folder. Once you choose which security principals may gain access to a resource, you then assign a set of permissions to each entry in the list. There are a number of permissions in any networking environment; Table 15-3 lists a few of the most common permissions found in the Microsoft world.

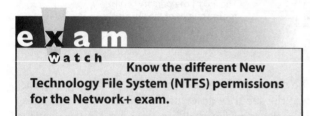

e x a m

ⓦ a t c h **Know the different New Technology File System (NTFS) permissions for the Network+ exam.**

Securing the Registry

Part of securing a Windows system is also securing the Windows Registry. The Registry is a central database of all the user and computer settings on the system. If this information were accessible to a malicious user, the results could be disastrous and could cause the system to

User-level security allows you to select which users have access to the resource.

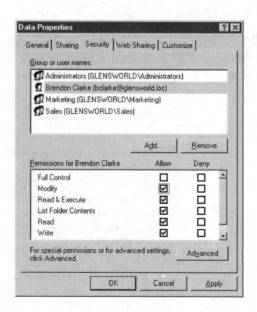

| TABLE 15-3 | Common NTFS Permissions Assigned to Files and Folders |

Access Permission	Description
List Folder Contents	This is a permission assigned to a folder that allows a user to view the contents of the folder but not necessarily to "read" the contents of files in the folder.
Read	This is a folder and file permission that enables a user to open and read the contents of files.
Read & Execute	This is a folder and file permission that allows users to read the contents of files and to execute a program.
Write	This is a file and folder permission that allows a user to modify the contents of a file (write to it) or to create a new file or folder within that folder.
Modify	A folder or file permission that includes all the permissions mentioned previously. Having the Modify permission allows a user to read, execute, delete, list folder contents, and write to the contents of the folder or file.
Full Control	A folder or file permission that gives a user all permissions possible. If you assign the Full Control permission, the user will be able not only to modify the contents of the file, but also to change the permissions on the resource.
Special Permissions	Special permissions are permissions outside of the preceding list. You can assign custom permissions, such as allowing a user to change permissions but not to modify the file.

be dysfunctional. Because of the risk involved in accessing the Registry, Microsoft does not even list the utilities provided to modify it with the rest of the administrative tools. You can use the regedit.exe to modify the Registry and set permissions in it.

There are two ways to secure the Registry. The first way is to secure the folder that holds the Registry files; the second way involves securing each section of the Registry. Let's look at securing the Registry files. The Registry files are stored in the systemroot\system32\config folder, so you can secure the Registry by securing this folder—which is done for you by default. Figure 15-7, which shows the default permissions in Windows Server for the config folder, reveals that authenticated users (users who have logged on) have only the List Folder Contents permission. This means that they can only see that the files are there—they can't modify them.

The second method of securing the Registry involves giving or not giving users specific permissions to a particular area of the Registry. You can control these permissions by using regedit.exe in Windows operating systems. Once you start regedit.exe, you can right-click a folder (known as a key) and then choose permissions, as shown in Figure 15-8.

Once you choose the permissions command, you can modify the DACL for that section of the Registry. To make sure that users can only read a section of the Registry and not

FIGURE 15-7

Default
permissions on
the config folder
allow users to see
the Registry but
not modify it.

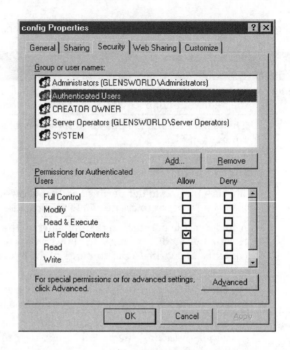

FIGURE 15-8

Changing
permissions in
the Windows
Registry

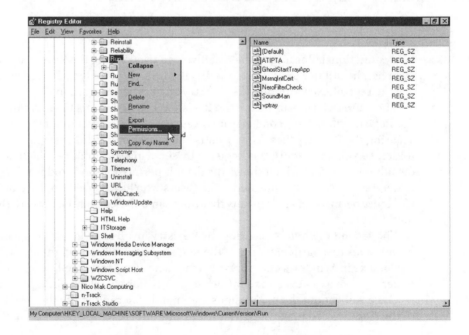

FIGURE 15-9

FIGURE 15-9

Ensuring that
authenticated
users have only
Read permission

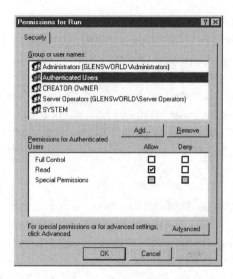

modify it, you can indicate that authenticated users have only the Read permission in the permission list but not the Full Control permission. The Full Control permission would allow a user to create and delete items from the Registry. The Permissions dialog box is shown in Figure 15-9, and Exercise 15-1 demonstrates how to secure the Registry with permissions.

EXERCISE 15-1

Video

Setting Permissions on Registry Keys

In this exercise, you will log on to Windows as a user named Bob, who does not have access to modify the Registry. You will subsequently log on as a network administrator and configure Registry permissions so that Bob can modify the contents of the Run area of the Registry. Keep in mind that you normally would not allow users to modify the Registry and this part of the exercise is simply for demonstration purposes.

1. Log on to Windows 8 as Bob. If you do not have a Bob account, you must create one.
2. Select Start, type **regedit**, and press ENTER.
3. In regedit, navigate to Hkey_Local_Machine\Software\Microsoft\Windows\ CurrentVersion\Run.
4. Right-click the Run folder, and choose New | String Value.
5. An error message should display because Bob does not have permission to modify the Registry.

6. Log off the system and then log on to Windows 8 as an administrator account.

7. Select Start, then type **regedit**, and press ENTER.

8. In regedit, navigate to Hkey_Local_Machine\Software\Microsoft\Windows\CurrentVersion\Run.

9. Right-click the Run folder, and choose Permissions.

10. In the Permissions dialog box, select the user's ACE and assign the Full Control permission. This allows Bob to create an entry only in the Run portion of the Registry.

11. Click OK.

12. Log off as administrator.

13. Log on to Windows 8 as Bob.

14. Select Start, then type **regedit**, and press ENTER.

15. In regedit, navigate to Hkey_Local_Machine\Software\Microsoft\Windows\CurrentVersion\Run.

16. Right-click the Run folder and choose New | String Value.

17. Type **test** and press ENTER. You should be able to create the entry this time because users were assigned Full Control of the Run portion of the Registry.

Configuring User Rights

In the Windows world, actions that users can perform on the network and on their computers are controlled by a feature known as user rights. Remember that a right is an operating system privilege to perform a specific task and that your rights are stored in your access token after you have logged on. As the network administrator, if you need to change a user's rights—for example, you want to allow users to be able to change the time on their computers—in Windows you may modify the Local Security Policy of the Windows system. If you want users to change the time on all computers on the network, you would change the domain security policy, which controls the security settings for the entire domain. To change the user rights within the domain security policy, go to the Group Policy Management Console on your domain controller and alter the Default Domain Policy.

When editing the default domain policy, you should see a Local Policies item on the left. If you expand that by clicking the plus sign and then select User Rights Assignment, you will see all the users' rights that can be modified (as shown in Figure 15-10).

A number of user rights are displayed on the right side of the screen. If you want to modify a user right, you simply double-click the right and then define the policy and add users or groups to the right to specify that you want those individuals to perform that particular operating system task. Figure 15-11 displays adding the users group to the Change the System Time right.

FIGURE 15-10

Looking at
user rights
assignments

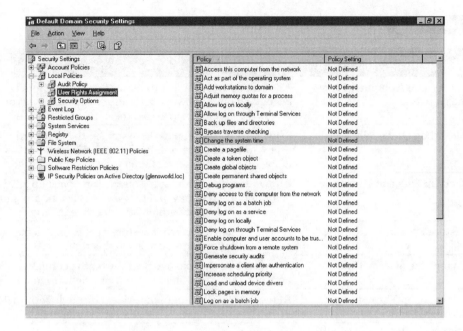

FIGURE 15-11

Assigning the
Change the
System Time right
to all users

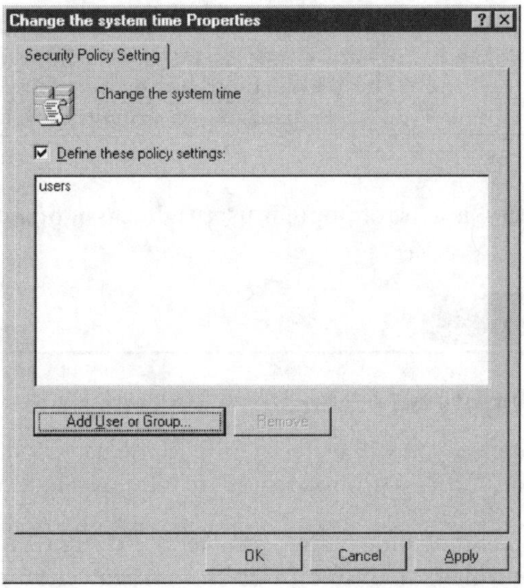

TABLE 15-4	Popular User Rights in Windows

User Right	Description
Access This Computer From the Network	Allows a user to connect to the system from across the network, but not by logging on to the system locally. By default, everyone is allowed to access the system from across the network.
Allow Log On Locally	Allows users to log on to the system at the keyboard if they have a valid user name and password. By default, only administrators have the right to log on locally to servers. Everyone has the right on a Windows client.
Back Up Files and Directories	Allows users to run backup software and back up any file on the computer or server, even if they do not have permissions to the file. By default, only network administrators have this right.
Restore Files and Directories	Allows a user to perform a restore operation of a backup. By default, only network administrators are given this right.
Change the System Time	Allows the user to change the time on the computer. By default, only network administrators are given this right, even on client systems.
Allow Logon Through Terminal Services	Allows users to log on to the system through Terminal Services.
Manage Auditing and Security Logs	Allows users to manage the audit log and security log contained in Windows Event Viewer.
Shut Down the System	Allows users to shut down a Windows system. If users do not have this right, they will be unable to choose the Windows shutdown command.
Take Ownership of Files and Other Objects	Allows users to take ownership of files, folders, and printers. If an individual takes ownership of a resource, that individual controls access to the resource. By default, only administrators can take ownership.

Table 15-4 is a list of popular user rights assignments and their meaning.

EXERCISE 15-2

Video

Modifying User Rights on a Windows System

In this exercise, you will learn to modify the user rights on a Windows system. Be sure that you have an Authors group created in Windows before starting this exercise.

1. Depending on whether you want to change the security of a single system, a domain controller, or all systems in the domain, choose one of the following commands:

    a. **Windows Client** Start | Administrative Tools | Local Security Policy

    b. **Domain Controller**   Start | Administrative Tools | Domain Controller Security Policy

    c. **Entire Domain**   Start | Administrative Tools | Domain Security Policy

2. Under Security Settings (on the left), expand Local Policies and then select User Rights Assignment.

3. To allow the Authors group to back up files, double-click the Back Up Files And Directories policy at the right. List who currently has the right to do backups:

_____

_____

4. Click the Add User Or Group button and add Authors to the list of those who can do backups.

5. Choose OK and then close the policies window.

Configuring Auditing

A major part of configuring network security is making sure that if a user tries to access a protected area of the network, or a hacker tries multiple times to crack a user's password, you are aware of the malicious activity. Configuring auditing on your network server, whether it is Linux or Windows, will allow you to identify suspicious activity on the server and take corrective action. Configuring auditing is a two-step process—you first need to define your audit policy, and then you need to monitor for suspicious activity day in and day out by reviewing the security log. Most auditing software can alert the administrator (usually through e-mail) of suspicious activity. For important network servers, it's always best to have audit logs e-mailed to the administrator (otherwise, a hacker who compromises a machine might clear the audit logs).

Defining the Audit Policy

The first step to configuring auditing is to define your audit policy. When defining your audit policy, you want to enable auditing for specific events within the operating system. An event is something that happens within the system and is usually invoked by a user. For example, logging on or logging off the network is an event. Accessing a folder is also an event. So you need to determine which events you wish to be notified of, and believe me, you need to be extremely picky as to which events you enable. The important thing to remember is that the more events you audit, the more information that is collected, and you don't want to collect unnecessary information because it will hide the important audited data.

In the Windows world, there are a number of events you can enable auditing for, and when you enable auditing, you have to decide whether you care about the success or the failure of such an event. For example, do you care whether someone successfully logs on to the network

TABLE 15-5 Auditing Events in Windows

Audit Event	Description
Audit account logon events	Logs an entry each time a user logs on to the system or domain, if auditing is enabled on the domain controller. If you want to monitor when users fail to log on to the network, you would enable this policy on the domain controller and monitor for failures. An entry will be recorded on the domain controller, but not the local workstation, because the logon request is sent to the domain controller.
Audit account management	Enable this event if you want to be notified when a user or group is created or modified. This is a great event to enable the success of because you can monitor when a user account is created. If you enable auditing on account management, you will become aware when a hacker has created a backdoor account, if in fact he got that far. This event also tracks the resetting of user passwords and group membership changes.
Audit directory service access	Audits access to Active Directory objects if auditing is enabled on a particular Active Directory object.
Audit logon events	If you want to audit the event that a user attempted a logon to the domain from the workstation and to record the audit data on the workstation, you would enable this event. If you were to enable audit account logon events instead of this event, there would be no data recorded on the local system when a user logs on to the domain, because the local system did not attempt to answer the logon request.
Audit object access	You can audit folders, files, and printers if you enable this audit policy. Auditing folders, files, and printers is a two-step process—you would need to enable this policy and then enable auditing on any folders or files you want to audit.
Audit policy change	If you enable this event, it will allow you to monitor any changes to the security policy, such as auditing and user rights.
Audit privilege use	Audits anyone who takes advantage of any rights they have been given. For example, if you give Bob the right to back up files and directories, you may want to know when he actually does a backup to prevent him from performing an extra backup and taking private corporate data home with him.
Audit process tracking	Handles events that deal with programs, such as monitoring when a program activates, when a program exits, and indirect object access.
Audit system events	Enables auditing for system startup and shutdown events; also audits any event that affects the security log or the system security as a whole.

or fails to log on to the network? I am going to choose "we care to know if someone fails to log on to the network." Table 15-5 displays a list of the various events in Windows that you can enable the success or failure of.

To enable auditing on a Windows domain controller, you would configure the Default Domain Controllers Policy by launching the Group Policy Management Console from the

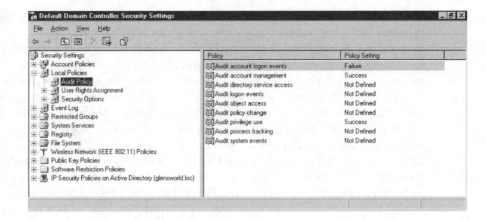

FIGURE 15-12

Configuring
auditing on a
Windows server

Tools menu of Server Manager. Within the policy, expand Local Policies and then select
Audit Policy (as shown in Figure 15-12).

Once you have enabled auditing, you need to monitor the security log for the recording
of such events. One of the biggest mistakes network administrators make is to put a lot of
focus on ensuring that they have enabled auditing, but then never look at the audit log. As a
result, they never know whether their security has been compromised, thereby defeating the
purpose of auditing!

**Make sure that each day you allow enough time to monitor the security log for
suspicious activity. A good idea is to take the first 30 minutes of your morning
to review, archive, and then clear the security log while you have your morning
coffee.**

Monitoring the Security Log

Once you have enabled auditing, you should monitor the security log in Windows Event
Viewer, because that is where all audited data appears. Figure 15-13 shows the Windows Event

FIGURE 15-13

Reviewing the
security log on a
Windows server

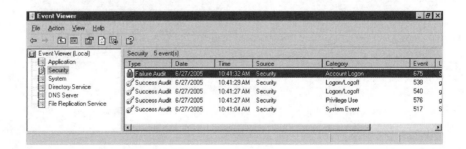

Viewer in Windows 2003. In the Event Viewer, you can review the various events, save the contents of the log to a file for your own records, and then clear the log to start a clean one for the day. It is important to archive the log in case you need to go back to it at a later time. A lot of security problems are not noticed until long after the event has occurred. Windows also allows you to store the log file to any location, including on another secured host.

To review the security log in Windows Server 2012, start Server Manager and then select Tools | Event Viewer. Once in the Event Viewer, expand Windows Logs and select the Security log on the left side, and you will see all the security events. The events with a lock are failure events, and events with a key are successful events. Figure 15-13 displays the security log on a Windows Server, and Exercise 15-3 demonstrates how to enable auditing of account management and failures to log on.

Notice in Figure 15-14 that once auditing has been enabled, you can see that a user has failed to log on to the network on June 27, 2005, at 10:41 A.M. When reviewing the security log, if you need more information about the event, double-click the event, and the properties appear, as shown in Figure 15-14.

In Figure 15-14, you can see the date and time someone failed to log on (at the top), but in the description you can see that someone tried to log on with the gclarke user account. Notice that we also have the IP address of the machine at which the person sat to try to log on. This information can help you track down the individual.

FIGURE 15-14

Viewing details on a failed logon

EXERCISE 15-3

Implementing Auditing in Windows

In this exercise, you will implement auditing on a Windows system. Although this lab has been written for a Windows Server 2012 domain controller, you can apply the same general steps for a Windows Server 2008 system.

1. Ensure that you have the 2012ServerA VM running.

2. To enable auditing, on 2012ServerA go to Server Manager and choose Tools | Group Policy Management.

3. Expand the Forest node, then the Domains node, then the certworld.loc node, and then Group Policy Objects.

4. Right-click Default Domain Controllers Policy and choose Edit.

5. In the Group Policy Management Editor, expand Computer Configuration | Policies | Windows Settings | Security Settings | Local Policies, and then select Audit Policy.

6. Perform the following to configure auditing:

    a. Double-click Audit Account Logon Events and choose Failure.

    b. Double-click Audit Account Management and choose Success.

    c. Ensure all other auditing is disabled.

7. Once you have configured auditing, you can close the Default Domain Controller Security Policy window and then start a command prompt.

8. Type **gpupdate** to force policies to refresh.

9. Log out of 2012ServerA and then try to log on to the system using the user name administrator and the wrong password.

10. Log on to 2012ServerA with an administrative account. Create a new user account in Active Directory with the Active Directory Users and Computers tool.

11. To review the auditing data, you can go to Server Manager and choose Tools | Event Viewer. Once in Event Viewer, expand Windows Logs and select the Security log.

12. Review the security log for the failed logon (should have a lock icon) and for the success of the account being created (should have a key icon).

Implementing Network Security

Most organizations and individuals have an Internet connection allowing them to communicate with the outside world. Although this provides access to a wealth of information, there are a number of security risks involved in connecting directly to the Internet. As a general rule, you should always put another device between you and the Internet, and that device is known as a firewall.

Network Access Security

In order to implement a highly secure network environment, you must start by controlling the type of traffic that can enter and leave the network and control the systems and devices that can make a connection to the network.

Controlling Traffic

To control which traffic enters or leaves different parts of your network, you will configure rules on your firewall or routers known as access control lists (ACLs). The ACL is a list of rules either permitting or denying different pieces of traffic from the network. You will learn more about ACLs in the upcoming paragraphs, but the general idea is that the router or firewall receives a packet and then typically allows or denies the packet based on the source or destination IP address (IP filtering), or the source and destination port (port filtering).

Network Access Control

Network access control (NAC) is a hot technology today, and it allows you to control who gains access to a wired or wireless network based on the state of the connecting system, which is known as *posture assessment*. With network access control, you can specify conditions that a system must meet to gain access to the network. If those conditions are not met, you can send them to a restricted network, which allows them to remedy their system.

For example, you may require that for a system to connect to the network, it must have antivirus software installed, with the antivirus definitions up to date. You may also require that the system have a personal firewall enabled. If any of these conditions are not met, the NAC system places the client on a restricted network, where they can typically apply patches or, in this case, perform an update of the virus definitions.

When connected to the restricted network, the client has no access to network resources because communication to the private company network from the restricted network is controlled. Figure 15-15 displays a network access control environment.

FIGURE 15-15   Network access control is used to place health requirements on systems connecting to the network.

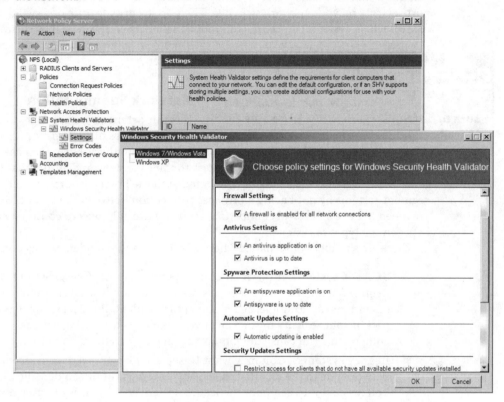

There are many scenarios where NAC is being used today, as demonstrated in the following examples:

- **Connecting to wireless**   When connecting to a wireless network, the NAC system may require you to accept the terms of wireless network usage before you are given access to the network.

- **Patch status**   A common scenario where NAC is being used is when a client connects to a network, either locally or through VPN, the client's health is checked to ensure it has antivirus software installed, virus definitions are up to date, and the system is up to date with patches before the client is allowed to connect to the network.

- **Connecting to a switch**   If the switch is 802.1x compliant, it can be configured to ensure that the connecting client is authenticated by an authentication service (such as RADIUS) before allowing the client access to the network. You will learn more about 802.1x later in this chapter.

Port Security

Another common method used to control who can gain access to the network is to implement port security on your network switches. The port security feature of a switch allows you to control which systems can connect to individual ports on the switch by their MAC address. To refresh your memory on port security, review Chapter 7.

Network Segmentation

It is important to ensure that you separate different types of systems, or environments, from one another to help increase security. For example, a hotel that allows wireless access to their guests would ensure that the systems from the wireless network are not connected with the hotel corporate systems. You typically segment systems by not having a physical connection between the two networks, or if you need to have a physical connection, then you use a firewall to control communication between the types of systems.

There are a number of scenarios where it is important to implement network segmentation:

- **SCADA systems/industrial control systems**   *Supervisory Control And Data Acquisition (SCADA)* is a special system used in industrial environments to monitor operations, for example, at a manufacturing plant. Physical security is an important part of your security in such an environment, as tampering with any of the SCADA components can cause the monitoring and alarms to malfunction.

- **Legacy systems**   You may want to separate legacy systems from the rest of the network due to the fact that the legacy system is running older software or protocols. You may want to segment the legacy system because it is older or not as secure as newer systems and having it connected to the same network as newer systems would lower the security of the newer systems. You could place Windows XP and Windows Server 2003 in the category of a legacy system.

- **Separate private/public networks**   You will learn more about zones in the next section, but you may want to separate the private network (your LAN) from any untrusted public network (the Internet) to help reduce chances of attack from the Internet.

- **Honeypot/honeynet**   You will learn more about honeypots in the "Intrusion Detection Systems" section of this chapter, but as a quick explanation, a honeypot is a system designed to attract a hacker to attack it instead of a production system. You want to ensure you segment the honeypot on a different network than the production network so that a hacker who is trying to hack into the honeypot does not see the production system.

- **Testing lab**   Any test environment should be segmented from the production network. One good reason is the test lab will typically use the same IP addresses and computer names that the production systems are using, so you want to make sure it is not on the same network (IP and name conflicts).

- **Performance optimization and load balancing**   You may choose to segment systems as a way to load-balance some of the work. Instead of having all users connect to one server for service, you place that service on two different servers, which are each on a different network. This way, each network is being serviced by one server with half the traffic. You could also load-balance traffic by having a separate switch or wiring closet for each floor and have that floor connect to a layer 3 switch in order to segment the traffic of each floor from one another.

- **Security**   One of the biggest reasons to segment is for security purposes. You want to control which systems are able to communicate with other systems, so you divide the systems across multiple network segments and control communication between those segments. VLANs are a great tool to use for segmentation.

- **Compliance**   You may need to segment systems across different segments for compliance purposes. A vendor may not support a product unless it is separated from different types of systems. Regulations governing your organization may also have compliance requirements that involve controlling communication to systems that hold sensitive data.

Firewalls

One of the best techniques for securing the network is to use firewalls to control what traffic is allowed to enter or leave the network. You will learn more about firewalls in Chapter 16.

CERTIFICATION OBJECTIVE 15.04

Securing Communication

As more companies go online, the need to protect data becomes more prevalent. The information technology industry has striven to provide a more secure data transfer mechanism because TCP/IP was not designed as a secure network protocol. You can keep up to date with worldwide vulnerabilities affecting all vendors by visiting the website for the Computer Emergency Response Team at www.cert.org. Data needs to be protected during a transfer and guaranteed that it is sent to its recipient unread and unmodified. Because of this need, encryption services have grown in popularity. Multiple encryption implementations have been published and are now available to the public. Several standards have also come about that deal with encrypting data in transit, such as Secure Sockets Layer (SSL) and Internet Protocol Security (IPSec).

To understand encryption, you must first learn how it works. You will also be introduced to some specific methods and algorithms used for encryption services. In addition, the main standards that have been defined will be explained, as will a few other data protection methods.

Defining Data Encryption

Many different types of data encryption are available with each methodology, providing different advantages and varying levels of security. To date, there are a number of complex encryption standards that have not yet been broken, along with other standards that use simple encryption methods and have been cracked, but can still provide a level of security if used appropriately. Encryption can be defined as the process of taking plain-text data and converting it to a meaningless format that is unreadable, better known as cipher text. Once the data has been transformed into cipher text, anyone wishing to decrypt the content needs to know the encryption key to convert the data back to plain text, as shown in Figure 15-16.

The encryption key is passed through a mathematical algorithm to encrypt the contents of the data. There are a limited number of encryption algorithms, so if a hacker knows the algorithm, that is not considered a security issue, but if a hacker obtains the encryption key, that is a compromise of network security. There are two popular forms of encryption: symmetric key encryption and asymmetric (public key) encryption, each of which is discussed in the following sections.

Symmetric Key Encryption

The most basic form of encryption is *symmetric key* encryption, so named because both the sender and the receiver of the data use the same key to encrypt and decrypt the data. The

FIGURE 15-16 Encryption standards convert plain text to cipher text.

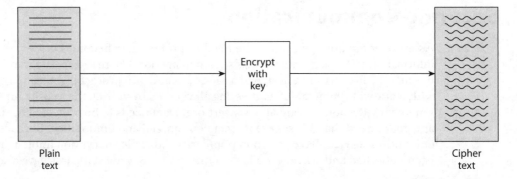

problem with symmetric key encryption is that you must have a secure way to transport the encryption key to individuals you wish to exchange data with. If you do not use a secure method to send the key to a recipient, someone may intercept the key. This makes encryption useless, because now the interceptor can decrypt the data, knowing the key. In addition, if you are using encryption techniques for multiple recipients, you may not want one person to have access to another's data. Now you must keep multiple single keys per person, which can become extremely cumbersome.

Asymmetric Encryption

A second form of encryption is *asymmetric* encryption, which uses a public key/private key pair for the encrypting and decrypting of the data. Asymmetric encryption requires two mathematically related but separate keys in order to perform the encryption/decryption work.

With asymmetric encryption, the public key is freely distributed to anyone you choose. The second key, the private key, is kept in a secure location and is used only by you—hence, the term "private." Both keys are required to send data securely over a network structure. For example, say you want to send data to Bob by encrypting the content. You would retrieve his public key and encrypt the data with it. Once you have encrypted the data, you can send it over the wire, knowing that anyone who intercepts the message would need the related key (Bob's private key) to decrypt the message. Once you send the information on the wire, nothing but the related private key can decrypt the message—not even the public key you have. And because Bob is the only person who possesses the related private key, he is the only one who can decrypt the message, as shown in Figure 15-17.

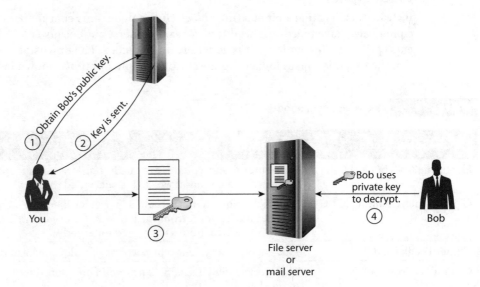

FIGURE 15-17

Encrypting data with a public key/private key structure

This system works well because it enables the public key to be sent over an insecure communications channel while still maintaining an appropriate level of security—remember that it would be difficult to share the key securely with symmetric encryption.

Encryption Methods

When encrypting data, different methods can be used. Each has its own advantages and drawbacks, and some methods work in cooperation with others to provide an overall solution. The more common methods are discussed and explained here.

Stream Cipher

Stream cipher algorithms encrypt data one bit at a time. Plain-text bits are converted into encrypted cipher text. This method is usually not as secure as block cipher techniques, but it generally executes faster. In addition, the cipher text is always the same size as the original plain text and is less prone to errors. If an error occurs during the encryption process, usually this affects only a single bit instead of the whole string. In contrast, when block ciphers contain errors, the entire block becomes unintelligible.

Block Cipher

Instead of encrypting a bit at a time, *block cipher* algorithms encrypt data in blocks. Block ciphers also have more overhead than stream ciphers, but because block cipher handles encryption at a higher level, it is generally more secure. The downside of block cipher is that the execution takes longer. Numerous block cipher options (shown in Table 15-7) are

TABLE 15-7   Block Cipher Methods

Block Cipher Mode	Description
Electronic Codebook (ECB)	Each block is encrypted individually. If information reappears in the same text, such as a common word, it is encrypted the same way.
Cipher Block Chaining (CBC)	Feedback is inserted into each cipher block before it is encrypted. It includes information from the block that preceded it. This ensures that repetitive information is encrypted differently.
Cipher Feedback (CFB)	This enables one to encrypt portions of a block instead of an entire block.
Output Feedback (OFB)	This works much like CFB. The underlying shift registers are used somewhat differently.

available, such as Electronic Codebook (ECB), Cipher Block Chaining (CBC), Cipher Feedback (CFB), and Output Feedback (OFB).

Padding

When encrypting data, plain-text messages usually do not take up an even number of blocks. Many times, padding must be added to the last block to complete the data stream. The data added can contain all ones, all zeros, or a combination of ones and zeros. The encryption algorithm used is responsible for determining the padding that will be applied. Various padding techniques are available and used, depending on the algorithm implementation.

Encryption Standards

As encryption has become more popular, the need for industry standards has arisen. Standards for different implementations and algorithms have been defined to move the industry in the same direction. The most popular standards are discussed here with a brief history and explanation.

DES and AES

The *Data Encryption Standard (DES)* was created and standardized by IBM in 1977. It is a 64-bit block symmetric algorithm and is specified in the American National Standards Institute (ANSI) X3.92 and X3.106 standards for both enciphering and deciphering operations, which are based on a binary number. In addition, the National Security Agency (NSA) uses it as the standard for all government organizations. There currently exist 72 quadrillion (72,000,000,000,000,000) encryption keys for DES, in which a key is chosen at random. DES uses a block cipher methodology to apply a 56-bit symmetric key to each 64-bit block. An additional form of DES, known as triple DES, runs the information through three mathematical operations using three different 56-bit keys to create 168-bit encryption. Like DES, 3DES is a block cipher.

The *Advanced Encryption Standard (AES)* has replaced 3DES as the new standard for symmetric encryption algorithms. AES is a block cipher that supports 128-bit, 192-bit, and 256-bit encryption.

RSA

Ron Rivest, Adi Shamir, and Leonard Adleman (RSA) were the individuals responsible for creating the RSA standard at MIT, which defines the mathematical properties for using the public key encryption methodology. The algorithm randomly generates a very large prime number that is used for the public key, which is then consequently used to derive another prime number for the private key via mathematical computations (prime numbers have no pattern). Many forms of RSA encryption are in use today, including the popular PGP. PGP (Pretty Good Privacy) has worked well in the past. Some vendors have included implementations of RSA in their core application code. Versions 4–7 of Novell NetWare have RSA encryption built into the client and server to provide a secure communications channel.

Methods of Securing Traffic

The Network+ exam requires you to be familiar with a number of technologies, along with their related terms, that can be used to secure network traffic. Securing network traffic refers to techniques that can be used to encrypt the network traffic that is sent along the wire (or in the air) between the two systems.

Digital Signatures

Digital signatures are used to verify that a message was sent from the appropriate sender and that it has not been tampered with. When using digital signatures, the message is not altered, but a signature string is attached to verify its validity. Digital signatures usually use a public key algorithm. A public key is used to verify the message, whereas the private key is used to create the signature. A trusted application is usually present on a secure computer somewhere on the network that is used to validate the signature provided. This computer is known as a certificate authority and stores the public key of every user on the system. Certificates are released containing the public key of the user in question. When these are dispensed, the certificate authority signs each package with its own private key. Several vendors offer commercial products that provide certificate authority services. For example, Microsoft Exchange Server can be set up to provide certificates to mail clients by using digital signatures. Lotus Domino also employs this strategy to authenticate client workstations to the server. Employing this methodology doesn't mean you're protecting your data completely, but you will know if it has been tampered with.

It is important not only to encrypt data traveling across the network, but also to encrypt it when it gets stored as a file—the lack of file encryption leads to theft of data, which is what we hear about increasingly. On Windows, certificates can be used to encrypt files on an NTFS partition through a feature known as the Encrypting File System (EFS). When implementing EFS in Windows 2000, only the user who encrypted the file can decrypt the file and use it, but in the later Windows operating systems, you can select additional persons who can decrypt the file. With EFS, the recovery agent always has the capability to decrypt a file as well, and by default, the Administrator account is the recovery agent. The benefit of having the recovery agent is that if the person who encrypted the file is no longer available, the recovery agent can decrypt the file so that the organization can access the data. The disadvantage in some Windows versions is if the recovery agent user account is compromised, so is all of the encrypted data.

Internet Protocol Security

Internet Protocol Security (IPSec) is a fairly new security protocol that can be used to encrypt all IP traffic, as well as take part in authentication services and ensure the integrity of data sent across an IP network. One of the things that is so exciting about IPSec is that if you enable it by means of an IPSec policy, you will not need to configure different encryption methods for each type of application you run on the computer—all IP traffic is encrypted by IPSec once the policy is implemented. For example, because IPSec encrypts all traffic, you do not need to configure a separate encryption technology for your web server, FTP server, and Telnet server. They all run on top of TCP/IP, so IPSec can be used to secure traffic presented by each application.

When you enable IPSec, you can use one of the default built-in policies. The IPSec policy is used to determine the type of traffic to be encrypted and the method used to encrypt the traffic. The three default IPSec policies are as follows:

- **Client (respond only)**   If asked to communicate securely, this system will respond by using IPSec, but it will never request or initiate secure communication.
- **Server (request security)**   When enabled, this system will request to use IPSec to secure traffic; if the remote system does not support IPSec, the system will communicate insecurely.
- **Secure server (require security)**   This system will communicate with a remote system only if the remote system supports and uses IPSec.

Secure Sockets Layer

Secure Sockets Layer (SSL) is a session-layer protocol that encrypts data sent from any higher-layer program, such as FTP, HTTP, Simple Mail Transfer Protocol (SMTP), and so on. SSL has become the standard method of encrypting traffic between a web client and a web server, ensuring that malicious users cannot capture such traffic and read it.

SSL can work only with guaranteed transports—or basically anything using the TCP protocol—and is made up of two protocols: SSL Handshake and SSL Record:

- *SSL Handshake* is used to create a secure session between the two systems that are communicating. This includes all methods and parameters used for the encryption.
- *SSL Record* is used to encrypt all data packets, including the SSL Handshake data packets.

SSL is mainly used on e-commerce websites during the exchange of personal information such as credit card numbers because SSL can encrypt the traffic between the client and the server.

Point-to-Point Tunneling Protocol

The *Point-to-Point Tunneling Protocol (PPTP)* is a VPN protocol used to create an encrypted tunnel over a TCP/IP network such as the Internet.

PPTP and L2TP are VPN protocols. PPTP uses MPPE to encrypt VPN traffic and uses TCP port 1723. L2TP uses IPSec to encrypt VPN traffic and uses UDP ports 500, 4500, and 1701.

All data that passes through the tunnel is in an encrypted format. The Point-to-Point Tunneling Protocol was dominant in older Microsoft VPN solutions and used Microsoft Point-to-Point Encryption (MPPE) to encrypt the traffic that passed through the tunnel.

Layer Two Tunneling Protocol

The *Layer Two Tunneling Protocol (L2TP)* is similar to PPTP, in that it creates a tunnel over the Internet between two points using PPP data packets encapsulated in TCP/IP protocol packets (for regular networks, you can also use IPX/SPX and NetBEUI). While using IPSec for encryption, the combination will create a VPN. L2TP is supported by Windows 2000 and higher operating systems, but does not support implementation over Asynchronous Transfer Mode (ATM), X.25, or Frame Relay networks.

Kerberos

Kerberos is a distributed authentication security protocol using private keys that verify the validity of a user during logon and will repeatedly do the same every time a request is made. This is useful when a user accesses the network from a workstation that is not secure. A workstation might be in a public kiosk, and anyone may be allowed to log on to the network as a guest, but regular users may visit the kiosk to log on using their individual user accounts.

WEP

The *Wired Equivalent Privacy (WEP)* protocol is used to encrypt wireless traffic from a wireless client to the wireless access point. Once the data reaches the wireless access point, it is decrypted and then sent along the wired network if needed. WEP uses a symmetric key configured on the access point and then on each client used to encrypt the network traffic. It has been proven that a WEP encryption key is fairly easy to break with products such as Airsnort or WEPCrack.

WPA

Wi-Fi Protected Access (WPA) is the answer from the wireless community to provide more security with wireless communications now that WEP has been proven to be vulnerable to hackers. WPA has improved upon WEP by offering two key features:

- ■ **Improved encryption** WPA scrambles the encryption keys by passing them through a hashing algorithm and then performing an integrity check to verify that the keys have not been tampered with. The protocol used to scramble the keys is the Temporal Key Integrity Protocol (TKIP), which builds off WEP devices. Typically, only a software upgrade is needed for WEP devices to use WPA.
- ■ **Authentication** WPA uses Extensible Authentication Protocol (EAP) as the authentication protocol, which allows for more secure authentication using public key encryption and authentication. WEP currently does not offer a method of authentication.

WPA has been superseded by the more secure WPA2. For more information on wireless protocols such as WEP, WPA, and WPA2, read Chapter 10.

802.1x

Wireless security has generated much interest within the IT industry because it is such a convenient technology. It doesn't need cables all over the place, but still, because of the lack of physical security, some form of authentication is needed to find out who is connecting to the wireless network.

The 802.1x standard provides an authentication technique that leverages EAP and RADIUS to authenticate a user connecting to network devices such as a VPN server, Ethernet switch, or a wireless access point. Figure 15-18 displays a typical 802.1x authentication infrastructure.

In the figure you can see that the wireless client is connecting to the wireless access point. The wireless access point, which is the RADIUS client in this scenario, sends the request to the RADIUS server for the user to be authenticated. The RADIUS server challenges the wireless client for a user name and password. After the wireless client supplies the user name and password, the RADIUS server authenticates the client, and the wireless access point allows the wireless client to access the network.

Note that other examples of RADIUS clients are an Ethernet switch to authenticate someone connecting to a wired network and a VPN server to authenticate users connecting remotely to the network.

FIGURE 15-18   802.1x using a RADIUS server to authenticate a wireless client

Wireless client

Wireless access point

RADIUS server

Is user authenticated?

Yes: Authenticated

CERTIFICATION OBJECTIVE 15.05

Fault Tolerance and Disaster Recovery

This section introduces two significant topic areas: fault tolerance and disaster recovery. Fault tolerance is the concept of duplicating devices such as drives, power supplies, and network links so that if those components fail, another one becomes operative right away. If, for some reason, your fault tolerance plan is not effective, a disaster recovery procedure would be in place to help you recover from such failures.

Fault Tolerance

Fault tolerance is the concept of ensuring that systems will continue to function because you have created a solution that involves having backup copies of power supplies, hard drives, and network links. If one of the links goes down, there would be another link ready to kick in at any time, reducing downtime and ensuring an available solution to clients on the network. The following is a list of widely used fault-tolerant components found on the network:

- **RAID solutions** *Redundant Array of Independent Disks (RAID)* is the concept of storing redundant data on additional drives in case one drive in the RAID solution should fail. RAID solutions can apply to hardware or software. The hardware solution involves having a RAID controller that controls the RAID array, whereas in a software solution, the RAID solution is managed by software such as the network operating system. The software solutions are cheaper, but the hardware solutions offer better performance and are more flexible. For more information on RAID volumes, refer to Chapter 14.

- **Power** A number of network devices, such as servers, support a fault-tolerant power source, such as a power supply, in case the original power supply fails.

- **Battery backup/UPS** One method of ensuring a system or device has fault tolerance on power is to ensure you supply an alternative power source, such as a battery, as a backup power source. Most networks will have uninterruptible power supply (UPS) devices to provide battery backup to servers, switches, and routers.

- **Network link** In a number of networking environments, a fault-tolerant network link is created to ensure that one network location can communicate with another location at all times or that there is a constant connection to the wide area network (WAN) environment or Internet. A number of business applications require a network link at all times; therefore, when you design the network infrastructure, you should decide whether the organization requires a fault-tolerant network link.

The goal of fault tolerance is to ensure that you eliminate all single points of failure. To determine single points of failure, you look at a resource and ask yourself, "If this component fails, will it still operate?" If the answer is no, then you need to ensure there is an alternative component. For example, if the network card in the server fails, can clients still communicate with the server? Because the answer is no, we need to ensure we add a second network card to the server. The following are some considerations that should be made when considering single points of failure:

- **Critical nodes**   All critical nodes should be fault tolerant. If a critical node fails, a standby server should become available so that users do not notice the critical system has become unavailable. Clustering technology is a great solution for critical nodes, which offers additional servers that can act on behalf of the critical node when it fails.
- **Critical assets**   All critical assets should have fault tolerance. For example, the network switch and router are critical to network operations, so you want to be sure to have fault-tolerant solutions configured with them so that if a switch fails, there is a second one that can take over the responsibility.
- **Redundancy**   The key point with eliminating single points of failure is ensuring you have redundancy on all critical components to the functionality of the network and business operations.

Disaster Recovery and Business Continuity

Disaster recovery is a matter of ensuring that you can help the company recover from any kind of disaster. When preparing for disaster, you need to make sure that your disaster recovery plan includes backup and restore plans, contact information for product vendors, and step-by-step instructions on how to recover each part of your information systems. The step-by-step plan should contain the location of backup tapes, specify which tapes to restore in different scenarios, and list the steps for rebuilding servers, including detailed information on what to do when a disk fails and how to replace and rebuild the data.

A number of disaster recovery documents overlook key elements, such as the location of software and CD keys needed to rebuild the system. Be sure that contact information for hardware and software vendors is included in the plan so that if you need to replace an item such as a disk, you can contact the vendor.

Along with detailed recovery steps, a disaster recovery plan should contain detailed information on backup and restore strategies, offsite storage, hot and cold spares, and hot and cold sites.

The disaster recovery plan is designed to ensure the business can still operate, but it is more focused on the recovery of assets such as servers, routers, and switches. The company should also have a business continuity plan, which includes the disaster recovery plan, but also includes a number of other considerations that need to be made in order to continue business operations in case of disaster. Some examples of considerations that should be documented in the business continuity plan are

- **Successors** In case of a disaster in which upper-level management ceases to exist, you want to ensure you have designated successors to run the company.
- **Alternative sites** In case of a disaster in which the company location becomes unavailable, you want to ensure you have an alternative location to continue business operations.

Backup and Restore Strategies

Chapter 14 discussed various backup and restore strategies and emphasized the need to guarantee that a strong backup plan is in place to aid disaster recovery. If you have not created a strong backup plan that specifies what to back up and how frequently, you may not be able to recover from disaster. Be sure to review your backup strategy and make certain that you have all the necessary data stored on backup media. You should periodically verify that you can actually restore data using a test environment. Further, make sure that you know and have documented the restore strategy to implement when disaster strikes.

Offsite Storage

It is absolutely critical that you store a copy of the backups offsite in a secure location. You cannot totally rely on the backups stored on your own site because they will be of no value if the building burns down, destroying all your servers along with the tape backups stored at the location. You must make certain a copy of the backups is stored offsite.

Hot and Cold Spares

When preparing for recovery, organizations typically maintain spares of equipment ready to be used in case of device failures. For example, they may have a spare power supply, hard drive, or network card available in case the original one fails. You can also have spare switches and servers available in case one of those devices fails. By having the spare available, you don't need to wait for a part to be delivered to your facility after a device has failed, creating excessive downtime. With a spare available, downtime is minimized. There are two types of directions that you can take with spares, as follows:

Be sure to know the difference between a hot spare and a cold spare for the exam.

- **Hot spares** A hot spare is a spare component that is typically connected and powered on in case the primary device should fail. When the primary device fails, failover kicks in, allowing the spare device to take over the workload immediately. No time is needed to connect the device or turn it on—hot spares are ready to work.

■ **Cold spares**   A cold spare is a device that is not powered on and is usually sitting on a shelf in a server room. A cold spare involves an increase in downtime because the device must be connected and powered up before it can take over the function of the original device.

Hot, Warm, and Cold Sites

Disaster involves more than your servers and the data on them; you need to ask yourself, "How can I continue business in the event of a disaster? What if my building burns down? Where can my employees perform their work and continue business operations?" You need to investigate whether your organization will invest in an additional work location, known as a site, in case the original office building becomes unavailable because of fire, flood, or an extended power outage.

When deciding on an alternative location, or site, to continue business operations in the event of a failure, you must choose between a hot site, a cold site, and a warm site. Each site type is explained as follows:

■ **Hot site**   A hot site is an alternative location that provides adequate space, networking hardware, and networking software for you to maintain business operations if disaster strikes. This hardware and software should include any data that your staff would need in the event of a disaster, so the provider of the hot site should ensure that the data is up to date and the hot site is ready 24/7 if your organization needs it.

■ **Cold site**   A cold site is an alternative location where you typically have arranged to have the space available, but not the networking hardware or software. Providing the hardware and software would be your responsibility in the event of a disaster. A cold site takes time to prepare following a disaster because only the space is made available.

■ **Warm site**   A warm site occupies the middle ground between a hot site and a cold site. It is an alternative location with office space and spare networking equipment, such as a server and backup devices, so that you can quickly restore your organization's network in an emergency.

CERTIFICATION OBJECTIVE 15.06

Guidelines to Protect the Network

A number of concepts can be applied to your network to help secure the company and its data. This section is intended to provide a best-practice guide to guarding your corporate investments. Although it is not designed to be a complete list, this section outlines common practices that should be followed to help create a more secure infrastructure.

One of the most important things to understand about network security is that you should take a layered approach to securing network data. In other words, don't focus too much on just one area of protection, but implement all layers of protection. This section outlines common mitigation techniques to help reduce the likelihood that your organization will be attacked.

Physical Security

Physical security plays an important role in any security plan. If someone can get physical access to a system, you can pretty much guarantee that they could bypass the logon screen and gain access to confidential data stored on the system. It is important that you take the necessary steps to ensure physical access to systems is controlled.

The following is a list of physical security measures that should be considered:

- **Physical perimeter security**   In high-secure environments, a fence is placed around the perimeter of the location and a guard at a gate is used to control who gets access to the premises.
- **Swipe cards**   Within the facility you can control access to different areas with swipe cards or keypad locks.
- **Locked doors**   It is important that critical systems be locked in a room and access to that room be controlled. Servers should be placed in a locked server room so that physical access to the servers can be controlled.
- **CMOS settings**   You can change a number of complementary metal-oxide semiconductor (CMOS) settings on the system that deal with physical security. For example, you can ensure that the system cannot boot from a CD-ROM. If someone can boot from a CD-ROM, that person can load his own operating system and potentially bypass security. You can also disable ports, such as universal serial bus (USB) ports, in CMOS, which will ensure someone is not using a thumb drive to take data away.

Firewalls

One of the first things you should do to protect your network from Internet attacks is to make sure that you have a firewall between your corporate systems and the Internet. In addition, you should create a *demilitarized zone (DMZ)*, which is an area on the network where you have selected certain data from the Internet to pass through and reach selected services, such as a web server. Figure 15-19 displays a DMZ created by configuring two firewalls; one firewall allows HTTP traffic destined for port 80 to pass through it, and the second firewall connects to the private LAN and allows no traffic to pass through it— essentially protecting internal resources.

FIGURE 15-19 · A DMZ is used to publish servers while maintaining security through controlled access to those servers. The DMZ is also used to protect the private LAN.

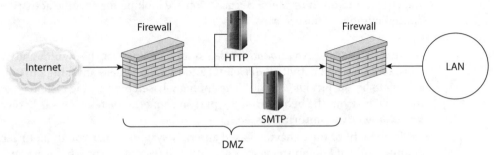

When designing your firewall strategy, do not be afraid to create multiple layers of firewalls and allow certain traffic to pass through different resources. Also, when using multiple firewalls, be sure to use different vendors for each firewall so that if there is a vulnerability in a firewall and a hacker learns this and bypasses the security of the first firewall, the hacker cannot get past the second firewall using the same technique. For additional security, consider installing personal firewall software on every device on the LAN.

Intrusion Detection Systems

As part of your security best practices, you may consider installing an intrusion detection system. As you learned in Chapter 3, an *intrusion detection system (IDS)* is a security device that monitors system or network activity and then notifies the administrator of any suspicious activity. The IDS is an important device to complement the firewall because it will notify you not only of suspicious activity against the firewall, but also of suspicious activity inside the network.

Analysis Methods

How the IDS determines that there is suspicious traffic depends on the type of analysis the IDS performs. The following outlines the different methods that an IDS uses to determine if there is suspicious traffic.

Signature Based   With a *signature-based* IDS, a signature file lists what is considered suspicious activity. When the IDS captures activity, it compares the activity against the signature database, and if there is a match, it sends out notification of an intrusion.

For example, you may have a system that notifies when a number of SYN messages are sent from a single IP address to a number of ports on the same target system within a short period. This is a classic signature of a port scan.

The benefit of a signature-based system is it has few false-positives—meaning minimal false alarms—because a signature-based system bases everything on the signatures that you configured on the system. Because you are looking for specific activity, you will have a limited number of false alarms.

Anomaly Based   An *anomaly-based* system means that the system understands what is considered normal activity (a baseline) and then considers anything outside that normal activity to be "suspicious" activity. The anomaly-based monitoring system typically determines the baseline from the behavior of the person using the system. This is known as a *behavior-based anomaly* monitoring system.

The benefit of the behavior-based anomaly system is that you do not need to configure a definition file of known suspicious activity; the system learns what is normal based on the users' activity. The drawback of a behavior-based system is that anything outside the norm is considered suspicious, which results in a large number of false alarms (false-positives).

Heuristic   *Heuristic* analysis identifies malicious activity based on past experience and is very popular with antivirus software. With virus detection, the goal of heuristic analysis is to detect new, unknown viruses. The virus protection software typically runs the program in an isolated area known as a virtual machine. The virus protection software then analyzes everything the program does when it executes, looking for malicious activity such as file overwrites, signs that the program is replicating itself, or signs that it is trying to hide itself.

Types of Intrusion Detection Systems

When implementing your intrusion detection system, you have a choice of implementing a host-based IDS or a network-based IDS. The following is an overview of the difference between the two types:

- **Host based**   Host-based intrusion detection systems monitor the local system for suspicious activity. A host-based IDS is typically a piece of software installed on the system and can only monitor activity on the system it is installed on.
- **Network based**   A network-based IDS monitors network traffic for suspicious behavior. It has the capability of monitoring the entire network and comparing that traffic to known malicious traffic patterns. When a match is found, an alert can be triggered. A network-based IDS can be software loaded on a system that monitors network traffic, or it can be a hardware device.

Intrusion detection systems can be either active or passive. An *active* IDS will monitor activity, log any suspicious activity, and then take some form of corrective action. For example, if a system is doing a port scan on the network, the IDS may log the activity but also disconnect the system creating the suspicious action from the network. Note that an active IDS is now known as an *intrusion prevention system (IPS)*.

A *passive* intrusion detection system does not take any corrective action when suspicious activity has been identified. The passive IDS will simply identify the activity and then log to a file any information needed during an investigation. The passive IDS does not take any corrective action.

Honeypots and Honeynets

Another common network component that makes up part of the security infrastructure of a network is a honeypot. A *honeypot* is a system that is placed on the private network or in a DMZ, and is designed to lure the hacker away from production systems and to the honeypot. The hacker spends time trying to hack into the honeypot while you are logging the activity and having the host-based IDS installed on the honeypot send you notification of the hacker's existence!

Most companies make the mistake of not securing the honeypot because they want the hacker to break into the honeypot, but if you make it too easy for the hacker to compromise the honeypot, the hacker may walk away, sensing a trap. It is critical that you challenge the hacker by hardening the honeypot and that you implement security controls to make the system appear as if it may have value.

Another common security term is honeynet. A *honeynet* is an entire network that is designed to appear as a production network, but is solely there to lure the hacker away from the real production network.

on the **Ⓙob**

Another purpose of a honeypot is to identify the presence of a hacker and learn the approach the hacker takes to compromise the system. It is critical to ensure that you have high levels of logging enabled on the honeypot so you can collect the hacker's activity.

Patch Management

A number of people believe that if they have a firewall they are safe from network attacks—a belief that most hackers hope for. The firewall can help protect us against data or services that we have not requested, but what about services that we ask for, such as e-mail? Hackers can attack the system by sending an e-mail that includes an attachment, hoping you open the attachment, which will then attack your system. This is why it is so important that you not open or run any program from an e-mail whose source you are not familiar with.

on the **Ⓙob**

It is important to note that most vendors, including Microsoft, will never send you an e-mail with an attachment to download. Microsoft has stated that they will send you the URL of a file and downloading it is up to you.

I have received e-mails in the past that appeared to be from Microsoft asking me to run update.exe, which was attached to the e-mail. The hacker doing this was very smart, because the e-mail used the look and feel of the Microsoft site so that it appeared to actually come from Microsoft. The e-mail stated that update.exe would fix a security vulnerability within the operating system, but I knew better and did not run update.exe!

An important part of securing your system is to make sure that you are constantly updating your virus definitions so that your system can protect you from any new known viruses.

Along the lines of updating virus definitions, you will want to make sure that you keep up to date on operating system patches and product updates. For example, if you are running a Windows server along with Exchange Server and SQL Server, you must certainly test and apply any patches or updates for each of the products. This is a highly critical step to perform!

A few years ago I was asked to do a security audit on a hotel. During the audit I plugged into a network jack that was available to guests in the hotel. Once I got the IP address, I typed a few Microsoft commands, such as **net view /domain,** and saw the domain for the corporate network! I also performed a Remote Procedure Call (RPC) exploit known as kaht2 on the server and was connected to the server instantly. So within 45 seconds I went from knowing nothing about their network to potentially taking full control of it. Needless to say, the hotel failed the audit!

The lesson here is that the network consultant who configured the network violated every best practice. First, the hotel guest network should never be connected physically to a corporate network. If there is a physical connection, there may always be a way to get access to the data. Second, the server was installed but had never had an update or patch applied to it! If the administrator had run Windows Update on the server, the RPC exploit would not have been successful.

The bottom line here is that you must constantly update your antivirus software and apply any fixes or patches for your server operating systems and network devices. These fixes are provided because of flaws in the products, and hackers are aware of these flaws and use them to gain control of your network. Deny them the opportunity by taking the flaw away!

Hardening Devices and Systems

When patching systems, you must also harden network devices and network servers. Hardening a system or a device involves removing unnecessary features that you are not using. For example, after installing a Windows 2000 Server you will notice that Internet Information Services (IIS) is installed by default. If you are not planning on hosting websites on the server, you should uninstall the IIS service—this is the concept of hardening.

Hardening an operating system or network device is a time-consuming process because you have to research the operating system or device and find out what software is installed by default. You then must verify whether you actually need that feature and, if not, remove it. This process involves a lot of paperwork, and you really must do your homework to determine what is needed and what is not; otherwise, you could cause the system or device to be dysfunctional by removing the wrong operating system component.

Hardening a server and then applying any updates or patches to the server is a very effective method of securing the server. It is not the be-all and end-all of network security, but combined with firewalls and data encryption, it can go a long way to securing your environment.

As part of your hardening practice, you will want to make sure that you have renamed any built-in accounts, such as the Administrator account. Once you have renamed the account, you may even create a new user account named "Administrator" and assign a really strong password to this account. The benefit is that a hacker who obtains the password for that account will only have "user" privileges on the system and also needs to figure out which of your accounts is the real Administrator account.

You must also make sure that all accounts are using strong passwords. For more information on creating a password policy, refer to Chapter 13. To audit users' passwords and be certain that their passwords are strong, you could use a password auditor such as LC4.

Data Encryption

In this chapter you have learned about various technologies used to secure network traffic, such as SSL for web traffic or IPSec for all IP traffic. If you want to make sure that a hacker cannot read the traffic on the network, you need to encrypt your traffic to protect its confidentiality.

If you have a wireless network, you need to enable some form of encryption, such as WEP. Remember that WEP encryption has proved to be crackable; use it only if you don't have another method of encrypting wireless traffic, but try to implement another form of encryption if possible.

Another really important point to make about a hacker's capturing network traffic is that on a wired network, the hacker must be connected to the network. If you enforce rules of physical security, you can protect network traffic. For example, many companies will not allow anyone with a laptop to connect to the physical network because they know that a laptop connected to the network can run a number of security hacks and potentially yield access to corporate data.

Make sure that you have a policy in place that limits who can connect to the network with devices such as laptops. You can enforce this by deactivating network ports until someone wants to use any of them. Even then, the user must be granted permission by management, and the port will be activated for only that MAC address.

Policies and Procedures

The first step that any organization should take in helping to prevent security incidents from occurring is to ensure that they have created a strong security policy. A security policy is a document that outlines all the company dos and don'ts and is how the technical team configuring the security controls knows what to configure. For example, when configuring a password policy, you should refer to the company security policy (the password policy portion of the security policy) and check to see what the company rules are surrounding passwords and the password policy.

Network Security Policy

The security policy is a large document made up of many subpolicies, with each subpolicy governing a specific area of security within the organization. The following are a few policies that should be found in the security policy or network policy:

- **Acceptable use policy (AUP)**   The AUP specifies what is considered acceptable use of Internet, e-mail, and mobile devices such as smart phones. Employees are typically asked to sign an acceptable use agreement stating that they agree to the terms.
- **Password policy**   The password policy specifies password requirements such as password strength, frequency of password changes, and if account lockout is to be enabled.
- **Incident response policy**   An important part of the security policy is the incident response policy, which informs the security team within an organization of the steps they need to take when a security incident occurs.
- **Firewall policy**   The firewall policy specifies what type of traffic is or is not allowed to pass through the firewall.
- **Remote access policy**   The remote access policy specifies under what conditions employees are allowed to log into the network from a different location. For example, the company may specify that remote access is only allowed through the approved VPN solution.

Consent to Monitor

One of the important tasks of the security officer of the company is to ensure that the employee reads the acceptable use policy and signs the document. The company should also have a monitoring statement indicating that all employee activity is being monitored, including Internet sites visited, e-mail messages sent and received, and all system and network activity. It is important to ensure that you set zero expectation of privacy so that employees know the company is monitoring all activity. This monitoring statement may be part of the AUP so that when that document is signed, the employee also signs that they are aware all activity is being monitored—we call this consent to monitor.

Standard Business Documents

Security doesn't just involve aspects of network or computer security; it covers all aspects of business operations to ensure that the company is protected against ceasing business operations. Part of protecting the company comes from the business side; there are a number of business documents that should be used to protect the interest of the company. The following outlines some common business documents:

- **SLA** A *service level agreement (SLA)* is a contract between a provider of a service and the client that determines the quality of service that needs to be delivered.
- **MOU** A *memorandum of understanding (MOU)* is a document that describes an agreement between two parties. The agreement describes the relationship between the two parties and what each party is responsible for.
- **MSA** A *master service agreement (MSA)* is an agreement between two parties that identifies the terms of future transactions between the two parties. You can include standard terms defining the relationship in the MSA, but transaction-specific terms can be negotiated per transaction. The general terms of the agreement do not need to be repeated with each transaction because they are in the MSA.
- **SOW** A *statement of work (SOW)* document describes the type of work, any deliverables, and the timeframe for the work to be completed, and is presented to a client to be agreed upon before the work is started.

Data Breach and First Responder

A data breach is a security incident that involves a security risk to information that could be considered sensitive to the organization. A data breach can take many forms: it may be the result of a hacker compromising a system, or it could be due to an employee accidentally e-mailing the information outside the organization. A data breach could also occur as a malicious action involving the employee stealing the data on a USB drive.

The first responder is a person trained on how to properly respond to security events. They typically are responsible for assessing the situation to determine if a security incident has occurred and are responsible for containing the event. For example, if the system has been hit with a virus, the first responder will disconnect the system from the network to ensure the virus does not spread to other systems.

Adherence to Standards and Policies

One of the most important actions employees can take to help protect the company from a security incident is to read company policies and ensure they follow any standards and policies that have been set by the company. As a security professional, you need to ensure employees are following these policies and ensure you enforce them. One of the best ways to ensure employees are following company policies is to educate them on the value of the policy—give examples of the effect of not following the policy. For example, you may want to explain to employees that they are asked to not share passwords because what happens when the employee they shared the password with no longer works at the company? Most companies will disable the account of the ex-employee, but will not think to ask everyone to reset their passwords if they have shared their password.

Vulnerability Testing and Penetration Testing

The last point I want to make about network security is the fact that a company should ensure that regular vulnerability testing or penetration testing is performed.

Vulnerability Testing

Vulnerability testing is the testing of a system to identify mistakes in the configuration that could make the system vulnerable to attack. Vulnerability scanners are available that can scan your network, making you aware of common security mistakes and unpatched systems. These vulnerability scanners can inform you of such things as

- The number of network administrator accounts
- Group memberships
- Patches or updates that have not been applied
- Weak passwords used by user accounts
- Common security practices not followed

This list is a small example of the features available from vulnerability scanners such as the Microsoft Baseline Security Analyzer (MBSA) or GFI's LanGuard. You can download both of these tools from the following URLs:

- **MBSA**   A free download from Microsoft's website (www.microsoft.com/downloads).
- **LanGuard**   A commercial tool that provides a wealth of information about the system being assessed and security-related issues (www.gfi.com).
- **Nessus**   Originating in the Linux environment, Nessus is a common vulnerability assessment tool that also has a Windows version (http://www.tenable.com/).

LanGuard is my favorite of the three and does a better security assessment of your network infrastructure. LanGuard reports a long list of items to you, such as a list of user accounts, groups, permissions, open ports, services that are running, and missing patches. The benefit of a security scanner is that it can scan the entire network and report all of these issues to you in one screen—for all the systems on the network! Figure 15-20 displays LanGuard.

FIGURE 15-20

FIGURE 15-20

LanGuard is a security scanner that reports on a number of security issues.

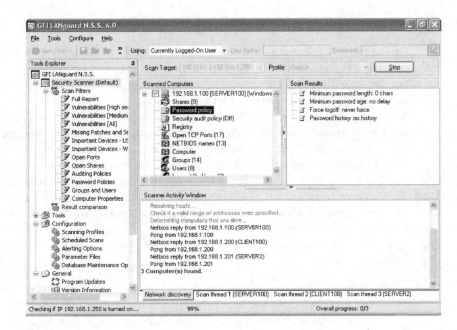

Another common program that can help you identify security issues is nmap, which stands for network mapper. Nmap is more of a port scanner than a vulnerability scanner, but is a great way to identify systems on the network running different services. For example, the following nmap command performs a TCP scan on the entire 10.0.0.0 network for any systems that have Remote Desktop enabled (port 3389):

```
Nmap -sT 10.0.0.0/8 -p 3389
```

Penetration Testing

Penetration testing is a method of testing the security of a system by actually performing the attacks that a hacker would to see if you can compromise the system. If the attacks work, then the system is not secure and needs to be secured. Penetration testing is known as *active* testing in the sense you are actually attacking the system! This is different than vulnerability testing, as vulnerability testing checks the configuration of a system and does not try to exploit it. Vulnerability testing is known as *passively* testing the system.

It is important to note that management may frown upon active testing (penetration testing) when testing the security of the system. Management may ask you to perform security testing, but request that you do a vulnerability test because it is safer due to the fact you are not actually trying to attack a production system.

End-User Awareness and Training

One of the most overlooked security measures that can be taken within any organization is training and awareness. It is vital to the success of any security protection program that all employees within the organization are given seminars that make employees aware that their actions could cause security incidents.

One of the best examples I can give is an employee password. Passwords should be changed frequently, and when they are changed, they should be strong passwords (mix of letters, numbers, symbols, and case). If I were the security manager for a company, I would ensure that all employees saw a demonstration of how easy a program such as LC4 can crack simple passwords, but at the same time has difficulty cracking strong passwords. This style of training and awareness will show the value of policies such as frequent password changes and the need for strong passwords. If we don't make the employees aware, they won't really care.

You can use a number of methods to train employees. The following are a few popular delivery methods:

- **Lunch and learn**   A popular method of raising awareness is to have small one-hour sessions during lunch hour. These sessions, termed lunch and learn, are typically short sessions focused on one topic. For example, today there may be a session on protecting passwords, and tomorrow the topic may be physical security.

- **Intranet site**   You could create training videos and post them on an intranet site for employees to watch. These are typically not as effective, because you need to ensure you have control measures in place that verify employees are watching the videos. You could also post documents on the intranet that explain security best practices.

- **Awareness seminars**   Instead of relying on lunch time, you could allocate time in the day for short awareness seminars. This is the same idea as the lunch and learn, but you are not using up the employees' lunch time.

- **Training courses**   A training course is a longer version of awareness seminars and normally goes into a lot more detail. Typically, the network administrators will need to be educated on how security compromises are happening and how to protect against them. These courses could range from three to five days in length.

This section has introduced a few best practices relating to securing network resources. Network security is a huge topic and can't be covered in just a few pages, so I hope that I have given you worthwhile information on just a few quick points. If you are interested in learning more on network security, I recommend reading *CompTIA Security+ Certification Study Guide, 2nd Edition (Exam SY0-401)* published by McGraw-Hill Professional.

CERTIFICATION SUMMARY

In this chapter you learned some best practices for securing your network. It is important to remember to implement security in layers and not to rely on just one method of securing your systems.

You have learned about a number of operating system features that are used to secure systems, such as authentication and authorization. Authentication is the process by which a user presents logon credentials that are then verified by the network server against a database; if the credentials are correct, the user is allowed to access the network. After a user has been authenticated, an access token is generated that is used to authorize the user to access various network resources. A network resource uses an access control list to determine who is allowed access.

A firewall is a device used for protecting one network from a second interconnected network, such as the Internet. Firewalls compare the data passing through them with rules set up to allow or deny access. There are several architectures for firewalls; three of them are dual-homed host, screened host, and screened subnet. A dual-homed host firewall has two network interfaces and acts as a gateway between the two networks. A screened-host firewall has a screening router placed between the public network and the dual-homed host firewall. This provides an additional level of security against outside intrusion. A screened subnet firewall, meanwhile, puts a screening router on either side of the firewall host. This provides protection on both sides of the host.

Three firewall types are in use: packet-level firewall, application-level firewall, and circuit-level firewall. The packet-level firewall controls data at the network and transport layers. The type that works at the application level acts as a proxy and controls the top three layers of the OSI model. A circuit-level firewall works like an application-level firewall, but operates at the transport layer. Additional security features have been added to firewalls to provide better service, such as support for VPNs and caching and better management tools. Proxy servers can also function as firewalls and can be used to enhance Internet access, as well as function as firewalls by filtering ports.

Data security has become increasingly important as networks are becoming interconnected. Data encryption provides a way to ensure that the data is kept secure. Encryption is the process of taking plain-text data and converting it into a format that is unreadable. A key is used to encrypt the data and then to return the data to a readable format. Two types of encryption are in use: symmetric and asymmetric (public key/private key). Two common encryption methods include stream cipher and block cipher. Two standards for encryption have been accepted: the Digital Encryption Standard (DES) and Ron Rivest, Adi Shamir, and Leonard Adleman (RSA). Both use different methodologies and are in wide use today. Digital signatures can be used to verify that a message arrived without being tampered with. Digital signatures do not encrypt a message. Instead, they attach a signature that can be verified against a certificate authority. Windows versions since Windows 2000 use certificates to encrypt files on an NTFS volume.

You have learned a number of different disaster recovery concepts, including backing up data and storing a copy of the data offsite. You also learned that there are two types of spares for equipment such as hard drives or other network components—hot spares and cold spares. A hot spare is connected to the system and has power already supplied to the device so that if there is a failure in the original device, the hot spare can take over right away. The cold spare is typically close by but not connected to the system at the time of the failure. Because the spare is not readily available without any kind of changeover time, it will take longer to recover from the failure. You have also learned that companies serious about disaster recovery are likely to have an alternative location set up in case of a disaster affecting the original location. There are hot, cold, and warm disaster recovery sites. A hot site is a fully furnished site that has servers and a copy of the corporate data ready to go in case of disaster. A cold site is a company just paying to have the facility available; a warm site includes the facility with a server and backup devices ready for the restore operation.

You have also learned a number of guidelines to protect the network, such as patching systems and keeping them up to date and using firewalls to protect the network and its data. It is extremely critical that you keep your knowledge up to date about known vulnerabilities within the operating systems you are supporting. Be sure to perform a vulnerability scan on your network frequently with a product such as Languard.

TWO-MINUTE DRILL

Understanding Attack Types

❑ Social engineering attacks are when the hacker tries to trick a person into compromising security through social contact such as an e-mail or phone call.

❑ Denial-of-service attacks result in the system crashing or being so busy servicing requests from the hacker that it cannot answer requests from valid clients.

❑ There are three main types of password attacks: dictionary, hybrid, and brute-force attacks.

❑ Spoof attacks are when the hacker alters the source address to make the data look like it came from a different source. There are different types of spoof attacks: IP spoofing, MAC spoofing, and e-mail spoofing.

❑ A buffer overflow attack typically results in the hacker getting shell access to the system with administrative permissions.

Understanding System Security

❑ When a user logs on to the network, an access token is created that contains the user account and any groups the user is a member of; the token is then used to authorize the user to access resources.

❑ Security descriptors are broken down into several components: the system access control list (SACL), the discretionary access control list (DACL), an owner, and a primary group.

❑ The DACL is a list that shows the users and/or groups allowed to access the object and the level of permissions applied.

❑ User-level security, used in all new Windows operating systems, allows administrators to select which users can access a resource and specify the permission they have.

❑ Share-level security is available on client operating systems such as Windows 95 and Windows 98, which place a password on the share. Anyone who knows the password can access the resource.

❑ Share-level security is easy to implement and maintain on small peer-to-peer networks. However, users must remember the password for each shared resource.

❑ You can secure the Registry for Windows systems by using regedt32.exe and setting permissions on different areas in the Registry.

❑ Auditing allows you to monitor the security of the system and any administration activity performed.

❑ A permission is a level of access to a resource, whereas a right is a privilege within the operating system to perform an operating system task.

Implementing Network Security

❑ Network access control (NAC) is a set of technologies that can be used to determine the health of a system before allowing that system to make a connection to a wired network, wireless network, or VPN solution.

❑ NAC considers a system to be healthy based on whether the system has a firewall enabled, is up to date with patches, and has antivirus software installed.

❑ You should ensure you separate (segment) the network in order to control communication between different parts of the network, or different classifications of systems.

Securing Communication

❑ Symmetric encryption uses the same encryption key for encrypting and decrypting traffic.

❑ Asymmetric encryption uses a different key to encrypt the traffic from the one it uses to decrypt it.

❑ There are multiple methods of securing communication; you need to choose the best method for your situation.

❑ Encryption can be defined as the process of taking plain-text data and converting it to cipher text.

❏ Internet Protocol Security (IPSec) allows for encryption of all data on an IP network by configuring an IPSec policy.

❏ The Secure Sockets Layer (SSL) is used to encrypt website information transferred between a user and the web server (online credit card information is encrypted this way).

❏ The Layer Two Tunneling Protocol (L2TP) and Point-to-Point Tunneling Protocol (PPTP) are VPN protocols that are used to encrypt traffic between a VPN client and the VPN server.

❏ Kerberos is a distributed authentication security mechanism used by Windows Active Directory for user validation.

Fault Tolerance and Disaster Recovery

❏ Fault tolerance is a matter of ensuring that your systems will still function when a component fails because you have another component ready to take over the work. RAID is an example of a disk fault-tolerant solution for your data.

❏ Disaster recovery is the concept of ensuring that you can recover from any type of disaster by preparing for it. You can prepare for disaster by building a disaster recovery plan, which contains step-by-step procedures for recovering a system from different failures.

❏ You can create an alternative site for your organization as part of your disaster recovery plan. There are three types of alternative sites: hot, cold, and warm sites.

❏ There are two types of spares when it comes to having standby components: hot spares and cold spares. A hot spare is a component that is connected and powered on, ready for failover; a cold spare must be powered up to be made available.

Guidelines to Protect the Network

❏ Place your web servers, FTP servers, and mail servers in a DMZ to protect them from the outside world.

❏ Make sure that you patch all systems and devices. Patching a system or device helps remove known vulnerabilities from the system or device, which in turn helps secure it.

❏ Review your firewall rules to be certain that you are allowing only needed traffic through.

❏ Physically secure servers behind a locked door in a controlled-access server room. If a hacker can get physical access to the system, the system can be compromised.

❏ Encrypt the traffic of sensitive data so that it cannot be captured and analyzed by network intruders. You can use such technologies as SSL or IPSec to secure network traffic.

❑ Be sure to spend time hardening your servers. Hardening a server involves removing unnecessary services from the system. The less software running on the server, the fewer security holes.

❑ Make sure that you perform a vulnerability scan of the network with tools such as LanGuard on a regular basis.

SELF TEST

The following questions will help you measure your understanding of the material presented in this chapter. Read all the choices carefully, because there may appear to be more than one correct answer.

Understanding Attack Types

1. What type of attack involves the hacker altering the source address of a packet?

A. Buffer overflow

B. Dictionary attack

C. Social engineering attack

D. Spoof attack

2. What type of password attack involves using dictionary words and appending numbers to the end of those words?

A. Brute-force

B. Dictionary

C. Hybrid

D. Buffer

Understanding System Security

3. What portion of the Windows security subsystem handles both local security policies and user authentication, and generates audit log messages?

A. Local Security Authority (LSA)

B. Security Accounts Manager (SAM)

C. Security Reference Monitor

D. None of the above

4. What portion of the Windows security architecture maintains the database used for storing user and group account information on a local Windows 8 system?
   A. Local Security Authority (LSA)
   B. Logon Process
   C. Security Reference Monitor
   D. Security Accounts Manager (SAM)

5. What access control list object determines which users and groups have permissions to an object?
   A. System access control list (SACL)
   B. Discretionary access control list (DACL)
   C. Owner
   D. User

6. Which of the following allows a user to modify the contents of a file?
   A. Read and Execute
   B. Read
   C. List Folder Contents
   D. Modify

7. A user's credentials are checked against a database of accounts that are allowed to access the network. This process is known as _____.
   A. Authorization
   B. Authentication
   C. Rights
   D. Permissions

Implementing Network Security

8. What type of device analyzes packets that attempt to enter the network and then either allows or denies the traffic, based on rules?
   A. Encryption
   B. Firewall
   C. Router
   D. None of the above

Securing Communication

9. Which encryption scheme uses the same encryption key to decrypt the data as the one that encrypted it?
   A. Asymmetric
   B. RSA standard
   C. Symmetric
   D. Public key algorithm

10. Which of the following is classified as an encryption method? (Choose all that apply.)
    A. Stream cipher
    B. Data cipher
    C. Byte cipher
    D. Block cipher

11. Which block cipher mode encrypts each block individually during the encryption process?
    A. Electronic Codebook (ECB)
    B. Cipher Block Chaining (CBC)
    C. Cipher Feedback (CFB)
    D. None of the above

12. What encryption standard is based on a fixed 56-bit symmetric key encryption algorithm?
    A. RSA
    B. DES
    C. CPA
    D. DSE

13. What technology uses certificate authorities to verify that a message has not been tampered with?
    A. RSA encryption
    B. Local Security Authority
    C. Digital signatures
    D. None of the above

Fault Tolerance and Disaster Recovery

14. Which disaster recovery site provides only the facility, but no equipment or copy of the original data?
    A. Hot site
    B. Warm site
    C. Blue site
    D. Cold site

15. Which disaster recovery site provides the facility and ensures that the site has an up-to-date copy of the data necessary to have a fully functional site?
    A. Hot site
    B. Warm site
    C. Blue site
    D. Cold site

16. What type of spare component has power supplied to it and is ready to take over if the original component fails?
    A. Cold spare
    B. Network spare
    C. Warm spare
    D. Hot spare

Guidelines to Protect the Network

17. Which of the following pieces of software provide a vulnerability scan of the network? (Select two.)
    A. LanGuard
    B. Norton AntiVirus
    C. Microsoft Baseline Security Analyzer
    D. Microsoft AntiSpyware
    E. Spybot

18. After installing a network operating system, what should you do before placing the machine on the network to help secure it?
    A. Harden the operating system.
    B. Disable the firewall.
    C. Configure e-mail.
    D. Build user accounts.

19. After hardening the operating system, what should you do to ensure that your server has all security fixes applied to it?
    A. Install antivirus software.
    B. Install antispyware software.
    C. Patch the server.
    D. None of the above.

Performance-Based Question Review: See the performance-based question sample from the author included with the accompanying media.

SELF TEST ANSWERS

Understanding Attack Types

1. ☑ **D.** Spoof attack is the term used for when the hacker alters the source address of the packet. There are different types of spoofing, depending on what source address is being altered: IP spoofing, MAC spoofing, and e-mail spoofing.
   ☒ **A, B,** and **C** are incorrect. A buffer overflow attack is when too much information is sent to an application, and as a result the hacker can run arbitrary code. A dictionary attack is a form of password attack using a word list file, and a social engineering attack is when the hacker calls or e-mails an individual and tries to trick them into compromising security.

2. ☑ **C.** A hybrid attack, like a dictionary attack, uses a word list file, but also tries popular modifications on the words, such as adding a number to the end of the dictionary word.
   ☒ **A, B,** and **D** are incorrect. A brute-force attack is when all the possible character combinations are calculated to try to figure out a password. A dictionary attack uses a word list file, but doesn't try variations of the word. There is no such thing as a buffer password attack.

Understanding System Security

3. ☑ **A.** The Local Security Authority (LSA) handles these functions above the Security Accounts Manager and Security Reference Monitor. Those services are used to provide specific functions for the LSA.
   ☒ **B, C,** and **D** are incorrect. SAM is a local database of users and groups. The Security Reference Monitor is used to validate a user right to perform a task and permission to access resources.

4. ☑ **D.** The Security Accounts Manager (SAM) is the database of users and groups contained on a local Windows system.
   ☒ **A, B,** and **C** are incorrect. The LSA initiates the authentication process in Windows and validates against the SAM database. The Logon Process is applied to allow a user to log on and be verified. The Security Reference Monitor is used to validate a user right or permission to access resources.

5. ☑ **B.** The discretionary access control list (DACL) determines which users and groups have permissions to an object.
   ☒ **A, C,** and **D** are incorrect. The SACL controls security auditing. The owner maintains ownership of the object, and a user is not a valid ACL object type.

6.   ☑   **D.** The Modify permission is the permission that allows a user to modify (and delete) a file.
☒   **A, B,** and **C** are incorrect. Read and Execute allows a user to read the contents of a file and execute a program from that location. Read allows the user only to read the file contents, and List Folder Contents allows a user to see the files that exist in a folder but not read the contents.

7.   ☑   **B.** Authentication is the process of logging on to the network.
☒   **A, C,** and **D** are incorrect. Authorization comes after authentication and involves determining whether a user can access a resource after being authenticated. Permissions and rights are methods of authorization.

Implementing Network Security

8.   ☑   **B.** A firewall is used to secure the internal network from the outside world by rules configured on the firewall that specify which packets to drop and which packets to allow through.
☒   **A, C,** and **D** are incorrect. Encryption converts plain text to cipher text. A router is used to provide routing functions to the network, but it may have firewalling features.

Securing Communication

9.   ☑   **C.** In symmetric encryption, both parties use the same key to encrypt and decrypt the data.
☒   **A, B,** and **D** are incorrect. Asymmetric encryption has two related keys—one is used to encrypt and the other decrypts.

10.   ☑   **A and D.** Stream cipher and block cipher are valid encryption methods.
☒   **B and C** are incorrect because data cipher and byte cipher do not exist.

11.   ☑   **A.** The Electronic Codebook (ECB) mode encrypts each block individually, but the Cipher Block Chaining and Cipher Feedback modes do not.
☒   **B, C,** and **D** are incorrect because the Cipher Block Chaining and Cipher Feedback modes do not encrypt each block individually.

12.   ☑   **B.** The Data Encryption Standard (DES) uses this algorithm.
☒   **A, C,** and **D** are incorrect because the RSA uses a different type of algorithm, and CPA and DSE are not valid encryption standards.

13.   ☑   **C.** Digital signatures technology does not encrypt the message—it only verifies that it arrived without being tampered with.
☒   **A, B,** and **D** are incorrect because RSA is an encryption standard and the Local Security Authority is a Windows NT subsystem.

Fault Tolerance and Disaster Recovery

14. ☑ **D.** A cold site provides only the disaster recovery facility. The equipment and data are the responsibility of the company using the facility.
☒ **A, B,** and **C** are incorrect. A hot site provides the facility and the equipment, and it will ensure that an up-to-date copy of an organization's data is available in case of disaster. A warm site provides the facility and the backup equipment to perform a restore when needed. There's no such thing as a blue site.

15. ☑ **A.** A hot site provides the facility and the equipment, and it will ensure that an up-to-date copy of an organization's data is available in case of disaster.
☒ **B, C,** and **D** are incorrect. A cold site provides only the disaster recovery facility. The equipment and data are the responsibility of the company using the facility. A warm site provides the facility and the backup equipment to perform a restore when needed. There's no such thing as a blue site.

16. ☑ **D.** A hot spare is connected and already has power supplied to it so that there is minimal delay for failover.
☒ **A, B,** and **C** are incorrect. A cold spare is not connected and immediately available. When needed, it must be connected and powered up to become available. The other choices are not types of spares.

Guidelines to Protect the Network

17. ☑ **A** and **C.** LanGuard and the Microsoft Baseline Security Analyzer are examples of vulnerability scanners that allow you to audit the network for security-related problems.
☒ **B, D,** and **E** are incorrect because they are not vulnerability scanners.

18. ☑ **A.** After installing the network operating system, you should harden it, which involves removing unnecessary services. Removing unnecessary services helps secure the system, because each additional piece of software running provides more security holes for a hacker to find.
☒ **B, C,** and **D** are incorrect. You would not disable the firewall, as you may allow unwanted traffic to the system. Also, unless needed, you would not configure e-mail or additional user accounts on the system. The less software installed and the fewer accounts that exist mean fewer ways for a hacker to get into a system.

19. ☑ **C.** After hardening the operating system, you should patch the server to apply security fixes to any software running on the server.
☒ **A, B,** and **D** are incorrect because they are not ways to apply security fixes to the system.

Chapter 16

Network Security Practices

T he new Network+ certification exam has expanded on its security topics and has opted to test candidates in different areas of security than in previous versions of the exam. The new Network+ certification exam will test you on networking hardening techniques, physical security, firewalls, and the basics of computer forensics. This chapter is designed to give you the background needed in those areas.

CERTIFICATION OBJECTIVE 16.01

Implement Network Hardening Techniques

Network hardening involves looking at different methods of creating a more secure environment with regard to the network and any devices that exist on the network. In this section you will learn different techniques used to harden the network environment.

Security Policy and Access Control Models

When looking to harden the network environment, be sure to review the company security policy for different network features or techniques that are required to be implemented. For example, you may find that the security policy dictates that any systems used by non-employees must be connected to a guest network, which is to not have any connection to the production network. This will force you to look at creating network segments and zones as a hardening technique. You may also find that the security policy specifies that all company systems, including employee desktops, laptops, and servers, must have antivirus software installed and definitions must be up to date.

The security policy should also have requirements for systems connecting to the network. For example, all systems connecting to the network must be fully patched and equipped with antivirus software. There are a number of technologies related to network access control models you need to be familiar with:

- **802.1x** This is the network access control method that involves having users authenticated via a Remote Authentication Dial-In User Service (RADIUS) server in order to get a connection to a wireless network, wired network, or even a virtual private network (VPN) connection into the network.

- **Posture assessment** This is determining the security state of a system before allowing it to connect to your network. For example, you should verify the system is fully patched, has antivirus software, and has a firewall enabled before allowing it to connect to your network. An unprotected system that connects to your network could introduce viruses to your network.

- **Guest network** A guest network is a valuable network segment that you can have to allow visitor Internet access, but it will not be connected on the same network segment as your corporate systems.

- **Persistent vs. non-persistent agents** When implementing access control, the agent is the software component that checks the health of your system (if it has antivirus software, is patched, and has a firewall). A persistent agent is agent software that resides on the client making the connection, and a non-persistent agent is software the client runs (usually from a browser) as they are connecting so the agent can perform the checks, but the software does not permanently stay with the client after they disconnect.

- **Quarantine network**   If a client does not meet access control requirements, for instance, if they are not up to date with patches or their virus protection is not up to date, they can be connected to a temporary network known as a quarantine network. The quarantine network allows the client to do their updates and then they can connect to the production network.

- **Edge vs. access control**   Having users and computers simply authenticate to the network is not enough security today. It is important to ensure that the system or device being used to make the connection is in a healthy state (is patched, is virus protected, and has a firewall enabled) before they are granted network access. This is the importance of edge security. Edge security is placing security checks on the client as they make the connection to the network, whether that be when connecting to the switch, connecting to the wireless local area network (LAN), or remotely connecting through VPN. The combination of authentication and performing the health check on connection increases your security posture.

Antimalware Software

In today's day and age, there is a wealth of different types of malicious software (malware) that are designed to do harm to your computer systems. Malware comes in different forms; the following is a quick description of the types of malware you may be exposed to:

- **Virus**   A virus is malicious software that can cause damage to a system by deleting files or using up resources such as central processing unit (CPU) cycles, causing the system to perform poorly.

- **Spyware**   Spyware is malware that is designed to track and report your online activity.

- **Worm**   A worm is a self-replicating virus that replicates across the network, either by itself or by attaching to a universal serial bus (USB) drive.

- **Ransomware**   Ransomware is malicious software that takes control of your system and does not give control back until you pay a fee.

When looking at hardening systems, one of the things you want to consider as well is how you will protect this system from malicious software. To protect from malicious software, you will install an antimalware product such as Windows Defender.

A number of other considerations need to be made when it comes to virus protection, and one of those considerations is where you will install antimalware. The following are some key systems or devices you should install antimalware on:

- **Host-based**   You should install antivirus or antimalware software on each system on the network, including desktops, laptops, and servers.

■ **Network-based** You can also install network-based antimalware software that checks different types of network traffic for malicious content. For example, you may have an appliance that scans all e-mails that come into the company for virus and spam messages. The appliance will discard the e-mail if it has a virus or is spam related instead of forwarding the e-mail to the e-mail server of the company. The key point with a network-based virus protection solution is that the processing is happening on the premises and you have to manage the network-based appliance.

■ **Cloud/server-based** With cloud-based antivirus software, the actual virus definitions and scanning for viruses are provided by a service in the cloud. In this case, there is no antivirus software installed on the desktop—only a small agent program that communicates with the antivirus service in the cloud. The big benefit of cloud-based antivirus software is centralized administration. For example, you could manually invoke a virus scan from the cloud to a group of desktops (or all of them).

Switch Port Security

One of the key techniques to harden the network is to ensure you leverage features of the switch that add to the security of the network. For example, most switches have a port security feature that allows you to control which systems can connect to any given port on the switch. When you limit which systems can connect to a port on the switch, you do it by listing the Media Access Control (MAC) address of the system. This is a great solution where a network jack on the wall is in a public area like a reception area and you want to ensure unauthorized systems cannot connect to the port and gain network access. You may also consider disabling the port if it is not being actively used by employees.

The network switch has other features you can leverage that add to the security of the network. The following outlines some key features you should look to enabling when hardening the network:

■ **DHCP snooping** DHCP snooping is a set of features on a switch that can help harden your Dynamic Host Configuration Protocol (DHCP) infrastructure. DHCP snooping can be used to ensure clients are receiving Internet Protocol (IP) addresses from only authorized DHCP servers.

■ **ARP inspection** ARP inspection, also known as dynamic ARP inspection (DAI), is a switch hardening feature that allows the switch to block malicious Address Resolution Protocol (ARP) messages that hackers use to poison the ARP cache on systems in order to perform a man-in-the-middle attack.

■ **MAC address filtering** When configuring a switch, you can control which systems can connect to the switch by their MAC address. This feature is typically known as port security.

■ **VLAN assignments**   When looking to harden the network environment, you can configure your network for multiple VLANs and then assign ports to specific VLANs. The VLANs act as communication boundaries and are a great way to control communication between types of systems on the network.

Disable Unneeded Network Services

One of the important aspects of network hardening is to ensure you disable any unneeded network services from servers, desktops, and devices. After installing a server, verify any default protocols and network services that are installed. After inventorying these items on each server, determine if those services are needed. For example, many years ago when network administrators installed a Windows Server, the server came installed with Web Server by default. If you didn't take the time to assess the default services installed, you would have never noticed that web server software was installed on your file servers by default!

The critical point to remember is that hackers exploit systems by leveraging vulnerabilities built into software—and the more software you have loaded on a system, the more vulnerabilities that exist! Your goal is to reduce the attack surface by removing unnecessary software and network services. If you are not hosting a website on a server, then be sure to verify that there is no web server software installed. If you are not providing fully qualified domain name (FQDN) name resolution, then you do not need to have the Domain Name System (DNS) service installed on your servers. Be sure to remove unnecessary network services from a server after installation.

Network Segmentation and Access Lists

One of the best ways to harden the network is to ensure that you separate it into different network segments. Breaking the network into segments allows you to use a firewall or access control list on a router to limit the communication between different network segments. For example, a hotel would want to ensure that their employee computers are on a network separate from the computers of guests in the hotel rooms. In this situation, we would usually create a "corporate" network and a "guest" network. We would ensure that systems on the guest network cannot communicate with systems on the corporate network.

Another example where you can use the concept of a guest network is with a wireless network. You may configure the wireless access point with two wireless networks: one for employees and the other for visitors needing Internet access. Because you do not know the state of the visitors' systems (they could have a virus), you do not want them to connect to your regular wireless network, so you create a guest wireless network for any visitors.

Once you have created the different network segments, which are networks separated by firewalls or routers, you can then configure access lists that allow you to control traffic that can travel between those two networks. The access list is a rule added to the firewall or router that allows or denies traffic based on criteria. Examples of criteria used to configure an access list are

- **Web/content filtering** A feature designed to allow you to control what type of content someone can view on the Internet. You can typically limit information by protocol, by the uniform resource locator (URL), and by keywords.

- **Port filtering** A feature designed to allow you to control what traffic can pass through the firewall or router by the Transmission Control Protocol (TCP) and User Datagram Protocol (UDP) port numbers. For example, if I only want to allow web traffic, I would allow TCP ports 80 and 443, but deny all other traffic.

- **IP filtering** Allows you to control traffic that can pass from one segment to another via the source or destination IP address.

- **Implicit deny** Most access control lists on firewalls and routers have an implicit deny, which means if you have not built a rule that allows traffic through, then the traffic is denied by default. It is important to verify the default rule with all products and make sure the default is to deny all traffic; then you add the exceptions for traffic you want to pass through the firewall or router.

Use Secure Protocols

When hardening the network environment, it is important to ensure that you are using secure protocols for network communication. Secure protocols encrypt the network traffic so that if someone is eavesdropping they cannot see the data in plain text. A malicious person can use a packet sniffer to capture network traffic, which allows them to view the packet data in plain text—for example, a credit card number that was entered into a website.

When hardening the network, determine what type of traffic is being transmitted on the network, and if that traffic is not encrypted, then replace the protocol with a secure version of it. For example, if the corporate Intranet site is using Hypertext Transfer Protocol (HTTP), which is unsecure, then use Hypertext Transfer Protocol Secure (HTTPS) instead, which is the secure replacement to HTTP and does encrypt the traffic.

The following is a listing of common secure protocols that should be used to encrypt different types of traffic on the network:

- **SSH** The *secure shell (SSH)* protocol can be used as a replacement to Telnet, which is typically used by administrators to remotely administer routers and switches. Be sure to disable Telnet as a protocol on routers and switches and use SSH instead.

- **SNMPv3** SNMPv3 is a secure replacement to the *Simple Network Management Protocol (SNMP)*. SNMP is a management protocol, allowing you to manage IP devices such as routers and switches. The original SNMP protocol did not have security as one of its goals, so the newest version, SNMPv3, focuses on offering security features such as packet encryption, integrity of messages, and authentication.

- **TLS/SSL**   Two protocols used to encrypt communication are *Secure Sockets Layer (SSL)* and *Transaction Layer Security (TLS).* SSL has been used for years to encrypt web, File Transfer Protocol (FTP), and e-mail traffic. TLS is the successor of SSL and is designed to secure communication between systems.

- **SFTP**   *Secure FTP* is used to encrypt FTP traffic and should be used as a secure replacement to the unsecure FTP protocol.

- **HTTPS**   Web traffic using HTTP that contains sensitive information should be replaced with the secure replacement protocol, HTTPS.

- **IPSec**   The *IP Security (IPSec)* protocol is used to encrypt all IP traffic and is a great solution for encrypting server-to-server traffic.

CERTIFICATION OBJECTIVE 16.02

Physical Security Controls

One of the most important security concepts to follow when trying to secure your company environment is to implement different types of physical security. Physical security ensures that an individual cannot get physical access to a computer or device—the philosophy you should follow is if someone can get physical access to a device, they can compromise security.

Securing the Premises

The first line of defense in physical security is at the perimeter of the facility premises. It is critical in highly secure environments that you control who gets access to the company property even before they reach the building. Two popular methods of controlling access to company property are by using fences and guards.

Perimeter Fencing

In highly secure environments, look at putting a fence around the perimeter of the property to deter intruders from trespassing. With a fence around the perimeter, you are forcing anyone who wants access to the facility to go through the main gates, where you implement security checks on everyone entering or leaving the facility.

The height of the fence you put in depends on what your goal is. If you are looking to deter a casual intruder, then you typically go with a fence that is three to four feet high.

Keep in mind that a four-foot fence is easy to climb, so if you are looking to deter a casual climber, then the recommended fence height is five to seven feet. A determined intruder would have no problem figuring out how to climb a seven-foot fence, so to deter such an intruder, the recommended fence height is eight feet plus three lines of barbed wire on top tilted at a 45-degree angle toward the intruder.

Security Guards

When you implement the fence around the perimeter of the network, you will need to have a security gate with guards checking anyone entering or leaving the premises. The guards at the gate will verify that a visitor is expected at the facility and then typically give them a "visitor" ID badge to be worn at all times. Employees entering the facility will need to display their employee ID badge to get access. The ID badge will have the employee name and a photo of the employee.

The guard at the gate will monitor persons leaving the facility and try to ensure that equipment is not being stolen from the facility. Adding a security guard to your physical security plan has the added bonus that the guard can identify abnormal activity or anything out of the norm. I talked to one customer who said that if employees are leaving with a laptop or other computer equipment, the equipment is verified at the gate on the way out. The guard verifies the employee is allowed to leave with the equipment and makes them sign out the equipment. This is used to hopefully eliminate internal theft of company assets.

Depending on the level of security required by your company, you may have guards positioned throughout the facility ensuring that no security incidents occur. The guards should be trained to watch for ID badges on all persons walking through the facility and to question anyone who does not have an ID badge. At one customer's facility where I was given a visitor badge and put it on, the gentleman who authorized me to be there said, "No, you have to attach it on your left side." The organization strictly enforces that all personnel wear the badge in the same place so that security can easily see it.

Mantraps

No physical security discussion would be complete without discussing a mantrap. A mantrap is an area between two doors—with the second door not opening until the first door is closed. This helps prevent *piggybacking* or *tailgating*—which is when someone tries to slip in behind you after you have unlocked a door. The concept here is that you would not open the second door if someone you didn't know entered the mantrap area. An alternative form of a mantrap is a C-shaped cylinder which rotates between two openings and can be stopped halfway to prevent an intruder from proceeding. The C-shaped entrance is the size of a telephone booth.

Depending on the environment, the mantrap area may have a secure window looking into the mantrap. On the other side of that window a security guard monitors anyone who enters or leaves the facility.

ⓦatch **A mantrap is used to help prevent tailgating by trapping individuals in an area between two doors. The second door will not unlock until the first door is closed.**

Video Monitoring

A big part of physical security today deals with implementing *closed-circuit television (CCTV)* or other video monitoring technologies such as *IP cameras.* CCTV involves having video cameras set up to monitor areas of the facility and having that information sent to computer screens in a central security area where security personnel are monitoring for suspicious activity. CCTV monitoring systems in the past have sent the video to VHS tapes or to other recording equipment.

ⓦatch **Remember that CCTV systems capture video and send it to a *specific* system or set of displays. It is popular to have these video feeds** **sent to a control room where security personnel are monitoring the screens for suspicious activity.**

Today's monitoring systems are a little more advanced and are not really considered closed circuit because the owner of the equipment can now connect to the camera from across the Internet to view the captured video live. Most monitoring systems today can also record the captured video to remote locations across the network, such as to a central server.

Network Closet/Server Room

Once you have controlled access to the building, you also want to ensure that you control who has access to the network closet or server room. With regard to physical security, you should ensure that the network closet containing communication equipment is locked and only a limited number of personnel have access to that network closet. You should also ensure that the server room, which contains servers, routers, and switches, is a locked facility with a limited number of personnel who have access to that room as well. Most server rooms and communications closets use rack systems that support locking the door to the rack to prevent someone from gaining access to the network equipment located in the server room or communications closet. This is a great additional layer of security to protect your equipment from someone who may have gotten access to the room.

Access Control Methods

We stressed that you should ensure you have the network equipment such as servers, routers, and switches in a locked area. That locked area is either a communications closet (also known as a network closet) or a server room. There are a wide range of locking mechanisms you can use for these secured areas that are introduced in this section.

Door Access Controls

One of the most popular methods of controlling access to a facility or room is to implement a locking system on the doors. Conventional locks are easy to pick and susceptible to a bump key attack. A *bump key* is a normal key that has been filed down to fit into a lock—the key is inserted into the lock and pulled out one notch. When the key is tapped, it causes the pins in the lock to align and then unlock the door.

Keypad   You can purchase pick-resistant locks (for a higher cost), which give you the added security that the lock will not be easily compromised, but most companies use electronic locking systems in today's high security environments. The electronic locking systems are also known as an *electronic key system*. With the electronic key system, employees are given a *token* device or swipe card, which has their access code encoded in it. When the employee swipes the token or card past the electronic sensor, the door unlocks.

Cipher Locks   You can also have a cipher lock, known as an *electronic combination lock*, which allows employees to type a personal identification number (PIN) number into the lock to gain access. With these cipher locks, you need to enter the code before accessing the facility, and the code may sometimes require you to press multiple numbers at the same time. For example, the code may be press 3, then 2 and 4 at the same time, followed by 7. I have seen electronic keypads that do not have numbers on the buttons until you press the start button. Once you press the start button, the system randomly generates the placement of the numbers so that if someone watches your finger position, it will not help them guess the access code. The electronic combination locks are also known as *cipher locks*.

With either of the electronic locking systems, the company can control which areas an employee has access to based on the access code. These systems can also log access, including the date and time that the employee accessed the facility or different areas of the facility.

Proximity Readers/Key Fob

A proximity reader is a sensor device that reads the access code from a token or card. The two major types of proximity readers are user activated or system sensing. With a *user-activated* proximity reader, the employee would key in a code or swipe the access card by the sensor to gain access to the facility. A *system-sensing* proximity reader system continuously sends out an interrogating signal that the user's access device would respond to by sending the access code to the sensor for the door to unlock.

A key fob is a keychain-like device that is used to swipe across a sensor in order to get access to an area of the building, network closet, or server room. There are also key fob token devices such as an RSA token, which continually regenerates codes that last for 60 seconds. The code is then used in conjunction with a user's password to authenticate to the network.

Biometrics

Biometrics is a form of authentication that can be used with physical security that involves a user using a characteristic of themselves to unlock a door. Examples of biometrics are using a retina scan to unlock a door, using a fingerprint scan to unlock the door, or even voice recognition to unlock a door. Many laptops today and mobile devices use fingerprint scanners to authenticate a person before allowing them access to the device.

CERTIFICATION OBJECTIVE 16.03

Implementing Firewalls

A huge part of network security is ensuring that you control communication from one part of the network to another. Firewalls or access control lists on routers can be used to create rules that control communication from different parts of the network.

There are a number of different types of firewalls you should be familiar with for the Network+ certification exam:

- **Host-based vs. network-based**   A *host-based* firewall is firewall software installed on a system designed to control traffic to that system. A *network-based* firewall is a firewall device that is designed to control traffic that enters or leaves the network.
- **Software vs. hardware**   Firewalls can either be software installed on a system to control traffic that can pass through the network interfaces of the system or it can be a hardware device.
- **Application aware/context aware**   Firewalls can be aware of application-specific traffic and block it from an application. Firewalls can also be context aware in the sense that they know when traffic is being sent at an inappropriate time.

■ **Small office/home office firewall**   Many small office/home office (SOHO) devices, such as a home wireless router, have firewall features that are designed to protect your LAN from external traffic that originates on the Internet.

■ **Stateful vs. stateless inspection**   *Stateful* packet inspection firewalls filter traffic that is not being sent in the context of the communication, whereas *stateless* does not have that capability. You will learn more about stateful packet inspection later in this chapter.

■ **UTM**   *Unified Threat Management (UTM)* is a security device that offers many security features, such as firewall, VPN, gateway antivirus, antispam, intrusion prevention, and content filtering.

Firewall Architecture

Firewalls are designed to protect systems on one side of the firewall from systems on the other side by analyzing packets that reach the firewall and determining whether the packet is allowed to pass through. Firewalls can be either software-based solutions or their own hardware device. A software-based firewall is installed on a system and then configured to control traffic that passes through.

You configure rules on the firewall that indicate which traffic is to pass through and which is to be blocked. For example, as a general rule, you should configure the firewall to block all traffic, meaning that no traffic can pass through the firewall. This is often referred to as an *implicit deny* rule. Once you have configured the "default" rule of blocking all traffic, you can configure exceptions to the rule, allowing selected traffic to pass through. For example, if you have a web server that you want to expose to the Internet, you would block all traffic except TCP port 80, the port on which web server traffic runs (shown in Figure 16-1). It should be noted that Cisco devices such as routers and firewalls have an implicit deny rule automatically. So if a rule in the access control list does not allow the traffic in, then the traffic is denied.

FIGURE 16-1   Firewalls allow selected traffic to pass through the firewall.

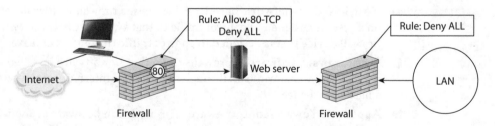

Before we consider how to create these firewall rules, let's look at some firewall configurations that are currently used in networking environments.

Dual-Homed Host Firewalls

A *dual-homed* host firewall consists of a single computer with two physical network interfaces that act as a gateway between the two networks. The server's routing capability is disabled so that the firewall can handle all traffic management. Either application-level proxy or circuit-level firewall software is run on this system to pass packets from one side of the dual-homed system to the other. You must be careful not to enable routing within the network operating system that will be used as the dual-homed system, or you will bypass your firewall software and simply be routing data. Figure 16-2 shows a dual-homed host firewall configuration.

exam watch

It is important to note that this chapter is focused on network-based firewalls, which are firewall devices or systems that protect the entire network. For the Network+ exam, you need to be familiar with network-based firewalls and with host-based firewalls. A host-based firewall only protects the one system and is personal firewall software installed on that one system. Personal firewalls should be used on systems in situations where the employee is connecting the company system to an untrusted network.

Screened-Host Firewalls

Screened-host firewall configurations are considered by many to be more secure than the dual-homed firewall. In this configuration, you place a screening router between the dual-homed host and the public network. This enables you to provide packet filtering before

FIGURE 16-2

A dual-homed system acting as a firewall has two network interfaces.

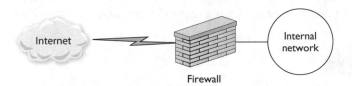

FIGURE 16-3 A screened-host firewall configuration adds an extra layer of network security by adding a screening router to implement packet filtering.

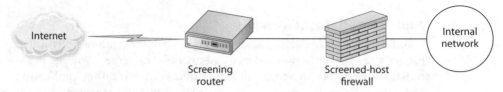

the packets reach the dual-homed computer, thereby adding an extra layer of network security. The dual-homed computer can then run a proxy to provide additional security to this configuration. Figure 16-3 shows a screened-host configuration.

Screened Subnet Firewalls

A *screened subnet* firewall configuration takes security to the next level by further isolating the internal network from the public network. An additional screening router is placed between the internal network and the dual-homed firewall. This provides two additional levels of security. First, by adding a screening router internally, you can protect the dual-homed firewall host from an attack by an internal source. Second, it makes an external attack much more difficult because the number of layers that an attacker must go through is increased. Normally, the outside screening router will be configured to pass any data that has passed the filter rule to the dual-homed firewall, which will perform more tests on the incoming traffic. Once the incoming traffic has passed the test performed by the dual-homed system, the traffic may then be sent to the internal screening router, where additional tests on the packet are performed. The internal screening router is typically configured to accept only data from the dual-homed firewall, ensuring that hackers can't skip past the outside firewall layers. Figure 16-4 shows the screened subnet firewall configuration.

Firewall Types

Three types of firewalls can be used: packet-level firewall, application-level firewall, and circuit-level firewall. Each uses different security approaches, thus providing advantages

FIGURE 16-4

A screened subnet uses two screening routers and a firewall.

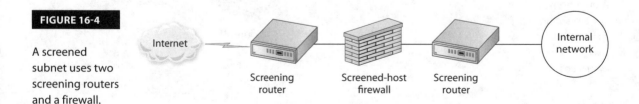

over the others. When you have a complete understanding of the features and the type of security needed from a firewall, you can determine the implementation that bests fits your environment.

Packet-Filtering Firewall

A *packet-filtering* firewall is usually a form of screening router that examines packets based on filters set up at the network and transport layers. You can block incoming or outgoing traffic according to TCP/IP address or port address rules, so packet-level firewalls map to OSI layers 3 and 4 (network and transport layers, respectively). For example, you may choose to disable all incoming traffic but enable outbound traffic. You can also set up rules that will enable certain types of requests to pass, whereas others are denied. The information that rules can be based on includes source address, destination address, protocol type, and source and destination port address.

For example, if you intend to allow all incoming traffic from any system that is destined for port 80 on your web server's IP address of 24.15.34.89 while disabling all other inbound traffic, you may configure a packet-filtering rule such as the following:

Direction	Protocol	Source Address	Destination Address	Source Port	Destination Port	Rule
Inbound	TCP	Any	24.15.34.89	Any	80	Allow
Inbound	TCP	Any	Any	Any	Any	Deny

Typically, the first rule that applies to the packet is what happens with the data. For example, with the first rule, if we have any inbound traffic destined for port 80 on IP address 24.15.34.89, it would be allowed through, but any other traffic would be compared against the next rule, which would deny the traffic at the firewall.

⊚ a t c h   A packet-filtering firewall uses an *access control list (ACL),* which is a list of rules on the firewall that are used to decide which traffic is allowed to pass through.

Stateful Packet Inspection Firewall

Packet-filtering firewalls look like a great type of firewall at first, but they are not all that intelligent because it is easy for a hacker to spoof a packet so that it meets the rules of the firewall. For example, if you open port 80 on a packet-filtering firewall, any packets destined for port 80 will bypass the firewall.

Like packet-filtering firewalls, a *stateful packet inspection firewall* can filter traffic based on the source and destination IP address or port number, but can also look at the context of the conversation and determine if the packet is supposed to be received at that point in the conversation. If the firewall receives a packet in the correct context of the conversation and the packet follows one of the rules, it allows the packet into the network.

For example, if a hacker tries to send malicious commands to the firewall with a destination port of 80 and the hacker has not performed a three-way handshake first, the stateful packet inspection firewall says, "Nope, sorry, you are not allowed in because I don't see that we have established a connection." Stateful packet inspection firewalls know that before TCP communication can occur there needs to be a three-way handshake.

Application-Level Firewall

The *application-level* firewall understands the data at the application level. Application-level firewalls operate at the application, presentation, and session layers of the OSI model. Data at the application level can actually be understood and monitored to verify that no harmful information is included. An example of an application-level firewall is a proxy server. The proxy server can analyze the application data in the packet and decide if it is allowed through the firewall. This is different from a packet-filtering firewall, which can only analyze the headers of the packet, including information such as the source and destination IP addresses and port numbers.

In addition, clients often must be configured to pass through the proxy to use it—ideally, after they have authenticated themselves properly. Proxy servers are also used to mask the original origin of a packet. For example, an Internet proxy will pass the request on, but the source address listed in the packet will be that of the proxy server and not of the client that made the request. The overall server doesn't just filter the packets; it actually takes in the original and retransmits a new packet through a different network interface.

Circuit-Level Firewall

A *circuit-level* firewall is similar to an application proxy except that the security mechanisms are applied when the connection is established. From then on, the packets flow between the hosts without any further checking from the firewall. Circuit-level firewalls operate at the transport layer.

Other Firewall Features

As firewalls have evolved, additional feature sets have grown out of—or have been added to—the feature set of a firewall. These features are used to provide faster access to Internet content and better security mechanisms to help protect network resources. A few features that are implemented on firewall products, or are their own stand-alone products, are discussed in the following sections.

NAT/PAT

Most routers and firewalls support *Network Address Translation (NAT),* which allows the device to translate the source address of any outbound traffic from your internal systems to the public IP address used on the NAT device. This gives you the financial benefit of allowing multiple internal systems to access the Internet with only one IP address, and gives you the security benefit of hiding the internal addresses from the Internet. Most implementations of NAT also do *Port Address Translation (PAT)*, where not only the source IP address is replaced, but also the source port address. To review NAT and PAT, check out Chapter 9.

Caching Servers

Caching servers are used to cache Internet content on a server within your local LAN, so that if additional requests are made for the same content from a client, the content is delivered from the caching server—not retrieved from the Internet a second time. The benefit of such a technology is that you can conserve bandwidth on your Internet connection because the additional request for a resource that has been cached does not create network traffic on the Internet connection, but instead uses bandwidth on the LAN. There is no problem using LAN bandwidth, because LANs are typically much faster than a company's Internet connection.

Proxy Servers

By definition, a *proxy server* is a server that performs a function on behalf of another system. The employees who want to access the Internet perform the actions they normally would with their browser, but the browser submits the request to the proxy server. The proxy server then transmits the request on the Internet and receives the results, which are sent to the original requester. The benefit of a proxy is that anyone who captures the traffic sent out on the Internet would have the IP address of the proxy and not that of the internal network systems. Some proxy servers implement caching features as well, allowing the administrator to filter the websites that are allowed to be viewed by internal clients.

Stateful vs. Stateless Firewalls

A typical packet-filtering firewall is known as a *stateless* inspection firewall because it simply allows or denies traffic based on the header of the packet (source/destination IP address or source/destination port number). It is possible that the attacker could alter the addresses in the header so that it fits into the rule placed on the firewall and then the firewall allows the packet into the network. In this example, the hacker has simply made up the packet and it really has no context.

A *stateful* packet inspection firewall will look at the packet and the context of the conversation and if that is the packet that is supposed to be received at that point and time, it allows the packet into the network.

Content Filtering

Another feature available with a number of proxy servers and firewalls is content filtering. Content filtering allows you to filter what information users are allowed to see when using an application. For example, we may allow web traffic out of the private network onto the

Internet, but we want to make sure that users on the network are not surfing inappropriate content. At the proxy server or firewall we create content filters that deny any traffic with certain content. For example, we may deny any webpages with the word "sex" in them.

Zones and Firewall Placement

Firewalls allow the network administrator to divide the network into different network segments known as *zones*. When creating your firewall plan, you will typically create three zones:

- **Private zone (LAN)** The firewall placed in front of the LAN creates a private zone and will ensure that no inbound traffic from any other network is sent into your network through the firewall.

- **DMZ** The *demilitarized zone (DMZ)* is an area between two firewalls that allows selected traffic through from a public network such as the Internet. The DMZ is where we place any servers that need to be reached by the general public, such as a web server, FTP server, or DNS server. The DMZ is typically an area sitting between an external firewall connected to the Internet and an internal firewall connected to the LAN.

- **Public zone** The public zone is any network not controlled by the network administrator. The best and most popular example of a public zone is the Internet.

watch For the Network+ exam, know that as part of segmenting the network, you should at least divide the network into two zones—the private zone and the public zone. The private zone holds your network resources that are segmented from untrusted networks in the public zone.

Configuring Access Control Lists

The foundation of a firewall product is to be able to create rules, known as access control lists (ACLs), on the firewall that will either allow or block traffic based on characteristics of the traffic entering (inbound) or leaving (outbound) the network.

IP and Port Filtering

IP filtering is having the capabilities to allow or deny traffic based on the source or destination IP address stored in the IP header of the packet. Port filtering is another major part of building firewall rules. It is extremely important for you to be comfortable with the protocol (either

TABLE 16-1			
	Port Number	**Protocol**	**Description**
Popular Ports Used by Network Services	20	TCP	FTP server data
	21	TCP	FTP server control
	25	TCP	SMTP server
	53	TCP	DNS zone transfers
	53	UDP	DNS zone queries
	80	TCP	Web server
	3389	TCP	Terminal Services (RDP)
	110	TCP	POP3
	23	TCP	Telnet

TCP or UDP) and the port number used by an application when administering firewalls. Some of the popular port values and associated protocols for popular network services are listed in Table 16-1.

Direction of Transfer (Inbound or Outbound)

When creating a firewall rule, you not only need to supply the layer-3 and layer-4 address information, you also need to specify the direction of the traffic. Most times you will focus on inbound traffic for each of the firewall rules, but you may also control outbound traffic.

Source or Destination Address

On the firewall, we can filter packets based on the source or destination IP address contained in the IP header of the packet. This is a critical tool along with the port number (layer-4 header), because if you want to allow traffic into your network only from one of your other locations, you can specify the source address of your other location in the firewall rule.

A nice feature of layer-3 filtering is that if you detect an intruder accessing the company network from the Internet, you can block any data coming into the network from the IP address of the intruder to help secure your data.

e x a m

ⓦ a t c h   **Ensure that you know the popular port numbers for the Network+ exam.**

Implicit Deny

Before configuring the rules on the firewall to control what packets are allowed to enter the network, you typically set the default rule. The default rule is what you want the firewall to do with packets that are not governed by a specific rule on the firewall—the answer should be drop all packets except the packets matching your specific rules. Most routers and firewalls will have an implicit deny rule, which means they automatically drop all packets except the packets you specify.

Virtual Wire vs. Routed

Most firewall solutions act as a routed hop in the sense that they function like a router between networks or network segments. Another type of firewall is a transparent firewall, also known as a virtual wire firewall, which runs at layer 2 (no routing) and that has each interface connected to the internal network. This is a great way to filter or inspect traffic traveling on the LAN or network segment.

EXERCISE 16-1

Video

Enabling the Windows Firewall

In this exercise you will enable the firewall feature on Windows Server 2012 to block all traffic, with the exception of allowing clients to reach the web server that you are hosting and to allow clients to access your server using Remote Desktop.

Determining Ports to Open

In this part of the exercise you will determine which ports are used by services such as web servers and terminal servers so that you can open those ports on your firewall once it is enabled.

1. First plan which ports need to be opened on the firewall by filling in the following table:

Service	Port Number	Protocol (TCP/UDP)
HTTP		
SMTP		
RDP (Terminal Services)		

2. Once you have determined the three ports that will be enabled, on your Windows Server 2012 system, go to Control Panel | System And Security | Windows Firewall | Advanced Settings.

3. Choose Inbound Rules. Note the default list of applications that can pass through the firewall (they are identified with a green check mark).

4. To open a port on the firewall, right-click Inbound Rule and choose New Rule.

5. Choose Port to open a port on the system and then choose Next.

6. Choose TCP and then type the port number of 80 and choose Next.

7. Choose Allow The Connection (notice that you can also block the connection).

8. Ensure all network profiles of Domain, Private, and Public are selected so that the firewall rule applies to those profiles and then choose Next.

9. Type a name of **_LAB_HTTP** and then choose Finish. You should see the rule listed at the top of your inbound rules.

10. Now perform the same steps to create a rule called _LAB_RDP, which allows TCP 3389 communication.

11. Close all windows.

CERTIFICATION OBJECTIVE 16.04

Basic Forensics Concepts

The new Network+ certification exam has expanded on its security topics to include the basics of computer forensics. In this section you will learn about the role of the first responder to a security incident and the basics of computer forensics.

First Responder

As a *first responder* to a security incident, your first goal is to contain the incident. For example, if you are responding to a user's complaint that their system seems to be slow and you notice after arriving that it may be due to a virus, then disconnect the system from the network (by disconnecting the network cable from the computer) so that the virus does not infect other systems on the network. The only thing worse than dealing with an infected computer is dealing with multiple infected systems!

If you find that the systems on your network are replicating a worm virus out to the Internet,

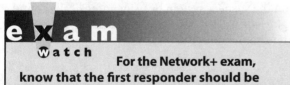

exam

watch   **For the Network+ exam, know that the first responder should be focused on containing the security incident so that it does not become a bigger problem.**

you may have to power off the entire switch or maybe even disconnect from the Internet so that the virus does not replicate from your network out to everyone else on the Internet.

Evidence Collection

Evidence is a critical aspect of any court case or corporate investigation, and as a result evidence must be handled with great care. It is important to first secure the area and to limit how much you change the crime scene and any digital evidence. Modifying the scene or the evidence is known as *contamination* and may result in the evidence not being admissible in court. If you are the first responder and your only goal is to assess whether a security incident has occurred, then you may need to escalate the incident to the security team when necessary.

Before you arrive where you will be collecting evidence, it is important that you first familiarize yourself with the situation so that you can plan for the type of evidence that you are looking for. For example, you need to know if you are looking for a computer, maybe a laptop, or a smart phone that could have potential evidence. Being prepared is the key!

Seize the Evidence

Note that if the system is on, and it is acceptable to perform a live analysis, you can run forensics tools to capture the contents of memory before powering off the system. In a corporate case this may involve waiting for a time after hours when the employee is not around and then taking the employee's workstation. Or, depending on the nature of the violation, you may seize the computer and mobile device immediately. When dealing with a public case, it is important that law enforcement obtain a search warrant for any items that need to be seized.

It is critical during seizure of the evidence that you document the scene, including making your own notes, labeling the evidence, and taking pictures of the scene.

Acquire the Evidence

Once the evidence has been seized, you can then *acquire* the evidence. Acquiring the evidence involves taking an image of the evidence so that you can do your investigation from a copy of the evidence and not from the original evidence. It is critical that you acquire a bit-level copy (raw sector-by-sector copy) of any drives on the suspect system by using forensically sound imaging software. *Forensically sound* imaging software is software designed for computer forensics and does not make any modifications to the source drive.

Analyze the Evidence

After you have acquired the image of the suspect's drive and generated the hash value, you are ready to start your forensics analysis. You should create your analysis only on a copy of the evidence and never on the original evidence.

When performing your analysis, you will use forensics software to locate data on the drive, including deleted files. Depending on the nature of the case, you may wish to look through the suspect's e-mail, Internet history, and deleted files to locate files of interest.

Documenting the Scene and Your Steps

It is critical that you document all of your steps after arriving at the scene. Be sure to take pictures of the area where the evidence is. For example, if you're responsible for seizing a computer from a suspected criminal's home, be sure to take photos of the area where the computer is before you touch anything. You may also capture video of your investigation steps with a video camera or screen-capturing software.

Document and photograph anything that is connected to the computer as well. For example, you may notice that an external drive is connected to the system. Be sure to photograph not only the external drive but also the connectors on the back of the computer showing that the drive is connected to the computer.

When performing the analysis on the evidence, be sure to document each step you perform. It is critical that if you find the evidence, you can explain the steps you took to find the evidence and that you can reproduce the results over and over again.

For the Network+ exam, know that term used for acquiring electronic data, analyzing the electronic data, and searching through it for evidence is known as e-discovery.

Handling Evidence

In the computer forensics field it is critical that you handle your evidence with great care, as you will need to prove that the evidence was in a secure location at all times and the evidence itself was not tampered with.

Chain of Custody

When collecting evidence, it is critical that you document and label each piece and store the evidence in evidence bags. When documenting the evidence, record what the item is, where the item was discovered, the label ID number, the date and time the evidence was collected, and who collected the evidence.

It is critical that you have a chain of custody form created for each piece of evidence so that you can record where the evidence is at all times. If an authorized investigator takes the evidence out of secure storage at a later time, then that needs to be recorded in the chain of custody so that you can account for everyone who had access to the evidence.

**watch** For the Network+ exam, know that the chain of custody is a document that records where the evidence is at all times. It is imperative that you have a chain of custody in place for the evidence so that you can account for its whereabouts at all times.

Data Transport/Preserving the Evidence

When collecting the evidence, not only must you document each piece of evidence and create a chain of custody, but you must also ensure that you take steps to preserve, or protect, the evidence. The evidence should be placed in secure containers and then transported immediately to a secure storage location.

With digital evidence, you will need to ensure that the evidence is protected from damage from magnetic fields and also protected against electrostatic discharge (ESD). ESD is a common way that computer chips are destroyed, so be sure to protect computer components.

watch Evidence should be documented and stored in a secure location with limited personnel having access to it.

Ensure that the evidence is stored in a secure cabinet and that the secure cabinet is located in a secure area with limited personnel access. You will need to prove that only authorized individuals had access to the evidence.

Forensics Report

During the analysis of the evidence, most forensics software allows you to bookmark items of interest and to have them added to a report that you can generate. It is critical as you are performing your investigation that you are planning the report on your findings by logging all of your steps and marking items of interest. The report may contain any of the following:

- **Items of interest** Your report should list any items of interest from the image. This may include e-mail messages, images, movies, or deleted files.
- **Log of actions taken** Some forensics software log each action you perform within the software. This could be very useful in validating the actions you have taken.
- **Result of the investigation** The report should have a summary concluding the result of the evidence found. For example, if you have a deleted file that contains potentially incriminating evidence, then it should be noted.

Legal Hold

Legal hold is a common term used today to ensure that users cannot delete digital evidence while performing an investigation. For example, you suspect that an employee is sending confidential data to a competitor via e-mail, so you place a legal hold on their mailbox and e-mail messages to ensure that they cannot delete any messages from their mailbox before you get a chance to review their e-mail.

CERTIFICATION SUMMARY

In this chapter you learned about important security concepts such as hardening the network, implementing firewalls, physical security, and basic forensics concepts. This section identifies some key points to remember.

Network hardening involves a number of techniques to create a more secure network environment. You should start with reviewing the company security policy for requirements on how clients are allowed to connect to your company network. You can then implement features on the switches to control what clients can connect and also enable switch features to detect suspicious traffic on the network, such as rogue DHCP messages and harmful ARP messages.

A firewall is a device used for protecting one network from a second interconnected network, such as the Internet. Firewalls compare the data passing through them with rules set up to allow or deny access. There are several architectures for firewalls; three of them are dual-homed host, screened host, and screened subnet. A dual-homed host firewall has two network interfaces and acts as a gateway between the two networks. A screened-host firewall has a screening router placed between the public network and the dual-homed host firewall. This provides an additional level of security against outside intrusion. A screened subnet firewall, meanwhile, puts a screening router on either side of the firewall host. This provides protection on both sides of the host.

The new Network+ exam has added physical security and basic forensics concepts to the exam. Be sure to know different methods to control physical access to your environment and the value of physical security. Also know the role of the first responder and the chain of custody when dealing with digital forensics.

TWO-MINUTE DRILL

Implement Network Hardening Techniques

- ❑ You can use 802.1x to authenticate clients using RADIUS who are connecting to a wireless network, wired network, or VPN server.
- ❑ Switches have a number of security features that can create a more secure network environment, such as port security, which allows you to limit the MAC addresses that can connect to a port on the switch.

❏ Use VLANs on the switch to create different network segments, allowing you to control which clients can communicate to other systems on the network.

❏ Always have a guest network for untrusted systems.

Physical Security Controls

❏ Cipher locks should be used over conventional key systems. Cipher locks have a keypad that allows you to enter a PIN number to unlock the door.

❏ Electronic locking systems can log the time someone has gained access to the facility.

❏ A mantrap can be used in high secure environments to control access to an area of the building. The mantrap is an area between two doors where the second door does not open until the first door is closed.

Implementing Firewalls

❏ A firewall protects the network by analyzing packets trying to pass through it and either allowing or denying the packet.

❏ Traffic can be controlled through the firewall by building a firewall rule that specifies the traffic that can pass through by source, destination IP address, or port address.

❏ A screened-host firewall places a router between the firewall and the Internet that filters and analyzes the traffic before it reaches the firewall.

❏ A dual-homed firewall is made up of a computer with two network interfaces that filters traffic from one interface to the other.

❏ A DMZ is a network segment that allows selected traffic through the firewall to the DMZ. The DMZ can host the web servers and the e-mail server for a company, but it does not host any private corporate servers—they are located behind an additional firewall.

Basic Forensics Concepts

❏ Be sure to document and photograph the scene when you arrive and note the location of digital assets such as computers, laptops, phones, and cameras.

❏ Record all evidence in a chain of custody document and log who is handling the evidence at all times.

Q SELF TEST

The following questions will help you measure your understanding of the material presented in this chapter. Read all the choices carefully, because there may appear to be more than one correct answer.

Implement Network Hardening Techniques

1. Your manager is looking to harden the network environment by ensuring clients are receiving IP addresses only from authorized DHCP servers and wants to prevent malicious ARP messages on the network. What features should you enable on the switch to accomplish these goals? (Select two.)
    A. MAC address filtering
    B. DHCP SNOOPING
    C. VLAN assignments
    D. ARP inspection
    E. DNS inspection

2. After installing a network operating system, what should you do before placing the machine on the network to help secure it?
    A. Harden the operating system.
    B. Disable the firewall.
    C. Configure e-mail.
    D. Build user accounts.

3. After hardening the operating system, what should you do to ensure that your server has all security fixes applied to it?
    A. Install antivirus software.
    B. Install antispyware software.
    C. Patch the server.
    D. None of the above.

4. You are assessing the security of the network infrastructure and have noticed that administrators are using Telnet to access network devices remotely to administer those devices. What change would you recommend?
    A. Use SFTP.
    B. Use HTTP.
    C. Use HTTPS.
    D. Use SSH.

Physical Security Controls

5. Your manager would like to implement a security system that can be used to secure the server room but at the same time audit who enters the server room. What technology would you use?
    A. Give each employee a key to the server room.
    B. Use an electronic locking system and give each employee a separate code.
    C. Give employees a key to the server room and ask them to record an entry in the paper-based log by the entrance.
    D. Ask Jane to store the key in her desk and log anyone who uses the key.

6. Which of the following represents the use of a biometrics device?
    A. A key fob
    B. PIN number
    C. Retina scan
    D. Proximity card

Implementing Firewalls

7. What type of device analyzes packets that attempt to enter the network and then either allows or denies the traffic, based on rules?
    A. Encryption
    B. Firewall
    C. Router
    D. None of the above

8. What kind of firewall provides a single computer with two physical network interfaces?
    A. A dual-homed host firewall
    B. A screened-host firewall
    C. A screening router
    D. A screened subnet firewall

9. Which component(s) is/are included in a screened subnet firewall configuration?
    A. Single screening router
    B. Host firewall server
    C. Circuit application
    D. Two screening routers

10. Which type of firewall is used to provide security based on rules governing the network or transport layers?
    A. Packet level
    B. Application level

    C. Circuit level

    D. None of the above

Basic Forensics Concepts

11. What is the role of the first responder?

    A. Contain the incident.

    B. Capture an image.

    C. Analyze the digital data.

    D. Perform e-discovery.

12. Your manager suspects that Sue is sharing confidential information with a local competitor. What is the first thing you should do?

    A. Back the e-mail up.

    B. Seize Sue's laptop.

    C. Seize Sue's phone.

    D. Place a legal hold on the e-mail.

Performance-Based Question Review: See the performance-based question sample from the author included with the accompanying media.

SELF TEST ANSWERS

Implement Network Hardening Techniques

1. ☑   **B** and **D.** In order to protect against unauthorized DHCP servers on the network, you can enable the DHCP snooping feature on the switch. You can also enable ARP inspection to help protect against malicious ARP messages.

☒ **A, C,** and **E** are incorrect. MAC address filtering is a feature of a switch that filters traffic based on the destination MAC address of the frame. VLAN assignments is a great feature of a switch that allows you to separate your systems into different communication boundaries. DNS inspection is not a feature of a switch.

2.   ☑   **A.** After installing the network operating system, you should harden it, which involves removing unnecessary services. Removing unnecessary services helps secure the system, because each additional piece of software running provides more security holes for a hacker to find.
     ☒   **B, C,** and **D** are incorrect. You would not disable the firewall, as you may allow unwanted traffic to the system. Also, unless needed, you would not configure e-mail or additional user accounts on the system. The less software installed and the fewer accounts that exist mean fewer ways for a hacker to get into a system.

3.   ☑   **C.** After hardening the operating system, you should patch the server to apply security fixes to any software running on the server.
     ☒   **A, B,** and **D** are incorrect because they are not ways to apply security fixes to the system.

4.   ☑   **D.** You would ensure that administrators are encrypting traffic between their administrative workstations and the network devices by using SSH. SSH is a secure replacement to the unsecure Telnet protocol.
     ☒   **A, B,** and **C** are incorrect. SFTP is a secure replacement to FTP and HTTPS is a secure replacement to the unsecure HTTP protocol.

Physical Security Controls

5.   ☑   **B.** One of the benefits of using an electronic locking mechanism is that they typically log when someone gains access to the facility.
     ☒   **A, C,** and **D** are incorrect, as they do not offer valid logging methods.

6.   ☑   **C.** Examples of biometrics used to gain access to a facility are a retina scan, voice recognition, and a fingerprint scan.
     ☒   **A, B,** and **D** are incorrect, as they do not involve using a characteristic of one's self to gain access to a facility.

Implementing Firewalls

7.   ☑   **B.** A firewall is used to secure the internal network from the outside world by rules configured on the firewall that specify which packets to drop and which packets to allow through.
     ☒   **A, C,** and **D** are incorrect. Encryption converts plain text to cipher text. A router is used to provide routing functions to the network, but it may have firewalling features.

8.   ☑   **A.** A dual-homed host firewall contains two physical network interfaces.
     ☒   **B, C,** and **D** are incorrect because a screened-host firewall passes data through a screening router first and then onto the firewall. A screened subnet firewall provides two screening routers with a firewall in between, providing an extra layer of security.

9.   ☑   **B and D.** A firewall and two screening routers are required in a screened subnet configuration.
     ☒   **A and C** are incorrect. These items are not included in a screened subnet firewall configuration.

10. ☑   **A.** The packet level controls the network or transport layer within packets, creating rules that allow or deny traffic based on IP address (layer 3) or port number (layer 4).
☒   **B, C,** and **D** are incorrect because the application-level type controls the layers above the transport level and the circuit-level type works at the transport layer.

Basic Forensics Concepts

11. ☑   **A.** The goal of the first responder is to contain the security incident and ensure the incident does not become a bigger problem.
☒   **B, C,** and **D** are incorrect. SFTP is a secure replacement to FTP and HTTPS is a secure replacement to the unsecure HTTP protocol.

12. ☑   **D.** Placing a legal hold on Sue's mailbox ensures that she cannot delete messages from her mailbox while you start your investigation.
☒   **A, B,** and **C** are incorrect, as they do not represent actions to take in this situation.

Chapter 17

Monitoring the Network

O nce the network is up and running you will need to take the time to monitor network resources to ensure that the network stays healthy and responsive. Monitoring network resources may require you to monitor network traffic, open ports on a system, or simply monitor percent usage of network components in order to identify when something is overloaded.

This chapter looks at where to go to monitor network resources and the types of characteristics to monitor. You are also introduced to a few monitoring tools that are used by network administrators day in and day out!

CERTIFICATION OBJECTIVE 17.01

Monitoring and Logging

An important aspect of managing and maintaining a network environment is to ensure that you perform adequate monitoring and logging of activity to help you troubleshoot problems.

Monitoring

Monitoring network resources is a task that most network administrators seem to forget about. It is critical to set up the network and have everything working fine, but you need to ensure you monitor network activity so that you know what is going on with the network or if something is wrong with it.

There are a number of tools that you can use to monitor network resources for each of the different operating systems (OSs) and devices.

SNMPv1/v2/v3

Simple Network Management Protocol (SNMP) is used to remotely monitor network devices. In order to use SNMP, the protocol needs to be enabled on the network device and then connected to it with an SNMP client. With SNMP you can monitor the device and get statistics from it or remotely manage the device. Note that originally SNMPv1 did not encrypt communication, but starting with SNMPv2 the traffic can be encrypted.

To use SNMP to monitor a device or server you will install SNMP agent software on the device or server. On your administration workstation you will install SNMP management software, which then connects to all the agents so that you can monitor all devices from a single location. The management software can tell you things like the type of device you are monitoring, IP address, free disk space, open files, network statistics, and the ARP table, to name a few possible items.

There are a number of concepts related to SNMP you need to know for the exam:

- **Management information base (MIB)**   This is the system that defines the types of information (called objects) that can be retrieved by a device. An MIB is a hierarchy of objects, with each object identified by an object ID (OID).
- **Trap**   A trap is a message from the SNMP agent to the manager that lets the manager know about an event that occurred on the SNMP-enabled device.
- **Get**   A get is a type of SNMP message that is used to retrieve a piece of information from an SNMP-enabled device. When a get command is used, the OID representing the piece of information requested is passed into the command.

■ **Walk**   A walk, or SNMPwalk, is an application that is used to retrieve an entire hierarchy of information instead of just the single piece of information that would be retrieved with get.

Syslog

Syslog is a technology supported by a number of different servers and devices that allows the network device to send messages to a central syslog server, which stores event information in a central log so that you can monitor all of the devices from one location.

The list of monitoring tools and logs could go on and on; the following are some critical logs and tools you should know for the Network+ exam:

■ **System logs**   Most servers and devices have system logs where system information, warnings, and error messages are stored. You should review the system logs on a regular basis. In Windows, you can review the system log by using the Event Viewer.

■ **History logs**   History logs are past log files on the server or device. It is important that you regularly save the system logs to history logs and then clear the system log. This allows you to find past events for specific days as you have archived the logs and keeps the system logs from getting too large.

■ **General logs**   When monitoring any application activity, it is important to see if the application logs activity to a log file or if it can be configured to log activity to a log file. Most networking applications and services can take advantage of logging, which can help you troubleshoot problems.

■ **Traffic analysis**   Network administrators commonly use an application that captures traffic as it travels along the network and then summarizes it for you. These programs will typically identify what systems are generating the most traffic on the network and how much broadcast traffic exists on the network.

■ **Network sniffer**   A great program to use for monitoring network traffic is a network sniffer, also known as a packet sniffer or protocol analyzer. A network sniffer will capture all the network traffic on your network segment (collision domain) and allow you to browse through the details of the traffic to identify issues.

e**x**a m

ⓦatch   Be sure to know the purpose of SNMP and syslog as monitoring tools. SNMP is an application-layer protocol that can be configured on most devices to allow you to monitor the device. Syslog is a technology that can centrally log information to a syslog server.

Logging

As mentioned earlier, an important form of information that is extremely valuable when troubleshooting network issues is log files. Most operating systems and server software maintain a record of activity in a log file. For example, if you are using Microsoft's web server, Internet Information Services (IIS), by default, it logs any visits to your website in a text file. The benefit of having the information in a log is that if you notice suspicious activity with the system, you can look at the log file and view information such as the date and time someone visited the site, their IP address (client IP), what page they requested, and what program they used (User-Agent). Figure 17-1 displays a web log from an IIS server.

The following are default locations in Windows that you can use to find log files:

- **Microsoft Web Server** Stores the log files in the c:\windows\system32 \logfiles\ w3svc1 directory.
- **Microsoft FTP Server** Stores the log files in the c:\windows\system32 \logfiles\ msftpsvc1 directory.
- **Windows Clustering** Stores the log files in the c:\windows\system32 \logfiles\ cluster directory.
- **Firewall log** If you turn on logging in the Windows Firewall in the Advanced Settings page, you can log dropped packets to the default log file of c:\windows\ pfirewall.log.

FIGURE 17-1   Looking at a web server log file

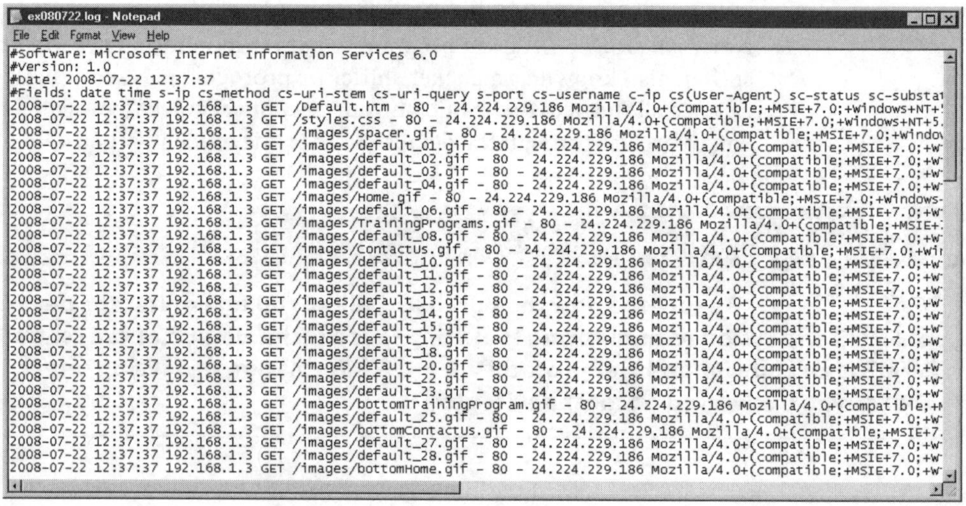

- **Audit logs**   Stores the log entries in the Security Log of the Windows Event Viewer. The files for the Event Viewer are stored in the c:\windows\system32 \config folder, but you will use the Event Viewer to view the log entries.

UNIX and Linux also use a number of log files to record activity on the system. The following are some popular log files in Linux:

- **Linux system log file**   Most system and kernel messages are logged into the /var/log/messages text file. For example, failed logins or newly detected hardware messages show up in this file.
- **Linux last login file**   The /var/log/lastlog file lists the user name, IP address, and date/time of user logins. Use the **lastlog** command to view this data.
- **Linux Apache Web Server logs**   Apache stores error and access log files under /var/log/apache2. Since these are text files, use any text editor to view them.

A number of log files are created with each operating system and application. Be sure to spend some time and find where the software you support logs information.

CERTIFICATION OBJECTIVE 17.02

Monitoring Tools

There are a number of tools that you can use to monitor network and server performance. Two of the most popular tools in the Windows environment are Network Monitor to monitor network traffic and the Performance Console to monitor the health of a system.

Packet/Network Analyzer

A packet or network analyzer, such as Wireshark, Microsoft's Network Monitor, or tcpdump for Linux, can be used to monitor and analyze network traffic. A tool such as Network Monitor is outstanding for monitoring network activity and troubleshooting network performance. Network Monitor is a good choice if you are troubleshooting communication problems and you need to see the details of the packets. To aid in the analysis of captured data, you can download a number of add-ins known as "Experts" for Network Monitor. For example, you can use the Top Users' Expert to identify the heaviest users of network bandwidth.

Switched environments usually require configuring traffic from all ports in the switch to be mirrored to a specific port where the administrator is running Network Monitor;

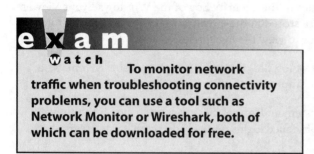

w a t c h   **To monitor network traffic when troubleshooting connectivity problems, you can use a tool such as Network Monitor or Wireshark, both of which can be downloaded for free.**

otherwise, the administrator is capturing only traffic sent and received through the port the administrator is plugged into.

You have used Network Monitor (shown in Figure 17-2) at different points in the exercises throughout this book to analyze network traffic, so you have seen how powerful a tool it is to help you understand and troubleshoot network problems by displaying the contents of packets running on the network.

Port Scanner

A port scanner, such as SuperScan or NMAP, is a useful monitoring tool that allows you to scan a system and determine what ports are open on it. The importance of being able to know what ports are open is that certain ports are used by certain services, so if you know the port that is open, then you know what services are running on the system. For example, let's say that management approaches you and says, "There is a new vulnerability with SQL Server. Can you locate all the SQL Servers on the network?" The answer is yes! You could easily use a port scanner to search for port 1433 (the SQL Server port)—any systems with that port open are most likely running SQL Server.

FIGURE 17-2   Looking at network traffic with Network Monitor

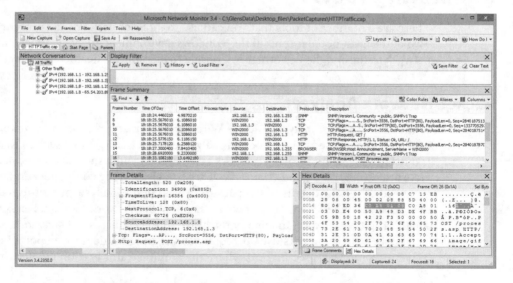

EXERCISE 17-1

Using a Port Scanner

In this exercise you will download, install, and use SuperScan, a popular port scanner for Windows.

1. Download SuperScan 4.1 from www.mcafee.com and run it as administrator.
2. Type the starting IP address as **10.0.0.1** and the ending IP address as **10.0.0.10** and then choose the -> button to add the IPs to the list of scanned systems.
3. Click the Play button at the bottom to start the scan.
4. When the scan is completed, choose View HTML Results to see what ports are open on each of those systems (note that if a firewall is running on those systems, you may not see any results).

System Monitor

Another useful Windows tool is the Performance Console. System Monitor (seen in Figure 17-3), a component of the Performance Console, is used to monitor the system's health and to troubleshoot performance-related problems. A performance baseline of normal activity should be established before using any type of performance tool. You can use System Monitor for a variety of tasks, including the following:

- Identifying bottlenecks in the central processing unit (CPU), memory, disk input/output (I/O), or network I/O
- Identifying performance trends over time
- Monitoring real-time system performance
- Monitoring system performance history
- Determining the system's capacity
- Monitoring system configuration changes

Using System Monitor

When monitoring the system's health, you are trying to determine why the system is running slowly. There are four areas of potential bottlenecks on a system:

- **Processor**   The processor may be overworked if you are running too many processes at the same time or running processor-intensive applications. If you determine that the processor is being overutilized (typically above 85 percent

FIGURE 17-3   Using System Monitor on a Windows server

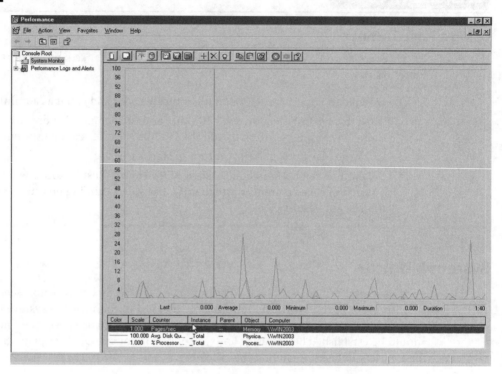

utilization), you may need to upgrade the processor, add another processor, or enable processor hyperthreading (if your processor supports hyperthreading).

■ **Memory**   You may notice that the system is getting sluggish because you do not have enough memory. If you don't have enough memory, the system will be doing a lot of paging—that is, swapping information from memory to disk and then disk to memory; this puts a lot of workload on the system. To reduce paging, always add more random access memory (RAM).

■ **Hard disk**   The hard disk is another area of potential bottlenecks. Because the hard disk is servicing all requests for files on the server, you may want to make sure that you have a fast disk or multiple disks to service the request.

■ **Network**   The network card is a potential bottleneck as well, especially on a network server because it is answering all requests for network resources. You should make certain that you have the fastest network card possible.

When using System Monitor, you will be required to add counters to the monitoring tool. A counter is an element of the computer that you want to monitor. For example, a good counter to measure is percent utilization of the processor to help you determine if the processor is being overworked. The percent utilization counter is a characteristic of the processor object—an object is a component of the system, and a counter is a characteristic of the object. You may add a counter to System Monitor by right-clicking in the detail screen and choosing Add Counters.

When you click the + sign to add a counter, a dialog box appears asking you to select the counter to add. You can choose the object from the drop-down list and then choose the characteristics of that object (as shown in Figure 17-4). You will notice that there are hundreds of objects to measure, and as you add more software to the system, the list of objects will increase. For example, if you add SQL Server to the system, there will be objects and counters to keep a close eye on the health of SQL and your databases.

FIGURE 17-4   Adding a counter to System Monitor

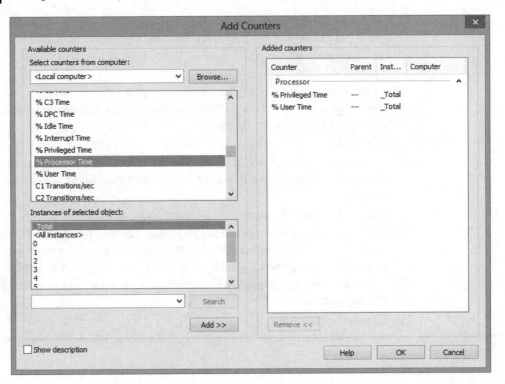

EXERCISE 17-2

Using System Monitor

In this exercise, you will use System Monitor to monitor the health of the CPU and memory in Windows Server 2012.

1. To start the Performance Console, go to Server Manager and then choose Tools | Performance Monitor.

2. Select Performance Monitor on the left. At the bottom of the screen you will see one counter already added to the console. Fill in the following table using information from those counters.

Object	Counter

3. To delete the existing counters at the bottom of the screen, select the counter and press DELETE on the keyboard. You will add the counters manually yourself.

4. To add a counter, click the + button on the toolbar at the top of the screen in System Monitor.

5. In the Add Counters dialog box, in the Available Counters section on the left side of the dialog box, expand the Memory object. Ensure that Pages/sec is the counter you are adding by having it selected in the counter list.

6. Click Add.

7. Let's add the % Processor Time so that you can be sure your processor is not being overworked. Expand the Processor object, and then select % Processor Time as the counter.

8. Click Add to add the counter to Performance Monitor.

9. You have added two counters: the Pages/sec counter to monitor how much paging is occurring on the system and the % Processor Time counter to view how much of the processor is being used. Click OK to close the Add Counters dialog box.

10. Start up another program, such as Outlook, to see whether you get any activity in System Monitor.

11. Close all applications.

Event Viewer

Windows-based operating systems such as Windows clients and Windows servers each have an error log mechanism called the Event Viewer that is critical to the diagnosis and resolution of problems within those operating systems. It is recommended that you consult the Event Viewer during the troubleshooting process, watching for the critical, red-X error entries that have occurred.

The Event Viewer is an application that reads the binary log files stored in the <windows directory>\system32\config folder. You will not need to go to the config folder to view the logs, however, because the Event Viewer console retrieves the information from the files located in that folder for you. Windows allow the creation of event subscriptions, which can forward specific log events to a central logging server. UNIX and Linux systems can also do this using the syslog daemon. There are three main types of logs within the Windows-based operating systems that you should monitor on a regular basis:

- **The system log** Records events that are provided by the Windows operating system and contains error messages that typically deal with device drivers failing to load, services failing to start, or general information about something that happens within the OS, such as purging a printer.

- **The security log** Contains all security-related events when auditing has been enabled. If you have audited events such as the failure to log on, success or failure to access a file or folder, or the success of account management, this is where that information would be recorded.

- **The application log** Contains events that have been generated by applications that run on top of the operating system. For example, if you install SQL Server or Exchange Server on the system, those applications typically record their errors in the application log.

EXERCISE 17-3

Video

Checking Event Logs

If you are having a problem with a Windows system, you can view one of three logs depending on the type of problem. This exercise will show you how to view the system log for problems with the Windows Server 2012 network operating system. You can see an example of this in the video for this exercise on the accompanying media.

1. To start the Event Viewer, go to Server Manager and then choose Tools | Event Viewer.
2. Expand Windows Logs on the left side to locate common Windows logs.

3. To view the system log, click System on the left side. You can see the contents (each entry representing a different event) of the system log on the right side. You can see different types of events such as information events (displayed with a blue "I" icon) or an error event displayed with a red "!" icon.

4. To investigate an event, such as an error, you can view the details at the bottom of the screen or double-click the entry to view the details.

5. A dialog box opens, and you will need to try to decipher the information presented. Notice that you can see information such as the date and time the event happened, the user causing the event, and the computer that was involved in the event.

6. Once you read the event information, you can close all the windows and start fixing the problem.

Other Monitoring Tools

The Network+ certification exam is sure to test you on common monitoring tools. Some other tools that you need to be familiar with are

- **Interface monitoring tools**   Interface monitoring tools allow you to view statistics on each of the network interfaces on a device. This statistic information can give you an idea of the bandwidth that is being utilized on each interface. Tools such as Performance Monitor, Resource Monitor, and Network Monitor allow you to monitor network statistics and utilization.

- **Top talkers/listeners**   There are monitoring tools out there, such as Cisco's NetFlow, that can give you a summary of which systems are generating the most traffic on the network and sort it by either the total number of packets or the total number of bytes. Identifying top talkers can be useful to identify denial-of-service (DoS) attacks or to identify the need for load balancing. Network Monitor is another example of software that can show top users (also known as top talkers) and top protocols using Network Monitor Experts.

- **Alerts (e-mail and SMS)**   Alerts are a great monitoring tool, as you can configure software to send an alert based on certain conditions or thresholds. You can configure the alert to notify you either via e-mail or text messages to your mobile device (SMS). Alerts are a common feature of many monitor tools such as Cacti, Xymon, and Nagios that can monitor networks and servers and generate alerts when abnormalities occur.

- **Packet flow monitoring**   Packet flow monitoring is useful to watch the pathway that packets are taking and to ensure that your network elements such as routing tables and access control lists are working properly.

■ **Security information and event management (SIEM)**   Security information and event management systems are products (typically software) that allow you to monitor security information and events from a single system—in real time! SIEM products offer centralized monitoring and reporting of security information and events across a number of devices on the network.

Environmental and Power Monitoring

Another common tool you can use to monitor network components is an environmental monitor. It is critical to monitor equipment temperature, as you may experience problems with equipment if it overheats. An environmental monitor, also known as a temperature monitor, will send alerts if the temperature gets too high.

There are other types of monitors as well—you can use a *humidity monitor* to monitor the humidity of the environment. You can also use *power monitors* to monitor power levels and ensure that adequate power is provided to systems and devices.

CERTIFICATION OBJECTIVE 17.03

Monitoring Techniques to Track Problems

In this section you will learn about monitoring best practices and methods of tracking problems.

Monitoring Best Practices

A number of best practices can be followed to aid in diagnosing problems while monitoring systems. The following are critical to successful monitoring:

■ **Baseline**   Ensure that you capture a baseline of a system's health (resource usage) while under normal working conditions. If you notice a system is not running well, you can compare the existing resource usage to the baseline to verify there is a problem with the health of the system.

■ **Bottleneck**   Look for bottleneck areas, such as processor usage, network bandwidth usage, memory usage, and disk IO. Each of these is a common area where a system or network gets overutilized.

■ **Log management**   Ensure that you are reviewing logs, but also archive logs (if needed) and then purge them so that you do not have a buildup of logs. A number of tools are available that can be used to centrally archive logs from multiple servers—Splunk is an example of such a tool.

■ **Graphing**   You can use graphing tools to help you report on monitored data. Visually graphing performance data can help employees understand performance goals and performance baselines much better.

Monitoring Utilization

When monitoring network devices and servers, it is critical to keep a close eye on their health. It is common for network devices and servers to be overutilized in four major categories:

■ **Bandwidth**   You may find that network servers and devices are overloaded with requests and as a result the bandwidth of their network interfaces is being pushed to the max. You can optimize bandwidth by teaming multiple network cards together (also known as bonding) so that the bandwidth of multiple network cards is used as one. Another option is to upgrade the network hardware to faster components. For example, you could upgrade your 1 Gbps network cards to 10 Gbps network cards.

■ **Storage**   You may find that the disk drive types you are using cause a bottleneck. Be sure to use the fastest disk technology and ensure that the disks you are purchasing for network devices are not rated as desktop drives. To improve performance, look to using redundant array of independent disks (RAID) 0 in order to write data across multiple drives in parallel. Adding more drives to the RAID array increases the number of spindles in use, which increases performance by allowing data to be retrieved and written to the drive at the same time.

■ **Network device CPU**   Closely monitor the CPU of the network device and ensure that it is not being overwhelmed. This could be a potential bottleneck if encrypting communication, as encryption is CPU intensive.

■ **Network device memory**   Monitor the available memory on a network device to ensure there is adequate memory. Also look for devices that have large data caches to improve performance.

Interface Monitoring

When it comes to networking, one of the critical components to monitor is the network interface. When monitoring the network interface, you look for information such as if a link is present or how many packet errors were received on the network interface. The following outlines some key characteristics to watch for on an interface:

■ **Link status**   Looking at the link light on the interface should tell you if there is a physical link. Green means there is connectivity!

■ **Errors**   Monitor the number of errors on the interface. A large number of errors indicates that the network card could be bad.

- **Utilization** As mentioned earlier, monitor the utilization of a network card to verify that it is not being saturated with too much data.

- **Discards and packet drops** Watch for a large number of discards or packet drops, as this could indicate congestion on the network, signal degradation, or faulty network hardware.

- **Interface resets** Interface resets is when the counters on the interface are reset to start from 0 again. Interface counters track packets sent, packets received, packets dropped, and errors on the interface. If you have not reset the interface in a while, you could be looking at old statistics.

- **Speed and duplex** It is important to ensure that the speed (10/100/1000 Mbps) of the interface on a network device matches the speed of the interface on the other end of the communication channel. The same applies to the duplex setting—you will need to ensure that the duplex setting is the same at both ends of the communication channel. These are typically set to auto-negotiate so that systems will detect what is being used and use that. A number of Simple Network Management Protocol (SNMP) tools that can monitor interfaces on the switches, routers, and servers such as Cacti and MRTG.

CERTIFICATION SUMMARY

In this chapter you have learned about the importance of monitoring network resources to help prevent problems later on down the road. This chapter has introduced you to the difference between monitoring and logging, a number of monitoring tools, and some best practices for monitoring.

TWO-MINUTE DRILL

Monitoring and Logging

❑ A number of log files are created with each operating system; be sure to spend some time and find where the software you support logs information.

❑ Most Windows software logs to the c:\windows\system32\logfiles folder.

❑ Review the logs on a regular basis.

❑ SNMP is used to monitor and manage SNMP-enabled network devices. The information that can be retrieved is provided by the management information base (MIB).

❑ Syslog is a technology that can have all logs for all your systems and devices sent to a central location.

Monitoring Tools

❑ A packet sniffer is used to capture and analyze network traffic.

❑ Port scanners can be used to scan multiple systems and identify ports that are open.

❑ System Monitor is used to monitor the health of a system.

❑ Event Viewer is a Windows tool used to monitor the event logs of a system, such as the security log, system log, and application log.

Monitoring Techniques to Track Problems

❑ To effectively monitor a system for health problems, you should first establish a baseline.

❑ Be sure to review the logs regularly and clean old log entries out of the log file.

❑ When monitoring systems and devices, watch for overutilized bandwidth, storage, CPU, and memory on a system or device.

SELF TEST

The following questions will help you measure your understanding of the material presented in this chapter. Read all the choices carefully, because there may appear to be more than one correct answer.

Monitoring and Logging

1. Where does Windows Server store IIS log files?
   A. C:\logs
   B. C:\windows\system32\logfiles
   C. C:\iislogs
   D. C:\windows\iislogs

2. Internet downloads have become extremely slow, and Bob would like to monitor activity and get some bandwidth statistics. What tool should he use?
   A. PPTP
   B. IPSEC
   C. SNMP
   D. SMTP

3. Jeff is responsible for managing three Linux servers and two Windows servers. He would like to review all logs on these servers from a central location. What technology should he use?
   A. Syslog
   B. SNMP
   C. Baselines
   D. Port scanner

Monitoring Tools

4. Bob is the network administrator for Company ABC and is troubleshooting why one of his switches is constantly shutting down at the same time each day. Which of the following tools should Bob use to help diagnose the problem?
   A. Port scanner
   B. Environmental monitor
   C. Cable tester
   D. System Monitor

5. A few of the systems on your network are performing slowly, and you suspect that there may be a virus on the network. Which of the following tools could you use to capture and analyze the network traffic?
   A. Port scanner
   B. System Monitor
   C. Cable tester
   D. Packet sniffer

Monitoring Techniques to Track Problems

6. Jeff, a senior network administrator, is monitoring network traffic and notices that the network is running at about 74 percent capacity. Which of the following could be used to determine if 74 percent capacity is normal or not?
   A. Syslog
   B. SNMP
   C. Baselines
   D. Port scanner

7. You are monitoring network traffic and notice a large amount of packet loss. Which of the following could cause this large amount of packet loss?
   A. Faulty network hardware
   B. Port mirroring
   C. Port security
   D. Wrong version of software

Performance-Based Question Review: See the performance-based question sample from the author included with the accompanying media.

SELF TEST ANSWERS

Monitoring and Logging

1. ☑ **B.** The IIS log files are stored in the \windows\system32\logfiles folder. There is then a separate subfolder for each service. If you host multiple websites on the web server, there will be a folder per website with the logs for that website.
   ☒ **A, C,** and **D** are incorrect because they are not where IIS stores the log files.

2. ☑ **C.** SNMP is a protocol that can be loaded on devices and systems that allows you to monitor or manage the device across a TCP/IP network. SNMP allows you to review information about a device, including statistics such as bandwidth utilization.
   ☒ **A, B,** and **D** are incorrect because they are not monitoring protocols.

3. ☑ **A.** Syslog is a technology that allows you to configure each device and system on the network to send their log data to a syslog server.
   ☒ **B, C,** and **D** are incorrect. SNMP is a monitoring protocol, a port scanner is used to identify open ports on a system, and baselines are used to identify potential health issues with a system.

Monitoring Tools

4. ☑ **B.** It is possible that the switch is shutting down at the same time each day because it is overheating. You can use an environmental monitor or temperature monitor to determine if the device is overheating.
   ☒ **A, C,** and **D** are incorrect. A port scanner is used to identify open ports on a system, a cable tester is used to determine if there is connectivity from one end of the cable to another, and System Monitor is used to monitor the health of a system.

5. ☑ **D.** A packet sniffer is used to capture and analyze network traffic. You can use the packet sniffer to locate suspicious traffic on the network, such as traffic generated by a virus.
☒ **A, B,** and **C** are incorrect. A port scanner can be used to identify open ports on a system. System Monitor is used to identify health issues with a system, and a cable tester is used to test connectivity from one end of the cable to another.

Monitoring Techniques to Track Problems

6. ☑ **C.** A baseline is recorded when the system is operating normally so that you can compare to the baseline at a later time if the system is not performing well.
☒ **A, B,** and **D** are incorrect. Syslog is a technology that allows you to centrally store logs from multiple systems and devices. SNMP is a monitoring and management protocol for TCP/IP networks, and a port scanner identifies open ports on a system.

7. ☑ **A.** Faulty network hardware is one of the reasons why you can have a large amount of packet loss.
☒ **B, C,** and **D** are incorrect. Port mirroring is a feature that allows you to copy all data to a specific port on the switch. Port security is a feature that allows you to limit which systems can connect to a port on a switch. Having the wrong server version does not affect traffic on the network but does affect compatibility with other available products or features.

Chapter 18

Troubleshooting the Network

K nowing how to deal with network problems when they arise is one of the most important parts of operating a network. In this chapter you will learn a methodology to find and diagnose problems in a systematic and logical manner.

CERTIFICATION OBJECTIVE 18.01

Managing Network Problems

Data communication is still not bulletproof. Many things can go wrong when you are networking several different types of computers, mainframes, printers, and network devices using different operating systems, protocols, and data transfer methods. When problems occur, you need not only an understanding of each of the devices on your network, but also an understanding of the network as a whole. Learning how each device coexists with and contributes to the network provides you with a strong foundation for understanding how and why network-related problems occur and how to resolve them. For example, if you don't understand how a router works, you will be quite overwhelmed when one segment of your network cannot communicate with another segment. However, if you have a very good understanding of routers and routing and one segment of your network cannot communicate with another segment, you will immediately know that there is a problem with routing—that possibly a router is malfunctioning. It is helpful to classify the types of problems you are having and to ask yourself questions concerning the problem in order to stimulate your network problem-solving abilities.

Does the Problem Exist Across the Network?

When you first encounter a problem, it is important to determine its scope. Does this problem occur with a specific machine, or does the problem exist across the network? You need to narrow down the problem as soon as possible. If more than one computer is having the same problem at one time, it is obvious that you have a network problem, not a computer-specific one. This phase of the problem-solving process often requires you to check the status of other computers on the network to determine whether they are having the same problem.

If you are having a network-related problem, the symptoms are helpful in determining its cause. In the example of one segment of the network not being able to communicate with another segment, you could quickly determine that you had a routing problem. Another symptom is that everyone on a floor in your building may lose connectivity to the rest of the network. The cause of this situation is likely a problem in the communications closet for the floor; likely a problem with the switch or the connection from the backbone to the switch since the entire floor has lost connectivity with the rest of the network. Another symptom is that one department of the company on a twisted-pair Ethernet network can no longer communicate with the rest of the network. The cause is most likely a problem with the switch used to connect this group. As you know, a switch connects groups of computers. The switch itself is then connected to the network backbone, and in this case, the connection to the network backbone from the switch might have been severed.

As you can see, quickly determining the scope of a problem is the first step in gathering information about the nature of it.

Workstation, Workgroup, LAN, or WAN Problem?

To continue the discussion on determining the scope of a problem, larger networks present even more possibilities for error. Not only are you faced with computer-specific problems, but you also can have problems within your workgroup, your local area network (LAN), or even the wide area network (WAN).

For example, say that accounting department users employ a terminal-based order-entry system to transfer orders to corporate headquarters. This system operates through terminal sessions on user computers across the WAN to the corporate mainframe. One day the connection on a user's computer is not working. How can you diagnose such a complicated issue? First, you need to determine whether the problem is occurring with a workstation, a workgroup, the LAN, or the WAN. You continue by going over to another computer and trying the connection. You find that this computer is having the same problem. Therefore, the problem is not computer specific. Luckily, the same order-entry program can be used to acquire the monthly sales orders from another terminal session, this time at the regional headquarters. You find that the user is able to connect to the regional headquarters' mainframe with no problems. Therefore, you have proved that you can at least get out to another remote location, but you still haven't determined the cause of the problem.

As it stands now, you could be having a routing problem with the corporate headquarters, a name resolution problem, or a mainframe connectivity problem. You can test the routing problem theory by trying to communicate with another computer on the corporate headquarters' network. For example, you could ping another computer on this network by using the Ping utility and pass it the IP address of a system on the remote network. You receive a response from this computer. This response determines that you don't have a routing problem to this remote network. Next, you get the IP address of the mainframe and attempt to ping it:

```
Pinging 207.149.40.41 with 32 bytes of data:
Request timed out.
Request timed out.
Request timed out.
Request timed out.
```

You have found out why the order-based software is not working—the system it connects to is not responding and is likely down. You're sure that corporate headquarters is aware of the problem, so you decide not to pester them. You can check back every so often to determine whether the problem has been fixed. Luckily, it's their problem, not yours!

It is beneficial to know the IP addresses of some of the core servers on your network so that when you do connectivity testing with Ping, you will not need to dig up those addresses.

See how quickly you can determine the scope of the problem? It took only a few minutes to determine whether you had a workstation, workgroup, LAN, or WAN problem. Unfortunately, all problems won't be this easy to fix, but armed with the troubleshooting methodology presented here, you are on your way to solving any network problem that occurs.

Is the Problem Consistent and Replicable?

Sometimes you are faced with weird problems that are not so easy to solve and that require you to gain more information beyond the scope of the problem. You might already know you are having a LAN or WAN problem, for example, but you need more information to get you down the road to solving the problem. Next, you need to ask yourself, "Is the problem consistent and replicable?" and determine a way to replicate the problem.

For example, let's say that when someone in the purchasing department sends a job to the printer, it takes over five minutes for the job to print. As in the preceding section, we need to find out if more than one computer is having this problem. We send a print job from another computer only to discover that the print job once again takes five minutes to print. We now have a consistent problem that is replicable. The problem is not computer specific because we were able to replicate it on another computer.

When we take a look at the print server's health, we notice that its processing power and memory utilization are high—we need to know why, but at least we have found the source of our problem. Chances are, if we can free up system resources we will have a better-performing print server.

Once again, notice how quickly we narrowed down the problem to a possible source. Furthermore, notice how we used logic to determine the cause. We went to the next logical source in our printing problem—the print server. We didn't immediately go to the router and check to see whether it was routing correctly, and we didn't go to the domain controller to check whether the user had rights to print to this printer. We used logical troubleshooting methodology to arrive at the solution to the problem.

Standard Troubleshooting Methods

As you learned in the preceding section, it is important to isolate the subsystem involved with a problematic process. When you work with a problem internal to one computer, you learn to isolate the subsystem involved. For example, say that your system is not detecting your primary hard drive. What subsystem do you check? You check the disk subsystem, which includes the hard disk drive, the drive controller, and the drive cable. You wouldn't begin your troubleshooting by removing the video card and the CD-ROM drive.

You must apply this methodology to solving network-related problems as well. In the preceding section, you knew you had a printing problem, so your troubleshooting remained focused on the printing subsystem; you tracked the problem by following the flow of information. You would have been led to a problem outside the printing subsystem if you researched the problem and found out that everything you did on the network, not just printing, took five minutes.

CERTIFICATION OBJECTIVE 18.02

Network Troubleshooting Methodology

When you are troubleshooting network problems, it is important to follow a logical troubleshooting methodology. Always assume that the problem is a simple one. It might sound counterintuitive, but the simple solutions are most likely to elude you. As your experience grows, you can easily find yourself caught in a web of always assuming that the problem is more complicated than it actually is. When that happens, it can result in an excessive waste of troubleshooting time. Don't forget to ask yourself three basic troubleshooting questions:

- Did the device ever work?
- When was it last known to be working?
- What has changed since then?

Remember this: as an administrator, you are a "doctor." Your patients are computers and networking equipment. As with any doctor, your first step to finding a cure is making a proper diagnosis. Use logic and the scientific method, and do not forget to use one variable at a time. To put it in plain English: fix one thing at a time!

Always remember to start with the simplest things before checking the more complicated items. Most of the time, the problem is caused by something simple. It's easier to check simple items than complicated ones, and doing so can save a great deal of time. Complicated items can take hours to check, whereas simple items can take only seconds or minutes. A process you can follow to help you troubleshoot a problem is presented in the seven steps to troubleshooting that follow:

1. Identify the problem.
2. Establish a theory of probable cause.
3. Test the theory to determine the cause.
4. Establish a plan of action to resolve the problem and identify potential effects.
5. Implement the solution or escalate as necessary.

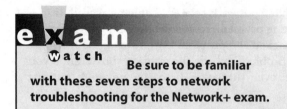

6. Verify full system functionality and, if applicable, implement preventative measures.

7. Document findings, actions, and outcomes.

Later in this chapter you will learn about some of the tools available for diagnosing and correcting network problems. Let's look at the seven phases of the network troubleshooting methodology in a little more detail.

Step 1: Identify the Problem

The first phase is to identify the problem. This typically involves you receiving a complaint from a user on the network stating that they are having issues. You need to identify the problem by performing the following steps:

- **Gather information** Start by collecting information about the problem. You can assess the state of the system when you arrive at the client's location. Collecting information involves using programs on the system to identify the problem or making an assessment of the state of the system. For example, you may use ipconfig in Windows to determine the TCP/IP configuration of the system.

- **Identify symptoms** It is important to identify the symptoms of the problem. Doing so allows you to know the exact effects the problem is causing. You'll use this information later to determine that the problem has been resolved, because these symptoms will disappear.

- **Question users** After your initial assessment of the problem, you should question the user to determine how the problem was initially discovered. You may ask the user things such as what program they were using, if the program was used before, and when they first experienced the problem.

- **Determine if anything has changed** One of the biggest questions you need an answer to when troubleshooting problems is what has changed on the system or network since the last time the system or network worked appropriately. You may find that a piece of software or network device was recently installed, which is causing the problem.

- **Duplicate the problem, if possible** When trying to identify the problem, it is important to try to duplicate the problem as much as possible. If you can cause the error to happen again, that will help you understand the process.

- **Approach multiple problems individually** When troubleshooting a system or network device that seems to be having multiple problems, you should focus on one problem at a time and make a single change at a time to verify what technique has worked.

Step 2: Establish a Theory of Probable Cause

The next phase is to determine the probable cause of the problem. In this phase you should list all potential causes and then prioritize them by how likely each one is. It is important to ensure that you come up with multiple causes of the problem and then rate them by the most probable to cause the issue. Also be sure to consider multiple approaches to address how the problem occurred and how each cause potentially could be solved.

For example, if a client is unable to access an Internet resource, it could be because their system has connectivity issues, or it could be because the office router is having issues. If you notice that others in the office are surfing the Internet, then the office router is fine and that probable cause should be eliminated.

It is important to ensure that you *question the obvious!* Too many times I see technicians look for complicated causes of the problem when it could be something as simple as the cable having disconnected from the back of the computer.

Step 3: Test the Theory to Determine Cause

Once you have determined the most probable cause of the problem, you then want to test your theory by correcting it. For example, if you suspect the system is experiencing network issues because the cable is not seated in the network card properly, disconnect and reconnect the cable. If you have network access once the cable is reconnected, then you have verified that the network connection was the issue.

When testing your theory, you may need to swap out parts with known functioning parts. For example, if you suspect that the network card is bad, you may have to disable the onboard network card and install a new network card in the system.

During this phase you have two considerations:

- **Once the theory is confirmed, determine the next steps**   If you have determined that the network card is bad, then you would resolve the problem by identifying that a new network card should be installed.
- **If the theory is not confirmed, re-establish a new theory or escalate**   If you install a new network card and there is still no network connectivity, then you must work on a new theory. For example, maybe network connectivity is not occurring because port security has been enabled on the switch port you are connecting the system to. If you cannot resolve the problem, you must escalate it to the next layer of support.

Step 4: Establish a Plan of Action to Resolve the Problem and Identify Potential Effects

After you have identified the problem and the cause, it is time to implement a solution. For example, if port security has been configured on the switch controlling which Media Access Control (MAC) addresses can connect to the port, then you will need to add the MAC address of the system to the port security list on the switch.

After you establish your plan of action, you must then take time to identify what effects the change you propose will have on the network. It is critical that you plan ahead by identifying the potential effects of your action. For example, if you chose to disable port security so that you could connect a station to the switch, then you may have created a security risk to the organization, because anyone can now connect to that port on the switch.

on the **Job**

Any time you make a change to the system, ask yourself what potential effects your change will create. It is important to get in the habit of identifying problems before they occur.

Step 5: Implement the Solution or Escalate as Necessary

Once you have identified the solution to the problem, it is time to implement it. Because you have thought out the solution and any negative effects it may have on the system, you are most likely prepared for positive and negative results.

If the solution is out of your control, you may have to escalate the situation to the next layer of support. For example, if you are troubleshooting a problem where a client cannot connect to a system called server1.companyxyz.com, and you determine that the problem is a name resolution problem, you may need to escalate to the Domain Name System (DNS) server administrator so that he or she can build the appropriate host record in DNS in order to solve the problem.

Step 6: Verify Full System Functionality and, If Applicable, Implement Preventative Measures

Once you have implemented the solution—fixed the problem—be sure to verify that your solution has actually fixed the problem and also has not caused any new problems with the system or network. Too many times I have seen technicians solve a problem only to introduce three new problems to the system along the way. Your solution should fix the problem, not introduce new problems!

After implementing the solution and verifying you have not introduced any new problems to the system or network, you should implement preventative measures to avoid this problem in the future. For example, if a system was infected with a virus and you have cleaned the virus off the system, it is important to ensure that virus protection software is installed on the system to prevent future infections. You also should ensure that the virus definitions are up to date within the virus protection software.

Step 7: Document Findings, Actions, and Outcomes

After verifying that the system is fully functional and your solution has not introduced any new problems, you are ready to update your troubleshooting documentation. In this documentation you record the initial problem, the symptoms, any corrective action you took, and the final outcome.

This documentation acts as a great troubleshooting resource for other technicians in the office if you store the information in a database that technicians can search. Instead of new technicians spending four hours troubleshooting a problem, they can search the database and hopefully find that the problem has already been solved, and the solution is at their fingertips within minutes!

Other Methodology Steps

When troubleshooting network issues, there are two other principles that should be followed:

- **Top-to-bottom/bottom-to-top OSI model**   When troubleshooting, it always helps to follow the layers of the OSI model, whether it is from bottom to top or top to bottom. For example, when troubleshooting network issues, I like to check the physical stuff first, then verify the link light on the network interface card (NIC) and switch, then start verifying the IP configuration, and eventually check out software settings.
- **Divide and conquer**   Separate all the problems and deal with each problem individually. This allows you to stay focused and work one problem at a time.

Sample Troubleshooting Situations

To follow up on the troubleshooting steps, let's look at an example of a network issue and the troubleshooting steps you can use to help you diagnose the problem.

In this example, you get a call from a network user who says she cannot print to the laser printer in her department but has no problem accessing the servers or any other PC. She was able to print to the printer yesterday but is unable to print to it today. In fact, no one in the department is able to print to the printer, which is a network printer. The user verifies that the printer is turned on; she has even powered off the printer and turned it back on. No error messages are displayed on the front panel. What do you do?

The first step of troubleshooting is to identify the problem and its symptoms, which have just been reported by your caller. You have also determined the affected area; in this case, the whole department that uses the laser printer is affected.

As part of identifying the problem you also determine what has changed. You would consult the log (if one exists) of what has been performed on the printer or the print server from the time it worked yesterday. While searching, you might find that the network interface card in the printer was changed at the end of the day yesterday. You check the printer and determine that the NIC was improperly configured.

In step 2, you would determine that the most probable cause of the problem is that the NIC was not configured correctly, so it cannot be contacted by the print server to receive print jobs. You may also identify that the TCP/IP settings on the network card of the print server are configured incorrectly as a potential cause. You need to be open to all possible causes, but be sure to determine the most probable cause.

For step 3, you want to test your theory on the probable cause by looking into the network card configuration. In step 4, you establish a plan on how you are going to configure the network card correctly. Don't forget to identify any negative effects your changes may have on the system or network.

In step 5, you implement the changes you have planned. After consulting the documentation for the printer configuration, you change the settings as they should be to allow proper connectivity. If you had determined that the IP address settings were incorrect in the preceding step, you would configure the addressing information correctly now.

For step 6, you would test the result by waiting to see whether the print jobs that have been sent to the print server will start spooling to the printer. After about a minute, the printer starts printing all the spooled print jobs. This step also dictates that you determine any adverse effects your change has made, but if there were none before the NIC was changed (except the problem for which the NIC configuration was corrected), all should be fine.

The last step is to add to the printer's documentation that the configuration was done improperly and has been redone. You might also document the correct settings once more to make sure that this problem does not occur again.

CERTIFICATION OBJECTIVE 18.03

System or Operator Problems

In some cases, it is very clear whether a system or operator error has occurred. A system error can be classified as an error on the part of a computer or network device or process that was not associated with a user's direct actions. This error can be a result of hardware failure or of something involved in the process of transferring or manipulating data. An operator problem is the result of a user's action, such as not logging on correctly, connecting to the wrong server, or printing to the wrong printer. The sources of most operator-related problems are obvious. However, operator problems can stem from misconfiguration of a device, program, or service by the initial operator—the network administrator. If a device is misconfigured, it might not be apparent until the device is promoted to a production area and fails in the process. For the Network+ exam, you need to understand the various ways a system or network device error can occur, the symptoms of such an error, and how to go about resolving the problem. First, you need to learn the areas that will provide you with a clue as to the problem's nature.

CERTIFICATION OBJECTIVE 18.04

Checking Physical and Logical Indicators

When you begin troubleshooting a network-related problem, several indicators can help you determine the source. These indicators are a combination of physical and logical elements. On a physical level, you can determine many things about the nature of the problem with the device in question by looking at its various indicator lights, error displays, and monitors. Let's look at these tools now.

Link Lights

Link lights are invaluable in determining whether a network connection is present. A link light is a green or amber light-emitting diode (LED) that shines if the networking device detects a network connection. Many network devices, such as routers, switches, and network cards, are equipped with link lights for this very reason. Most network cards have two lights—a link light, which remains on while there is a physical network connection, and a light that displays the current activity of the network card and pulses as data is transferred to and from the computer or device. This second light can be an obvious indicator that the device is functioning on the network. Link lights on some network connectivity devices (e.g., switches) won't light up if the wrong type of cable is plugged in (e.g., crossover cables are sometimes required to cascade switches together). If you are troubleshooting a network-related problem, it is best to start by examining the device's link light to determine whether a network connection is detected.

w a t c h   **The link light and the activity light are great aids when troubleshooting network issues and will definitely appear on the Network+ exam.**

Collision Lights

Troubleshooting network issues can also be determined by collision lights on a hub. Collision lights show whether a specific connection is having problems caused by packets colliding with one another. Collision lights can sometimes be the same as activity lights;

the activity light is green when sending or receiving data and turns yellow or orange when a collision occurs.

A collision results in the loss of the packet being received and the packet being sent. Sometimes a faulty cable or hub can cause packets to be generated from other packets or electrical interference. Sometimes called chatter, these disruptive packets can cause major collisions and can even halt an entire network due to collisions of all packets. Administrators and technicians need to watch these lights to verify that network chatter is not occurring.

Power Lights

Even more rudimentary than the link light in the network troubleshooting area is the power light. Simply put, absence of a power light means either no power is present in the device or the power light is burned out. If the power light is not present, check that the device is receiving proper power. If it is not, you should check the power supply, the power cable, or the wall connector. If you have verified that all these are working, the device could literally be dead. In this case, you will have to replace it.

Error Displays

An error display is a means of alerting you to a malfunction or failure in a device. This display can be a visual error dialog box on a computer when the error occurs or an LED error display on a network device. Such error messages should describe the problem that is occurring; however, they might not provide the necessary course of action required to solve the problem.

The error display might refer to an error code that you must look up in order to determine the cause of the problem and the ways to resolve it. Referring to documentation for the device is helpful when you're troubleshooting a network device, because each manufacturer has its own special procedure to resolve a physical or logical problem. Sometimes you must check the error codes on the manufacturer's website because they cannot easily or immediately be deciphered.

Error Logs and Displays

Similar to the error display is the error log, which maintains a listing of errors encountered on a device. This error log should contain the time the problem occurred, the nature of the problem, and, quite possibly, the procedure for resolving the problem. Unfortunately, error logs usually don't contain enough information to solve a problem, and you must consult documentation to diagnose and resolve it. However, error logging is important because it can help you determine when the problem occurred, what might have caused the problem, and what other processes are affected by this problem. Often, error displays give a visual alert of the problem and log the error into the error log for future reference. Many entries in the error log are not critical-stop errors. Some entries are warnings that do not currently indicate a problem but are worthy of your attention. Other entries, such as those indicating when the computer was restarted or when a service started or stopped, are purely informative.

Performance Issues and Optimization

There are a number of terms in the Network+ objectives that you need to be familiar with pertaining to network performance, bandwidth, and availability. This section will introduce you to those terms and also give you a tour of two popular network troubleshooting tools.

For the exam, you'll need to know about VoIP, SIP, and RTP. *VoIP* **is used to send voice over an IP network.** *Session Initiation Protocol (SIP)* **is an application-** layer protocol used to create, manage, and terminate the VoIP session. The *Real-time Transport Protocol (RTP)* **is used to send the VoIP packets.**

QoS

Quality of Service (QoS) is used to control the network bandwidth that is used by different applications or users. QoS is critical to high-bandwidth applications, such as Voice over IP, or streaming multimedia, where the network engineer will need to ensure that enough bandwidth is available to those applications in order for them to function correctly.

QoS ensures available bandwidth by assigning priority to traffic according to type.

Traffic Shaping

Traffic shaping is when the network administrator controls network traffic in order to reach a desired level of performance on the network. With traffic shaping, the network administrator will delay packets for delivery according to certain criteria, such as the type of traffic, which then leaves the bandwidth available for mission-critical applications.

Caching Engines

A *caching engine* is another method to optimize traffic. When you add a caching engine device to the network, it will download content from the Internet and store it in memory for other clients that request the same content.

You can purchase such a device from Cisco. When you use the caching engine, you need to configure the router to forward the request to the caching engine first so that the engine can decide if a trip to the Internet is required or if it already has the content cached.

High-Availability Concerns

When dealing with networking applications such as web applications, e-mail servers, database servers, or even something as simple as a file share, you will want to look at ways to ensure high availability. *High availability* means that you are taking steps to ensure that the service is always available. There are a number of technologies that aid in high availability.

High-Availability Clusters   Clustering is a popular high-availability solution. A typical example has two servers—called nodes—in the cluster. One of the servers is called the primary node, while the other is the secondary node. The primary node is the server that is available, and the secondary node is in a standby state and is not used unless the primary server becomes unavailable.

An example is your e-mail server. This is a critical service on the network, and users typically have fits of rage if the e-mail server goes down! Your job is to ensure e-mail is always available, so you install two servers in a cluster that is running your e-mail server software. Your e-mail server software is running on both nodes in the cluster with the e-mail data on a drive shared by both nodes.

When the primary server fails, the secondary server automatically becomes the active node and can then service any request from clients wishing to access their e-mails. The clustering technology takes care of automatically detecting when the primary node fails and then making the secondary node the active node.

Load Balancing   A very common method of increasing performance of network resources, such as popular e-commerce websites, is to load-balance the website. Load balancing means that you will install the website on multiple servers, and then the requests for the site are distributed among all servers in the load-balancing solution.

The load balance happens as the load-balancing software accepts the request and then uses an algorithm to decide which server to forward the request to. The benefit of a load balance is that if you have a large number of requests coming into the site, you don't have one poor server that is bogged down with requests.

Fault Tolerance

We talked about fault tolerance previously in the book, and I just want to stress that high availability and fault tolerance are two totally different things. High availability is about ensuring the service is available, such as the e-mail server, whereas fault tolerance ensures that the data the e-mail server accesses is available through data redundancy.

If you implement fault tolerance without high availability, the e-mail data may be protected through fault tolerance, but if the e-mail service actually fails, then there would be no way to access the fault-tolerant data. High availability will ensure the fault-tolerant data is accessible by having a secondary server with the e-mail service running. This secondary server will come online automatically if the primary e-mail server fails.

CARP

Another method of providing redundancy is with the *Common Address Redundancy Protocol (CARP).* With CARP, multiple systems are configured as a group, which makes up a virtual address. One of the systems in the group (the master) answers requests sent to the virtual address of the group, with the other systems acting as backup systems.

Physical and Logical Issues

When it comes to troubleshooting networking issues, you will need to troubleshoot the physical aspects of the network, such as devices and cables, but also the logical aspects of the network, such as invalid IP address settings or virtual LAN (VLAN) issues. This section will identify different physical and logical issues you may encounter.

Troubleshooting Copper Cable Issues

Most of the physical issues you will encounter deal with cabling problems. To solve cable connection issues, you will use the visual indicators mentioned earlier, such as the link light and activity light.

You may encounter a number of other issues that deal with cabling, such as

- **Attenuation**   Attenuation is the degradation of the signal as it travels great distances. If you find that you cannot communicate with a system that is quite far away, it is possible that you have exceeded the maximum cable length for that type of cable. You can put a repeater in the middle to regenerate the signal or use a different cable type.

- **Collisions**   If you find you have a lot of collisions on the network, it could be because you have too many systems on the network segment and may be using a hub device. Upgrade the hubs to switches, because each port on the switch is its own network segment, meaning the data will not collide with any other data because it is the only system on the segment.

- **Open impedance mismatch (echo)**   High impedance can cause signal bounce, which could cause communication issues. This signal bounce could be due to a miswired cable or an incorrect connector. Using a cable tester or analyzer will determine if there is connectivity between the two ends of the cable. If there is not, then you will need to recrimp the cable.

- **Bad connectors**   You may experience issues with connectivity due to the connector on the cable going bad. The contacts on the connector may not be making contact with the copper wire in the cable or the pins in the NIC.

- **Incorrect termination**   You may have a problem with the cable if you have mismatched the 568A and 568B standards. For example, if you are looking to create a straight-through cable, then wire both ends for 568A, but if you are looking to create a crossover cable, then one end is wired as 568A and the other end is wired as 568B.

- **Bad wiring**   Another common problem with network cables is bad wiring, especially if the cables were made in house. You may find that the wires are in different order at either end of the cable or not making contact with the pins in the connector.

- **Split pairs**   Split pairs is a result of improper wiring, where the wire pairs are punched down to the jack or connector in the wrong order.

- **Shorts (open short)**   A short in the network cable could cause network downtime. When experiencing connectivity issues, use a cable analyzer to identify if there is a short in the cable.

- **Split cables**   When splitting cables, such as your TV and Internet line, you may experience issues due to signal loss. If this happens, be sure to purchase a quality cable splitter or look to a signal amplifier to increase the signal.

- **DB loss**   DB loss is the term used to measure the strength of the signal when it was sent compared to when the signal was received at the other end of the communication. To have no loss of signal power would be 0 DB (decibels). You could be experiencing DB loss because of interference or quality of connectors and splitters being used.

- **TX/RX reversed**   Related to my bad wiring point, you may find that you have the transmit (TX) wire and receive (RX) wire reversed on the cable. A common cause of this is when trying to use a straight-through cable to connect similar devices together. You need to use a crossover cable in this example.

- **Cable placement**   When troubleshooting connectivity issues, ensure that the cable is not running along power lines or other sources of interference.

- **EMI/RFI interference**   You may receive interference from external components. Be sure to wire the network cable away from power cables and other interference sources.

- **Distance limitation**   When troubleshooting connectivity issues, always look at the distance of the cable and ensure you are not exceeding the maximum distance of the cable type. You may need to install a repeater to amplify the signal if the cables are too long.

- **Crosstalk (near and far)** Crosstalk is interference from adjacent wires. If you experience a lot of signal degradation, it could be due to crosstalk. To fix the problem, look at using another cable type that has more layers of shielding, but you may also experience crosstalk from wires within the cable if they are damaged. Near end and far end represent the distance from the measuring connector. For example, crosstalk occurring close to the connector would be considered *near end*, whereas crosstalk at the other end of the cable would be *far end*. A *time domain reflectometer (TDR)* can be used to identify crosstalk within the cable (more on tools later in this chapter).

exam

- **Bad SFP/GBIC** It is possible that you have a bad small form-factor pluggable (SFP) transceiver or cable. Try replacing the cable and transceiver to see if they are the issue.

Troubleshooting Fiber-Optic Cabling Issues

Like copper cabling, fiber-optic cabling can have the light signal weakened for a number of reasons. The following are things to consider when troubleshooting fiber-optic cabling:

- **Attenuation/Db loss** Attenuation in fiber-optic cabling is the reduction of power in the light signal due to components such as cable splices and connectors. Ensure that you minimize the number of these components the light travels through.

- **SFP/GBIC (cable mismatch)** It is possible that the *small form-factor pluggable (SFP)* transceiver or the *gigabit interface converter (GBIC)* has the wrong connector types for the cable. You will need to match the transceiver with the appropriate cable types.

- **Bad SFP/GBIC (cable or transceiver)** It is possible that you have a bad SFP transceiver or cable. Try replacing the cable and transceiver to see if they are the issue.

- **Wavelength mismatch** Fiber optics implementation allows you to break the light signals into multiple wavelengths; it is important to make sure that the equipment supports a common wavelength setting.

- **Fiber type mismatch** You could experience issues with communication over the fiber cable if you are using the wrong type of fiber optic. You cannot mismatch multimode fiber with single-mode fiber.

- **Dirty connectors** You could have signal degradation due to dirty connectors. It is important to ensure that the connectors are kept clean.

- **Connector mismatch** Ensure that you have the correct connector types for the fiber-optic implementation.

■ **Bend radius limitations**   There are many reasons why the light passing through fiber cabling can lose strength, and one of those is when the cable is bent. Fiber has a minimum bend radius and, if not followed, can result in bend loss.

■ **Distance limitations**   Each type of fiber implementation is limited to a maximum distance, so be sure to not exceed the maximum distance of multimode and single-mode fiber.

Troubleshooting Logical Issues

I find that most of the problems with networking deal with logical issues, such as administrative errors when assigning IP addresses or placing a system in the wrong VLAN. The following is a list of popular logical issues that cause problems on networks:

■ **Speed and duplex mismatch**   If you have a problem with a system connecting to the network, double-check that the speed and duplex settings of the card are set correctly.

■ **Incorrect VLAN assignment**   It is possible that miscommunication is occurring if you place a system on the wrong VLAN. Remember that a system on one VLAN cannot normally talk to a system on another VLAN unless you are routing between VLANs.

■ **Incorrect IP address**   One common logical issue is when the IP address of a system is typed incorrectly. When troubleshooting, check the IP addresses of all parties involved.

■ **Duplicate IP**   Verify that the IP address of the system is not being used by another system on the network.

■ **Incorrect gateway**   If you have trouble communicating off the network, this is typically a routing issue. Check the default gateway settings on all the systems to verify they are pointing to the IP address of the router.

■ **Wrong DNS**   If you can communicate by the IP address but not the DNS name of a system, you most likely have a name resolution problem. Check the IP address you have configured on the system as the DNS server entry.

■ **Wrong subnet mask**   If you have the wrong subnet mask typed into the TCP/IP properties, this could cause miscommunication. When you check the IP address of a system, also verify that you are using the correct subnet mask.

■ **Broadcast storms/switching loops**   Loops on the network will typically bring the network down. This is why Cisco switches use the *Spanning Tree Protocol (STP)* protocol: it prevents loops by placing one of the ports in the loop in a blocking state. If you have intermittent problems with the network where systems seem to just lose connections, then it could be a loop issue. Check how you have everything wired, and remove the cable that creates a loop.

■ **Missing IP routes**   If you find all clients on the network cannot communicate with systems on another network, then you most likely have a routing problem. Check the routing table on the router and ensure there is a route to the network you are trying to reach.

■ **Wireless issues**   There are a number of potential wireless issues. Your wireless client could have connected to the wrong wireless network automatically. Check to ensure that you are connected to the correct wireless network. If you are losing your wireless connection a lot, then you most likely are getting interference from cordless phones or the microwave.

■ **End-to-end connectivity**   When troubleshooting network issues, be sure to verify end-to-end connectivity, which is ensuring that communication between the two parties can occur and is reliable. For example, if troubleshooting why FTP is not working with the server in the head office, first verify that you have connectivity with that server by using the Ping program.

■ **Hardware failure**   You could be experiencing problems with the physical hardware itself or maybe a component in the hardware device, such as a faulty port.

■ **Misconfigured DHCP**   You may have misconfigured the Dynamic Host Configuration Protocol (DHCP) server. Verify the DHCP scope settings, including the range of addresses you wish DHCP to hand out and any reservations and exclusions.

■ **Misconfigured DNS**   You may have misconfigured the DNS server. Verify the DNS records and ensure that systems are referencing the correct system for DNS.

■ **Incorrect interface/interface misconfiguration**   You may have misconfigured an interface. Check the IP address settings and other interface settings, such as speed and duplex settings.

■ **Cable placement**   Verify that the cable is not running alongside power cables or other sources of interference.

■ **Interface errors**   Check the interface status and errors to help diagnose the source of the problem.

■ **Simultaneous wired/wireless connection**   You could be experiencing network issues due to having multiple network cards enabled at the same time. Look at disabling one of the connections and then verify connectivity.

■ **Discovering neighboring devices/nodes**   You may experience problems discovering neighboring devices or nodes if a firewall is preventing discovery protocol traffic or the Windows system has the Link Layer Discovery Protocol (LLDP) disabled.

■ **Power failure/power anomalies**   If you are having power-related problems, it is possible that the device or component is not getting enough power to function properly. Use a multimeter to check that adequate power is being supplied.

- **MTU/MTU black hole**   In the networking world, a black hole is an area of the network where the packets are dropped and never make it through that area. One of the reasons for the dropped packets is that the maximum transmission unit (MTU) size of the network is smaller than the size of the packet. For example, an Ethernet network has the MTU set to 1500 bytes, and any packets greater than that size are discarded.

- **NIC teaming misconfiguration**   Verify that the network adapters have been configured in the NIC team properly. You may need to remove the adapters and then add them again to the NIC team.

- **Active-active vs. active-passive**   If you are experiencing performance-related issues in a network load-balance environment, ensure that you have an adequate number of nodes in the load-balance solution to handle the workload.

- **Multicast vs. broadcast**   A number of technologies rely on sending broadcast messages out on the network. If you have a router separating the network, this may be preventing broadcast messages from reaching an intended destination.

Troubleshooting Security Issues

There are a number of common security-related issues that could prevent communication between systems:

- **Misconfigured firewall**   A misconfigured firewall could be blocking traffic you do not want to block or allowing traffic you do not want to allow.

- **Misconfigured ACLs/applications**   A misconfigured access control list (ACL) on a firewall or router may be allowing unwanted traffic to travel into your network.

- **Malware**   Malware may be present on the system, causing the system to act in an unwanted manner. Be sure to install antivirus software and keep its virus definitions up to date.

- **Denial of service**   A system may be unresponsive due to the results of a denial-of-service attack. Be sure to place your systems behind a firewall to control traffic that can reach the system.

- **Open/closed ports**   A common security issue is having too many ports open on a system. A port is opened by software that is installed on the system. Review the open ports and then terminate the application that opens an unwanted port.

- **ICMP-related issues**   Ensure that you are blocking Internet Control Message Protocol (ICMP) echo request messages at the firewall so that someone cannot flood you with ICMP messages (known as *ping of death*). You may also experience problems with ping reply messages from remote systems if you cannot reach your default gateway.

- **Unpatched firmware/OSs**   A huge security concern is having unpatched firmware and operating systems, because an unpatched system likely has known vulnerabilities that can be taken advantage of to gain access to a system.

- **Malicious users**   Be sure to protect your network from malicious users. This includes trusted users who may perform a malicious action without knowing it and untrusted users who intentionally perform a malicious action. Be sure to monitor for systems that are using packet-sniffing software, as they could be seeing sensitive information.

- **Authentication issues**   There are a number of security issues related to authentication. You want to make sure any protocols that transmit passwords are encrypting the passwords. Also, if a user is having trouble logging in, then check the account settings and reset the password. Also verify your Terminal Access Controller Access Control System (TACACS) or Remote Authentication Dial-In User Service (RADIUS) server settings to verify the systems are configured properly. Also, be sure to modify the default passwords on all devices.

- **Improper access/backdoor access**   Keep the systems patched to ensure that any vulnerabilities that can give someone improper access or access to the system through a backdoor are minimized.

- **ARP issues**   Ensure that you monitoring for suspicious or malicious Address Resolution Protocol (ARP) traffic on the network to help protect against it. If troubleshooting miscommunication, verify the ARP cache and its contents.

- **Banner grabbing/OUI**   Ensure that your servers and devices are responding with generic messages when responding to banner grabs. A banner grab is when someone makes a connection to a port and the system responds by telling the version of the product that is running, letting them know where to focus their exploits.

- **Domain/local group configurations**   Ensure that you have configured security policies to lock down the domain environment or local system. Configure policies such as the account policy, security settings, and user rights.

- **Jamming**   Jamming is when a device is used to purposely interfere with, or block, wireless communication.

Troubleshooting WAN Issues

When troubleshooting networking issues, you are sure to run across network problems related to the WAN environment. The following are some key issues to watch for that relate to troubleshooting WANs:

- **Loss of Internet connectivity**   Verify the WAN connection and check the IP address settings on the WAN interface.

■ **Interface errors**   The WAN interface uses different protocols; for example, if the WAN port is a serial link, you should verify the correct layer-2 protocol is running, such as Port-to-Port Protocol (PPP) or High-Level Data Link Control (HDLC).

■ **Split horizon**   To help prevent loops on the network, you can implement a feature known as split horizon. Split horizon prevents the routers from sending the packet back in the direction it was received from.

■ **DNS issues**   When troubleshooting the WAN, verify your DNS configuration. Check to see if you have the correct forwarders configured and references to the root DNS servers exist.

■ **Router configurations**   Anytime you are troubleshooting WAN issues, always verify the router configuration. Verify any firewall/ACL settings that may be blocking traffic and ensure that Network Address Translation (NAT)–related features are correctly configured.

■ **Customer premise equipment**   When troubleshooting WAN connections, be sure to verify the customer premise equipment. This includes verifying connections with the smart jack, at the demark point, loopback links, the channel service unit/data service unit (CSU/DSU), and any copper line drivers or repeaters.

■ **Company security policy**   WAN issues could sometimes be the result of network features that have been implemented that limit connectivity. Verify with the company security policy whether throttling and blocking access outside the network is permitted. Also check the policy for a fair access policy, looking to see if everyone is to be given the same utilization limits.

■ **Satellite issues**   When troubleshooting a WAN environment using a satellite link, verify the performance of the link and determine if the amount of latency is to be expected.

CERTIFICATION OBJECTIVE 18.05

Other Symptoms and Causes of Network Problems

It may sound obvious, but you need to closely examine the symptoms of a network problem in order to determine the cause. Now that you have seen the various causes for network problems, let's look at Table 18-1, which identifies some network-related problems and the appropriate solutions.

You've seen some examples of the most common problems you will encounter in your networking professional journey. You are beginning to see that the same problems will continue to arise, but the causes and solutions could be different.

TABLE 18-1	Network Problems and Potential Solutions

Problem	Potential Cause
I cannot connect to a computer on a remote network.	This sounds like a routing issue. Check to see whether you can connect to a computer on your local network. If you can connect, try to ping the router or another host on the remote network. You need to determine whether the host or the link to the host is down.
No one can communicate on the entire network.	When no one can communicate on the network, you have some work cut out for you. One of the major reasons the network may be down is due to a broadcast storm. A broadcast storm occurs when you have connected multiple switches in a loop, which is not allowed. For example, you can connect switch A to switch B, and then switch B to switch C, but do not connect switch C to switch A, as that would create a loop.
It takes way too long to connect to a network resource.	Make sure that the network is not being overloaded. Most network devices, such as switches and routers, display a percentage of bandwidth being used; check this display to determine whether the network is being saturated. You can also use network monitoring software to do the same thing. Further, you should determine who and what is being affected. Maybe you are experiencing a broadcast storm on one segment and not another.
A domain controller cannot be found.	Is anyone else receiving this error? This is most commonly a local workstation issue, either an incorrect TCP/IP configuration or a problem with the network adapter or cable. Make certain that the network card has a link light and the cable is firmly plugged in. You should also try replacing the cable to the workstation. Ensure the station is configured to use the correct DNS server.
A device in my system is not functioning and I can't connect to the network.	This sounds like a network card configuration error. Make sure that the NIC is configured correctly. Be sure that the correct driver has been loaded for the network card and then verify speed and duplex settings on the card. What has changed since this adapter worked correctly?
No one in this department can communicate, but other departments can.	Make sure that the switch is not locked up. Resetting the switch usually fixes this problem. Sometimes an incorrectly configured network adapter causes it. Communication issues can arise because a network card on a system or a port on the switch has the wrong speed or duplex setting set.
No one can access the Internet.	This problem can be caused by many things, but make sure that there is no problem with the Internet gateway, if you are using one; this gateway is a computer that acts as an intermediary between the Internet and your local intranet. This problem also could be a routing issue if you are using a dedicated connection to the Internet. Verify that the router or gateway is functional, and try pinging key computers on remote networks and the Internet. Use Tracert to connect an Internet host to see if the problem is with your network or your Internet provider's network.

(Continued)

TABLE 18-1	Network Problems and Potential Solutions (*Continues*)

Problem	Potential Cause
I can't reach the mainframe using its hostname.	Make sure that you are not having a name resolution problem. Did this problem just start occurring? Test for connectivity by pinging the host. If you can connect to the host using an IP address instead, you definitely have a name resolution problem. If you can't connect with an IP address, try pinging another computer on that network. Maybe you are having routing problems.
Our Token Ring network suddenly locked up.	Someone on the network is beaconing. Therefore, the nearest active upstream neighbor (NAUN) is having a problem. The network cannot continue until the problem is fixed. Sometimes the problem occurs because a bridge is locking up too.

Recognizing Abnormal Physical Conditions

The key to recognizing abnormal physical conditions on the network is knowing what a normal physical condition is. Normal conditions are determined when you establish a baseline of normal activity. Such a condition could be different from one network to another. For example, it could take your network only three seconds to spool up a print document, but it could take another network one minute to spool up a document of the same size. This doesn't mean that the second network has a problem; it could be merely a normal physical condition for that network. The following are things to look for when you attempt to determine whether an abnormal condition is occurring on your network:

- Printing takes longer.
- Authentication takes longer.
- You are receiving more errors than usual.
- Connecting to remote resources takes longer, if you can connect at all.
- You are losing connections to resources.
- Network applications are not running.

To determine whether these situations are abnormal occurrences on your network, you need to ask yourself a few questions:

- How many users are affected by this problem?
- Is the problem consistent?
- Is the problem replicable?

- Was there a recent upgrade to the network or computer?
- Has any of the equipment been moved?
- Have we encountered this problem before?
- Has anyone else attempted to fix the problem?
- How many applications is this problem affecting?
- Are there new users or computers on the network?
- Is this a busy or congested time of day?
- Which products are involved?

Your mind should be going at top speed, thinking of what could have contributed to the problem. With knowledge of what constitutes a normal network environment, you can determine rather quickly what is not normal.

Isolating and Correcting Problems in the Physical Media

Experienced network administrators know that cabling is one of the most common causes of network failure. For this reason, you should check cabling first during your network troubleshooting process. Most often, the cable that is damaged is the cable from the workstation to the wall jack. This cable receives the most abuse. Sometimes you can fix the problem by simply plugging the cable back in, if it has become loose or fallen out.

If you have determined that a cable could be the culprit of a network-related problem, the next logical step is to test your hypothesis by replacing the cable with a known good cable. The results are simple to assess: if you can communicate once again, the old cable was bad. If once again you cannot communicate, you need to continue troubleshooting or find another cable to test.

There are devices you can use to determine whether cables have gone bad, but these can be expensive. Most of the time you can swap out cables to determine whether they are bad. Table 18-2 lists some common cable-related problems and their solutions.

W a t c h   **The information in this section is important for the exam. Make sure you know the symptoms of cable problems and how to correct them.**

Checking the Status of Servers

Checking server status is critical because servers can be plagued with ongoing problems that are not so obvious, and if the problems are not corrected, they can become worse. There are

TABLE 18-2   Common Cable Problems

Cable Problem	Likely Solution
None of the workstations on the network are able to communicate with each other. They use a thinnet coax Ethernet to connect to each other.	The backbone has been severed. Find the point at which the bus became severed and reconnect it.
You have a brand-new unshielded twisted-pair (UTP) cable, but the workstation is still not able to communicate on the network. The workstation worked with your test cable.	The brand-new UTP cable might be a crossover cable. Use a cable tester to verify the cable is wired correctly and then obtain a regular UTP cable if it is not.
A workstation was just moved to a new location and is no longer able to communicate on the network. There is nothing wrong with the workstation's configuration.	Cables were damaged in the move. Replace each cable one at a time to find the problematic cable.

many ways to continually monitor the status of your servers, and each is operating system specific. Some general monitoring tasks are listed here:

- Check error logs.
- Check services.
- Verify connectivity.
- Monitor the performance and the network.
- Verify backup logs, including test restores.
- Test alerts.

The error logs can give you an indication of a failed device or service and a good idea of how to fix the problem. The errors listed vary from critical to informational. Some errors, such as a service failing to start, warrant immediate action. A service failing to start can be critical, and it often has dependencies that require the running of another service to allow the services themselves to run.

on the **Job**

It is important to develop a maintenance plan for your network and to include in that plan daily tasks such as monitoring the event logs for potential problems. Make it part of your early-morning or end-of-day routine.

You can test for connectivity with a server using utilities such as Ping to determine whether the server is responding to network requests, and performance and network monitoring can determine whether the server is overloaded or is broadcasting unnecessarily. An overloaded server can increase the length of time needed to fulfill network requests.

If you are backing up a server, which is always recommended, you need to verify that the backups have finished successfully. This is imperative, because in the event of an emergency, you will need to recover data from the backup tapes. You must also do test restores to make sure that the data can be restored correctly and that you understand the restore process. A disaster is the worst time to discover that your backup routine hasn't been working correctly.

Finally, you can configure your server to send alerts to specific computers or users in the event of emergencies or when the system encounters thresholds that you have predefined. A threshold is a peak in the rate of activity about which you would like to be notified so that you can correct the situation. Setting thresholds includes baselining your system so that you know the normal rate of activity.

Checking for Configuration Problems

When you are bringing a new server online or configuring a server with a new service such as DNS or Windows Internet Naming Service (WINS), it is imperative that you begin by verifying that the configuration is correct. Sometimes you will incorrectly configure a server and it will continually deteriorate or it will not work at all. You must make sure that the base operating system, TCP/IP, networking, error logs, and memory allocation are configured correctly. You must also correctly configure the additional services that run on top of the operating system. You will frequently have an application or database server that also runs a backup service, such as ARCserve or Backup Exec.

When you are configuring the backup server, you might have to reboot the machine for changes to take effect. This means downing a critical server for a few minutes, thus breaking connections with all users and services that are currently using that machine. You might have to do this during off hours; be very careful about configuring services for mission-critical machines during business hours.

on the job

It is important to have a change log book beside the servers and to train your network administrators to record any of their changes in the log book. This will help you identify potential causes of problems by having a history of the changes and who made them. Note that many large companies have a change management process that must be followed, which typically involves changes being approved by a management group and then scheduled and documented prior to being implemented.

It is important that the following services be correctly configured because they have the capability to affect the entire network, not just the local server—a catastrophe waiting to happen. Most networking environments rely on one of the services discussed in the following sections.

DNS

DNS is now a requirement of most networking environments, such as Microsoft Active Directory and any Internet-based application. Configuring DNS for these environments requires a great deal of planning. You need to gather the following information prior to installing the service:

- Your domain name
- The IP address of each server for which you want to provide name resolution
- The hostname of each server

This information must be correct; otherwise, your network will experience ongoing name resolution problems that will be difficult to diagnose. This is especially the case with hostname-to–IP address mappings. DNS entries can be entered manually, so you must be very careful not to enter a wrong IP address or hostname. You will not be prompted with an error message informing you that you have entered an incorrect IP address.

WINS

WINS is much like DNS in that it provides name resolution; however, DNS resolves hostnames to IP addresses, and WINS resolves NetBIOS names to IP addresses. WINS does not require you to manually enter mappings before you begin—this is because WINS is a dynamic service that can add, modify, and delete name registrations dynamically, saving valuable time for the network administrator. At times you will want to add a static mapping for important clients or servers.

WINS, like DNS, has many configuration possibilities. Although most WINS configuration parameters will not be covered on the Network+ exam, you will be required to know how to configure each client to point to the WINS server in a WINS environment.

The Hosts File

As you have learned, when you use DNS, you must manually add hostname-to–IP address mappings in order to resolve hostnames. With the hosts file, you also have to manually configure a database with these exact mappings. Unlike DNS, which uses a centrally located database of hostname mappings, the hosts file resides on every computer. This makes the process of updating the hosts file very difficult. The hosts file is usually located under %systemroot%\system32\drivers\etc.

All the DNS rules apply to the hosts file: you must be careful to enter the correct hostname-to–IP address mappings. A helpful tip for configuring the hosts file is to copy to the remaining hosts the newly created file that you have guaranteed to be accurate. This step ensures that you don't make any clerical errors on each of the remaining machines.

Checking for Viruses

If you have ever been a network administrator in the midst of a virus attack, you know how frustrating the situation can be. Once the virus gets in from the outside, whether from the Internet, a user's home computer, or the local intranet, it poses a huge problem. But how can you eradicate the viruses before they come into the network? A server running a virus-scanning program can make all the difference in applying "preventive maintenance."

Many companies engage in multipronged attacks against viruses, including continually scanning for viruses on the file and messaging servers and installing virus-scanning software on every workstation. Both precautions are critical for stopping the spread of viruses. The server can catch viruses coming in from the messaging servers, such as Microsoft Exchange, and from files stored on the file servers. The workstation virus-scanning programs can catch viruses on users' machines before the viruses get a chance to replicate to the servers and to other users' computers on the network. The virus-definition files must be updated on a continual basis. Many virus-scanning utilities enable workstations to automatically update the virus definition files from a central server, which means you, the network administrator, do not have to visit every workstation once a month to apply the new definition files.

Checking the Validity of the Account Name and Password

Usually, you configure services or applications to log on with a certain account in order to perform their functions. A number of services usually use the built-in system account, but if the service requires logging on to a remote computer, it requires an account name and password that resides in the network account database, such as Active Directory. Some services require administrative privileges or membership in certain groups on the network to accomplish their tasks, so you will need to make sure that the account a service is using is the correct account, has the appropriate level of rights, and is in the correct groups. You must document these special system and service accounts and remember not to delete or tamper with them in any way. If you mistakenly disable, delete, or affect the account details, you could find yourself with a service or application that fails to start—a problem that is often very difficult to diagnose.

I have seen network administrators install applications and specify their own administrator account for the service to use. When the network administrator leaves the company, his account is disabled or deleted, and, mysteriously, some of the programs fail. If the other members of the department were not aware of this configuration, they could be scratching their heads for days wondering why this program or service does not work anymore.

Rechecking Operator Logon Procedures

The most obvious problems often involve logging on. If a user mistakenly tries to log on to a network or domain in which he doesn't have an account, he will be denied, and he will call you, the network administrator. Users often forget their passwords or the fact that the password is case sensitive. After three attempts (or however many times you have configured the system to accept guesses), the user is normally locked out and will need to contact you to re-enable the account.

Sometimes users return from vacation to find that their accounts have been disabled or their passwords have expired. You may need to reset a user's password when he or she returns from vacation so that the user can access network resources. Figure 18-1 shows how to change the user's password in Microsoft's Active Directory.

Selecting and Running Appropriate Diagnostics

To build a strong network, you need to run diagnostics to search for bottlenecks or problematic situations. These diagnostics may reveal problems or limitations that you can fix before they get too bad.

You need to choose diagnostic programs that correlate with your specific network needs. For example, you can purchase extensive protocol-analyzing and packet-sniffing products, but they would be overkill for a 20-node network. Often, the free diagnostic products, such

FIGURE 18-1

Resetting a user's password

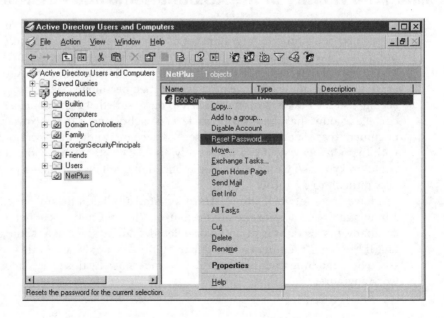

as Performance Monitor and Network Monitor, are capable of determining computer and network problems.

Whichever tool you choose, you must spend plenty of time with the product to determine the most effective way to deploy it. You must also be trained to analyze the results and determine what needs to be adjusted in order to remedy the situation. It will take more than one trial to establish a reliable baseline of activity for your testing.

For example, running a diagnostics or performance test at 8:00 A.M., when all the users are logging on, gives entirely different results from running the diagnostics at noon, when they are at lunch. Taking snapshots of activity from various periods of the day, week, and month gives you the most accurate assessment of your network. The longer you spend baselining your network, the more accurate the results. From there, you can begin assigning thresholds to chart and alert for abnormal activity. Furthermore, you are training yourself to read the various diagnostics so that you can quickly determine how, why, and where a problem is occurring. The following section gives more examples of devices that can help you troubleshoot your network.

CERTIFICATION OBJECTIVE 18.06

Network Troubleshooting Tools

In most network troubleshooting sessions, there comes a time at which a simple isolation of problems is just not feasible. In that situation, it's time to use some electronic tools to determine your problem and its source. This section discusses the most common network troubleshooting tools and how they are used.

Cable Crimper, Wire Stripper, and Punch-Down Tool

A tool that will prove to be useful from time to time is a cable crimper, like the one shown in Figure 18-2. A cable crimper should have the actual crimping tool to "crimp," or close, the connector on the end of the cable, along with a wire cutter to cut the ends of the wire and a wire stripper.

The crimper typically has a wire cutter, but you can also get a separate wire cutter or wire snips as a tool to cut wires. These are useful tools to have if working with cabling on a regular basis.

A *punch-down tool* is used to connect the twisted-pair cabling to the back of a patch panel—a critical tool when wiring the building or even troubleshooting wiring problems! Figure 18-2 shows a punch-down tool beside the crimper.

FIGURE 18-2

A network cable crimper and punch-down tool (inset)

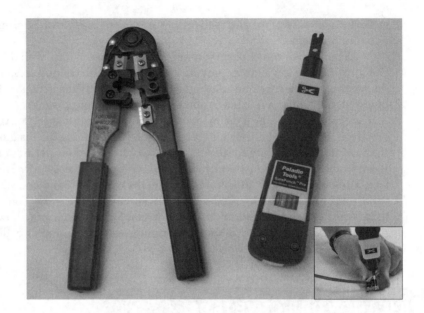

Cable Tester, Certifier, and Butt Set

You should also have some cable testers handy to help you determine whether the cable is crimped properly. A cable tester should have two parts to allow it to plug into each end of the cable, and it should have light indicators that light up as it tests for connectivity from one end of the cable to another on each wire (see Figure 18-3).

The tester should have a light for each wire in the cable. It will light up an indicator for each wire, one after the other—you will need to watch the lights light up at both ends and make sure that the order is the same on both parts of the tester. If the order is different, you have an incorrectly positioned wire and you will need to recrimp an end.

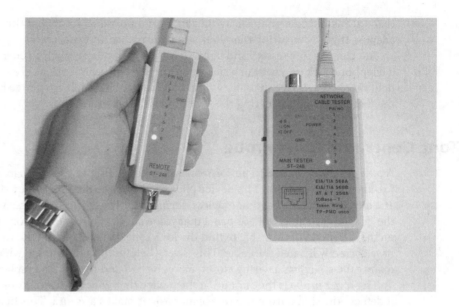

FIGURE 18-3

Testing wiring of a cable

Crossover Cables

A *crossover cable* appears to be just another twisted-pair cable, but two wires are crossed, which makes the cable not fit for plugging into a computer and a hub for normal use. The crossover cable is used to directly connect two computers to each other, without the use of a hub. This can be extremely useful when you are troubleshooting a system and want to have it disconnected from the network but also need to be able to connect your own system because it has diagnostic tools on it.

A crossover cable is also used to interconnect some hubs and switches. If you were to substitute a crossover cable for a regular twisted-pair cable to connect two hubs, it would not work correctly (there would be no link light for that port). Therefore, it is important that you mark your crossover cables or use a different color cable to designate a crossover cable. Many companies use gray cables or blue cables for regular network cables (straight-through) and have their crossover cables use either red or yellow color. You will not need many crossover cables, and you can make them yourself if you have the correct pinout.

Loopback Plug, Line Testers, and Light Meter

A hardware loopback adapter is a way to test the ports on a system without having to connect to an external device. For example, you can use a serial loopback adapter to verify that a transmitted signal is leaving your serial port and returning through the loopback adapter, thereby ensuring that your serial port is working correctly.

You can use line testers and light meters to verify items such as current and voltage on a telephone jack or a network jack to ensure that the connections are working properly. A light meter is a device that allows you to test for items such as voltage by having lights on the meter light up indicating the levels of voltage present.

Tone Generator/Toner Probe

A *tone generator* is used to perform tests on phone and network lines in what is referred to as a fox-and-hound process. The device clips to a wire, terminal panel, or standard modular jack and aids in the identification of wires during the wire-tracing process. You begin by attaching the "fox" to the cable, jack, or panel that you want to trace, and you continue with the "hound" on the other end of the cable to find the fox's tone. When you find the tone, you know that you have correctly located the cable. This is very helpful for determining which cable in a group of many cables, such as a wiring closet, has gone bad and needs to be replaced.

The *toner probe* is the "hound"-type device that you move alongside the cables, and when it detects the signal from the tone generator, it makes a sound. This helps you identify the correct cable in a batch of cables.

TDR and OTDR

A *time domain reflectometer (TDR)* is used to troubleshoot problems with a cable by sending a signal down the cable, where it is reflected at some point. The TDR then calculates the distance down the cable that the signal traveled before being reflected by measuring the amount of time it took for the signal to be returned. If this distance is less than your overall cable length, a cable problem exists at that distance from your location. (Yes, this means that it is in the most inconvenient location possible. It is a law of networking that when something breaks, it will be in the worst possible place to fix it.) The TDR can also be used to test for shorts and breaks in the cable. This is something that an oscilloscope (next discussion) can do as well, and many times the oscilloscope will have a TDR integrated into it.

Optical time domain reflectometers (OTDRs) are similar to TDRs, but are used to test the performance of fiber-optic cables.

Oscilloscopes

Oscilloscopes and toner probes can determine when there are shorts, crimps, or attenuation in a cable. An *oscilloscope* formats its output in a graphical format. They are commonly used to test cables that have been recently run through walls to ensure that there are no problems with the cables before you use them.

Multimeter

A *multimeter* (shown in Figure 18-4) is a common device used to measure voltage, or when troubleshooting cabling issues, it can measure resistance (in ohms). A normal cable without any problems should measure a resistance of 0 ohms, but if the cable is broken or has faults in the wiring, it will measure higher resistance.

FIGURE 18-4

A multimeter can detect cable issues by measuring resistance.

Software Troubleshooting Tools

There are a number of different software tools that you can use when troubleshooting network problems. You may find yourself using tools such as protocol analyzers, throughput testers, and connectivity software.

Protocol Analyzer and Wi-Fi Analyzer

Protocol analyzer and *packet sniffer* are used interchangeably by network administrators as both are used to capture network traffic so you can analyze the traffic and determine the cause of a problem. Technically, however, a *protocol analyzer* is used to analyze traffic from a particular protocol, whereas a *packet sniffer* captures all network traffic.

A *Wi-Fi analyzer* is typically software that you use to detect wireless networks and display characteristics of the wireless network, such as the strength of the signal, the Service Set Identifiers (SSIDs), and potentially the MAC addresses of the clients that are connected to the wireless network. You can also use a spectrum analyzer, which takes the Wi-Fi analyzer a step further by analyzing the spectrum and displaying interference information from the radio level.

Throughput Testers, Speed Test, and Looking Glass Sites

Throughput testers are designed to test upload and download speeds on your network or Internet connection. This will help determine if you are getting the speeds you are paying for and help you identify issues with bandwidth. You can also get throughput testers that test your hard drive performance.

When troubleshooting networking-related issues, it is very useful to perform speed tests of the WAN or Internet connection. In today's day and age, with voice and video being carried across the Internet, we are becoming more dependent on high-speed Internet connections. To verify that you are getting the correct Internet speeds, you can use a *speed test site* such as www.speedtest.net. You can also use sites such as www.dnsstuff.com to run a number of tools to verify IP address information, ping tests, and DNS configuration.

Looking glass sites are great troubleshooting tools, as they provide routing and diagnostic information for protocols like Border Gateway Protocol (BGP) from computers outside of your network.

Connectivity Software

Connectivity software is designed to ensure that a certain type of connectivity exists between a client and a server. For example, if you are troubleshooting why a Microsoft Outlook client cannot connect to the Microsoft Exchange Server, there is a Remote Procedure Call (RPC) ping connectivity tester that you can run. When using the RPC ping utility, if it cannot communicate from the client system to the server, then the Outlook client will not be able to communicate with the server either, because Outlook also relies on RPC communication.

w a t c h   **There are other network troubleshooting tools to know about for the exam, such as multimeters or voltage event recorders to monitor voltage. A butt set is used to test telephone lines. *System &***   ***Network Integrated Polling Software (SNIPS)* monitors network activity from a UNIX system. And temperature monitors are used to monitor the temperature of computer components.**

CERTIFICATION SUMMARY

In this chapter you have learned quite a lot that not only will help you on the Network+ exam, but also will give you a troubleshooting methodology that you can use for the rest of your career. You have learned the general model for troubleshooting, which involves establishing the problem symptoms, identifying the affected area of the network, determining what has changed, selecting the most probable cause, implementing a solution, testing the result, recognizing possible side effects of the solution, and documenting the solution.

You have learned to ask yourself questions such as these:

- Does the problem exist across the network?
- Is this a workstation, workgroup, LAN, or WAN problem?
- Is the problem consistent and replicable?

You have learned the physical and logical indicators of network problems, such as link, collision, and power lights, as well as error messages and error logs, which give you a good indication of the problem that is occurring.

Finally, you have learned about the various network tools that are available to you to obtain more information about the problem, to solve the problem, or simply to make your networking life a little bit easier.

TWO-MINUTE DRILL

Managing Network Problems

❑ Learning how each device coexists and contributes to the network will provide you with a strong foundation for understanding how and why network-related problems occur and how to resolve them.

❑ When you first encounter a problem, it is important to determine its symptoms.

❑ You need to determine whether the problem relates to a workstation, workgroup, LAN, or WAN.

❑ Determine whether the problem is consistent and replicable.

❑ It is important to isolate the subsystem involved with the problem process.

Network Troubleshooting Methodology

❑ When you troubleshoot network problems, it is important to follow a logical troubleshooting methodology.

❑ Having others troubleshoot the problem as a team will give you many different perspectives and theories as to the cause of the problem.

❑ Sometimes it is possible to re-create the problem, learning exactly why and how it occurred.

❑ It is critical to know the seven steps to the network troubleshooting methodology for the Network+ exam.

❑ Often, there is more than one way to correct a problem, each with its own set of related issues and consequences.

System or Operator Problems

❑ In some cases, it is very clear whether a system or operator error has occurred.

Checking Physical and Logical Indicators

❑ When you begin troubleshooting a network-related problem, several indicators are available that will help you determine the problem.

❑ Link lights are invaluable in determining whether a network connection is present.

❑ Collision lights can help determine whether a network element has failed and is causing chatter.

❑ Even more rudimentary in the network troubleshooting area than the link light is the power light.

❑ An error display is a means of alerting you to a malfunction or failure in a device.

❑ Similar to the error display is the error log, which maintains a listing of errors encountered.

❑ Network Monitor is an outstanding tool for monitoring the network performance of your system.

❑ Performance Monitor tracks the use of resources by the system components and applications.

Other Symptoms and Causes of Network Problems

❑ Experienced network administrators know that cabling is one of the most common causes of network failure.

❑ Make sure that you know the symptoms of cable problems and how to correct them.

❑ There are many ways to continually monitor the status of your servers, and each is operating system specific.

❑ When you are bringing a new server online or configuring a server with a new service such as DNS or WINS, it is imperative that you begin by verifying that the configuration is correct.

❑ Make sure that you know the definition of WINS, DNS, the hosts file, and the LMHOSTS file. You won't be expected to know any in-depth information about each, just the purpose of each.

❑ A server running a virus-scanning program can make all the difference in keeping viruses out of your network.

Network Troubleshooting Tools

❑ To build a strong network, you need to run diagnostics to search for bottlenecks or problematic situations.

❑ A hardware loopback adapter is a way to test the ports on a system without having to connect to an external device.

❑ A TDR is a device that sends an electronic pulse down a cable. The pulse then travels until it is reflected back, and the distance traveled is calculated. This process is similar to the way sonar works.

❑ An oscilloscope can determine when there are shorts, crimps, or attenuation in a cable.

❑ Network monitors and protocol analyzers monitor traffic on the network and display the packets that have been transmitted across it.

SELF TEST

The following questions will help you measure your understanding of the material presented in this chapter. Read all the choices carefully because there might be more than one correct answer. Choose all correct answers for each question.

Managing Network Problems

1. A few computers on the engineering segment are having problems reaching the AutoCAD design segment on the network, but they can access all other segments. What is your initial diagnosis of the problem?
   A. It's a default gateway issue.
   B. It's a routing issue.
   C. The computers are having cable problems.
   D. A hub is locked up.

2. All users on a coaxial bus topology network have suddenly complained that the network is not functioning and they can no longer access resources on the local or remote networks. What is your initial diagnosis of the problem?
   A. It's a routing issue.
   B. It's a default gateway issue.
   C. The network is no longer terminated.
   D. A hub is locked up.

3. You think you are having problems with the UNIX server in another region. Two users have already complained this morning. What would be the next logical step in your troubleshooting methodology?
   A. Check the router.
   B. Check the switch.
   C. Use netstat on your system.
   D. Ping the UNIX server by IP address.

4. You have a workstation that you moved from one cubicle to another. Nothing on the workstation was changed, but the computer refuses to connect to the network at the new cubicle but seems to work fine still at the old cubicle. Which of the following is a likely cause?
   A. The network drop has not been activated in the wiring closet.
   B. The cable was damaged in the move.
   C. The TCP/IP configuration is incorrect.
   D. The network adapter was damaged in the move.

Network Troubleshooting Methodology

5. You are experiencing problems on a coax bus network. How can you quickly determine where the problem is occurring?
    A. Divide the network in half, terminate it, and find which side is still not functioning. That is the affected area. Continue this process until the break is found.
    B. Use a network packet sniffer to determine where the packets eventually stop responding. This will tell you which computer is the closest to the break.
    C. Use a fox-and-hound process to determine the location of the break in the network backbone.
    D. Use Network Monitor to determine what is causing the broadcast storm. One computer's faulty network card is the likely culprit and must be found.

System or Operator Problems

6. Steve, a user on your network, just got back from a two-week vacation. He calls you first thing Monday morning. Which of the following are most likely the reason for Steve's call? (Select three.)
    A. He forgot his password.
    B. His account has been disabled.
    C. His password has expired.
    D. A coworker changed Steve's password while he was on vacation.

Checking Physical and Logical Indicators

7. You came to work on Monday morning only to notice that you are having network problems. Your domain controller, which also functions as a database server, appears to be having problems. How can you further investigate the situation?
    A. Check the error log.
    B. Ping the server to see if it responds.
    C. Run diagnostics on the server.
    D. Restart the computer and then begin troubleshooting.

8. You have made system configuration changes to one of your servers. How can you tell if the changes have made a difference?
    A. Watch the server closely for a few hours, especially during peak usage.
    B. Run Network Monitor to perform an assessment of the current system activity and compare that with your previous baseline, taken before the configuration change took place.
    C. Run Performance Monitor to perform an assessment of the current system activity and compare that with your previous baseline, taken before the configuration change took place.
    D. Check the Event Viewer for errors, warnings, or any indicators that system degradation has occurred.

9. Which of the following is the most reliable indicator that a network server could be overloaded?
    A. The activity light on the network card is constantly lit.
    B. Performance Monitor shows network requests are backing up in the queue.
    C. Network Monitor shows too many packets are leaving this server.
    D. The computer is very slow to respond when you log on.

10. Which of the following is not a good recommendation when it comes to performing a baseline of your network?
    A. Monitor traffic at different times of the day.
    B. Configure the snapshots to take place at midnight each night.
    C. Monitor traffic for days, even weeks.
    D. Take as many traffic snapshots as possible.

Other Symptoms and Causes of Network Problems

11. You can't seem to surf the Internet or connect to the servers in a remote office location, but you can communicate with systems on your local LAN. What would you do to verify what the problem is?
    A. Run ipconfig.
    B. Ping the router.
    C. Ping a local server.
    D. Ping a local workstation.

12. During any network troubleshooting call, which should you check first?
    A. The printer
    B. IP address
    C. Cabling and connections
    D. User

Network Troubleshooting Tools

13. How can you eliminate complicated cable problems in your troubleshooting process?
    A. Visually inspect the cables.
    B. Use a "fox and hound" to find cables in a tangled mess.
    C. Examine cables with a TDR to find any problems.
    D. Swap suspect cables with known good cables.

14. What is the best tool to determine where a break has occurred in a cable?
   A.   A tone generator
   B.   A spectrum division analyzer
   C.   A time domain reflectometer
   D.   A fox and hound

Performance-Based Question Review: See the performance-based question sample from the author included in the accompanying media.

SELF TEST ANSWERS

Managing Network Problems

1.   ☑   **B.** It's a routing issue. If you have a very good understanding of routers and routing, and one segment of your network cannot communicate with another segment, you will immediately know that there is a problem with routing—possibly a router is malfunctioning.
     ☒   **A, C,** and **D** are incorrect. Segments are usually created by routers or bridges, and one of these will be the issue when one segment has problems contacting another. Default gateways are used to connect to the gateway or router that is used to contact other segments. Since some segments in the question can be contacted, the default gateway is fine. Since some PCs can be contacted, the hub is not locked up.

2.   ☑   **C.** The network is no longer terminated. One segment of the network is not able to communicate with another segment; therefore, you should quickly determine that you have a routing problem. Another symptom is that everyone on the coaxial-based bus network is not able to communicate. The cause of this problem most likely lies with the network bus backbone, which requires terminators on each end.
     ☒   **A, B,** and **D** are incorrect. The terminator is a problem with bus networks and should be checked whenever the whole network is the issue. If none of the PCs on the local segment can be contacted, the problem is not a router or gateway. Hubs do not simply lock up, so this is not the issue.

3. ☑ **D.** Ping the UNIX server by IP address. You can test the routing problem by trying to communicate with another computer on the corporate headquarters network. For example, you can ping another computer on this network or use a program that connects to a computer on this network.

   ☒ **A, B,** and **C** are incorrect. Ping allows you to determine whether the problem is the server, a router, or another network device.

4. ☑ **A.** Chances are that the network drop was not activated at the new cubicle. For security reasons, the unused ports on the network may be disabled and need to be enabled when used.

   ☒ **B, C,** and **D** are incorrect because the workstation works when connecting to the old cubicle.

Network Troubleshooting Methodology

5. ☑ **A.** Divide the network in half, terminate it, and find which side is still not functioning. The best example of this is in thinnet coax. Determine the midpoint of the cable and place a terminator on each end. One half of the cable should now be working, and it is obviously not the source of your problem. Repeat this step until you solve the problem.

   ☒ **B, C,** and **D** are incorrect because using a sniffer or fox-and-hound tool would require about as much work, but moving the terminator would allow you to find the source of the problem with no extra tool other than the terminator, which is readily available. These tools might not be available to all technicians. Network Monitor might not always determine which computer is causing the problem. If the problem is in a cable rather than a computer, Network Monitor will be of no help.

System or Operator Problems

6. ☑ **A, B,** and **C.** He forgot his password, his account has been disabled, or his password has expired. You need to intervene to correct the situation.

   ☒ **D** is incorrect because a coworker cannot change Steve's password while he is on vacation.

Checking Physical and Logical Indicators

7. ☑ **A.** Check the error log. Error logs usually don't contain enough information to solve a problem, and documentation must be consulted to diagnose and resolve it. However, checking the error logs is important because you can determine when the problem occurred, what might have caused the problem, and what other processes are affected by this problem.

   ☒ **B, C,** and **D** are incorrect. Pinging the server verifies that TCP/IP is running and functional on the server, and if there are no calls from users unable to contact the server, this is not an issue. Running diagnostics can help, but you are not sure what diagnostics to run. Diagnostics can be run on all the physical hardware, the database, or the network. Restarting the computer and troubleshooting the system still require you know where to start troubleshooting.

8. ☑ **C.** Run Performance Monitor to perform an assessment of the current system activity and compare that with your previous baseline, taken before the configuration change took place. Performance Monitor can be used for a variety of purposes, including the following: identifying bottlenecks in CPU, memory, disk I/O, or network I/O; identifying trends over time; monitoring real-time system performance; monitoring system performance history; determining the capacity the system can handle; and monitoring system configuration changes.

☒ **A, B,** and **D** are incorrect. Visual inspection of system performance is not a very good measure. It is hard to visually determine CPU and hard disk performance as well as other system resources. Network Monitor does not show system degradation or problems. Event Viewer shows only system-generated errors, not performance issues from configuration changes.

9. ☑ **B.** Performance Monitor shows network requests are backing up in the queue. Performance and network monitoring can determine whether the server is overloaded or broadcasting unnecessarily. An overloaded server can increase the length of time needed to fulfill network requests.

☒ **A, C,** and **D** are incorrect. A constant network light shows that the network, or even the server network card, is overburdened. Network Monitor is used to check for an overburdened network, not a server. When logging on, if you do not give the system enough time to start, services could still be in the process of being loaded, which can cause slow logon issues, but this does not mean that the server is overburdened.

10. ☑ **B.** Configure the snapshots to take place at midnight each night. Taking snapshots of activity from various periods of the day, week, and month gives you the most accurate assessment of your network. The longer you spend baselining your network, the more accurate the results. If you are taking network activity snapshots only at midnight, you are not getting an accurate assessment of the normal network activity that occurs throughout the day.

☒ **A, C,** and **D** are incorrect because they are all good recommendations.

Other Symptoms and Causes of Network Problems

11. ☑ **B.** When you can communicate with systems on the local network but not remote networks or the Internet, the problem is typically related to the router. As a result, you should ping the router to see if it is up and running.

☒ **A, C,** and **D** are incorrect. You may run ipconfig, but you don't really need to because you are communicating with other systems on the local network. There is no need to ping a local server or workstation because you know that you can already communicate with systems on the local LAN.

12. ☑ **C.** A number of network issues arise because of faulty cables or cables being accidentally disconnected. Always check the simple stuff like connections first!

☒ **A, B,** and **D** are incorrect because they are not items that you would check first. You may verify the IP address, but you check that the network cable is plugged in first.

Network Troubleshooting Tools

13.   ☑   **C.** Eliminate complicated cable problems by examining cables with a TDR to find any problems.
       ☒   **A, B,** and **D** are incorrect. Visually inspecting a cable cannot determine whether the cable is faulty. You need more advanced tools to determine this. Using tools saves time and money if you catch a potentially faulty cable before it is put into production.

14.   ☑   **C.** Use a TDR or an oscilloscope to find the exact spot where the cable is broken. If you don't have access to such a tool, you might be able to replace the cable without determining the exact area of breakage.
       ☒   **A, B,** and **D** are incorrect. A tone generator is used to determine the two ends of a specific cable within a large bulk of cables. A spectrum division analyzer is used with fiber-optic cables to determine their quality. A fox and hound is the same as a tone generator.

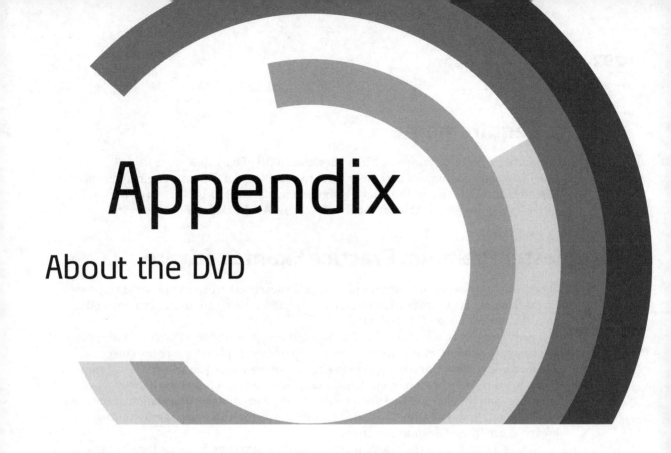

Appendix

About the DVD

The DVD included with this book features additional bonus content not available in the print book, including

- Total Tester customizable practice exam software, including a pre-assessment test
- How to Score Your Pre-assessment PDF
- Video training from the author
- Performance-Based Questions PDF
- Video demonstrations of the performance-based questions
- The Glossary for the book in PDF format
- Lab Book PDF containing all of the labs from the book plus a separate PDF with the lab book answers, and the files to complete the labs
- Quick Review Guide PDF that gathers all the Two-Minute Drills from the book in one place for accelerated review
- PDF copy of the book for studying on the go

System Requirements

The software requires Windows XP or later and 30MB of hard disk space for full installation, in addition to a current or prior major release of Chrome, Firefox, Internet Explorer, or Safari. To run, the screen resolution must be set to 1024 × 768 or higher. The PDF files require Adobe Acrobat, Adobe Reader, or Adobe Digital Editions to view.

Total Tester Premium Practice Exam Software

Total Tester provides you with a simulation of the live exam. You can also create custom exams from selected certification objectives or chapters. You can further customize the number of questions and time allowed.

The exams can be taken in either Practice Mode or Exam Mode. Practice Mode provides an assistance window with hints, references to the book, explanations of the correct and incorrect answers, and the option to check your answer as you take the test. Exam Mode provides a simulation of the actual exam. The number of questions, the types of questions, and the time allowed are intended to be an accurate representation of the exam environment. Both Practice Mode and Exam Mode provide an overall grade and a grade broken down by certification objectives.

To take a test, launch the program and select the exam suite from the Installed Question Packs list. You can then select Practice Mode, Exam Mode, or Custom Mode. After making your selection, click Start Exam to begin.

Installing and Running Total Tester

From the main screen, you may install Total Tester by clicking the Total Tester Practice Exams button. This will begin the installation process and place an icon on your desktop and in your Start menu. To run Total Tester, navigate to Start | (All) Programs | Total Seminars, or double-click the icon on your desktop.

To uninstall the Total Tester software, go to Start | Settings | Control Panel | Add/Remove Programs (XP) or Programs And Features (Vista/7/8), and then select the Total Tester program. Select Remove, and Windows will completely uninstall the software.

Pre-assessment Test

A pre-assessment test has been included in Total Tester as a separate question pack, and the DVD includes a PDF guide on how to interpret the results of your pre-assessment. Answer all of the questions in the time allotted and use the Total Tester score report and the How to Score Your Pre-assessment PDF to gauge your areas of relative strength and weakness before beginning Chapter 1 of this book.

Video Training from the Author

Video MP4 clips provide detailed examples of key certification objectives and exam topics in audio video format direct from the author of the book. You can access the videos directly from the table of contents by clicking the Videos link on the main page.

Performance-Based Questions PDF and Video Demonstrations

A PDF containing all the performance-based questions referenced in the book is included on the DVD. To access the PDF, click the Performance-Based Questions link on the main menu and then select the Performance-Based Questions PDF link. Read through the Performance-Based Questions PDF before watching the video demonstrations.

Video MP4 clips provide animated examples of the performance-based questions in audio/video format with overview and explanation from the author of the book. You can access the video demonstrations directly from the main menu by clicking the Performance-Based Questions link on the main page and then selecting the Video Demonstrations link.

Lab Book, Lab Book Answers, and Lab Files

A PDF containing all of the labs from the book and a separate PDF containing all of the lab book answers are also included. The corresponding lab files and sample website files for use in the labs have been provided as well. Click the Lab Files And Solutions link on the main page to access these resources.

Quick Review Guide PDF

A PDF containing all of the Two-Minute Drills from the book has been included for your review.

Glossary

The Glossary for the book is included on the DVD in PDF format and includes detailed definitions of key terms.

PDF Copy of the Book

The entire contents of the print book are provided as a PDF on the DVD. This file is viewable on your computer and many portable devices.

To view the PDF on a computer, Adobe Acrobat, Adobe Reader, or Adobe Digital Editions is required. A link to Adobe's website, where you can download and install Adobe Reader, has been included on the DVD.

> **Note: For more information on Adobe Reader and to check for the most recent version of the software, visit Adobe's website at www.adobe.com and search for the free Adobe Reader, or look for Adobe Reader on the product page. Adobe Digital Editions can also be downloaded from the Adobe website.**

To view the PDF on a portable device, copy the PDF file to your computer from the DVD, and then copy the file to your portable device using a USB or other connection. Adobe offers a mobile version of Adobe Reader, the Adobe Reader mobile app, which currently supports iOS and Android. For customers using Adobe Digital Editions and an iPad, you may have to download and install a separate reader program on your device. The Adobe website has a list of recommended applications, and McGraw-Hill Education recommends the Bluefire Reader.

Technical Support

Technical support information is provided as follows, by feature.

Total Seminars Technical Support

For questions regarding the Total Tester software or operation of the DVD, visit www.totalsem .com or e-mail support@totalsem.com.

McGraw-Hill Education Content Support

For questions regarding the PDF copy of the book, e-mail techsolutions@mhedu.com or visit http://mhp.softwareassist.com.

For questions regarding book content, e-mail customer.service@mheducation.com.
For customers outside the United States, e-mail international_cs@mheducation.com.

INDEX

B

C

D

E

N

Q

R

T

U

V

W

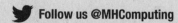